3D GAME ALCHEMY

FOR DOOM, DOOM II, HERETIC, AND HEXEN

WHAT'S NEW IN THIS EDITION

This book is the second edition of the best-selling *Tricks of the DOOM Programming Gurus*. You'll find dozens of areas that have been added and updated, including the following:

■ Hexen editing techniques, including special codes, scripting language, and more

■ "Towards a Total Conversion" (Chapter 25), and "Changing the Face of DOOM" (Chapter 21), written by the creator of *Aliens*-TC

■ Additional reference material for all games

■ Revised WAD-building lessons

■ Expanded information on playing the included game levels

■ "Special Visual Effects" (Chapter 24)

■ Two new chapters on special sectors and sector types

Plus the CD-ROM includes exciting new software such as:

■ Full registered version of WadAuthor, the powerful Windows-based graphical level editor—a *3D Game Alchemy* exclusive

■ DoomShell 5, the ultimate game level front end—found only on this CD-ROM

■ More than 3,000 new game levels for DOOM, DOOM II, Heretic, and Hexen

■ The *Alchemy* graphics library for creating your own game levels—found only on this CD-ROM

■ New and updated tools and utilities

■ Updated version of WADED, the DOS level editor

■ Expanded examples for the WAD-building lessons

SAMS PUBLISHING

201 West 103rd Street,
Indianapolis, Indiana 46290

3D GAME ALCHEMY

FOR DOOM, DOOM II, HERETIC AND HEXEN

Steve Benner *et al.*

This book is dedicated to all the forgotten pioneers of DOOM editing. Their early quests led us to where we are today.

COPYRIGHT © 1996 BY SAMS PUBLISHING

SECOND EDITION

International Standard Book Number: 0-672-30935-1

Library of Congress Catalog Card Number: 96-67718

99 98 97 96   4 3 2 1

Interpretation of the printing code: the rightmost double-digit number is the year of the book's printing; the rightmost single-digit, the number of the book's printing. For example, a printing code of 96-1 shows that the first printing of the book occurred in 1996.

Composed in Goudy and MCPdigital by Macmillan Computer Publishing

Printed in the United States of America

TRADEMARKS

Publisher and President: Richard K. Swadley

Acquisitions Manager: Greg Wiegand

Development Manager: Dean Miller

Managing Editor: Cindy Morrow

Marketing Manager: John Pierce

Assistant Marketing Manager: Kristina Perry

Acquisitions and Development Editor
Wayne Blankenbeckler

Software Development Specialist
Wayne Blankenbeckler

Production Editor
Kristine B. Simmons

Copy Editors
Cheri Clark, Anna M. Huff,
Karen Brehm Letourneau,
Lisa M. Lord, Angie Trzepacz,
Faithe Wempen

Technical Reviewers
David Jaskolka, Vincent Mayfield,
Larry Richardson

Editorial Coordinator
Bill Whitmer

Resource Coordinator
Deborah Frisby

Technical Edit Coordinator
Lynette Quinn

Formatter
Frank Sinclair

Editorial Assistants
Carol Ackerman, Andi Richter,
Rhonda Tinch-Mize

Cover Designer
Tim Amhrein

Book Designer
Alyssa Yesh

Copy Writer
Peter Fuller

Production Team Supervisors
Brad Chinn, Charlotte Clapp

Production
Mary Ann Abramson, Ginny Bess
Carol Bowers, Georgiana Briggs,
Mona Brown, Michael Brumitt,
Jeanne M. Clark, Michael Dietsch,
Jason Hand, Michael Henry,
Louisa Klucznik, Ayanna Lacey,
Clint Lahnen, Paula Lowell,
Donna Martin, Casey Price,
Laura Robbins, Bobbi Satterfield,
SA Springer, Susan Van Ness,
Mark Walchle, Todd Wente

OVERVIEW

CONTENTS

INTRODUCTION

DOOM, from id Software, is a remarkable computer game, played by countless people all over the world. It has monopolized hundreds of millions of hours of computer time in businesses, schools, and homes. DOOM has become the yardstick by which other computer games are measured, even if those games are not intended to compete with DOOM directly. Now DOOM's sequels—DOOM II, Heretic, and Hexen—have extended the legacy.

Many things set DOOM apart, but one particular feature that is virtually unique to DOOM created the need for this book. The makers of DOOM have granted permission for people not only to play the game for free in a full-featured shareware version, but also to add to the registered version and share the results with other players. The original developers of DOOM do, however, state a couple of pre-conditions, if you're going to make changes, create your own new graphics or sounds, or create an entire new DOOM world. First, you have to use a registered version of the game. (After all, fair's fair, and this enables you to purchase a game engine, enjoy DOOM, and then set about driving others crazy with your own levels.) The other important requirement is that you do not distribute any material that has been extracted from the main files that come with the game itself—this belongs firmly to the original designers and cannot be given or sold to others. This book will show you just how much you can do while honoring these requirements.

From the beginning, people have done much more than merely make changes to DOOM's supporting files. Many people have worked to create utility programs and editors to make it easier for *anyone* to carry out the changes. These people become experts at working the magic necessary to construct the supplemental (WAD) files that drive the DOOM engine.

In this book, the experts lay before you the secrets of their particular craft—DOOM alchemy—which also, of course, includes a study of DOOM II, Heretic, and Hexen. You will quickly find that this is not a book about playing these games, nor is it a book about playing add-ons for these games. Nor is it documentation for a particular WAD file or utility program. This book will not only teach you the ins and outs of one of the greatest computer-game phenomena of all time and introduce you to some of the most highly acclaimed add-ons available, it will also teach you to develop your own worlds with a Master Alchemist always at your side. In short, it will set you on the path to enlightenment whereby, with hard work, perseverance, and, of course, a good deal of general carnage and other such fun along the way, you might one day become a full DOOM Alchemist yourself.

You will be presented with some of the best WADs that are currently available—WADs that have stood the test of time to become the world's favorites—as well as the very latest masterpieces, hot from the alembics of some of the most renowned WAD-masters. Technical information on the development of these WADs (as well as an exclusive library of new graphics ready for you to use) will help you in developing your own worlds.

This book also includes a multitude of editors and other tools for you to use. You will learn about many of these tools from the people who actually created them.

Because no book or CD-ROM could ever contain all the files that can be found or used, the final episode of the book contains information on where you can go online to obtain more DOOM files. There is also information on how and where you can distribute your own WAD files. (If you are interested in DOOM, there are definitely a lot of places to go and people to see.)

A CD-ROM is provided to help supplement what you will find in the book. Unlike every other DOOM-related CD-ROM currently available, the *Alchemy* CD-ROM was created by asking each of the actual developers of DOOM tools or WAD files to include their products. On this one disc, you will find everything you need to create your own complete DOOM worlds.

In addition, as the second edition of *Tricks of the DOOM Programming Gurus*, this book has been fully revised and updated to bring you the latest tricks and specialist discoveries about the innermost workings of DOOM and the games it has spawned. Information on Heretic has been greatly expanded since the first edition, and Raven Software's latest adaptation of DOOM, Hexen, also features fully.

All the technical information presented in this book has been tried and tested by practicing Master Alchemists. They have worked long and hard to ensure that what you have before you is the purest form of their particular Philosopher's Stone—as complete and accurate a distillate of DOOM, DOOM II, Heretic, and Hexen alchemy as can be found anywhere. Much of the arcane knowledge assembled here is newly discovered; some of the Hexen information in particular is presented to the world for the first time.

The revisions extend to the CD-ROM as well. Here you will find many new WADs, not only for DOOM and DOOM II, but also for Heretic and Hexen, with plenty of new mayhem and carnage to occupy both single-player and group-player aficionados for countless gore-soaked hours (as well as a sophisticated, yet simple-to-use program, DoomShell, that will let you get in on the action straight-away).

You will also find that the Master Alchemists have been hard at work, extending and improving their editors and other utilities. The very latest tools are brought to you on the *Alchemy* CD-ROM. Readers familiar with the first edition will find updated versions of their favorite DOOM-editing tools here, whereas old hands and newcomers alike will be thrilled with the new tools that are presented for the first time in this edition. The CD-ROM provides fully registered versions of the popular DOS-based editor WADED and the exciting new Windows-based editor WadAuthor so that you can dive straight in and begin brewing up your own DOOM, DOOM II, Heretic, or Hexen concoction. Of course, you'll find plenty of recipes to try.

So, read on. And happy DOOMing, whatever your preferred flavor!

ACKNOWLEDGMENTS

Sams Publishing would like to acknowledge the Master Alchemists who helped to make this book possible. They are Vincenzo Alcamo, Matthew Ayres, Steve Benner, David Bruni, Justin Fisher, Robert Fenske, Jr., Robert Forsman, Jason Hoffoss, Jens Hykkelbjerg, Piotr Kapiszewski, Greg Lewis, Steve McCrea, Denis Moeller, Olivier Montanuy, Ben Morris, Raphaël Quinet, Jeff Rabenhorst, Jack Vermeulen, Lisa Whistlecroft, John Williston, and Kirk Yokomizo. Without their time, assistance, guidance, wisdom, and patience, this book would not have been feasible. Only those truly devoted to their craft can and will take the time to create the software you'll find featured in this book.

Sams Publishing would also like to acknowledge and thank id Software, responsible for bringing DOOM and DOOM II to the world, and also Raven Software, creators of Heretic and Hexen. Without these games, this book would not be possible.

As lead author of this book, I would like to add my own voice to that of Sams Publishing in thanking the many people who have helped bring this second edition to fruition. I'd like to thank the countless individuals who have helped and encouraged me personally in this endeavor. Many I have come to count amongst my friends, but there are others—too many to mention, and some whose names I do not know. All have generously provided invaluable assistance throughout the preparation and production of this book. Whether adapting their utilities to suit my whims, testing out my crazy ideas, or merely discussing some of the more obscure features of this arcane craft we share, they have each given selflessly of their time and expertise. In particular, I'd like to thank those on the DOOM-editing mailing list who helped me to start out on the DOOM-editing road myself and without whose patient explanations I would never have made it so much as halfway here. I hope that this book and its CD-ROM will help others as much as those early contributors to DOOM-editing helped me and also that it provides its readers with as much fun as I've had putting it together. (But without any of the headaches!)

I would like to express my gratitude to my family and friends for enduring my total immersion in this project (albeit with a certain degree of bemusement on occasions). Inevitably some have found themselves drawn in deeper than they might have wished. In particular, special mention must go to my partner, Lisa Whistlecroft, for true devotion above and beyond the call of duty. As proofreader, play-tester, co-author, and builder of several of the sample WADs, she has made no small contribution to this book herself. In addition, her love and everyday support has been vital to the book's successful completion. And she doesn't even *like* DOOM!

My thanks go to Jane Rowe for dealing with the deluge of e-mail messages and coordinating the effort in obtaining the new levels and utilities for the CD-ROM. Thanks also to Dave Dobson and Robert Edge for their services as WAD mercenaries.

Finally, I would like to offer my sincere thanks to all those people at Sams who have nursed me through this latest birth with understanding and forbearance (to say nothing of a rare good humor!) and whom I have come to look upon as friends. They are the real creators of this book. It is the result of their vision that you hold in your hands.

Steve Benner, February 1996
(S.Benner@lancaster.ac.uk)

EPISODE

MISSION 1: INTRODUCING DOOM... AND BEYOND

MISSION 2: THE ALCHEMY CD-ROM

1

KNEE DEEP IN DOOM

WHAT IS DOOM?

DOOM. Who would have thought this one word would become the standard by which all other games would be judged? What is DOOM? DOOM is a phenomenon. DOOM is a fast-paced, virtual-reality, 3D type game created by id Software. DOOM is also much, much more—as we hope to show you in this book.

DOOM and its follow-ons are state-of-the-art computer games. They are all tremendously popular and great fun to play. This book, however, is not a player's manual. This book is for designers and developers who want to create their own levels for DOOM and the games based on it. Many features of these games are discussed, and many of the best editors and other utilities are examined in detail. Every effort is made to present proven techniques for what you can do with DOOM—from how to create your own single- or multiplayer levels to changing the graphics and even altering the way the game plays. This book is an in-depth study of DOOM and its clones. It is technical in its scope. This book guides you through the complex world of DOOM and takes a little of the mystery out of the game. It also shows you how to continue reaping enjoyment from the game long after you've completed all of its levels.

GENESIS

In DOOM, you use quick reflexes and wits to maneuver through and around myriad mazes, monsters, and acid pits. The capacity to involve other players—whether in Cooperative or Deathmatch play—creates additional dimensions to an already multifaceted playing experience. The object of the game is simple: survival. Making it through DOOM alive is never easy, but trying is always fun—provided that you enjoy being shot, fried, crushed, clawed, chewed, poisoned, and dissolved in acid!

— By David Bruni and
Steve Benner

More than two years after DOOM's first appearance, however, it is now sometimes difficult to decide just what is and is not DOOM! Where did DOOM begin and where will it end? We begin this book by addressing these questions. Let us start by reviewing the early history of the game before turning to look at the variety of games that can now be said to compose that singular phenomenon known as DOOM.

As with many other computer games, DOOM's origins lie in another game altogether—in this case, Wolfenstein 3D. Here's a brief look at it.

DOOM'S ROOTS—WOLFENSTEIN 3D

The game Wolfenstein 3D was an instant hit when it was released. The first of its kind, the game won many awards for its originality, its game characteristics, and above all, its realistic rendering of characters and locales. It also won many fans because it was extendable (with a little hacking) and available in a shareware version. This shareware version allowed you to try a cut-down version of the game for free to see whether you liked it before deciding whether to buy the full registered version.

The designers of Wolfenstein 3D were conscious of many of its limitations, however. In this game, for instance, a room's walls must be arranged at 90 degree angles to each other. The walls were actually four-sided blocks with the same graphical design on all four sides. The way you made levels for Wolfenstein 3D was by placing these blocks on a fixed grid. Each square on the grid represented an area approximately 8 feet square. Wolfenstein 3D also had fixed floor and ceiling heights, making all the rooms seem boxlike and confining—great for its intended Colditz Castle kind of scenario but of very limited use beyond that. It wasn't long before Wolfenstein 3D's programmers were back at work, extending its capabilities. The result of those labors was a new product—DOOM.

THE BIRTH OF DOOM

DOOM was a natural development of Wolfenstein 3D, showing improvements in all aspects of its design. Although DOOM clearly has its roots in the earlier game, DOOM is like Wolfenstein 3D on steroids. There can be no doubt that Wolfenstein 3D revolutionized the computer-gaming world. DOOM, on the other hand, turned that world on its head.

From an environment in which everything was built on one plane and used fairly crude walls, DOOM transported the player to a seemingly fully three-dimensional world, rich in graphically textured surfaces with staircases, moving floors, and lighting effects. Rooms, it seemed, could be any size, shape, or height. Further, this new world was populated with a truly spine-chilling array of enemies, all designed to awaken a player's most deeply rooted fears. Using precision-crafted animations, realistic sound, and other special effects, everything about the new game was designed to get the adrenaline flowing and the blood pumping. With a more visceral approach to the entire game and by again having a cut-down, prerelease, shareware version available over the Internet, the game was a worldwide success story before it had sold a single copy!

But what made DOOM such an advance over its forerunner?

FEATURES OF DOOM

The DOOM engine wasn't merely a rehash of the Wolfenstein 3D engine. Instead, it was rewritten from the ground up and vastly improved. The data structures used to notify the gaming engine of the design of its world were completely redesigned too, and in such a way as to allow much more flexible use. Later episodes of this book show you just how flexible (or not!) this use can be.

Floor and ceiling texturing were added to DOOM to make it more realistic than Wolfenstein 3D. Sky textures were added as well to give an outdoor feel. The sky textures were a welcome addition to DOOM; outdoor areas are easy to make, and they add the illusion of vast spaces. Also added were special animated floor and ceiling patterns that give the appearance of movement, allowing areas of water or even noxious fluids to be created. The opening mission of DOOM introduces a player to these new features of the game immediately, as you can see in Figure 1.1.

Figure 1.1.
An early scene from DOOM.

Many more wall patterns are available in DOOM than were available in Wolfenstein 3D. Some of these look (and act) like switches, changing their appearance when thrown. DOOM handles all of this automatically. Some wall textures are see-through, walk-through, and shoot-through. Interesting effects can be achieved with these textures, as you will see in later portions of this book.

DOOM also introduced significant improvements to the way its world could be laid out. Floors and ceilings could now be at any height, allowing the game environment to be enriched with stairways, pits, windows, ledges, and as many other types of nooks and crannies as the designer could want. (Well, almost!)

Floors that moved, carrying players (and monsters) along with them; ceilings that descended, crushing whatever was beneath them; tripwires and switches; exploding barrels—these are just some of the things that contributed to the runaway success of DOOM. And all of these features are readily available to the add-on designer.

For many players, though, the abundance of new scenery elements paled into insignificance beside DOOM's other major new feature—the capability to play with or against other players by running multiple copies of DOOM on computers connected through their serial ports or over a network. Not only could players team up with one another to defeat the game's bad guys, but they also could forget about the game's monsters altogether and fight each other if they preferred—for with the coming of DOOM was born Deathmatch.

DEATHMATCH

DOOM's great step forward was to make it possible to play against a real opponent rather than just the game itself. Deathmatch is regarded by many as the true test of your DOOM playing abilities. Whereas the monsters in DOOM aren't sneaky (well, not very), most of your Deathmatch opponents probably will be.

You haven't done DOOM until you've done Deathmatch; it's a whole new ball game, and it takes the DOOM experience to a new level. Later chapters in this book discuss the issues involved in designing your own Deathmatch levels. Figure 1.2 illustrates the main objective of a Deathmatch tourney.

Figure 1.2.
Another buddy bites the dust.

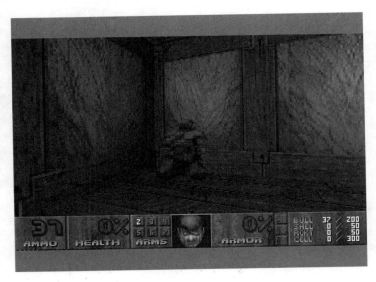

Besides competing against buddies, players can also play cooperatively with them, working together to solve the game's puzzles and battle the bad guys. Although DOOM's new, sophisticated playing environs alone would have made the game a worthy successor to Wolfenstein 3D, it was the addition of Cooperative and Deathmatch play that really marked DOOM as a major advance in virtual-reality gaming. With these additions, DOOM's designers effectively created three games in one. There was one more aspect of DOOM guaranteed to ensure its long-term playability and popularity—its extendability.

DOOM'S EXTENDABILITY

It had been possible for the user to design and build new levels for Wolfenstein 3D; however, a considerable amount of effort often was required, and the scope for add-ons was limited. With DOOM, this all changed. DOOM's newly designed data structures, isolated from the game engine code in special data (WAD) files, made it a simple matter to create whole new gaming scenarios—when the rules of construction were understood, of course. The designers of DOOM helped out here by making available the specifications of their data files and encouraging the development of utility programs, written by the game's enthusiastic followers, for the creation and manipulation of these files. It wasn't long before the first editors appeared (see Figure 1.3) and the craft of DOOM-editing began.

Figure 1.3.

Changing things with DEU, a popular DOOM editor.

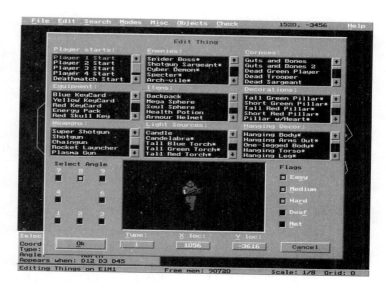

With DOOM, many people's ideal virtual-reality computer game came into being. It took only a single look at the game to know it was a major improvement over Wolfenstein 3D. A more detailed look, however, made it clear that this game was here to stay. After all, what could possibly follow it?

DOOM'S SEQUELS

No matter how sophisticated a computer program is, it will have shortcomings. DOOM, of course, is no exception. Since its first release, DOOM's programmers have continually striven to improve the game, adding new features and refining existing ones, as well as making the game available on various computing platforms. This book is concerned only with versions of the game produced for the IBM-PC market, but even here, a confusing number of versions of the game are now in circulation. In addition, various sequels have appeared, produced both by the original developers and by third-party programmers under license from id Software. It is worth spending a little time reviewing the various PC versions of DOOM available, detailing their differences.

DOOM: THE ORIGINAL

As already noted, the original release of DOOM was made in a shareware version, featuring a single episode. This release was designed to enable a player to try out the game free, become hooked, and thus want to buy the complete registered version of the game for the full three-episode experience. Naturally, the shareware version does not have all the features contained in the full release. Many of the monsters and the more powerful weapons are missing. In addition, id Software requested that the utility authors take steps to prevent their programs from operating on the shareware version, as a further incentive for people to buy a full copy of the game. In accordance with id's wishes, the shareware version is not be considered further in this book—only the various incarnations of the full product.

DOOM V1.0

The first release of DOOM, although awesome in its potential, was somewhat flawed. It contained numerous bugs and didn't function too well over a network. This version also had problems associated with the version of the DOS extender used for the game. It was rapidly replaced.

DOOM V1.1

For all intents and purposes, v1.1 was the first major release of DOOM, although it too contained numerous bugs. Copies of this version, however, are still in circulation.

DOOM V1.2

Version 1.2 of DOOM was released a couple of months after the first registered release of the game, and it was also supplied as a patch to the earlier version. This version featured modem DOOM for the first time. It also had a new upper difficulty setting, Nightmare, in which monsters move faster and respawn at their starting positions some time after the player has killed them. DOOM v1.2 is regarded by many as the first really stable version of the game, and some developers still prefer to work with it, claiming that it contains fewer bugs than the later versions.

DOOM V1.4

Six months or so after DOOM first appeared, v1.4 was made available. Although virtually no new features were visible to players, developers soon discovered that new features had, in fact, been implemented in the heart of the program. The game had gained capabilities that the designers at id Software were not themselves utilizing in their levels but that were nevertheless available for others to use. It soon became clear that this version was something of a test-bed for an upcoming major release from the game's designers: the release that was later to become DOOM II.

Version 1.4 overcame some of the game's original design restrictions and cleared out other irritating little bugs. Not surprisingly, some new bugs had been introduced, but generally these were not sufficient to stop the DOOM-editing community from warmly welcoming this release.

DOOM V1.666

Version 1.666 of DOOM was supposedly the final upgrade to the original game when it was released in September 1994. In this version, all the new capabilities added to the game in readiness for its reappearance as DOOM II were fully implemented (although the new graphics weren't available in DOOM, of course—DOOM II would have to be purchased to acquire those). This release was marred by various small faults that took several new versions (which appeared in rapid succession) to fix.

DOOM V1.9

The current definitive version of DOOM is v1.9. Spokespersons for id Software say this is the last. Absolutely. Definitely. For sure. Upgrade patches to this version are available for registered owners of the earlier versions.

DOOM II—THE SEQUEL

DOOM had been such an instant, runaway success that it was probably inevitable that id Software would follow it with a sequel before long. It was probably equally inevitable that this sequel would disappoint many people, as sequels so often do. DOOM II: Hell on Earth was released in October 1994 and was available only in a full, commercial version. In place of DOOM's three-episode structure, DOOM II used a linear structure of 32 levels, but it continued with the same storyline used in its predecessor. It introduced seven new monsters, a new combat shotgun, and many interesting new textures. Of course, it also made full use of the new features that the programmers had added to the new engine.

With hindsight, it is now possible to observe that much of the initial disappointment felt by many people occurred because most of the new game's features had already been made available in the v1.4 release of DOOM. Many people had hoped for another massive change in standard, comparable to that between Wolfenstein 3D and DOOM, rather than the gradual development that had occurred.

Such expectations were entirely unreasonable, of course, given the timetable in which DOOM II was produced. In fact, DOOM II is a worthy successor to DOOM in many ways. It preserves and enhances the atmosphere of its predecessor, but its layout and number of monsters make it many times harder than DOOM. The levels in DOOM II are more complicated and require puzzle-solving skills similar to those needed in Wolfenstein 3D. There are more buttons, tricks, and brainteasers in DOOM II. The new monsters are truly fearsome, and the new double-barreled combat shotgun is a superb weapon, well worth having (see Figure 1.4).

DOOM II's designers also decided to have a bit of fun. In honor of its roots in Wolfenstein 3D, DOOM II boasts two secret Wolfenstein 3D levels. You have to see them to believe them! Even the old SS guards are there (see Figure 1.5).

Figure 1.4.

One of DOOM II's new monsters, about to find out what the new weapon can do.

Figure 1.5.

A Wolfenstein 3D SS guard in one of two secret DOOM II levels.

TIP: If you haven't found your way to these secret levels (and don't object to cheating) just type `idclev31` or `idclev32` while playing the game to check them out.

Then, of course, there are other reminders of the programmers' earlier computer game successes. (If you don't know what I'm talking about, I won't spoil things by telling you; you'll have to play the game to completion to find out!)

DOOM II has appeared in two major versions:

- Version 1.666, the first release of DOOM II. This tends to be the version supplied on CD-ROM.
- Version 1.9, a bug-fixed "definitive" release, available as a patch. Interestingly, this version's executable file is identical to that of DOOM v1.9.

There are no significant differences between these two versions in terms of capabilities.

LATER DOOMS

In addition to the two major releases of DOOM, other DOOM-related releases have come from id Software, including The Ultimate DOOM and DOOM II: Evilution.

THE ULTIMATE DOOM

The Ultimate DOOM is a special four-episode release of DOOM. The first three episodes are the same as the regular game, but the fourth, "Thy Flesh Consumed," is an all-new nine-mission episode. The game contains no new elements, however, and the release is numbered v1.9.

DOOM II: EVILUTION

DOOM II: Evilution is a special release of DOOM II, featuring a completely new set of 32 levels. In fact, this release is a major success story for a group of DOOM alchemists. This series of levels is the result of a collaborative effort involving DOOM enthusiasts from around the world. It was all set to be released free of charge as TNT: Evilution when id Software stepped in and bought the rights, proving that perseverance and hard work can indeed pay dividends!

DOOM-SPAWN: HERETIC

For a true extension of the DOOM engine, you must look beyond the immediate stable of id Software to the work done under license by Raven Software. This company took a fairly early version of the DOOM engine and adapted it from the Space Marine scenario of DOOM to a more medieval-warrior-and-wizards feel to create the product called Heretic. In so doing, they introduced additional elements to the play, such as the capability of the player to fly (which requires suitable power-ups, of course) as well as the capability to look up and down, a feature sorely lacking in DOOM.

Apart from a change in the way power-ups are acquired and used (the player can store them in an inventory until they are needed), Heretic includes few real changes to the engine's capabilities. Heretic uses the same add-on file structure as DOOM and is therefore just as extendable. It has proved less popular, however. I suspect that this is largely due to the increased number of keystrokes covering the new actions. These keystrokes interfere with the smooth gameplay that makes DOOM such fun. Also, the magical weapons lack the raw, visceral feel of DOOM's very physical weaponry, and many of the monsters lack any real character. Heretic does not support the lower screen resolution mode of DOOM and DOOM II, and consequently its graphics are generally sharper and more detailed. After extended play, however, many people find these more detailed environments more tiring on the eyes. Heretic also lacks the richness and variety of DOOM and DOOM II's graphical palette, limiting the kinds of gaming environments that can be built.

The increased utilization of the vertical element in Heretic makes it an excellent Deathmatch environment, however, as you can see in Figure 1.6. Being able to fly over your opponents definitely adds a new dimension. Being able to turn them into chickens is also great fun!

Figure 1.6.

Looking down on an opponent in Heretic.

hERETIC Despite its different character, Heretic can be viewed as a DOOM variant. Its data file structure is sufficiently close to DOOM's for most of the editors and utilities developed for DOOM to function equally well with Heretic files. Throughout this book, therefore, any statement made about the original DOOM can be regarded as equally applicable to Heretic, unless specifically modified by additional remarks contained within Heretic note boxes such as this one.

BEYOND HERETIC: HEXEN

Whereas many DOOMers saw Heretic as yet another disappointment—again, no major leap forward was made—Raven Software's subsequent release, Hexen, rather took the world by surprise. Although clearly based on the DOOM engine, Hexen has taken that engine about as far as it is possible to go and still have it recognizable as DOOM.

The first thing a player notices when playing Hexen is the game's new adaptation to a role-playing scenario. In Hexen, players can opt to be one of three classes of characters:

- Fighter
- Mage
- Cleric

The use and function of various game artifacts change with a character's class. Different types of objects become available, and different game play is encountered. Immediately, the player has a wider choice of gaming options.

The next feature that impresses itself on the player of Hexen is the range of atmospheric effects that are possible. These have been extended considerably from DOOM and even Heretic. A thunderstorm is clearly raging around the player in the opening level. The synchronized lightning-flash and thunder-crack is an effect that DOOM could never have managed, as too are the leaves being blown from the trees around you. (See Figure 1.7.)

Figure 1.7.
A flurry of leaves in Hexen.

Another surprise is in store for you as soon as you operate the first door: a crack opens down its center, and its two halves *swing away from you* with an eerie creaking sound. DOOM's doors all operate vertically; nowhere will you find walls capable of moving sideways. Hexen seems full of them—some when you least expect them (see Figure 1.8).

Figure 1.8.
Hexen swinging into action!

In fact, Hexen is full of surprises. Time and time again, the seasoned DOOM player will be caught off guard as the environment fails to operate as expected. Greatly improved textures, monsters, and general design all help to make Hexen seem almost as far beyond Heretic as DOOM was beyond Wolfenstein 3D.

Only when you look at the changes to the underlying data structures, however, do you discover just how much more advanced than DOOM Hexen is. Just about every structure has been expanded to provide the designer with almost limitless control and flexibility (within the limits imposed by the basic 3D engine itself). You discover that Hexen scenery and objects are, in fact, programmable; Hexen WAD files include scripting facilities. And then there are those moving walls!

Hexen is likely to be the culmination of the evolution of the DOOM game engine. So extended are Hexen's data structures that the game is barely recognizable, deep down, as DOOM.

Despite its many differences, Hexen is treated as a standard DOOM variant in this book. Where there are differences between Hexen and DOOM, your attention is drawn to them by means of Hexen note boxes such as this one.

MORE SEQUELS?

More DOOM clones are believed to be not too far over the horizon. A second Heretic release is promised, supposedly with five episodes rather than three. A new game called Strife is also expected soon. This too will be based on the DOOM engine. At the time of writing, however, no firm information is available about these developments.

THE COMING QUAKE: THE DEMISE OF DOOM?

It has been known for a long time that the developers and programmers at id Software have been working hard on a true successor to DOOM, code-named Quake. Outside of id Software's offices, almost nothing is known for sure about this venture. Many promises have been made, however. A fully three-dimensional game world is one promise. This would overcome what most designers view as the severest limitation of the DOOM engine. (You will learn more about this limitation in Chapter 9, "Measuring and Mapping DOOM.") Complete access to all game parameters is another pledged feature, along with fully programmable object and game world behavior. These capabilities would provide a much greater degree of control over the game than has been seen before. Perhaps the current developments in Hexen offer some indication of what to expect, but we will have to wait and see.

EXIT: MOPPING UP AND MOVING ON

This chapter provides an introduction to the phenomenon that is DOOM. It gives a brief history of the game to date and reviews the various versions of DOOM and related games that are available for the PC.

The next chapter gets down to the business of driving the main DOOM engine. It deals with all the command-line switches that the game uses to change the way it operates, and it introduces the runtime switches (cheat keys!) that are available. It also shows you how to record your own demos to impress both family and friends with your DOOM-playing prowess!

2

RUNNING DOOM

This chapter details the ways in which a player can control and modify the running of DOOM, many of which you might not have discovered from simply playing the game. The chapter first looks at the command-line switches, which can be used to make DOOM start in a particular way, and then at the hidden play-time controls (or cheat keys), which enable you to take control of the way the game behaves during play. Finally, you are shown how you can make DOOM record and play back demos or take snapshots of the screen to impress your friends.

STARTING DOOM

You can pass many parameters to DOOM directly from the command line when you start the game. These parameters control various aspects of the way in which the game plays. There are controls to make DOOM play without monsters or to make the monsters automatically respawn after they have been killed or to take you straight to a particular level, for instance. Before looking at the full list of these parameters, though, take a quick look at how to activate them.

USING COMMAND-LINE SWITCHES

Command-line switches can be used in various ways with DOOM. These are the main methods:

- Direct from the DOS command prompt
- In batch files
- In response files
- Via a front-end utility

Which method you adopt is a matter of your own preference and depends on how comfortable you are working with DOS. These methods are detailed separately in the following text.

— By Steve Benner and David Bruni

> **NOTE:** This chapter assumes that you have DOOM, DOOM II, Heretic, or Hexen correctly installed and operational on your computer. If you are experiencing problems in getting your chosen game to run, you should first check the readme file that came with your copy of the game. If that doesn't help, you are advised to contact the Technical Support team for your particular game. You can find their telephone number and e-mail address in the readme file in your game directory.

USING COMMAND-LINE SWITCHES DIRECTLY

The simplest way to use a command-line switch to pass a control parameter to DOOM (or one of its clones) is simply to add the appropriate switch to the command you type to start the game. To start DOOM with all sound output disabled, for example, you type this:

```
doom -nosound
```

Here, the `-nosound` command-line switch causes DOOM to disregard its normal configuration file and operate with all music and sound effects turned off.

Command-line switches can be used in combination, like this:

```
heretic -warp 2 3 -nomonsters
```

Here, Heretic is being started at Episode 2, Mission 3 (using the `-warp` switch) with no monsters present.

This method of using command-line switches is simple and easily understood, but it can be tedious, especially if you find yourself using the same command-line switches over and over. In such cases, you should consider one of the alternative methods of using switches.

USING BATCH FILES

If you find yourself using one particular string of parameters quite often, you should consider turning the string into a batch file. For instance, as you develop a WAD file, you will play-test it repeatedly. Typing a 25-character string to start the game can get tiresome, and you will become prone to making typing mistakes. It's much easier to save the string as a batch file and give it a one- or two-letter name, such as this one-line file, which might be saved as A.BAT:

```
doom -file arachno.wad -devparm -warp 3 2
```

With such a file, you can simply type A at the DOS prompt and press Enter, and DOOM starts with an external WAD file called ARACHNO.WAD, at Episode 3, Mission 2. You can use such a file to make your development of this add-on WAD easier. Also, when you've finished your WAD file and you're ready to distribute it, you can include the batch file (renamed to something like ARACHNO.BAT) with the WAD file so that anyone who obtains the WAD can use your batch file to start the game. Not all DOOM players know the correct syntax to load a WAD file successfully, so this technique saves everyone a lot of time and effort.

More information about using external WAD files with DOOM is given in Chapter 3, "Extending DOOM." To learn more about batch files, consult the reference manuals that came with your copy of DOS.

USING RESPONSE FILES

An alternative method of passing parameters to DOOM is to use a response file. This is a text file containing all the parameters you want to pass to the game. A response file can contain up to 100 command-line arguments, which should be more than enough for all practical purposes. Each parameter must be on its own line with a carriage return at the end of the line. The parameters are typed just the same as if you were loading them from the command line. A response file that achieves the same result as the preceding A.BAT batch file example contains these lines:

```
-file arachno.wad
-devparm
-warp 3 2
```

If this file was called, say, A.RSP, you use it to control DOOM by starting the game by typing this:

```
doom @a.rsp
```

Unlike batch files, which must have a .BAT extension, response files can be given any extension you want. Only v1.4 of DOOM and later (plus all versions of the other game variants) will work with response files. They are useful if you are working with a number of different variants of the game and want a convenient way to start any one of them in your favorite configuration.

> **TIP:** You can usually achieve maximum flexibility by using batch and response files in combination.

USING FRONT-END UTILITIES

If the very thought of typing strange and unmemorable commands at the DOS prompt or creating bizarre and esoteric text files fills you with dread, you will probably be happier accessing DOOM command-line switches through the agency of some front-end utility. The DM utility supplied with DOOM (and all of its clones) is one such front end designed to simplify the launch of Deathmatch and Cooperative play sessions.

Other third-party utilities provide access to most of the other command-line switches. You can find details of one such utility supplied with this book in Chapter 5, "Playing New Levels."

CAUTION: Be warned that whichever of the preceding methods you choose to use, you might be thwarted in your attempt to pass command-line switches to DOOM if there are intervening batch files in use in your particular setup. If you find that your command-line parameters are persistently ignored by DOOM, check that any batch files that are handling your commands are utilizing the replaceable parameters (%1, %2, and so on) responsibly. Again, consult your DOS manuals for details about batch files and replaceable parameters if you are in doubt.

AVAILABLE COMMAND-LINE SWITCHES

This section provides full details of all of DOOM's available command-line switches and the parameters they pass to DOOM.

NOTE: Not all command-line switches are available (nor do those available work the same way) in all versions of DOOM. This section details only the way in which switches work in v1.666 of the game and later.

The command-line switches can be divided into a few categories:

- General configuration control switches
- Multiplayer game control switches
- Developers' control switches
- Demo control switches

You are free to mix any number of switches from any number of categories.

GENERAL CONFIGURATION CONTROL SWITCHES

The command-line options for controlling the general configuration of DOOM are listed in Table 2.1. They make DOOM ignore the configuration file created when the SETUP program was run. They are useful if you just want to change some of the setup parameters temporarily and don't want to run SETUP to do it.

Table 2.1. DOOM's general configuration command-line switches.

Switch	Function
@filename	Specifies a response file from which more command-line options should be read and acted on.
-avg	Restricts operation of the game to 20 minutes. Useful for tournament play. (See also the -timer option.)

Switch	Function
-cdrom	Tells the game that it is running from CD-ROM, causing it to read its configuration and saved game files from a directory on drive C, rather than the directory containing the game. (Works only with variants of the game that can be supplied on CD-ROM.)
-config filename	Loads an alternative configuration file. This is mainly for playing the game from a remote network drive, where different machines connected to the drive require different configuration files to be used.
-episode episodeNo	Causes the game to begin straight at the first mission of the specified episode number, without waiting for the player to access the New Game menu (valid only for DOOM and Heretic). The episodeNo used should be in the range of 1 to 3 (4 is also allowed in Ultimate DOOM).
-file wadname	Causes the game to load the specified PWAD file. This name must be complete with the .WAD extension, and a path must be included if the file is not in the same directory as the game. Chapter 3 contains more information about loading and using external PWAD files.
-loadgame game_number	Causes the game to load and start a saved game from the specified Save Game slot. Valid game_numbers are 0–5. Note that games saved from one version of DOOM cannot be loaded into other versions.
-nojoy	Disables use of the joystick.
-nomouse	Disables use of the mouse.
-nomusic	Turns off the music.
-nosfx	Turns off the special-effects sound (such as your gun firing, as well as all the sounds that monsters make).
-nosound	Turns off all sound.
-timer minutes	Causes the game to exit the current level after the specified number of minutes. This option is used for tournaments, in which each player or group is given the same length of time in which to compete.
-turbo boost	Increases the speed at which the player moves while playing the game. Valid numbers are 0–250. This switch is intended for use in Deathmatch; other players are notified of your speed boost. Note that the use of this option in single-player games is regarded as cheating!

SWITCHES TO CONTROL MULTIPLAYER GAMES

The options for controlling the operation of multiplayer games are listed in Table 2.2. These options are frequently combined with options from other categories.

Table 2.2. DOOM's multiplayer game control switches.

Switch	Function
-altdeath	Starts Deathmatch using DM v2.0 rules. These rules make all the items such as health kits, ammunition, and armor respawn 30 seconds after they are taken by a player. The Invulnerability Artifacts and Blur Artifacts do not respawn. This makes it possible to play a single level for an infinite amount of time without running out of ammo or health. The new Deathmatch rules also make committing suicide illegal, and you receive a negative frag for doing this. The old rules permitted you to commit suicide if you were low on health to keep your opponent from being able to kill you easily. (This switch does nothing in Heretic, because Heretic operates with DM v2.0 rules all the time.)
-deathmatch	Starts the game in Deathmatch mode. If this option is not used, the game starts in single-player mode unless the -net option has been specified, in which case the game starts in Cooperative mode. The reason you would use this in a single-player game would be to test the Deathmatch start locations.
-net *players*	Starts the game in Multiplayer mode, with the specified number of players. To be valid, *players* must be in the range of 1 to 4. The game starts in Cooperative mode unless the -deathmatch option is also specified.
-nodes *players*	Works as -net. If no *players* parameter is given, DOOM assumes 2.
-port *port_no*	Specifies the port to use, enabling more than one group of players to play over the same network simultaneously.

SWITCHES FOR USE BY DEVELOPERS

The developers' options for controlling the operation of DOOM are listed in Table 2.3. These options are frequently combined with options from other categories.

Table 2.3. DOOM's developers' control switches.

Switch	Function
-debugfile *id*	Causes the game to dump debugging information into a file called debug*id*.txt.
-devparm	Puts DOOM into developer mode. Only in this mode can other command-line developer options be activated in DOOM. In this mode, the game engine continually updates a display of black and white pixels along the very bottom of the display. These indicate the game's current frame rate. This feature was used to check slow-down during play and to test the game on

Switch	Function

various speeds of machines during its development. This option can be used only in DOOM and DOOM II. In the other variants of the game, this switch has been disabled, but the developers' options that it provides access to have been made immediately available.

`-warp episode mission`
`-warp map`

Causes the game engine to start play immediately on entry to the game at the specified level. The first form of the option is used in DOOM or Heretic to select an episode and a mission number. DOOM II and Hexen use the second form of the switch to select the level number. Valid values for each parameter are *episode*, 1–4; *mission*, 1–9 (9 is the secret mission of each episode); *map*, 1–32 (31 and 32 are the secret levels). The `-warp` option must be active before the following command-line switches have any effect:

`-fast`   Causes the monsters to react the way they do in Nightmare mode. They shoot at you and move up to three times faster than normal. It does not affect their respawning, however.

`-nomonsters`   Starts a game without any monsters present. This option is good for debugging single-player levels and for playing Deathmatches when you don't want to be bothered by monsters.

`-respawn`   Causes the monsters to respawn without your playing in Nightmare mode. (This has no effect in Hexen.)

`-skill level`   Selects a skill level at which to start playing, from 1 to 5.

`-class type`   Only available in Hexen, this option selects a player class for the game being started. Permissible values for type are 0=Fighter, 1=Priest, and 2=Mage.

`-wart episode mission`   Causes the game engine to load an external PWAD file called `EepisodeMmission.WAD` from a directory called `\DOOM` on the current drive and then warp straight to the specified episode and mission. This shortcut can be useful when you're developing new levels. It works only in DOOM, and no other game variant.

You learn more about using external PWAD files in the next chapter.

SWITCHES FOR CONTROL OF DEMOS AND SCREEN SHOTS

The final category of command-line switches is those controlling the capture of the action in rolling demo (LMP) files and taking screen shots. This topic is fully covered later in the chapter, but the available command-line switches are summarized in Table 2.4.

Table 2.4. Command-line switches for demo control.

Switch	Function
-devparm	This option must be specified if you want to take snapshots of the screen while playing DOOM or DOOM II. With this option active, the F1 key no longer brings up a help screen, but saves a screen shot to disk. The file is called DOOM*xx*.PCX, in which *xx* is a two-digit number. (The game engine determines the next free number itself each time you press F1.) This switch works only in DOOM and DOOM II; if you want to take screen shots in Heretic and Hexen, use -ravpic instead.
-ravpic	Enables the F1 key to take screen shots in Raven Software's variants of DOOM. The resulting files are called HRTIC*xx*.PCX or HEXEN*xx*.PCX. Obviously, this switch is not used in DOOM or DOOM II.
-maxdemo *size*	Specifies the size in kilobytes of a demo file that you record. If you don't specify a -maxdemo size, the demo defaults to 128K.
-playdemo *filename*	Plays back a previously recorded demo LMP file. You don't need to include the .LMP extension in the filename.
-record *filename*	Causes the game engine to record the next game you play until either the amount of memory specified using -maxdemo is reached or you die or quit the game. The recording is made to the specified file. You don't need to include the .LMP extension in the filename.
-recordfrom *slot filename*	Causes the game to record a demo from the specified saved game slot (0–5) into the specified .LMP file.
-timedemo *filename*	Causes the game engine to play back the specified demo file, calculating its length. When you return to DOS, the game reports two numbers, GAMETICS and REALTICS. The game frame-rate can be calculated from the formula (GAMETICS÷REALTICS)×35.

MAKING PROGRESS

The preceding section looked at the command-line options available for changing the way the DOOM engine starts. Sometimes, though, you might want to change the way the game operates while you are playing it. To allow this kind of control, DOOM's programmers built in access to certain special developers' modes.

THE DEVELOPERS' MODES

During the development of a computer game, there are times when a designer needs to check out one particular aspect of the way a design plays without having other aspects of play complicate matters. To facilitate this need, programmers add codes to the game that access certain game features or turn others off. Often, these codes are not removed when the game makes it onto the market; they are merely kept secret. Gamers call these codes *cheat codes* because as well as serving their intended purpose of aiding the developer, they can be used to provide a player with an unfair advantage, allowing the game to be completed much faster.

DOOM and its clones all have the original developers' codes left active for you to use. Each variant uses different codes and in slightly different ways. Before telling you what all of these codes are, though, I will describe the effects that you can achieve by using them.

BECOMING INVINCIBLE

In God mode (also known as Degreelessness), the player can never be harmed by anything during play. You can use this mode to observe the way monsters or other harmful elements of the game behave without constantly having to battle to stay alive long enough to watch! This is handy for examining the way large groupings of monsters act. DOOM notifies you (and anyone watching) that you are playing in this mode by changing the player's status picture at the bottom of the screen, as shown in Figure 2.1. Just look at those eyes! (Of course, you can also use this mode to romp your way to the end of each and every level of the game, but personally, I don't see the point. Do you want to play DOOM or don't you?)

Figure 2.1.
Playing in God mode.

ACQUIRING GOODIES

DOOM and DOOM II's Very Happy Ammo code provides a player with all keys, full health, weapons, and ammo. This mode enables you to check out areas of a WAD without having to visit the places that would normally provide the means of opening intermediary doors and gathering weapons and ammunition. Raven Software's variants of the game require the use of several codes, each handling the acquisition of keys, health, and ammunition separately. (DOOM allows the chainsaw to be acquired separately from the other weapons—just why is a complete mystery to me!)

I suppose you could also use these codes if I'm Too Young To Die is too hard for you!

 Heretic has a separate code to invoke Power-up mode. This works exactly as though the player had just used Tyketto's Tome of Power.

In addition to the codes for acquiring full-scale armament, each game has codes for acquiring other power-ups during play. Obtaining specific individual artifacts in this way is useful for testing how these power-ups contribute to the flow of the game. This speeds the development of a WAD because it helps the WAD designer try out different combinations of artifacts without having to constantly change their layout in the map.

NO CLIPPING

When No Clipping is turned on, the game suspends all player collision detection, enabling you to walk through solid walls and other objects. In this mode the player cannot interact with any of the DOOM environment. Doors, lifts, and switches cannot be activated, and no objects can be picked up. This mode is useful for quick dashes from one area to another, without the bother of sticking to passageways, but it has little practical use beyond that.

INCREASING MAP INFORMATION

Another useful developers' code is one that provides increased information while you're viewing the game's auto-map. The first time this code is used, the game engine shows the entire map regardless of how much of the level the player has actually seen. The map displays all lines as if the player had seen them (not the way they would appear if the all-map power-up were to be used). If you type the code a second time, all objects (monsters, obstacles, missiles, and so on) show up on the map also. This second mode is handy for observing the way monsters track the player through a level so that you can refine their placement or the shape and layout of corridors and so on. Type the code a third time to return the map to normal.

WARPING AROUND

When testing a multiple-level WAD file, you can use the Warp code to warp straight to the start of that level. By using this code, the developer can check out many different levels without having to complete preceding levels or restart the game.

Another effect of this code is to reload the specified level from disk. This is handy if you are working in a multitasking environment with DOOM running at the same time as an external WAD file editor. In such an environment, this code makes it possible to switch back to the editor to fix an error noticed during play and then switch back to DOOM and reload the level without restarting the game. Hexen makes this operation even easier with its additional code to re-initialize the current level.

OBTAINING YOUR LOCATION

The Report Location code causes the player's exact location to appear on the screen as a hexadecimal display of the game coordinates of the player's center-spot. It is of little practical use, although it can be used to report the location of display or design faults in areas that are without convenient landmarks. This code is most likely a debugging code left behind from the early development stages of the game.

CLEARING MONSTERS (HERETIC AND HEXEN)

Heretic and Hexen have codes for clearing all monsters from a level. These are handy if you forget to specify -nomonsters at the command line. They're also pretty satisfying to use!

CHANGING THE PLAYER (HERETIC AND HEXEN)

Heretic also has a code to turn the player into a chicken. Hexen has an equivalent that turns the player into a pig. Don't laugh—automorphing is bound to come in handy one day! In Hexen there is also a code to enable the player to change class during play—useful for checking out how parts of a level play for each player class without having to start the level over.

ADDITIONAL MISCELLANEOUS CODES

To make up for the lack of frame-rate information in Heretic and Hexen (because of the removal of the -devparm command-line switch) these games provide an additional code (ticker) to access this information, should you ever need it. The code is really intended for use by the games' programmers, but it is useful to gain a quantitative measure of how fast (or otherwise) your level is playing. Levels with more scenery to display and more monsters to move around play slower than less open levels with fewer monsters.

Hexen also lets you activate a script from a keyboard code, provided that you know its number (this must be typed immediately after the code). Hexen's scripts are the subject of "Hexen's Scripting Language," a chapter on the CD-ROM.

Hexen's *noise* code provides additional information about the game sound settings.

NOTE: You will see examples of the way the more important codes are used to help the WAD developer in later chapters of this book.

THE DEVELOPERS' CODES

Table 2.5 shows the codes that you can use in each major game variant to access the various modes that have just been described. To activate any of these codes during the game, simply type it while playing. You don't need to press Enter after any of them. To deactivate a cheat code, you can usually just retype the code.

Table 2.5. Developer mode access (cheat) codes.

Mode	DOOM	DOOM II	Heretic	Hexen
God mode	iddqd	iddqd	quicken	satan
Very happy ammo	idkfa	idkfa	–	–
All weapons	–	idfa	rambo	nra
Acquire chainsaw	idchoppers	idchoppers	–	–
All keys	–	–	skel	locksmith
Full health	–	–	ponce	clubmed
Acquire item	idbehold	idbehold	gimme	indiana
All puzzle pieces	–	–	–	sherlock
No clipping	idspispopd	idclip	kitty	casper
Map information	iddt	iddt	ravmap	mapsco
Warp	idclev	idclev	engage	visit
Restart level	–	–	–	init
Report location	idmypos	idmypos	–	–
Kill all	–	–	massacre	butcher
Power-up	–	–	shazam	–
Run script	–	–	–	puke
Change class	–	–	–	shadowcaster
Automorph	–	–	cockadoodledoo	deliverance
Frame rate check	–	–	ticker	ticker
Sound information	–	–	–	noise

Some of these codes require additional typing to achieve anything. The Warp code, for example, needs two digits after it. In DOOM and Heretic, these two digits are interpreted as an episode and a mission number (in that order). In DOOM II and Hexen, the two digits specify a level number directly.

The item acquisition codes also require that you press extra keys after entering the code to indicate which item you want. Table 2.6 shows which keys are used to obtain specific items in each game variant.

Table 2.6. Code keys used to acquire items.

Key	Item Acquired
DOOM/DOOM II Items (Accessed with `idbehold`)	
S	Berserk Pack
I	Invisibility (Blur) Artifact
V	Invulnerability Artifact
A	Computer Map
R	Radiation Suit
L	Light Amplification Visor
Heretic Items (Accessed with `gimme`)	
A	Valador's Ring of Invisibility
B	Shadowsphere
C	Quartz Flask
D	Mystic Urn
E	Tyketto's Tome of Power
F	Torch
G	Delmintalitar's Time Bomb of the Ancients
H	Torpol's Morph Ovum
I	Inhilicon's Wings of Wrath
J	Darchala's Chaos Device

The Hexen `indiana` code gives the player 25 of every available artifact.

In Raven Software's games, acquiring an item does not automatically activate it; the item is merely added to the player's inventory for later use. This is equally true if the item is acquired using the developers' acquisition code. Additionally, this variant of the game engine prompts for a numerical key to be pressed after the item code has been entered. This number specifies how many of the chosen items to add to the current inventory.

Take care not to use DOOM cheat codes in Heretic because they can have some disastrous consequences. No, I'm not going to tell you—you'll have to find out for yourself!

RECORDING YOUR PROWESS

This final section on running DOOM is concerned with capturing evidence of your gaming prowess. You might want to do this to prove a point to your friends, provide a demonstration of some playing technique, or simply change the rolling demonstration that plays when no one else is playing.

If you have access to CompuServe or a similar online service, you've probably noticed some demo files that have been uploaded. These files include everything from demos of people playing through a whole level using nothing but their fists to examples of how to defeat the Final Boss of Level 30 in DOOM II. Also available are multiplayer demo files that help determine who's the better of two players and establish who owns the bragging rights.

You can make two kinds of recordings:

- Static screen shots
- Running demos

The latter type is the more common (very little can be done with a static screen shot, after all).

TAKING SCREEN SHOTS

Taking a screen shot is easy in DOOM: You just have to remember to turn developer mode on with the `-devparm` (or `-ravpic` in Raven Software's games) command-line switch. After you've done this, a single press of the F1 key is enough to record the current screen to disk in 256-color PCX format. Naming of the files is handled automatically by the game engine; see Table 2.4 earlier in this chapter for details.

NOTE: DOOM records the image as it would appear without any gamma correction. Raven Software's games apply the level of gamma correction in use at the time F1 is pressed.

RECORDING DEMOS

You have already seen that a command-line switch is used to cause the game engine to record a game session. A typical recording string is something like the following:

```
doom -record filename
```

This command makes a recording with a size of 128K, the DOOM default. The recording you make is stored in a file with a .LMP extension (you don't need to type this as part of the *filename* you specify to DOOM). When the recording reaches its predesignated size, the game quits back to DOS. Alternatively, you can stop the recording at any time by pressing Q or F10. If you want to make a longer recording, you can add the `-maxdemo` parameter to the end of the command line to specify a size in kilobytes.

```
doom -record filename -maxdemo 1024
```

This command permits the recording of a 1M demo file of approximately one hour in duration.

> **CAUTION:** If you use `-maxdemo` and DOOM crashes to DOS with a `Z_MALLOC` error, you don't have enough memory for the size of the demo file you specified. You need to decrease the `-maxdemo` size.

If you're recording a Deathmatch, both players must use the same command-line parameters for the recording to work. The game ends for both players when the recording stops.

PLAYING BACK DEMOS

To play back a demo, use the `-playdemo` command-line switch like this:

```
doom -playdemo filename
```

If the demo is a recording of a Deathmatch, you can see the other player's view of the game by pressing F12.

> **CAUTION:** A demo will only play back correctly if you use identical versions of both the game *and* the WAD file that were used to record it.

DISTRIBUTING DEMOS WITH PWAD FILES

A good way of showing off a WAD you have designed and built yourself is to record a demo of it and incorporate the demo in the WAD. This demo then takes the place of the built-in demo that runs before you start playing DOOM. It's a good way to demonstrate your WAD file before people play it. You can also reveal a few of the level's secrets in the demo file if you want to.

Details of how to go about incorporating demos in your own WAD files are given in a later chapter after you've learned some more about the WAD files themselves.

EXIT: MOPPING UP AND MOVING ON

This chapter provides details of how DOOM's operation can be controlled through command-line switches at startup or by developers' (cheat) codes during play. It also shows how recordings can be made of play in progress.

The next chapter examines how the DOOM experience can be prolonged by extending DOOM itself with add-on PWAD files.

3

EXTENDING DOOM

So you've played DOOM through to the end. You've played it through to the end again, this time in Nightmare mode. So that's it, is it? You've seen all that DOOM has to offer? Wrong! The fun is just starting.

One of the greatest things the designers of this game did was to make the format of its data files open to other designers, encouraging the development of add-ons for it. This chapter shows you how to extend your copy of DOOM, explaining how you can tap into a virtually limitless supply of (free!) extra levels. It also shows you the possibilities for you to contribute to the flood of add-ons yourself. Finally, it outlines the kinds of changes you can make to personalize the way DOOM plays for you. After reviewing the contents of this chapter, you will start to appreciate what a complete game DOOM is.

ADD-ON LEVELS

From the outset, DOOM was designed with extendability in mind. Its underlying data files are structured to make adding to them easy. These data files are termed WAD files (probably because they contain great wads of data). This review of DOOM's extendability begins with an examination of just what WAD files are and how they are used.

WAD FILES: WHAT ARE THEY?

There are two basic kinds of WAD files:

- IWAD (Initial WAD) files
- PWAD (Patch WAD) files

The internal structures of these two kinds of WAD files are essentially identical. All that varies is the way the game engine uses them.

— By Steve Benner

THE IWAD FILES

The IWAD files are the main data files used by the game engine. In fact, for any given version or variant of DOOM, there is only ever *one* IWAD file. This file, supplied by the game designers, is placed in your main game directory by the installation program. This very large file contains virtually all the data for every level of the game. The IWAD file that comes with DOOM is about 11M in size. Hexen's IWAD is over 20M! Every time the game starts, it expects to have access to this file.

PWAD FILES

Patch WAD files are files supplied by other designers to supply additional information to the game engine. Ordinarily, no patch WAD is in use. You can make the game engine use one, however, by starting it with the `-file` command-line switch, as explained in Chapter 2, "Running DOOM." When this switch is specified, DOOM first locates and reads its particular IWAD file. It then reads the PWAD files specified after the `-file` command-line switch, using the information in this file to supplement (patch) the information found in the IWAD.

This scheme enables PWAD files to be kept reasonably small because they contain only the information that is to be changed. Further economies in the size of PWAD files are made by organizing information in a clever way so that even a small amount of patch information can make a big difference in what the game engine displays.

WAD CONTENTS

Full details of the use of PWADs to construct your own levels are given later in this book (Episode 2, Mission 1, "A Hell of Your Very Own"), but it is worth an overview here of just what WAD files contain. This information should give you a better feel for what you can—and cannot—achieve by manipulating them.

In essence, WAD files contain all the information necessary to tell the game engine how the game world is arranged and how that world should be drawn on-screen. To achieve this, a WAD contains the following information:

- Map layout information, organized by level
- Object layout information, organized by level
- Music
- Sound effects
- Pictures of wall, floor, and ceiling textures
- Pictures of objects (sprites)
- Supporting screens (help and inter-level screens, and so on)

As already noted, the main IWAD file contains all the information required to play the standard game, so it contains all the preceding items of information. (Perhaps now you see why it is so big!) Patch WAD files need to contain only the information they are changing. Typically, this is only map and object layout information, although it is possible to add new music and sound effects to a WAD also. Note, incidentally, how this elegant scheme removes any need to distribute any bulky pictorial information in a PWAD file. Provided that you are happy to use the graphics supplied with the game, you need distribute no graphics in your own PWADs at all. It is possible to substitute your own graphics, however, should you want to. Figure 3.1, for example, shows Steve McCrea's all-new wall textures in his TRINITY.WAD, and Figure 3.2 shows some of Bill Neisius's replacement monster sprites in action.

Figure 3.1.

All-new surface textures in TRINITY.WAD.

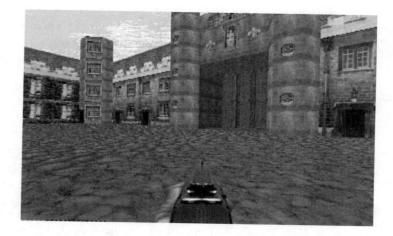

Figure 3.2.

PacDOOM sprite replacements in action.

NOTE: Because of the wide range of information types that WAD files can hold, many utility programs exist for the manipulation of these files. Some of the best of these have been assembled on the CD-ROM that accompanies this book. You will find details of what the CD-ROM contains and how to access it in Chapter 4, "Using the CD-ROM."

USING PWADS

You have already seen that to make DOOM add a PWAD file to the main IWAD, you need only start the game with the -file command-line switch. In fact, this switch enables you to add any number of WADs with each successive WAD contributing its own set of patches. To do this, simply list the names of the files you want to use after the -file switch:

```
doom -file mywad.wad wad2.wad d:\wads\space.wad
```

In this example, DOOM adds the WADs MYWAD.WAD and WAD2.WAD from the same directory as DOOM and SPACE.WAD from the \WADS directory on drive D. These three WADs might contain information about different levels, replacing three of the game's standard levels, for instance. On the other hand, one might hold information about a level, whereas another contains replacement sounds, and the third replaces just part of the standard game, such as the player's face in the status bar.

An alternative method of loading PWAD files is to utilize a front-end utility program (or launcher). Such programs simplify the process of starting DOOM with a PWAD by enabling you to build and maintain lists of your favorite add-on levels and start these with a click of a mouse or the press of a single key. Chapter 5, "Playing New Levels," covers this topic in more detail and shows you how to access the add-on levels supplied on the CD-ROM that accompanies this book.

 CAUTION: You should be able to see that because of the way PWAD files operate, it is not a good idea to load a PWAD file designed for use with one variant of the game into a different variant. Attempting to do this creates references to resources that the game engine cannot resolve. The result is a crash back to DOS or a total lockup of your computer.

HACKING THE EXECUTABLE

Although the PWAD add-on scheme is very flexible, certain aspects of the game still remain unalterable through WAD patches. Some of the game's controlling data remains buried deep in the heart of the main DOOM.EXE executable file. Fortunately, many of the more interesting items of information have been located and identified, and utility programs exist to enable you to tinker with this data, changing the way DOOM plays.

WHAT CAN BE CHANGED?

Many things can be changed by altering the information contained in the data sector of the DOOM executable. These are the important ones:

- Basic characteristics of monsters and game artifacts
- Basic characteristics of weapons
- Animation (frame) sequences for game actions
- Game-time text messages

There are no doubt others, as yet undiscovered. A more detailed introduction to changing the data in the DOOM executable file can be found in Chapter 6, "Hacking It." This subject also features prominently in Episode 2, Mission 2, "Towards the Land of the Gods."

> **CAUTION:** Note that if you change the data within the DOOM executable file, you are not making a temporary alteration to the game data, as is done when you're playing external PWADs. Instead, you are changing the fundamental way that DOOM operates. The effects of such alterations will manifest themselves in *all* subsequent games you play with the altered version of the game until you restore the altered data. Be sure, therefore, that you have a copy of the original version of the executable put away somewhere safely, in case you need to reinstall it.

EXIT: MOPPING UP AND MOVING ON

This first mission of the book provides an introduction to the phenomenon of DOOM and shows how much more there is to it than merely the game itself. You are shown its history, evolution, and a brief glimpse of its future. You see the range of playing options provided and the means at your disposal for changing them. Finally, you learn about DOOM's extendibility and see its potential for adaptation.

In the next mission, the attention turns to the CD-ROM—*Alchemy*—that accompanies this book. You briefly look at the range of add-ons for DOOM contained on the disc, and you are shown how to get the most from these and from the remaining missions in this book.

USING THE CD-ROM

The previous mission of this episode was concerned entirely with DOOM and its successors. In this mission, I turn the attention away from DOOM itself for a little while and concentrate on the CD-ROM and the book. You learn how they can enhance your enjoyment of the game and provide you with many hours of gore-soaked pleasure.

In this chapter, you find out how to install all the software from the *Alchemy* CD-ROM. Whether you want to play or edit game levels, you must first install software from the CD-ROM.

Most of the tools and utilities are DOS-based. You install these through a DOS installation menu program. The registered version of WadAuthor is a Windows program, as are some of the other editing tools; you install these programs from within Windows.

DOS INSTALLATION

The DOS installation menu enables you to install the DOS-based software to your hard drive. This software includes the following:

- DoomShell, the graphical interface that enables you to easily play game levels from the CD-ROM
- WADED, the DOS level editor used in most of the book's editing lessons
- The sample WAD files used in the level-building lessons
- The *Alchemy* graphics library from Justin Fisher
- Other level editing and hacking utilities

Insert the *Alchemy* disc in your CD-ROM drive and follow these steps to run the DOS installation menu.

— By Steve Benner and
Wayne Blankenbeckler

NOTE: The DOS menu program is a graphical application. It requires the use of a mouse. Most systems are set up to automatically load mouse drivers upon startup. If your system doesn't automatically load these drivers, load them before running the program. See your system manual for more information if you're not sure how to load your mouse drivers.

1. From the DOS prompt, change to the drive that contains the CD-ROM disk. For example, if the disc is in drive D, type **D:** and press Enter.

2. Type **INSTALL** and press Enter.

3. The DOS installation menu appears. The initial screen contains buttons for the various programs and categories of software on the CD-ROM. Click any of these buttons to proceed with your selection.

4. When you choose to install a program or files to your hard drive, a separate installation program begins. You can choose the hard drive where the files are installed.

5. After the installation of your selection is complete, you are returned to the installation menu program. To exit, click the Exit button or press the Esc key.

If you've installed DoomShell to play levels from the CD-ROM, go to Chapter 5, "Playing New Levels," for more information on using this software. If you installed WADED or another level utility, go to Chapter 6, "Hacking It," for more information on where to start in the book.

NOTE: Be sure to read the Read Me First file in the root directory of the CD-ROM. It contains important information about the disc including any late-breaking information that might not be in this book. Windows users, open the \README.WRI file. DOS users, open the \README file.

WINDOWS INSTALLATION

To install the registered version of WadAuthor and other Windows-based software, insert the *Alchemy* disc in your CD-ROM drive and follow these directions:

NOTE: If you're running Windows 95 and you have the Autoplay feature enabled, the setup program automatically starts after you insert the disc in your drive.

Windows 95 users: Double-click the My Computer icon on your desktop. Double-click the icon for your CD-ROM drive and then double-click the SETUP.EXE program.

Windows 3.1x users: From the Windows Program Manager menu, choose File | Run. Type **x:\SETUP** and press Enter, where *x* is the letter of your CD-ROM drive. For example, if the disc is in drive D, type **D:\SETUP** and press Enter.

Follow the on-screen instructions in the setup program. WadAuthor is automatically installed unless you deselect this option during the installation. You also have the option of installing other Windows tools. A program group named Doom Alchemy is created when the setup program has finished.

For more information on where to start learning about level editing, see Chapter 6, "Hacking It."

ORGANIZATION OF THE CD-ROM

The CD-ROM is organized into a number of subdirectories, reflecting the different types of files contained on it. You don't need the following information on the contents of the CD-ROM to play game levels or install any of the programs; the DOS or Windows installation programs enable you to easily do these things.

- **WadAuthor**—Installation files are in the \WAUTHOR directory.
- **WADED**—Installation files are in the \WADED directory.
- **DoomShell 5**—Installation files are in the \DSHELL directory.
- **WAD files (game levels)**—These game levels are arranged in directories according to the game they are designed for: \DOOM, \DOOM2, \HERETIC, and \HEXEN. In each of these directories are subdirectories named DMATCH, COOP, and PATCH. These subdirectories contain game levels designed for Deathmatch or Cooperative play and patches for selected WADs. To find out more about how to play the WADs straight from the CD-ROM, turn to the next chapter, "Playing New Levels." If you're one of those more discerning readers who would like to dive straight into the *very best* of the WADs, then you might want to review Chapter 38, "Worthy WADs," before looking at Chapter 5 and making a start.
- *Alchemy* **graphics library**—This specially produced library of graphics is available to owners of this book for adding to their game level creations. The files are located in the \LIBRARY directory.
- **Utilities**—The special utility programs discussed in the book, and many that aren't discussed, are organized in subdirectories beneath the \UTILS directory. You will find a file called INDEX.TXT in this directory, giving a full list of the programs included.
- **Sample WAD files from lessons:** The \SAMPLES directory contains all the sample WADs and other files referenced throughout Episode 2, "Creating Your Own DOOM." You will find these files in subdirectories arranged by chapter. You can copy these files to your hard disk from the DOS menu program or access them directly from the CD-ROM. See Chapter 5, "Playing New Levels," for information on manually opening and playing a single WAD file.
- **Extra Documentation**—The \XTRADOCS directory contains special documentation for several editing and utility programs, written especially for this book by the authors of the programs. These documents are in Adobe Acrobat format; the Acrobat reader is included on the CD-ROM. See the section titled "Installing Acrobat Reader" for more information.

NOTE: In addition to the files and programs discussed in this book, the CD-ROM includes many other useful utilities and reference files. See the README.WRI file (Windows) or README file (DOS) for complete information on the CD-ROM's contents.

All other directories on the disc can be ignored; they contain software for the menu programs that ease the process of installing software from the CD-ROM.

INSTALLING ACROBAT READER

To read the special documentation provided in the \XTRADOCS directory, you need to install the Adobe Acrobat Reader software that's included on the CD-ROM.

I recommend that you install and use the Windows version of the Reader, if at all possible, because it is superior to the DOS version. Run the ACROREAD.EXE program in the \ACROBAT\WINDOWS directory to install this software.

To install the DOS version of the Reader, change to the \ACROBAT\DOS directory on the CD-ROM and run the INSTALL.EXE program from a DOS prompt.

The \ACROBAT directory contains a simple tutorial on using Acrobat Reader in Windows Write format only. This tutorial is also available from the Acrobat Reader help menu.

EXIT: MOPPING UP AND MOVING ON

Now that you know what can be found on the CD-ROM, you should have a better idea of which section of this book to turn to next. Here is a summary:

- To find out more about the best WADs on the CD-ROM, look at Chapter 38, "Worthy WADs."
- To find out how to play the WADs on the CD-ROM, look at Chapter 5, "Playing New Levels."
- To find out about the DOOM editing utilities and how to start using them, turn to Chapter 6, "Hacking It."

PLAYING NEW LEVELS

This chapter provides details on how to play the add-on levels from the *Alchemy* CD-ROM.

You will find all the WADs on the CD-ROM located in sensibly named subdirectories—\DOOM, \DOOM2, \HERETIC, and \HEXEN. If you want, you can play most of them by starting DOOM with the `-file` command-line parameter, as explained in Chapter 3, "Extending DOOM." However, this is the difficult way.

The DoomShell 5 program, specially created for this book, enables you to easily play any level from the CD-ROM with the click of a button. You can also set parameters such as "No Monsters," choose the mission and level to start, and much more.

You can also use DoomShell to play with (or against) friends. You can control all aspects of the game prior to startup with its single, easily operated control panel. Using DoomShell, you'll never need to remember a single command-line option ever again! Of course, DoomShell is already aware of the multitude of levels contained on the *Alchemy* CD-ROM, so it can quickly tell you about and launch you into any new level that takes your fancy.

INSTALLING DOOMSHELL

Getting DoomShell up and running is as easy as using it. Simply run the DOS installation menu (see the preceding chapter for details). Click the Install DoomShell 5 button, and the installation program begins.

If you're the curious type and you insist on manually installing software, you can run the INSTALL.EXE program in the \DSHELL directory. You need to have your mouse active before you run this installation program; see your system manual if you're not sure how to load your mouse drivers.

— By Steve Benner and Wayne Blankenbeckler

1. The first thing you see is an introductory screen. Click the Proceed button.

2. Next, you are asked where you want to install the software. The default is C:\DOOMSHEL. If you want to install to a different location, type it in the text entry box. Click the Install button when you're ready to proceed.

3. You see a message informing you when the files have been installed.

 NOTE: This special version of DoomShell is not freeware or public domain; it is only for purchasers of this product. It cannot be distributed in any way except on the *Alchemy* CD-ROM.

STARTING DOOMSHELL

Once DoomShell is installed on your hard disk, follow these steps to start it:

1. From the DOS prompt, change to the drive where you installed the software. If you installed to the default location, type **c:** and press Enter.

2. Change to the directory where DoomShell is installed. If you chose the default location, type **CD \DOOMSHEL** and press Enter.

3. Type **SHELL** and press Enter.

 CAUTION: Do not start DoomShell by running the DOOMSHEL.EXE; the program will not work properly with DOOM or other games if you do this.

The first time you start DoomShell, it displays a configuration screen. The screen asks you to confirm the drive letter of your CD-ROM drive. DoomShell automatically tries to detect this letter; if it's correct, click the OK button. If not, type the correct letter and click OK.

 NOTE: If you ever need to change this configuration setting, start the program by typing **SHELL -s** (the -s parameter must be lowercase). This enables you to reset the CD-ROM drive setting.

Next, you need to tell DoomShell where your copies of the games are kept. To do this, click the Game button in DoomShell's main control window (see Figure 5.1).

Figure 5.1.

DoomShell's main control window.

Game button

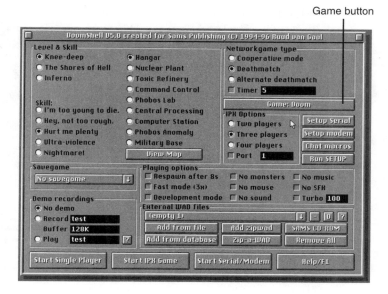

Clicking the Game button brings up the game selection window shown in Figure 5.2. If the right-hand side of this window does not show the correct location of the games you want to play, click the name of one that is wrong and then click the Locate button to bring up the locate window shown in Figure 5.3. Use this window to locate the main executable file of the particular game you have selected (DOOM.EXE, DOOM2.EXE, HERETIC.EXE, or HEXEN.EXE) and then click OK. This returns you to the game selection window, where you can repeat the operation for any other games that you have.

Figure 5.2.

DoomShell's game selection window.

Figure 5.3.

DoomShell's game location window.

Once you've told DoomShell where to find all the game variants you want to use, click the Select button in the game selection window to select the one you'd like to use first. DoomShell returns you to its main control window.

 TIP: If you need help with using DoomShell, click the Help button on the main screen or press the F1 key. This displays a help file that contains information on using DoomShell, cheat codes for the games, solutions to common problems, and more.

PLAYING THE LEVELS ON THE CD-ROM

To play the levels on the CD-ROM from DoomShell, you should first select the game variant you want to play, as just described, and then click the Sams CD-ROM button. When you do this, another window appears from which you can choose the type of game you want to play—Single Player, Cooperative, or Deathmatch (see Figure 5.4).

Figure 5.4.

Using DoomShell to access the DOOM II Deathmatch WADs from the CD-ROM.

When you've made your choice from this window, DoomShell presents you with a list of add-on levels in the chosen category for the selected game. In addition to the name of the WAD, the list provides a brief description to help you better identify the levels. Figure 5.5 shows Necromania highlighted.

Figure 5.5.

A selection of WADs ready for play.

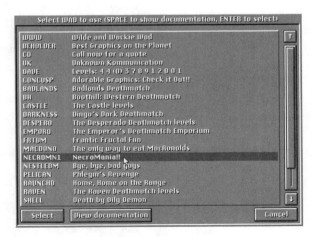

You can move the highlight bar using the cursor up and down keys or click an entry with the mouse. Scroll buttons on the right side of the list enable you to scroll up or down through the list.

If you'd like to know more about a level than the short description gives in this window, move the highlight bar to the WAD that takes your fancy and click the Show Documentation button or double-click the WAD listing. DoomShell presents the WAD author's documentation file for you to browse (see Figure 5.6).

Figure 5.6.
Browsing Necromania's documentation in DoomShell.

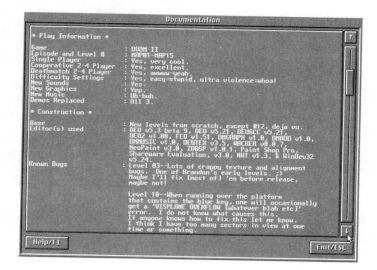

Click the Exit/Esc button to return to the WAD selection window. To select a WAD to play, move the highlight bar and click the Select button (or press Enter). DoomShell returns you to its main control window with the chosen WAD added to the play list (see Figure 5.7).

Figure 5.7.
Necromania ready to play in DoomShell's main control window.

The selected WAD file, ready for play

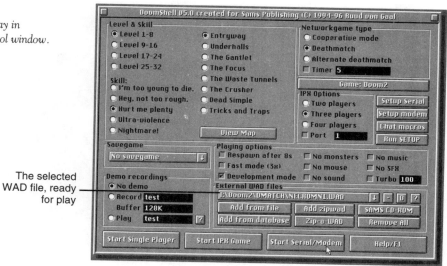

From the main control window, you can select any of the game's startup settings (described in detail in Chapter 2, "Running DOOM"), choose which map in the WAD file you'd like to play, or even preview a map—see Figure 5.8. (You wouldn't use this feature of DoomShell to cheat, now, would you?)

Figure 5.8.
Previewing the layout of a DOOM II level with DoomShell.

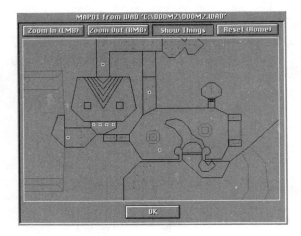

When you're ready to play, click one of the principal play buttons along the bottom of the screen to start the type of play you want—Single Player, Networked (IPX), or Modem play. DoomShell starts the game you've chosen with the WAD and settings that you've selected. Off you go; watch out and enjoy yourself.

MAINTAINING A DATABASE OF WADS

When you've finished playing and quit the game, DoomShell once again takes control. If you have just played a WAD for the first time, DoomShell presents you with a form to fill in (see Figure 5.9) to provide the WAD with a DoomShell database entry. This database enables you to keep a record of how you rate each WAD and also makes your favorite WADs more easily accessible for future play.

Figure 5.9.
Recording your rating of a WAD with DoomShell.

Start your database by filling in your comments and the difficulty and overall rating scores that you would give to the WAD you have just played. Click the Record button to file the details away. (You can click the Forget It button if you'd rather not have the WAD's details recorded.)

To recall your database later—to review an entry or select a WAD from it—use the D button on the main control window. Figure 5.10 shows a sample database window.

Figure 5.10.
DoomShell's WAD database window.

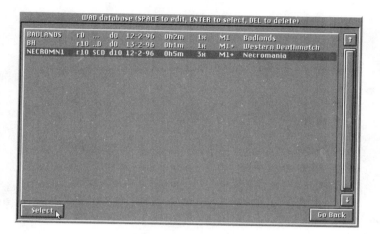

Incidentally, you can use this database feature with any new game level, not just those on the *Alchemy* CD-ROM.

EXIT: MOPPING UP AND MOVING ON

This chapter showed you how to dive straight in and start on the carnage using the DoomShell utility supplied with the *Alchemy* CD-ROM. It also introduced you to DoomShell's capability to build your own database of favorite levels. If you'd like to learn more about what else is on the CD-ROM, just turn to the next chapter.

HACKING IT

This chapter discusses the provision that this book makes for those readers who are interested in the true alchemy of DOOM—the means to make their own DOOM worlds, alter the way DOOM behaves, or work other magic upon their favorite game.

In this chapter, you will find guidance on where to continue your reading and what kinds of utilities are on the *Alchemy* CD-ROM. The chapter will also show you how to install the utility programs from the CD-ROM for use on your computer.

WHERE TO START

There are many changes that you can make to DOOM and countless ways of going about it. The previous chapter showed you the easiest way—simply playing other people's add-on levels. Although this is great fun and can extend the life of the game almost indefinitely, if you do no more than this, you are missing out on the true potential of DOOM and its siblings in building your own add-ons. This is where the product really comes into its own.

The purpose of most of this book is to lead you through the mysteries of DOOM hacking, clearing away the mists that veil the paths to successful DOOM editing and thereby helping you attain the status of Master Alchemist in your own right.

Where to start? The answer hinges on how much you already know and what you want to achieve. To help you decide which part of the book to look at next (or to help you find what you're looking for, if you know what interests you) let us take a look at how this book addresses the needs of each reader.

— *By Steve Benner*

STARTING MAKING LEVELS

If you want to produce your own new levels but have no knowledge of what this entails, then look no further than the next chapter for an introduction to the wonders of the map editor. The chapters that follow throughout the rest of Episode 2, Mission 1, "A Hell of Your Very Own," lead you step by step through the basics of WAD building. At the same time that the theory of DOOM-world construction is presented, a graded series of "WAD sorties" guides you through the practicalities of the art and shows you how to produce working WADs of your own. Figure 6.1 shows a scene from the sample WAD constructed in the WAD sorties (and available on the CD-ROM if you just want to play it instead).

Figure 6.1.
A view of ARENA.WAD, produced in Episode 2, Mission 1 of this book.

MORE ADVANCED EDITING

If, on the other hand, you are already experienced in the art of WAD building and are more interested in advanced editing topics, you should find much to interest you in Episode 2, Mission 2, "Towards the Land of the Gods." This mission covers the more advanced material in a more general way, providing you with some general tips and rough rules to help direct your own experimentation. Turn to this mission for information on the following topics:

- Creating and using your own graphics in DOOM
- Changing the fundamental behavior of the program by hacking at the data in the executable file
- Altering the way monsters react in certain areas of your WADs by introducing reject table tricks
- Creating unusual (and perplexing) visual tricks in your WADs
- Carrying out total conversions on DOOM to create an entirely new DOOM experience
- Designing WADs intended specifically for Deathmatch play

As an advanced user, you might also be interested in checking out Episode 3, "The Tools of the Gods." Here are presented all the major software tools that are supplied on the CD-ROM. You will find them divided up by function:

- Genesis tools—map editors and other tools for creating new DOOM worlds
- Synthesis tools—tools for creating new game elements or behavior beyond the "mere" laying out of a map
- Metamorphosis tools—tools for changing one WAD into another with a minimum of effort

Included in Episode 3 is Chapter 32, "The *Alchemy* Graphics Library," a guide to the exclusive library of DOOM-related graphics that has been prepared especially for this book by Justin Fisher (of *Aliens* TC fame!).

INFORMATION REFERENCE

Even if you are an old hand at DOOM hacking and editing, you will still find much of value in this book; Episode 4, "The Day After the Apocalypse," contains a vast amount of essential reference data. All the special codes and characteristics of DOOM and its game variants are presented in tables for convenient access—just the ticket for those vital editing moments when you need that last little snippet of information. Episode 4 of the book also details where to go out and about on the Internet if you want to collect even more DOOM-related information—and where to go to contribute to it yourself!

INSTALLING THE EDITING SOFTWARE

If you want to use any of the software utilities described in the various sections of this book, you will first need to install them on the hard disk of your computer.

Most of the editing tools and hacking utilities are DOS based. You'll install these through the DOS installation menu. The registered version of WadAuthor is a Windows program, as are some of the other tools; you'll install the Windows programs from within Windows.

For your convenience, all these programs can be installed from an easy-to-use installation program. See Chapter 4, "Using the CD-ROM," for complete instructions on how to install the software under DOS or Windows.

EXIT: MOPPING UP AND MOVING ON

This chapter outlined the structure of those sections of this book concerned with altering DOOM by building your own add-ons. It explained how to install the various utility programs that are provided for carrying out those tasks.

This completes the introductory material of this book. It is now time for the real fun to start, so buckle on your armor or grab your gauntlets. Let's go build some WADs.

EPISODE

MISSION 1: A HELL OF YOUR VERY OWN

MISSION 2: TOWARDS THE LAND OF THE GODS

2

CREATING YOUR OWN DOOM

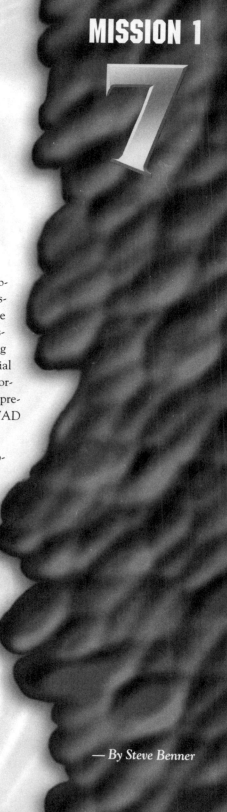

PRELIMINARY RECONNAISSANCE

By now, you should know what DOOM is capable of, and you are probably itching to start building your own hair-raising scenario. In this mission, you will learn how to do just that. This mission's primary objective is to introduce you, through each of its various chapters, to the main aspects of WAD development. This mission starts with the simple laying out of the lines of the map and progresses through each of the essential features of a WAD in turn. Throughout, you will be led on a series of sorties designed not only to enable you to try out for yourself the features presented in the briefings, but also to produce a complete, fully featured WAD of your own.

In this first chapter of this mission, you will find a checklist of the equipment you'll need. You will be shown how to prepare your tools and receive some elementary training in their use. You will also be led on a quick reconnaissance sortie into the domain of the WAD builder.

BEFORE YOU START: CHECKING YOUR KIT

You must have four important things before you can start building your own WADs:

- A copy of DOOM
- The appropriate software editing tools
- A design idea
- A lot of patience

To begin, each of these essentials are looked at in turn.

— By Steve Benner

DOOM ITSELF

Before you can venture forth on a WAD-building expedition, you need, of course, a copy of id Software's DOOM program—the full registered version. The shareware versions are not adequate for PWAD development; they are incomplete. No editors work with these versions, and versions later than v1.4 cannot use PWADs in any case. You can use any major release of the registered version, though. (DOOM v1.2 lacks some of the features added to later revisions and runs up against its limits more quickly than other versions. Many WAD designers still prefer to work with it, however, believing it to have fewer bugs than later releases.) Not surprisingly, id Software recommends the use of the latest version of the game, currently v1.9.

Alternatively, you can work with one of the later DOOM variants—DOOM II, Heretic, or Hexen. Throughout the chapters of this mission, you can usually assume that any reference to DOOM applies equally to all variants. When this is not the case, note boxes for specific variants detail the differences.

NOTE: The sample WADs that are developed during the course of this mission assume that you are using at least v1.2 of DOOM. The additional features provided by the later revisions of the game are covered in the text but are not included in the examples, although particular instances in which the newer features could be employed are mentioned in passing. If you are using DOOM v1.4 or later, you might want to utilize the new features where you see fit, as you work through the sample WADs.

DOOM II For readers with DOOM II, a parallel series of sample WAD files is supplied on the accompanying CD-ROM. The details of how these WADs differ from the ones described in the text are given in DOOM II note boxes like this one in the appropriate WAD sortie sections.

HERETIC For readers with Heretic, an additional parallel series of sample WAD files is supplied on the accompanying CD-ROM. The details of how these WADs differ from the ones described in the text are given in Heretic note boxes like this one in the appropriate WAD sorties and also by the appearance of settings marked in brackets [like this].

Hexen Readers wanting to work with Hexen are given less assistance than readers working with other variants of the game. There are two main reasons for this difference: first, the main editor used in this mission's sorties does not (yet) work with Hexen WADs—the file structure is too different from that of DOOM. Second, building WADs that make full use of Hexen's features is a little more complicated than building WADs for DOOM, and it is best done after you have acquired some familiarity with creating WADs for one of the other variants of the game.

If you want to learn to build WADs by using Hexen, however, there is no reason why you should not. You can use the Windows editor WadAuthor covered in the sorties, or you can choose one of the other WAD editors included on the CD-ROM—details of these are given in Chapter 29, "Other Genesis Tools." You will need to manage with less direct instruction but you should find enough information to be able to cope.

EDITING TOOLS

In addition to a copy of the game engine itself, you need access to some WAD-editing tools. First and foremost, you need a map editor (also known as a WAD editor or mission editor). This editor enables you to lay out your map and to populate it with goodies and baddies. In addition, you might also need a nodes builder. Before you can submit a map to DOOM (or any of its variants), it must contain a structure known as the binary space partition or nodes tree. This fearsome-sounding structure holds the results of some essential pregame calculations. It lightens DOOM's math-loading and enables the graphical engine to function better in real time.

Throughout this mission, I describe WAD-production using Matthew Ayres's WADED program. I chose to use this editor because it provides a good selection of features without overwhelming the user. It also has a fully automatic nodes builder, making the generation of useable WADs a simple matter. It works with DOOM II and Heretic, and being a DOS-based editor, it requires nothing more than a PC that is capable of running DOOM, plus a mouse. A special registered version of WADED is supplied on the CD-ROM that accompanies this book, ready for use.

If your computer has 16M of RAM or more and you have Windows 3 (or above) or Windows 95, you might prefer to use a Windows-based WAD editor. A preregistered version of WadAuthor is supplied on the CD-ROM that accompanies this book, and some guidance in the use of this editor is provided in the WAD sorties, although not to the same level of detail as with WADED. Both of these editors are fully documented in their own chapters (Chapter 27, "WadAuthor," and Chapter 28, "WADED") if you need any extra help using them.

You do not need to use either of these editors for your WADs if you don't want to (although the early WAD sorties are easier to follow if you do). One of the beauties of WAD-editing is that with the structure of the files being standardized and editors so readily available, it is possible to try out a range of editors or even routinely employ several, using each for whatever features you particularly like. Feel free to chop and change, or pick one that looks good from its description and stay with it, just as you fancy. The choice is yours.

Various other tools are available to allow full customization of your DOOM WADs, but for now, you should proceed without them. The use of these more advanced tools is covered in the next mission of this book, "Towards the Land of the Gods." All the sample WADs developed in the current mission can be produced by using any of the map editors on the accompanying CD-ROM, together with any external nodes builder that the editor might require. No other utilities are needed at this stage.

THE DESIGN

With the right tools at hand, building a DOOM WAD can be a fairly easy task. Finding an effective blend of design elements and producing a good DOOM WAD can be much more tricky!

You probably already have some ideas about what you want in your WADs and are just dying to try them out. Before you get too carried away, however, you need to be aware that although the number of features available in DOOM is very large, it is by no means limitless. There are, in fact, a large number of design restrictions within which you must work—restrictions imposed by limitations in the game engine, as well as by the structure of the WAD files themselves. To produce good, playable missions, you need to not only be fully aware of these restrictions but also learn how to work around them.

I suggest that you hold off trying to produce your own killer design right away and that you start instead by following the sorties quite closely. The final WAD you produce this way is relatively simple and straightforward in its design, but I hope you find that it is still fairly exciting and challenging to play. By building the WAD according to the game plan prescribed here, you will encounter all the major design elements of DOOM WADs in an ordered and structured sequence. The potential pitfalls for would-be WAD designers are many and various. By staying close to the plan throughout this mission, you will learn to recognize them and thus avoid them when you do set off alone.

PATIENCE IS A VIRTUE

The final essential in WAD-making is patience—and you might need a lot of it! Like many computer-related tasks, WAD-building can be simple to perform but complex to master. You can expect to spend many hours switching to and fro between your editor and the game engine as you lay out, test, and refine your creation until you produce something you feel can be released to the world. Expect to make mistakes, and be prepared to spend long hours tracking them down and rectifying them.

Remember that most of the available WAD-editing utilities are produced not by large and successful software houses but by keen individuals working largely in their spare time. This is not to say that these programs are of poor quality; many are produced to high professional standards. Do bear in mind that the resources available to these eager young programmers might not have permitted rigorous testing of all the component parts; programs might have been released hurriedly, perhaps so that people could start to use them quickly, and they might be a little less than complete. You might find, for example, that a user interface is not as polished as you would like; or documentation might be lacking, requiring you to indulge in some trial-and-error guesswork before you can benefit fully from some of the utilities. You might even find that some programs crash more often than you want. You should not be put off by these cautionary words; most of the programs supplied on the CD-ROM are very powerful and easy to use after you have mastered a few basics. If you protect your work with frequent backups, you should be just fine.

Bear in mind, too, that even now, WAD-editing is very much a pioneering activity, and it requires you to have something of a pioneering spirit to get the most from it. Many of the "rules" of WAD structure and design have been formulated by amateurs working long hours, discovering things by experimentation. The nuances of WAD design are far from settled, and there is still much to discover. You should feel free to explore and experiment with the capabilities of the DOOM engine yourself. Be prepared for a certain amount of frustration and confusion if you venture too far into uncharted territory alone. Your WAD-building adventure begins, though, in the relative safety of the well-charted areas of WAD production.

PREPARATION FOR THE SORTIES

Before you can set out on even the first reconnaissance sortie, you need to gather some tools and prepare them for use. It's time to do that now.

COLLECT THE GOODIES FROM THE CD-ROM

The CD-ROM that accompanies this book contains many WAD-building utilities. To make the business of starting easier, however, I selected two editors that are particularly good for setting out on the WAD-building road. WADED is covered in detail in this mission's WAD sorties. It is my preferred editor if I'm working in DOS. For maximum hand-holding in the chapters ahead, I recommend that you start with this editor.

If you're confident that you don't need full guidance in the use of the editor and want to work in Windows rather than DOS (or with Hexen), you might want to use WadAuthor as your editor instead.

Alternatively, of course, you can use any other editor that strikes your fancy. You find details of what else is offered in Chapter 29, "Other Genesis Tools." Your choice might well be determined by the capabilities of your computer, the operating environment you prefer to use, and the game you want to work with. If you opt for one of these other editors, you should have the relevant documentation files on hand in case you need to look up how to carry out certain tasks.

CONFIGURING THE EDITOR

After you pick your editor (or editors), you should install it, following the instructions given in Chapter 4, "Using the CD-ROM."

Whichever editor you choose, before you can use it to start editing maps, you will need to provide it with some additional information—the location of your main IWAD files. Even though you might not intend to change the main maps, editors need to read information from these files and therefore cannot operate unless they can find them. Hence, you must configure your editor before you can start using it.

NOTE: You must have a registered copy of each game you want the editor to work with because editors do not work with IWADs from shareware or demo versions of the games. Editors usually ask you where you keep each game's main IWAD file. Table 7.1 gives the usual names of the IWAD files supplied with each major variant of DOOM. You need to preface these names with the path to each of the IWAD files you have (or want to work with). An editor should need to be told this information only once because it stores the information in its configuration files.

Table 7.1. Names of the IWAD files for the main game variants.

Game	IWAD Filename
DOOM	DOOM.WAD
DOOM II	DOOM2.WAD
Heretic	HERETIC.WAD
Hexen	HEXEN.WAD

NOTE: The nature and purpose of IWAD files are explained in Chapter 3, "Extending DOOM."

PREPARING WADAUTHOR

If you are working with WadAuthor, little setup is required. The program prompts you for a configuration file to use (to specify which variant of the game you want to work with) and leads you through any necessary changes to the configuration file. After this is complete, you are ready to start a new map. See Chapter 27 for more information on using WadAuthor. Online help is also available within the program.

PREPARING WADED

If you intend to work with WADED, you might want to write yourself a couple of simple batch files to make switching between the editor and DOOM a little easier. I use some simple ones like those given in Listings 7.1 to 7.4.

Listing 7.1. EDITWAD.BAT.

```
@echo off
cd \doom\waded
waded %1.wad %2 %3
cd ..
```

Listing 7.2. TRYWAD.BAT.

```
doom -file waded\%1.wad %2 %3 %4 %5 %6 %7 %8 %9
```

Listing 7.3. EDITWAD2.BAT.

```
@echo off
cd \doom\waded
waded -2 %1.wad -2 %2 %3
cd ..
```

Listing 7.4. TRYWAD2.BAT.

```
@echo off
f:
cd \doom2cd
doom -cdrom -file e:\doom\waded\%1.wad %2 %3 %4 %5 %6 %7 %8 %9
e:
```

These batch files ensure that my WADs are always kept in a convenient directory (the same as my editor), and they also minimize the amount of typing I must do to move between the editor and the game engine. Copies of these batch files are available on the CD-ROM in the \BATCH directory. You might want to use them as templates for batch files of your own.

CAUTION: The batch files presented here are examples only. You will need to adapt them to match where the games and editor are installed on your computer. Consult your DOS manuals if you are in doubt about the use of batch files.

After you have suitable batch files in place, you can start the program (by typing the name of the batch file you created for the purpose) and complete the set-up screen (as explained in Chapter 28, if you are using WADED). You should then be ready to begin creating your first WAD.

WAD SORTIE 1: A QUICK FIRST WAD

With an editor sitting there in front of you ready to use, I expect that you want to try it out immediately. Let us immediately head out on a quick-and-dirty WAD-editing sortie together. At this stage, I don't want to weigh you down with too much theory, explanations, or design issues. For now, treat this as a reconnaissance trip. You can worry more about where you are heading (and where you've been) later. The main text of this sortie describes the steps involved if you are using WADED. Sidebar text covers the use of WadAuthor to achieve the same results.

THE OPENING VIEW

After WADED has gone through its opening initialization sequence, you are presented with its main editing screen. If you didn't specify a WAD to work on, WADED presents the opening map of the main game: DOOM or Heretic's E1M1, or MAP01 if you're working with DOOM II. Figure 7.1 shows how this looks.

NOTE: Readers using a game other than DOOM have a different map displayed, but everything else should be more or less the same.

Figure 7.1.

WADED's main editing screen, as seen at startup.

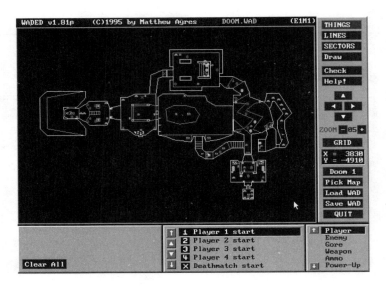

Most of the display is taken up by the main map, but to its right, down the side of the screen, are several buttons (all but the top one of which are blue). Also in this right-hand button bar is an X,Y indicator box, showing the location of the mouse pointer whenever it is positioned over the map window.

At this stage, do not bother yourself with what all the buttons do; I will cover that in due course. For now, just follow the instructions, and don't worry too much if you do not understand what the steps are actually achieving—again, all will be revealed shortly.

WadAuthor's Opening View

After you select a configuration file with which to work, WadAuthor merely presents you with an empty Windows frame. All you should see at this stage is the name of the game you chose to work with displayed in the status bar at the bottom of this frame.

CLEARING THE CURRENT MAP

 NOTE: Throughout the book, the term *clicking* means clicking with the left mouse button, unless otherwise indicated.

Start by clicking the fourth button from the top, at the right of the screen—the one labeled Draw. As you click this button, the map display changes somewhat, and a new button bar appears along the bottom of the screen under the map display. Of these buttons, the one labeled Lines in the leftmost Draw column should be red with all the others blue. Click the Scratch button to remove the E1M1 (or MAP01) map from the screen (don't worry, you won't affect your game's main IWAD here). When asked, confirm that you want to start from scratch. You should now have a completely empty map area. The Lines button should still be red. WADED is now ready to accept your new map.

Starting a New Map in WadAuthor

To start a new map in WadAuthor, just choose the File | New menu option, or press Ctrl+N. WadAuthor opens a new window, as shown in Figure 7.2.

Figure 7.2.

A new WAD window in WadAuthor.

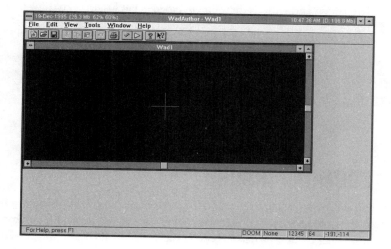

A FEW PRACTICE LINES

You might find that WADED's drawing technique is just a little different from that used by other drawing packages. This is because it is geared to WAD production and is often making assumptions about what you will draw. It is probably worth taking a little time now to become familiar with its behavior.

Start your drawing by clicking once somewhere in the map area (it does not matter where). You should notice that a small magenta square appears under the mouse pointer. If you now move the mouse pointer, the square turns red and is left behind, and another red square follows the pointer. Between these two squares stretches a magenta line with a small tick mark at its center. As you move the pointer, the X,Y indicator at the right side of the screen updates as usual, and another indicator box in the lower portion of the screen displays two other values: the length of the line you currently have attached to your pointer and the angle at which that line is running.

If you click some distance away from the location of the first click, you find that the red block under the pointer turns magenta, and at the same time, the line between the two blocks turns from magenta to a pulsating red. When you move the mouse away from this new point, however, the block turns red again, and the line turns magenta, loses its central tick mark, and no longer follows the pointer. Instead, a new tick-marked line appears, stretched between a new red square at the mouse pointer and the location of your last click. WADED continues to add squares and lines to your map each time you click until you click back on one of your existing red blocks or at some point on one of your lines (which turns red before you click to let you know that you are about to make contact with it).

The normal way of ending a drawing in WADED is to close a shape (by contacting with existing blocks or lines), but you can also terminate the drawing process by clicking (anywhere) with the right mouse button. This action erases the current line in progress but leaves everything intact up to your last left-button click.

At this point, you might want to practice drawing some lines and shapes in the map-editing area for a while.

Drawing in WadAuthor

You don't need to worry about drawing lines in WadAuthor because this editor works differently—it builds shapes for you. You will see how later in this chapter.

ZOOMING AROUND

When you have a few squiggles and assorted shapes on your map, you might also want to try out WADED's map-scrolling buttons (clustered in the center of the right-hand button bar) as well as the ZOOM – and + buttons just under them. The cursor keys on the keyboard also scroll the map display. The Home key is worth trying out; it recenters your drawing in the map display, which is useful if you've done a lot of scrolling off to one side.

Notice too, incidentally, that you can still access and use the scroll and zoom buttons while you are drawing lines. WADED might stretch the current line disconcertingly off the screen to follow the pointer, but you do not confuse it by using these buttons at the same time.

For now, don't concern yourself with how to move or erase lines that you have placed.

Zooming Around in WadAuthor

The + and – keys on the keyboard zoom WadAuthor's display of the map much like they do in WADED. The cursor keys work the same way too. The Home key works a little differently: in addition to centering the map in the display, it also auto-scales the display so that the whole map fits in the current window. Of course, you need to have some lines on your map before you try out this action.

STARTING FOR REAL

When you are comfortable with the process of drawing and viewing your lines in WADED, click the Scratch button again, and confirm the deletion of your recent doodles. Check that the ZOOM level is set to 05 and that the (Draw) Lines button is still red. (Just click it if it isn't.) You are now ready to start on your first WAD.

This first WAD is very rudimentary—nothing more than the bare essentials. It consists of a simple hexagonal room with a pillar in it.

Figure 7.3 shows how your first map should look when you've finished; the next section leads you through the drawing process.

Figure 7.3.

The map you are aiming for.

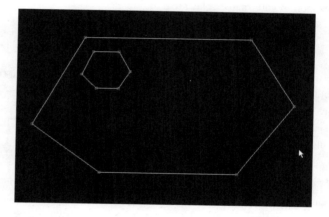

DRAWING YOUR FIRST MAP

CAUTION: Do not be tempted to speed up the production of your first WAD by skipping any stage of the instructions that follow. All the stages are essential.

Begin your drawing by clicking at the point indicated in Figure 7.3. The exact location of your first click does not matter, but you should allow space for drawing to the right of (and also a little to the left of) and below your starting position. You can, of course, scroll the display later if you find that you need more space, but life might be a little easier if you plan not to need it.

Having placed the first point of your map, move the mouse to the right and draw a horizontal line (Angle: 90) that is 900 units or so long. (Don't worry if WADED won't enable you to have a line of exactly 900 units. This is normal.) This is line 1. Now add successive lines of the lengths and angles given in Table 7.2. Again, don't worry about getting the values precisely as specified.

Table 7.2. Four more lines for the first hexagon.

Line	Angle	Length
2	147	450
3	218	500
4	270	750
5	307	460

Finish this part of the drawing by connecting back to the first point you placed. You should now have a magenta hexagon in your map display area.

Drawing the First Hexagon in WadAuthor

Creating the initial hexagon is even simpler in WadAuthor. Using the right mouse button, click anywhere in the map window to bring up a floating menu. Choose New Polygonal Sector from this menu; specify 6 sides and a radius of 600 in the dialog box that subsequently appears. Click OK, and then press Home to make the hexagonal shape fit in the display. The shape of the hexagon will not be the same as that shown in Figure 7.3, but don't worry about that for now.

Now add another, much smaller hexagon to WADED's map, as explained next. Start by positioning the mouse about 50 units east and 60 units south of the first point you placed. Before clicking, make sure that none of your current lines shows red (if one does, you are too close—move a little farther away). Then draw the new lines detailed in Table 7.3.

 CAUTION: As you draw, take care not to get so close to any of the lines of the larger, outer hexagon that WADED tries to connect any of your new lines to it. You must start over if such a connection happens.

Table 7.3. Lines for the second hexagon.

Line	Angle	Length
7	90	136
8	150	130
9	214	115
10	270	120
11	315	113

Line 11 should end in such a position that the line needed to close the hexagon is more or less parallel to the adjacent line of the larger hexagon (line 6). Complete the new hexagon by connecting line 12 to the start of line 7. Again, take care that you connect to the starting point of the inner hexagon, not to any point of the outer one.

You should now have two magenta hexagons. At this point, you should select the Make Sector button, located in the center of the lower screen section. This button turns red as the (Draw) Lines button turns blue. Position the mouse pointer anywhere within the larger hexagon but outside the smaller one, and then click once. Both hexagons turn to a pulsating red color. Notice that when you move the mouse away from both hexagons now, they turn white. Take care not to click anywhere else on the map while the Make Sector button is red.

Adding the Second Hexagon in WadAuthor

Add the second hexagon in WadAuthor in the same way as the first: Click with the right mouse button anywhere inside the first hexagon. Select New Polygonal Sector from the menu, and this time specify 6 sides and a radius of 80. Check that the new hexagon is contained wholly within the first. If it is not, simply move the mouse to its center and drag it until it is.

COMPLETING THE MAP

Next, click the THINGS button, located in the top-right corner of WADED's screen. The lower portion of the screen changes to a largely blank area on the left with two scrolling lists to the right of this area. The far-right scrolling list should have the entry "Player" highlighted, and the central list should have "Player 1 start" highlighted, as shown in Figure 7.4.

Figure 7.4.
WADED's Things selection boxes, with "Player 1 start" selected.

Position the mouse pointer somewhere inside the larger hexagon, about 40 units in from one of its southwestern corners. Click once with the *right* mouse button. A small number 1 should appear on your map, enclosed in a green rectangle, as shown in Figure 7.5. Various details (which you can ignore for now) should also appear in the lower-left information box.

Adding a Player 1 Start in WadAuthor

To add a Player 1 start to your map in WadAuthor, move the mouse to just inside the southwestern corner of the large hexagon, and click with the right mouse button. This time, select New Thing from the pop-up context menu. You should be able to just click OK in the next dialog box because

WadAuthor should be showing a Player 1 start as the default Thing to place. As you do this, WadAuthor displays a picture of the player close to where you clicked the mouse on the map, as shown in Figure 7.6.

Figure 7.5.

WADED's map after a Player 1 start has been placed.

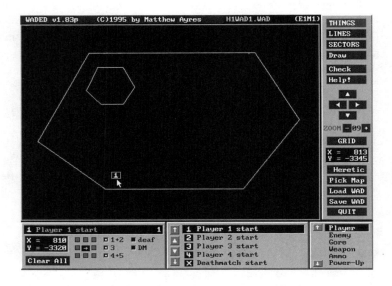

Figure 7.6.

The completed first map in WadAuthor.

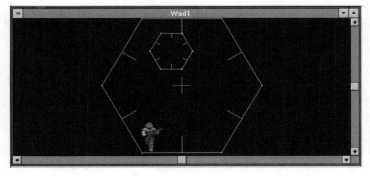

ɦERETIC Because of a minor bug in WADED, Heretic users must carry out an additional step at this point. Before proceeding with the current sortie, click the button labeled SECTORS, located in the right-hand button bar (it will turn red). Notice that the words CEIL3_5 and FLOOR4_8 are shown in cutouts in the SECTORS attributes box at the bottom of the screen, as shown in Figure 7.7. Click each of these words once; they should change to FLOOR03 as you do this.

Failure to carry out this additional step results in Heretic's crashing back to DOS with the message R_FlatNumForName: FLOOR4_8 not found when you try to start a new game with your WAD. You will learn more about the cause of this trouble later.

Figure 7.7.
WADED's SECTORS attributes box, with details that Heretic users need to change.

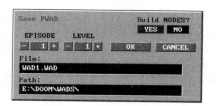

SAVING THE WAD

You now have enough of a map to try out in DOOM. Click the Save WAD button (located toward the bottom of the right button bar) to make the pop-up box shown in Figure 7.8 appear in the center of the screen.

Figure 7.8.
WADED's Save WAD pop-up box.

Click the File entry box in this pop-up box; type a name for your WAD (perhaps WAD1.WAD), and press Enter. Check that the path is OK, and change it if necessary (if you do this, you need to press Enter again after typing the new path). Notice which level your WAD plays as—the default is E1M1 (MAP01 in DOOM II). I suggest that you leave this set as it is for now. Make sure that the Build NODES? YES button is red.

NOTE: You can save your WAD with any standard DOS filename, provided that it has a .WAD extension (WADED adds one if you omit it), although DOOM.WAD is probably not a good choice! You will find that WADED works best if you leave the path setting to its default—usually the WADED directory.

When you are happy with the settings in the Save WAD pop-up box, click OK. WADED rapidly displays a sequence of messages (mostly too quickly for you to read) and then saves your WAD. You can now leave the editor (click the Quit button) and start DOOM to try out your handiwork.

Saving the WAD in WadAuthor

To save the WAD in WadAuthor, select the File | Save menu option. Supply a name and choose a directory for your WAD.

TRYING YOUR NEW WAD

Don't forget to start DOOM with an appropriate `-file` command-line switch (or use the batch file I recommended earlier). On startup, DOOM advises you that the game has been modified (by the addition of your new WAD) and that you are now on your own as far as help from id Software is concerned.

You can then try out your new map by starting a new game of the appropriate episode. You should find yourself located in one corner of a hexagonal room with a pillar somewhere to your left.

Trying the WAD in WadAuthor

If your computer has sufficient memory (8M or more), you can use WadAuthor's Tools | Run Map menu option to load the game with your WAD. Otherwise, you must quit WadAuthor and start the game as usual. This option works better under Windows 95 than Windows 3.1x.

If DOOM starts with a standard map rather than your own, check that you did indeed start DOOM with the `-file` switch, that you typed the appropriate path to your WAD file, and that you typed its name correctly. Check also that you are starting the same episode and mission (or level, in DOOM II) as you specified when you saved your WAD. Table 7.4 lists the common reasons a WAD won't load and how to avoid the causes. If all else fails, go back to your editor and follow through the instructions again—but more carefully this time!

Table 7.4. Reasons the game engine won't use your map.

What You Did	What Happens	The Cure
You forgot the `-file` parameter.	If you don't tell DOOM to use an external WAD, it won't bother. You will know when this is the cause because DOOM won't pause to tell you that the game has been modified.	Always start DOOM with the `-file` parameter to use your own WADs. Use a batch file to start DOOM with the `-file` command in it, so that you won't forget it.

What You Did	What Happens	The Cure
You used an incorrect filename or path.	If DOOM can't find your WAD, it won't be able to load it. DOOM II will warn you if it is unable to load a WAD file; earlier versions of DOOM won't.	Check your typing carefully. Don't forget that if you're starting DOOM with a batch file, your default directory might not be what you think. DOOM insists that the full name of the WAD be given, including the .WAD extension. Again, use a batch file to manage these things for you.
You gave a invalid WAD name.	If DOOM doesn't recognize your file as a WAD, it won't use it.	WADs must have the .WAD file extension, so always save WADs with one.
You used a higher mission number in your WAD.	DOOM always starts a new game from the first game of the episode unless you use the -warp or -wart command-line parameters, so that's what you'll get if you saved your map as a higher mission.	Save the WAD with an opening mission number, or use appropriate command-line parameters to reach it. If you're convinced you used the correct command-line parameters, you might need to return to the editor to check.

With luck, though, your WAD loaded and started without trouble, and you can now take a walk around your first DOOM (see Figure 7.9) or Heretic (see Figure 7.10) scenario. Not bad for a few minutes of work, eh? Future WAD sorties build on this first simple one-room WAD.

WAD Differences in WadAuthor

Because of differences in the ways WADED and WadAuthor operate, the WAD produced in WadAuthor is different from that produced in WADED (and supplied on the CD-ROM that accompanies this book). In fact, just about everything looks different, as you can see in Figure 7.11. The room is a different size and shape, the walls and the floor are painted differently, the player starts facing a different way, and most striking of all, the pillar is missing! Don't worry about these differences; they are normal. The cause is explained later in this chapter.

Figure 7.9.

A view of your first DOOM WAD.

Figure 7.10.

A view of your first Heretic WAD.

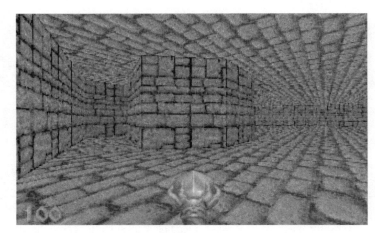

Figure 7.11.

A view of your first DOOM WAD, produced by WadAuthor. Where's the pillar?

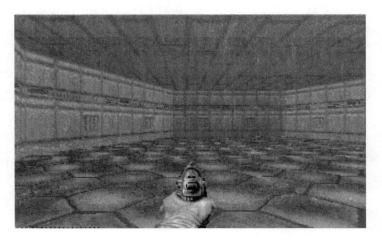

TECHNIQUES FOR EDITING AND TESTING WADS

Now that you have seen just how easy it is to produce a working WAD, you are probably keener than ever to dive in and make a real start. Before you do, however, you should review some of the practicalities of WAD development, starting with the mechanics of moving between editor and game engine.

MOVING BETWEEN THE EDITOR AND DOOM

By now, you probably have a feel for what is involved in putting together and testing a WAD file, and you have already experienced something you will probably spend a lot of time doing from now on: moving to and fro between the editor and the game engine. Because this process can be such a large part of DOOM WAD development, it is worth learning how to make this operation as simple and painless as possible.

If your PC has sufficient memory and can run DOOM under Microsoft Windows, you might want to take advantage of the task-switching capabilities of that environment. Many designers like to cut down on the time spent waiting for programs to load by starting their favorite editor in one window and running DOOM in another, then simply switching between the two with a couple of keystrokes. For many, this is the ideal way to work. To do this, you need plenty of memory—enough to run Windows, DOOM, and your editor simultaneously. You would probably need 16M as a good working minimum.

> **TIP:** You can reload a changed level into DOOM without quitting the game by using the Warp-to-level cheat code during play. (The cheat codes are detailed in Chapter 2, "Running DOOM.")

On the other hand, it is perfectly feasible (and some would say decidedly safer) to stay entirely within the confines of DOS. In this case, however, you must resign yourself to a lot of waiting as your various programs load. You can make life somewhat easier by using some carefully constructed batch files, such as those listed earlier, but you still spend a lot of time waiting for programs to start. You therefore might want to adopt a couple of working habits that make switching back and forth less tiresome. Some of these practices are briefly discussed in the following sections.

OPTIMIZING THE EDIT-SAVE-TEST CYCLE

In whatever manner you decide to operate your editor, you should resist the temptation to draw up too much of your map at one time. Learn to gauge the amount of detail you can add to your map before you need to test it. This can make a big difference in the speed at which you work. If you draw too little of your map, you spend a disproportionate amount of your working time waiting for programs to switch. If you draw too much, you run the risk of having so much to test that you miss some of the problems, or you might find a mistake that requires a lot of undoing, thereby wasting a lot of your previous edit. If you can find the right frequency, switching between the two tasks might also help keep your mind fresh longer.

As you follow the examples in this book, you should develop a feel for just how much you can add to a map before you need to test what you have done. You will also learn which things need (and take) the most testing.

Along with developing an edit-save-play strategy that optimizes the switching between editor and engine, remember that you can utilize the time spent waiting for programs to load by taking stock of where you are in the current stage of development of your WAD and planning your next step.

KEEPING NOTES

Throughout the WAD-development process, you will find it useful to keep a notebook handy. Along with sketching out your WAD before you start, you should keep a list of the things you add during each edit so that you know exactly what you need to test during the next play session. As you wait for the game engine to start, decide on a logical strategy for working through everything that needs to be tested in this session. Make sure that you test all your new additions before going back to the editor to fix any errors you spotted or put in any changes you thought of as you played your WAD. Of course, write down the problems you encounter and ideas you have while testing so that you have a list to work from when you return to the editor. Yes, you're right—it is just like programming.

USING AN APPROPRIATE MAP NUMBER

For convenience in starting your new WAD in DOOM, you are advised to save your WADs as startup games, at least during the developmental stages. This means saving them as E1M1, E2M1, or E3M1 in DOOM or Heretic or as MAP01 in DOOM II or Hexen. That way, you can go straight to your WAD to test it when you begin the game. Even if you are working on a multimap WAD, you should develop each map in a separate WAD file initially, and when the maps are all complete, use a utility such as WADCAT to assemble your multimap WAD for final testing and distribution. This technique keeps your WAD files small and quicker to load (and reduces the damage that can occur if you have an accident with the editor).

DECIDING WHEN TO ADD MONSTERS

Opinions differ as to what stage of WAD development is the right point to start adding monsters and such, largely because of the added effort of checking a WAD populated with enemies. Many developers leave adding the bad guys until almost the end. I prefer to add some creatures to my WADs quite early on, usually so that I can check whether the various geographic components work well together as a combat arena. I find that the easiest way of checking sightlines and firing lines is to put some monsters around the place and see how they behave. When WAD-building, you can easily be seduced into producing clever scenery that looks very pretty but turns out to be virtually useless when it comes to fighting in that arena. It is especially tempting when working with a map editor to build rooms and corridors that map out some grand design when viewed as a map but turn out to be boring to play. I find that adding creatures to the map as I go keeps me concentrating on the real business at hand: providing the player with a survival challenge.

After you start populating your WAD with hazards, be it with monsters or harmful scenery elements, the business of moving through it, testing its general playability, and looking for faults becomes more difficult and time-consuming. At this stage, you find that the task of testing your work is easier if you learn the proper use of the developmental aids that id Software has provided: the command-line switches and the so-called cheat codes. (Other players might use these codes to cheat during play. But you, of course, use them only as they were intended—as aids to play-testing. Quite a different matter!)

USING SWITCHES AND CHEATS

Full details of the various command-line switches and cheat codes available in DOOM and its clones are presented in Chapter 2, "Running DOOM." Those that are particularly useful during play-testing are worth recapping here.

The -nomonsters switch is useful for walk-through testing when you simply want to look around and inspect your scenery, layout, and so on. Having to battle monsters as you move through your WAD just distracts you from the real task at hand, and the job quickly becomes more of a chore than a pleasure.

TIP: The drawback of the -nomonsters switch is that you must quit the game and reload it to switch the monsters back on. An alternative is to make all the test monster-placings applicable only to the higher difficulty settings; you can then play-test without monsters simply by restarting the game at a lower difficulty setting. You learn how to do this later.

The (double) Enhanced Map Information cheat code is useful for checking out monster behavioral patterns. Use this code and watch the map to check that monsters move around your layout and hunt the player as you intended. Of course, if you spend a lot of time simply observing the monsters from locations where they can see you, you probably need to use God mode to stay alive long enough to see how they behave. Very Happy Ammo is useful for the later stages of your design when you are trying to decide how much of what kind of weaponry and ammunition to make available and also for moving quickly through areas that have keyed doors.

Users of Heretic or Hexen need to use several codes to make up for the absence of a single Very Happy Ammo code, but the idea is the same.

You might be tempted to use No Clipping to take shortcuts through your map to areas you are working on that are far from the start. I do not recommend the use of this cheat in this way. You will find that the game plays very differently with this cheat active. You will not get a proper feel for your geography while you are using it. In my view, it is much better (and usually simpler) to relocate the player's start position on your map so that you are already positioned at a convenient point when the WAD starts. The No Clipping cheat is useful, however, for occasional quick trips through a WAD to check small fixes to the scenery.

Other codes can be usefully employed at various times during the play-testing process, but the ones mentioned here are generally the most useful. You should always bear in mind just what is available, though, and be sure to use whatever speeds up your play-testing.

THE IMPORTANCE OF PROPER FILE MANAGEMENT

The final point to make about the WAD-production process is really just a matter of common sense: don't forget to make regular backups of your work in progress. Even the best of editors can occasionally get into something of a tangle. Often the only way of dealing with these tangles is to give up, load an earlier version of the WAD file, and rebuild your work from there. If you follow the strategy outlined here—of working only in fairly small and manageable chunks and saving each major edit to a new file—then even when the worst does happen, you should never end up losing too much work.

EXIT: MOPPING UP AND MOVING ON

This concludes the preliminaries. It is now time to take stock and move on.

In this chapter, you outfitted yourself for the WAD-building adventure ahead. You had a chance to build and play a simple WAD and were given some hints on the most painless ways to proceed.

In the next chapter, you will find an explanation of the steps you have just taken, an introduction to the basic elements of WADs, and more details about the use of WADED.

RECONNAISSANCE DEBRIEFING

In the preceding chapter, you experienced the thrill of producing your own WAD. This chapter examines precisely what you did. Here, you are introduced to some of the fundamental constructs of all WAD files. You learn what the various map components are and how they interact.

You are also led on two further WAD sorties, which teach you more about using WADED to edit both the lines of your maps and the things located in it.

SECURING THE SECTOR

In the preceding chapter, you produced a simple one-room WAD without too much effort. The WAD was built without much explanation, either. It is time now to review the actions you took in that first session and explain why you were instructed to take them and what you achieved by them. You might find it helpful to restart the editor with that first WAD before reading on.

DIVIDING SPACE INTO SECTORS AND VOID

Believe it or not, probably the single most important step you took in building your first WAD was making the mouse click in the middle of your "room" after selecting WADED's Make Sector button. This one action brought all your other actions together and created the single room of this simple WAD. What you really created with that mouse click was a special division of DOOM space known as a sector. The extent of a

— *By Steve Benner*

sector is determined by the lines that bound it; when you made that mouse click, WADED used the 12 lines that bound the space in which you clicked to mark out this WAD's single sector.

WHAT EXACTLY IS A SECTOR?

The game engine regards the sector as the fundamental building block of DOOM WADs. Sectors enable the engine to distinguish game-space from void space—space within the map area that is not utilized during the game. In essence, they provide the engine's point of access to all the information about any particular location on the map.

So important are sectors, in fact, that many editors (such as WadAuthor) take the approach that maps should be constructed entirely from them. Maps are built in these editors by the creation of new sectors with a specified number of sides, which can be rearranged later.

Any point a player can reach must belong to a sector if the game engine is to handle the view from that point correctly. Any point on the map that is not assigned to a sector is regarded by the game engine as belonging to the void.

In your first WAD, you created a single sector consisting of a hexagonal "ring." The game engine saw and displayed this space as a single room. As far as DOOM was concerned, there was nothing outside the sector's enclosing walls or even within the hexagonal pillar.

You can think of a sector as simply a designer-defined area of the DOOM map. That area is of a specific extent, defined by a series of lines. To mark off such an area without ambiguity, a sector's bounding lines must completely enclose the space. There can be no gaps in the lines, as illustrated in Figure 8.1.

Figure 8.1.
Closed and unclosed shapes.

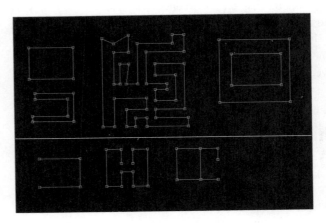

The upper four shapes are all valid closed shapes—they could all form sectors (the rightmost shape could form one or two sectors). The lower three sets of lines form unclosed shapes. These unclosed shapes cannot form sectors, and they crash both WADED and DOOM if you try to use them. WadAuthor does its best to keep sectors closed by always drawing the complete shape for you. It will let you delete lines later, however, so you should take care that you never leave shapes open as a result of later edits.

LOOKING AT THE DIVISION OF SPACE

If you have WADED loaded and your WAD1.WAD map on-screen, you can readily observe this division of the map into sectors and void.

Click the Draw button and then the Make Sector button. Now, while taking care not to click the mouse button, move the pointer around over the area of the map. Whenever the pointer is over space that belongs to a sector, the bounding lines of that sector show up as pulsating red lines. You should find that the only time any lines are highlighted in your WAD is when the pointer is over the annular space of your single room, at which time all the lines are highlighted. Whenever the mouse pointer is outside your large hexagon or inside the small one, it is in the void, and all lines show as white. (You can also observe a similar effect in WadAuthor, but the smaller hexagon's lines will light up whenever the pointer enters it.)

ATTRIBUTES OF SECTORS

Each sector has a specific set of attributes that tell the DOOM engine how that space looks and behaves during play. It is important to remember that a sector's attributes are applied across its entire extent. A sector's main attributes consist of the following items:

- Floor details
- Ceiling details
- A brightness level
- A special characteristic

You learn all about these attributes later; they are considered here only briefly. Note that no information is given here about your WAD's walls. You find out more about them later, too.

Viewing Sector Attributes

In WADED, you can view a sector's attributes by clicking the SECTORS button in the right-hand button bar. (You can safely click the map again now.) In the bottom section of the screen, the settings of the currently selected sector appear, as shown in Figure 8.2.

In WadAuthor, a sector's attributes can be accessed with a double-click inside the sector.

Heretic users who completed the preceding chapter's WAD sortie have already seen this attribute box and know that its settings are not exactly as shown in Figure 8.2.

Figure 8.2.
WADED's sector-attribute box.

FLOOR AND CEILING

The *floor* of a sector is the horizontal plane that forms the lower boundary of the sector in space. It is the surface on which the players (and most monsters) walk while they are in that area of the map. The *ceiling* is the horizontal surface forming the sector's upper boundary.

These surfaces are truly horizontal and cannot slope. You will learn more about this topic and other limitations of DOOM space later.

A sector's floor and ceiling each possess two definable properties:

- A height
- A texture

The *height* value specifies the surface's absolute vertical placement in the range –32768 to +32767. Naturally, the ceiling is normally placed higher than the floor, and the difference between the two heights provides the apparent height of this area of the map, as seen by the player.

The *texture* value consists of an eight-character name that tells the game engine which pattern to render on-screen when showing this particular surface.

SECTOR BRIGHTNESS

A sector's *brightness level*, expressed as a number between 0 and 255, determines how brightly anything occupying that sector (including the floor and ceiling textures) is displayed on-screen.

SPECIAL CHARACTERISTIC

The *special characteristic* (or *type*) of a sector determines whether the game engine does anything special with it. Examples might be making the lights flicker or damaging a player in the sector. Most sectors have no special characteristic set.

Chapter 13, "Special Sectors," looks at this property of sectors. The next WAD sortie takes a closer look at other sector settings within your own embryonic WAD.

> **NOTE:** The following WAD sortie builds on the WAD produced in the last sortie of the preceding chapter. If you did not accompany me on that sortie but want to come along on this one, you should use WAD1.WAD (DOOM), D2WAD1.WAD (DOOM II), or H1WAD1.WAD (Heretic) from the CD-ROM as your starting point.

WAD SORTIE 2: CHANGING SECTOR ATTRIBUTES

You are probably wondering how your WAD managed to acquire ceiling, floor, and brightness settings without your having to specify any values for these attributes. The answer is that WADED, like many editors, generally supplies sensible defaults for all values you do not specify. Of course, WADED also provides the facility for you to specify all these settings yourself. You might want to change some of them now.

Assuming that you are running WADED with WAD1.WAD loaded, click the SECTORS button in the right-hand button bar. Click anywhere inside your only sector, and its attributes are displayed at the bottom of the screen. The sector identification number is shown at the far left of the Attributes bar, with the current value of the special characteristic next to it. You can ignore these values for now. Next to the Special value is displayed the sector's brightness level (called Lighting by WADED) and, to the right of that, the current ceiling and floor heights, as well as the names of the textures in use by those surfaces.

Sector Settings in WadAuthor

Access a sector's settings in WadAuthor by double-clicking within the sector. The use of the Sector Settings dialog box that this action invokes should be obvious. If not, click the Help button for a description.

CHANGING SETTINGS

To change any of the numerical settings, you can use the + or – buttons alongside the particular value, or you can click the value itself and directly type a new value and press Enter. Try reducing the sector's lighting level to 144, say, and bring the ceiling down a little to 120.

You might also fancy a change of floor texture. In the lower-right corner of the screen to the right of the attributes area, you see a list of eight-character names arranged in alphanumerical order, as shown in Figure 8.3. These are the available floor and ceiling textures.

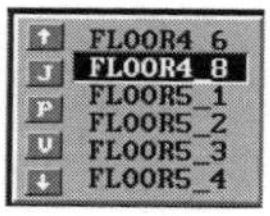

Figure 8.3.
WADED's SECTOR floor/ceiling texture list box.

The precise content of this list depends on the variant of the game you are using. Figure 8.3 shows part of the list you see if you are using DOOM. DOOM II has a similar list with some names the same and others different. The textures used by Heretic and Hexen are unique to those games.

The arrows to the left of the names enable you to scroll this list up and down.

TIP: Use the right mouse button on the arrows for rapid scrolling.

The J button enables you to jump to a particular part of the list—you click the button and then enter an initial letter. The P button brings up a larger pick list from which you can select a texture.

WADED provides various ways to view the textures. You can use the V button to see the currently highlighted texture; you can use the mouse to right click a texture name in the list; or you can use the appropriate button in the pick list to preview textures. When you're previewing a texture using any of these techniques, WADED removes the map-editing screen and displays a single "tile" of the chosen texture in the middle of the screen, as shown in Figure 8.4.

Figure 8.4.
WADED's preview of floor/ceiling texture MFLR8_1.

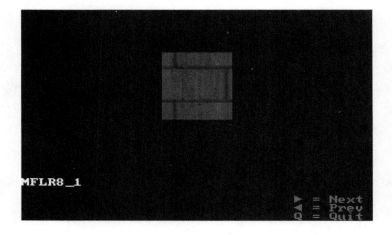

Here, you can use the left- and right-arrow keys to view other textures, or you can press the Q (or the Escape) key to return to the editor. The texture you last viewed is highlighted in the textures list box.

You can change the current floor texture as described next. With the main map-editing screen visible, scroll through the list of texture names until, say, MFLR8_1 [FLOOR01 in Heretic] becomes visible. Click the entry to select it. Now click your sector's floor-texture field, located in the sector attributes bar (where it currently says FLOOR4_8 [FLOOR03 in Heretic]). With this mouse click, the sector's floor-texture name field changes to the new name.

HERETIC In addition to using FLOOR01 rather than MFLR8_1, Heretic users might want to change the ceiling texture to FLAT516 by selecting that name in the list of textures and then clicking with the mouse in the sector's ceiling-texture field (currently FLOOR03).

Changing Sector Settings in WadAuthor

If you are working with WadAuthor and your map is not for Hexen, you might want to change the main hexagonal sector's settings to match those being used by readers with WADED. Table 8.1 gives the values to use. You also need to change the smaller hexagonal settings to match.

Table 8.1. Hexagonal sector settings in WAD1.WAD.

Attribute	DOOM/DOOM II	Heretic
Lighting	144	144
Ceiling height	120	120
Ceiling texture	CEIL3_5	FLAT516
Floor texture	MFLR8_1	FLOOR01

Save this WAD as WAD2.WAD and try it out. The differences might be slight, but you have now changed the way your room looks.

DRAWING THE BATTLE LINES

Although the sector might be regarded as the DOOM engine's starting point in its interpretation of your WAD, you began your drawing with something rather more fundamental: a series of lines. In fact, map lines consist of even smaller units: the vertices between which the lines themselves are stretched.

LINES AND VERTICES

Lines and vertices are simple elements to understand. Each vertex is nothing more than an X and a Y coordinate, representing a point location on the DOOM map. Lines are marks on the map running between two of these vertices. Lines cannot exist without a vertex at each end.

Linked Creation of Lines and Vertices

With WADED, you don't need to worry about the creation of vertices because this is handled automatically each time you draw a line. WADED shows vertices as small squares on your map. You have already seen that each line you draw has such a square at each end.

WadAuthor takes this idea one stage further. This editor creates an entire *sector* for you, complete with all necessary lines and vertices. You can then point to and select any individual component of the sector and manipulate it as you want.

THE HANDEDNESS OF LINES

It is important to realize that lines in DOOM WADs are regarded by the game engine as vectors. In other words, they are deemed to run in a particular direction *from* one vertex (the starting vertex) *to* another (the finishing vertex). Most editors (WADED included) watch the way you draw your lines and take the vectoring information from your actions.

This vectoring of the lines can also be regarded as a handedness; lines are said to have *right-hand* sides and *left-hand* sides. Both WADED and WadAuthor (along with most other editors) show a line's right side by means of a small tick mark. To appreciate what this signifies, imagine yourself standing on a line's starting vertex (as made by the mouse click that started the line) looking toward the line's finishing vertex. This line's right side lies to your right. Simple really, but confusing sometimes—hence the tick.

LINEDEFS AND SIDEDEFS

It so happens that lines in DOOM WADs are actually composite structures consisting of more than just start and end points. Each line has its own particular attributes (you learn more about these in due course), which are held in a data structure called a linedef (short for "line definition"). In addition, each linedef has information attached to each of its sides, in a pair of additional structures known as sidedefs (short for "side definitions"). A line can have both a right sidedef and a left sidedef to tell the DOOM engine how it appears to the player when viewed from either side.

To economize on space in the WAD, if a line can possibly be seen from only one of its sides (like all the lines in your first WAD), then only one sidedef is needed, and the second can be omitted. By convention, single-sided lines have only a right sidedef. Lines that can be viewed from either side must have a right and a left sidedef, or an error occurs.

WADED's Treatment of Lines

For simplicity, WADED does not distinguish between linedefs and their attached sidedefs, calling the composite structure a line. This is a great convenience; WADED is usually smart enough to know exactly how many sidedefs each of your linedefs needs, and it handles the generation of all the appropriate information automatically. It is often helpful, however (especially when trying to track down map faults), to bear in mind that all map lines are really tripartite structures, consisting of a linedef and (potentially) two sidedefs.

You will encounter more about the roles of these structures in Chapter 10, "At the Sector's Edge."

Line Handedness in WADED

Although WADED is aware of the direction in which you drew your lines, it is also smart enough to know that a single-sided line's only sidedef should be on its right side. As you build sectors, WADED might flip single-sided lines around to ensure that their right sides are always used. Don't be concerned, therefore, if you find that lines in your WAD do not always appear to run in the direction you remember drawing them. WADED is just trying to make life easier for you.

CONTROLLING THE THINGS

In addition to the lines of the map—whose principal role is to mark out the sectors—WADs can contain a number of items that are not part of the geography but represent the various objects the player encounters when the WAD is played. These map items are termed Things. These Things are placed on the map by the designer to indicate where they will be when the WAD is started. Some Things might subsequently move with the progression of the game.

THINGS

You probably have a fair idea already what the family of DOOM Things includes. Monsters are Things, as are all weapons, bonuses, and ammunition supplies. Also included are several other items you might not immediately think of as Things. These are the main categories of Things available in DOOM and DOOM II:

- Player start positions
- Enemies
- Gore (pools of blood, dead monsters, and so on)
- Weapons
- Ammunition
- Power-ups (health and armor bonuses and so forth)
- Keycards
- Obstacles (barrels, pillars, and so on)
- Miscellaneous (currently just the teleport destination)

Heretic and Hexen add sounds to this list, divided into two subcategories. Atmospheric Sounds add atmosphere to a map, and if used, they sound at random intervals throughout the playing of the level. Environmental Sounds are associated with specific map locations and appear louder the closer the player is to them.

You will learn more about the use of Things as you progress through this mission. A discussion of the uses for the more important categories of Things appears in Chapter 19, "Populating Your Nightmare," and a full list of all Things available in each of the variants of the game is given in Chapter 34, "Essential Thing Information."

 CAUTION: The only really essential Thing that every map of every WAD must have is a single Player 1 start position. Without one of these, the WAD crashes the game engine when you attempt to start a new game.

ATTRIBUTES OF THINGS

Each WAD Thing can possess several attributes the designer can set:

- A facing angle
- Skill-level options
- A deaf guard option
- A multiplayer option

Hexen uses an extended WAD Thing structure that provides these additional attributes:

- A dormant guard option
- A starting altitude
- An identification code
- A special action code

 NOTE: Not all categories of Things can utilize all available attributes, even though they possess them.

FACING ANGLE

The *facing angle* attribute determines the direction in which the Thing is facing at the start of the mission. Only player starts, monsters, and teleport destinations use this attribute. All other categories of Thing look the same from all directions. (Have you noticed how corpses turn around as you walk around them?) The default facing angle is East.

SKILL-LEVEL OPTIONS

The *skill-level* options determine at which difficulty-level settings of the game the Thing appears. There are fewer difficulty levels than you might expect. These are the levels:

- Level 0 ("I'm too young to die" and "Hey, not too rough")
- Level 1 ("Hurt me plenty")
- Level 2 ("Ultra-Violence" and "Nightmare")

Note the joining together of the "I'm too young to die" and "Not too rough" skill levels, as well as the "Ultra-Violence" and "Nightmare" levels. The differences within each of these groupings are achieved by mechanisms other than Thing availability. All Things could be set to appear (or not) at any of the three difficulty levels independently.

Heretic and Hexen give different names to their difficulty-level settings, but I'm sure you see the correspondence.

DEAF GUARD OPTION

The normal behavior of enemies is to remain asleep at their posts until they either see a player or hear a sound made by a player. The *deaf guard* option enables you to set particular monsters to awaken only on seeing the player (or being hit by a shot). This attribute has no meaning for any other category of Thing.

You learn more about the way sound propagates in Chapter 19, "Populating Your Nightmare."

DORMANT GUARD OPTION (HEXEN ONLY)

Hexen's *dormant guards* are very heavy sleepers: these can be awakened only by special activations, which are under complete control of the designer. You learn more about these special activations in "Programming the Action," a chapter on the CD-ROM.

MULTIPLAYER OPTION

The *multiplayer option* enables the use of Things that appear only in Cooperative or Deathmatch multiplayer games. This option is useful for the addition of obstacles to prevent player access to items such as teleports and for creating a different distribution of weapon and ammunition supplies for multiplayer games.

Hexen provides much more flexible control over the appearance and non-appearance of Things with the capability to set whether or not particular objects should appear in Single-player, Cooperative, and Deathmatch play independently. In addition, the designer can control whether items appear when the player is playing as Fighter, Cleric, or Mage, allowing the game to play differently in each case.

STARTING ALTITUDE (HEXEN ONLY)

In Hexen, each Thing can have a *starting altitude* specified. The Thing is placed at this height above its sector's floor at inception of the level containing it, and it is immediately subjected to gravity (and begins to fall).

SPECIAL ACTION ATTRIBUTES (HEXEN ONLY)

The *identification code* and *special action code* attributes added to Things in Hexen are part of that game's greater WAD programmability. This feature of the game is discussed at length in "Programming the Action," a chapter on the CD-ROM.

HIDDEN EXTRAS

For the sake of completeness, I should mention that there are other essential resources that every WAD needs in order to operate. Principally, these are those resources:

- The blockmap
- The BSP (or nodes tree)
- The reject table

Hexen WADs also require these resources:

- A mapinfo lump
- A behavior resource

These resources are considered briefly next.

BLOCKMAP

To speed up the collision-detection process during play, DOOM requires the map to be divided into a series of blocks. These blocks provide the game engine with a list of lines for their particular area of the map. Without this blockmap, all lines would become completely walk-through, and DOOM would become a very strange game indeed. The No Clipping cheat code operates, in fact, by telling DOOM to stop consulting the blockmap. Editors should build a blockmap automatically without your needing to worry about it.

BSP (NODES TREE)

The binary space partition has already been mentioned as an essential WAD resource. It is needed to enable the game engine to display all the WAD scenery in real time. This structure is calculated from the lines you draw. Some editors include the generation of the nodes as an integral part of their operation; others require a separate nodes builder to be used before the WAD can be used.

NOTE: The symptoms of a faulty nodes tree vary greatly. Sometimes the WAD simply refuses to play with DOOM crashing to DOS (or worse). Usually, however, you find that the WAD simply displays oddly with some walls missing or with transparent stripes or flickering patterns. This topic is discussed in Chapter 33, "The Anomalies."

THE REJECT TABLE

The reject table (or map) provides DOOM with some shortcuts for working out whether monsters can see the players as they all move around. The purpose of this structure is to save the DOOM engine from some math calculations during operation of the game, thus speeding up play. Most editors produce an empty reject table. This enables the WAD to operate but not optimally. Unless your WAD contains many monsters and many sectors, however, this is not a problem for you. A special utility, known as a Reject Builder, is needed to produce a fully optimized reject table. More details of this utility and what can be achieved by using it are given in Chapter 23, "Reject Table Tricks."

Blockmap, Nodes, and Reject Generation in WADED

When WADED reads a WAD file, it discards the blockmap, generating a new one when you save the edited file to disk. It needs to rebuild the nodes, though, only if you have entered Draw mode at all.

Also, because node generation can be a lengthy process on a large WAD, WADED makes this step optional at the point of saving. The value of the Build Nodes? option that appears in the Save WAD pop-up is set to NO as you load a WAD and changes to YES if you add or move any lines on the map. The option can usually be trusted to be in the most appropriate setting automatically, but if in doubt, set it to YES.

If you suspect your WAD of having a faulty nodes tree, load it into WADED, press B to force an immediate build of the nodes, and then resave the WAD.

WADs produced or edited with WADED have an empty reject table.

HEXEN'S MAPINFO LUMP

Because Hexen does not use a linear progression of maps like other DOOM variants but permits the player to teleport between levels, it requires an additional WAD resource to keep track of the interconnections and the players' progress through them. This is the *mapinfo lump*. A good Hexen editor gives you full access to this resource, which is covered in detail in "Programming the Action," a chapter on the CD-ROM.

HEXEN'S BEHAVIOR RESOURCE

Hexen's designer-programmed actions are stored in the WAD in a special area known as the *behavior resource*. Editors rarely provide direct access to this area. This topic is covered in detail in "Programming the Action."

WAD SORTIE 3: MOVING THINGS AROUND

NOTE: This sortie builds on the WAD produced in the preceding one. If you did not produce that WAD, you should use WAD2.WAD (DOOM), D2WAD2.WAD (DOOM II), or H1WAD2.WAD (Heretic) from the CD-ROM as your starting point here.

So far, you have seen how to add new lines to a map but not how to move lines or how to reshape your layout. If you would care to start the editor again, I show you how to do this, along with a few other useful things.

SPEAKING OF THINGS...

Because WADED always starts in Things mode, it is worth taking a look here at Thing placement in a bit more detail. You have already seen how to place a Thing into a WAD; you did this when you set your Player 1 start position just before saving your first WAD.

WADED's Thing placement process is simple. Click the THINGS button at the top of the right-hand button bar. (If you've just started WADED, this step is unnecessary.) Then scroll the far-right list box at the bottom of the screen until the desired category of Thing is visible, using the left mouse button to select it. Do this now to select the Obstacle category.

The scroll box to the left of the Thing-category list shows a list of Things that belong to the currently selected category. The box displays a descriptive name of the Thing and shows the icon that WADED uses to indicate this Thing's position on the map. If you're using DOOM or DOOM II, scroll this list box's highlight down quite a ways, to the entry labeled Tall, Techno Column. Readers working with Heretic should scroll the highlight down to the entry for Demon-brazier. Now, to place the chosen obstacle in your room, move the mouse pointer to the location you want it to occupy (the middle of the large hexagon, perhaps?), and click once with the *right* mouse button.

Note that a copy of the gray, spherical icon used to represent the techno-column's position appears on your map, surrounded by a green rectangle. WADED uses this green rectangle to indicate which of the Things on the map is currently selected. A Thing becomes selected as it is placed or subsequently when the left mouse button is clicked on its icon. A selected Thing's details appear in the details box at lower left. Figure 8.5 shows how the WADED screen looks after placement of a techno-column.

Figure 8.5.

The WADED edit screen with Tall, Techno Column selected.

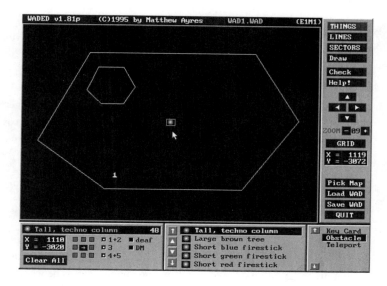

 TIP: If you don't like the names WADED uses for the Things in the scrolling list boxes, you can change them. You should find a text file called WADED.T in your WADED directory. Edit this file to change the names. Don't change any of the other information about the Things, though, or your WADs will not work properly and could crash DOOM.

Adding Things in WadAuthor

To place a new Thing in WadAuthor, right click the map where you want to place the Thing. Then select New Thing from the context menu to bring up the Thing Properties dialog box. Use of this dialog box should be obvious. If it is not, click the Help button for a description of its fields and their uses.

CHANGING A THING'S ATTRIBUTES

In WADED, details of a selected Thing's attributes appear in the Thing's details box in the lower-left part of the screen. On/Off check boxes enable you to alter the various options of the currently selected Thing. The Thing's facing angle is shown by means of a white arrow, which is surrounded by some gray blocks. Click an appropriate gray block to change the facing angle of the selected Thing.

There is no point in changing the way your obstacle faces, because this will have no effect on the way it appears to the player. You might want to select your current Player 1 start position, though, and change the way your player faces at the start of the game.

TIP: Although the only essential thing your WAD must have before you can play it is a Player 1 start, if your WAD is ever to be used in multiplayer mode, it also must have the requisite number of additional Cooperative and Deathmatch Player starts. Even if you have not designed the WAD with multiplayer use in mind, you should make sure that such positions are provided so that your WAD is at least useable in multiplayer mode. It is easy to forget to add such starting positions later, so I suggest that you add them now. Place start positions for each of the other Cooperative players alongside Player 1. Also, place four Deathmatch start positions around your central obstacle. Make sure that they start up with their backs to each other, won't you?

MOVING THINGS AROUND

You can move a Thing around on the map simply by using the left mouse button to drag it to where you want it. Try placing a Cyberdemon [Weredragon in Heretic] (of the Enemy category) somewhere in your WAD. Drag it around a bit, and try to decide where you want it to be when you start the WAD. You can put a few items of gore about the place for practice, if you must.

HERETIC Heretic users can also embellish their WADs with the addition of an atmospheric sound or two. You might want to add one to your embryonic WAD now. Choose the Sounds category, locate and select the item called Water Dripping, and then right-click anywhere in your WAD to cause the sound of dripping water to be played at random intervals during the playing of the WAD.

It is perfectly possible to place or drag Things into void space, but doing so is singularly pointless. (Void space, remember, is space that is not assigned to a sector.) The player can never see into the void, so decorations placed there are wasted. The player can never enter the void, so bonuses placed there can never be collected. Monsters there awaken at the player's first shot, but because they can never enter any sector space, they can never be encountered (although the player hears them wandering around the void trying to get in!) and so are never killed. DOOM won't mind about this waste, but it notices that the player has not encountered the items left suspended in the void and reports the score appropriately at the conclusion of the level.

There is an exception to this general rule, however, and that is with the placing of Sound Things in Heretic and Hexen. Because these items are never actually encountered by players, it doesn't matter where on the map they are placed. Atmospheric Sounds are used and heard *throughout* the level, whether they occupy sector space or void. Environmental sounds become quieter the further the player moves from them. If you want to mask the source of these sounds and make it hard for a player to locate them, place them in void space so that a player can never come close to them.

DELETING UNWANTED THINGS

Have you found a good spot for that Cyberdemon or Weredragon yet? No, you're right, it is probably not a good idea to have one here. In WADED, click the monster's icon on your map with the right mouse button. Poof! (Don't you wish it was that easy to be rid of them during play?) In WadAuthor, left click the monster's icon to select it and then press Delete.

MOVING LINES AND VERTICES AROUND

CAUTION: WADED's map-editing operations can rarely be undone. You might want to save your WAD before going on in case you make a mess of it experimenting with the following operations.

To move map elements other than Things around, you need to click first on the Draw button in the right-hand button bar. The three buttons that then appear in the Move/Del column of the lower button bar should be self-explanatory by now. If you click this column's Vertices button, WADED enables you to select and move vertices (they are the square blocks at the ends of your lines, remember?) around the map by dragging with the left mouse button. You might want to try this operation, refining the shapes of your hexagons a little.

CAUTION: Do not move any vertex so far that a nearby line turns red. If you do this by accident, move it away again *before* releasing the mouse button. If you do release the mouse button while a line is red, the vertex you are moving becomes connected to the red line. This action cannot be undone.

Also, if you move a vertex too close to another vertex and release the mouse button, WADED asks whether you want to merge the two vertices. Ordinarily, this action can be useful by enabling you to connect otherwise-disconnected lines. Not here though. It also cannot be undone.

Selecting the (Move) Lines button enables you to select and move lines around as you just moved vertices. Notice that when you're moving lines, WADED preserves the angle and length of the line being moved, but it resizes and reorients any that are connected to the vertices at its ends.

As you've probably guessed, the (Move) Sector button permits the movement of entire sectors. Because you have only one sector in this WAD, it doesn't achieve a great deal here, of course.

Moving Map Elements in WadAuthor

You can move any map element around in WadAuthor by simply pointing to it and dragging it with the left mouse button. WadAuthor moves all the map elements that show as cyan when the mouse button is pressed. By default, objects moved in this way are snapped to a fairly coarse grid. You might want to adjust this grid setting to 8, or turn Snap to Grid off altogether. (You can make these setting changes from the context menu, which you bring up by right clicking anywhere in your map windows.) You might then want to reshape the two hexagons of your WAD to better match the shapes shown in the preceding chapter.

DELETING MAP ELEMENTS

 CAUTION: If you want to keep the changes you just made, save your WAD now if you have not already done so. Your next experimentation is likely to destroy essential information in your WAD. Use the name WAD3.WAD to keep your WAD names synchronized with mine.

To delete unwanted lines or vertices in WADED, you must have the appropriate Move/Del column button selected, just as if you were going to move the element. Then, a single click with the right mouse button on the offending element is all that is needed to delete it. In WadAuthor, select an element with the left mouse button and then press Delete to achieve the same effect.

Use this feature with extreme caution at all times. Deleting map elements can have far-reaching effects. Remember that deleting a vertex affects its connected lines; at least one line is always removed as well. Deletion of a line might leave a sector open (and therefore in error). You must redefine sectors that are damaged in this way, which might result in extra work.

TIP: Plan all modifications to your map for minimal removal of existing lines. Try to reuse lines instead of deleting them. Later WAD sorties show you how.

You might want to experiment with the line- and vertex-deletion capabilities of your editor for a while now, just to see how they operate. Don't attempt to put any lines back afterward, however. Just quit the program without saving the WAD when you have finished. Load DOOM and try out the last WAD you saved. This should be your reshaped room with an obstacle at its center and whatever other items you scattered around. (You did remember to remove all major monsters, didn't you?) Heretic users should also hear water dripping from time to time.

EXIT: MOPPING UP AND MOVING ON

This chapter showed you how lines are used to divide DOOM space into sectors within the void. You also learned that lines have a handedness and that they really consist of linedefs with a vertex at each end and sidedefs attached to their sides. You saw that sectors are responsible for supplying floor, ceiling, and lighting information to DOOM. In addition, you got a fleeting glimpse of some of the more esoteric wonders that lie at the heart of WAD files, and you learned a little about some of the objects that populate DOOM levels. You also had further lessons in the operation of WADED and have made some cosmetic changes to your embryonic WAD. (See Figure 8.6.)

Figure 8.6.

Oops! You should have taken it out while you could!

In the next chapter, you will learn more about the way in which DOOM space is measured and organized.

MEASURING AND MAPPING DOOM

From the preceding chapter, you know that DOOM's map area is divided into sectors and void space. This chapter's briefing discusses sectors in more detail, explaining their true role and showing you why they are needed and how you should use them. It provides some useful rules for the layout of your maps.

Continuing previous WAD sorties, you will also begin a tentative expansion of your embryonic WAD by adding a new passageway as well as another room. You will discover too that there are pitfalls along the way.

The briefing starts with an exploration of the nature of DOOM space itself, showing you just what is and is not possible within it. Take note that vital information is contained here about the limitations that the DOOM engine imposes on your design. Ignore it at your peril!

UNDERSTANDING DOOM SPACE

The lines of your first WAD were laid out in a fairly arbitrary manner in the blank space of your editor's map-editing window. You drew them with little regard for position. The lengths you used were largely arbitrary, too. Before you can decide how to draw any of your own lines, you need to know how DOOM space is measured and how big it is. You also need to know something of its limitations.

DOOM METRICS

The basic unit of measurement in DOOM is essentially the pixel. Understand that this is not a screen pixel but the smallest picture element of a DOOM engine graphic. The sizes of all DOOM elements are expressed in terms of the number of such pixels, or blocks of color, it takes to paint them.

— By Steve Benner

This measurement system is used throughout the entire WAD world. Map coordinates follow this scheme, so a wall that is, say, 128 units long has exactly 128 blocks of color along its length.

Figure 9.1 shows a close-up view of some features of the DOOM world. The individual blocks of color that compose them can be quite large—look in particular at the closest area of the door and at the nearby Trooper.

Figure 9.1.

A close-up view of some DOOM pixels.

Deciding how pixel measurements convert to real-world units is a little tricky. It seems that the folks at id Software have distorted their game world somewhat, making exact comparisons with the real world difficult. The best rule of thumb seems to be that each horizontal unit in the game approximates 2 centimeters in the real world, with the vertical unit being nearer to 3 centimeters, in keeping with the PC screen-pixel's 3:2 aspect ratio. Vertical scaling is generally more difficult to judge, though, because it seems to vary with the distance of objects from the viewer and is distorted by the different zoom levels the player can select. Although you need to have some idea of DOOM's scaling if you are trying to reproduce some real-world setting in your WAD, you will find that, in practice, you rarely need to know the equivalent real-world sizes of DOOM objects. As you progress, you quickly learn to start gauging DOOM space for yourself. (You will find more about the implementation of real-world settings later in this chapter.)

All Things in DOOM (including the player) have specific heights and widths (expressed as a diameter). This limits the space into which they can fit. The full details of these limitations and the consequences of ignoring them are the subject of Chapter 12, "Putting Sectors to Work."

THE EXTENT OF DOOM SPACE

Map coordinates can range from –32768 to +32767. Therefore, in theory at least, DOOM maps could be quite large—this range gives the gaming space a theoretical maximum area equivalent to over 1 kilometer square. In practice, however, other engine limits are encountered long before this space is filled. As a rough guide, you should aim to keep the extent of your maps below 500,000 square units so as not to exceed the size limits of several DOOM resources.

CAUTION: Don't get too carried away with the vastness of DOOM space and start building huge open areas. Not only are they boring to play, but they also have a tendency to be rendered poorly on-screen, owing to limitations in the game engine and current display technologies. As a rough guide, aim to keep walls shorter than a couple of thousand units long and rooms less than 500 units high (preferably even smaller if you are using DOOM v1.2). Chapter 33, "The Anomalies," shows you why!

2D OR 3D?

A common misconception among DOOM players is that their gaming world is fully three-dimensional. As a designer, you must understand the fallacy of this notion. DOOM space is what is normally termed pseudo-three-dimensional (sometimes termed 2D). The map consists of a series of items (lines, vertices, and Things) placed into a two-dimensional playing grid. Particular areas within that grid are then notified to the engine as being at specific elevations.

You have already seen how lines are arranged to create special divisions of DOOM space called sectors. These line and sector structures hold the information about the division of the playing grid and the various elevations of its parts. This is why areas not defined as sectors are deemed void by the game engine; there is simply no information whatsoever about them in the WAD.

PRACTICAL CONSEQUENCES

The main consequence of this pseudo-3D nature of DOOM space is its incapability to permit any location on the map to possess more than one vertical elevation. What this means for the designer is that no sector (or part thereof) can ever overlap any other sector. This imposes a severe limitation on permitted designs. Rooms over one another are not possible, for example. Corridors or passageways that cross at different levels are out, as well as archways through which players can pass while enemies lurk over their heads.

This particular spatial restriction is often the one that is hardest for designers to come to terms with when planning their WADs. It can be difficult to limit one's imagined geography in this way. Of course, many real-world environments are immediately excluded. Gone is any chance of implementing your favorite office or school block, for instance.

Fortunately, there are some simple rules of layout, which, provided that you follow them, should keep you out of trouble. It is worth looking at these rules in some detail.

CORRECT LINE LAYOUTS

Perhaps the single most important key to trouble-free DOOM maps is the correct laying out of lines. This really boils down to a full understanding of the role of sectors and hence to the correct employment of them in your design. Spelling out the guiding rules for line layout first, however, should make the whole issue of the correct use of sectors more obvious.

NEVER CROSS LINES

The first guiding principle in laying out your maps is that no lines must ever cross. If they meet, all lines must be connected by means of a vertex. This rule ensures that all division of space on the map occurs unambiguously and that unique floor and ceiling heights can be assigned to each location through the use of appropriate sectors.

Following are some examples to illustrate this rule. Figure 9.2 shows some line layouts that are not permitted. The errors are all caused by illegal line crossings. These attempted line crossings are sure-fire indicators of the designer trying to overlap sectors at differing heights.

Figure 9.2.
Illegal DOOM line layouts.

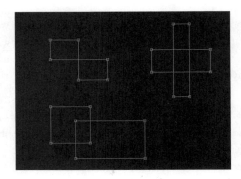

Figure 9.3 shows the correct way to lay out these areas. Note that the connections break up the space in a way that discourages you from thinking of areas that physically overlap. Areas that previously might have been thought of as two sectors are now clearly seen to be three or even five.

Figure 9.3.
The correct way to lay out lines.

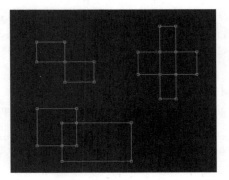

THINK OF WALLS AS VOIDS

The second guiding rule for correct line layout requires you to remember the simple fact that the lines of your maps have no thickness. This means that a line is not a wall. It can be the surface of a wall but never the wall itself. The wall is never really part of the map; what the player might perceive as a wall is formed by the void behind the lines. It often helps to think of lines as paint, or as wallpaper, hung to hide the void beyond.

Figure 9.4 shows how this rule is applied to create two adjacent rooms off a single corridor. Notice how all the walls have been drawn explicitly with two lines, not just one.

Figure 9.4.

A line layout that produces a pair of adjacent rooms with a wall between them.

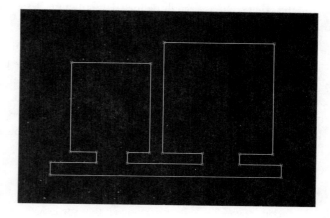

AVOID UNCONNECTED LINES

The final guideline for trouble-free maps is to avoid lines that are not connected at both ends to other lines. Although such lines are not illegal in DOOM, they are rarely used, and until you fully understand their use, you should avoid them. This removes any risk of your sectors failing to close and also helps reinforce the preceding guideline.

NOTE: Failure to observe the guidelines that are presented here will have serious consequences when it comes to trying out your maps. If you ever present a WAD to DOOM in which a sector is unclosed, the game engine will crash back to DOS with the error message Z_CheckHeap: Size of block does not touch next block. A good editor should spot this error in the making and warn you of it. Often, however, the editor will become as confused as DOOM by what you are doing and crash (or lock up) itself. If you find this happens to you, check your line layouts carefully for violations of the guidelines.

ROOMS VERSUS SECTORS

You might feel that I have been using the word "room" interchangeably with the term "sector," and consequently you might be wondering how these two ideas relate to each other. You might even be equating them in your mind.

So far, I have used the word "room" rather loosely. This is because a room (as I use it in this book) is a perceptual construct within a WAD design. It is important to appreciate that a room really exists only in the mind of the players who are guiding their game-world alter egos through the virtual environment of a WAD (and, hopefully, in the mind of the designer who planned it). It has no matching data construct in the hard, numerical world of the DOOM WAD file.

The sector, on the other hand, is a rigidly defined data structure, designed to inform the DOOM engine about the disposition of virtual floors and ceilings within its map space.

In planning and designing your DOOM battleground, you are free to think in terms of rooms, corridors, stairways, caves, ledges, and whatever other spatial entities are appropriate to the environment you are modeling. When it comes to implementing the WAD that holds your design, you must break your map into sectors for the purpose of informing DOOM how your world should be arranged. You need a new sector each time you need to change the ceiling height or texture, floor height or texture, brightness level, or special sector characteristics. The proper use of sectors to provide playing spaces will become more apparent as you progress deeper into this mission.

NOTE: The following WAD sortie builds on the WAD produced in the last sortie of the preceding room. If you did not come along on that sortie but want to accompany me on this one, you should use WAD3.WAD (DOOM), D2WAD3.WAD (DOOM II), or H1WAD3.WAD (Heretic) from the CD-ROM as your starting point.

WAD SORTIE 4: BREAKING THROUGH THE WALLS

With the lessons of this briefing in mind, you can now begin the expansion of your embryonic WAD. To demonstrate the need for walls to have thickness, I will lead you through the addition of some territory beyond the confines of your initial hexagonal room, starting with a short passageway. The opening into the passageway is narrower than the passageway itself to create some apparent walls for the hexagonal room.

You should load your editor with WAD3.WAD as a starting point.

SYNCHRONIZING WADS

Before you start, you need to check that the shape of your room is a close approximation to mine. Look at Figure 9.5 and compare it with your own map. The important feature to have the same is the line that marks the southeast wall of the hexagonal room. Mine is about 500 units long and runs at an angle of 230. As long as your shape looks similar to the one in the figure, you should be OK. Use your knowledge from earlier sorties to adjust the vertex positions if you need to change the layout of your lines to match mine.

Before you start drawing the new section in WADED, you might find it helpful to adjust the ZOOM factor to 08 and scroll the view of your map so that the line of that crucial southeastern wall of the main hexagon is toward the left of the screen. This way, you leave yourself some space in which to work to the right. Make sure that you have the Draw button clicked along with (Draw) Lines.

Figure 9.5.

The suggested starting shape. (This is my WAD3.WAD.)

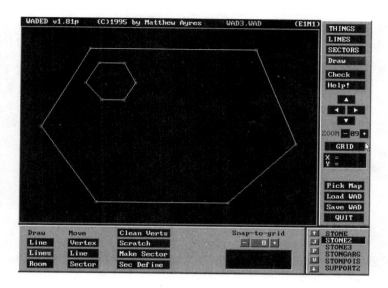

DRAWING THE NEW PASSAGE

To begin the new part of the map in WADED, move your mouse pointer to the center of the southeastern line of your main hexagon. This is where the new passage joins the main room. When the mouse pointer is properly in contact with the existing line, the line changes to the familiar pulsating red. When this happens, click once with the left mouse button to create a new vertex that is connected to the existing line and splits it into halves. When you move the mouse, you find that you are in the process of drawing a third line from this new vertex.

Add the lines listed in Table 9.1 to your map. Again, measurements and angles are approximate. Note, however, that the first line should be perpendicular to the one you have just split, and the second should be perpendicular to the first (and thus parallel to the split line).

Table 9.1. Some new lines for your map.

Line	Angle	Length
1	140	50
2	50	74
3	140	110
4	90	448
5	180	192
6	270	672
7	320	96
8	50	96

These additions should leave you with just one line to draw to complete the new shape, shown in Figure 9.6.

Figure 9.6.
The new addition to the southeast corner of the map.

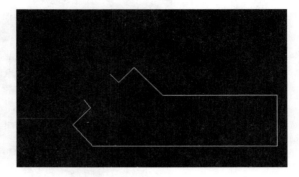

The final new line needs to reconnect with the original southeastern wall of the hexagon. Aim to do this about halfway along the line that runs southwest from the new shape's starting point. Your final line must connect with the original hexagon wall, so make sure that the appropriate line shows red before you click it. If your connection is successful, WADED terminates the drawing process, because it recognizes that you have produced a closed shape.

NOTE: If the drawing process does not terminate with your last click, you failed to connect your last vertex to the original line. You can easily salvage this situation. Click (anywhere) with the right mouse button to terminate the drawing process. This action should leave everything intact up to your final vertex. Click the (Move) Vertices button and then drag your errant final vertex onto the line to which it should have connected. As this line turns red, release the mouse button, and the desired connection is made.

You might also want to confirm that the vertex with which you began this new section connects properly. With (Move) Vertices selected, try moving it a little and check that all three lines move with it. If they don't, simply drag the vertex to the point on the original line where you want it connected, and release the mouse button as the line turns red.

The original southeast line of your hexagon is now split into three sections by the addition of the two new vertices. You might find, in fact, that this line is now no longer the nice straight line it once was. Use the appropriate buttons in the Move/Del column, and reposition any of your new area's lines or vertices if they are not to your liking.

TIP: You can make diagonal lines easier to place in WADED by reducing the Snap-to-Grid setting while drawing. Generally, though, this is best left set at 8.

Adding the New Lines in WadAuthor

Add the new shape in WadAuthor by first clicking with the right mouse button below and to the right of the main hexagon. Use the context menu to add a new polygonal sector with 10 sides (the radius is unimportant). Then move this figure's vertices to produce a polygon of approximately the same size and shape as the new area, shown previously in Figure 9.6. Move this shape into the approximate position it is to occupy, just outside the southeastern wall of the main hexagonal room.

Next, split the line forming the southeastern wall of the main hexagon by clicking the line once with the left mouse button to select it, then clicking with the right mouse and choosing Split Linedefs from the context menu. Repeat this operation so that the original line is divided into three.

Finally, connect the new area to the hexagonal room by merging two lines—the new central section of the hexagon's southeastern wall and that line of the new area which is closest to it and parallel with it. To merge the two lines, select one of the lines by clicking it with the left mouse button. Hold down the Ctrl key and left click the other line. This action should give you two lines that show yellow when you move the mouse away (see Figure 9.7). Use the right mouse button to bring up the context menu and choose Join Linedefs. The two areas now join. You can make any final adjustments to the shape that might be necessary before saving the map.

Figure 9.7.

Preparing to join sectors in WadAuthor.

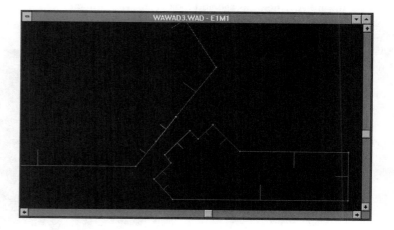

You might discover that diagonal lines are tricky to get just right in most editors. If you have lines that you need to run parallel or perpendicular to each other, or that need to be of particular lengths, it is often best if you can arrange for these lines to run east-west or north-south on the map. Drawing them is easier this way, and you might find that this method causes fewer problems for the nodes builder and the game engine too—more good reasons for planning your WAD on paper first.

MAKING A NEW SECTOR

In WADED, notice that all your new lines are still magenta. WADED uses this color to warn you that these lines are not yet part of any sector; they therefore mean nothing to the game engine and cause an error if you try to play this WAD. When you are happy with the layout of your lines, click the Make Sector button and then click once somewhere within your new shape. All the enclosing lines of your new shape should turn red as WADED incorporates them into a new sector.

Click the SECTORS button (in the right-hand button bar). Now click in each of your two sectors in turn. Observe that WADED has transferred the attributes from your original sector to your new one. The only item that changes in the lower region of the screen as you select each sector is the Sector identification number shown at the far left.

WadAuthor users just need to change the settings of the new sector to match those of the adjoining hexagonal sector.

ADMIRING YOUR NEW WALLS

Save your latest additions as WAD4.WAD. (Make sure that WADED knows it has to build the nodes before you OK the Save WAD pop-up.) Then you can load DOOM to try out your extended WAD. Take the player over toward your new passage and look carefully at the entrance to it. Admire those nice, thick walls. (See Figure 9.8.)

Figure 9.8.
A view of your new walls.

ADDING ANOTHER ROOM

Now that you have seen how simple it is to extend your map by adding new sectors, you are no doubt eager to add some more. You should be confident enough to add another room without too much help from me, so start your editor again with WAD4.WAD as your starting point.

Figure 9.9 shows the basic shape of a new room, this time connected to the original hexagon's southwest wall. In WADED, you might find that a ZOOM factor of 8 is useful before you start. As before, begin your new drawing at one of the points of connection with the existing hexagon, working around the shape to the other point of connection. I won't give you specific details of the new room, except to say that its long southern wall should be made about 1,100 units long. You can copy the rest of the shape from the figure. (WadAuthor users might find it most convenient to start with a new rectangular sector and then split some lines to reshape it as required.)

Figure 9.9.

The new shape for the southwest corner of the map.

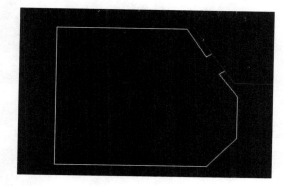

After the shape is complete, use Make Sector in the usual way to create a new sector out of it. To add a little variety, make this new room a bit brighter than the first. Click the SECTORS button in the right-hand button bar and then click anywhere in the new sector. Increase the Lighting level to 224. Raise the ceiling height to 160 as well, and change its texture to CEIL3_6 [FLOOR08 in Heretic]. Then save the WAD as WAD4A.WAD and take a look at it.

EXAMINING THE NEW ROOM

Take the player into the new room and have a good look around. Everything might seem OK at first, but if you look closely, you might see that, in fact, there are problems this time.

First, examine the ceiling. In the DOOM and DOOM II sorties, I deliberately chose a pattern that has lights in it (see Figure 9.10) in an attempt to provide an explanation of the increased light level in this new room. For the Heretic example (shown in Figure 9.11), on the other hand, I simply chose a grating type pattern as the closest match to the DOOM ceiling. (Heretic, with its more medieval setting, does not offer strip lighting for the ceiling, of course!) In all cases, however, notice how poorly the chosen pattern works where it meets a diagonal wall. (Your version might not be as bad as mine; it depends on the exact location of your walls.)

What about the opening between the two rooms? That hasn't worked very well this time, has it? The floor appears fine, but the ceiling is definitely odd. Do you remember that you set the ceiling of the new room higher than the old ceiling? There seems to be some visual confusion over this in the opening, doesn't there?

Figure 9.10.

A messy junction of rooms (DOOM example).

Figure 9.11.

The same messy junction in Heretic.

NOTE: WadAuthor users won't have the same problems here: your editor is doing more work for you. Load the sample WAD from the CD-ROM if you want to see what trouble WADED users are having!

Finally, take a close look at the walls as you move through the opening. Notice how the mortar lines of one room don't meet properly with those from the other room. What on earth could have gone wrong?

EXIT: MOPPING UP AND MOVING ON

In this chapter, you learned some salutary lessons about the limitations of DOOM space, found out more about laying out lines, and saw how easy it is to extend a WAD by adding new sectors. You also saw how easy it is to make a mess of things. You now have some real mopping up to do!

Take heart, though, because the next chapter leads you some way toward a solution to the present problem by revealing some more facts about DOOM's lines. It also sheds some light on the mystery of how the walls are painted.

AT THE SECTOR'S EDGE

In the preceding chapter's editing sortie, you successfully broke out of the single room of your first WAD (although you did so without any real explanation of how it was achieved or of exactly where your old wall went). The mission was not a complete success, however, in its attempt to add another room to your growing WAD. You discovered that DOOM's walls don't always automatically look right on their own.

This chapter provides you with some more explanations of what you have been doing with your editor and how much it has been doing by itself. A further sortie attempts to correct some of the problems that earlier sorties of this mission introduced to your developing WAD.

The briefing starts with a look at how lines really work.

A CLOSER LOOK AT LINES

So far, you have had no detailed information about what lines do in DOOM WADs. You have been told that they always run between vertices, that they consist of a linedef with a couple of sidedefs attached, and that they define the extent of sectors. You have not been given any real details of what these structures are, what they do, or how they do it. It might have been apparent to you that your current lines are providing DOOM with the walls of your rooms. Yet you have been told that your lines are not the walls themselves. You broke out of the walls of your first room without deleting (or even apparently changing) any of your original lines. You are probably wondering, therefore, how all of this fits together.

Start WADED with your latest WAD, and I'll show you.

— By Steve Benner

WHAT LINES REALLY DO

The principal role of the lines in DOOM WADs is really very simple. It is to tell the game engine about the *edge* of a sector. Remember that the sector is DOOM's basic division of space. You have seen how, in essence, each sector has a floor, a ceiling, and a light level. At the edge of each sector, something must happen to those three items. Lines tell DOOM precisely what that something is.

THE LINEDEF STRUCTURE

You know already that a linedef runs between two vertices. This determines both where the line lies on the map and also its handedness. In addition, each linedef provides a set of attributes that tell the game engine how the line should be treated during play.

Viewing Linedef Attributes

In WADED, you can view all a line's attributes (remember that linedefs and sidedefs are treated as one entity in WADED) by clicking the LINES button located toward the top of the right-hand button bar. When you select this button, the Line Attributes bar is displayed in the lower portion of the screen below the main map-editing area. (See Figure 10.1.) Click any of your lines to select it and view its attributes.

In WadAuthor, double-click a line to access the line's properties. Take care to click on the line itself, and not in the sector next to it; otherwise, you get the sector properties instead.

Figure 10.1.
WADED's Line Attributes bar.

Many of a line's attributes are under automatic editor control. For now, look, but don't change anything!

LINEDEF ATTRIBUTES

Most *linedef attributes* are single-bit (on/off) flags that determine a line's main characteristics. These are the on/off characteristics:

- Two-Sided/See-Through/Shoot-Through
- Impassable
- Secret on Map
- Blocks Sound
- Not on Map

- On Map from Start
- Blocks Monsters
- Upper Unpegged
- Lower Unpegged

NOTE: Most editors use slightly different terms, but the correspondence should be obvious.

THE LINEDEF SPECIAL ACTION CHARACTERISTIC

In addition to the previously listed simple attributes, each linedef possesses a special action characteristic, which enables it to trigger particular actions during play. This characteristic is the subject of several later chapters, so you can ignore it for now.

LINE FLAGS

The simple attributes of linedefs (which I term *line flags* from now on) warrant further inspection.

TWO-SIDED / SEE-THROUGH / SHOOT-THROUGH

The *Two-Sided/See-Through/Shoot-Through flag* (or just *Two-Sided flag*, as it is more conveniently termed) serves many purposes, as you can tell from its name. It is used principally to inform the game engine whether or not there are sectors on both sides of a line (although it does not need to reflect the true state of affairs here). This information is used by the graphic engine to decide whether there is anything more to draw beyond this line. It is also used to determine whether monsters can see through the line and the fate of bullets and shotgun pellets (but not rockets or plasma) that reach the line.

There are other ramifications for lines flagged as two-sided, as you see shortly. For now, you should leave the manipulation of this flag strictly to your editor.

IMPASSABLE

A line's *Impassable flag* determines whether players or monsters can cross the line: they never can cross a line that has this flag set. If there is no sector beyond a line, this flag is redundant and DOOM ignores it, whatever its setting. Note that this flag has no effect on the passage of bullets or projectiles.

Editors' Automated Flag Waving

WADED automatically adjusts all the lines' Two-Sided and Impassable flags as needed, provided that you build your sectors with the Make Sector button. (You will see another way of making sectors later.) A quick inspection of the lines of your map should show you that virtually all your current lines have their Impassable flags set; however, you should also be able to spot two that haven't. WadAuthor also adjusts lines' Two-Sided flags as sectors are linked together with a Join Linedefs command.

SECRET ON MAP

Lines with the *Secret on Map flag* set appear as standard impassable lines on the DOOM auto-map during play. This flag is used to hide secret doors and such from the players before their discovery. Secret areas are the subject of Chapter 18, "Let's Get the Hell Out of Here!"

BLOCKS SOUND

Setting a line's *Blocks Sound flag* limits the transmission of sound from sector to sector, thus preventing any nondeaf monsters from waking and hunting the player when the first shot is fired. Such lines do not stop sound dead, though—you learn more about sound propagation in Chapter 19, "Populating Your Nightmare."

NOT ON MAP

Lines with their *Not on Map flag* set do not appear on DOOM's auto-map at all, even if the player acquires the computer-map power-up. This flag enables you to hide any lines from the player that you feel might cause confusion. It also permits the hiding of special action lines so that no clues to their presence can be gleaned from the map.

ON MAP FROM START

Lines with their *On Map from Start flag* set appear on DOOM's auto-map when the level starts, even though they might not yet have been "seen" by the player. You can use this flag to give the player clues about secret locations by hinting at additional map areas. This flag should rarely be needed in a well-designed WAD.

BLOCKS MONSTERS

The *Blocks Monsters flag* enables a line to block the movements of monsters without impeding the player. You will have occasion to use this flag in later sorties.

UPPER/LOWER UNPEGGED

A line's two unpegged flags contribute to the way in which patterns are painted on the vertical plane that the line represents. The purpose and use of these two flags are covered in detail in the next chapter. Before you learn the use of these flags, though, you need to know how the walls get painted in the first place.

PAINTING THE WALLS

You have now seen how linedefs tell the DOOM engine how each line contributes to the operation of the game. On its own though, a linedef says little about the way lines look. For that, DOOM needs to consult the sidedef.

THE ROLE OF THE SIDEDEF

To fully understand the role of sidedefs, you have to appreciate that each sidedef belongs to a sector as well as to a linedef. Lines therefore need as many sidedefs as they have sectors bordering them. It is the sidedef that truly connects each sector to its surrounding linedefs and is responsible for informing the game engine about the view of that line from its particular sector. The graphical engine consults the appropriate sidedef whenever it needs to render a sector's boundary on the screen. The connection of the sidedefs through their linedefs then provides the links out to adjacent sectors and the data required to render fully all the surfaces in the player's field of view at any moment.

This interconnection and mutual ownership of data structures might sound complex, but it provides the DOOM engine with a quick and convenient way of obtaining the information it needs in order to display its world.

THE SIDEDEF STRUCTURE

Sidedefs provide details of the view of their particular sector edge by supplying texture names to the DOOM engine in a similar manner to the way that the sector structure supplies texture names for its floor and ceiling. Because of the added complication brought about by the potential vertical displacement of adjacent sectors, sidedefs need to provide a little more information than just a single texture name. Each sidedef might be called on to supply up to three texture names, depending on the precise disposition of the floors and ceilings of adjacent sectors. Each sidedef therefore consists of three texture slots, each of which holds one texture name.

These are a sidedef's three textures:

- The normal (or main) texture
- The upper texture
- The lower texture

Additionally, each sidedef supplies a horizontal (X) and vertical (Y) displacement value that allows for the precise alignment of the specified textures at the time of painting. (A discussion of the intricate details of texture alignment is deferred until the next chapter.)

Viewing Sidedef Information

As has already been noted (as shown previously in Figure 10.1), when you select WADED's LINES button to view the linedef attributes, you are also presented with any sidedef data in the same information bar. The sidedef information for the currently selected line appears in two columns, just to the right of the full column of linedef flags. Each sidedef column consists of three text field boxes with two blue numerical value buttons under them. The leftmost of these two columns displays data from the line's left sidedef, if one exists (these fields are empty if the line is single-sided), and the rightmost column displays the information from the line's right sidedef.

WadAuthor also displays sidedef information at the same time as the rest of a line's attributes. Access this by double-clicking a line to bring up the Linedef Properties dialog box. The right-hand side of the dialog box shows the line's sidedef information, one side at a time. (WadAuthor calls the right side of a line its *front* and its left side its *back*.) Note also how this dialog box shows which sector each sidedef belongs to.

A SIDEDEF'S THREE TEXTURES

A sidedef's three textures can supply all the information that is ever needed to successfully render any DOOM wall surface. This situation is illustrated in Figure 10.2, which shows all the possible vertical arrangements of two adjacent sectors.

Figure 10.2.
Locations of textures on lines between sectors.

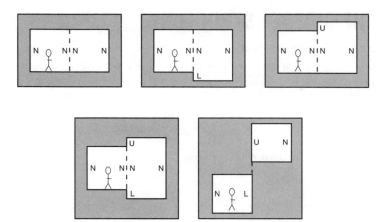

In all cases, a dashed line shows the two-sided line lying on the boundary between the two sectors. Letters indicate which texture slot provides the appropriate pattern for all visible wall surfaces. Remember that each sidedef supplies the engine with the details of what is seen when viewed from within its particular sector.

THE NORMAL (OR MAIN) TEXTURE

A single-sided line can have nothing beyond it. DOOM knows, therefore, that when rendering any visible portion of such a line, it needs to apply paint between the current sector's ceiling and its floor to completely block off any further view. It obtains the name of the pattern to use as this paint from the line's normal-texture slot.

The outer walls of the sectors in Figure 10.2 (with letter Ns adjacent to them) consist of lines of this type.

A line with a sector on each side of it needs to have the relative heights of the floors and ceilings of these sectors taken into consideration before anything can be painted. In these cases, the normal texture is applied only to the gap between the *lower* of the two ceilings and the *higher* of the two floors. Again, Figure 10.2 shows these areas with a letter N, this time on the dashed lines between the sectors. Note that one such letter occurs on each side of these lines. Each provides the view of that space from its own side.

NOTE: DOOM does not permit all wall textures to be applied to a two-sided line's normal texture. You should be able to tell from Figure 10.2, though, that you are unlikely to want any texture there in most situations. (The application of textures to two-sided lines is discussed in detail in later chapters.)

After the normal texture has been dealt with, other portions of the wall might still need to be painted, as happens when a sector's floor is lower, or its ceiling is higher, than its neighbor's. The other two texture slots are used to provide the paint for these additional areas.

UPPER TEXTURE

The *upper texture* is used to paint the wall area between a sector's ceiling and any lower adjacent ceiling. Figure 10.2 marks these areas with the letter U.

LOWER TEXTURE

The *lower texture* is used to paint the wall area between a sector's floor and any higher adjacent floor. Figure 10.2 marks these areas with the letter L.

NOTE: DOOM's decision about whether a line has anything beyond it is based only on the setting of the line's Two-Sided flag. It does not count the line's sidedefs. An incorrect setting of this flag therefore drastically affects the way the line displays.

LEAVING OUT THE PAINT

In some cases, you want a line to be completely transparent—as with most of the normal textures on the two-sided lines shown in Figure 10.2. Most lines between adjacent sectors are like this, in fact, to enable a player to see from one sector to the next. DOOM uses a null or transparent texture setting to achieve this. This special value is designated by means of a dash character (–) in the appropriate texture slot.

This special texture (which is really a lack of texture, of course) causes the engine to paint whatever is in view beyond the line, rather than painting some pattern in the line's vertical plane. It can therefore be used only in a location where there is another sector to be seen through it; otherwise, you are inviting a view of the void—an action you will always regret. An inspection of Figure 10.2 should indicate which locations these are.

More Automatic Line Changing

When you build sectors up against each other, as you did in the preceding WAD sortie, most editors automatically make all the changes to your lines that are deemed appropriate. Usually this means making any lines that are common to the two sectors passable, two-sided, and transparent. "But," you might ask, "what if I wanted an impassable wall between my two adjacent rooms?" In such a case, don't build the wall out of a single line. Use two single-sided lines with a void between them, just as I showed you in the preceding chapter.

PUTTING PAINT IN THE RIGHT PLACES

As you can undoubtedly appreciate, with a WAD's potential for complex geometric arrangements, it is vital that the graphical engine be supplied with correct and complete information if it is to perform its task of rendering the DOOM world correctly on-screen. It is important that you learn to recognize the areas where texture information is crucial, if you are to avoid problems with the way your WADs appear.

ESSENTIAL TEXTURES

The biggest cause of serious problems in the on-screen rendering of DOOM WADs is the omission of essential textures. By this, I mean the use of the *transparent* texture in an area of wall that has nothing to see beyond it. You should regard having a texture as essential in the following places:

- The main texture of any single-sided line
- Any upper texture where the current sector's ceiling is higher than its neighbor's
- Any lower texture where the current sector's floor is lower than its neighbor's

Again, look back at Figure 10.2 if you can't immediately see why trying to look through these areas is not a good idea.

Discussion of the full consequences of omitting essential textures is deferred until the next chapter. For now, just note where the presence of a texture is crucial, and try to ensure that you don't omit textures from these locations.

Essential Texture Notification in WADED

WADED alerts you to essential textures by marking such slots in the Line Attributes bar with a red background (rather than the usual black). It only marks slots in this way that are essential by virtue of the relative elevations of adjacent sectors; it assumes that you will take care of the main texture of single-sided lines yourself. WADED always assigns a main texture to a line as you draw it—it is not unreasonable, therefore, for WADED to assume that you know what you are doing if you subsequently remove it.

NOTE: The following WAD sortie builds on the WAD produced in the preceding chapter's sortie. If you did not accompany me on that sortie but want to come along on this one, you should use WAD4A.WAD (DOOM), D2WAD4A.WAD (DOOM II), or H1WAD4A.WAD (Heretic) from the CD-ROM as your starting point.

WAD SORTIE 5: FIXING THE MESS

Now that you understand something of the way in which lines work, you should take a more detailed look at your WAD to see how WADED has handled line settings so far (that is, when left to its own devices). The causes of the problems might even become apparent.

LOOKING AT THE LINES

With WAD4A.WAD loaded and the LINES button selected, try clicking a few of your lines in turn. Notice that just about all your lines are flagged as impassable (unless you built the WAD in WadAuthor), have no left sidedef (shown by the left-textures column being entirely empty), and have STONE2 [GRSTNPB in Heretic] as the right main-texture with the transparent texture (–) in the right upper- and lower-texture slots. In other words, all your lines represent impassable surfaces, painted with a stonelike texture from ceiling to floor. I hope this sounds reasonable!

If you inspect the line that separates the main hexagon from the passage in the southeast corner, however, you see that this is different from most of your other lines. This line is flagged as two-sided, having right and left sidedefs, with the transparent (–) texture assigned to all slots (or just the two normal slots, if you built the WAD using WadAuthor). This is, therefore, a line through which the player can both see and walk—it is an opening in the "wall" of impassable lines around it. This is the line that WADED changed when you used Make Sector to add the southeastern passage to the family of sectors in your WAD or that WadAuthor changed when you linked the sectors. Your editor made this hole in the wall for you by switching two flags (impassable and two-sided) and removing the paint from the right normal.

You might have already noticed that WADED gave you a visual clue to the action it took. Look carefully at this particular line on your map, and you see that it is displayed less prominently than your other lines. WADED always uses this dimmer color and thinner linestroke to distinguish two-sided lines from single-sided ones on your map so that you can always tell at a glance which is which.

THE OFFENDING LINE

Turn your attention to the equivalent line in the southwest wall of your hexagon—the one that connects the hexagon to the new room off to the southwest. You can spot now, I hope, that this line is two-sided, even before you click it. When you do click it, observe that its settings are identical to those of its counterpart in the southeast wall. Notice that here WADED marks the left upper-texture slot with a red background. This color is a warning that a texture is missing from this line.

Remember that you made the ceiling of the new room quite a bit higher than the ceiling of the hexagonal room. When viewed from inside, the new room has a step down along this line from the level of its ceiling to the level of the adjacent ceiling. DOOM must be told what to paint on the vertical surface of this downward step. (Of course, it has no such requirement when the southwest room is being viewed from within the hexagonal room. From there, the step up on the other side of the line is hidden by the hexagonal room's lower ceiling—hence the need for two sidedefs in these situations. Again, refer to Figure 10.2 if you're having difficulty visualizing this.)

It would be sensible, I suppose, to fill this missing texture with the same texture used for the neighboring walls. I'm getting tired of the default stone pattern, however, as I'm sure you are, so I suggest that you look for an alternative. It would be nice to use a new texture for the whole of the new room, wouldn't it?

CHOOSING A WALL TEXTURE

While you're viewing lines in WADED, a list of available wall textures is displayed in the lower-right corner of the screen. This list box operates in exactly the same way as the floor/ceiling texture list box that appears when you are viewing sectors. (WadAuthor provides a browse list of textures if you press F2 when the Linedef Properties dialog box is active.) Notice how STONE2 [GRSTNPB in Heretic] is the currently selected texture. Using the right mouse button, click any entry in the list box to preview it on-screen, just as you did with the floor textures. The preview of a wall texture (Figure 10.3 shows DOOM's STONE2) is similar to that of a floor tile; however, the graphic is generally bigger, and a little more information is displayed. The next chapter examines wall textures in more detail, so I won't dwell on the subject here.

Take a look at the texture that appears immediately after the default wall texture in the list: STONE3 in DOOM/ DOOM II, GRSTNPBV in Heretic. This would seem like a good texture to introduce into the new room—it is related to the texture of its neighbor's walls but is different.

TIP: Don't get carried away introducing new textures at random through your WADs. Overuse of textures makes your WADs look amateurish. Think through your use of textures. Make changes gradually and with reason. Texture changes that the player hardly notices or that appear as a natural progression usually work best.

Figure 10.3.
WADED's preview of the wall texture
STONE2.

CHANGING LINES EN MASSE

Now that you have a new texture for the new room, it needs to be applied to all the lines that make up this southwestern sector. Selecting all of these lines in turn and changing the entry in all of their right normal-texture slots sounds rather tedious, though, doesn't it? Fortunately, WADED provides a shortcut, in the form of its MULTI button. I will show you how to use it.

Click the MULTI button. It turns red, and any line you had selected reverts to its normal color. In addition, all the information in the Line Attributes bar changes to xs (or green dots in the case of the flags). Click a line now and notice that even though you have selected it in the usual way (it has turned red), none of its attributes is displayed. If you click more lines, you see that each new line becomes selected in addition to earlier selections. Click a line that is already selected, and it becomes deselected. In this mode, you can now select each line you want to change. Click all nine lines you added to form the new room in the southwest corner of your map. Do not include the two-sided line linking this room with your hexagon. Make sure that no other lines are included in your selection before going on; click any that are to deselect them.

When you have selected all nine lines, make sure that the new texture is selected in the wall textures list box, and then click once with the left mouse button on the middle texture-field of the right-hand column of line textures. The X that was there should be replaced by the name of the new texture. WADED gives you the chance to change your mind about multi-line operations such as this and does not effect the change until you click the APPLY button.

NOTE: If you decide you don't want to make any multi-line changes, you can click MULTI again to return to single-line selection without applying any changes.

When you are sure that you have the correct nine lines selected and the new texture name is displayed in the appropriate texture field, click APPLY. WADED makes the changes you have requested and then returns to its normal single-line selection mode. The line you had selected immediately before clicking the MULTI button is the current line.

Selecting and Changing Multiple Lines in WadAuthor

You can select multiple lines in WadAuthor too. Left-click the first line you want to select and then Ctrl-click to add further lines to the selection. Alternatively, to select all the lines of a single sector, just click inside the sector. Press Alt+Enter to view the selected lines' properties. Any changes you make in the Properties dialog box are applied to all the selected lines. It would be a good idea to use this technique now to change the textures used on all of your lines and not just those of the southwest room to match those in the sample WAD (STONE2 in DOOM/DOOM II, GRSTNPB in Heretic). Don't attempt to fix the hexagonal room's pillar yet, though; that is dealt with shortly.

Now select the line that runs across the entrance to your newly painted room. Apply the new wall texture to the upper essential texture slot. Right, that's one problem solved.

FIXING THE OTHER PROBLEMS (MAYBE)

One of my other complaints about this room is the poor ceiling texture. I don't like the way the lights disappear into the walls. You can rectify this situation by applying a new ceiling texture. Click SECTORS to access sector attributes; click in the southwest sector to show its attributes and find a better texture to apply to the ceiling. In DOOM, you should find that TLITE6_6 works quite well. Heretic users might prefer to stay with FLAT516 (as used in the hexagonal room), utilizing the change of light level to create variation in the ceiling's appearance. In a later sortie you find an explanation for the increased light level here.

When you've made this change, save the file as WAD5.WAD (there should be no need to build the nodes) and try out the WAD. Is that opening into the new room any better now? (See Figures 10.4 and 10.5.)

Figure 10.4.
Better (in DOOM/DOOM II)—but still not right!

Figure 10.5.
Slight improvements in the Heretic version.

Never mind. Soldier on. It's time to look at the problem more closely.

REEXAMINING THE PROBLEM

What is it that looks odd about your gap through the wall now? Well, there is still a problem with the matching of the mortar lines. There remains a discontinuity where the lines on the hexagonal room's walls meet those coming through the gap. You didn't expect these to change with the latest modification, though, did you? The vertical step down from the higher level of the southwest room's ceiling to that of its neighbor does appear in the view now. (Figures 10.4 and 10.5 each show this.) The mortar lines on this wall section (as it now appears) don't align too well with its neighbors' lines, however. It looks to be in a rather odd place; wouldn't you expect that step down to occur in a plane flush with the inner surface of the southwestern room's walls? Maybe it is time to return briefly to the drawing board and rethink this area of the WAD.

First, ask yourself what makes this opening different from the opening at the other side of the hexagonal room. You experienced no difficulties there, so why are there problems here? The answer, of course, lies in the change of ceiling height across the opening. The southeastern opening uses the same floor and ceiling heights as the main room. In fact, it uses the same floor and ceiling textures as well as the same lighting level. There was no necessity to create a new sector there at all—you could have merely extended the hexagonal room sector around the new shape.

Don't worry, though. Developing the WAD the way you did was expedient, and nothing much is wasted as a result. You could recombine the lines into one sector, but there is little to be gained by so doing. As it is, you can always change either sector independently of the other should you ever want to. I'd leave things as they are.

Having identified the problem as the change in ceiling height, I examine the solution afresh.

RETHINKING THE SOLUTION

Consider what is really wanted here: a hexagonal room connecting to another room through an opening in the wall. Now, how many sectors is this? The WAD currently implements this in two sectors. Would it not be better as three? Consider the following setup:

- The hexagonal room
- The southwest room
- The hole in the wall

This way, each area can have its own ceiling height, with the interconnecting hole handled independently of the two rooms.

Your WAD is suffering from a case of insufficient sectors! This is quite a common fault in the WADs of beginners. It generally demonstrates that the novice has yet to grasp fully the correct use of sectors.

Now return to your WAD, wiser than you were. You need to change the way the two rooms interconnect.

REBUILDING THE INTERCONNECTION

Reload WADED with WAD5.WAD. Enter Draw mode and amend the interconnecting gap between the hexagonal room and its southwestern neighbor. This gap currently has a single line between the two rooms, marking the line of the hexagonal room's southwest wall. There are two vertices that, if connected to each other by a line, would provide another line, parallel to the first, and fulfill a similar role in completing the line of the southwestern room's northeast wall. Add this missing line.

You now need to create a new sector out of the small rectangle you have just completed that represents the interconnecting area through the wall between the two rooms. Use Make Sector to do this. This action "steals" this area away from the sector that currently owns it (the old southwestern room) and creates a new sector out of it. After you have done this, move the mouse pointer away into the void somewhere, and notice that WADED is now displaying your new line in the brighter color that signifies a single-sided line. If you now move the mouse into the remaining area of the southwestern room, you see that the southwest sector is no longer closed—the new line has not automatically been incorporated into it. Click somewhere in the southwest room to make WADED correct this error. You should see that doing this makes your new line two-sided.

You should now select SECTORS (in the right-hand button bar) and inspect the new interconnecting sector. Notice that it has inherited the settings from the adjacent hexagonal room, even though this area originally belonged to the sector to the southwest. (The reason for this odd behavior are explained in a later sortie.) Click LINES and inspect the textures of the new line. Notice how this time WADED has supplied something for the essential upper texture. It might not be particularly appropriate, but at least it has tried. Change this texture to match the main texture of its neighboring lines. Then save the WAD as WAD5A.WAD and try it out.

CAUTION: If you are using Heretic, it is *essential* that you change the upper texture used on your new line. Failure to do so results in Heretic's crashing with the message R_TextureNumForName: STARTAN3- not found when you try to play your new WAD. WADED's default texture, STARTAN3, is a DOOM texture; Heretic wants nothing to do with it!

Using WadAuthor to Fix the Interconnection

To fix the interconnection in WadAuthor, start by creating a new rectangular sector of 64 units square somewhere *inside* the southwest sector. Drag this over to the opening between the southwest sector and the hexagonal sector and then use Join Linedefs three times in the following ways: Join the new sector's eastern edge to the line that currently divides the hexagonal sector from the southwest sector. Join the new sector's northern edge to the northern wall of the opening between the hexagonal and the southwest sectors and the new sector's southern edge to the opening's southern wall. Readjust the lines and vertices to restore the correct shape to the two rooms and the interconnection.

Finish the changes by making the new sector's settings match the hexagonal sector's settings, and apply textures to its walls to match those of its neighbors.

Examine the "improved" doorway (see Figure 10.6). It does look a little better when viewed from the southwest, doesn't it? The lintel is now flush with the walls, which improves its appearance somewhat, but the mortar lines still don't match up. If you look closely and compare the current WAD's view through the gap with the earlier view, you see that the mortar alignment problem through the gap has changed, but not noticeably for the better. With Heretic, there's an odd effect visible at the ceiling, as shown in Figure 10.7.

Figure 10.6.
The rebuilt interconnection (DOOM/ DOOM II).

Figure 10.7.
*The Heretic WAD's new inter-
connection.*

MODIFYING THE INTERCONNECTION

Try one more modification. Reload WAD5A.WAD, click SECTORS, and select the small interconnecting sector you just made. Reduce the ceiling height to 104. Doing this creates another essential texture. Can you figure out where it is?

That's right—it's on the boundary between the hexagonal room and the interconnecting doorway sector. Note that the left upper texture of this line is still marked as having a texture in use. You can delete this texture if you want by simply clicking it with the right mouse button (although leaving it does no harm—DOOM does not attempt to use it).

Note that this line's right upper texture is now marked by WADED as essential by WADED (although it hasn't bothered to supply it!). You should be able to work out for yourself why this texture is essential. (The fact that WADED doesn't supply one can be ascribed to a bug.) Apply the default stone texture here (STONE2 in DOOM, GRSTNPB in Heretic) and then save as WAD5B.WAD—no node-building should be necessary. Quit and then try the WAD.

You should find that this action has produced an opening that looks (structurally) better from both sides—although it has now completely messed up all the mortar-line alignments around the opening! It would seem that there are still some things to learn here.

EXIT: MOPPING UP AND MOVING ON

In this chapter, you learned a lot about the way lines work in DOOM. You learned how they can be made to produce both walls and the openings in them. You found out how and where paint can be applied, and you learned to recognize where it is needed. You saw how to access some more features of WADED, and you moved away from the ubiquitous stone of your first WAD's walls.

Your latest sortie also made some progress toward correcting the faults around your WAD's doorway. What you need now is the lowdown on how textures are applied to the walls so that you can mount a full-scale rescue attempt on this area of your WAD. You will find everything you need in the next chapter.

THE LOWDOWN ON TEXTURES

So far in this mission, you used various floor, ceiling, and wall textures to paint the "hard surfaces" of your WAD. You saw that although it might be easy to specify their use, making them look right is not always so simple.

This chapter provides you with the full lowdown on DOOM textures. You will see and use textures that act as more than mere paint. You are also shown something of the full richness of the texture palette that has been provided by the designers at both id and Raven Software.

In addition, the rules for applying textures are discussed in full, along with the consequences of transgressing those rules. By the time you reach the end of this chapter, you will know how to apply textures to any of your WAD's surfaces and have them look just right.

This chapter also leads you on three WAD sorties, building on the WADs produced in previous chapters. During these sorties, you will see something of DOOM's great outdoors with the addition of a court-yard to your WAD. At long last, you are also shown how to cure the problems of texture alignment that have been plaguing your WAD throughout the past few sorties.

CEILING AND FLOOR TEXTURES

Your first introduction to textures in this mission involved tiles for ceilings and floors. These ceiling and floor textures make a good topic with which to begin a full survey of DOOM textures.

— By Steve Benner

FLATS

Figure 11.1 shows a sample view of a DOOM floor or ceiling texture. The graphic itself is a 64×64 block of pixels. All floor and ceiling textures use graphics of this size.

Figure 11.1.

A close-up view of a single occurrence of the FLOOR5_1 floor texture.

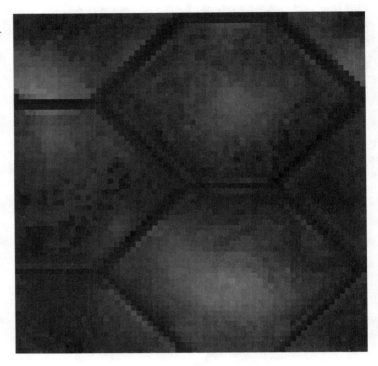

These simple, square, graphical textures are often termed floor and ceiling *flats* or *tiles* to distinguish them from the more complex wall textures that you encounter later in this chapter. The DOOM game engine allows flats to be applied interchangeably to floors or ceilings. You might find, however, that not all textures look equally good on both surfaces—and some might look downright odd if used inappropriately.

Because flats are all of a standard size, DOOM's graphical engine applies them in a standard way to floor and ceiling surfaces. A flat's exact position is determined from the map's X,Y coordinate grid; flats are always placed starting at a coordinate that is a multiple of 64.

As well as being positioned firmly on this grid, tiles are always oriented the same way, along a north-south axis. The flat's first pixel (the colored block in its upper-left corner when viewed as in Figure 11.1) is copied to the appropriate surface at the starting coordinate. Subsequent pixels are transferred to adjacent locations to the east (working across the graphic) and south (working down the graphic). If the same texture is applied to both the floor and the ceiling of a sector, these two surfaces appear as mirror images of each other. Each pixel on the ceiling is the same color as the pixel on the floor directly below it.

Because floors and ceilings are locked to the coordinate system in this way, their patterns are rendered with no reference to walls or other map elements (except that these areas are clipped by their sector boundaries, of course). This methodology ensures that adjacent sectors having the same floor or ceiling heights can have their textures connected smoothly across the boundary between them, whatever the shape or orientation of that boundary. It also means that if the designer is not careful, walls might cut blithely across features in the ceiling or floor textures, making them look odd. Remember the abortive attempt to use the CEIL3_6 texture in the southwestern room of your WAD, back in WAD Sortie 4?

Note that the only way of changing the way in which floor and ceiling textures line up with your sector boundaries is to reposition your map lines to make them clip the flats differently. The flats themselves cannot be moved or rotated.

Assistance with Flat Alignment in WADED

To assist in the placement of lines for the best alignment of flats, WADED supplies an optional grid overlay, which shows where flats are placed in your map. You activate and deactivate this overlay by using the GRID button, located in the right-hand button bar. Use this grid to position your lines along the joins of the flats to ensure the best painting of floors and ceilings.

SEEING THE SKY

The preceding chapter taught you that walls can be assigned a transparent texture (or have texture omitted, depending on how you care to think of it) to allow sectors beyond the walls to be visible through them. You are possibly wondering whether there is an equivalent transparent texture for ceilings, one that enables the player to see out to the sky and the rest of the outside world. After all, you have seen something like this in DOOM, haven't you?

The answers are "Yes" and "What outside world?" DOOM is capable of displaying the sky and distant mountains and such, but don't think that such "outside" elements exist anywhere on your map (or anywhere else, for that matter).

When you want your players to see sky, the ceiling texture to use is F_SKY1. As its name suggests, this texture provides something rather more special than transparent paint—it provides sky (mountains and buildings too, sometimes). This shouldn't surprise you. After all, what use would transparent paint be on the ceiling? There is nothing beyond the ceiling to see, only void. And, as you find out shortly, that is not a pretty sight.

The sky texture in Hexen is called F_SKY.

If you try to preview F_SKY1, however, you might be a little surprised by what you see. (See Figure 11.2.)

Figure 11.2.
The surprise preview of F_SKY1.

"Where is the sky?" you might ask. "And how could they get it all into a 64×64 tile anyway? It surely wouldn't work!" I can see that I'm going to have to convince you.

> **NOTE:** The following WAD sortie builds on the WAD produced in the last sortie of the preceding chapter. If you did not accompany me on that sortie but want to come along on this one, you should use WAD5B.WAD (DOOM), D2WAD5B.WAD (DOOM II), or H1WAD5B.WAD (Heretic) from the CD-ROM as your starting point.

WAD SORTIE 6: ADDING AN OUTDOOR SECTOR

This WAD sortie extends your existing map by leading you through the steps needed for the addition of an outdoor courtyard area.

BREAKING OUT

Start by adding just three new lines to the south wall of the southwest room, as shown in Figure 11.3. These eventually form the exit from the southwest room to the new courtyard. (WadAuthor users should know by now just to create a new sector and join two lines.)

Figure 11.3.
Three new lines for the WAD.

The short ends of the rectangle are about 56 units long. The long dimension isn't critical, but don't make it too long; 360 units is fine.

DEFINING THE COURTYARD

After adding these three lines, with WADED in (Draw) Lines mode, find and select the texture called BROWN1 [CSTLRCK in Heretic] in the scrolling texture list in the bottom-right corner of the screen. (Yes, you've guessed it. This selection changes the wall texture that WADED uses for your next lines to something new. I think it's time for a bit of a change, don't you?) Now draw the additional lines shown in Figure 11.4. These lines form the courtyard's enclosing walls. (WadAuthor users should change the wall textures after creating the new sector.)

Figure 11.4.
More new lines for the WAD.

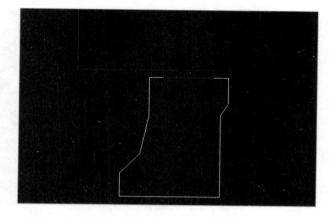

Don't worry about the precise size or shape of this area (but don't encroach too far to the west: I have other things planned for there), just make it match the basic form shown in Figure 11.4.

When you've added all the new lines and are happy that everything connects properly in WADED, click Make Sector. Click next in the new, small rectangle to break out of the southwest room; and then in the larger shape, to add the courtyard area to the list of sectors. Click SECTORS (at upper right) and then somewhere in the new area that is to be the courtyard. This should be Sector 5.

TIP: If you always build your sectors sequentially in this way, working out from existing sectors, WADED has something to build from (a neighboring sector) and assigns more useful values to the various attributes by copying them from the adjacent sector.

Heretic users in particular benefit from this technique because they find that it prevents WADED from using its default sector settings for floor and ceiling textures. WADED's defaults are all DOOM textures and crash Heretic if used in a Heretic WAD.

TAKING THE ROOF OFF

Now, using the right mouse button, click once in the ceiling-texture field of the courtyard sector. This is WADED's shortcut for applying F_SKY1. (WadAuthor users must type the name or select it from the F2 browse window.) The floor texture MFLR8_1 [FLOOR01], inherited from the inner rooms, is rather inappropriate for a courtyard, so I suggest you change it while you're here. I think you'll find that FLAT1_1 [FLOOR03 in Heretic] fits the bill nicely. Because it's a bright, sunny day in the land of DOOM, why not take the lighting level up to 255? Then, save the file as WAD6.WAD (you might find that the nodes are taking a little longer to build by now) and try it out.

Now do you believe me? I know that the transition between sky and building doesn't look right yet (see Figure 11.5), but you have a chance to fix that in a moment. For now, I just wanted you to see the sky.

Figure 11.5.
Behold! The sky!

FAKING THE GREAT OUTDOORS

Now that you have seen the reality of F_SKY1, you need to know how to use it. Some aspects of this texture can be confusing, so I set you straight on these points first.

SOURCES OF CONFUSION WITH DOOM SKIES

You have already observed the principal confusing aspect: the absence of the flat itself from the list of ceiling textures. The reason that there is no ceiling flat for this texture is the obvious one: a realistic and believable rendering of the sky could not be obtained by tiling a 64×64 graphic. Not surprisingly, therefore, DOOM doesn't use one. (Exactly what it is that you see when previewing F_SKY1 remains something of a mystery—probably a dummy entry in the flats table to keep the graphics engine happy.)

To add to the confusion, the sky textures (for, as you see, there is more than one) can be found lurking among the wall textures. Preview the wall texture called SKY1, and you see the sky graphic used in your preceding WAD. Wall textures SKY2 and SKY3 should look familiar, too. (Remember, you need to be in LINES mode to preview wall textures in WADED or have the Linedef Properties dialog box open in WadAuthor.)

NOTE: The names used for the sky textures in DOOM II and Heretic are the same as those used in DOOM, but the textures look different. Hexen has more than three sky textures.

This leads me to the final point of confusion: the fact that there are several separate graphics for portraying the sky but only one ceiling-texture name for obtaining them.

All of this confusion can be cleared up when you realize that F_SKY1 is not a texture at all. It is a special name used to trigger a different ceiling-painting technique. To utilize it properly, you need to understand how it works.

HOW IT ALL WORKS

This is how the process operates. When the game engine comes to paint a ceiling marked as F_SKY1 (or F_SKY in Hexen), it checks first to see what the current episode is (or level, in DOOM II). From this information, the engine decides which sky texture to use. SKY1 is used for Episode 1, SKY2 for Episode 2, and SKY3 for Episode 3. (DOOM II spreads out the three sky textures over its 30-odd levels in a similar manner.) You therefore can only choose which of the three sky textures you want to appear in your WAD by choosing the episode (or level) that your map appears in.

> Hexen handles the selection of sky textures differently from all other variants of the game. Details are given in "Programming the Action," a chapter on the CD-ROM.

Having located the appropriate texture (stored among the wall textures, remember), the graphical engine pastes it into the ceiling space of the appropriate sector. Rather than performing the graphical transformations necessary to create the normal ceiling perspective, however, the graphical engine pastes the texture onto the screen area, pixel for pixel, starting at the top of the screen and working down (clipped, of course, by any other textured surfaces in view at the time). The player's viewing direction is used to determine the horizontal screen displacement of the graphic so that the sky (and any associated distant vista) appears to rotate correctly as the player turns. No other scaling is ever performed on this graphic, thus giving it the appearance of being at an infinite distance from the player at all times.

> In Raven Software's games, the sky textures are handled a little differently from the way described previously. Because these variants of the DOOM engine provide the player with the ability to look up and down, the rendering engine does not always paste the sky graphic onto the screen starting at its topmost row of pixels. Heretic and Hexen's SKY textures are in fact extended vertically: they are 256×200 pixels in size, rather than the normal 256×128. For the normal, horizontally looking view of the sky, the engine begins painting the screen using the 73rd row of pixels from the top of the graphic. Additional rows above this point become used (so that the sky appears to move down) as the player looks up.
>
> This variation in the sky painting method makes no difference to the practical use of the F_SKY ceiling texture, but there are other ramifications for the use of SKY textures in these games, which are mentioned shortly.

USING THE SKY TEXTURE EFFECTIVELY

When this process is properly understood, use of the F_SKY1 texture becomes a fairly simple and straightforward matter. Look back at your sample outdoor area, shown previously in Figure 11.5. If you ignore the details of the sky graphic and imagine ceiling tiles placed over the area it occupies, you should be able to see quite easily that the sky does indeed act as a replacement for the ceiling, in that it occupies precisely the same area as tiles would. Notice how the plane of the "outdoor ceiling" runs continuously into the ceiling of the adjacent "indoor" area. It does so because the ceiling heights are the same in all three of the sectors in view.

To create an illusion that the "building" the player has just left has height beyond its ceiling, as a real building would have, the outdoor sector must have its ceiling raised. Why? To make the sky higher—and, therefore, the wall below it taller. This change creates an upper texture in the step down from this higher sky to the ceiling of the adjacent indoor sector. By using a pattern appropriate to the outside surface of the building as the texture for this step down, you can create the upper facade of the building. Used with care, this technique can produce reasonably realistic-looking buildings. It does need care, however, because this facade is just like those of a Western movie set: flat, with nothing of substance behind it. Allow the player too close to its edges and the player sees around the edges, giving the trick away.

Another useful characteristic of the F_SKY1 painting technique is that the sky texture used is always rendered at a constant brightness, regardless of the brightness level specified for the sector. This technique allows the use of variations in lighting level in outdoor sectors to simulate areas of shade without making the sky look odd as a consequence. However, the incapability of applying sloping shadow areas to walls can limit the usefulness of this technique, as you will see shortly.

USING THE SKY TEXTURE IN OTHER PLACES

F_SKY1 can be applied to the floor, but not surprisingly, it produces an odd effect there. Remember that the display position of a texture applied as F_SKY1 is always reckoned from the top of the screen. Being 128 pixels high, it needs to repeat before it reaches the space set aside for it on the floor. The result is generally somewhat less than attractive and never realistic—the effect does bear experimentation, however.

 CAUTION: Never apply F_SKY1 to both ceiling and floor of a sector simultaneously. The engine cannot cope with this situation, and the result is a mess!

Similarly, any of the SKY textures can be applied to walls, where they look and act like any other wall texture. They do not behave as if they had been painted as sky; they simply look like a picture of the sky painted on the walls—which, of course, is what they are.

The nonstandard (256×200 pixel) size of Raven Software's SKY textures makes them unsuited for creative use on walls. As you will learn shortly, the DOOM graphical engine uses only the upper 128 pixels of any texture that it is required to paint onto a wall surface. Preview the SKY textures in WADED to see how they appear when cut down to this size. You should notice that the lower part of the graphic is missing.

WAD SORTIE 7: IMPROVING THE OUTDOOR SECTOR

NOTE: This sortie builds on the WAD produced in the preceding sortie. If you did not produce that WAD, you should use WAD6.WAD (DOOM), D2WAD6.WAD (DOOM II), or H1WAD6.WAD (Heretic) from the CD-ROM as your starting point here.

If you want to start your editor again, I will show you how to improve the appearance of the outer courtyard by applying some of these techniques.

You have learned that to create the appearance of a building adjoining the courtyard, the ceiling of the outdoor sector needs to be raised. If the ceiling of the entire courtyard area were to be raised, however, it would also have the effect of raising all the enclosing walls, because they are formed by the bounding lines of this sector. I want these walls to stay the height they currently are: any higher and this space would start to feel cramped and the walls would look artificially high. To achieve the desired effect, the current single courtyard sector needs to be divided into various new sectors, each responsible for different sections of the outer walls. This action enables the heights of these wall sections to be varied independently of each other.

PRESERVING THE EXISTING WALL HEIGHTS

The walls along the western and southern boundaries are fine as they are. To prevent them from being changed when the main sector's ceiling is raised, you must place them in a sector of their own. To achieve this result, you must add more lines to your map.

TIP: Users of WadAuthor might want to investigate that editor's Motifs capabilities before proceeding. Details are contained in Chapter 27, "WadAuthor," and the package's own online help. Creating a Courtyard motif from the current settings of the courtyard sector will save you some time in the coming sortie.

In WADED, start at the vertex in the northwestern corner of the courtyard. Draw a line from this vertex at an angle of about 135 until you are a little ways, 80 units or so, from the western wall. Add lines sufficient to mark off an area of the courtyard sector that contains all its western and southern walls. The exact shape is unimportant, but aim to keep the new area fairly thin so as to consume as little of the main courtyard sector as possible. End the drawing at the vertex in the southeastern corner of the courtyard as in Figure 11.6. Leave enough room at this southeastern vertex for additional lines to be added to permit similar treatment of the eastern walls later. (WadAuthor users need only create a new polygonal sector with an appropriate number of sides somewhere within the courtyard sector, and then join lines as needed.)

Figure 11.6.
Lines to bring down the western and southern walls of the courtyard.

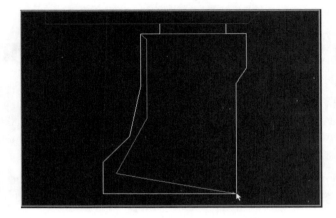

BUILDING THE FACADE

When the addition of these lines is complete, click Make Sector, and then click first in the larger central area of the courtyard before clicking in the thinner western strip.

This order of clicks causes WADED to redefine the larger area as a new sector first and then, with your second click, reconsolidate what remains of the original Sector 5 (together with the appropriate sides of your new lines) into the outer strip. This method ensures that the settings for Sector 5 (the original courtyard) are preserved for the area close to the western and southern walls—unfortunately, the new main courtyard area gets its settings from the interconnection to its north. You therefore need to select SECTORS mode and change the settings of this main courtyard area.

If you are confused by Make Sector's seemingly arbitrary creation of sectors, be patient. Chapter 12, "Putting Sectors to Work," provides a full explanation of its operation.

You need to change the ceiling texture to F_SKY1, the floor texture to FLAT1_1 [FLOOR03 in Heretic], and the lighting level to 255. Take the ceiling up to 216.

In this particular sector, it is probably worth lowering the floor a touch, to make the change in floor pattern between the indoor and outdoor areas more natural. Therefore, take the floor down to –16. This change, of course, changes the sector's elevation relative to the other outdoor sector to its west and south, so you need to reduce that sector's floor to match. In turn, this modification alters the apparent wall heights that these changes were designed to preserve, so be sure to bring the outer sector's ceiling down by 16 units as well, to 144.

TIP: Yes, all of this sector juggling can be tedious and time-consuming—another good reason for you to plan your maps on paper first!

Finally, to complete the facade of the building, apply BROWN1 [CSTLRCK] to both essential textures of the line shared by the courtyard and the gap through the wall.

UPPER TEXTURES BETWEEN F__SKY1 SECTORS

You might be worrying about some other texture locations that you know to be essential and to which you have not yet applied texture: the upper textures of the eastern side of the lines dividing your two courtyard sectors. You might be wondering just how these areas can be dealt with. After all, you don't want to see any textures here—they would seem to be hanging in thin air, wouldn't they? And yet, you have been taught that such textures are essential. If you inspect these lines now, you will see that WADED thinks so, too—it has marked the lines in red. But what can you put there that won't look odd?

The answer is that it doesn't matter what you put there—DOOM won't use it anyway! Another change in the painting technique invoked by the use of the F_SKY1 texture is that upper textures between adjacent sectors with F_SKY1 specified for their ceilings are not painted. This enables the designer to vary the ceiling heights of outdoor sectors to alter the heights of surrounding walls and still have the sky effect work correctly.

MODIFYING THE EASTERN WALL

This might be a good point to save your WAD. Call it WAD7.WAD. Before trying it out, though, you should make a few more changes.

The modifications you have just made should have created a raised wall to the north of the outside courtyard, while keeping the western and southern walls as they were. The eastern wall has not been given its own sector, however, so it is now at the same height as the "building" to the North. In my opinion, it would be better to have this wall closer in height to the other outer walls, so this eastern area needs to be split away from the main courtyard sector too. You could introduce a little visual interest to the courtyard by varying the wall's texture as well; one of the vine textures would go well here. Vines tend to look a bit odd growing out of paving stones, though, so while you're adding a sector to bring the walls down, why not put it to use by letting it create a border to the paving?

CAUTION: You might need to set WADED's ZOOM factor to 9 or above to complete the next set of modifications without making spurious connections to existing lines.

Separate the eastern wall from the main courtyard by making another new sector. In WADED, start at the extreme southeast vertex, and draw a series of lines parallel to and about 32 units away from the lines that mark out the eastern wall of the courtyard. (WadAuthor users should be able to work out for themselves how to make their WAD keep pace here.) These should connect to the existing lines at the south and north ends of the eastern wall. The short lines that connect the new series of lines to the existing ones should run at an angle of about 45 degrees to the others in order not to cross or connect to other lines. It is imperative that your new sector takes none but the eastern walls away from existing sectors; otherwise, the desired height effects will be spoiled.

This time, apply Make Sector first to the new thin strip before clicking in the main courtyard area to redefine that sector's reduced area. (This sequence prevents you from having to change all the main courtyard sector's attributes yet again!) Set the floor height of the new thin sector to –20. (The vine border should be a little lower than the stone of the courtyard, don't you think?) A ceiling height of 108 brings the walls down, as desired. (You need to enter these values from the keyboard in WADED, rather than by using the mouse.)

Set the floor texture to FLAT10 [FLAT516 in Heretic] to provide something suited to the task of nurturing a vine, and set the ceiling to F_SKY1. Reduce the lighting to 144. (This vine will be in the shade of the wall.)

Now that you have finished adjusting the sector attributes, switch to LINES mode and apply the BROVINE texture (available only in DOOM—see following note box) to the main texture slot of the courtyard's eastern wall sections.

DOOM II / **HERETIC**   If you are working with DOOM II or Heretic, you must find a substitute for DOOM's BROVINE texture. DOOM II's dead vine texture, BROVINE2, is suitably in keeping with the wasted nature of DOOM II's geographical features, and it can be used to good effect here. ROOTWALL is the closest equivalent that Heretic can offer.

This just leaves the new western lines of the vine-border strip. If you inspect these lines, you will discover that WADED has done something odd here. It has given you some textures you do not want and left off a texture that is essential. You need to work along all of your new lines in turn, removing everything from their western sides and changing the essential (eastern) lower textures to BROWN1 [CSTLRCK] (I suggest). Think carefully about which side of the line is which when it comes to changing the textures.

CAUTION: If you are working with WADED and Heretic, pay particular attention to *all* the two-sided lines bordering the large central sector of the courtyard. Before saving the WAD, you should inspect these lines carefully for any occurrences of the STARTAN3 texture, which **HERETIC** WADED will most likely have added to some texture slots it considers essential. Make sure that you remove these textures (or change them to another appropriate texture if you find that the texture is indeed essential). Heretic will crash if you leave so much as a single occurrence of this texture in your WAD (even if it never needs to be displayed).

Now save your WAD as WAD7A.WAD and try it out. Head straight out to inspect your courtyard. You should find that it is still surrounded by walls of about the same height as before but that you now have an improved facade to the building to the north. If you look carefully, however, you might notice that there is something a little strange at each end of the new vine-border. When the border is viewed from certain locations, strange "notches" appear in some of the surrounding walls. (See Figure 11.7.)

Figure 11.7.
Evidence of an outdoor sky-drawing bug in the DOOM engine.

This effect is the result of a bug in the DOOM rendering engine. It occurs with certain configurations of low-ceilinged sectors using F_SKY1 for their ceiling and having void beyond. The solution is usually to create an additional sector, also with F_SKY1 for the ceiling, adjacent to them. This sector often can be utilized to produce an effective shadow zone. Let's try that approach here.

ADDING AN AREA OF SHADE

Restart your editor with WAD7A.WAD. Then add a sector to extend the area of shade that is currently confined to the vine-border a little way over the paving. This action has the combined effect of improving the appearance of the courtyard's shaded area and providing a buffer sector to remove the upper texture sky bug around the vine-border.

The new sector should start and finish at the same vertices as the preceding one: the southern and northern ends of the eastern wall. Again, start drawing in WADED at the extreme southeast vertex. By setting the ZOOM factor to a minimum of 11 and making sure that WADED does not show any of your existing lines in red until you are ready to connect to existing vertices, you can draw the connecting lines running as close to the northern and southern boundaries of the courtyard as possible without having them connect. (Users of WadAuthor might need to turn off Snap to Grid to add this area.)

The rest of the lines should run parallel to the eastern wall, somewhere to the west of the western edge of the vine-border sector. Remember that you are drawing the shadow line that would be produced by the sun if it were due east and quite high in the sky. Figure 11.8 shows the final arrangement of lines you are aiming for.

After successfully drawing the new lines in WADED, use Make Sector to create a sector out of the thin area of shade. You then need to click in the (ever-shrinking) main courtyard area to force it to acquire its share of the new lines. Change your new sector's floor to FLAT1_1 [FLOOR03] (the ceiling should already be F_SKY1). Change its floor height to –16 and its ceiling height to 216, to match the main courtyard sector. Leave its brightness at 144.

Figure 11.8.

The lines necessary to implement the courtyard fully.

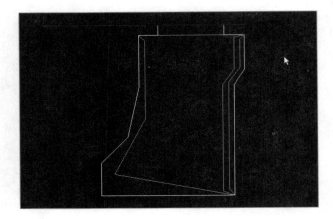

 Again, readers working with Heretic and WADED need to check for the occurrence of STARTAN3 on *all* the two-sided lines of the large central courtyard sector.

FIXING THE INTERCONNECTION

Finally, reduce the ceiling of the interconnection between indoors and out to a height of 128. This change creates an essential texture inside the room. Apply STONE3 [GRSTNPBV] to that texture, to match its neighbors. You might also want to change the interconnection's ceiling texture, because lights will look a bit odd here. You should find that CEIL5_2 [FLAT509] is OK. Finally, save the WAD as WAD7B.WAD and try it out.

REVIEWING YOUR HANDIWORK

Again, head straight out to inspect your courtyard. In passing, you might notice that, unlike your previous opening in a wall, the one out to the courtyard has ended up looking OK from inside the building (in DOOM and DOOM II, at least). When the opening is viewed from the outside, though, the texture alignment isn't too good around the opening. Apart from that, everything else should look fine. (See Figure 11.9.) (Well, maybe the shady area isn't perfect, but it's about as good as DOOM allows.)

To deal with the remaining texture alignment problems in this WAD, you need to know more about the way DOOM paints the walls.

Figure 11.9.
The new improved courtyard.

WALL TEXTURES REVISITED

Now that you've seen how floors and ceilings are painted, I can reveal the intricate details of how textures make it onto the walls, starting with a closer look at the wall textures themselves.

THE DIFFERENCES BETWEEN WALL AND CEILING TEXTURES

You have seen that ceiling and floor flats are all the same size: 64×64 pixels. If you care to preview a few wall textures, however, you will quickly see that wall textures vary widely in size, in both their horizontal and their vertical dimensions. Figure 11.10 gives you an idea of the variety: the familiar STONE2 is 128 pixels square; STEP1 is just 32 pixels wide by 8 pixels high; BROVINE is a comparatively massive 256 by 128 pixels; and LITE4 is 16×128.

Figure 11.10.
A collection of wall textures.

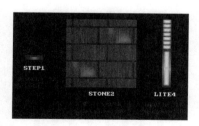

The differences between flats and wall textures go beyond variation in size, however. If you watch carefully as WADED's texture previewer draws the BROVINE texture, you will notice that instead of supplying the image in a smooth sweep from left to right (as it does when showing SKY1, for example), the texture previewer shows the image in a series of scattered patches that, after they are assembled, are finally overlaid with the image of a vine.

Readers using DOOM II need to watch the BROWNPIP texture being previewed to observe a patchiness similar to BROVINE's; Heretic users should preview GRSTNPBV.

This effect is brought about by the way in which wall textures are stored. To optimize the use of space in the main IWAD file (where all of these textures are stored), wall textures are broken down into a series of common graphical *patches*. The textures themselves are then created as an assemblage of these smaller patches. In this way, many different wall textures can be created by careful repetition, juxtaposition, and overlapping of a surprisingly small number of graphical elements.

The patches themselves can be virtually any size, although the final texture height must not exceed 128 pixels. Some wall textures are made up of just a single large patch (CEMENT1, for instance), whereas others (such as LITE3) are produced from many repetitions of the same small patch. This multi-patch characteristic of some wall textures can limit their use, as you will see shortly.

The final main difference between flats and wall textures is that it is possible for wall textures to have transparent areas within them. The preceding chapter introduced you to the notion of the transparent texture, which provides completely see-through lines on your map. That, of course, is not any special texture, but an absence of texture altogether. You will find, though, that there are wall textures that in effect use a transparent paint to produce holes through which a player can see. Preview the texture MIDGRATE [GATMETL] to see an example of these see-through textures. (See Figure 11.11.)

Figure 11.11.
The MIDGRATE (left) and GATMETL (right) see-through textures.

SUMMARY OF TYPES OF WALL TEXTURE

In summary, then, these are the textures that can be applied to a line's various texture slots:

- The transparent texture (really, no texture): Nothing is rendered here, except the view beyond the line.

- A solid texture: The texture completely covers the specified area.
- A see-through texture: The texture has holes in it through which the view beyond the line is rendered.

Wall textures are capable of a couple of other special effects, which you will learn about toward the end of this chapter.

THE CONSEQUENCES OF OMITTING ESSENTIAL TEXTURES

So far, you have been told that essential textures are so-named because they block a player's view of the void. You have been warned that to allow a player to view the void is to court mishap and disaster. It is time that you were told the true extent of the dangers inherent in viewing the void.

MISSING ESSENTIAL UPPERS/LOWERS

You have already seen the effect of omitting essential upper textures. Provided that the lower edge of such an upper texture remains *above* the player's eye level *and* the ceiling of the sector beyond is at least partly visible to the player, DOOM fills the entire gap with ceiling texture from the sector beyond. This process produces visual confusion, as you should remember from one of your early WADs. Other than that, though, the result is not serious—indeed, if you hunt around, you will find that id Software has missed quite a few of such upper textures from their own WADs. If the lower edge of the upper texture is below the player's eye level, however, or the ceiling of the sector beyond is too high to be visible, the effect is the same as if a main texture had been omitted.

The effect of a missing lower texture is similar. In this case, provided that the upper edge of the lower texture is *below* the player's eye level *and* the next sector's floor is at least partly visible to the player, the adjacent sector's floor appears to be at the level of the current sector's—until the player reaches it, in which case the step up comes as a surprise!

MISSING ESSENTIAL MAIN TEXTURES

The effect of a transparent main texture on a single-sided line is much more serious—even disastrous. It results in what is known as the Hall of Mirrors (HOM) effect. Instead of leaving the line's space empty, the graphical engine fills it with copies of various other parts of the current view, producing a flickering display of seeming reflections, reminiscent of the fairground amusement from which the effect derives its name. It is extremely disturbing for the player to encounter the Hall of Mirrors effect in a WAD. It cannot be used to any constructive effect, and most players will simply see it as a fault (which, of course, it is).

Raven Software's variants of the game use a different video mode from the original game and consequently do not exhibit the Hall of Mirrors effect in the same way. In these games, there is no flickering of the image. Nevertheless, the effect is still disturbing and is to be avoided.

Avoid this effect by making sure that you never omit any essential main textures.

HOM can result from other faults in the WAD; these will be covered in due course. If the effect always manifests itself on the same wall segment wherever it is viewed from, you should suspect a missing essential there and check your texture assignments carefully.

SEE-THROUGH ESSENTIALS

See-through textures used as essentials produce another type of fault known as the Tutti-Frutti effect. The solid parts of the texture are shown correctly, but the gaps through which the player can normally see are filled with pixels of random color. This effect can sometimes be put to decorative use in a WAD, but mostly it just looks wrong. You can best avoid this effect by ensuring that all essential textures are covered by completely solid coloring.

> **TIP:** If you want to place a grating in a wall that appears to look into a pitch-black room, create a small sector behind the grating with a brightness level of 0. Set the grating line's Impassable flag to prevent the player from passing through it.

TEXTURE PLACEMENT

Now that you know more about the nature of wall textures and what happens if they are omitted from your lines, the precise details of the process whereby the paint is applied to the walls can be considered.

The process of painting a line's textures begins with the game engine obtaining the name of the line's main texture and then assembling the appropriate set of component patches into the graphic to be used. What the engine does with that graphic depends on the setting of the line's Two-Sided flag. Let's consider the simpler case of the single-sided line first.

PAINTING SINGLE-SIDED LINES

Because a single-sided line lies at a single sector's boundary with only void beyond it, such lines can only ever possess a main texture. DOOM renders a single-sided line on-screen by pasting the graphic for its main texture into the upper-left corner of its space, at the point where this space meets the ceiling. The pattern is repeatedly applied, like tiles, horizontally and vertically until the entire wall space, from left to right and ceiling to floor, is covered. Figure 11.12 illustrates this process schematically for the simple graphical pattern shown at the left of the figure.

This process might sound straightforward, but in fact, it works correctly only with textures of the right size: the graphic must be either precisely 128 pixels tall, or tall enough to fill the space without vertical repetition. This is because the DOOM engine gets its vertical repetitions correct only if they occur at 128-pixel intervals. The use of graphics that need to be repeated at intervals other than 128 pixels leads to small gaps in the rendering.

These gaps fill with multicolored graphical noise, producing the so-called Pink Bug effect. Like Tutti-Frutti, it can sometimes be used as a decorative effect, but it generally should be avoided. To avoid Pink Bug, ensure that you use textures 128 pixels high on single-sided walls, or textures that are at least as tall as the wall space into which they will be painted.

Figure 11.12.
*The process of painting
a single-sided wall.*

The Graphic

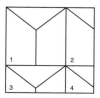

NOTE: If a line's Two-Sided flag is clear, the line is treated by DOOM as single-sided, even if there is, in fact, a sector on the other side of it. It therefore is painted over its full height using the preceding method, with complete disregard for adjacent ceiling and floor heights.

PAINTING TWO-SIDED LINES

The graphics engine handles two-sided lines in a different manner. The painting starts in the usual way with the main texture. If no texture is given, the space is left clear, as you have seen. Otherwise, the specified graphic is applied, as a tile, in the upper-left corner of the main texture space. Note that this will be at the ceiling only if no upper texture is required on this side of the line. The main texture pattern is repeated horizontally, just as with single-sided lines, but it is not repeated down the vertical dimension of the wall. This might leave a horizontal strip of the wall unpainted. This strip is treated as transparent (which is perfectly OK on a two-sided main texture, remember).

After considering the main texture, DOOM paints a two-sided line's other textures as necessary. The lower texture is painted in the same manner as the main texture of a single-sided line. The painting starts at the upper-left corner of the lower texture space and repeats horizontally and vertically until the space is filled.

The upper texture is painted in a similar manner, with the exception that here the pattern is painted first at the lower-left corner of the upper texture. The graphic is repeated horizontally to the right, as usual, and vertically upward until the space is filled.

Figure 11.13 illustrates schematically DOOM's default method of painting a two-sided line's (potentially) three textures, using the same simple graphical pattern used in Figure 11.12.

Again, if vertical repetitions are needed to fill the space of the upper and lower textures, they will occur correctly only when the graphics used there are precisely 128 pixels tall.

Figure 11.13.
DOOM's default method of painting a two-sided line.

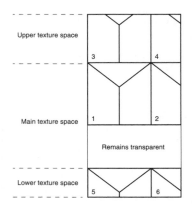

Upper texture space

3   4

Main texture space

1   2

Remains transparent

Lower texture space

5   6

> **CAUTION:** Although it is possible for a line with sectors on each side of it to have its Two-Sided flag clear—such lines are treated as if there is nothing beyond them, remember—it is vital that lines which have their Two-Sided flag set really do have two sidedefs. DOOM crashes if led to expect sectors that are not present!

SPECIAL TREATMENT OF TWO-SIDED LINE MAIN TEXTURES

You need to be aware that DOOM gives special consideration to the main texture of a two-sided line. Remember that these lines, by definition, connect adjacent sectors. They therefore represent an interconnection between one space and another; as such, one would ordinarily expect these main textures to be transparent. If they carry a texture at all, it is most likely to be one of the see-through textures of the grid and grating variety. Such textures would look strange if tiled vertically, so the engine doesn't tile textures used here. Instead, it just repeats the patterns horizontally as needed.

More significantly, however, this part of the graphics engine cannot cope with wall textures that consist of complex, overlaid patches. It handles single-patch wall textures (which is what all the see-through textures are) and textures that, when assembled, have all of their patches placed side-by-side horizontally and without overlap. Other arrangements of patches cannot be used.

If you use a texture composed of overlapping patches, or patches that are arranged vertically, as the main texture of a two-sided line, a serious error occurs. Whenever DOOM is asked to display such a texture, it pours weird streams of color down from the offending wall space, often to the bottom of the screen. At the same time, the PC slows to a crawl. This is known as the Medusa effect (so-named because the player sees snakes and is turned to stone!). Medusa makes the WAD unplayable while the offending space is in view. To eliminate it, you must ensure that all the main textures of your two-sided lines either are transparent or do not consist of vertically positioned or overlapping patches. This restriction does not apply to upper or lower textures because semi-transparent textures are not normally used there.

Although Raven Software's adaptation of the DOOM engine is not as prone to the drastic slow-down associated with the Medusa effect, it still exhibits the effect to some extent if you violate the restrictions just outlined. Fortunately, Heretic has proportionally fewer multi-patch textures, so there are plenty of wall textures you can use with impunity.

USES FOR SOLID TEXTURES ON TWO-SIDED LINES

The treatment of two-sided lines just outlined—the lack of vertical repetition of the main texture and the limitations on what those textures can be—is neither as strange nor as restrictive as it might at first appear. As already noted, the textures that are usually applied here—the grids and gratings—you would not normally want tiled, and you will rarely want a solid texture to occupy a gap between sectors.

The only time you might want to employ a solid graphic as a two-sided main texture is in the creation of a secret entrance or sniper ambush spot, as used in the hidden upper passage of the original DOOM's E1M1. Such locations leave the player open to attack from monsters (or, in Deathmatch play, other players) who cannot be seen and whose presence is given away only when they open fire. You make these spots by placing a solid main texture on one side of a line while leaving the other transparent. The solid texture prevents a player from seeing through the side that carries it, but from the other side, the line remains transparent. Remember also that the Two-Sided flag is more properly termed the Two-Sided/See-Through/Shoot-Through flag. Setting this flag enables players and monsters to shoot through the line's main texture space without impediment. (Now you see why this creates an ambush spot!)

NOTE: Monsters can see both ways through all two-sided lines, regardless of texturing. It is not possible, by using standard map-editing techniques, to set up locations where the player can snipe at monsters unseen. The effect can be created, however, with the use of a reject map builder, as is demonstrated in Chapter 23, "Reject Table Tricks."

Remember that a line's impassability is also determined by a flag. Unless you set this flag, a two-sided line can be passed through—by player or enemies—regardless of the main texture. The "magic" or "secret" entrances that appear in various locations of the main DOOM.WAD—such as the curtains of fire through which a player can walk—are made in this way, too.

In summary: Remember that not all the available textures can be used to create locations such as the ones just described. If you want a two-sided main texture to look solid, it must consist of either single or side-by-side, non-overlapping patches, and because it will not be vertically tiled, it also needs to be tall enough to fill the space completely.

TEXTURE ALIGNMENT

As you have already observed in your own WADs, the game engine's default application of wall textures does not always result in the desired rendering of the walls. Having had the default mechanism described, you can no doubt see why. All is not lost, however, because DOOM provides the designer with some controls over the paint-application process, allowing surfaces to be rendered in ways other than the default painting method.

To demonstrate how these controls work, I will use two different wall textures: MARBLE2 and BRNSMAL1. Figure 11.14 shows these textures. MARBLE2 is a fairly standard 128×128 solid graphic. It is useful here because it has easily identifiable upper and lower edges. BRNSMAL1 is a 64×64 see-through texture.

Figure 11.14.
Wall textures MARBLE2 and
BRNSMAL1.

DEFAULT WALL TEXTURE ALIGNMENT

Consider the application of the MARBLE2 texture to a wall that is taller than 128 units. The texture will be applied from the ceiling down, repeated as necessary until the floor is reached. The texture is 128 pixels tall, so there will be no problem with Pink Bug. Above and below an opening in the wall, though, something different will happen. Figure 11.15 illustrates the result of the application. The walls on either side of the central opening consist of straightforward single-sided lines. The central opening itself is a two-sided line, with a pitch-black sector beyond it. MARBLE2 is used above and below the opening; the line's main texture is set to BRNSMAL1. The figure shows DOOM's default rendering of this configuration.

You can see that where the wall is solid, the pattern has been applied from the ceiling down and repeated over the full height of the wall. The upper texture of the two-sided line, however, has been painted upward from its meeting with the main texture. The main texture itself has been painted from its upper edge but without vertical repetition of the pattern. As a consequence, the grating appears to be suspended from the top of the opening. Beneath the opening, on the line's lower texture, the marble pattern is applied from the bottom of the main texture down.

Figure 11.15.
DOOM's default painting around an opening.

Sometimes, this default method of applying the paint achieves the desired effect. Usually, though, as here, it spoils the alignment of the upper and lower textures. You probably recognize this effect from your own WADs.

CHANGING DOOM'S PAINTING METHOD

DOOM provides two mechanisms for changing its wall-painting method. The first is termed *unpegging*, and the second is texture *offsetting*. I will first explain what these terms mean and how the mechanisms are accessed, before considering how they can be employed.

UNPEGGING

By default, lines are said to have their textures *pegged* to their surfaces. In other words, the graphical patterns are painted on their surfaces starting from a particular location. These reference locations are at the top of the main texture space for the main and upper texture patterns, and at the bottom of the main texture space for the lower. Naturally, this greatly affects the way in which textures align from one wall section to the next. You might recall from the preceding chapter that two flags control a line's pegging: the Upper Unpegged flag and the Lower Unpegged flag. Note that these are linedef attributes; they therefore affect both sides of a line.

TEXTURE OFFSETTING

A texture *offset* is a displacement that can be applied to the horizontal and vertical position of a texture's starting point. By using such displacement, you can shift a texture any number of pixels in any direction on any wall. This mechanism provides you with fine control over the graphic's placement. Again, you might recall from the preceding chapter that each of a line's two sidedefs supplies X- and Y-offset values for texture displacement. These values enable textures to be aligned independently on each side of a line. Note, however, that the offset is applied to all texture slots on that side of the line.

UNPEGGED TEXTURES ON TWO-SIDED LINES

You have seen that, by default, a two-sided line's upper texture is pegged to its lower edge. By setting the *Upper Unpegged* flag, you can unpeg this texture from the structure of the line and have the paint applied from the sector's ceiling instead. This action forces the upper texture to be applied in the same way as it would be on any adjacent single-sided lines, causing their patterns to line up.

Setting a line's *Lower Unpegged* flag causes the line's lower texture to lose its pegging to the bottom of the main texture. Again, the unpegged texture's placement is reckoned from the ceiling, bringing its pattern into alignment with any adjacent single-sided line.

Confusingly, setting the Lower Unpegged flag also changes the painting of a line's *main* texture. Remember that any graphic in this space is normally "hung" from its top and might have transparent space below it. Setting a line's Lower Unpegged flag causes this graphic to be placed at the bottom of the main texture space instead. It still does not repeat vertically, so there might now be a transparent area above the graphic. Figure 11.16 shows how the earlier wall opening is rendered when both upper and lower textures are unpegged.

Figure 11.16.
The effect of unpegging upper and lower textures.

UNPEGGING SINGLE-SIDED LINES

It is possible to set the unpegged flags of single-sided lines, even though they have neither upper nor lower textures. The effect is precisely the same as happens to the main texture of a two-sided line when unpegging is used there. Setting the Lower Unpegged flag causes the line's main (and only) texture to be applied from the floor up, rather than from the ceiling down. Changing the Upper Unpegged flag has no effect on the rendering of single-sided lines.

In Figure 11.17, the wall to the left of the corner has had its Lower Unpegged flag set, whereas the wall to the right uses the default painting method.

Figure 11.17.

The effect of lower unpegging on single-sided lines.

NOTE: The Upper and Lower Unpegged flags feature prominently in a later chapter of this book.

Examining Other Combinations of Unpegging

If you want to look at the effect of other combinations of unpegging around openings in walls, examine the sample WAD called MWALLS.WAD (the DOOM II version is called D2MWALLS.WAD) on the CD-ROM that accompanies this book. It shows all the possible combinations of the unpegged flags for the sample opening described previously. A similar example that uses different textures and is suitable for Heretic is supplied as H1MWALLS.WAD.

USING TEXTURE OFFSETS

On occasion, simple unpegging does not achieve the precise alignment effect a designer wants. Examples would be the small but deliberate misalignment of textures used to give hints of the presence of secret doors; or the adjustment of textures across, rather than up and down, a wall—centering a texture between two adjacent walls, for instance. In cases like these, total control over texture alignment is needed.

To provide this level of control, each sidedef allows the specification of individual X- or Y-offsets. These values can be positive or negative numbers in the range –128 to 127. The X-offset produces a shift of the texture to the left (negative values to the right), whereas the Y-offset produces a shift upward (negative values downward) of the texture, in each case by the specified number of pixels.

COMBINING UNPEGGING WITH TEXTURE OFFSETTING

The use of these two texture-alignment mechanisms is not mutually exclusive. The graphical engine applies any X- and Y-offset values specified in the sidedefs after all pegging information has been acted on, so the offset values can always be used to effect small adjustments to the alignment of your textures.

WAD SORTIE 8: TIDYING UP THE WALLS

NOTE: This sortie builds on the WAD produced in the preceding sortie. You should note, however, that the precise solutions to the texture alignment problems discussed here are greatly dependent on the particular textures used in the WAD. If you have opted not to use the suggested textures in earlier sorties, you might find it helpful to follow this sortie using the appropriate sample WAD from the CD before inspecting your own WAD to determine the exact way to deal with its problems. If you have not produced WAD7B.WAD, or yours differs from the one built up in preceding sorties, you should use WAD7B.WAD (DOOM), D2WAD7B.WAD (DOOM II), or H1WAD7B.WAD (Heretic) from the CD-ROM for this sortie.

With all the previous information at your fingertips, you should now be able to perform a simple walk-through of your WAD, noting the alignment problems that exist and deciding on a method for fixing them. So start the game with your latest WAD (or with the appropriate WAD from the CD-ROM), and I'll walk through the level with you.

Because wall textures can vary so much in size and form, the precise solution to any texture alignment problems varies with the actual textures in use. For this reason, the fixes required if you have been building for DOOM, or DOOM II, will be somewhat different from those required if you are working with Heretic. I will consider each of these cases separately, starting with DOOM/DOOM II.

FIXING THE FIRST OPENING (DOOM/DOOM II)

The first problem area is around the southwest exit from the hexagonal room. You should now recognize the alignment fault over the opening as a pegging error. The upper textures need to be unpegged on both sides of this opening. Make a note to do this when you next return to the editor.

The second fault with this exit is the alignment of the mortar lines through the gap. Here you have a major problem. Simple realignment of the textures on the short through-wall sections cannot solve the fault, because, as a careful inspection will show you, the mortar lines of the hexagonal room do not line up with those of the southwest room. Now, you could just cheat at this point and apply some kind of neutral texture through the interconnection and hope that no one notices the alignment fault between the two rooms. You wouldn't learn much by doing that, though, so on this occasion at least, you should do things properly!

From the earlier description of the texture-application process, you know that textures are always applied to single-sided lines from the ceiling down. Look at the walls of these two rooms, and you will see that this is indeed the case here. The misalignment of textures on each side of the opening is a result of an awkward difference in ceiling height. Now, you could realign all of one room's textures, but to do this would require the adjustment of the Y-offset of the textures on all of that room's walls. This process would be tedious in the extreme. Fortunately, there is another way out here—why not just change a ceiling height?

The STONE2 and STONE3 textures have four courses of "bricks" up their 128-pixel height. (You can verify this for yourself by using WADED's previewer, if you want; for now, just trust me.) A quick bit of math tells you, then, that the mortar lines of these graphics occur at 32-pixel intervals up each texture. Provided, therefore, that you make sure that these two rooms' ceiling heights differ by an integral multiple of 32, these textures should align automatically.

The current difference is 40, so the problem can be fixed by changing one of the ceiling heights by 8 units. Now, the hexagonal room contains a techno-column that just fits between ceiling and floor and, in addition, has a further sector beyond it, which is fine the way it is. It would therefore make more sense to apply the change to the southwest room's ceiling, bringing it down 8 units to 152. Make a note of this for your next edit, too.

The same mathematics can be applied to the interconnecting sector, too, of course. Its walls are painted, like all the rest, down from its ceiling. The current difference between this ceiling height and that of the hexagonal room is 16. That's 16 pixels short of the 32-unit interval needed to make the textures align properly. Bringing the interconnection's ceiling down by this amount can make the opening rather low, however. It would be better to apply these 16 units as a Y-offset on the two troublesome lines. Forcing the wall textures down 16 pixels requires a Y-offset of −16. Make another note and then proceed to the next opening, the one out to the courtyard.

FIXING THE FIRST OPENING (HERETIC)

Heretic users reading the preceding section might be wondering what all the fuss is about: Depending on the exact size of your opening and the walls on either side of it, the opening between the hexagonal room and the room to its southwest might not look too bad. This is because the texture used in Heretic does not have the regular, dressed stone appearance of the one used in the DOOM and DOOM II versions of the sample WAD. If you look very closely over the opening from within the hexagonal room, you might notice some poor alignment of blocks—or you might not. You should make a note to unpeg this upper texture when you return to the editor to see whether it can be improved, though.

From within the southwest room, the texture over the opening certainly looks wrong, though, doesn't it? This error can be fixed by unpegging the upper texture so that its placement matches that of its neighbors. Take a close look at the area over the opening, though (see Figure 11.18). Notice how it is larger than the size of the plain stone-work above the frieze-work. Merely changing the pegging would result in the top four pixels of the frieze-work detail continuing to run over the doorway. This would probably make the opening look odd (although you might decide that it wouldn't!). You can deal with this situation in several ways. First, you could simply change the texture used over the door to the plain GRSTNPB version of the texture. Alternatively, you could change the size of the area of wall above the opening, either by reducing the ceiling height of the southwest room by, say, 8 units, or by raising the height of the ceiling of the opening itself. I will leave the exact solution here to you.

Figure 11.18.
Problems around the first opening in the Heretic WAD.

You might also be having problems around this opening with the frieze-work being cut into by the left edge of the opening through the wall. Remember that wall textures are always painted from left to right, which means that this texture is being painted from the leftmost end of the wall. To meet the opening correctly, the wall to the left of the opening must be an exact multiple of the width of the pattern: 64 pixels. You might need to reshape the southwest room (or the opening through the wall) to arrange this layout.

Turning now to the through-hole walls, the main problem with these is that the frieze-work detail looks odd. It is located at the wrong height and, in any case, does not fit conveniently in this location—the walls are not thick enough for it. The simplest solution here probably is to change the texture to the GRSTNPB texture used in the hexagonal room. This change does not address the problem of mortar line continuity through the gap, but unfortunately, that problem has no simple solution, given the irregular block pattern used in this texture. This is one of those times when you'll have to make do with things as they are!

FIXING THE SECOND OPENING (DOOM/DOOM II)

From inside, the next opening looks fine in DOOM, doesn't it? Remember, though, that you have just made a note to bring this room's ceiling height down. This opening will no longer look right after that fix, so make a note to unpeg this upper texture as well. I suggest that you don't bother realigning this opening's through-textures, though; STONE3 looks a bit odd here, anyway. I recommend that you replace both side-walls' main textures with BROWNHUG. (No, you're not cheating, just refining the design!)

Moving out into the courtyard now, take a look at the final problem area, the other side of the opening to the courtyard. The misalignment of the upper texture here can again be fixed by unpegging. The lower texture looks OK to me as it is. It doesn't align with the textures on either side, but I think that makes it look more like a step. I vote that it should stay the way it is, so the changes already noted should be sufficient to fix this opening in DOOM and DOOM II.

FIXING THE SECOND OPENING (HERETIC)

Again, this opening doesn't look too bad in Heretic—just how bad is largely a matter of personal preference. The main faults, to my eyes, are from the courtyard side, where the textures to the sides of the opening look somewhat lost. These might look better aligned with the textures making up the walls surrounding the courtyard. The current misalignment is caused by the difference in ceiling heights, so you need to apply a Y-offset of −72 to the appropriate sides of all three of the lines making up the northern boundary of the courtyard. You also need to unpeg the upper texture over the opening so that it aligns properly with its neighbors, too.

You might also want to change the through-wall texture to something like SQPEB1.

FIXING THE REST OF THE COURTYARD (DOOM, DOOM II, AND HERETIC)

So is that everything that needs fixing? It depends on how great a perfectionist you are. The vine texture doesn't continue perfectly around the bend in the eastern wall, but this effect is barely noticeable and certainly not worth the effort involved in fixing it. Of course, if you want to calculate the X-offsets that need to be applied to two of the vine wall-sections to produce a seamless join, I'll not stop you. There is one other little change I would make, though, to something you have probably not seen. Press Tab and take a look at the auto-map. Notice how the lines marking off the western and southern walls of your outdoor area show up. I would be inclined to hide these lines by setting their Not on Map flag; that way, the map-watching player is not likely to waste time trying to determine their significance during play.

So, notebook at the ready, load your editor and try making a new WAD8.WAD, with all of these problems fixed.

Applying Texture Offsets

To adjust the Y-offset of a texture in WADED, you need first to be in LINES mode. You can then bring up the texture-offsets pop-up box (shown in Figure 11.19) by clicking any of the four offset buttons (which appear below the lower texture slots). The pop-up shows the X- and Y-displacements of left and right sidedefs (in that order). Each value can be changed by means of the + and − buttons beside them.

Texture offset values are accessible in WadAuthor through the Linedef Properties dialog box.

Figure 11.19.

WADED's texture displacement settings pop-up.

MOVING ON

When you have made all the changes, try out your new WAD8.WAD. I hope that with these latest revisions, all the previous defects in your WAD have been cleared up and you are ready to move on and extend your design further. There are still a few more details you should know about textures, though.

ANIMATED TEXTURES

All the textures you have seen so far have been flat and static, just like paint. But DOOM also provides a family of textures that are rather more exciting than ordinary paint—they are animated.

USING ANIMATED TEXTURES

After all you have just read about textures, you might be surprised to learn that the use of animated textures is simplicity itself. There are animated textures for walls as well as for floors and ceilings; their names appear in the lists of available textures along with the static ones you are familiar with. You can use animated textures like any other texture. Apply them to the appropriate surface, and the DOOM engine does the rest.

 NOTE: It is not possible to tell animated textures from static textures in most editors' texture lists.

DOOM performs the animation by cycling around a series of texture names. You specify the entire animation sequence by specifying any name within it. You don't have to choose a texture from any particular point of the sequence to get the complete animation. Note, however, that DOOM steps all animated textures on to their next "frame" at the same time. So areas that are given different textures from within the same animation remain out of phase by the same amount throughout the game.

ANIMATED FLOOR/CEILING TEXTURES

Table 11.1 lists all the animated floor-texture sequences available in DOOM and DOOM II.

Table 11.1. DOOM and DOOM II's animated floor-texture sequences.

Sequence	DOOM	DOOM II	Description
BLOOD1, BLOOD2, BLOOD3	X	X	Blood, maybe?
FWATER1, FWATER2, FWATER3, FWATER4	X	X	Water

Sequence	DOOM	DOOM II	Description
LAVA1, LAVA2, LAVA3, LAVA4	X	X	Lava
NUKAGE1, NUKAGE2, NUKAGE3	X	X	Nukage slime
RROCK05, RROCK06, RROCK07, RROCK08	—	X	Pulsating red cracks between rocks
SLIME01, SLIME02, SLIME03, SLIME04	—	X	Blotchy brown slime
SLIME05, SLIME06, SLIME07, SLIME08	—	X	More uniform brown slime
SLIME09, SLIME10, SLIME11, SLIME12	—	X	Fine-texture version of RROCK05 (yes, really!)

RAVEN SOFTWARE'S ANIMATED FLATS

Heretic and Hexen also have animated floor textures. This aspect of the original DOOM engine has been extended in Raven Software's adaptations. As well as animating, some of the textures have a Splash effect with an associated sound effect. The Splash effects are triggered by any player, monster, or other object landing from a greater height onto a floor that carries the appropriate texture. Table 11.2 lists all of Heretic's animated floor-texture sequences, together with their visible and audible Splash effects.

Table 11.2. Heretic's animated floor-texture sequences and special effects.

Sequence	Splash Effect	Splash Sound	Description
FLATHUH1, FLATHUH2, FLATHUH3, FLATHUH4	Splash of fire	Sizzle	Molten lava
FLTFLWW1, FLTFLWW2, FLTFLWW3	Splash of water	Splash	Flowing water
FLTLAVA1, FLTLAVA2, FLTLAVA3, FLTLAVA4	Splash of fire	Sizzle	Hot rock
FLTSLUD1, FLTSLUD2, FLTSLUD3	Small splash	—	Slime and mud of slime
FLTTELE1, FLTTELE2, FLTTELE3, FLTTELE4	—	—	Pulsating teleporter symbol
FLTWAWA1, FLTWAWA2, FLTWAWA3	Splash of water	Splash	Still water

If you want to examine these textures in use, take a look at the sample WAD called H1ANIFLO.WAD on the CD-ROM that accompanies this book.

Table 11.3 lists all of Hexen's animated floor-texture sequences, together with their visible and audible Splash effects.

Table 11.3. Hexen's animated floor-texture sequences and special effects.

Sequence	Splash Effect	Splash Sound	Description
F_084, F_085, F_086, F_087, F_088	—	—	Blue portal (landing)
X_001, X_002, X_003, X_004	Splash of fire	Sizzle	Molten lava
X_005, X_006, X_007, X_008	Splash of water	Splash	Water
X_009, X_010, X_011	Splash of slime	Gloop	Muddy slime
X_012, X_013, X_014, X_015, X_016	—	—	Red portal (active)

USING ANIMATED FLATS

Some animated floor textures are generally associated with areas that damage players who linger in them. The damaging aspect of these areas is not a product of the textures themselves—except for Hexen's X_001 lava texture, which *does* automatically cause harm to any player who enters the sector where it is used. Usually, an animated floor is just that—an animated floor! You will learn more about sectors' harmful effects on players in Chapter 13, "Special Sectors."

Like all flats, the animated floor textures can be applied to ceilings, but they rarely look convincing—somehow, slime just doesn't look right up there.

ANIMATED WALL TEXTURES

Table 11.4 lists all the animated wall-texture sequences available in DOOM and DOOM II.

Table 11.4. DOOM's animated wall-texture sequences.

Sequence	DOOM	DOOM II	Description
BFALL1, BFALL2, BFALL3, BFALL4	—	X	Falling curtain of blood
BLODGR1, BLODGR2, BLODGR3, BLODGR4	X	—	Nukage slime dripping from ruptured pipework
BLODRIP1, BLODRIP2, BLODRIP3, BLODRIP4	X	X	Blood dripping from ruptured pipework

Sequence	DOOM	DOOM II	Description
DBRAIN1, DBRAIN2, DBRAIN3, DBRAIN4	—	X	Dancing red and yellow blotches
FIREBLU1, FIREBLU2	X	X	Pulsating red and blue flame
FIRELAVA, FIRELAV3	X	X	Dense curtain of flame
FIREMAG1, FIREMAG2, FIREMAG3	X	X	Dancing red and blue flames
FIREWALL, FIREWALA, FIREWALB	X	X	Wall of fire over embers
GSTFONT1, GSTFONT2, GSTFONT3	X	X	Stone gargoyle spouting blood
ROCKRED1, ROCKRED2, ROCKRED3	X	X	Glowing red-hot rock
SFALL1, SFALL2, SFALL3, SFALL4	—	X	Falling curtain of nukage slime
SLADRIP1, SLADRIP2, SLADRIP3	X	—	Nukage slime pouring from grating

NOTE: The texture called FIRELAV2 is not part of the FIRELAVA sequence. It is a static texture.

Heretic also has animated wall textures, but fewer of them. They are listed in Table 11.5.

Table 11.5. Heretic's animated wall-texture sequences.

Sequence	Description
LAVAFL1, LAVAFL2, LAVAFL3	Falling wall of lava
WATRWAL1, WATRWAL2, WATRWAL3	Waterfall

No sounds are associated with animated wall textures in Heretic. You will need to place a Thing of type Environmental Sound: Waterfall close by if you want these features to make a noise.

Hexen has a much wider range of animated wall textures than Heretic. They are detailed in Table 11.6.

Table 11.6. Hexen's animated wall-texture sequences.

Sequence	Description
CLOCK01, CLOCK02, CLOCK03, CLOCK04, CLOCK05, CLOCK06, CLOCK07, CLOCK08	Hour hand of clock (texture steps only after a full cycle of CLOCK11)
CLOCK11, CLOCK12, CLOCK13, CLOCK14, CLOCK15, CLOCK16, CLOCK17, CLOCK18	Minute hand of clock (performs full cycle in 8 seconds)
GEAR02, GEAR03, GEAR04, GEAR05	Rotating gears
GEAR0A, GEAR0B	Oscillating gears
TPORT1, TPORT2, TPORT3, TPORT4, TPORT5, TPORT6, TPORT7, TPORT8, TPORT9	Swirling teleport mirror
X_FAC01, X_FAC02, X_FAC03, X_FAC04	Wall of flames
X_FIRE01, X_FIRE02, X_FIRE03, X_FIRE04	Pulsating lava wall (like flat X_001)
X_SWMP1, X_SWMP2, X_SWMP3	Swamp life
X_SWR1, X_SWR2, X_SWR3	Sewer outfall
X_WATER1, X_WATER2, X_WATER3, X_WATER4	Wall of water (like flat X_005)

Most animated textures are not designed to tile vertically and so need to be used on walls of an appropriate height. Many animated textures look odd if used on short walls using the default rendering operation—you need to set the Lower Unpegged flag in most cases to ensure that their lower surfaces align with the floor. Additionally, some (particularly in Hexen) are short textures that manifest the Pink Bug effect if used on an essential texture space that is too high for them.

Animated wall textures can be used on any texture slot. If you have more than 40 areas using animated textures in any one map, however, the game engine crashes. Some of the Hexen textures are also see-through textures, and those should be used only on two-sided main texture slots.

NOTE: Versions of DOOM prior to v1.4 and all versions of Heretic do not animate the main texture of a two-sided line. This restriction has been lifted in later versions of DOOM, DOOM II, and Hexen.

There are several additional wall textures in Hexen that are clearly part of an animation sequence but that do not automatically animate if they are used. These textures require scripts to perform the animation (usually with other accompanying actions). These are the subject of "Programming the Action," a chapter on the CD-ROM.

SCROLLING TEXTURES

In addition to animated texture sequences, some surfaces can be made to scroll their textures in a particular direction. This topic is discussed in Chapter 14, "Activating Sectors."

EXTENDING THE TEXTURE PALETTE

Rich though the texture palettes provided by id and Raven Software are, at times they just seem to lack the precise type of texture you want. Often you want to customize the appearance of your walls, floors, and ceilings to match the scenario of your WAD better. Tools are available to enable you to do this. The techniques involved go beyond simple editing of the map, however, so this topic is deferred until the next mission of this episode, "Towards the Land of the Gods."

EXIT: MOPPING UP AND MOVING ON

In this chapter, you learned more about DOOM's palette of textures for ceiling, floor, and wall surfaces. You learned how the DOOM engine's sky works and saw how to add realistic outdoor areas to your map. You learned, too, how the DOOM engine goes about painting its world and precisely what happens if it isn't provided with all the textures it needs in order to fill the gaps. You saw how to make the game engine paint the walls exactly as you want them by utilizing the alignment mechanisms provided. You had a taste of the use of those mechanisms as you fixed all the remaining problems in your own WAD. Finally, you were told that DOOM's paint doesn't need to be static but can be animated.

In the next chapter, as well as trying out some animated textures, you start to expand your map with new sectors as you learn the techniques for implementing many of the standard elements of the DOOM world.

You also receive some of your final lessons in the use of WADED.

PUTTING SECTORS TO WORK

By now, you should be familiar with the role of the sector in DOOM WADs and be comfortable with its use and structure. In this chapter, you will be shown how sectors are put together to form the common types of elements that make up the traditional DOOM world. The various sorties in this chapter lead you through the addition of many new areas to the WAD that has been developed in earlier sorties of this mission.

Remember, though, that WAD-building is more of an art than a science—there are no fixed ways of producing anything. Consequently, you will not be given rigid rules or instructions for the implementation of every scenery element you will ever want. This chapter is intended as a gallery of ideas. Use it as a starting point for planning your own maps.

AREA DESIGN

Part of the secret of successful WAD-building is learning to plan and construct your sectors. You have already seen that with WADED, for instance, the careless and haphazard addition of sectors within your WAD can cost you a lot of time in redefining line and sector settings. You will find that the same holds true with all other WAD editors. No matter which you use, you will find that before you start work with the editor, careful planning of your WAD (and its sector layout in particular) will pay dividends when you finally do begin.

PLANNING THE MAP

In planning your WADs, you should remember that no matter how beautiful (or ugly, if that's what you prefer) you make your WAD, it is unlikely to be much admired unless it plays well. Keep this thought uppermost in your mind at all stages of design.

— By Steve Benner

In particular, you should question your motives for the introduction of every new area. Ask yourself, "Why am I creating this area? What will it contribute to the game?" Keep a mental tally of how many times you reply, "For decoration" or "To add atmosphere." Ornamentation is undoubtedly a significant aspect of any design, but if it becomes more important to you than creating a functional space in which to hide weapons or to ambush opponents, you are probably spending too much time using your editor and not enough time playing what you produce there!

After you've answered the fundamental question of what your new map area is really for, you can turn to the more practical questions of how it should look, from the specifics of textures to the overall design scheme. How high will it be, how wide, how long? Will it be brightly lit or should it be dark? How high above other areas should it be? Will it have overlooks? Should it be hidden? Will it contain any tricks or traps?

In considering your approach to these design questions, you should be fully aware of all the features of the DOOM world that are available for exploitation. You also need to know about DOOM's inherent design restrictions.

APPEARANCE

The look and feel of your map will develop as you go along. You've seen some of this already. You know a little bit about textures and lighting levels, and you will see some more specific and atmospheric examples of these capabilities as this episode progresses. You can use these aspects of your map's appearance for more than simply adding atmosphere, however. DOOM's lighting levels can vary from very bright (a setting of 255) to pitch black (a setting of 0). Obviously, dimly lit areas can be used to make the players' task harder; it is easier for you to hide things in the dark—be they goodies, switches, traps, monsters, or the pathway itself. Try to use lighting levels realistically—take a close look at the way lighting levels are utilized throughout DOOM's E1M1 for an excellent example of this. Also, try to vary the lighting levels through your WAD so that players don't get too accustomed to (or bored with) playing at a particular light level. Areas of darkness can be much harder to play when they follow immediately after well-lit areas.

Exercise careful thought in your use of textures too. Aim for more than mere decoration. Beside lending atmosphere to your WAD, textures can create challenges of their own—some enemies are harder to spot against some surface colorings, for instance. Textures are also invaluable in providing clues to various aspects of your design, clues about such things as hazards, traps, and secret locations. Observant players will soon pick up on your textural pointers and will enjoy your level all the more. Of course, you can always throw the occasional false pointer into the mix to trip them up every now and then!

There are no hard-and-fast rules about the basic appearance of your map areas. If you've played many WADs, you already know what particular design aspects you like. If you can't decide, perhaps you should play some more and give it additional thought.

LARGE AREAS OR SMALL?

The sizes of the various areas of your map will be influenced by the functions you see these areas fulfilling. Do you intend to give the player a large open space in which to charge around and battle many foes simultaneously?

Will you force the player to take on a few monsters at a time by confining the action to a smaller space? Do you want to restrict the player's options for movement or escape? Is this one of those twisty mazes that do their best to disorient and confuse the player? Will this area be built to contain a particularly unusual menace?

The effectiveness of many of the weapons in DOOM is related to the geography in which they are used. The geography also affects the way monsters behave, particularly in their tracking of the player. You should test these aspects of your design fairly early in the design process, especially before you have too many lines and sectors to rearrange if you find that things are not working well.

To create map areas that function correctly, you need to know something of the way DOOM's objects and its geography interact. You need to know what can fit where in the DOOM world. You also need to be aware of the movement constraints that DOOM applies to both players and enemies.

SIZE CONSIDERATIONS

If you want areas of your map to contain particular objects, you need to make sure that the areas are large enough to hold whatever you place there. You need to know something, therefore, of how things are measured and the restrictions on where they fit.

THING METRICS

You should remember from Chapter 8, "Reconnaissance Debriefing," that all Things have both a diameter and a height. These two values determine an object's "extent"—how much map area it needs and what headroom it requires.

NOTE: The metric values for all of DOOM's Things are given in Chapter 34, "Essential Thing Information."

The term "diameter" as it is applied to Things is misleading, for it implies that Things are circular, whereas in fact, they are square. This square is always oriented with the map's coordinate system, regardless of the direction in which the Thing faces. You need to take this fact into account when calculating where Things will fit, particularly for those Things that can move around, such as players and monsters.

THING COLLISION DETECTION

A Thing is deemed to be in contact with anything that touches or overlaps the square space it occupies. The consequences of these contacts depend on the type of Thing involved. Players who touch on bonuses obtain them; monsters reaching walls change direction; players or monsters colliding with Things that are classed as obstacles find their progress barred.

Things that move around (players and monsters) can only enter gaps that are wider than their diameter (allowing for the fact that it is really a square) and at least as tall as they are.

NOTE: The game engine shows an inconsistency here. Height restrictions do not operate as tightly as width restrictions!

Note that for the purposes of inter-object collision detection, DOOM regards all Things of the obstacle category as being of infinite height. Players can never leap over a barrel, for example, no matter how far below them it is.

The height restriction has been lifted in Hexen. In this game variant, the player *can* leap over barrels. In fact, all of Hexen's obstructions now have a finite height, enabling the player to pass over (or under) them if the relative vertical placements permit it.

The fact that Things' extents are square and do not rotate complicates the WAD designer's job. You have to bear in mind that players and monsters are wider when moving at angles other than one of the cardinal directions. Thus, wider gaps are needed between obstacles if the player is to pass between them at angles other than due north, south, east, or west, as Figure 12.1 shows.

Figure 12.1.
Gaps might be smaller than they look.

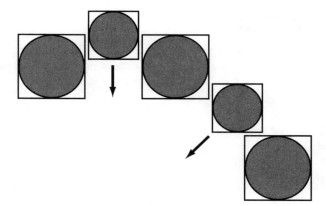

In this figure, the smaller circles represent players who are moving in the directions shown by the arrows. The larger circles represent obstructions (such as barrels). Notice how the real (square) extents of these items interact very differently from the way their visible (circular) shapes would suggest. The player moving due south between the obstacles can pass freely through a gap that would seem to be much narrower than the one that the other player is about to find impassable.

OVERLAPPING THINGS—STUCK MONSTERS

Most editors allow Things to be placed anywhere on the map, even if they are actually too large for the chosen spot. Any object larger than the space in which it is placed, however, looks unsightly. The entire object is rendered on-screen by the engine, even though it is visually too large for the space it is in. As you can imagine, this usually looks odd.

If your objects are purely decorative, such as pillars, lamps, firesticks, and so forth, it is largely up to you how tight a fit you want to make them. Objects growing out of walls, ceilings, or floors are likely to be viewed as errors, but that should be the only consequence of carelessly placed decorations and bonuses. On the other hand, the consequences of placing player and monster start positions in tight spaces can be much more serious.

If you place monsters or players in spaces where they do not fit, you will find that they stick tight and are unable to participate in the game. Stuck monsters cannot attack a player, but they can be injured and killed, either by a player or by other monsters if they get caught in crossfire. This effect has been used intentionally in some WADs—usually to "glue" several powerful monsters together. None of these monsters can attack the player, who sets about disposing of them and then suddenly discovers that the final monster becomes free to attack— usually just as the player runs out of ammunition!

Stuck players are there for good—or until they think to use the no-clipping cheat code! This is not an effect that many players view as worthwhile.

REACHING GOODIES

If you are placing bonus items around your map, you normally need to make it possible for the player to get at them. You therefore need to ensure that the player can either enter the area (eventually!) to collect the booty, or reach in to grab it. Players are 56 units high and have a diameter of 32 units, so they can enter only areas that are at least 56 units high by 33 units wide. As you've seen, this width restriction can be imposed by walls or by impassable Things.

Note that in Heretic, when the player has been turned into a chicken (and you DOOM guys can stop laughing; it happens!) or has been reduced to a pig in Hexen (something that is not discussed in polite company), it is possible to enter smaller places. In these guises, the player is reduced to 24 units high but retains the normal 32-unit diameter.

It is possible for players to reach the distance of their radius (16 units on the coordinate system axis) into areas they cannot wholly enter, provided that the area's floor is not above their head—in other words, it must be less than 56 units above the floor on which they are standing (as long as they aren't masquerading as animals at the time).

RESTRICTIONS ON A PLAYER'S VERTICAL MOVEMENT

From playing DOOM, you should know that there is a restriction on the height that a player can step up from one sector to the next. This height restriction is 24 units—any greater and the engine refuses to enable the player to continue onward. There is no limit on the downward distance a player can fall without taking damage.

The rules on vertical motion have been changed in Hexen: a player can still step up only 24 units, but can now jump up 64. In addition, it is no longer possible to fall far without being harmed as a result.

In the preceding section, you were told that a sector must be 56 units high if a player is to enter. Whenever the player tries to step from one sector to another, DOOM checks that there is a gap of this size between the higher floor and the lower ceiling of the two sectors. Therefore, if you are building stepped sector sequences, bear in mind that the player cannot pass up or down the steps if any floor-to-ceiling space between adjacent sectors is less than 56 units high.

In Raven Software's adaptations of the game, Inhilicon's Wings of Wrath provide the player with the added ability to fly. This, in effect, gives a player the freedom to move any distance in the vertical direction whenever the power-up is active. If you make this power-up available in your WAD, therefore, you need to be aware that any part of a sector into which a player can physically fit becomes potentially reachable during the game. This can have implications in your positioning of goodies and in the construction of your scenery in general.

MONSTER MOVEMENTS

Sector sizes are also important for determining monster behavior. Whenever monsters are awake, they tend to track players. Even when the player is not in their line of sight, awakened monsters remain aware of the direction of players and generally head toward them, unless they are constrained in some way or are distracted—usually by being struck with weapon fire from other monsters who can see the player.

Like players, free-roaming monsters cannot enter spaces that are smaller than they are. They also demonstrate a reluctance to enter spaces that are a tight fit for them; the smaller the gap, the more reluctant a monster is to enter it. For completely unimpeded movement, a monster needs a sector to be at least twice as wide as the monster's own diameter.

Monsters can climb stairs just as a player can—all monsters with legs can step up 24 units but no higher. They are more careful than players about coming down, however (a topic that will be explored in more detail shortly).

MONSTERS' REACH

Again, like players, clawed monsters (such as Imps) can reach into sectors they cannot enter—not to collect goodies, of course, but to savage players! For a player to be safe from such a savaging, monsters must be constrained far enough away for their (square) extent not to touch the player's.

CAUTION: Monsters can inflict clawing damage from any distance below the player, so don't confine a player to a tall, narrow pillar in an Imp-infested pit unless you want survival to be impossible!

SIZING FOR BETTER TEXTURE ALIGNMENT

You have already seen the final sizing consideration: fixing sector sizes to ensure better texture alignment. In addition to the alignment problems you have experienced yourself, some textures look strange when replicated up or along walls. Often you need to limit your sectors to certain absolute sizes (as well as grid locations) to use particular textures effectively or to minimize problems with their alignment.

Usually, however, the choice of textures, and the adjustment of the map to make them work properly, is completely subordinate to the size and shape that the area needs to be in order to play well. If you have areas that already work well but find that you cannot get the textures to look right with any of the available alignment mechanisms, it is usually best to look for another texture to use rather than to compromise your WAD's playability for the sake of its appearance.

HEIGHT CONSIDERATIONS

Although the structure of the DOOM world precludes the arrangement of floors immediately above one another, this does not mean that you need to build your WADs without regard for the vertical dimension. You can (and indeed should) make good use of height variations throughout your WAD. Not only does this add realism to the overall feel of the game, but it also is important to keep players looking all around them—above and below, as well as from side to side and behind. Heretic and Hexen's added facility for looking up and down make the utilization of height variations of particular importance in those variants of the game. The improved viewing capabilities introduced by Raven Software (as well as the added power of flight) have expanded the usefulness of DOOM's vertical dimension enormously; be sure to take full advantage of it.

DIVIDING ROOMS INTO SECTORS

After you've answered the fundamental questions of what an area is for and how it needs to be arranged, you can start to think about how it might need to be divided into its component sectors. You already know a lot about this topic.

WHEN DO YOU NEED ANOTHER SECTOR?

Back in Chapter 8, you learned about the fundamental role of the sector in the WAD, and you learned to distinguish the WADster's sector from the DOOMster's "room." By now, you should be comfortable with the use of sectors and should know when you need to create a new sector. It is worth summarizing here, however, the occasions when an area of the map needs to be in a sector of its own:

- When it needs to have a different ceiling height from its neighbors
- When it needs to have a different ceiling texture from its neighbors
- When it needs to have a different floor height from its neighbors
- When it needs to have a different floor texture from its neighbors
- When it needs to have a different lighting level from its neighbors
- Any combination of these situations

These are the reasons you are already familiar with. There is another reason:

- When it needs to be able to do something special

The next chapter, "Special Sectors," deals with these special activities of sectors. The current chapter is confined to considerations of the kinds of scenery components (alcoves, staircases, and so on) that require only simple floor, ceiling, or lighting changes for their implementation.

Note that all the areas covered in the rest of this chapter are no more than perceptual elements of a map. Within the WAD, they are implemented either as individual sectors or as particular arrangements of sectors, but there is nothing particularly special about them.

SIMPLE SECTORS

Many areas of the map require (or at least benefit from) additional sectors within or adjacent to them, acting as both decorative and structural features. These sectors are frequently simple in form. They generally fall into one of several fairly loose categories.

PILLARS AND COLUMNS

Pillars and *columns* provide useful cover for players in otherwise open rooms. They are also useful devices for restricting the movement of monsters, particularly flying ones that cannot be constrained by stairs. Pillars can be added either by leaving void areas marked out within the room sectors (as you saw in the first WAD sortie) or by means of their own sectors, with suitably elevated floors. Which method is adopted depends largely on the appearance you want the pillars to have: if the pillar is to reach from floor to ceiling (as most do), the easier and more economical method in terms of space is to use the void.

ALCOVES, LEDGES, AND PLATFORMS

Alcoves are small areas generally set into the walls of larger rooms or passageways. *Ledges* are longer, thinner areas, usually running along the walls of rooms. They are frequently at a considerable height from the main room floor, and if the player is to enter them, they need to have some mechanism or provision for access. *Platforms* are usually raised areas within rooms.

All of these areas are common components of DOOM WADs, and they provide good spots for scattering bonuses, power-ups, and, of course, enemies. Trying to locate the access points to these locations (or even just spotting the locations themselves) can be a major element in playing rooms that contain them. As well as providing good ambush points, alcoves are suitable locations for secret switches and such—which you will learn more about shortly.

You should already know enough about sectors to see how all of these areas can be implemented. Each is likely to need nothing more than an appropriate sector, set as necessary into or alongside a larger sector. You will see the building process in the next WAD sortie.

POOLS, PONDS, AND PITS

Pools are areas containing liquids through which a player can pass, with or without taking harm. *Ponds* are usually deeper, and their higher sides can trap the player, forcing a hunt for an exit—usually in the form of a single step or a lower side somewhere. *Pits* are deep areas from which players can expect to have major difficulties extracting themselves. Pits might need to have some special sort of escape provided if you don't want the player to be trapped in them forever.

Again, these types of areas should already be familiar to you. They are used as traps for the unwary, as areas that wreak havoc if the player falls into them, or simply as obstacles that need to be skirted.

The techniques for building these areas should already be obvious to you. They are simply sectors with appropriately lowered floors. Pools and ponds generally have animated textures on these floors. Often, these areas cause harm to players who spend time in them. (You will see how to implement these harmful effects in the next chapter.)

STEPS

Steps are a common feature of DOOM WADs. You have one in your own WAD already. Additional sectors functioning as steps are needed to enable the player (and/or monsters) to move freely between sectors with a difference of floor height greater than 24 units. They provide changes in the vertical levels of your WAD, preventing the player from always having to fight on the flat, which thus makes for a more interesting game. You have already seen that they can affect monsters' behavior too. Steps are also a convenient means of making floor texture changes look better.

> **NOTE:** The WAD sortie that follows builds on the WAD produced in the last sortie of the preceding chapter. If you did not accompany me on that sortie but want to participate in this one, you should use WAD8.WAD (DOOM), D2WAD8.WAD (DOOM II), or H1WAD8.WAD (Heretic) from the CD-ROM as your starting point.

WAD SORTIE 9: ADDING ALCOVES, PLATFORMS, AND POOLS

Having described some basic map elements, I think it would be useful for you to add a few of them to your WAD. By doing this, you will get a better feel for the way in which sectors can work together and will become more conversant with WADED's methodology for adding sectors to your map.

WADED'S TREATMENT OF SECTORS

So far, you have been using WADED's sector-creation facilities strictly according to my dictates. I will now explain the way these operate so that in the future you will be able to work out the correct way to use them for yourself.

CREATING/FIXING SECTORS IN WADED

The operation of WADED's Make Sector facility can sometimes be very confusing, even to experienced users of the program. The confusion arises because it is not always obvious when the clicking action will make a new sector and when it will simply "fix" an existing sector by incorporating extra lines into it. The methodology behind Make Sector is actually quite straightforward—the key to its operation lies in the color of the lines surrounding the area of the mouse click.

Make Sector recognizes three significant combinations of lines surrounding the mouse pointer:

- **At least one magenta line is present:** Under these circumstances, WADED knows that you have added at least one new line to the map. It assumes therefore that you want to add a new sector, either by adding one in the void or by dividing an existing sector.

- **All lines are white:** With Make Sector active, if an area with the mouse pointer in it is completely surrounded by white lines, that area must currently be void space. Consequently, WADED assumes that you want a new sector created out of this void space.

- **At least one red (but no magenta) line is present:** For there to be any red lines around the area, the mouse pointer must be in at least the remains of an existing sector; but because there are no magenta lines present, no new lines can have been drawn. Under these circumstances, WADED assumes that the existing sector is merely being rebuilt, and it therefore does not create a new sector but ensures that the area's lines are incorporated into the same (existing) sector.

MAKE SECTOR'S AUTOMATIC SIDEDEF GENERATION

Make Sector alwaystries to generate appropriate sidedefs for all the lines that make up the sector on which it operates. It does this by checking each of the lines composing the boundary of the sector as follows:

- **Line is magenta:** Magenta lines have no sidedefs. (That is why they are magenta.) WADED therefore adds a right sidedef to this line and then, if necessary, flips the line so that this side faces into the sector that has just been created. WADED also sets this line's Impassable flag.

- **Line is white:** A white line already has one sidedef. This sidedef, however, is on the opposite side from the current sector. A new left sidedef is therefore added to the line; its Two-Sided flag is set, and its Impassable flag is cleared. If a new sector has just been created and this is the first white line encountered, Make Sector takes the settings from the existing sector on this line's right side as the default settings for the new sector.

- **Line is red:** A red line already has a sidedef on its appropriate side. WADED makes sure that this sidedef belongs to the correct sector but makes no other change to the line.

TIP: Although it shouldn't make any difference, you will find that Make Sector usually works best if you draw lines in a way that requires the minimum number of them to have their directions changed. For best results, draw complete sectors in a clockwise manner.

AUTOMATIC SECTOR SETTINGS

As mentioned previously, Make Sector generates settings automatically for new sectors. If a new sector is bounded by any line that is already a member of a sector on its other side, Make Sector creates the new sector with its neighbor's attributes; otherwise, a set of arbitrary values is assigned.

Heretic users are probably already well aware of the shortcomings of WADED's arbitrary sector settings. Even in Heretic mode, the program always assigns *DOOM* textures to the floor and ceiling. If left in, these texture names crash Heretic when a new game is started with the WAD. If you find that Heretic crashes back to DOS with the message R_FlatNumForName: *xxxx* not found, check the floor and ceiling textures of any sectors that you have made (or fixed) using Make Sector since the last successful use of your WAD.

Note also that each time WADED adds a second sidedef to a line, it also sets the line's Two-Sided flag. Unfortunately, it takes this rather too far: contrary to DOOM's rules, the current version of WADED insists that a line's Two-Sided flag always must match the true number of sidedefs. If the user switches off this flag on a two-sided line, the program sees this action as a request to delete the left sidedef. This it does, destroying the integrity of the sector that owned the left sidedef. (WadAuthor also shares this bad habit!)

The correct order for drawing lines, using Make Sector, and setting sector attributes takes some getting used to; therefore, the next few WAD sorties continue to provide guidance on this function's use. Gradually, this guidance will be withdrawn, but by then you should be fully conversant with this aspect of the program.

NOTE: There is an additional sector-defining function in WADED: the Sec Define button, located below the Make Sector button. This feature can be awkward to use, but it is useful for minor amendments to the WAD's sector information. Its use will be demonstrated in a later WAD sortie in this chapter.

WADAUTHOR'S TREATMENT OF SECTORS

WadAuthor's methodology for creating new sectors makes its settings much easier to predict. A new sector inherits its settings from the sector in which the right mouse click was made to trigger its inception. Sectors created inside other sectors this way automatically have their bounding lines two-sided. Sectors created in the void, on the other hand, have their bounding lines single-sided. These sectors take the settings from the currently selected Motif (or the Default Motif, if one has not been selected).

> **NOTE:** Now you know why the first WAD you produced in WadAuthor had no pillar in the hexagonal room. You might want to fix that as the first step in this sortie. The easiest way is to set both floor and ceiling of the small inner hexagon to the same value. Don't forget to assign textures to the essentials that this action creates.

ADDING ALCOVES

The areas to be added in this sortie are relatively straightforward. Start WADED with WAD8.WAD and begin with a simple alcove or two, as described in the following text.

> **TIP:** Feel free to save your WAD at appropriate times during this sortie. Use a series of names such as TEMP9A, TEMP9B, and so on.

At this stage, the alcoves you are adding might appear purely decorative in function. I have plans for them later, however, so don't let that worry you after all I've said about decorations!

ENTRANCE DOOR

The first addition is something that, in my opinion, no WAD should be without: an explanation of how the player got to the start position. I always feel that a player's materialization at some arbitrary point in the middle of a room detracts immediately from the realism of the situation. Therefore, this WAD will have an entrance door. The door will be firmly locked with no hope of escape through it, but at least the player will have some point of reference from the start of the WAD.

All that is needed for this entrance is a simple alcove of an appropriate size to hold the right textures. For this job, I consider the textures given in Table 12.1 to be the right ones.

Table 12.1. The textures for the entrance.

Surface	Texture [Heretic]
The locked door	DOOR3 [METL2]
Side walls	LITE3 [METL2]
Floor and ceiling	FLAT18 [FLOOR28]

Preview these textures and note their sizes: DOOR3 is 64 pixels wide and 72 pixels high. This texture needs to fill the alcove's back wall completely; its size therefore dictates the width and height of the alcove. LITE3 is 32 pixels wide; this provides the depth of the alcove. FLAT18 looks to be composed of two tiles, each 64 pixels wide by 32 deep. Either half of this flat will therefore fit conveniently on the floor and ceiling of the planned alcove, but you will need to ensure that the alcove is drawn squarely in either the northern or the southern half of one of the map's grid squares. At this point, if you are using WADED, you might want to turn on the grid, and you might find that a ZOOM factor of around 10 helps also.

The suggested Heretic textures are a little different in size from the DOOM textures, but you should be able to see how well they will fit in the spaces for which they are recommended. METL2 works quite well in the size of gap suggested, although you might want to go for a better fit by increasing the height of the alcove to 96. (Preview the texture to see why.)

The new alcove is to be added toward the western end of the south wall of the main hexagonal room. Start by adjusting the line that marks the southern wall so that it lies along one of the east-west grid lines (or precisely halfway between two, if that is easier). Then add the new lines for the alcove in a clockwise sequence, with each running along conveniently located grid lines. Remember that you want the new sector covering exactly one-half of one of the grid squares; this automatically makes it 32 units deep and 64 units wide.

Apply Make Sector to the new alcove, and then set the new sector's floor height to 8 and its ceiling to 80. (It needs to be 72 units high, remember.)

NOTE: The line on the northern edge of the alcove is not a new line and therefore was white when you used Make Sector. It consequently will be made two-sided and its new sidedef incorporated into the new sector, while its other side will remain as it was. The sector on the other side of this line (the main hexagonal room) provides the settings for the new sector and is itself left untouched. It will therefore need no repair after Make Sector is used on the new alcove.

The lighting level of the new sector can be left at 144. Apply the appropriate textures to the alcove's surfaces. A couple of essential textures need to be dealt with where the alcove meets the main room. STONE2 [GRSTNPB] would seem appropriate for these textures. Unpeg the upper and lower textures here to ensure that the textures align correctly with the adjacent walls. Finally, put the player start positions close enough nearby to suggest that this is the door through which they've arrived.

PASSAGEWAY ALCOVES (DOOM/DOOM II)

 These alcoves are handled differently in Heretic; instructions will be given shortly.

The next additions to the WAD will be a pair of alcoves in the southeastern passageway. I'd like these to face each other in the section of the passage that runs southeast to northwest, just out of the hexagonal room. One of these alcoves is to have the SW1GARG texture on its back wall, and the other is to have SW1LION. Both of these textures are 64 pixels wide, so each alcove needs to be this width. Their depth is not crucial; a value of 24 units or so will be fine.

You should be able to add the appropriate new lines and create these two new sectors without any further instructions from me. Getting the lines the right length here might prove tricky—just do your best. Reducing the Snap-to-Grid setting to 4 or so might make the job a little easier. The grid won't help you much—you might want to turn it off.

 NOTE: The same remarks about the use of Make Sector apply to these alcoves as they did to the preceding one.

I want each alcove to be 72 units high; after you've made the new sectors, bring the ceiling height down appropriately. The rest of the sector settings can be left the same as those of the passageway. Use STONE2 for the side walls of the alcoves to match the passageway. You need a Y-offset of −16 to keep the mortar lines continuous here. The upper essential should be STONE2 also, and, as you know by now, need to be unpegged. Finally, apply the SW1GARG and SW1LION textures as required to the back walls of the alcoves. If you preview these textures and visualize how they will be rendered on a wall that is 72 pixels high, you will see that the default rendering will cause a problem. These textures have important details that need to be kept at the correct height from the floor. They therefore need to have their Lower Unpegged flag set so that they are rendered from the floor up.

This completes the addition of alcoves to the DOOM/DOOM II version of the WAD. You can save it and try it out now, if you want. Heretic users, read on…!

PASSAGEWAY ALCOVES (HERETIC)

If you're working with Heretic, there are no good alcove textures comparable with DOOM's SW1LION and SW1GARG. I therefore recommend using the METL2 texture, but this requires that the alcoves be built a little differently.

The METL2 texture is the same width as both SW1LION and SW1GARG, so you should draw the alcoves and make their sectors in precisely the same way as just described. Instead of making the alcove sectors 72 units high, however, make them 96 units high so that METL2's 32-unit pattern repeat can be used just three times on each alcove's back wall. Use GRSTNPB on the side walls of the alcoves, with a Y-offset of –24 to improve their alignment with the main corridor walls. Use the same texture over each alcove and mark it as unpegged. Finally, to add some interest to these alcoves (METL2 is a much more boring texture than either SW1LION or SW1GARG), click the THINGS button and place a Wall Torch (in the Obstacle category) against the back wall of each alcove. You can then save and try out your WAD.

ADDING A PLATFORM

The next addition to the WAD is a platform inside the hexagonal room. Figure 12.2 shows its position and shape: another hexagon in the northeastern corner of the main room. Draw the new hexagon in a clockwise manner in WADED (or merely created inside the hexagonal room in WadAuthor), keeping about the same distance from the outer walls of the main room as the pillar is in the other corner.

Figure 12.2.
Lines for a new platform in the hexagonal room.

NOTE: This time, if you are working in WADED, all the lines of the new area are magenta. Make Sector needs to be applied inside the new hexagon first so that a new sector is created from the new lines. All the new lines are created single-sided, however, so Make Sector needs to be applied subsequently to the original hexagonal room to make that sector take over the second sides of the new lines. The settings for the new sector are arbitrary.

Set this new sector's floor to BLOOD1 [FLTLAVA1] at height 32, the ceiling to TLITE6_5 [FLAT516] at height 104, and the lighting level to 160. Put STONE [GRSTNPB] on all essentials.

Notice that this new sector's floor is too high above the floor of the main room for the player to climb onto it directly. This platform will provide the player with the WAD's first puzzle—not a particularly difficult one, but a puzzle, nonetheless. It will house some security armor (100 percent armor) in DOOM/DOOM II, a Silver Shield in Heretic. You can place the appropriate item now, if you want. Put it close to the southwestern edge of the new sector, but not so close that the player will be able to reach it from the floor of the main room. It needs to be about 40 units in from the edge.

Now, to enable the player to gain this power-up, you must provide access to the platform. You should do this by adding a step, but don't make the presence of the step obvious. Tuck it away in the extreme northeast corner of the hexagonal room, between the platform and the main wall. Players will discover this step only by walking around the platform. The careless player might miss it altogether.

To implement the step, you should add a new line connecting the northeastern corner of the platform to the nearby corner vertex of the room. Then add another new line some way to the south, connecting the platform to a point on the main room's northeast wall.

 NOTE: In WADED, after using Make Sector on the new step sector, you will need to use it on the main room sector again, because this sector has acquired two new lines. You shouldn't need to use it on the platform sector again, though, because you haven't added any lines to that. Pass the mouse over it and watch the lines turn red to confirm this fact. By now, you should know what settings WADED will have given to your new sector.

 Heretic users should stick with the usual floor, ceiling, and wall textures for this new sector, just making changes to the lighting, floor, and ceiling levels as suggested next.

Set the new step's floor to FLAT20 at height 16. This setting provides the necessary step up to the platform. This floor texture is fairly granular and won't require careful alignment. Now, it is often considered polite to provide clues to the solution of DOOM's problems, and even though this is a fairly simple problem, I suggest that you do provide a clue here. Let this sector provide a hint of its existence by changing its ceiling (visible from the other side of the platform, unlike the step itself) and lighting level. Apply FLAT20 to the step sector's ceiling, and change its height to 112. Check that the lighting level is 160. Put STONE on the lower essentials and STONE2 on the uppers. The section of the original outer wall that this sector has acquired now needs a Y-offset applied to compensate for its new ceiling height. The texture needs to be moved up by the same amount as you brought the ceiling down; a Y-offset of 8 achieves this effect.

This completes the first puzzle area in your WAD. Try it out, if you want.

ADDING A POND

The final addition to your WAD in this sortie is another little puzzle for the player, this time located out in the courtyard. Figure 12.3 shows the shapes to add here. Draw them now.

 NOTE: In WADED, use Make Sector on the larger of the two shapes before applying it to the smaller, inner shape. Don't forget to use it also on the main courtyard sector afterward.

Figure 12.3.

Lines for the pond added to the courtyard.

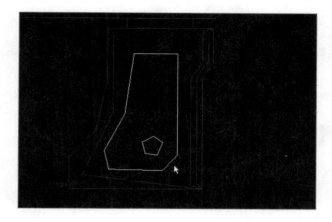

This new area is to be a pond. Its edges will be made too high for the player to climb out. Unless the player is to be forced to perish here, some form of escape mechanism is needed.

TIP: It is not good design practice to set dead-end traps for players. It might seem tempting to set a pond's edge height to 25 units in the full expectation that players will not notice it until they find themselves trapped. Remember, though, that this trap catches players only once—if you provide no escape mechanism from this trap, I would guess that a player would be unlikely to come back to discover what other neat ideas you've incorporated into your WAD!

The escape mechanism here will be a step, but not one that is simple for the player to use. It will take the form of a small island in the pond, carefully positioned so that it can be used as a step only when the player runs at it.

Use the settings shown in Table 12.2 for the two new sectors. Notice that the lighting level of the main pond sector is reduced just to make it look a little more threatening.

Table 12.2. Settings for the pond sectors [Heretic settings in brackets].

Sector	Lighting	Ceiling	Floor	Essentials
Pond	160	216 F_SKY1	–48 FWATER1 [FLTWAWA1]	BROWNHUG [SQPEB1]
Island	255	216 F_SKY1	–24 FLAT1_1 [FLOOR03]	BROWNHUG [SQPEB1]

You now need to save and play test the WAD a few times to get the size and the position of your island just right. Start with the island about 80 units from the eastern edge of the pond, and adjust its position and size until it's tricky, but possible, to use it to escape from the water.

TIP: WADED users might find the (Move) Sector facility useful here.

When you're happy with all of your latest additions, save your final WAD as WAD9.WAD.

USING STAIRS

In the preceding section, I discussed briefly the uses of steps. Often in DOOM WADs, steps are arranged in long runs, providing staircases between areas of widely differing floor elevations. These structures are required often enough, and are sufficiently interesting, to warrant a separate examination.

STAIRCASES

Staircases with twists and turns can provide limited visibility ahead and make for good constricted fighting areas. They also provide natural funnels to limit the attacks on a player, while providing no place to hide or run to. They are good for ambush spots too.

Staircases generally require no special design considerations. The maximum step-up size of 24 units applies here as elsewhere. Note, though, that there is no minimum tread width; the player can climb steps with treads as narrow as one pixel (provided that your editor will let you draw them)!

Don't get carried away with long stairways. DOOM has a limit on the number of surfaces it can render at any one time, and this limit is not very high: 128 in v1.2 and 256 in later versions. If you overload DOOM in this way, the engine renders only the first 128 (or 256) surfaces in view and then leaves the remainder unpainted—but filled with the Hall of Mirrors effect. It is not clear precisely how the surface count is reckoned. It would seem to be a count of the number of separate polygons of continuous texture. Intervening structures—such as pillars—cutting across the view of an otherwise continuous surface divide its space into two, for example. No matter how this limit is actually reckoned, though, stairways can quickly cause DOOM to reach it. If you consider that each step has the potential to add an additional 5 surfaces to the view, a 20-step stairway could provide DOOM v1.2 with most of its permitted surfaces.

ONE-WAY STAIRCASES

You already know that when a player moves from one sector to another, DOOM checks for a maximum step height of 24 units and a minimum gap of 56 units (the height of the player) between one sector's floor and the adjacent ceiling. Additionally, a gap must be at least 33 units wide for a player to pass into it. There is an interesting flaw in the method by which DOOM checks on these conditions when climbing and descending, a flaw that allows the construction of a useful addition to the repertoire of scenery elements: the one-way staircase.

When moving up from one sector to another, DOOM does not consider the destination sector's depth (that is, in the direction the player is moving). All that can prevent the player from making the upward step is the riser height and the size of the floor-ceiling gap. If the destination sector is not deep enough to take the player completely, it doesn't matter—the player simply does not move wholly into it but "overhangs" the preceding sector a little.

Coming down, however, the DOOM engine does not permit a step to be taken unless the player can move wholly (in other words, a full 33 units) into the destination sector. The engine therefore checks that the ceiling height is no less than 56 units above the player's current floor for the entire 33-unit distance ahead. Treads narrower than 33 units can thus be used with carefully calculated ceiling heights to produce stairs that players can ascend without problem—only to find themselves unable to reverse the maneuver.

Staircases that permit descent but not ascent are even easier to produce—simply include a step size that exceeds the 24-unit maximum.

TIP: As previously noted in the section on ponds, you should make sure that areas entered via one-way staircases have another means of exit. Generally, you should ensure that trap features such as this do not force players into positions from which there is no escape, particularly if they take no harm from being there. Players who are forced to die of boredom will not return to play your WAD again. It is considered polite to add a warning of some sort too!

MONSTER BEHAVIOR ON STAIRCASES

When designing staircases, you should bear in mind that steps and stairs have an effect on the way monsters follow the player. As you have already seen, all monsters with legs share the same restriction as the player when it comes to climbing: 24 units is the maximum height they can manage. Monsters are much more reluctant than most players about descending steps, however. They never step down more than 24 units, and in addition, they are fussy about steep stairs. Generally speaking, the greater the downward step-distance, the deeper each tread needs to be for monsters to be lured down them. Also, you might need to adjust the tread depth to suit the particular monsters you are using—the larger the monsters, the more wary of steep steps they are.

Experimentation has shown that on stairs with the maximum 24-unit risers, the treads need to be at least 0.85 of a monster's diameter before the monster will venture down them. This figure is for steps aligned with the coordinate system; those at an angle need correspondingly larger treads. Of course, you might want to use this fact to produce stairs that monsters are less likely to descend so that the player can fight the monsters from the comparative safety of the bottom!

Floating monsters are, of course, oblivious to the presence of steps, up or down, when it comes to chasing the player.

WAD SORTIE 10: STAIRWAYS TO HELL

NOTE: This sortie builds on the WAD produced in the preceding sortie. If you did not produce that WAD, you should use WAD9.WAD (DOOM), D2WAD9.WAD (DOOM II), or H1WAD9.WAD (Heretic) from the CD-ROM as your starting point here.

This sortie give you plenty of practice in the use of WADED's Make Sector facility. During the sortie, you will add a couple of stairways to your WAD. In particular, it will demonstrate how much easier it is to extend a WAD out from existing sectors into the void than it is to build within existing sectors. Start with WAD9.WAD and feel free to save your WAD as often as necessary during the course of this sortie, using a sequence of TEMP10A.WAD, TEMP10B.WAD, and so on, for the names.

EXTENDING THE SOUTHEAST PASSAGEWAY

For this addition, you will find it useful to have the grid turned on in WADED and the ZOOM factor set at about 10. Try to draw as much as possible in a clockwise manner. In WadAuthor, set the grid to 64.

With (Draw) Lines selected, but before drawing anything, select MARBLE3 [DOORSTON] as the default texture for the new lines. Then scroll your map so that the eastern end of the southeast passageway lies toward the bottom of the screen. The first new staircase is to be a one-way staircase heading north from the eastern end of this passageway. Figure 12.4 shows how the map will look after the new additions. Follow the instructions given next for the most efficient way of adding them in WADED (the additions are straightforward in WadAuthor). Delay using Make Sector until all the new lines are drawn. Again, you will be led through the most efficient way.

Figure 12.4.
The new lines for the staircase.

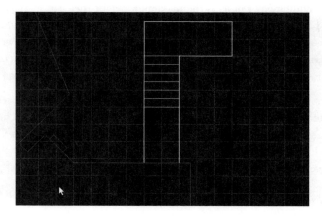

Start by adding a short corridor out through the north wall of the passageway. This corridor needs to be 128 units wide, so make sure that its western and eastern walls run along grid lines. Make it about 200 units long.

The exact length is immaterial, but, again, make sure that its northern edge runs along a grid line. This sets you up for easier construction of the stairs.

Now, to catch players, one-way stairs need to be less than 33 units deep. Utilize the grid, therefore, to add four more rectangles to the map, maintaining the new corridor's width of 128 units but making each rectangle only 32 units (exactly half a grid square) deep from north to south. Change the default texture to MARBLE1 if you're using DOOM or DOOM II (Heretic users can stay with DOORSTON). Then add two more rectangles of the same size as before. You should now have the lines (magenta in WADED) for six steps, as well as a corridor connecting the stairs to the original passageway.

Finally, add the lines for a new passageway running east from the northern end of the stairs. It should run a total of 320 units east from the western end and be 128 units north-south.

When you have all the lines drawn, you can think about creating the sectors.

MAKING THE STAIR SECTORS

In WADED, apply Make Sector to the southern corridor area first. Then, before making any more sectors, change the new corridor's ceiling height to 128, and apply DEM1_5 [FLOOR28] to both ceiling and floor. Put MARBLE3 [DOORSTON] on the essential texture over the new opening, and unpeg it.

Now use Make Sector on the next rectangle—the bottom step—and then inspect that sector's settings. Put DEM1_6 [FLOOR28] on its floor, and increase its floor height to 16. Now apply Make Sector to the second step. You should find that WADED has copied the first step's settings onto the second, and all you need to do is increase the new step's floor height to 32. Note how you are using Make Sector to transfer sector settings in your favor.

Continue in this manner, successively using Make Sector and adjusting each new sector's settings, before moving on to the next sector. Table 12.3 shows the settings to use for the sectors you are adding.

Table 12.3. Floor and ceiling settings for the new sectors.

Area	Floor Height	Ceiling Height
Southern corridor	0	128
Bottom step	16	128
Second step	32	128
Third step	48	128
Fourth step	64	144
Fifth step	80	240
Sixth step	96	240
Top corridor	112	240

Notice how the floor heights form an orderly progression, each rising 16 units above the preceding one. The ceilings don't follow the same progression, however—they start out 128 units above the floor at either end of the stairway, reducing to 80 units over the third and fourth steps.

With 16-unit risers, as here, a ceiling-floor height of 80 units provides a 64-unit gap between the ceiling of one step and the floor of the next step up. Consequently, a player will have no problem climbing these stairs. Coming down will be a different matter, however.

The treads of these steps are only 32 units deep. In considering the downward movement, therefore, the engine will have to look *two* ceilings ahead of the player's sector to determine the ceiling-floor gap 33 units ahead. Over the third and fourth steps, this gap reduces to 48 units. So after the player is over the third step, there will be no going back.

Of course, you could have built the entire staircase using a ceiling-floor height of 80 units. In such case, it would have been a one-way stair from top to bottom. But because I want to provide the player with a chance to notice what is happening here, the configuration you have just been given has only two "non-return" steps.

 Again, Heretic's different textures force readers with that game to do things a little differently. In the subsequent section, I will present the DOOM way of providing a clue to the one-way stairs before considering the Heretic solution.

FIXING THE TEXTURES (DOOM/DOOM II)

Now that all the sectors are made, you can fix the missing textures. Start with the riser of the bottom step. Make it MARBLE1. Do the same with the next two steps' risers. The next step is the dangerous one—it cannot be reversed—so give a clue to the hazard by using MARBLE3 on both essentials. This action places the clue on the step riser so that it is visible on the approach to the stairs. It also places the clue on the wall face above the step so that it is at the players' eye level when they attempt to descend the stairs—rather too late for them to do anything about the situation, but it might make them notice the clue the next time they see it!

NOTE: Preview the MARBLE3 texture to see how it provides a clue to the hazard ahead. Remember that only the top 16 pixels of the pattern are displayed on these textures.

Use MARBLE3 on both essentials of the next riser, but revert to MARBLE1 for the remaining risers. Finally, put MARBFACE on the western wall of the top corridor, just to add a threatening touch there.

Readers using DOOM or DOOM II can now save their WAD and rejoin me after the description of the Heretic stairs.

FIXING THE TEXTURES (HERETIC)

Heretic's paucity of textures prevents you from giving clues to hazards by using the multiplicity of different patterns just demonstrated. Far from being a nuisance, however, this feature actually makes the task easier! Place the DOORSTON texture on *all* the step risers (essential lowers, remember). Locate the risers to the fourth and fifth steps, and unpeg both their upper and lower textures. That's all you need to do!

It is not immediately obvious how this unpegging provides a visual clue, is it? Preview the DOORSTON texture for a hint. Or perhaps you can spot it in Figure 12.5.

Figure 12.5.
A *view of the one-way stairs in Heretic.*

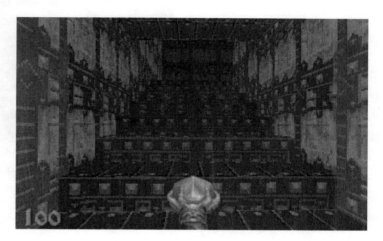

TRYING THE STAIRS

You can now try out your new one-way staircase. Of course, having ascended it, you must press Escape and restart the game to do anything else! Don't worry, though. The exit from this particular trap will be added in a later WAD sortie.

NOTE: Be wary of adding traps such as this to your WADs. Although they might work fine in single-player games—forcing the player to tackle particular areas of a WAD without hope of retreat or to find other routes through the WAD—they can cause complications during multiplayer games by limiting players' movements. This is not to say that these are bad things, just that you might need to take some extra care with these features if you intend your WAD to be used in Deathmatch or Cooperative play.

COMBINING STAIRWAYS AND PLATFORMS

Stairways are often used to provide a player with access to a platform that is at some height above a surrounding area. Such a platform provides players with a good view around—and exposes them to attack from all sides! I'll have you build a platform like this in the large room to the north of the courtyard. Figure 12.6 shows the configuration of lines to add. Once again, you will be led through the additions.

Figure 12.6.

New lines to add inside the southwest room.

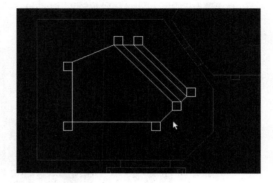

These lines represent seven pillars (the small squares) around a high platform reached by three steps from the floor of the main room. The seven pillars do not quite reach to the ceiling, and so they need to be made separate sectors rather than left as voids.

NOTE: Making the additions to this room is much easier in WadAuthor than in WADED. WadAuthor's cut-and-paste facility should make life simple indeed if you fix each new sector's settings as you create it.

Start with these seven small square pillars; they should all be exactly 64 units square. If you're using WADED, apply Make Sector to each pillar as you draw it, but do not fix the original outer area just yet. Next, draw the lines that link the squares and make up the perimeter of the new area. Work around in a clockwise manner. This should leave just three of the new lines undrawn. Before adding these, use Make Sector on the large area you have just marked out in the middle of the room. Don't bother with this sector's settings, though, because later operations will destroy them.

Now you should use Make Sector on what remains of the original southwest room sector. This room needs greater headroom because of the platform, so take its ceiling up to 184. (Note that this height preserves the 32-pixel increment that was needed in this room to make the doorway texture alignments work for the DOOM/DOOM II version of the WAD. Heretic users, however, will be less than impressed with this change.)

You can then draw the three additional lines marking the stairs climbing up to the new platform. You need to add these lines with care—this area is becoming a little complex for Make Sector's liking. Start by drawing the two lines that mark out the first step down from the platform, and make this step's sector before using Make

Sector to fix the large platform sector. (You have just added a new line to it, remember.) Finally, add the remaining line and make sectors out of the areas on each side of it.

Now work around all the new sectors, correcting any settings that differ from the ones given in Table 12.4. (WADED users will find the MULTI function available in SECTORS mode to be of use here. This function works in precisely the same way as the MULTI function available in LINES mode.)

Table 12.4. Sector settings for the new platform area [Heretic settings in brackets].

Lighting	Ceiling		Floor	
		Main Sectors, West to East		
144	256 [312]	CEIL5_1 [FLOOR10]	88	FLAT5_2 [FLOOR10]
144	256 [312]	CEIL5_1 [FLOOR10]	72	FLAT5_2 [FLOOR10]
144	256 [312]	CEIL5_1 [FLOOR10]	48	FLAT5_2 [FLOOR10]
144	256 [312]	CEIL5_1 [FLOOR10]	24	FLAT5_2 [FLOOR10]
		Pillar Sectors from NE Corner, Clockwise		
192	256 [320]	CONS1_1 [FLOOR08]	152 [136]	FLOOR4_8 [FLOOR03]
192	256 [320]	CONS1_7 [FLOOR08]	152 [136]	FLOOR4_8 [FLOOR03]
144 [192]	256 [320]	CEIL5_1 [FLOOR10]	152 [136]	FLOOR4_8 [FLOOR03]
192	256 [320]	CONS1_5 [FLOOR08]	152 [136]	FLOOR4_8 [FLOOR03]
192	256 [320]	CONS1_7 [FLOOR08]	152 [136]	FLOOR4_8 [FLOOR03]
192	256 [320]	CONS1_7 [FLOOR08]	152 [136]	FLOOR4_8 [FLOOR03]
192	256 [320]	CONS1_1 [FLOOR08]	152 [136]	FLOOR4_8 [FLOOR03]

Finally, apply the textures given in Table 12.5 (DOOM/DOOM II) or Table 12.6 (Heretic) to the new lines.

TIP: In WADED, you might find it easier to work with the wall textures required for the pillar essentials if you first scroll ICKWALL2 to the top of the scrolling list box by using the [and] (bracket) keys.

Table 12.5. Line textures needed for the new area in DOOM/DOOM II.

Lowers	Uppers: North Wall	East Wall	South Wall	West Wall
	Pillar Essentials, from NE Pillar, Clockwise			
STONE3	ICKWALL6	ICKWALL5	—	ICKWALL2
STONE3	ICKWALL2	ICKWALL2	ICKWALL2	—
STONE3	—	ICKWALL6*	ICKWALL5	—
STONE3	—	ICKWALL2	ICKWALL5	ICKWALL2
STONE3	GRAYBIG	GRAYBIG	GRAYBIG	GRAYBIG
STONE3	GRAYBIG	—	GRAYBIG	GRAYBIG
STONE3	ICKWALL4	ICKWALL2	—	ICKWALL7

Lowers	Uppers			
	Peripheral Line Essentials, from Long NE Boundary, Clockwise			
WOOD5	ICKWALL3			
WOOD5	ICKWALL1			
WOOD5	ICKWALL7			
WOOD5	COMPSTA1			
WOOD5	COMPSTA2			
WOOD5	COMPSTA1			
WOOD5	ICKWALL7			

*DOOM II does not have the ICKWALL6 texture—use ICKWALL5 in its place.

All the upper textures should be unpegged if you're building for DOOM or DOOM II. (Again, MULTI might come in handy in WADED.)

Table 12.6. Line textures needed for the new area in Heretic.

Location	Lower Texture	Upper Texture
Pillars	GRSTNPBV	CTYSTCI4
Peripheral lines	CTYSTCI4	CTYSTCI4

Three additional lines need WOOD5 [CTYSTCI4] added to their lower essentials—these are the risers formed by the last three lines you added to the map.

Finally, attach a railing to one edge of this platform. Apply the texture BRNSMALC [GATMETL2] as the main texture of both sides of the line running between the northwestern pillar and the next pillar to the east. Save the WAD and inspect your handiwork.

NOTE: You can find ready-built copies of this WAD on the accompanying CD-ROM as WAD10.WAD (DOOM), D2WAD10.WAD (DOOM II), and H1WAD10.WAD (Heretic).

INSPECTING THE PLATFORM

If all has gone well, the appearance of your WAD should have no major problems. It is probably a bit ragged in places, with some less-than-perfect texture alignments, especially around the tops of the pillars. Heretic users are most likely to be annoyed at the messy walls of the main room. They might also glimpse a problem in the view out to the courtyard from the top of the new platform—an unsightly gap between the top of the vine wall and the "bottom" of the sky. These will be the main problems to sort out in the next sortie.

If there are any glaring omissions of textures, make a note of where they are. You can return to the editor to check that everything matches what's given in the appropriate tables in a moment, but before doing that, take a good look at the grating texture you added. Not quite right, is it? Climb up onto the platform and try walking into the grating. You shouldn't be able to pass straight through it like that, should you?

To understand the cause of this problem and learn how to fix it, it is necessary to review see-through textures and the use of the two-sided line. The next section of this chapter does that, so if you have other problems with your WAD that need attention, return to your editor now and try to fix those first. I'll meet you when you're ready to correct that railing.

SECTOR EDGES—THE TWO-SIDED LINE REVISITED

It is time now to review the nature of the two-sided line, starting with its role in providing a link between sectors.

MOVEMENT THROUGH TWO-SIDED LINES

You already know that by definition, a two-sided line (a line with sidedefs on each side) lies on the boundary between one sector and another. By now you are used to passing freely from one sector to another through these two-sided lines.

What is it about these lines that enables a player to pass through? It's simply their two-sidedness: the fact that there is another sector on the other side to pass into. When determining whether a player can move through a line, DOOM first looks "through" the line to see whether there is anywhere for the player to go beyond it. If not, as happens with a single-sided line, progress comes to an abrupt halt. With two-sided lines, floor- and ceiling-height mismatches are required to prevent further progress—or, as you might recall, the line's Impassable flag needs to be set.

This explains why your players can pass freely through the railing texture and leap from your platform—the texture is placed on a two-sided line. To make this railing seem solid, you need to mark the line as impassable.

UNPEGGING OF TWO-SIDED LINES

Before heading back to the editor to make this fix, examine the grating texture used around the platform, and see whether you can decide what mars its appearance. (See Figure 12.7.)

Figure 12.7.
The prototype grating installation.

If, like me, you left the default pegging on this line, your grating texture will be aligned with the top of the gap. It would really look better on the floor, wouldn't it? If you agree, make a note to unpeg this line's lower texture. The real problem though, to my eyes, is that the grating looks unrealistic just petering out at the pillars. I'll take a closer look at the grating texture in use here.

DOOM'S MULTIPART TEXTURES: THE BRNSMAL_ SERIES

ɲɛʀɛʈɩɔ Heretic does not have any textures that glue together in quite the same way as DOOM's BRNSMAL_ series. The WEBx_F/B/M series come close; your next WAD sortie will feature these web textures rather than the railings. I suggest that you use the editor's texture browsing capabilities to inspect this series of textures and compare their properties with those of the series of DOOM textures described next.

Figure 12.8 shows the BRNSMALC texture that was used for the railing. Notice how the texture is open at both ends to enable it to be repeated as necessary to cover the entire length of a line. Also shown in the figure are two more textures in the BRNSMAL_ series: BRNSMALL and BRNSMALR. These textures provide the left and right ends of the open grating pattern. For these grating patterns to be used correctly, the main texture should have these end pieces attached.

Figure 12.8.
The BRNSMAL_ series of grating textures.

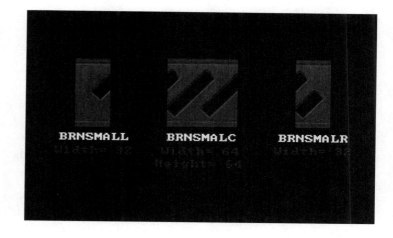

Notice the size of the two end textures: each is 32 pixels wide. It is clear that these particular textures do not repeat correctly horizontally; they each need to be on a line precisely 32 pixels long. Note also that they connect seamlessly to the center texture only if they meet that texture at the appropriate point in the pattern—in this case, on an exact repeat of the 32-pixel-wide main structure of the grating.

It's time to make these modifications to your WAD.

WAD SORTIE 11: PUTTING TEXTURES TO WORK ON TWO-SIDED LINES

NOTE: This sortie builds on the WAD produced in the preceding sortie. If you did not produce that WAD, you should use WAD10.WAD (DOOM), D2WAD10.WAD (DOOM II), or H1WAD10.WAD (Heretic) from the CD-ROM as your starting point here.

You have seen that to create realistic railings along the edge of your platform using the BRNSMAL_ series of textures, you need to reorganize the way in which the platform is structured. I'll go over the necessary restructuring in detail.

ᏙᎬᏒᎬᏆᏟ Even though the railing texture used in Heretic does not require all the modifications described here, I recommend that readers working with that game do, in fact, carry them out; they will be needed eventually.

CHANGING THE LINE

The first thing to do is to change some flag settings for the boundary line carrying the railing texture. The line needs to be impassable, and the texture should occupy the bottom of the gap, not the top, and so needs to be lower unpegged. You should set the appropriate flags now.

Then, to utilize the three textures that were just examined, you need to divide the line carrying the railing into three pieces of precise lengths. The two end sections must be 32 pixels exactly, whereas the central section must be a whole multiple of 32 pixels. Look at the line involved here—it isn't going to be easy to divide, is it? For a start, it is currently not of an appropriate length. The first task, then, is to make it an integral multiple of 32 pixels long.

The easiest way to do this is to make the line run true from east to west and then use the grid to get the lengths just right. So with the grid turned on, use Draw mode's Move functions to reshape this area to match that shown in Figure 12.9.

Figure 12.9.
The realigned platform area.

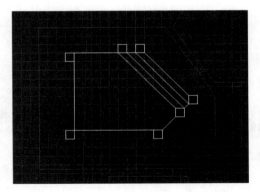

With this rearrangement, most of the pillar sectors now lie on the grid so that the interconnecting lines are generally multiples of 64 units. The line that is to carry the grating texture can now be split into three sections of the appropriate sizes. This is easily achieved in WadAuthor: split the line twice, moving the vertices at the split points to the appropriate distance from the pillar.

The operation is simple in WADED too. With the (Draw) Lines button activated, click the line at one of the desired split points, exactly 32 pixels in from one of its ends. This action splits the line, placing a vertex at the join. It also starts a new line, of course—in this case, a line you don't want. Click the right mouse button to abort it.

Repeat this operation 32 pixels in from the other end of the line, and you've done it. You don't need to use Make Sector, because you haven't added any new lines—you just split some existing ones. All the original line's settings—including sector ownership—have transferred to the new smaller sections, so no fixes are required to any sectors.

FIXING TEXTURES AROUND THE PLATFORM

Now, while you're at it, apply the same treatment to the two lines that make up the western and southern boundaries of the platform and fence off more of the platform area. This action forces the player to come and go via the stairs.

Heretic users have now done enough to try out the WAD. Do that now. (You'll find mine on the CD-ROM as H1WAD11X.WAD.)

What do you think? Not really very good, is it? The railings somehow don't fit too well. They do work as railings, though, don't they? They just look a little out of place. You should return to the editor and see whether things can be improved. Carry on with the next stage of this WAD sortie, but before doing so, replace the railings with cobwebs. The textures to use are toward the end of the textures list, and all start with the prefix WEB.

With the three platform edges split into correctly sized pieces, you should now be able to apply the necessary textures to create the required edges to the platform. Think carefully about which textures need to be applied at which ends (and on what sides) to produce the desired effect. If you're working with DOOM, you will probably discover something at this point that you'd never previously noticed about the railings when playing the game—I'll tell you what that is in a moment.

When you think you've got the application of the textures correct, save the WAD and try it out. Did you get it all right? The DOOM (and DOOM II) version of the platform should look something like that shown in Figure 12.10.

You should have realized (or discovered) that this series of textures only provides sufficient components to represent the view of the structure from one side. The railing therefore must be built looking the same from each side, which is not how it would appear in reality. But don't worry—it would take a very observant player to notice this anomaly.

If you are working with Heretic, you probably feel that your WAD is getting worse, not better, with each edit! You might, for instance, be wondering why you don't see any cobwebs. Don't worry about them at the moment; I will deal with them soon, I promise! First, though, I want to finish rearranging the platform.

Figure 12.10.

Your new railings in DOOM.

FURTHER ADJUSTMENTS TO THE PLATFORM EDGE

To my eyes, the western edge of the platform looks a little strange in the way it runs between the corners of the two western-most pillars rather than between the mid-lines of these pillars. I'll have you work at rearranging the way this edge of the platform is constructed. At first glance, this task might seem a little tricky, but it is actually fairly easy.

MOVING THE PLATFORM EDGE

First consider the northern end of the platform's western edge. Here it is a relatively simple matter to reform the edge's connection to the northwestern pillar. Start by splitting the line that marks the eastern face of this pillar. This gives you a square pillar with five vertices around its edges, rather than four.

Next, move the pillar's current southeastern vertex 32 pixels to the west, thus putting the connection between the pillar and the platform's western edge where you want it. You can now restore the original shape of the pillar by moving its new vertex south to become the southeast corner.

Having fixed the northern end of the platform's western edge, you can now turn your attention to its southern end. This area cannot be treated in the same way as the preceding one because both the western and the southern edges of the platform currently connect to the southwest pillar at the same vertex. This needs to be changed.

Here, then, it is necessary to delete the short line that connects the western edge of the platform to the southwest pillar. Do this in WADED by selecting (Move/Del) Line and then clicking the line with the right mouse button. Then use (Draw) Line to draw a new connecting line from the midpoint of the northern face of the southwest pillar to the southern end of the line marking the western edge of the platform. Make sure that the new line's right side faces the platform sector. Finally, straighten up the platform's edge by moving its central section to the west. Take care not to move the line north or south at all, because you need to keep the two end pieces 32 units long.

In WadAuthor, the process is a little different. Start by splitting the line that marks the northern face of the southwest pillar. Next, delete the short line that connects the western edge of the platform to this pillar, reconnecting the remaining line of the pillar's western edge to the new vertex in the middle of the pillar's northern face. WadAuthor should ask you to confirm that you want to merge objects as you complete this operation. (If it doesn't, turn on Snap to Grid and try moving the vertex again.)

ASSIGNING LINES TO APPROPRIATE SECTORS

After this modification in WADED, you will have a line that displays in magenta. This is the new line that you have added to your map and that currently belongs to no sector. You might be tempted to use Make Sector to bind this line into your existing sectors, but remember the way in which Make Sector works—if it encounters a magenta line, it creates a new sector. You don't want to do that here; all you want is to incorporate the new line into the existing sectors.

To achieve this effect, you need to use the Sec Define button. This is a fully manual sector-defining facility. It requires you to ensure that all lines have the appropriate number of sides before you use it, though. So go into LINES mode and set the Two-Sided flag of your new line. This action makes WADED add a left sidedef to the line. You can set the Impassable and Lower Unpegged flags at the same time.

Now, return to Draw mode and select Sec Define. Using the right mouse button, click somewhere in the area of the platform sector. (This action just selects an existing sector with which to work.) When you have the lines of the platform sector highlighted, left click your new line. A small pop-up with four options appears with the mouse pointer positioned beside it.

This pop-up enables you to add (or remove) any side of the chosen line to the currently selected sector. Note that this pop-up uses the terminology *front* and *back* (of line), rather than *right* and *left*. Click the Front button to add the new line's right side to the platform sector. Next, click the short eastern section of the northern face of the southwestern pillar, and make sure that its back (its left side) is transferred to the platform sector, too.

To assign the other side of your new line to the outer southwest room sector, right click somewhere in that sector to highlight it. Then left click your new line and add it back to this sector. You should find that WADED has worked out what you're doing by now and just adds the line to the sector as you click (without bothering with the pop-up).

Fixing Line Ownership in WadAuthor

If you look carefully as you move the mouse in WadAuthor, you will see that a correction is required here to the way the lines of the southwest pillar are assigned to sectors. Notice how the back of the short eastern pillar still belongs to the main room sector, not the platform sector it now borders. You need to correct this problem manually. Examine the linedef properties of one of the lines of the platform sector, to determine that sector's number. Then select the incorrectly owned line, and look at its properties in the Linedefs Properties dialog box. Change the number in the Sector field to that of the platform sector. Be sure you're editing the correct side of this line; it is the back that needs changing.

Figure 12.11 shows the final arrangement of lines in this area of the map.

Figure 12.11.
The final arrangement of lines around the platform room's southwest pillar.

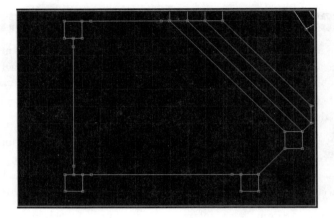

You can save the WAD as WAD11.WAD and try it out now if you want. DOOM and DOOM II users should find that the platform looks much better, apart from some ragged texture use on the platform's uppers close to the pillars. These are caused by the use of the COMPSTA_ textures on the uppers of lines that are only 32 units wide. These areas are best fixed by replacement of the COMPSTA_ texture with GRAY1 on the uppers of these lines. With these changes, your DOOM (and DOOM II) WAD should be fine. If not (you did remember those essentials textures on your new line, didn't you?), you can make whatever further corrections are necessary while I address the Heretic users for a moment.

FURTHER CORRECTIONS IN HERETIC

If you're working with Heretic, at this point you're probably wondering whether your WAD is ever going to be right! If you have used the line flags in the same way as was recommended in the earlier part of this sortie, your platform edges are no doubt acting very strangely now: they show no signs of any cobweb textures, yet they impede the passage of a player through the gap! You can, of course, correct this problem simply by changing the Impassable and Lower Unpegged flags of the lines marking all the edges of the platform. Indeed, it might have already occurred to you to do this, after you viewed the cobweb textures and realized that they need to be hung from the top of the gap they occupy. If you didn't realize (or do this) before, make a note now to clear the Impassable and the Lower Unpegged flags of all the lines marking out the edges of the platform.

Even if you did make this change, you will find that the cobwebs still look odd at the edges of the platform. This is because there is nothing for the cobwebs to hang between! This situation can be improved by the simple expedient of making the pillars around the platform reach all the way to the ceiling of the main room. Do this by setting their floors to 184. Add a Wall Torch to the back wall of each alcove so formed, and you should find that things suddenly start to look much better!

But what about the rest of the room—things are a little messy there still. In particular, the shield detail around the main walls no longer aligns well with the openings in its walls, so I suggest that you remove it by changing the GRSTNPBV texture to GRSTNPB. This texture can be left where it is, however, on the lower essentials of the pillars, because with the adjustment of the height of these sectors' floors, it now looks fine—with two exceptions. These exceptions are the faces of the westernmost pillars that were cut into two short lines with the last major edit of the WAD. The GRSTNPBV texture is a full 64 pixels wide and therefore does not sit well in a 32-pixel gap! Correct this problem by applying an X-offset of 32 to the appropriate half of each face. (I'll leave you to work out which is the appropriate half in each case.)

The final thing to fix in the Heretic WAD is that strange view out of the doorway to the south of the platform. This is caused by the fact that while the player is standing on the platform, the player's viewpoint is sufficiently high to permit the lower edge of the SKY1 texture to be seen over the lowest of the courtyard walls. The best way to correct this situation is to lower the ceiling of the sector that forms the opening so that the lintel then blocks this view. A setting of 112 should be fine.

Make these modifications (and any others to the platform decorations that you fancy) before proceeding with the rest of this WAD sortie. (The sample WAD, H1WAD11.WAD, on the CD-ROM has these modifications made.)

ADDING A SNIPER LOCATION

The last part of this sortie demonstrates the use of a solid texture on a two-sided normal texture to produce a sniper position. The sniper's lair will be located at the southern end of the courtyard area. For this, draw and create a new sector utilizing new lines running along the grid as indicated in Figure 12.12.

Figure 12.12.
Additional lines to add for a sniper's den.

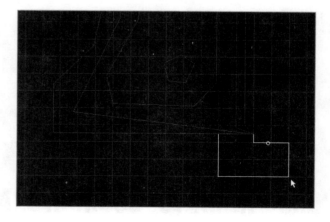

Having created this sector, you now need some way to keep whatever you use as a sniper inside it. Any monster placed here will be able to walk straight out through the sector's northern end—and will do so as soon as it sees a player, thus spoiling the secret. In addition, as the sector is now constructed, a player could easily blunder through this wall—an action that could result from using the escape route from the pond.

PREVENTING EARLY DISCOVERY OF THE DEN

Setting the line's Blocks Monsters flag would hold the sniper in place but would not prevent the player from finding the sniper's location by walking into it. Use of the Impassable flag is not a practical option here—that would make the line impassable for all time, and I want the player to be able to enter this sector eventually. Instead of using the flags, I recommend setting an appropriate difference of floor height between the sniper's den and the courtyard.

If the new sector's floor level is made 32 units higher than the paving stones outside, the player will be unable to step up into it, and the sniper will not step down out of it. All other sector settings can be left the same as for the courtyard for now.

Now, you want to hide this sector from the player by using a solid texture on the courtyard side of its northern-most line, making it appear as part of the southern wall of the courtyard. Currently, the rest of this wall uses the BROWN1 texture. This cannot be used on a two-sided main texture, however, because it consists of tiled texture patches—recall that this would cause the Medusa effect if used here. BROWN96 can be used, because it is a similar texture but is not tiled. Apply this texture to the main and essential lower texture slots of the outer side of the line that separates the sniper's den from the courtyard.

Used on its own, this one panel of BROWN96 would quickly give away the location of the sniper's den, so change the whole southern wall of the courtyard to this texture. Note how the width of the new sector was chosen carefully so that this line could take a complete width of this texture without betraying its presence with a seam.

 Heretic users can safely stick with the CSTLRCK texture in use on the southern wall of their courtyard. It will not cause the Medusa effect.

You also should set the Secret on Map flag of this line so that the map doesn't give the game away here.

Finally, place a Former Human Sergeant [an Undead Warrior in Heretic] in the new sector facing north, toward the courtyard. Set it to be present only at difficulty levels 4 and 5 so that the sniper will appear in only the top two skill settings. This action enables you to play-test the WAD at lower settings if you want to try it out without monsters in it. Save the WAD as WAD11A.WAD and start the game at the highest skill level to test the sniper's behavior.

OPENINGS IN WALLS, DOORWAYS, AND WINDOWS

The final part of this examination of plain and simple sectors considers the openings through walls that form doorways and windows.

DOORWAYS

You have already seen doorways formed from holes in the wall. They are generally short sectors with ceilings lower than the sectors on either side. Doorways containing real doors that open and close are the subject of the next chapter.

WINDOWS

Windows are a common feature of DOOM levels. They are really a variant on the simple doorway. They are made in the same way but have their floors brought up to a suitable level. Windows usually need both of their upper and lower textures unpegged to ensure that the walls above and below the opening line up correctly with the textures on either side.

You can simulate plate-glass windows by setting the Impassable flag on the lines composing them. (You can find an example of this effect in the large windows looking out of the first room in DOOM's E1M1 map.)

WAD SORTIE 12: COMPLETING THE PLATFORM ROOM

NOTE: This sortie builds on the WAD produced in the preceding sortie. If you did not produce that WAD, you should use WAD11A.WAD (DOOM), D2WAD11A.WAD (DOOM II), or H1WAD11A.WAD from the CD-ROM as your starting point here.

Let us now complete the construction of the southwest room by adding some windows to it.

CHANGING THE OPENING TO THE COURTYARD

You can construct the first window from the existing opening into the courtyard. Just take this opening's floor level up to 56, changing the texture to CEIL5_2 [FLAT510] at the same time. You have now created a new essential texture inside the room. Apply STONE3 [GRSTNPB] to this, setting the appropriate unpegged flag for proper texture alignment.

ADDING A NEW WINDOW

Next, add two new sectors to the north of the southwest room to form a window looking out over another, thin, outdoor area. (See Figure 12.13.) Make the new window sector about 550 units wide and 32 units deep.

Use STARGR3 [TRISTON1] on the northern walls of the new outdoor area. Put STONE3 [GRSTNPB] on the southern walls and around the window, remembering to unpeg the textures above and below the opening. Set the window sector's floor level to 56 and the ceiling to 120—this makes life easier with through-wall texture alignment. Put CEIL5_2 [FLAT509] on the floor and ceiling of the window sector.

Figure 12.13.

Two new sectors north of the southwest room.

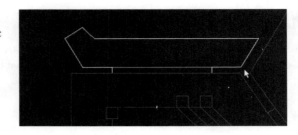

Finally, make the northern sector open to the sky by applying F_SKY1, and set its floor to FLAT1_1 [FLOOR03]. Adjust the brightness level to 255, the ceiling level to 216, and the floor to –64.

TESTING IT ALL

Now load up both courtyards with half a dozen Imps [mix Undead Warriors and Nitrogolems in Heretic] at skill levels 4 and 5. Then save the WAD as WAD12.WAD, and try out your platform.

Dreadful, isn't it? Hardly a sign of an enemy anywhere. But you know there's something in the southern courtyard because, more often than not, something kills your sniper for you! (You will notice this only if you have the sound effects switched on or if you watch what is happening with double Map Information cheat in operation.)

This design needs a bit of refining, don't you think? Try playing around with the height of the platform and the northern outdoor area to see whether you can improve things. Don't try to kill off anything yourself during this experimentation—just turn on God Mode and watch how your enemies attack you as you move around the platform and the rest of the southwest room.

The solutions to the problems you are experiencing here differ depending on which variant of the game you are building for. Take a look at the DOOM/DOOM II details first.

THE FINAL REFINEMENTS (DOOM/DOOM II)

Your experimentation might have shown you that with the northern sector's floor set at 16, Imps in that sector can see the player through the window when the player enters the southwest room. Setting the floor to 8, however, results in their being unable to shoot over the window's lower wall. Raising the floor level of the platform to encourage the Imps to shoot higher doesn't help any, either.

One solution to this problem is to leave the outdoor sector's floor at the lower setting of 8 units, placing the Imps here initially, and then adding another sector within the northern outdoor area. The new area should border the window and have a floor level of 32. The Imps then can spot only the players who climb onto the platform, not those who stay at the level of the main room's floor. When awake, however, the Imps will enter the new sector. From its greater height, they can fire unimpeded through the window, at players on the platform or elsewhere in the room. They can also step unimpeded into the window sector. If you want to prevent this situation, set the Blocks Monsters flag on the outer edge of the window sector.

You can also make an improvement by dragging the platform's northern pillars a complete grid square to the south and the three southeastern ones a complete grid square to the west. (Make room for the northwestern pillar to move by shortening the long section of the western edge of the platform by 64 units first.) This action reduces the size of the platform and flattens the Imps' firing angle, making it harder for the player to avoid their fire. Figure 12.14 shows the final layout of lines I used for this area of my WAD. All other sector settings I left as given in the earlier tables.

Figure 12.14.

The final arrangement of lines: my WAD12A.WAD.

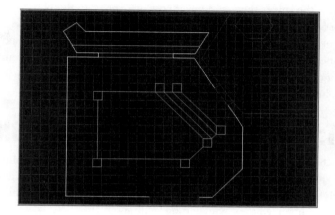

Finally, I reduced the number of Imps in the southern courtyard to two, placing one of them on the island in the pool. This way, one remains visible in the pool while the other comes close under the window wall—impossible for the player to dispose of, and a continuing danger when the player finally discovers how to enter the courtyard. With only two Imps in the courtyard, the sniper has less chance of hitting them accidentally and causing them to fire at him.

Other solutions in DOOM or DOOM II might be to change the sniper to an Imp, or to remove the southern courtyard Imps altogether and increase the number of snipers. But I will leave further experimentation in this area to you.

HERETIC REFINEMENTS

Heretic's Undead Warriors present a similar problem to DOOM's Imps but are somewhat taller and therefore require slightly different changes to the WAD. The additional sector added to the north of the window is still needed in the case of Heretic, but whereas this sector could be quite narrow in the DOOM case, you will find that it needs to be fairly wide (about 100 units or so) in Heretic to allow the Warriors space to fire. In addition, to allow for the Warriors' extra height, the floor of the northern-most sector should be set to –4, with the floor of its adjacent sector at 20.

The Heretic WAD benefits from the alterations to the platform outlined previously in the DOOM case, for the same reasons.

Even with these changes, the Warriors cannot quite manage to hurl their axes at the player who remains on the floor of the main room. I would address that situation by providing further problems for the player in the form of some Gargoyles (Plain or Fire, as you fancy) lurking just outside both windows, ready to enter the room when they are awakened. This tactic precludes the use of monster-blocking lines across either window, of course, but with the relative sector heights in use here, that should not matter.

Finally, I recommend a new mix of monsters in the southern courtyard. The Nitrogolems simply get into a scrap with the sniper there and never pose any threat to the player. A couple of Gargoyles and an Undead Warrior (or two) work much better here. Again, I've chosen to position one Warrior on the island in the pond, to encourage it to stay far enough from the window opening to continue to be able to keep the platform in its firing line. For this Warrior not to see the player on the floor of the main room, though, it is necessary to raise the floor of the southern window sector a touch, say, to 64. Again, you might want to experiment further with other solutions.

EXIT: MOPPING UP AND MOVING ON

In this chapter, you saw how sectors are used to build up the geography of your WAD. You were shown how sectors are commonly arranged to produce the static elements of WADs. You extended your own WAD considerably with alcoves, platforms, staircases, and windows; and by now you should be fully conversant with the use of your chosen editor's main editing facilities.

In the next chapter, you start to see some real action as you begin the introduction of special effects to your sectors.

SPECIAL SECTORS

So far, you have seen how you can put sectors to use in many ways simply by varying their basic size, elevation, lighting, and textural characteristics. Previous chapters have touched lightly on the fact that sectors possess an additional attribute: a special characteristic. In this chapter, you will learn about that characteristic and see how it can be used.

In this chapter's WAD sorties, the WAD that has been developing in previous chapters will be given some areas where a player will not want to linger!

SPECIAL SECTOR ACTIONS

A sector can be given special properties, or can be made to act continuously in certain ways, by the use of its special characteristic—a numerical attribute of a sector that has been ignored so far in your own sector settings.

THE SPECIAL CHARACTERISTIC OF SECTORS

A sector's special characteristic determines which special action that sector carries out. The actions themselves are hard-coded into the game engine and cannot be changed. Setting the special characteristic merely invokes them. The setting itself consists of a code number telling DOOM which of the available effects to employ. The effect is applied across the entire extent of the sector. Note that sectors possess only one special characteristic; such effects, therefore, cannot be used in combination within a single sector. When creating a new sector, most editors set its special characteristic to 0 by default, thus producing an ordinary sector with no special behavior.

— By Steve Benner

DOOM'S SPECIAL SECTOR TYPES

For the purposes of describing special sector actions, the available actions in DOOM and DOOM II can be divided into the following four categories:

- Damaging effects
- Lighting effects
- Miscellaneous effects
- Combined effects

Heretic has an additional three categories of special sector actions:

- Wind effects
- Current effects
- Slippery Floor effects

Hexen Hexen uses a completely different set of sector specials, with virtually nothing in common with any other variant of the game. Hexen's special sector actions are therefore the subject of a special section at the end of this chapter.

I'll look at each of these categories of actions in turn.

DAMAGING EFFECTS

Damaging special effects do harm to a player who enters the sector. There are three levels of damaging effects: high, medium, and low. The actual amount of harm done depends on the skill level at which the game is being played. Table 13.1 summarizes the effect of these three levels of damage.

Table 13.1. Harm done by the three classes of damaging sectors.

Damage Class	Lowest Skill Level	Higher Skill Levels
High Damage	–10 percent	–20 percent
Medium Damage	–5 percent	–10 percent
Low Damage	–2 percent	–5 percent

The harm a damaging sector does is applied once per second for as long as the player is in contact with the sector's floor. The harm values quoted in the table are applied to a player's health score, unless armor is being worn, in which case the damage is divided equally between health and armor. Damaging sectors affect only players; monsters are immune to their effects.

In Heretic, using these types of special sectors in conjunction with appropriate floor textures produces matching sound and visual effects. See the section on animated floor textures in Chapter 11, "The Lowdown on Textures," for more information.

Damaging effects in Hexen are caused not by the use of special characteristics, but by the use of a special floor texture, X_001—see the section on animated floor textures in Chapter 11 for more information. In addition, use can be made of this variant's special action codes and scripting capabilities. Details of these are given in "Hexen's Special Codes" and "Programming the Action," two chapters on the CD-ROM.

LIGHTING EFFECTS

DOOM's special lighting effects consist of blinking, flickering, and oscillating light levels within the sector. All of these lighting changes are generated by reference to the brightness level of the sector and the brightness levels of immediately adjacent sectors. The value specified for the sector's own brightness level determines the upper limit of the fluctuation, and its lower limit is taken from the lowest light level among all immediately adjacent sectors. If there are no adjacent sectors with a lower lighting setting, the sector's lighting usually fluctuates between its specified setting and total darkness. The available lighting effects are as listed here:

- Blink Off: Lighting is at the specified level most of the time, but it drops to the lower level momentarily.
- Blink On: Lighting is at the lower level most of the time, but it takes on the specified setting momentarily.
- Oscillate: Lighting moves smoothly from the specified level to the lower level and back again. If there is no adjacent sector with a lower light setting, this effect does nothing.

Additionally, some lighting effects are synchronized so that all the participating sectors adjust their lights together. Unsynchronized sectors change their lighting levels independently of each other.

MISCELLANEOUS EFFECTS

DOOM's miscellaneous effects provide some very special effects indeed. These are the miscellaneous effects:

- Timed Door Close
- Timed Door Open
- Award Secret Credit
- Kill Player and End Level/Game

These effects will be looked at in more detail in later chapters.

COMBINED EFFECTS

DOOM currently includes only one combined effect. It combines the Blink On lighting effect with High Damage. In Heretic, this effect has been extended even further; it will be covered in more detail shortly.

You will find a list of all the effects available in DOOM and DOOM II through a sector's special characteristic, and the codes required to produce them, in Chapter 35, "Special Sector Types." Usually, you don't need to remember all the code numbers for the various effects, however, because most editors provide a descriptive list from which you can choose the effects.

> **NOTE:** The next WAD sortie builds on the WAD produced in Sortie 12, at the end of the preceding chapter. If you did not complete that sortie but want to come along on this one, you should use WAD12A.WAD (DOOM), D2WAD12A.WAD (DOOM II), or H1WAD12A.WAD (Heretic) from the CD-ROM as your starting point. [Readers working with Heretic will find appropriate variations for their game marked in brackets.]

WAD SORTIE 13A: ADDING SOME SPECIAL SECTORS

In this sortie, you will get to try out some of these special effects by adding a few surprises for the player. As usual, you should build onto your latest WAD.

ADDING BITE

Obtaining that suit of armor (or shield) is a little too easy, isn't it? I'll make it a touch harder—or at least a touch more painful! In WADED, click the SECTORS button and select the hexagonal room's platform sector. Then set its special value to 5, either in the familiar way or by selecting the adjacent LIST button and selecting effect 5 from the pop-up list box that appears. (WadAuthor users should call up the Sector Properties dialog box and select Medium Damage from the Type pull-down selection list.)

Add a surprise to the outdoor pond too, by setting its special value to 7 (Low Damage). Who says water has to be harmless?

FLASHING AND FLICKERING LIGHTS

To try out the special lighting effects, add a new area to your WAD out from the southwest corner of the old southwest room (now the platform room). Figure 13.1 shows the new lines needed to add a staircase and passageway descending from this room.

Figure 13.1.

Lines for a new staircase and passageway.

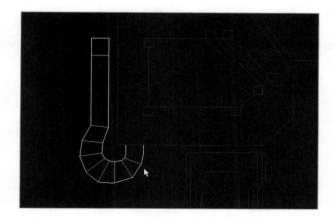

Draw the new lines using BROWN96 [CSTLRCK in Heretic] as the default texture. The precise shape of these new sectors is not important; you might want to refine the shape after play-testing it. One wall has the texture LITE3 [METL2] on it (see Table 13.2); you might want to make this wall the correct length to hold this texture. Also, the end sector needs to sit precisely within the grid squares for its ceiling texture to be rendered correctly.

By now you should be confident enough in the use of your chosen editor to construct these sectors without further help. Table 13.2 gives all the settings for the new sectors, working out in order from the platform room. Note how the floors form a progression downward by 16 units, with most other things staying the same. The wall textures given are for the left and right walls, as seen by a player progressing through the new sectors in the same sequence as given in the table.

Table 13.2. Sector settings for the new stairway and passage.

Lighting	Ceiling		Floor		Walls: Left	Right
		DOOM/DOOM II Settings				
144	120	FLOOR7_1	0	FLOOR7_1	BROWN96	BROWN96
176	120	FLOOR7_1	−16	FLOOR7_1	BROWN96	LITE3
144	120	FLOOR7_1	−32	FLOOR7_1	BROWN96	BROWN96
128	120	FLOOR7_1	−48	FLOOR7_1	BROWN96	BROWN96
112	120	FLOOR7_1	−64	FLOOR7_1	BROWN96	BROWN96
112	120	FLOOR7_1	−80	FLOOR7_1	BROWN96	BROWN96
96	120	FLOOR7_1	−96	FLOOR7_1	BROWN96	BROWN96
80	120	FLOOR7_1	−112	FLOOR7_1	BROWNHUG	BROWNHUG
80	24	FLOOR7_1	−112	FLOOR7_1	BROWNHUG	BROWNHUG
128	0	TLITE6_5	−128	FLOOR4_1	PIPE2	PIPE2

Table 13.2. continued

Lighting	Ceiling		Floor		Walls: Left	Right
			Heretic Settings			
144	120	FLOOR27	0	FLOOR27	CSTLRCK	CSTLRCK
176	120	FLOOR27	−16	FLOOR27	BANNER1	LITE3
144	120	FLOOR27	−32	FLOOR27	CSTLRCK	CSTLRCK
128	120	FLOOR27	−48	FLOOR27	CSTLRCK	CSTLRCK
112	120	FLOOR27	−64	FLOOR27	CSTLRCK	CSTLRCK
112	120	FLOOR27	−80	FLOOR27	CSTLRCK	CSTLRCK
96	120	FLOOR27	−96	FLOOR27	CSTLRCK	CSTLRCK
80	120	FLOOR27	−112	FLOOR27	CSTLRCK	CSTLRCK
80	24	FLOOR27	−112	FLOOR27	CSTLRCK	CSTLRCK
128	0	FLOOR09	−128	FLTLAVA1	BANNER1	REDWALL

The end of the corridor should have PIPE2 [REDWALL] on it also. Use STEPTOP [TMBSTON2] on the essential lowers of all steps and BROWNHUG [SQPEB1] on the essential uppers of the long section of the passageway. The essential upper over the new doorway should have STONE3 [GRSTNPB] on it, and it needs to be unpegged.

The Use of Short Textures on Step Risers

The STEPTOP [TMBSTON2] texture used on the risers of these stairs is one of several "short" textures provided for use in such places. These short textures are commonly only 16 or 24 pixels high. Remember that such textures do not tile properly if used in spaces that are too tall to take them. On stair risers, this generally does not cause any problems, because stairs must be kept below 24 units if the player is to climb them.

Be careful about the pegging of stair risers, however. Remember that if you unpeg the riser's lower texture, you are asking the game engine to recalculate this texture's placement from the sector's ceiling. Doing this with a texture that is other than 128 pixels high produces the Pink Bug effect on the riser.

When you have the sector layout to your satisfaction, you can set a couple of sectors' special characteristics. Users of DOOM and DOOM II should set the special characteristic of the sector that has the LITE3 texture on one of its walls to 1 (Blink off, randomly). Heretic users should set the special characteristic of the same sector (it is the first one to have BANNER1 on one of its walls) to 8 (Light Oscillates). You might also want to place a Chandelier in this sector, to explain the behavior of the light level here, and maybe an Environmental Wind sound, to suggest the presence of a draft.

Finally, set the special characteristic of the sector at the end of the corridor to 4 (High Damage, Lights Blink)—set it to 16 (High Damage) if you're using Heretic—before saving your WAD as WAD13.WAD.

This WAD sortie continues shortly for readers with Heretic. If you only have DOOM, read on and drool.

BEYOND DOOM'S SPECIAL SECTORS

One area of major change in the adaptations of the DOOM engine carried out by Raven Software is the action of the special characteristics of sectors. In Heretic, some of the standard effects were changed slightly and new ones were added. In Hexen, the whole special sector scheme was redesigned and many codes were dropped and changed. I'll look in turn at the way special sector behavior was changed in each of these two variants of the game.

HERETIC'S NEW AND CHANGED SPECIAL SECTORS

In addition to the standard DOOM special sector characteristics, Heretic provides some additional categories, as well as altering the behavior of DOOM's combined effect. The new and changed special characteristics all affect the way players or airborne objects behave in the sector. These are the additional categories:

- Low Friction effects
- Current (Scrolling Floor) effects
- Wind effects

I'll take a look at each of these new categories of effects.

LOW FRICTION EFFECTS

Heretic's Low Friction special sector setting causes the floor of any sector carrying it to have its friction substantially reduced, making it difficult for the player to alter speed or direction of travel while in the sector. This effect enables the designer to incorporate slippery areas, which hamper the players' movements, making fighting trickier and the area potentially more hazardous.

CURRENT (OR SCROLLING FLOOR) EFFECTS

The moving current effects provide Heretic with the capability to simulate flowing streams of water (or other liquids) by simultaneously scrolling the floor texture in a particular direction and imposing a corresponding motion on the player in contact with the floor of the sector. Currents are provided in five strengths:

- Very slow
- Slow

- Normal
- Fast
- Very fast

And they're provided in each of the four cardinal directions:

- East
- South
- West
- North

The movement is imposed only on players in these sectors, not monsters or other items placed within them. Note that the scrolling action that the floor flats undergo work seamlessly only if you use the textures specially designed for this movement (the animated floor flats). Use of any others results in strands of Tutti Frutti along the junctions between flats, for some reason.

WIND EFFECTS

The wind effects act on airborne objects (missiles, flying monsters, and players using Inhilicon's Wings of Wrath), blowing them in a specific direction while in the sector. This effect is provided in the strengths

- Weak
- Normal
- Strong

in each of the four cardinal directions, as with the scrolling floor effects. Unlike those effects, however, no associated texture motion is produced in conjunction with the wind. It is usually a good idea to place an Environmental Wind sound close by very windy sectors, to provide some indication of their presence.

NEW COMBINED EFFECT

Heretic takes DOOM's combined lighting and damage effect one stage further by adding a current effect to it as well. In addition to the flickering light level and the high rate of damage done to a player, a sector with this special characteristic scrolls its floor pattern and subjects anyone who enters it to a strong eastward drift as well!

Summary of Heretic Sector Specials

You can find a summary table of all of Heretic's special sector types and the codes required to implement them in Chapter 35.

HEXEN'S SPECIAL SECTOR TYPES

Hexen's new programmability resulted in many of the old special sector actions no longer being necessary, and consequently they have largely been dropped from this variant of the DOOM engine. Those that remain fall into three categories:

- Current (or scrolling floor) effects
- Stair-building effects
- Special lighting effects

I'll look at each of these effects in turn.

HEXEN'S SCROLLING EFFECTS

Hexen's scrolling floor effects operate in a similar way to Heretic's, except that the scrolling action now affects all objects within the sector, not just the player. In addition, the range of available directions of movement has been expanded to include NE, SE, SW, and NW. The effects remain available in three speeds.

STAIR-BUILDING EFFECTS

Hexen provides a new simplified way of controlling the way stairs can be made to build automatically. Examination of these effects is deferred until "Hexen's Special Codes," a chapter on the CD-ROM.

SPECIAL LIGHTING EFFECTS

If you have played Hexen, you know that it is capable of some spectacular special lighting effects. These include lightning and pulsed lighting effects. These will be looked at in detail after the next WAD sortie.

WAD SORTIE 13B: ADDING WIND AND CURRENTS IN HERETIC

NOTE: This WAD sortie continues the preceding one, for Heretic users, building on the WAD produced there. If you have a copy of Heretic but did not produce that WAD, you should use H1WAD13.WAD from the CD-ROM as your starting point here. Only true members of the Sidhe can complete this sortie, because it requires Heretic to play the result!

Before moving on to consider the special lighting effects that Hexen provides, readers who have been working through the WAD sorties with Heretic might want to try out some of the special effects available in that game. I'll have you use some of Heretic's special sectors to make the courtyard an even trickier place for the player.

Select the main courtyard sector (the one that encloses the pond sector), and set its special characteristic to 15 (Low Friction). This setting should have the player skittering toward that pond a little! You can also be a bit mean and provide the player with a gentle push or two in the wrong direction. To do so, select the western edge sector, and set the special characteristic here to 42 (Strong East Wind). Set the two eastern edge sectors' special characteristic to 51 (Strong West Wind) and that of the island sector to 45 (Strong North Wind). There is now virtually nowhere safe to stand in the courtyard, without a magical wind forcing the player inexorably toward that innocent-looking water!

You might want to place an Environmental Wind sound or two in the courtyard as a hint of the new hazard it contains (or you might not!). You also need to lower the floor of the window sector to the north of the courtyard so that you can try out the effect. (Make a note of its current setting so that you can put it back later.)

Before trying out the WAD, though, change the special characteristic of the sector at the end of the corridor added in the preceding WAD sortie to 4 (Random Blink; High Damage; Scroll East). This causes the lava floor used in that sector to flow to the east. You might want to reshape this sector a little as shown in Figure 13.2 (you need to add a vertex to split the sector's eastern wall) to provide somewhere for the current to take the player.

Figure 13.2.
*Reshaped sector at the end of the corridor
in the Heretic version of the WAD.*

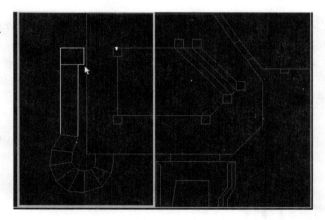

Save the WAD as WAD13A.WAD and try it out. Pity those poor DOOM folk not being able to join in the fun! It makes up a little for all those times they laughed at your being turned into a chicken.

HEXEN'S UNIQUE LIGHTING EFFECTS

As already noted, Hexen's lighting effects are somewhat more complicated than those of DOOM, or even of Heretic. Part of the secret of these additional effects lies in the use of special sector characteristics.

SPECIAL LIGHTING SECTOR TYPES

Hexen offers special sector types to produce these effects:

- Sky texture control
- Lightning intensity control
- Phased lighting control

Some of these effects are achieved directly through the use of special sector types, whereas others use the special characteristic of sectors in conjunction with other features of Hexen WADs.

SKY TEXTURE CONTROL

As part of Hexen's altered sky texture handling that was hinted at in Chapter 11, this variant of the game provides a mechanism for selecting a different sky in your outdoor sectors. A special sector type (200) notifies the game engine that a new sky is to be used. This sector type needs to be used in conjunction with Hexen's mapinfo lump, however, so discussion of this feature will be deferred until "Programming the Action," a chapter on the CD-ROM.

INDOOR LIGHTNING INTENSITY CONTROL

Ordinarily, lightning (with accompanying thunder clap) is available only in outdoor sectors in Hexen. Two special sector characteristic codes are provided to change this, however. One provides the full lightning effect, useful in areas immediately adjacent to outdoor areas where the lightning effect is active, whereas the other produces a reduced lightning effect, suitable for areas with windows, or only a little way indoors.

NOTE: The mechanism for the production of the lightning effect in Hexen levels is covered in "Programming the Action" on the CD-ROM.

PHASED LIGHTING CONTROL

The mechanism behind Hexen's phased lighting controls is often a little tricky to grasp. It will therefore be described in some detail.

HEXEN'S PHASED LIGHTING

Hexen's *phased*, or *moving*, lighting effects are a great improvement over the lighting level controls offered by DOOM. With this effect, the designer can create the illusion of pulses of light traveling down corridors, or around rooms and other areas of the map. Sectors that utilize phased lighting have their Brightness attribute used in a different way by the game engine. This value is either ignored altogether or is treated as a *phase index* value rather than as a lighting level. To understand how this phase index is used, you need to understand Hexen's built-in lighting cycle.

THE LIGHTING CYCLE

As part of its background processing, Hexen maintains a tally on the status of what is termed its *lighting cycle*. Think of this as a continuously running cycle of light and dark, a continuous oscillation of lighting level between total darkness and full light, taking about two seconds to complete. The game keeps a tally on how this cycle is progressing moment by moment by dividing it into 64 discrete intervals and maintaining a counter that tells it where in the cycle it currently is. This operation is achieved, in fact, by nothing more than a counter that runs continuously as the game plays, counting endlessly down from 63 to 0. When the counter hits 0, it resets to 63 and counts down again.

THE PHASE INDEX

Hexen provides the designer with a link to its lighting cycle through the use of its Phased Light special sector characteristic. Sectors with this characteristic have their lighting level determined only indirectly by their Brightness attribute. For such sectors, this attribute is treated as a *phase index*. Instead of supplying a light intensity level, this phase index tells Hexen precisely *when* in the internal lighting cycle the sector should be at maximum brightness. At any given instant, therefore, the sector's brightness is determined by comparing its phase index with the internal lighting cycle counter. The closer these two are, the brighter the sector is displayed. Thus, the sector passes from full brightness to total darkness and back again once every two seconds or so, at the same time as any other sector sharing the same phase index.

PRODUCING MOVING PULSES

By arranging for sequences of sectors with the Phased Light special sector attribute to carry a succession of different phase indexes, you can create the impression of a pulse of light traveling from sector to sector as each successive sector reaches maximum brightness and fades again. The jump in phase index between the sectors determines how rapidly the "pulse" of light passes from sector to sector and how sharp the cutoff is in light levels between adjacent sectors. (Note, however, that each sector is illuminated for exactly the same length of time, regardless.) Small steps in the phase index produce a rapidly traveling pulse, which diffuses through several sectors; larger step sizes make the pulse travel more slowly, and it will be narrower (in terms of sectors) with a sharper change in light intensity between sectors. Figure 13.3 illustrates this difference. The corridor to the player's left uses phase index steps of 1 between its sectors, whereas the corridor to the right uses the same number of identically sized sectors but with phase index steps of 8. Notice how much broader (and faster traveling) the pulse in the left corridor is.

 TIP: Best effects result from using small sectors, with steps in phase index of 8 or less. Using steps in excess of 16 quickly destroys the traveling pulse effect.

Figure 13.3.

Differences in pulse width and travel times caused by differences in steps in the phase index.

Pulsed lighting might sound tricky to produce, but, in fact, it is simple. Figure 13.4 shows the arrangement needed to create the illusion of a corridor with pulsed light traveling from west to east. In this figure, every sector that has a number in it uses a sector special of 1 (Phased Light). The numbers indicate the Brightness attributes applied in each sector to yield the appropriate phase index.

Figure 13.4.

Arranging phase indexes to produce a pulse of light traveling from west to east.

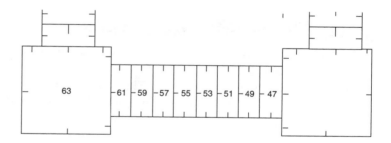

NOTE: Remember that the internal counter of the pulsed light cycle counts *down*. The light pulse will therefore seem to travel from *high* phase index numbers to *low*.

Notice how the sectors making up the corridor in Figure 13.4 have been made quite short to confine the lighting effect to a narrow pulse. The effect looks odd if you use it on sectors that vary greatly in length, because the light pulse will appear to travel faster through longer sectors unless you compensate by applying uneven phase index steps—often awkward to calculate. You will find that the effect works well on staircases.

AUTOMATED PHASED LIGHT GENERATION

The use of Hexen's Phased Light sector special just described can be a little tedious to arrange, especially for long sequences of sectors with pulsed lighting. Building such sequences requires the designer to calculate all the phase indexes needed to produce the desired effect, and these values then must be applied to all the sectors involved. Another drawback to this method is that it produces only a pulse of light traveling through an otherwise totally dark area. Raven Software therefore provides an alternative method for the installation of pulsed lighting in Hexen. This is an automatic method that makes the engine itself calculate the phase indexes needed. The method also enables the designer to specify a minimum ambient light level for each sector. This method employs a series of Lighting Sequence Control sector specials, detailed in Table 13.3.

Table 13.3. Hexen's sector specials for automated phased lighting control.

Code	Function
2	Start Lighting Sequence
3	Continue Lighting Sequence 1
4	Continue Lighting Sequence 2

USING LIGHTING SEQUENCE SPECIALS

To use Hexen's Lighting Sequence specials, you first need to designate a series of sectors, starting with a sector from which you want a pulsed lighting sequence to emanate. Set the special characteristic of this starting sector to the value 2 (Start Lighting Sequence). This sector's Brightness attribute is used to determine the lighting level that all other sectors in the sequence inherit as their *minimum* light level.

TIP: For best results, use a value in the range of 80 to 128 for the minimum (or ambient) light level in the sequence.

The rest of the sequence of sectors in the chain is indicated to the game engine by the use of an alternating sequence of 3 (Continue Lighting Sequence 1) and 4 (Continue Lighting Sequence 2) as sector special values. The chain is terminated by the use of any other sector special value. Figure 13.5 shows the sector special values that would be used to generate a pulsed lighting effect similar to the one illustrated previously in Figure 13.4. Notice how the presence of no special characteristic in the sector to the east of the end of the corridor terminates the sequence here.

Figure 13.5.

Deployment of sector special values for automated production of a pulsed lighting effect in Hexen.

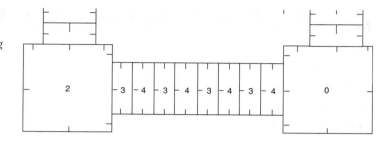

CAUTION: Failure to build lighting sequences correctly can prove catastrophic to your level. All the sequences of sector specials used to create pulsed lighting are collected by a special preprocessor as the level loads. These sector specials are subsequently replaced by appropriately calculated, internal phased lighting controls, before the level is passed to the game engine proper. Any sectors that are not so changed (owing to the sequence being incorrectly constructed) will cause a crash back to DOS when the player enters them.

In particular, make sure that the second sector in the sequence (the one adjoining the starting sector) has the correct Continue Sequence special (3). The accompanying error message—`P_PlayerInSpecialSector: unknown special 3` (or `4`)—indicates which type of lighting sequence special has been incorrectly placed. Bear in mind, also, that there must be no breaks in the chain of sectors—they must all share at least one line with the preceding and another with the succeeding member of the chain. Do not attempt to fork the chain, because this action also leaves uncollected special sectors that will crash the game.

All sectors other than the first sector of the sequence should normally have their lighting levels set to zero. As already noted, the lighting level set for the first sector in the sequence is propagated down the entire sequence by Hexen's special preprocessor when it generates the internal control structure. Any sector that has a nonzero Brightness attribute causes that value to be propagated as the minimum light level in subsequent members of the sequence.

The use of Lighting Sequence sector specials gives Hexen complete control over the generation of phasing indexes in these sectors. Normally, the lighting pulse should run from the starting sector into the rest of the chain, but occasionally, Hexen's preprocessor seems to misinterpret the sector chain and produces a pulse that runs the wrong way. Moving the starting sector to the other end of the chain sometimes cures this problem; other times, you just have to live with what you get, or revert to the manual method and enter the phase indexes yourself!

EXIT: MOPPING UP AND MOVING ON

This chapter has introduced you to the idea of active sectors. In it, you have learned how to provide some dynamic control to the lighting effects, and you have added some bite to your WADs. Heretic users also have discovered how to make floors slippery and arrange for players to be blown and buffeted about!

The next chapter provides further exploration of DOOM's active sectors and introduces you to the first of the moving sectors—the door.

ACTIVATING SECTORS

The preceding chapter introduced you to the special characteristic that some sectors can be given to make them behave in a particular manner. This chapter continues the investigation of active sectors by showing you sectors that can be made to move. It introduces you to the simplest type of moving sector—the door.

You will also continue to extend the WAD that has been developed in previous WAD sorties by the addition of a couple of doors.

TRIGGERED ACTIONS

In the preceding chapter, passing reference was made to an interesting pair of special sector types: the two time-triggered doors. It is worth looking in some detail at the way these doors operate. They provide a useful introduction to the operation of doors in general.

TIME-LOCKED DOORS

In DOOM, DOOM II, and Heretic, special sector type 10 provides a timed lock-out of an area. This operates by reducing the sector's ceiling height to the level of its floor 30 seconds into the game, thus effectively closing the sector to access from players and monsters alike.

Special sector type 14 provides the opposite effect, a timed opening of an area. This action takes place five minutes after the level starts. At this time, this sector's ceiling rises from its specified height (usually the same as the sector's floor) to a position just below the lowest adjacent ceiling, thus enabling the player to pass out through this sector (and allowing more monsters to pass in, of course!). Five seconds later, the sector closes again, this time for good.

As you can see, these two special sector actions are simple in their operation, but very effective. In fact, this mechanism of moving a sector's ceiling

— *By Steve Benner*

from one height to another is used a great deal in DOOM to achieve a number of useful WAD elements. It is, for instance, the mechanism by which all doors operate. The only difference between these two rather esoteric types of doors and the more common types is the activation mechanism they employ. The time-triggered doors are activated automatically at the appointed moment, whereas normal door types are triggered by the players (or occasionally by monsters) taking particular steps (often quite literally).

I'll consider these triggering actions in more detail and compare them with the actions taking place in special sectors.

TRIGGERED EVENTS VERSUS CONTINUOUS EVENTS

The actions of most of the special sector types can be viewed as continuous: sectors employing lighting effects have lights that fluctuate throughout the game, damaging sectors cause harm for as long as the player remains on their floor, and so on.

By comparison, the movements of doors triggered by players and monsters (and other events that will be examined in later chapters) are not continuous. They require particular actions to be carried out at particular locations.

Furthermore, the locations where these actions are performed might be at some distance from the sectors they affect. You are no doubt familiar with DOOM's switches and know that they frequently operate well away from the doors they open or the platforms they raise. For this reason, these triggered actions are not attached directly to sectors. Instead, they are attached to lines.

LINES AS TRIGGERS

You are familiar with the role of DOOM's lines. You know that they provide the game engine with vital information about the disposition and appearance of the edges of sectors. They can play a secondary role, also: they can act as triggers. You might recall from Chapter 10, "At the Sector's Edge," that in addition to flags, each linedef carries a special-action attribute. This attribute determines the nature of the triggering action that the line can carry out. It is another code number, like the sector's special characteristic. Usually a line has this value set to 0, meaning that it carries out no special activation. Lines with nonzero settings of this attribute are usually termed lines of special type.

Once again, the actions triggered by these special codes are determined by the game engine. You can only utilize what is provided, not add to or alter any of them. Just as sectors cannot possess more than one special characteristic, so lines cannot initiate more than one trigger action—although, as you will see, they can initiate that action in more than one location.

It is possible to use lines for their triggering action without having them contribute to the provision of sector-edge information. In this way, trigger lines can be laid out across sectors—as trip-wires, for example. The usual rules for placing lines still apply: they must run from vertex to vertex, and they cannot cross other lines. They do not need to form continuous or closed shapes, though, provided that the sector that contains them is itself properly closed. Lines used in this way need to be two-sided, with both of their sidedefs assigned to the enclosing sector. The use of such lines is demonstrated in later chapters.

Making Internal Triggers

To create trigger lines laid across sectors in WADED, you need to add the lines after you have used Make Sector to create the sector itself. You will need to make the new line two-sided manually and use Sec Define to add both of its sides to the appropriate sector.

Create this type of line in WadAuthor by adding a new rectangular sector and then deleting any unwanted lines.

INTRODUCING SPECIAL LINES

There is a very wide range of special line-types—sufficient, in fact, to fill several more chapters of this book! They all operate from the same basic activation mechanisms, however.

The operation of special lines has been almost completely changed in Hexen to provide a much more flexible approach to the control of triggerable actions. Two chapters on the CD-ROM, "Programming the Action" and "Hexen's Special Codes," provide full details of these changes, although many are indicated throughout the next few chapters in Hexen note boxes such as this.

TRIGGER TYPES

Each special line is triggered in a particular way, depending on the value of its special attribute. Four basic activation mechanisms are used among the line-types:

- Permanently active
- Spacebar activated
- Walk-through activated
- Impact activated

Additionally, each special action can be either repeatable or not. Repeatable actions can be performed any number of times; nonrepeatable actions can be carried out only once and then never again during the level. Some actions that are classed as repeatable can trigger events that can be repeated only provided that some other action subsequently returns things to an appropriate position first. (You will see an example of this in the next chapter, "Remote-Control Sectors.")

Some special line actions can be activated by monsters, but there aren't many of these.

Hexen gives the designer complete access to a line's triggering mechanism, permitting the type of activation to be specified line-by-line as part of each linedef's attributes. In this game variant, the designer is free to choose whether any particular line should be activated by players crossing the line, pressing the spacebar, pushing the wall, shooting at the line, or shooting across the line, or by monsters crossing the line. The designer can also specify whether activation of the line can be repeated.

ACTIVATION MECHANISMS

The action that is triggered by a line's special attribute is generally carried out on some associated sector. The process by which DOOM selects which sector to affect when a line is activated varies from action to action but falls into two basic categories:

- Local actions
- Remote actions

Local actions operate on the sector that owns the left sidedef of the active line. These actions all provide doors of some kind; their use will be examined shortly. Remote actions are more complicated. They are the subject of later chapters.

THE ODD ONES OUT: HORIZONTALLY SCROLLING TEXTURES

One special line action is completely different from all others. It requires no triggering and does not affect any sectors. In fact, it operates continuously and affects only its own line. It is special action 48—the horizontally scrolling texture. Any lines having this action automatically scroll their textures to the left (as viewed by the player) while the game is in progress. Note that because horizontal scrolling is implemented through a line's special attribute, lines using it cannot act as any other type of trigger.

Heretic adds another horizontally scrolling special action: 99. Any line with this special attribute scrolls its texture continuously to the right.

Hexen extends texture scrolling even further by supplying vertical as well as horizontal scrolling actions. See the chapter "Hexen's Special Codes" on the CD-ROM for more details.

OPEN (AND CLOSE) SESAME!

The remainder of this chapter concentrates on locally activated special lines. In id Software's parlance, these are all classed as manual door lines. The basic DOOM door is activated through the first of these manual door lines: special line-type 1.

THE BASIC DOOR

Special line-type 1 provides a repeatable, space- and monster-activated, local-action effect. It operates in this way: Whenever a player standing by this line presses the spacebar, the game engine raises the ceiling of the sector on the line's left side to a position just below that sector's lowest adjacent ceiling, thus simulating the opening of a door. This action is accompanied by the sound of a door opening. The ceiling stays in this position for five seconds and then lowers to the sector's floor again, thus effectively closing the door.

This action can be retriggered any number of times. The current motion or state of the door can be reversed with a further press of the spacebar. An enemy who simply approaches this line also causes the door to open.

Figure 14.1 shows how the door action is provided by the movement of a single sector's ceiling. The upper view is of the cross-section of a level with the player positioned close to a sector that has its ceiling set to the same height as its floor. Beneath is another view showing how this sector's ceiling could rise to provide an open door. Alongside these views is a sample map that can be used to implement this area. The arrows indicate which lines carry the appropriate special attributes necessary to permit the door to be opened from both sides.

Figure 14.1.
Implementation of a DOOM door.

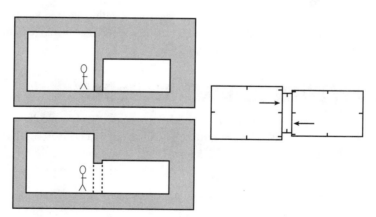

ENSURING THAT A DOOR WORKS CORRECTLY

To operate correctly as a door, the participating sector needs to be set up properly, of course. First, notice which way the door sector's activating lines face in Figure 14.1. A manual door line always moves the ceiling of the sector on its left side. If you have this line facing the wrong way, the ceiling of the sector in which the player is standing could be the one that is moved—usually with catastrophic effect! Make sure, then, that both of the lines that form the rising face of the door have their right sides facing out from the door sector itself.

Second, the sector needs to have its ceiling level set at an appropriate height. DOOM assumes that the first activation of a manual door line is to open the door; it therefore always takes the ceiling up. You should make sure, then, that all of your door sectors are created with their ceilings at the lower positions—usually at the same level as their floors. It doesn't matter to DOOM if you don't set all of your doors like this at the start, though. Even if a door is not completely closed at the beginning, the game engine still opens it properly when it is activated, and all doors close completely to the floor afterward, regardless of their starting position.

Players usually expect to be able to pass through doors they can open. Don't forget to allow for this movement, both in changes of floor height through your doors and in the final open height of doorways. The limit of the upward motion of a door sector's ceiling is determined by the height of the lowest ceiling adjacent to the door sector—the rising ceiling stops 4 pixels below this height.

For a player to be able to pass through the door after it has opened, you must allow for a minimum gap of 56 units between the door sector's floor height and the final resting height of its ceiling.

OTHER THINGS TO LOOK OUT FOR

The actual size and shape of the door sector is largely immaterial. The doors of most WADs tend to be a standard 64 or 128 pixels wide and 16 pixels deep, to take advantage of the standard door textures, but they do not need to be this size. Sectors of any shape can function as doors. All you need are appropriate lines accessible to the player with which to activate them.

Don't forget also that most doors need to be capable of being opened from both sides. Sectors that make up doors therefore need two manual door triggers, as illustrated in Figure 14.1. You can, of course, omit either of these triggering special attributes and make your doors capable of being opened from only one side, if that is what you want.

APPLYING TEXTURES TO DOORS

The designers of DOOM have provided many textures specifically for doors. (Heretic has far fewer of them.) The names of DOOM door textures generally start with DOOR or BIGDOOR. As already noted, most of these are 64 or 128 pixels wide by 128 pixels high. A few are somewhat shorter than the standard 128 pixels, however, and these door textures produce the Pink Bug effect if used in areas too large for them.

You should already have worked out that the door texture itself needs to be applied to the line's upper texture—the main texture is normally left transparent, to provide the doorway after the sector opens. If you place a solid texture on the main texture slot of a door line, the door seems to rise, but no opening appears beneath it. The player still can step through it, though. If you omit the texture from the door's upper slot, the result is usually HOM.

In its closed position, of course, the line's main texture occupies no space and therefore does not appear.

USING DOOR RECESSES

Although most door textures tile correctly vertically, they generally look odd if allowed to repeat very far up a wall. Figure 14.2 shows the effect. This door has been implemented using the arrangement of sectors shown earlier in Figure 14.1. Notice how the door looks wrong, running right up to the ceiling like this.

Figure 14.2.
The effect of placing door sectors directly on the side of tall rooms.

To avoid this unsightly implementation, doors out of tall rooms usually require additional thin sectors, 16 units or so deep, separating them from the main room sector. Each thin sector should have a ceiling height 128 units above its floor, to provide a recess in which the door then appears. Figure 14.3 shows the appropriate arrangement of sectors.

Figure 14.3.
Sector arrangement to provide a door in a recess.

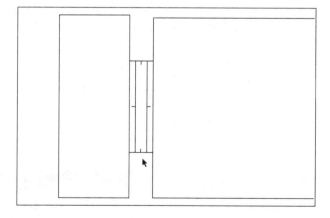

Figure 14.4 shows the improved appearance of the door brought about by this sector arrangement.

Figure 14.4.

An improved door in a recess.

PEGGING CONSIDERATIONS

The changes in ceiling height that simulate a door opening do not occur instantaneously, of course. For the action to look like a door opening, the textures associated with the door sector need to behave in an appropriate manner. It is the job of the texture pegs to ensure that this happens.

Consider first the face of the door, as viewed by a player opening it. Remember that the appearance of this face is provided by the line's upper texture. You should recall that the starting location for the painting of an upper texture is determined by the state of the line's upper unpegged flag. The pattern is painted either from the lower edge of the texture upward (when pegged) or from the ceiling downward (when unpegged).

DOOM opens doors by moving a sector's ceiling upward. A player viewing this action from a nearby sector observes the shrinking of the upper texture (the face of the door) and the growth of the main texture (the opening) below it. For this action to look natural, the shrinking upper texture must have its pattern rise as if being pushed into the ceiling.

To achieve this effect, the upper texture of the door face must remain pegged to its lower edge. If the upper texture were to be unpegged, the effect would be to cause the door face to remain stationary, with its pattern anchored at the ceiling adjacent to the door. Instead of appearing to move up into the ceiling, the door itself would look as though it was being eaten away by a gap rising from the floor. This effect looks unnatural. Make sure, therefore, that you clear the upper unpegged flag of all lines that represent door faces.

FURTHER PEGGING CONSIDERATIONS AROUND DOORS

Finally in this examination of the construction of simple doors, consider the sides of the sector making up the door. These are usually single-sided lines forming the "wall" through which the doorway passes. They therefore need only main textures. As the door opens, the height of these texture spaces increases.

You might recall from Chapter 11, "The Lowdown on Textures," that single-sided lines' main textures are usually painted from their sector's ceiling down. The implication for these side walls of the doorway, then, is that these textures would move with their sector's ceiling as the door opens. This movement would look unrealistic. The side walls should stay static as the door opens and closes. You can achieve this effect by setting the side walls' lower unpegged flag—you might recall that doing so causes these textures to be painted from the (static) floor up.

SUMMARY OF STEPS INVOLVED IN MAKING A BASIC DOOR

In summary, then, these are the steps involved in producing a basic spacebar-operated door:

1. Create appropriate sectors. Any shape will do for the door, but it needs two adjacent sectors for the doorway to connect between. Unless you particularly want a tall door, make sure that the sectors adjoining the door have ceilings no more than about 128 units from their floors; use recess sectors as necessary.

2. Make sure that the lines bordering adjacent sectors have their right sides facing out from the door sector.

3. Set the sector's ceiling height to the same as its floor.

4. Put appropriate door textures on the upper texture slots of the lines representing the faces of the door; clear their upper unpegged flags.

5. Put appropriate textures on the side walls of the door sector; set their lower unpegged flags.

6. Set the special attribute of each door face that you want a player to be able to activate to 1.

Although Hexen uses very different codes from other variants of the DOOM engine, the steps involved in constructing a basic door remain more or less the same. Readers who have played Hexen know, however, that it provides two very different kinds of doors from the kind just described: those that swing open and those that slide horizontally. These very special features of the Hexen engine are described in a chapter of their own—"Making Moving Scenery" on the CD-ROM.

The next sortie enables you to try out the construction of basic doors for yourself.

NOTE: The next WAD sortie builds on the WAD produced in Sortie 13, in the preceding chapter. If you did not complete that sortie but want to come along on this one, you should use WAD13.WAD (DOOM), D2WAD13.WAD (DOOM II), or H1WAD13A.WAD (Heretic) from the CD-ROM as your starting point.

WAD SORTIE 14: ADDING A DOOR

OK—so much for the theory. It's time to see how it is done in practice. Load your chosen editor with your latest WAD, and I'll lead you through the addition of a basic spacebar-operated door.

Many editors provide canned procedures for the automatic construction of doors. WADED is no exception— you have no doubt already noticed the Make Door button. Usually, though, just as much work is involved in customizing the appearance of such ready-made doors as is involved in building them from scratch! I recommend doing it manually.

ADDING A DOOR

The new door is to be placed across the opening into the stairway that you added to the southwest corner of the platform room in the last sortie.

In WADED, start by adding two new lines across the opening into the stairway. Place the first line 16 units south of the line currently dividing the platform room from the corridor. Add the second 16 units south of the first. The area between these two lines is to be the new door sector. Apply Make Sector as necessary, and then check that both of the new lines have their right sides facing out from the new door sector. If either of the lines has its tick mark pointing into the sector, select the offending line and press F to flip it over. Figure 14.5 shows the arrangement of lines you are aiming for.

Figure 14.5.
Lines for a door sealing off the corridor.

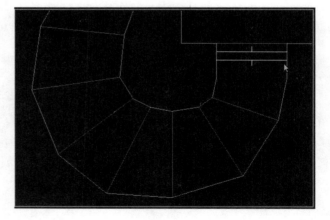

CAUTION: It is important that the node tree be rebuilt before you attempt to play a WAD that has had a line flipped in this way. WADED doesn't always notice this requirement, so you need to keep an eye out for it yourself. Remember this especially if you are loading a WAD into the editor just to fix a line that faces the wrong way. Make sure that the nodes are rebuilt as the WAD is saved.

The consequence of flipping a line without rebuilding the nodes is that the game engine becomes confused about which side of the line is in view. Visual turmoil results, with sectors being displayed at the wrong heights.

Adding the Door in WadAuthor

Adding the door in WadAuthor is simple: just insert a new rectangular sector in the appropriate location, joining the new sector's side walls to appropriate parts of the corridor. Check the ways the resulting lines face, as detailed previously for WADED, flipping any lines that need to be flipped.

Table 14.1 shows the settings needed for the changed areas.

Table 14.1. Sector settings around the new door [Heretic settings in brackets].

Sector	Lighting	Ceiling	Floor
Room alcove	208	120 FLAT3 [FLAT516]	0 MFLR8_1 [FLOOR01]
Door	128	0 FLAT3 [FLOOR10]	0 FLOOR7_1 [FLOOR27]
Top step	144	120 FLOOR7_1 [FLOOR27]	0 FLOOR7_1 [FLOOR27]

The alcove side-wall textures need to be changed to STONE3 [GRSTNB in Heretic] to match the rest of the platform room. Remember that this texture has a 32-pixel vertical pattern repeat. The difference in ceiling height between the alcove and the main room is 184–120 = 64 units. Thus, no adjustment is needed to keep these textures aligned with their neighbors (unless you're using Heretic, in which case the 32-pixel repeat does not apply; here you'll need to apply a Y-offset of 64).

To create the door, use BIGDOOR6 [GRSTNBW] as the texture facing into the room (on the upper texture, remember) and BIGDOOR7 [DOORWOOD] on the staircase side. Make sure that both of these textures are pegged. Set the special value to 1 (Local Door, Open & Close) for both of the lines with these textures so that the door can be opened from either side.

NOTE: WADED shows these locally activating door lines in cyan.

Put DOORTRAK [WOODWL] on the side walls of the door sector, with the lower unpegged flag set so that the textures don't move up and down with the door. Finally, save the WAD as WAD14.WAD and try it out.

Does it work properly? If not, check the way the door lines face, and make sure that you have used the correct value for the lines' special attributes. Then try again.

VARIATIONS ON THE THEME OF DOORS

In addition to the standard spacebar- (and monster-) activated door you built in the preceding sortie, a number of other active line-types provide variations on this door, implemented through the same mechanism. These doors are constructed in exactly the same way as the basic door you have just seen—all that needs to be changed is the activating line's special attribute.

DOORS THAT STAY OPEN

Line-type 31 in DOOM, DOOM II, and Heretic provides a door that works in the same way as a standard door but that, after it has been activated, remains open. Such doors are useful, of course, for committing the player to dealing with whatever lies behind them. Because the door does not close, any awakened monsters beyond the door can pursue the player.

Note that only players can open these doors.

DOORS THAT NEED KEYS

Table 14.2 gives the line-types that implement doors that require the player to have found and collected the appropriate key cards.

Table 14.2. Special attributes to provide key-coded doors.

Code	Action
26	Door requires blue key to open
27	Door requires yellow key to open
28	Door requires red (green in Heretic) key to open

Note that there is no difference between DOOM's standard and the skull keys—there are only three key types, not six as it might appear from playing the game. When the proper key is in the player's possession, these doors operate in exactly the same way as standard doors, except that monsters cannot activate them.

It is usual to provide some indication that a door requires a key before it will open, rather than simply relying on the game's text messages. The normal method in DOOM and DOOM II is to apply an appropriate texture to the reveals at either side of the recess into which such doors are usually set.

 NOTE: A *reveal* is the side wall of an opening or recess; it runs at right angles to the face of the window or door that occupies the opening.

Figure 14.6 illustrates how such doors might appear during the game. Note, though, that it is not the presence of the warning lights at the side of the door that causes the door to require a key, but rather the use of the appropriate special line-type as the face of the door sector.

Figure 14.6.
A *keyed door*.

Clues to the keyed nature of doors in Heretic are usually provided through the use of statues of a winged serpent, bearing an appropriately colored orb—commonly called "Door Gizmos"—as shown in Figure 14.7.

Figure 14.7.
A *keyed door in Heretic*.

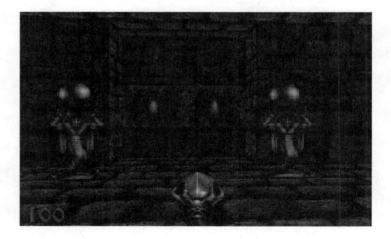

Table 14.3 gives the line-types in DOOM, DOOM II, and Heretic that provide keyed doors that stay open after they have been activated.

Table 14.3. Codes for latch-open key-coded doors.

Code	Action
32	Door requires blue key, stays open
33	Door requires red (green in Heretic) key, stays open
34	Door requires yellow key, stays open

Using Keyed Doors

The principal use of keyed doors is, of course, to force players to find and obtain an appropriate key before they can go on. The use of this feature in a WAD usually has an objective beyond the simple addition of another puzzle.

Keyed doors force an order to the players' progression though a map by locking them out of a new area until some other area has been played to completion. You should regard keys as rewards to the player for the completion of some specific task, or for finding the solution to some puzzle or other.

Use keyed doors as a way of keeping players concentrated on solving one puzzle before moving on to the next, or to ensure that players have located particular weapons before allowing them into more hazardous areas. Keyed doors should contribute to a player's structured completion of a mission, rather than be seen as impediments to his progress through it.

TURBO DOORS

DOOM v1.4 introduced a new type of door, not used in id Software's WADs until DOOM II: the turbo (or blazing) door. These doors work in the same way as the standard doors, except that they open and close much faster (and with a different sound). Their line-types (which, naturally, are available only in v1.4 of DOOM and later) are given in Table 14.4.

 Heretic, being derived from an early version of the DOOM engine, does not have locally activated turbo doors.

Table 14.4. Line-types for turbo doors.

Code	Action
117	Turbo open/close door
118	Turbo door, stays open

NOTE: DOOM has turbo versions of the keyed doors, too, but these are not locally activated doors; they are therefore the subject of the next chapter.

SECRET DOORS

Secret doors do not require any special implementation in DOOM. They are simply disguised or hidden from the player by being given standard wall textures as camouflage. Their presence is usually further kept from the player by setting their lines' Secret on Map flags.

NOTE: It is usually regarded as polite to give some hint of the presence of secret doors. This technique rewards the more observant players and removes the need for players to wander around trying all walls in the search for that elusive last secret location.

Secret locations are the subject of Chapter 18, "Let's Get the Hell Out of Here!"

SUMMARY OF LOCALLY OPERATED DOORS

Table 14.5 summarizes all the line-types in DOOM, DOOM II, and Heretic that provide locally activated doors. This table's activation category column indicates whether each action is classed as manual repeatable (MR) or manual nonrepeatable (M1).

Table 14.5. Special line codes for locally activated doors.

Action	Activation Category	Code
Open, pause, close	MR	1†
Open, pause, close; blue key	MR	26
Open, pause, close; yellow key	MR	27
Open, pause, close; red key	MR	28
Open and stay	MR	31
Open and stay; blue key	M1	32
Open and stay; red key	M1	33
Open and stay; yellow key	M1	34
Turbo; open, pause, close	MR	117*
Turbo; open and stay	M1	118*

Actions marked * are available in DOOM II and DOOM v1.4+ only.

Only the line-type marked † can be activated by enemies.

NOTE: If any player or monster is standing in the door sector as it closes, the ceiling's motion reverses (and the door reopens) when it contacts the obstructing object.

Setting Line-Type Codes

Once again, you should not need to remember the various code numbers responsible for providing each of these actions—most editors provide a list of special line-types for you to choose from.

WADED provides several lists of line-types grouped by action. You can access these lists by clicking the LIST button, located beneath a line's SPECIAL attribute field, which is displayed whenever you are in LINES mode. Each category of line-types can be selected by means of the selection buttons in each pop-up list.

Unfortunately, WADED's categorization of special line-types is far from perfect; its descriptions of their actions is often misleading and sometimes just plain wrong. (Many other editors share this affliction. It can be hard to come by the true answers to the arcane mysteries of the alchemy of DOOM!) Always use the numbers given in this book, therefore, instead of selecting codes that would seem, from WADED's description, to be closer to the required action.

Users of WadAuthor just have to trust that the descriptions given in the Linedefs Properties dialog box are correct (although you can edit the appropriate .WCF file if you think they are not, or if you want to change the description).

WAD SORTIE 15: ADDING KEYED AND SECRET DOORS

NOTE: This sortie builds on the WAD produced in the preceding sortie. If you did not produce that WAD, you should use WAD14.WAD (DOOM), D2WAD14.WAD (DOOM II), or H1WAD14.WAD (Heretic) from the CD-ROM as your starting point here.

In the preceding sortie, you added a basic spacebar-operated door to separate the platform room from the stairway leading out of it. In this sortie, you will add some other kinds of doors. First, you'll add a keyed door, leading into a new area of the WAD, south out of the original southeast passageway. This door will require the blue key to be found before it will open. It will give admission to another outdoor area of the WAD—this time with covered overhangs along its sides.

The second new door to add to the WAD is a secret door. It will be placed in the original outdoor courtyard, in the far southwestern corner, beyond the pond.

ADDING A KEYED DOOR

Start your addition of the keyed door by creating a recess in the south wall of the southeast passageway that is 16 units deep by 256 units wide. If you are working with DOOM or DOOM II, you should use DOORBLU on the short walls of this sector to indicate that the blue key is needed before it will open. Heretic users can either use BLUEFRAG in a similar way or can place a couple of Blue Door Gizmos at either side of the opening. Create another sector of the same size as this one to its south—this will be the door itself. Make sure that its lines face the correct way after you have used Make Sector on it.

Figure 14.8.
The lines for sectors through the keyed door.

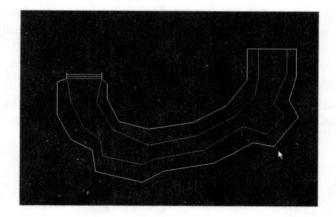

Place DOORTRAK [WOODWL in Heretic] on the short wall sections of your new sector, setting each line's lower unpegged flag. Next add the sectors on the other side of the door, as shown in Figure 14.8. Use STARTAN3 [CTYSTUC4] as the default drawing texture for all the lines beyond the door.

There are three major sectors beyond the door. Together they form a long curving outdoor space. The central sector is open to the sky, and the two sectors bordering it form covered areas. Table 14.6 gives the settings for all the new sectors.

As usual, whenever settings for Heretic differ from those given for DOOM, Table 14.6 shows the values in brackets. The ceiling textures used for both inner and outer recesses assume that you are using BLUEFRAG on the door reveals. If you are using Blue Door Gizmos rather than indicative textures, you might prefer to use METL2 on the walls and substitute FLOOR28 for FLOOR16.

Table 14.6. Sector settings for the areas around the keyed door.

Sector	Lighting	Ceiling			Floor	
Inner recess	144	112	CEIL3_5	[FLOOR16]	0 MFLR8_1	[FLOOR01]
Door	144	0	CEIL3_5	[FLOOR28]	0 MFLR8_1	[FLOOR01]
Outer recess	144	144	CEIL3_5	[FLOOR16]	0 FLAT1_2	[FLOOR03]
Outer central area	255	184 [232]	F_SKY1		0 FLAT1_2	[FLOOR03]
Outer edge areas	176	144 [192]	FLOOR7_1 [FLOOR27]		0 FLAT1_2	[FLOOR03]

Complete the new door area by applying textures for the faces of the door. Use BIGDOOR2 on both sides of the door in DOOM and DOOM II; in Heretic, put CHAINMAN on the inner face of the door, with DOORWOOD on the outer. There is an essential upper texture over the inner recess. Set this to match its neighboring walls, and set the upper unpegged flag to make sure that it aligns properly. Deal with the essential upper textures in the large outer areas by setting them to match the wall textures in use on the main walls of the outer area. Don't concern yourself with the alignment of the textures in the outer area just yet—there are some extensions to be carried out here later. You can tidy up then.

Finally, don't forget that if you want to be able to open and pass through this new door, you must either place a blue key somewhere in the WAD (right by the door would be a sensible place, for now) or play the WAD with the appropriate cheat code.

Try out this WAD now. Is it OK?

 NOTE: If you have a nasty case of HOM where your door should be, you have a missing essential texture. You did apply the door's texture to the *upper* texture slot, didn't you?

ADDING A SECRET DOOR

After you are happy with the keyed door, move on and add a secret door to the original courtyard.

For this area, you need new sectors at the southwest corner of the original courtyard as shown in Figure 14.9.

In order, from the courtyard itself, these new sectors will form the following areas:

- **An outer recess:** A door looks odd opening into the sky. This recess provides a more realistic setting. You might think it makes the presence of the door too obvious, though.
- **The door itself:** The door will be hidden by the application of a standard wall texture to match the rest of the western wall of the courtyard. After it has been opened, it will stay open. Again, make sure that this sector's lines face the correct way after you have created it.

■ **The inner room:** The development of the room to which access is gained by opening the door will be carried out later. Don't worry too much about its appearance for now. Because its ceiling is low, though, an additional recess on this side of the door is unnecessary.

Figure 14.9.

Lines for another secret area off the courtyard.

Use FLOOR4_1 [FLOOR04] on the ceiling of all of these new sectors, with FLAT1_1 [FLOOR03] on the floors. Table 14.7 has the remaining settings for the new sectors.

Table 14.7. Settings for the new secret area off the courtyard.

Sector	Lighting	Ceiling	Floor
Outer recess	176	120 FLOOR4_1	−16 FLAT1_1 [FLOOR03]
Door	176	−16 FLOOR4_1	−16 FLAT1_1
Inner room	144	120 FLOOR4_1	−16 FLAT1_1

Put BROWN1 [LOOSERCK] on all the new walls—including the uppers of the door sector itself and the upper essential over the outer recess—except the one that extends the southern wall of the courtyard into the outer recess (use BROWN96 [CSTLRCK] here to match its neighboring wall section) and the sides of the new door sector (use DOORTRAK [LOOSERCK], lower unpegged, as usual).

Apply a Y-offset of 24 to the two walls in the alcove to realign these textures to the rest of the courtyard. Then apply a Y-offset of 32 to the face of the door for better alignment, and also set this line's Secret on Map flag.

Complete the construction of the door by setting the special attribute of the line marking its outer face to 31. You don't need to worry about a trigger on the inner face of this door, because the player cannot reach it while the door is closed, and after it has been opened, it will stay open.

Finally, don't forget to reduce the height of the window ledge in the north wall of the courtyard to 0, temporarily, to allow access—or move the Player 1 Start position into the courtyard just to try out the new secret door. Save the WAD as WAD15.WAD and try out your latest additions.

EXIT: MOPPING UP AND MOVING ON

This chapter has brought you into direct contact with DOOM's doors for the first time. You have been shown how to construct doors in order for them to function correctly, and how to ensure that they look right while they operate. You have been taught about keyed doors, and the clues that can be provided to warn the player that keys are needed to open certain doors. Your own WAD should be coming along nicely by now.

I'll have you open some more doors in the next chapter when exploring the mechanism behind remotely operated doors and other effects. You will see how to use the various switches available in DOOM—the kinds the player can see as well as the ones that are hidden.

REMOTE-CONTROL SECTORS

In the previous chapter, you were introduced to the ability of lines to initiate certain actions in sectors. That chapter concentrated on *locally activated sectors*: sectors that have their actions triggered from one of their own lines.

This chapter focuses on *remotely activated sectors*. These sectors may have the triggers for their actions located at some distance from them. You have seen that all the local, manual-activated sector actions are, in fact, doors of one kind or another. In this chapter, you will discover more ways to make doors operate: you will be shown the use of wall-mounted switches and trip-wires.

The WAD that you've been developing from chapter to chapter in this mission will gain some additional doors during the forthcoming sorties. You will also begin developing a future area of maze with the introduction of some fairly complex light-switching arrangements. However, start your exploration of these remotely controlled sectors by examining the remote activation mechanism itself.

TRIGGERS AND TAGS

As you have already seen, a locally activated sector is connected to its initiating line through that line's left sidedef. It would be somewhat restrictive to force all activating lines to be connected to their target sectors in this way, though. DOOM, therefore, provides an additional way of connecting special lines to the sectors they affect. This mechanism is called *tagging*.

— By Steve Benner

TAGGED ACTIONS

The tagging of lines and sectors is a simple process. As well as having a special attribute, each of a WAD's lines and sectors also carries a tag number. Ordinarily, this tag number will be set to zero, meaning that the tag is not in use. Actions that use the tagging mechanism—all those provided by the remotely activating special line-types—operate by matching the tag of the activating line to that of a target sector, whenever the line is triggered. All sectors found with a matching tag are subjected to the action the line initiates.

The tag number itself is nothing more than an arbitrary identification number. Most map editors assign tag numbers automatically as needed; you should never need to know their actual value. All you need to do is set an appropriate special line-type, defining both the action that will occur and the method by which it will be triggered, and also indicate a target sector where you want the action specified by the line-type to be carried out.

Hexen Once again, Hexen does things a little differently when it comes to remote activations and tagging. It is now possible to tag *Things*, as well as lines, to sectors. In addition, the triggering mechanisms for actions have been completely reworked. A full discussion of Hexen's remote activation mechanisms appears in "Programming the Action," a chapter on the CD-ROM. The rest of the current chapter refers principally to the other variants of the game.

MULTI-ACTION TRIGGERS

DOOM does not insist that lines or sectors possess unique tag numbers. Indeed, you may not want them to: A single line can then initiate its specified action in several sectors simultaneously, just by having these sectors share the same tag number. Similarly, a sector (or a group of sectors with the same tag) can be made to undergo different actions by using more than one activation line with a common tag number. Therefore, you can, for example, have a line that opens several doors simultaneously, or have a door that can be opened from a number of different switch lines, or have a sector that can behave as a door, say, if one line is used, but as a crushing ceiling if activated from another.

Because a line has only one special attribute, it is not possible to have a single activation line trigger *different* actions. You could not, for example, have a trip-wire that opened a door behind the player at the same time it turned the lights out ahead. Furthermore, if you have sectors that share a common tag number, those sectors will remain linked for all actions applied to them through the tagging mechanism. It would not be possible, say, to have a line that caused a group of sectors to open as doors and to have a line elsewhere rigged to close just one of them.

The locally activating triggers explored in the last chapter operate independently of such groupings, though, because they do not use the tagging system. It is possible, therefore, to have a number of doors, each of which could be opened as a basic door, but can also be operated as a group by using shared tag numbers.

MULTIPLE ACTIVATIONS

Once you have more than one line trigger any particular sector, a potential for conflicting activation requests arises. DOOM has a simple way of resolving these. The rule, generally, is that if a sector is already involved in an activity, that action must finish before the sector can participate in any other kind of activity. Trigger requests are not queued. If a particular target sector is not available to participate as a line is triggered, then that sector will be left out of the action.

Additionally, some actions lock out all further actions on a sector, and others can entrain additional, untagged sectors in their activity. Some actions require their participating sectors to be set up carefully for them to be effective. Linking together sector actions to form complex arrangements of moving and changing sectors will be covered in more detail in Chapter 17, "Complex Moving Sectors."

MISSING TAG VALUES

Although tagging active lines to their target sectors is often made simple by map editors, it is always possible to make slips. The most common mistakes and their consequences include the following:

- **Not setting a tag number for a remote-activating line-type:** The precise result of this depends on the line-type involved. Some will simply not activate; others will locate all sectors with a tag value of zero (usually the majority of the sectors in the WAD) and apply the action to these. Needless to say, this can lead to some unexpected and often spectacular results when the line is activated. If you find that all your ceiling and floor heights have suddenly changed, for example, as you move around your WAD, suspect the presence of a line with a special line-type and a tag value of zero.

- **No sector has a matching tag number:** The outcome of this error again depends on the particular line-type. The usual result, though, is a crash to DOS when the line is activated. This error can easily happen if you have a special line tagged to a sector, then subsequently alter the sector's tag number by tagging it to a different line.

Many editors will provide internal consistency checks to alert you to the presence of these errors.

TOO MANY ACTIVE SECTORS

Note that the number of sectors that DOOM can have in motion simultaneously is limited to 30, which should be ample for most WADs. If this number is exceeded, DOOM will crash back to DOS with the message
`P_AddActivePlat: no more plats!`

TIP: If you find that DOOM gives a `no more plats!` error message when you know there should be nothing like 30 sectors in motion, you have probably forgotten to tag a trigger to its target sector—DOOM is trying to move all untagged sectors in your WAD simultaneously!

THE ACTIVATION MECHANISM

The precise mechanism for activating a line's special action varies from action to action. There are six basic categories of triggering mechanism, each with their own particular characteristics.

TYPES OF SWITCHES

Table 15.1 gives the categories into which all special line-types are divided. The table also shows the standard two-letter identifying codes usually given to these categories.

Table 15.1. Categories of special line-types.

Category	Code	Mode of Operation
Manual	M1/MR	Manual, local activated; action is triggered by the spacebar and may be one-off (M1) or repeatable (MR).
Trigger	W1	Walk-through activated; action does not repeat.
Retrigger	WR	Walk-through activated; action can be repeated any number of times.
Impact	G1/GR	Action is activated by being shot at; action may be a one-off (G1) or may be repeatable (GR).
Switch	S1	Spacebar activated; action does not repeat.
Button	SR	Spacebar activated; action can be repeated any number of times.

MANUAL ACTIONS

The locally activated (or manual) sector actions were the subject of the previous chapter, "Activating Sectors." They are mentioned again here for completeness.

TRIGGERS / RETRIGGERS

Walk-through triggers are activated as soon as the player steps over them. Consequently, they are useful only on two-sided lines. These lines can be either standard lines between sectors or lines added within sectors. Note that players are judged to have stepped over a line only when their center point makes a transition from one side to the other. This means that there will need to be a gap of at least a player's radius (16 units) on each side of any walk-through line for it ever to be activated.

NOTE: The player does not need to be in contact with the ground to activate these trigger lines; they will still operate even if they are flown through using Inhilicon's Wings of Wrath in Heretic or crossed while in the air after jumping from a ledge.

Walk-through lines often act as invisible trip-wires used to spring surprises on the player. These lines can be activated from either side. The retrigger actions will occur on each crossing of the line, but the trigger class of actions will happen only the first time the player crosses the line.

GUN-ACTIVATED ACTIONS

Impact-activated lines require the player to fire a gun (or aim a punch) at them. (Note that rockets and plasma fired at these lines have no effect. The fist and chainsaw will work on them, though!) Suitably armed monsters firing at these lines will also activate them. There are not enough of these types of action to warrant separate names to distinguish the one-off from the repeatable actions.

In Heretic, only the Staff, Gauntlets, Elvenwand, and Dragon's Claw can activate lines of this type.

SWITCHES AND BUTTONS

The final category of remotely activated lines requires the player to press the spacebar while next to and facing the line. Note that players cannot activate a switch or button that is not in front of them. In addition, these special lines can be activated only from their *right*. If a player attempts to operate a switch-line from its left side, nothing happens.

STACKING MULTIPLE ACTIVE LINES

A player does not need to be pressed against a switch or button line to activate it; if the player's center point is within 31 units of the line when the spacebar is pressed, the line's action will be triggered. It is not possible to trigger more than one line at a time, however. Once DOOM has encountered a line to trigger, it will not hunt for more. All attempts to have multiple lines triggered at once by placing them close together, or even stacking them "on top" of each other (by running them between the same pair of vertices) will fail.

In all such cases, DOOM takes the active line closest to the player as the one to trigger (in the case of more than one line running between the same pair of vertices, DOOM will select the one with the lowest number, usually the one drawn earliest) and only if the player is to its right and facing it. This blocking of spacebar-operated lines will be carried out by *any* intervening active line, regardless of its activation type. Therefore, a walk-through trigger placed to the right of a spacebar-activated trigger will need to be crossed before a player can operate the latter.

FAKING MULTIFUNCTION LINES

The capability of one active line to block another can be used to interesting effect in a WAD. When a non-repeating action is triggered during play, the game engine actually clears the special attribute of the triggering line, thus effectively rendering the line incapable of any further activations. This line becomes indistinguishable from any other non-triggering line in the WAD. It will therefore lose its capability to block the triggering of other nearby lines. You can use this to construct a special switch that appears to be change function each time it is used. This is achieved by constructing a series of "stacked" non-repeating actions. After each is activated and cleared by the game engine, the player becomes free to access the one beyond.

This technique enables the designer to either construct switches that seem to change function (as new types of active line are accessed) or limit the number of times a switch can be used (as each successive line is "used up"). To operate correctly, such stacked lines will need to be run between the same pair of vertices (which can be tricky to arrange with many editors) or placed side by side in an alcove, with a constraining line beyond them preventing the player from crossing any of them and thus accessing the lines out of turn. Three sample WADs— SW5.WAD (DOOM), D2SW5.WAD (DOOM II), and H1SW5.WAD (Heretic)—on the CD-ROM accompanying this book demonstrate how this technique can be used to produce a switch that will operate a door a limited number of times and give the player a little surprise the last time it's used.

SWITCH-LINE TEXTURES

Some "solid" surface is often needed for a switch or button line, if only to keep the player in the correct position to operate it. You should also use appropriate wall textures to give the player some indication that there is a switch line waiting to be activated.

GENERAL TEXTURES

Several textures are available to make switch-lines look like whatever they represent: a door face, a switch to be thrown, or a button to be pressed, for instance. Figure 15.1 shows some of them; use these textures to encourage players to use the spacebar to perform whatever action the line offers.

Readers working with DOOM or DOOM II have already used some of these textures in their own WADs—not only various door textures but also a couple of the switch textures. These latter textures are interesting because of their special properties and capabilities. Their use will be examined in some detail next.

SPECIAL SWITCH TEXTURES

The designers at id Software offer several special wall textures to simulate wall-mounted switches and buttons. The names of these textures all begin with SW1. If you look at a full list of the wall-texture names (you can do this in WADED by clicking the P button next to the texture list while in LINES mode), you will see that each SW1 texture has a matching SW2 partner. Together, each SW1/SW2 pair of textures provides the patterns for a switch or button in both untriggered (SW1) and triggered (SW2) states. Figure 15.2 shows one such pair of textures.

Figure 15.1.
A selection of wall textures to tempt the player to press the spacebar.

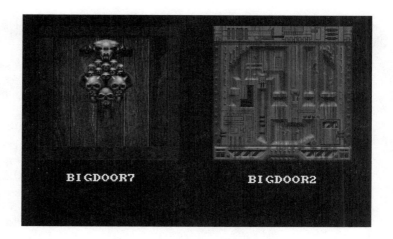

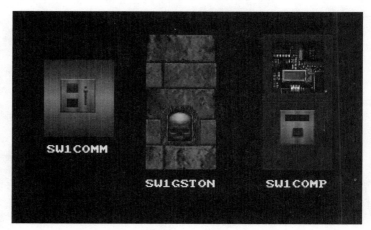

Figure 15.2.
The SWxBRN1 texture pair.

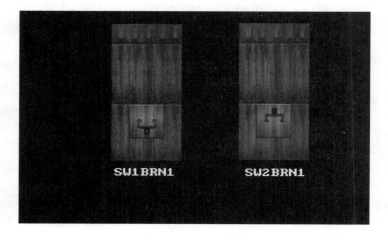

Heretic offers few such textures. It also has a different switch-texture naming convention, using "ON" and "OFF" suffixes rather than a state number.

The two textures SW1LION and SW1GARG, which you have already used in your WAD, fall into the switch texture category. You may have discovered that when they are used on their own, these textures do not automatically give you any switching action. They do not change to their partner pattern just by pressing the spacebar. Try playing your latest WAD again if you hadn't noticed this. Walk the player over to each of the alcoves and observe that these textures are quite static, whatever you do to them. (If you haven't been building this mission's WADs, WAD15.WAD on the accompanying CD-ROM—or D2WAD15.WAD if you have DOOM II—can be used here. The alcoves in question are in the passageway to the east of the player's starting position.)

 Readers using Heretic have not been using switch textures in the WAD sorties. It's easy to construct a WAD with a wall that does use them if you want to observe their static nature, or you can try H1SW1.WAD from the CD-ROM.

Used with appropriate special line-types, however, these lines will animate automatically. DOOM will change a SW1 texture to its matching SW2 counterpart whenever the player activates a switch or button line. DOOM also knows whether to change the texture permanently (for a switch action) or just temporarily (for a button action).

TIP: Do not be confused by the terminology into thinking that those textures that look like switches must be used on switch-type lines, while button-type lines require the pushbutton textures. Any SW1 texture will function correctly on either type of line.

Using an SW1 texture on a special line also causes DOOM to emit the characteristic "clunk" as the line is activated. This sound is produced whatever additional sounds may be associated with the action.

USING THE SWITCH TEXTURES

The SW1/SW2 texture pairs may be used on any suitable upper, lower, or main texture slot, as dictated by the particular sector arrangements. You will generally need to give some thought to the alignment and pegging arrangements required to keep the representation of the switch at the correct height; note that the precise switch position varies from texture to texture, so check this carefully.

Generally, lines that use these textures on their main slot will need to have their lower unpegged flag set to force the texture to take its alignment from the floor. If you cannot set a line's lower unpegged flag for some reason, you will need to apply appropriate Y-offsets. This can occur where the switch itself is required to take part in some movement or other—on a door face, for instance—or is located next to a floor that moves.

You may need to position the switch line in an alcove or other recess to limit the number of vertical and horizontal repetitions of the pattern. Multiple images of the same switch look silly and might confuse the player into thinking that more than one switch is present.

If you want a single switch to appear in the middle of a long wall without using an alcove, then you can break the long wall into more than one line, provided that the sector ceiling is low enough for the texture not to repeat vertically. The length of the line acting as the switch should be the same as the width of the switch texture. Most of the SW1/SW2 texture pairs provide switch images superimposed on the standard wall textures to allow you to do just this. Use the standard wall texture on the adjacent wall sections and a matching SW1 texture on the section carrying the switch action.

CAUTION: The superimposition of the switch image on standard wall texture makes the majority of SW1/SW2 textures unsuited for use as two-sided main textures. If you use them in this way, the result will be the Medusa effect, which is explained in Chapter 11, "The Lowdown on Textures."

MORE DOORS

The previous chapter examined locally activated doors, but let's look at DOOM's door mechanisms together with the remaining special line-types provided for their use.

SETTING UP REMOTELY ACTIVATED DOORS

The procedure for setting up remotely activated doors is similar to that used for basic doors. Here are the essential steps:

- Create appropriate sectors. For doors to look good, make the sectors adjoining the door have ceilings no more than about 128 units from their floors; use recess sectors if necessary.

- Make sure that door lines bordering adjacent sectors have their left sides facing into the door sector. This step remains necessary even for remotely activated doors. Odd effects result from getting this wrong. You can find all your ceilings (or even your floors) moving when you activate incorrectly made doors!

- Set the door sector's ceiling height to the same as its floor height so that the door starts in the closed position. Put appropriate door textures on the *upper* texture of the lines representing the faces of the door; check that the upper unpegged flag of each of these lines is clear. Use appropriate textures on the side walls of the door sector with the lower unpegged flag set.

- Choose an appropriate activating line for the door and set its special attribute to the required value (listed in Table 15.2 in the following section).

- Tag the activating line to the door sector.

The next WAD sortie will lead you through this process in detail.

REMOTELY ACTIVATED DOORS

Table 15.2 gives a full list of the codes for remotely activated doors. Note that not all types of doors are available in all activation categories and that Heretic has a code of its own.

Table 15.2. Special line codes for remotely activated doors.

| Action | Activation Category | | | | |
	W1	WR	S1	SR	GR
Door: open, pause, close	4†	90	29	63	-
Door: open and stay	2	86	103	61	46
Door: close	3	75	50	42	-
Door: close for 30 seconds, open	16	76	-	-	-
Turbo Door: open, pause, close	108*	105* [100]	111*	114*	-
Turbo Door: open and stay	109*	106*	112*	115*	-
Turbo Door: close	110*	107*	113*	116*	-
Blue-keyed turbo door	-	-	133*	99*	-
Red-keyed turbo door	-	-	135*	134*	-
Yellow-keyed turbo door	-	-	137*	136*	-

* Turbo doors are available only in DOOM v1.4 or later (but note that Heretic has a single kind of turbo door, which has a different code from DOOM's).

NOTE: Only the trigger indicated (†) can be activated directly by monsters. Suitably armed enemies can open a gun-activated door, though, if their fire misses its target and hits the appropriate trigger line.

If any player or monster is standing in any of these door sectors as the door closes, the door will re-open as soon as it encounters the obstruction.

You are already familiar with the majority of these door types. All that differs in most cases from basic doors are the activation mechanisms. There is, though, an additional category of actions to note: those that specifically make doors *close*. These special line-types can be used either to close a door that has been opened by one of the open-and-stay actions or to close a sector that was set open from the start. The target door will either close until re-opened by some *other* activating line or close for a timed period of 30 seconds. These latter types are commonly used to trap players in a hostile area, forcing them to face whatever it contains and letting them out again only if they survive long enough.

NOTE: The Door close triggers generate the sound of a door closing, even if the door was already closed when the line is activated.

SHOOT-'EM-UP DOORS

The only available impact-activated (or gun-activated) door does not close automatically, even though it is classed as a repeatable action (GR). If you want to have a door that the player must shoot at repeatedly to keep it open, you will have to tag another active line to this door to close it in some way between openings. A later sortie shows how you can do this.

NOTE: Many editors show the impact-activated door as a manual (locally activating) action and claim it is not necessary to tag lines using it to a sector. This is not the case, as you will quickly discover if you try it!

NOTE: The following WAD sortie builds on the WAD produced in the last sortie of the previous chapter. If you did not accompany me on that sortie but would like to come along on this one, you should use WAD15.WAD (DOOM), D2WAD15.WAD (DOOM II), or H1WAD15.WAD (Heretic) from the CD-ROM as your starting point. [As in earlier sorties, the variations required for Heretic are noted in brackets.]

WAD SORTIE 16: ADDING SOME MORE DOORS

It is time now to enhance your WAD with additional doors; let's begin with a trip-wire activated door.

ADDING A TRIP-WIRE ACTIVATED DOOR

The dark and winding staircase leading out of the platform room would seem an ideal location for a trip-wire activated door. This area is calling out for a door that opens as the stairs are descended, disgorging monsters into the stairway behind the player.

Figure 15.3 shows the sectors to add to set up a secret door off the stairway, with another room behind it.

THE NEW AREA

Notice how the new area has been divided into four sectors:

■ **The door into the room:** This door is to be opened by the player descending the stairs in the corridor outside it.

Figure 15.3.
Lines for a secret door and room off the dark stairway.

- **The central section of the room:** This section will have its lighting set so that it seems to be illuminated through the door by the lights in the corridor section outside.
- **Two "wings" of the room:** Either side of the illuminated central section are two darker sections. These are in the shadows cast by the sides of the doorway. They will be useful hiding places later for various goodies.

FIXING THE LIGHTS FOR THE NEW ROOM

Add the lines for these new sectors, using BROWN96 [CSTLRCK in Heretic] as the default wall texture. Before you apply Make Sector, though, you have a decision to make.

At the moment, the stair sector this new area will adjoin has a special characteristic in use: type 1. This blinks the lights off at random intervals. You need to decide what you want to do with this. Remember that the central sector of the new secret room will seem as though it is illuminated by the light source in the corridor outside. If you leave this blinking in effect, you will need to find a way of making the lights of the inner room and doorway flicker in synchronization with the corridor lights.

Special sector type 1 does not provide synchronized flickering. The lights blink randomly and independently in all sectors with the setting, so special sector type 1 cannot be used here—if it were, the result would look odd. Sector specials 12 and 13 each provide synchronized blinking of lights, but both of these effects are classed as blink-on; if used, the sectors will be at the lower lighting level most of the time and will blink to the higher level only momentarily. You need to decide, then, which effect you would prefer—synchronized blink-on, with these areas in semi-darkness most of the time, or steady illumination.

When you have made up your mind, apply the appropriate code to the existing corridor sector's special characteristic, then use Make Sector in each of your new areas in turn, starting with the door sector. You should find that the sector settings for the corridor are applied throughout all your new sectors this way. You can leave FLOOR7_1 [FLOOR27] on both floor and ceiling of the new sectors: Table 15.3 lists the remaining settings. Two sets of lighting figures are given in this table. The principal figure is used in areas with the blink-on special setting; the figures in parentheses should be used if the area is set for static lighting.

Table 15.3. Sector settings for the new secret areas off the stairway.

Area	Lighting	Ceiling	Floor
Door	176 (144)	−16	−16
Room (center)	144 (144)	88	−16
Room (wings)	112 (96)	88	−16

NOTE: Take special notice of the brightness levels used for these new sectors. The principal figures have been chosen carefully to keep the blink-on lighting effect working correctly throughout the new area. In this arrangement, the door and main room sectors both have neighbors with lower brightness settings. Had these been set to the same value, then the door sector would not have had a neighboring sector with a lower light level, and its light level would then drop to zero between blinks. This would look unnatural. When the values in the table are used, only the wings of the room have no neighbors with lower light levels, and it is acceptable for these areas to drop to total darkness.

Note also how the settings have been increased a little over the ideal static brightness settings to allow for the shorter illumination periods.

INSTALLING THE TRIP-WIRE

Now pick a suitable trip-line for the activation of this door; one of the stair risers around the corner from the door would seem to be a good choice. Enter LINES mode and click with the left mouse button to select your chosen trip-line. Set this line's special attribute to 2 to open a door as soon as a player walks over this line. Tell WADED which sector will be the door by right-clicking in the new door sector while your trigger line is selected.

Creating Tags in WadAuthor

Tagging lines to sectors is only marginally more complicated in WadAuthor. Press Ctrl+T, or choose the Tags... option from the Tools menu, to bring up the Tags dialog box. Click the Add button in this dialog box, which creates a new tag, then click once on the desired trigger-line to add its identification to the list of objects sharing the new tag. Click next in the sector that the trigger is to act upon, adding its identification to the list. Click OK to close the dialog box; that's all there is to it.

WADED and WadAuthor both mark tagged sectors in green whenever a trigger line is selected to show the link between them.

TIP: This tagging indication works the other way around, too. If you go into SECTORS mode and select the door sector, the trigger line will be shown in green. This feature saves you from having to remember which of your lines activate each of your sectors.

Once opened, this door will stay open for the rest of the game. In particular, it will enable whatever monsters you care to place in the room to either track the player (once they have been awakened) or lie in wait against the player's return.

BUILDING THE DOOR

Check that both the lines representing the faces of the new door have their right sides facing out from the door sector. You will probably have to flip one of these. (In WADED, select it and press F; use the context menu in WadAuthor.) Then apply BROWN96 [BANNER1] to the appropriate upper textures. This will be a secret door, so there should be no hint of its presence through texture changes. Set the Secret on Map flag for the outer face to prevent the map from giving the game away, too.

Now consider the texture alignment of the corridor-side door face. Because the player will discover the existence of this door soon enough, this face should contain no clue to the door's presence. You need to ensure, therefore, that its texture aligns precisely with its neighbors'. A casual consideration may lead you to think that no treatment is needed; it is easy to be misled into thinking that this wall section has not been changed substantially by the addition of the new sector. This would be wrong, though. The wall's texture is no longer provided by a *main* texture, but by an *upper*.

Remember that (pegged) upper textures are painted from their lower edge up (currently the floor, in this case), but the adjacent main textures are painted from the ceiling down. Consequently, these textures will align with each other only if the corridor is precisely the same height as (or a whole multiple of) the texture pattern: 128 pixels. It isn't, so the door-face texture will need alignment if it isn't to be obvious to the player.

Don't be tempted to just unpeg the upper texture. This would solve the texture alignment problem, but it would also spoil the effect of the door opening. You will need to use a Y-offset to adjust this texture alignment.

TIP: To work out the correct Y-offset needed to realign a door's face with its neighboring walls, use this formula:

Y-offset = height of door face – height of pattern + adjacent wall Y-offset

The door face is 136 units high here, the texture used on it is 128 pixels tall, and no Y-offset is in use on the adjacent walls. To keep its pattern in alignment with the walls, therefore, you will need to use a Y-offset on the outer face of the door of 136 – 128 + 0 = 8 units.

Finally, check that the short through-wall sides of the door sector have their lower unpegged flags set to prevent them moving with the door. (The current wall texture can be left on them, in my opinion.) Your new area should then be ready for a tryout. Put a couple of monsters in the new room if you want to see how they react to the player tripping the door. I'll leave a full consideration of the populating of this room until a later sortie.

REFINING THE DOOR ACTION

After trying this modification out, you may want to use a different line for the trigger. To do this, you will first need to break the link between the current trigger and the door. Do that in WADED by selecting the trigger line in LINES mode and right clicking in the door sector, just as you did to make the link. The green lines will disappear from the door sector to show you that the link has been broken. In WadAuthor, call up the Tags dialog box, select the appropriate tag number, and click once on the trigger line to remove it from the list of objects bearing this tag. You can then link another trigger to the door sector, just as you did your first.

CAUTION: After removing a tag from a line, don't forget to reset its special attribute back to 0. If you forget to do this, the line will continue to attempt to open a door—one that DOOM won't be able to find.

When you're happy with this area, I'll show you how to add a differently triggered door.

ADDING BUTTON-ACTIVATED DOORS

As already observed, if you've been working with DOOM or DOOM II, you have a couple of alcoves in your WAD with suitable SW1 textures on their walls, ready and waiting for the implementation of some switch-activated doors. (The alcoves are there in Heretic; they just don't have any switch textures on them.) Begin by hiding the marble corridor, which leads to the one-way staircase, behind another secret door.

CUTTING OFF THE STAIRCASE CORRIDOR

Add a new line in the staircase corridor some 16 units north of its junction with the southeast passageway. Use Make Sector on the new thin area you have just produced (the new door) and then in the corridor beyond it. The new sector's lighting level should be 144. Both the floor and ceiling should be at a height of 0 and have DEM1_5 [FLOOR28] on them.

BUILDING THE NEW DOOR

Flip any of the new door's face lines that are the wrong way around. (The new line is probably at fault here.) Then put MARBFAC3 [SKULLSB2] on the new line's essential upper texture. Use the same texture on the upper part of the passageway line as appears on the rest of the walls, keeping this texture's mortar lines aligned with those of the adjacent walls by using an appropriate Y-offset. Applying the formula presented earlier, you should find that this needs to be $120 - 128 + 0 = -8$.

This face of the door used to be the wall over the doorway. You will therefore need to change the line's pegging to something more appropriate. There is also a redundant texture to remove. Set this line's Secret on Map flag, too, to hide the new door on the auto-map.

Put DOORTRAK [WOODWL] on the through-wall side-lines of the new sector and set their lower unpegged flags. Now tag the rear wall of the northern of the two alcoves in the southeast passageway to the new door sector by selecting the alcove line and right clicking in the door sector (or using the Tags dialog box in WadAuthor). Set the switch line's special setting to 63 (SR Door: open and close) to provide a repeatable open-and-close door action from this line.

ADDING ANOTHER TRIGGER

You have now created a door that the player can open from the alcove switch any number of times. There is currently no way to open the door from the other side, however. Any player who makes it through this door before it closes will become trapped when it does close. (Using this door as a trap makes the one-way stair rather obsolete, doesn't it?)

You could set the special attribute of the inner face of this door to 1. That would allow the door to be opened from the staircase side as a standard door. Rather than doing this, though, I suggest a different approach: Put line-type 90 (WR Door: open and close) on the line forming the riser of the first or second step, tagging this to the door sector. In my opinion, this is a better solution than making a standard door, because a player may be tempted to try the door before proceeding up the stairs, just to see whether it can be opened from this side. A player who thinks it can't—as my proposed method will make it seem—will be relieved to discover that the door does, in fact, open as the stairs are climbed. The relief may be short-lived, however, if they fail to notice the stair-trap!

If, on the other hand, the player climbs the stairs without trying the door, the trigger on the step should at least make them jump, causing them to think that another door is opening somewhere. Of course, very fast players will not notice a thing, because they will have crossed the trigger before the door has even closed. They, of course, will have other things to worry about!

Alternatively, you may prefer to move the retrigger action to a stair riser beyond the stair-trap. This would give the player hope that there is a way back down the stairs. I think this makes the stair-trap less effective, though, as it now forces the player to climb the stairs, making the warning on the fourth step somewhat pointless.

CLOSING OFF THE HEXAGONAL ROOM

Finish the addition of button-activated doors with a new door that will lock the player in the hexagonal room at the start by closing off the gap into the platform room. All you need are two new lines across the doorway through the southwest wall of the hexagonal room, as shown in Figure 15.4.

To add these lines, you will probably need to turn the Snap to Grid setting down to 4 or maybe lower. You also need to take extra special care in WADED to ensure that the new lines connect properly to the opening's side-lines. As you have probably noticed, WADED sometimes has difficulty detecting that the mouse is over lines that run at an angle.

Figure 15.4.
The lines needed for a new door.

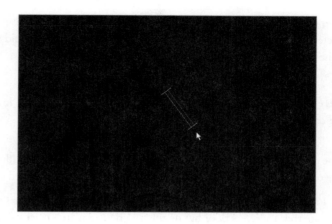

Only when you are convinced that your new lines connect properly at both ends should you apply Make Sector. Work from the new door sector out. You may find that you have to click in the new sector (and the two adjacent recess sectors) a couple of times to force Make Sector to handle them properly.

Table 15.4 has the settings for the three sectors that you have made out of the old opening through the wall.

Table 15.4. Settings for the three new sectors [Heretic settings in brackets].

Area	Lighting	Ceiling	Floor
Platform room recess	224	104 CEIL3_5 [FLAT516]	0 MFLR8_1 [FLOOR01]
Door	192	0 CEIL5_1 [FLOOR10]	0 MFLR8_1 [FLOOR01]
Hexagonal room recess	144	104 CEIL3_5 [FLAT516]	0 MFLR8_1 [FLOOR01]

Change the side walls of the recess in the hexagonal room to match their neighbors, taking care to leave the offset applied several sorties ago. Put DOORTRAK [WOODWL] on the side-lines of the door sector and set their lower unpegged flags.

BUILDING THE NEW DOOR

Make sure that the two-sided door lines have their right sides facing out of the door sector. Use BIGDOOR6 [GRSTNPBW] on the line facing into the platform room, but put STONE2 [GRSTNPB] on the side of the door facing the hexagonal room. You may need to apply an X-offset to both these textures to center them, as the gap is unlikely to be of a convenient length. Additionally, to have the hexagonal room texture align properly with its neighboring walls, it will need a Y-offset. Again, the formula presented earlier is used to calculate this: $104 - 128 + 16 = -8$ units.

This door will be opened from a switch, the one located on the rear wall of the second alcove in the southeast passageway. This is nicely out of sight of the door, and it may cause the player to wonder what it does. Put special line-type 63 (SR Door: open and close) on the back wall of the appropriate alcove and tag it to the new door sector. This door will stay open for only five seconds. You should find that the player will have to run across the hexagonal room to get through it before it closes.

NOTE: Readers with DOOM v1.4 or later may want to use line-type 114 (SR Turbo door: open and close) instead.

From the other side, the new door is to be capable of opening as a standard door, so set the special attribute of this face of the door to 1 (MR Door: open and close). There is no need to tag the line to the sector, of course.

Finally, I don't see any need to hide that this is a door by setting any lines' Secret on Map flags. Having the player aware that there is a door but unable to find the switch is effective enough!

ADDING A SHOT-ACTIVATED DOOR

The final new door in this sortie is to be an impact-activated door, located at the end of the passageway at the bottom of the stairs leading from the platform room—that should wake up those monsters lurking in the room behind the player! Figure 15.5 shows the extra lines needed to set up the new sectors that will provide the door and a room beyond it.

Figure 15.5.
Lines for an impact-activated door and room beyond.

The settings for the new sectors are given in Table 15.5. Don't forget to check the special characteristic setting here, as these sectors are likely to inherit one from nearby.

Table 15.5. Sector settings for the new door and room [Heretic settings in brackets].

Area	Lighting	Ceiling	Floor
Door	96	–112 FLOOR4_1 [FLOOR09]	–112 FLOOR4_1 [FLOOR06]
Inner room	128	24 TLITE6_1 [FLOOR09]	–112 FLOOR4_1 [FLOOR06]

Use PIPE2 [REDWALL] on all the new lines, but use PIPE4 [BANNER1] on the face of the new door. It will be needed on both the upper and lower texture slots here, because the door sector's floor is at a different height from the floor at the end of the passage.

If you are using DOOM (or DOOM II), change the texture on the end wall of the original corridor to PIPE4, too. This is a shot-up version of PIPE2 and is used in this area as a visual clue to the presence of the door and the nature of its activation mechanism. Using it on a wall alongside the real door makes the texture's presence more conspicuous but stops it from being immediately obvious which of the walls hides the door. Don't bother aligning the texture on the door face, though. There is absolutely no need to line the bullet holes up on the two wall sections, and the other adjacent wall has a different texture anyway. Put whatever you fancy on the inner face of this door, bearing in mind that only its lower four pixels are ever likely to be seen.

Heretic doesn't provide any texture comparable with DOOM's PIPE_ series, so repeat a previously used visual clue by using BANNER1 on the outer face of the new door. Decide for yourself whether you want to align this texture properly with its neighbor; it will depend on how much of a clue you feel like giving to the player at this point.

Hide the door on the auto-map by setting the Secret on Map flag of the appropriate line. As usual, make sure that the faces of the door have their right sides facing out from the door sector. Then use special type 46 (GR Door: stays open) on the outer door-face, explicitly tagged to the door sector.

The rear face of this door doesn't need any trigger mechanism, because the door will latch open. Don't forget, though, to set the lower unpegged flag of the door sector's side lines. Their textures can be left as they are.

Finally, save your WAD (as WAD16.WAD to stay in step with my numbering) and try out your latest additions.

LIGHT SWITCHES

Having seen how the remote triggering mechanism can be applied to an action you're familiar with—the door—you can now move on and look at other types of triggered actions. The first of these is the simple alteration of sector lighting levels with brightness-level switches.

BRIGHTNESS-LEVEL SWITCHES

DOOM and Heretic do not provide many options for player-triggered light-level changes. Table 15.6 shows what is available.

Table 15.6. Special line-type codes for brightness level switching.

| | Activation Category | | |
Action	W1	WR	SR
Switch lights off (brightness level 0)	35	79	139*
Switch lights on full (brightness level 255)	13	81	138*
Switch light level to match dimmest adjacent	104	–	–
Switch light level to match brightest adjacent	12	80	–
Make light blink on every 1.0 seconds	17	–	–
Line-types marked * require DOOM v1.666 or later.			

The new settings brought about by these actions replace the specified sector-brightness values, which are lost forever. Once it is changed through these actions, there is no way to restore a sector's original brightness setting, except by having an adjacent sector act as a copy of it (as will be demonstrated in the next WAD sortie).

NOTE: The actions of the brightness-level switches described here break the normal rule that sectors can only partake in one action at a time. Actions that affect the brightness level of a sector will always act immediately on their target sectors, regardless of any other action they are currently engaged in.

AUTOMATIC LIGHTING VARIATIONS

It is possible to build areas that have the lights switch on as players move into them and switch off again as they leave (or vice versa). All that is required is a careful arrangement of retriggering lines. Such features are also good for multiplayer games, because it is possible for players to turn the lights out on their opponents to give themselves the advantage. The next WAD sortie demonstrates part of the necessary arrangement of lines. You may wish to experiment further with it yourself after finishing your next WAD.

WAD SORTIE 17: TRIPPING THE LIGHTS—FANTASTIC!

NOTE: This sortie builds on the WAD produced in the previous one. Even if you did not produce that WAD, you can still follow this sortie by using the WADs supplied on the accompanying CD-ROM.

This sortie will explore just one possible arrangement of switched lights. The area in which this will be used will be developed in later sorties into a confusing maze area. These areas generally take a lot of time (and patience) to develop correctly. They can be a severe test of both the designer and the WAD editor. My advice is that you work on these areas in stages, perfecting each aspect of them in turn. You can begin by looking at the thinking behind the lighting design.

SWITCHED LIGHTS: THE THEORY

Figure 15.6 shows a schematic arrangement for the lighting "tricks" that will be played in the principal maze sectors.

Figure 15.6.
Schematic arrangement of triggers for the maze's lighting effects.

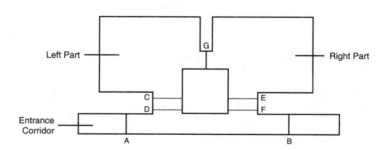

The maze comprises three main areas:

- An entrance corridor
- A left part
- A right part

The complexity of the maze shape has been omitted from Figure 15.6 so that you can better see and understand the scheme.

Each of these areas is rigged to have the lighting change as the player moves around. The effects are intended to operate as follows:

- The first time the player enters the entrance corridor, the lights of this corridor will go out. Switch line A is the trigger for this. The lights will remain on in the rest of the maze. The lights to this corridor can be turned back on only by locating the appropriate switch (line B). Once the lights have been turned back on with this trigger, they will stay on.

■ As the player enters the left part of the maze, the lights will go out. This is achieved by switch line C. Switch line D turns the lights back on when the player leaves this section of the maze. This happens each time the player passes over these lines. Notice how this arrangement has to differ from real light switches because of the nature of DOOM's line actions. Since each line can perform only one function, two lines are needed if the lights are to be turned both on and off. Furthermore, both lines are retrigger lines. Each will attempt to carry out its action every time the player crosses it, regardless of the current light settings. The arrangement of these lines is therefore critical. The lights in this part of the maze will always be in whatever state the last line-crossing left them in. When entering, the off-switch is the last triggered; when leaving, the on-switch has the final say.

■ The right part of the maze is rigged in the same way as the left, with switch lines E and F. These operate in exactly the same way as C and D respectively, but they act on the right part of the maze.

■ The right and left parts of the maze are linked through line G. This line is an ordinary, inactive line. To explore the right part of the maze with the benefit of the lights, then the player should enter the left part first but pass into the right section through this line. Leaving the maze by reversing this route will turn the lights back on in the left part, allowing that side to be explored with the lights on after re-entering it through line G from the right. However, if this area is constructed carefully enough, it could be quite a while before the player notices this tactic.

BUILDING IT IN PRACTICE

Figure 15.7 shows how the preceding idea has been used in my WAD17.WAD. (D2WAD17.WAD is the DOOM II equivalent; H1WAD17.WAD is the Heretic version.) The left part of the maze has been made a little more maze-like, and one or two details have been reworked slightly, but the three major divisions outlined in the preceding scheme should still be discernible. The locations of the seven lines that function as lines A to G are marked.

Figure 15.7.
WAD17.WAD's use of the lighting effects.

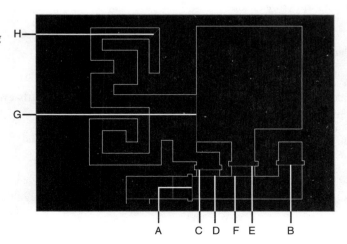

You may like to start the game with this sample WAD and walk through this area, observing its main features as they are described in the following sections.

THE ENTRANCE CORRIDOR

The new area has been added at the end of the marble corridor at the top of the one-way staircase. The corridor has been extended to the east, with the two "halves" of the maze area to the north of it. The main east/west section of the extended corridor has a trigger line just before the entrance to the maze. This acts like trigger line A in the preceding: As the player passes it, it plunges the eastern end of the corridor into darkness. A special line of type 35 (W1 Lights: off), tagged to the eastern sector of the corridor, has been used to do this.

At its eastern end, the corridor turns to the north to meet a short additional sector. The line bordering these two sectors has the trigger action 80 (WR Lights: match brightest adjacent) on it to turn the corridor lights back on. This action takes the new light-level setting from the adjacent sector with the highest brightness setting. Because the sectors at either end of this corridor have the same brightness level it originally had, the lights will always come back up to the starting level.

EXTRA WARNINGS

The walls of the corridor have the same textures on them as the walls of the corridor leading in from the staircase. Close to the lighting trigger lines, though, the corridor walls have been embellished a little to signal the presence of these triggers to the player. Not that there is really much that player can do to avoid them—the warning is really to unnerve the player a little. Having discovered what the warnings mean by crossing the first trigger, a player may hesitate before crossing others. Similar warnings have been placed at each entrance to the main maze, too.

The warning itself is provided by small alcoves placed next to each end of the lighting trigger lines. These alcoves have conspicuous textures on the back walls. Next to triggers that turns lights off, LITERED is used (in D2WAD17.WAD, BFALL1 has been used instead; REDWALL, in H1WAD17.WAD), and by the line that restores the main corridor lights, LITEBLU4 (SFALL1 in D2WAD17.WAD; MOSAIC1 in H1WAD17.WAD) is in use. I haven't bothered putting any notification against the lines that restore the inner maze lights; I thought players should discover these lines for themselves!

All the lines with these warning textures have the special attribute 48 (Effect: horizontal scroll) assigned to them to make them really noticeable. This should be enough to make most players wary of passing between them. The construction of the alcoves is finished by using BROWNHUG (METL2 in the Heretic version) on their side walls.

Note that these small alcoves have not been made into sectors of their own because they have no settings different from those used in the adjacent part of the corridor.

IN THE MAZE

The left and right parts of the maze have been drawn using the texture CRATE2 in the DOOM and DOOM II versions and SKULLSB1 in Heretic—although it doesn't really matter what is used here at the moment, because the full development of the maze itself will, no doubt, result in changes to these textures later.

The trip-lines required to turn the main maze lights off and back on again are provided by two lines across the entrances to each part. The inner lines of each half of the maze (lines C and E) use special line-type 79 (WR Lights: off) to turn the lights off as each maze sector is entered. The outer lines (D and F) use special line-type 80 (WR Lights: match brightest adjacent) to turn the lights back up again as the player leaves the maze this way.

In each of my implementations, I have made each of the areas between these pairs of trip-lines into sectors of their own and set their lighting levels to 144 to have them act as buffer zones between the outer corridor and the inner maze areas. This allows the retrigger that restores the lights to operate, regardless of whether the outer corridor is in darkness or not, by providing an illuminated adjacent sector for each half of the maze.

You could add a little extra sting in the tail of this lighting arrangement by dispensing with the buffer sectors, so that the inner maze areas border directly onto the corridor (or by tagging the triggers to the buffers as well as to their own half of the maze). Doing this would make the inner areas rather more complicated to explore until the player had discovered how to turn the outer corridor's lights back on. (I'll leave you to work out why!)

FURTHER EMBELLISHMENTS

Just to be really mean, I added an extra internal line to the inner area of the left part of the maze (line H in Figure 15.7). This has a special attribute of 104 (W1 Lights: off) and is tagged to its own half of the maze. In my maze, even if players work out how to get this far with the lights on, they will still have to find their way out in the dark.

You might like to wander around a bit through the various parts of the maze to satisfy yourself that it does indeed operate as described.

COSMETIC CHANGES

I made a few cosmetic variations by altering some floor and ceiling heights and a couple of textures. Table 15.7 gives the settings used for all the sectors in this area in the sample WAD17.WAD. (D2WAD17.WAD varies in the single regard already noted; H1WAD17.WAD differences are noted in brackets.)

Table 15.7. Sector settings for the entire maze area.

Area	Lighting	Ceiling	Floor
Original marble corridor	144	240 DEM1_5 [FLOOR28]	112 DEM1_6 [FLOOR28]
Short sector to east	144	248 FLAT2 [FLOOR29]	96 DEM1_6 [FLOOR28]
Eastern corridor section	144	240 DEM1_5 [FLOOR28]	96 DEM1_6 [FLOOR28]

Area	Lighting	Ceiling	Floor
Northern end of corridor	144	224 FLAT2 [FLOOR29]	112 DEM1_6 [FLOOR28]
Entrance buffers	144	224 FLOOR6_2 [FLOOR30]	96 DEM1_6 [FLOOR28]
Inner maze areas	144	240 DEM1_5 [FLOOR28]	112 DEM1_6 [FLOOR28]

MARBLE1 [DOORSTON in H1WAD17.WAD] is used on all upper essentials, with the upper unpegged flags set in all cases; NUKE24 [METL1] appears on all lower essentials. (NUKE24 is usually used on 24-pixel edges around nukage-slime pools, but it blends well here, too.) The side walls of the entrance buffers use MARBLE1 [DOORSTON], with Y-offsets of 16 units to ensure correct alignment with the walls of the corridor. Finally, I placed a few floor lamps [wall torches] around the place for effect, and to provide something for the player to navigate by in the dark! (The Heretic version of the WAD was also getting low on atmospheric sound effects, so I added some heartbeats to it.)

YOUR TURN

Once you have taken a look at one of these sample WADs for yourself, you should examine it in the editor, noting the main features of its construction. You may then like to experiment by building a similar area in your own WAD, with or without embellishments of your choice. Leave the maze areas fairly open for now—they will be developed later—and don't extend them out much further than the area they occupy in Figure 15.7.

A FINAL STAB IN THE BACK

Lastly, as a sort of coda to this chapter on remote-control sectors, you might want to add further development at the top of the one-way stairs, just to add to the player's misery in this area. I'm thinking of another room full of monsters to surprise them from behind. Figure 15.8 shows the arrangement.

Figure 15.8.
Lines for two new sectors at the top of the one-way stairs.

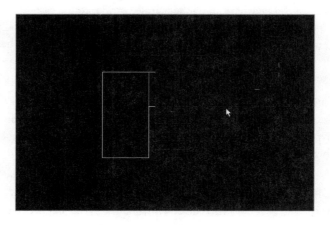

ADDING ANOTHER ROOM WITH A DOOR

Start by adding two sectors as shown in Figure 15.8. These represent a door sector (to be hidden, of course) behind the MARBFACE [DOORSTON] texture at the western end of the marble corridor and a room beyond it. Use STONE2 [CHAINSD] as the texture for the new lines.

Table 15.8 gives the settings for these two new sectors.

Table 15.8. Sector settings for the secret door and room. [Heretic settings in brackets]

Area	Lighting	Ceiling	Floor
Door	144	112 FLOOR6_2 [FLOOR30]	112 DEM1_6 [FLOOR28]
Room	96	208 DEM1_5 [FLOOR30]	112 DEM1_6 [FLOOR28]

The outer face of the door needs MARBFACE [DOORSTON] on its upper to preserve the original appearance of the corridor at this point, and this line should be flagged as Secret on Map. The inner face of the door should use STONE2 [CHAINSD] along with the through-door walls (the latter with their lower unpegged flags set). As usual, make sure that the right sides of the appropriate lines of the door sector face the correct way.

ΛΕRΕΤΙϹ As well as using CHAINSD on the inner face of the door to match the rest of the inner room, Heretic users will need to apply a Y-offset of –32 to this line to maintain alignment. They will also find that METL2 works best on the through-door wall sections.

TRIGGERING THE DOOR

The new door will be triggered in several ways: First, there should be a single trigger line of type 4 (W1: Door: open and close) somewhere along the marble corridor to the east. My WADs use the line to which the mouse arrow is pointing in Figure 15.8. Apply this special attribute to an appropriate line in your WAD and then tag it to the door sector. This line will act similarly to the trigger line on the darkened stairway out of the platform room, enabling monsters to ambush the player from behind. The door will open long enough for the monsters in it to see the player and awaken.

When this happens, the monsters in the room will move toward the player and should manage to leave the room before the door closes. By placing a standard line-type 1 trigger on the back face of this door, though, any who haven't emerged by the time the door closes but who are on the track of the player will be able to open the door when they reach it. Set the rear face of the door to line-type 1, therefore.

Why not just set the corridor trigger to a type that leaves the door open? Well, hopefully, the player will be too busy dealing with the monsters emerging from the room to bother too much about the door itself, initially. By the time the bad guys have been dealt with, and the player wants to enter the room behind it in search of loot, the door will be firmly closed. The trigger line that opened it at first will not now reopen it—it's a single-trigger action, remember—so the player must find another way to open this door.

Putting an impact trigger of type 46 on the face of this door will accomplish this. Do that now, tagging the outer face of the door to the door sector. Players can now re-open this door by firing at it. It may be a while before they think to try it, though. On the other hand, they may not need to think of it. Stray shots from the fight that has just taken place will, in all likelihood, have caused the door to open anyway!

Another retrigger line, this time of special type 75 (WR Door: close) tagged to the door sector and located somewhere in the corridor, will take care of this. With this modification, players who withdraw to fight from the eastern end of the marble corridor will close the door themselves when they do approach it. Again, it may be a while before they think to shoot at it to reopen it, as they will probably not realize that it was their shots that opened it before.

Finally, I added a further little surprise in the form of another line of type 75 to close the door as the inner room is entered. This may panic players a little; by now, they probably won't immediately think of trying to open the door in the normal way. Of course, there will need to be some goodies placed here to lure players far enough into the room to trip this line, but I'll leave that for another sortie.

The final arrangement of trigger lines for this new door is shown in Figure 15.9.

Figure 15.9.
Arrangement of triggers for the secret door at the top of the marble stairs.

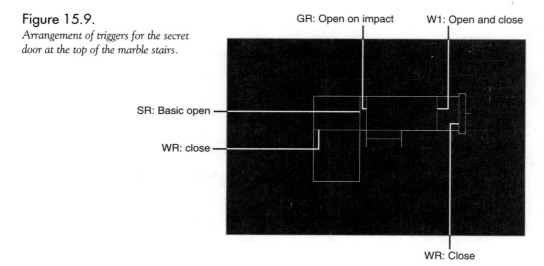

GR: Open on impact W1: Open and close

SR: Basic open

WR: close

WR: Close

The two lines to close the door (type 75) should both be added to existing sectors manually by using Sec Define—don't forget to use LINES mode to flag them 2-sided first—and then tagged to the door sector.

When you're happy with the arrangement of triggers in this area, add a few monsters to the room (just at difficulty levels 4 and 5, for now), then save this WAD as WAD17A.WAD and see how well it all works.

EXIT: MOPPING UP AND MOVING ON

This chapter introduced you to the idea of tags between lines and sectors as a way to provide sectors that can be activated from afar. You have now seen more of DOOM's doors and seen some fancy tricks with the lights.

The next chapter continues this theme of activating sectors remotely and shows you how surfaces other than the floors of sectors can be moved.

SIMPLE MOVING SECTORS

The previous chapter introduced you to the concept of the remotely activated sector. Exploring the range of actions these sectors can be made to undergo continues in this room. In particular, you will extend your repertory of effects that use moving ceilings and be introduced to those that involve moving floors.

The WAD sorties in this chapter will have you adding some additional traps for the unsuspecting players of your growing WAD. There are also a few cautionary words against setting traps for yourself!

I'll begin, though, with one of the most useful moving floor effects: the lift (or "elevator," as some readers probably prefer to call it).

LIFTS AND MOVING PLATFORMS

In earlier chapters, you have seen how DOOM produces the effect of a door by the simple expedient of moving a sector's ceiling from the level of its floor to some other higher setting. Lifts are produced by an equally simple process. They are obtained by moving a sector's *floor* from one level to another and back again. This creates a traveling platform that will carry whatever is standing on it.

HOW LIFTS OPERATE

DOOM's lifts all operate on the same basic principle. When activated, the floor of the lift sector moves down from its starting elevation to the level of the lowest adjacent floor. There, it pauses for five seconds before returning to its starting position. Appropriate sounds are produced as the lift starts to move and as it docks at each end of its travel.

— By Steve Benner

Once again, Hexen's programmable actions are somewhat different from those available in other variants of the game. This chapter, therefore, concentrates on the simple, sector-moving line-types available in DOOM, DOOM II, and Heretic. Hexen's more flexible scheme is explained in "Programming the Action," a chapter on the CD-ROM.

Note that DOOM expects to start the motion of all lifts by moving them downward. If a sector that has no lower floor next to it is activated as a lift, it will not move. Furthermore, lift sectors always return to their starting elevation.

Lifts always operate from their starting elevation to the *lowest* adjacent floor. They cannot be made to pause at the position of some intermediary floor. If you want to have a lift at the side of a tall room, say, operating between a high ledge and another ledge below it (but higher than the floor of the room), you will need to isolate the lift sector in some way from the main room to prevent it from continuing down past the intervening ledge to the floor below.

For a moving sector to function as a lift, players (and monsters) must be able to enter and leave the sector in both its upper and lower positions. Therefore, make sure you allow appropriate headroom and maneuvering space in and around these sectors, if you want players and/or monsters to be able to use them. Don't forget you will have to allow for the full travel of the moving floor.

If a lift's floor is prevented from returning to its starting position because of the presence of a player or monster—either because there is insufficient headroom in the floor's uppermost position or because the object overhangs the sides of the lift sector and thus touches an adjacent ceiling—then the movement of the lift will immediately reverse and the floor will return to its lower position. The lift will, however, persevere in its attempts to return to the starting position until it succeeds.

TURBO LIFTS

DOOM v1.4 introduced a high-speed version of the lift: the turbo lift, the lift effect's equivalent of the turbo doors. Apart from their higher speed, they operate in exactly the same way as standard lifts. They are not available in Heretic.

TRIGGERS FOR LIFTS

Table 16.1 gives the line-type codes that activate lift movements. Like all remotely activated effects, all lines using these special attributes must be tagged to an appropriate sector to provide the action.

Table 16.1. Special line-types providing lift actions.

| Action | Activation Category | | | |
	W1	WR	S1	SR
Standard lift	10	88	21	62
Turbo lift	121*	120*	122*	123*

*Turbo lifts require DOOM v1.4 and above and are not available in Heretic.

The majority of lift actions can be activated only by players. Line-type 88 (WR Lift), however, will also trigger a lift movement if a monster walks over it.

NOTE: In early versions of DOOM, line-type 88 could also be triggered by projectiles, such as rockets and Imp fireballs. This feature has been removed from v1.666 and later.

DECIDING TRIGGER POSITIONS

Often the hardest part of building a lift is determining a suitable triggering arrangement. You will recall that spacebar activators can be operated only from their *right* sides. This has major implications for building lifts, particularly if you want the lift to be capable of being operated from above and from below. Figure 16.1 illustrates the problem.

The upper part of this figure shows a common arrangement, with a lift linking two areas, the lower of which has its ceiling below the level of the upper area's floor. In Figure 16.1, the lift is in its upper (resting) position. As you can see, both the upper and lower corridors end at the same line—the line marked A.

This line would be a natural place to have the spacebar activate the lift. This cannot be made to work from both above and below the lift, however, as this would require line A to be active from both sides. An alternative method must be found for triggering this lift. There are a number of possible solutions, all of which are commonly used.

THE SIMPLEST SOLUTION

The simplest way of arranging triggers for a lift is to orient its lower sector boundary (line A in Figure 16.1) with its right side facing away from the lift sector and set this line to be a spacebar activator of the sector's movement. This enables a player to summon the lift from below while standing against the sector edge. The lift is set to trigger from above by means of a walk-through trigger action placed on the lift sector's upper boundary (line B in Figure 16.1). This causes the lift to descend as soon as a player steps into it from the adjacent upper area.

Case *i* in Figure 16.1 shows the arrangement of trigger lines. A right-angle tick mark on a line shows a spacebar-activated line's right side; oblique ticks mark walk-through trigger lines.

Figure 16.1.

Typical lift trigger arrangements.

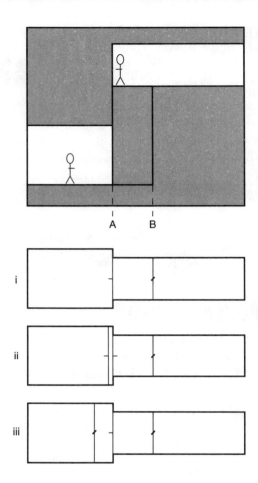

This configuration of triggers requires the player to think of activating the lift from below and provides automatic triggering from above. It can be used to build lifts that may not be obvious at their lower level, and thus are missed, or lifts that surprise the player who enters them from above with sudden, unexpected activation. (Readers familiar with the start of Level 5 of DOOM II may recognize this!) These lifts can also deliver monsters automatically from the higher to the lower level.

In building a lift in this way, remember that the walk-through line providing the upper trigger will operate in whichever way it is walked through. Players traveling up in this lift will, therefore, send the lift back down as they step *from* the lift at the top. You may regard this action as undesirable, or you may wish to use it so that the lift is sent back down to collect whatever is tracking the player along the lower level!

FORCING MANUAL OPERATION FROM ABOVE AND BELOW

To set up a lift that the player must activate manually from above *and* below, an additional trigger line is needed. If this line is positioned 16 or fewer units from line A, the difference in floor heights that occur at that line will prevent the player's center point from crossing the additional line. (Players are 32 units wide, remember.) By orienting these two lines with their right sides facing away from each other, and placing the same special attribute on each, the lift's lower boundary can be made to appear active from both sides. A player will be able to activate the lift from the "end" of either corridor. Case *ii* in Figure 16.1 illustrates this configuration of triggers.

It doesn't matter on which side of line A the new line is placed, if it's no further from it than 16 units and the two lines have their right sides facing away from each other. If the lines are placed further apart than a player's radius, the player can stand between the two lines and be on the left side of each—and thus not able to operate the lift!

A lift configured to use switches in this way cannot be activated by monsters.

FULLY AUTOMATIC LIFTS

A fully automatic lift is produced by using walk-over triggers on both the line of the upper boundary of the lift sector (as before) and on the approach to the lift from below. This also requires an additional line, of course. Note that here the activator used on the lower approach must be positioned more than 16 units from line A to give the player the space to cross it when the lift is in its raised position.

If the triggers are of the standard (non-turbo) variety, such a lift could be activated by monsters from either side. For effective use by monsters from below, however, the lower activator will need careful placement. It must be placed far enough from the lift to enable a monster to cross the activator and give the lift enough time to descend. The distance should not be so great, however, that the monster cannot reach the lift before it goes back up. If a monster cannot step straight onto the lift sector's floor when it gets to it, then it will turn and wander off in another direction. You may need to spend some time experimenting, using the Full Map Information cheat-code to watch the way monsters behave, to get these lines just right.

TRIPLE TRIGGER OPERATION

In the previous arrangement of active lines, players who step off the lift at the lower level will need to move forward to cross the lower activator if they wish to summon the lift back. As the lower activator will not normally be visible, few players will think to do this, especially if, having seen what is at the lower level, they decide they need to beat a hasty retreat! It is common, therefore, to arrange for the line-A boundary of the lift to provide an additional spacebar activator for summoning the lift from below. This triple-triggering is probably the most useful arrangement of lift triggers. It is shown in Figure 16.1 as case *iii*.

Note again that the lower walk-through activator must be positioned more than 16 units from line A. If it is any closer, neither of the triggers for summoning the lift from below will work. The walk-through trigger fails because there is no space for the player to walk through it; the spacebar trigger fails because DOOM will not permit the player to access it with the walk-through trigger that lies between the player and the line of the lift.

USING DIRECTION CHANGES

Lifts are generally good places to have a corridor change direction. This has two advantages. First, it can force the player to turn rapidly as the lift operates to face the hazard on the other level. Second, it can make the placement of triggers simpler.

Figure 16.2 shows a plan view of two corridors at different levels running at 90 degrees to each other. The corridors meet at a lift. Assuming the corridor from the south is the higher of the two, line U in Figure 16.2 could be used by players approaching from the upper level to operate the lift by using the spacebar. Line L can then be used as the spacebar activator for players in the lower corridor.

Figure 16.2.

Suggested trigger lines for a lift joining corridors at a corner.

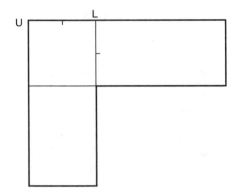

COMPLETELY REMOTE OPERATION

There is no reason, of course, for a lift's activating triggers to be positioned on or around the lift itself. They could be moved well away and placed on any standard trip or switch line. This can force players to hunt around for either the lift, the switch, or both. (They will usually need to make a run for it, too!)

ONE-WAY LIFTS

Similarly, there is no requirement for lifts to be capable of operating from above *and* below if you don't want them to. Remember that players can always jump from open-sided lifts (though they may hurt themselves doing this in Hexen).

TEXTURE CONSIDERATIONS AROUND LIFTS

As with all surfaces the user is expected to activate with the spacebar, it makes sense to use lift-like textures on the visible faces of lifts to alert the player to their presence. PLAT1 is the usual DOOM lift-face texture, although some of the door textures are suitable, as indeed are many of the standard wall textures.

More important than the textures themselves, though, is their application to the appropriate texture slots. Note that line A has essential textures on both sides: an upper when viewed from the lift sector itself and a lower when viewed from the bottom corridor. (See Figure 16.3.)

Figure 16.3.

The exposure of additional textures by the movement of a lift.

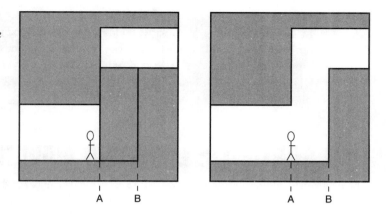

It is also easy to forget that moving floors expose additional surfaces. Figure 16.3 shows how a lift sector gains a completely new lower texture (along line B) when it moves to its lower position. Few editors will check the range of a lift's operation sufficiently to give you a warning of such so-called *latent essential* textures.

PEGGING CONSIDERATIONS FOR LIFTS

Pegging considerations around lifts are much easier than around doors. You usually want all textures to use the default arrangement. Ceiling relationships don't change with the operation of lifts, so the state of the upper unpegged flag is always immaterial. Lower textures are usually left in the pegged state, so that any visible outer face of the lift moves up and down with its floor, but the inner faces of the lift (the walls of the lift shaft, as it were) remain pegged to the static floors outside the lift sector and thus stay stationary.

STEPS INVOLVED IN BUILDING A LIFT

The steps involved in building a lift are as follows:

1. Make a suitable arrangement of sectors. The floor of the lift sector should be set at the upper limit of its travel.

2. Check that textures are applied to all lower texture slots that will be exposed by the movement of the lift.

3. Check that the lower unpegged flags of all lines bordering the lift are clear.

4. Decide on suitable trigger lines. The disposition of these will depend on the precise arrangement of the lift and adjacent sectors. Assign the appropriate special attributes to the trigger lines, and tag all these lines to the lift sector. Make sure that any spacebar-activated lines have their right sides facing the direction from which the player will approach them.

The next WAD sortie takes you through this process in your own WAD.

> **NOTE:** The following WAD sortie builds on the WAD produced in the last sortie of the previous chapter. If you did not accompany me on that sortie but would like to take part in this one, you should use WAD17A.WAD (DOOM), D2WAD17A.WAD (DOOM II), or H1WAD17A.WAD (Heretic) from the CD-ROM as your starting point. [Variations for readers using Heretic are noted in brackets.]

WAD SORTIE 18: LIFTS AND MOVING PLATFORMS

The first step in adding a lift to your WAD is to construct the upper and lower areas that the lift will connect. The lower level will be an entirely new area of your WAD, to the north of the platform room; the upper area will be an extension of the corridor that leads out of the platform room.

PREPARING THE NEW AREAS

Figure 16.4 shows how the new areas fit into the existing map.

Figure 16.4.
New areas in preparation for the installation of a lift.

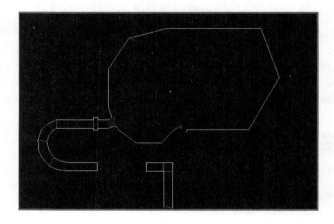

Begin by drawing a large open arena connected to the existing thin courtyard sector beyond the platform room's northern window. Make sure you draw this new area in a clockwise manner—don't worry about its exact size and shape—and connect it correctly to the existing sector. Use Make Sector on this large sector and lower its floor to –256 before continuing.

Next, set the default texture to GSTONE1 [GRNBLOK1 in Heretic]—this will make life easier later—and draw and make the first of the sectors that lead out of the large sector's southwest edge. Set this new sector's ceiling to –128 and its floor and ceiling textures to DEM1_5 [FLOOR19] before drawing and making the subsequent sectors of this new lower area of the map. It doesn't really matter how many lines or sectors you use to come around the corner; just aim to meet up with the existing corridor behind the impact-activated door, noting from Figure 16.4 how this is to be extended.

The full development of this lower area will be left to later sorties.

To draw the new area above the lift, change the default texture to PIPE2 [SPINE2] and add new sectors as shown in Figure 16.5, working from the room beyond the impact-activated door. In order, these new areas will be as follows:

- A second impact-activated door
- A short corridor beyond
- A third impact-activated door
- A further short corridor
- The lift

Figure 16.5.
New sectors as far as the lift.

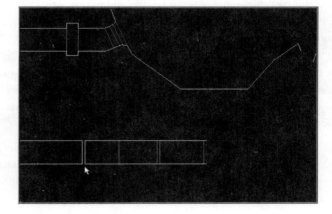

When fully drawn, the two new areas of the map should be left with a gap of about 24 units between them. Figure 16.5 has the mouse cursor pointing to this gap.

Table 16.2 gives the sector settings for the new areas above the lift. The lower areas can be left as they are, for now.

Heretic users should put FLOOR06 on both floor and ceiling of all these sectors, except for the lift sector itself, which needs FLAT509 on the ceiling and FLAT504 on the floor. The lift sector will also benefit from a floor height of –16.

Table 16.2. Sector settings for the extension to the upper corridor.

Area	Lighting	Ceiling	Floor
East Door	128	–112 FLOOR4_1	–112 FLOOR4_1
East Corridor	128	8 CEIL3_4	–112 FLOOR4_1
West Door	96	–112 FLOOR4_1	–112 FLOOR4_1
West Corridor	96	–8 CEIL3_3	–112 FLOOR4_1
Lift	96	–24 CEIL5_2	–104 FLOOR4_5

Finally, bridge the connection between the new areas of the map by adding the two missing lines and making the new sector. Set this sector's ceiling at –128 and its floor at –256.

MAKING THE LIFT

This lift is to be spacebar operated from above—its presence is not going to be too obvious—but automatic from below. To make the lift, set the special attribute of the western line of the lift sector to 62 (SR Lift), making sure that this line's right side faces east, into the upper corridor. Tag the line to the lift sector. This will enable the player to activate the lift with the spacebar from the upper level.

To make the lift come automatically to a player approaching from the lower area to its west, set the special attribute of the line at the western edge of the thin interconnecting sector to 88 (WR: Lift) and tag this line to the lift sector, too. Make sure this line is more than 16 units from the lift; otherwise, the player will not be able to cross it to activate it from the west when the lift is up.

You should now deal with the textures around the lift sector itself. As already noted, I don't want the presence of the lift to be too obvious from the upper corridor, but I think there should be some small visual clue to lead the player on here. The exact nature of this clue will vary depending on which game you are building for, of course. With DOOM, I recommend using the BROWNPIP texture, offset vertically in such a way as to suggest its continuation below the floor—a useful way to suggest that there may be something down there. With Heretic, you should continue the theme of using the banner textures to mark the route onwards. A similar device can be used at the end of the lower corridor to mark the lift's position from that side, but as the player will already know of its existence by then, this is less important. The rest of the lines for the lift sector can then be decorated in a suitably complementary manner: Table 16.3 gives the recommended textures and Y-offsets for the lines of the lift sector.

Table 16.3. Line texture settings for the lift sector.

| Line | DOOM | | Heretic | |
	Texture	Y-Offset	Texture	Y-Offset
Side walls	BROWN1	0	CSTLRCK	0
Upper end wall	BROWNPIP	32	BANNER2	−48
Lower end wall	PIPE4	0	BANNER1	20

CAUTION: Take care to apply the upper and lower end wall textures to the correct texture slots (upper and lower textures, respectively, but on opposite sides of the same line). If you accidentally apply either of these textures to one of the line's main textures, you can expect Medusa when the WAD is played.

To finish the lift, apply textures to the essentials at the eastern edge of the lift sector. There are three texture slots to deal with here. WADED will already be indicating two of them—those caused by differing floor and ceiling heights between the lift sector and the sector to its east. The third is a latent lower essential of which WADED is unaware: the face that will be exposed when the lift descends. I'll let you chose suitable textures for these faces yourself. Finally, don't forget to check that the lower unpegged flags of all lines are clear, as appropriate.

FINISHING THE CORRIDOR TO THE LIFT

Before you can try out your new addition, you need to finish the approach to it by setting appropriate triggers and tags for the two new impact-activated doors. If you're working with DOOM or DOOM II, you should use PIPE4 on the upper textures, with different X- and Y-offsets applied so that the bullet holes aren't always in the same place on every door. Readers working with Heretic should use the BANNER5 texture, applying a Y-offset only if one is necessary to make the texture sit correctly in the space.

Don't forget to set the Secret on Map flags for each of these door faces too, to prevent the map from betraying their presence. You can leave the default drawing textures on the through-door side walls.

IMPROVING THE CORNER: MAKING A BLOOD POOL (DOOM/DOOM II)

If you're working with DOOM (or DOOM II), you might like to try a modification of the hazardous area of this corridor just outside the original impact-activated door by putting the BLOOD1 texture on the corner sector's floor, as some warning of the harmful effect of standing in this sector. Next, add some explanation of the presence of blood here by splitting this sector's eastern wall so that it has a small section somewhere that's 32 pixels length. Put BLODRIP1 on this small section of wall. This texture has a blood-splashed lower edge and will need its neighbors to be set to the matching PIPE1 so it doesn't look odd.

This change creates a further problem, though. You now have a single blood-splashed wall that even in the lower lighting conditions of this sector will look a little odd surrounded by clean walls. Some adjacent textures need to be changed to match. These currently carry a hint to the player on how to proceed further, though, by the presence of their bullet holes. It would be nice to be able to preserve this hint.

The wall that is really the impact-activated door presents no problem—it uses both upper and lower textures. Its lower texture can be changed to PIPE1, with a Y-offset of –16 to move the pattern's lower edge down to the floor of the blood pool. PIPE4 can be left on the upper, as these two textures will meet with a correct match. The lower texture between the corner sector and the corridor to the south can be changed in a similar manner.

That just leaves the northern wall. There is a problem here because DOOM does not offer a texture that has both a blood-splashed lower edge and bullet holes. It seems as though this visual clue may have to be sacrificed. Rather than do this, though, why not treat this wall in the same way as the western edge of the pool? If you turned the northern wall into a door, you could use its upper and lower textures to hold the two different patterns needed to satisfy the various visual requirements.

To do this, draw a new sector to the north of the corner as shown in Figure 16.6. Only a single sector is needed: it will act as both door and room. For now, just make the room—don't bother setting up the door trigger; that will be taken care of later.

Figure 16.6.
A new sector to the north of the "improved" blood pool.

The new sector's floor and ceiling heights should be set at –96 (32 units above the floor of the blood pool). Set the lighting level to 96, and use FLOOR4_1 as the floor and ceiling texture. The walls can be whatever you fancy. Use PIPE1 on the essential lower texture beneath the face of the new door, applying an offset of –32 to compensate for the raised floor of the new door-room. Put PIPE4 back on this line's upper. Don't forget to remove the damaging special characteristic that the new sector will have inherited from its neighbor.

AMENDMENT TO THE CORNER LAVA POOL (HERETIC ONLY)

If you're working with Heretic, the area discussed in the previous section doesn't need any improvement, as it was developed into a nicely hazardous lava pool several sorties previously. To keep the series of WADs in step, however (and because it will provide a useful hiding place later), I recommend that you do add the new room to the north of this pool, as indicated in Figure 16.6. Use REDWALL for its walls, setting floor and ceiling to –96, with FLOOR09 on both. You should also take care to remove any damaging sector special inherited from the neighboring sector. Use REDWALL on both the upper and lower essentials of the line facing into the lava pool—no Y-offsets are necessary. Don't worry about a trigger to open this room; you'll set that up in a later sortie.

ANOTHER LIFT

Finally, before trying out the WAD, add another lift to make it easier to get back from the large open arena at the end of the new passageways. Mark off a small portion of the arena where it adjoins the thin sector to its south, as shown in Figure 16.7 (near the mouse cursor).

Figure 16.7.
Lines for another lift.

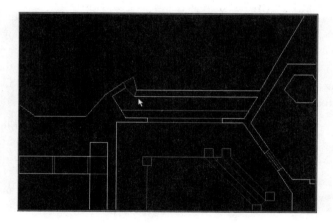

The new sector should be given the same settings as the area adjoining it to the south, so use Make Sector in the new sector before applying it in the large open arena. Then flip one of its northern lines around so that its right side faces into the arena sector to the north. Give this line a special attribute of 62 (SR Lift) and tag it to the new small lift sector. Deal with all of its essentials.

Before saving it as WAD18.WAD and trying it out, you might also like to make it a little easier to test this WAD by moving the Player 1 Start position nearer to the area of interest. You should find that you can do a circular trip out from the platform room, through all your new sectors, and finally arrive back through the platform room's northern window. You may find you have some essential textures to fix along the way, but everything should work fine.

HERETIC The differing sector heights used in the Heretic version of the WADs being constructed in this series of sorties prevents the player from reentering the platform room via the northern window, since the sill height is too great. Remember that this height was set in Sortie 12 (Chapter 12, "Putting Sectors to Work") after careful experimentation with the behavior of the monsters located hereabouts. The best way of permitting the player back in through this window is probably to make Inhilicon's Wings of Wrath available to the player who makes it to the arena—which may also make the lift up from the arena unnecessary also?

OTHER MOVERS

Apart from doors and lifts, DOOM provides several additional triggers for activating simple floor and ceiling movements. These actions come into the general category of *movers*.

SIMPLE MOVERS

All movers operate between their current height and some target height. Most are designed to act in one direction only, either up or down, in a single, once-only movement. The movement itself will be accompanied by a grating sound that continues until the movement finishes. Players (or monsters) trapped by these movers in gaps too small for them will stall the movement while they remain in the sector. The sound of the action will continue, however, and the movement will go on to completion as soon as the cause of the obstruction leaves the sector.

The trapping sector itself will not prevent players or monsters caught in it from moving, although its motion relative to adjacent sectors may, of course, make it impossible for them to leave. Trapping players in this way is not a good design feature because it requires the game to be aborted—never a popular move.

SIMPLE FLOOR MOVERS

Table 16.4 gives details of all of DOOM's simple floor-moving actions. Although there are many different varieties, not all types are available in all activation categories, and it can require some careful planning of your relative sector changes to make effective use of what is available. Unless otherwise indicated in the table, all floor movers operate at about half the speed of a lift.

Table 16.4. Simple floor movers.

Action	Activation Category				
	W1	WR	S1	SR	G1
Absolute Movers					
Raise floor by 24 units	58	92	-	-	-
Raise floor by 512 units (lift speed)	-	-	140*	-	-
Raise floor to match next higher floor	119*	128*	18	69	-
Turbo version of the preceding	130*	129*	131*	132*	-
Raise floor by shortest lower texture	30	96	-	-	-
Relative Movers					
Move floor up to lowest local ceiling	5	91	101	64	24
Move floor down to lowest adjacent floor	38	82	23	60	-
Move floor down to highest adjacent floor	19	83	102	45	-
Move floor down to 8 units above highest adjacent floor (turbo)	36	98	71	70	-

Actions marked * are available only in DOOM v1.666 and later (and not in Heretic).

ABSOLUTE MOVERS

Absolute movers will move in only one direction to the finishing height. Note that those that move up by a constant amount do so per activation and will move even if doing so takes the sector's floor above its own ceiling. It is probably wise to prevent this from happening by somehow limiting the number of times that players can access the trigger.

The actions that move a floor to its next higher adjacent sector will act cumulatively. The floor will move up to successively higher levels on each activation until there are no more higher neighboring floors.

USE OF SHORTEST LOWER TEXTURE

The actions that raise floors by the amount of the shortest lower texture determine how far to move by inspecting the textures used on the sidedefs facing out from the active sector. The game engine looks at the height of the patterns in use on the lower texture slots of all of these sidedefs and moves the sector by the height of the smallest short texture it finds there. If there are no textures of less than 128-pixel height in use on these lower slots, then the sector moves 72 pixels instead. (No, I don't know why.)

NOTE: Remember that a short texture is any texture fewer than 128 pixels tall.

Note that the distance to move is determined from the height of the texture itself, not the space it is occupying, and is therefore independent of relative sector elevations. This action is designed to provide steps that rise out of the floor. The short lower texture usually provides the pattern for a riser. Bear in mind that raising the sector to a height where more than one vertical tiling of the short texture is required to render the space it occupies will cause the Pink Bug effect. A short texture could, however, be used on a face that will never be visible to act as a control of how far the sector will rise on each activation. Once again, this action can drive the floor above a sector's own ceiling if allowed to repeat too many times.

RELATIVE MOVERS

Relative movers take their target positions from adjacent sectors. These may be above or below the sector's current floor level. The game engine has specific expectations of the direction in which each particular action will move the floor. These are indicated in Table 16.4. If the target position lies in the direction opposite to that which is expected, the movement will still occur, but it will be instantaneous and (virtually) silent. If these actions occur out of the players' sight, this limitation may not matter to you.

MOVING CEILINGS

In comparison to moving floors, there are surprisingly few actions that create simple moving ceilings. Table 16.5 gives the list of what is available. These actions differ from doors in their speed (they are much slower) and their accompanying sound, which is the standard grating noise associated with movers.

Table 16.5. Simple ceiling movers.

Action	Activation Category			
	W1	WR	S1	SR
Move ceiling up to highest adjacent ceiling	40	-	-	-
Lower ceiling to floor	-	-	41	43
Lower ceiling to 8 above floor	44	72	49*	-
*Line-type 49 lost this function in v1.666 of DOOM; see Table 16.8.				

The first of these actions (40) behaves as a relative mover. If the highest adjacent ceiling is below the target sector's ceiling, then the ceiling will come down instantly.

Again, as with simple floor movers, the presence of players or monsters in the active sector can prevent the action from completing until the sector is vacated. This does no harm to the player or monsters.

The next section examines moving ceilings and floors that *do* harm anything caught between them. Before that though, the next WAD sortie leads you through adding some simple movers to your WAD.

WAD SORTIE 19: SOME SIMPLE MOVERS

NOTE: This sortie builds on the WAD produced in the previous one. If you did not produce that WAD, you should use WAD18.WAD (DOOM), D2WAD18.WAD (DOOM II), or H1WAD18.WAD (Heretic) from the CD-ROM as your starting point. [As usual, Heretic variations are detailed in brackets.]

In this sortie, you will develop the area beyond the lift and add some simple movers. Before that though, there are a couple of movers to add to the platform room.

A WAY INTO THE SOUTHERN COURTYARD

So far, whenever you have wanted to examine additions to the southern courtyard, you have had to lower the floor of the window sector in the editor before playing the WAD. Let us create a switch to do this during play. This switch will be positioned in the secret room that was made a couple of sorties ago off the southwest stairway, just outside the platform room.

The modifications needed to make this change are straightforward. Start by putting a SW1BROWN texture on one wall of the secret room. (I suggest putting it somewhere on a short wall in one of the shadowy wings, where it may go unnoticed.)

Heretic users will need to use the SW1OFF texture rather than SW1BROWN for the switch. You may need to partner it with sections of METL2.

Take whatever steps are necessary to center a single instance of the switch texture horizontally on your chosen wall. Set the special attribute of the line carrying the switch texture to 102 (S1 Floor: move down to highest adjacent) and tag the line to the platform room's southern window sector.

Note that the secret room's height is somewhat small for the switch texture to look good here; the image of the switch will be very low if the default alignment is used. Changing that alignment will spoil the match of the other component of this texture, though, and will draw more attention to it. The best solution here is to reduce the floor level of this wing of the room, so take it down to –32. Put a suitable texture on the essential lower texture this produces and the changes in the secret room are complete.

Don't forget to check that the tagged window sector's floor is set at 56 [64 in Heretic] units—otherwise this switch will have no work to do! You should check that the lower texture of the wall under the window is pegged so that it appears to open correctly. However, because the player is unlikely to make it back in time to see this action occur, and because the lower texture is unpegged to provide better texture alignment, I suggest you leave it as it is.

MODIFYING THE NORTHERN WINDOW

You also need to modify the platform room's northern window by making it start closed and arrange for the player to trigger its opening. It would be nice to have the ceiling rise from the window sector's floor position, but the only actions that achieve this are door actions—which would be inappropriate—and a ceiling mover that ends at the height of the highest adjacent ceiling.

The ceiling mover could be used, but it would be tedious to set up. Because this mover takes the ceiling to the *highest* adjacent sector, using it would require the closed window sector to be isolated from both the outdoor sector and the room sector. This would require splitting the existing window sector into three long thin areas: a new window sector down the middle, with the remains of the original window sector on each side of it, cutting it off from the sectors with high ceilings and providing the desired target ceiling height. Furthermore, the presence of the window would be suggested by the remaining recess visible from inside the room; although this could be disguised with the use of suitable textures, it would still be less than satisfactory.

A simpler solution is to use a moving floor, starting at the current window sector's ceiling level. This solution will still require splitting the existing window sector to provide the final floor height, but it will need to be split into only two sectors, not three.

Using a fairly high ZOOM factor, divide the current opening into the platform room down its long center line to turn it into two long thin sectors, as shown in Figure 16.8. Use Make Sector on the southern new sector first. Set its lighting level and ceiling and floor textures to match the original sector's. Set its floor and ceiling levels to match the outer window sector's ceiling height.

Figure 16.8.
Modification of the platform room's northern window.

Put STONE3 [GRSTNPB] on the appropriate lower texture of the new line. You may need some offsets applied to the through-wall textures to keep the bricks looking right here.

Finally, choose a line to act as a trigger to open the window. (I suggest the line of the second step up to the platform, so that the window opens as the player climbs the steps.) Tag the chosen line to the new sector, using a special attribute of 19 (W1 Floor: down to highest adjacent).

You might like to try out these modifications before continuing with the development beyond the lift.

DEVELOPING THE LOWER AREA OF THE WAD

Figure 16.9 shows how the corridor area beyond the lift can be developed. You might like to try working on this area, using the description that follows.

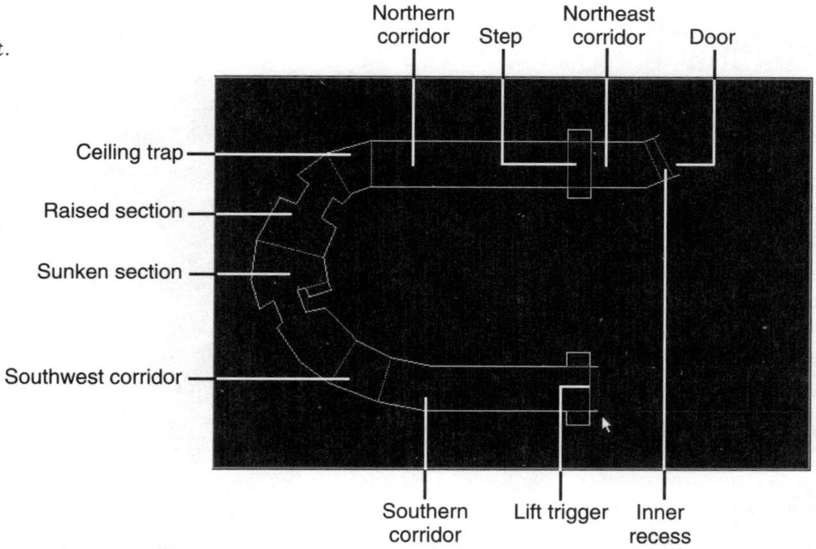

Figure 16.9.
Sectors beyond the lift.

The area beyond the lift (the lift is indicated by the mouse cursor in Figure 16.9) has been broken up into a number of sectors to provide variations in floor and ceiling height, a puzzle (or two), and alcoves for switches.

Starting at the lift and working around the room, the new areas are as follows:

- Lift trigger sector
- Long southern corridor (with switch alcoves)
- Southwest corner section
- A sunken section of corridor (with another switch alcove)
- A raised section of corridor
- Northwest corner section (ceiling trap)
- Long northern corridor
- A small step (with switch alcoves)
- Short northeastern corridor section
- Door recess
- Door

The location of these areas is marked in Figure 16.9. There is also another door recess between the door and the large outer arena, but that will be left as it is for now and will not be discussed further in this sortie.

Before setting up any of these areas, it might be helpful for you to know something about how they will function.

THE CORRIDOR

Overall, the corridor provides a long, curving connection between the bottom of the lift and the outer arena, as you have already seen. The intention now is to develop that area into something more than simply a long tube from one place to another. Its curving form will be used to limit the distance that players can see ahead; variations in floor height will be introduced to make the player unsure as to whether the area is leading them further down in level or back up. (This, combined with the curving nature of the corridor, is a good way of disorienting even those players with good spatial sense, and disorienting players is a good way of making them nervous!)

Sudden and erratic changes in corridor width, combined with the general shift in direction, will also be used, partly to add to the disorienting nature of the corridor, but also to provide nooks and crannies in which to hide various things and to keep the player distracted.

THE PUZZLE

One section of the corridor—termed the *sunken* section throughout this description—will be set with its floor much lower than the next section along. It will be set so low, in fact, that further progress will be barred until the player finds a way to raise this floor. A floor mover will be used here, of course, activated from a suitable switch.

THE TRAP

The arena beyond this corridor area will, in due course, contain a heavy concentration of enemies. It will start sealed off from the corridor by a door. After opening this door, and seeing what is beyond, players may wish to retreat back into the corridor for a time! The benefit to be gained from this maneuver will be limited here by two aspects of the current development. First, the door will be made to stay open, so any monsters spotting the player will be free to follow him down the corridor. Second, a ceiling trap will be sprung to close the corridor against retreat. The player will not be forced into springing this trap, though—merely encouraged. There will be two switches at the door end of the corridor: One will open the door, the other will spring the trap. The first time this area is played, it's a fairly safe bet that the ceiling will be lowered.

ADDITIONAL SWITCHES

This area will also be used to provide the switch that opens the additional room off the blood (or lava) pool added in the previous sortie. The implementation shown in Figure 16.9 also provides another switch alcove for later use.

MAKING THE CHANGES

The development of this lower area requires the existing walls to be broken into quite a few new sections and the long corridor divided into appropriate sectors. The exact forms and shapes of these is not important, although there are a number of aspects of the development that will work better visually if certain sizes are used.

First, the various alcoves all use textures that are 64 pixels wide. These will sit best if the alcoves are made exactly 64 units wide. Secondly, the ceiling trap uses MARBFAC_ textures in various locations: on the outside wall of its sector and on the face closing off the long northern corridor after the trap has been sprung. These textures are 128 pixels wide and, again, will look best if used on correctly sized lines. (The Heretic WAD uses different textures but their sizes are the same.)

Table 16.6 gives the sector settings for each of the areas in this development, working along the corridor from the bottom of the lift toward the arena door. Also given in this table is a column of Y-offset values. These are the vertical texture alignment values that are required to maintain the correct alignment of lines facing into the sector that use GSTONE1 (or a derivative) anywhere on them.

The Heretic version of the WAD uses the GRNBLOK_ family of textures instead of the GSTONE_ ones, but the settings are mostly the same. Figures in brackets in Table 16.6 indicate where Heretic settings vary from those required for DOOM and DOOM II.

This texture is used almost exclusively on this area's walls. All the GSTONE_ textures need careful alignment (the vertical brick spacing is not constant for these textures) so the walls don't look odd from sector to sector—especially with as many variations as this area has. When you set up this area, you should check the table to see whether a Y-offset is specified. If it is, this offset should be applied everywhere that a GSTONE (or GRNBLOK) texture faces into the sector (which means most of the lines, I'm afraid).

Table 16.6. Sector settings in the corridor beyond the lift.

Area	Lighting	Ceiling	Floor	Y-Offset
Thin sector beyond lift	144	−216	−320	24
Long southern corridor	144	−216	−320	24
Alcoves off the above	128	−248 [−224]	−320	0
Southwest corner section	144	−216	−336	24
Sunken corridor section	144	−192	−336	0
Alcove off sunken corridor	144	−224	−312	−32
Raised corridor section	144	−192	−288	0

continues

Table 16.6. continued

Area	Lighting	Ceiling	Floor	Y-Offset
Northwest corner (ceiling trap)	208 [224]	−160	−288	—
Northern corridor section	144	−160	−288	16
Step (by alcoves)	144	−160	−272	16
Alcoves off first step	112	−176	−272	0
Short northeast corridor	144	−128	−264	−16
Door recess	144	−128	−256	−16
Door	255	−256	−256	—

DEM1_5 [FLOOR19] is used on all floors and ceilings.

Additional set-up details for each sector are given in the same order in the following section.

LONG SOUTH CORRIDOR WITH SWITCH ALCOVES

In the DOOM and DOOM II versions of the WAD, each of the switch alcoves just beyond the lift use SW1HOT as the texture for their rear walls, with the lower unpegged flags set. Their side walls also have this flag set. The one on the northern side of the corridor is tagged to the secret room next to the blood pool above the lift, with a special attribute of 103 (S1 Door: open). The other alcove currently provides no switching action. The lines between the corridor and these alcoves should have GSTONE1 (unpegged) on their upper essentials, with the Y-offset appropriate for the sector into which they face. (See Table 16.6.)

HERETIC Owing to Heretic's paucity of switch textures, these alcoves will use the same technique used in an earlier sortie for a switch alcove: the METL2 texture is used on each alcove's rear wall, with a wall torch placed at the back of the alcove. This change requires a higher ceiling than used in the DOOM version of the WAD, as indicated in Table 16.6. GRNBLOK1 is used on the upper essentials over these alcoves.

SOUTHWEST CORNER SECTION

This sector has a lower essential where it borders the previous corridor section to its east; NUKE24 [METL1] is used here. GSTONE1 [GRNBLOK1] is used on the essential upper texture, with its upper unpegged flag set and an appropriate Y-offset.

SUNKEN CORRIDOR SECTION

Embellishments have been added to the sunken area of the corridor by adding protruding wall sections. The faces of these narrow areas carry the GSTSATYR [GRNBLOK3] texture for variation. This effect will look best if the texture is centered in its wall space; use the formula (length of texture – length of wall) ÷ 2 to calculate what X-offset to apply. Don't make the corridor too narrow, here, will you?

GSTONE1 [GRNBLOK1] is used on the lower essential where this sector adjoins the next sector to its north, with the lower unpegged flag set. The switch to move this sector and allow further progress down the corridor is tucked away in an alcove around the back of the protruding section of the eastern wall. The line separating this alcove from the sunken area has GSTONE1 [GRNBLOK1] on its upper and lower essentials, both unpegged. Figure 16.10 shows a view of this part of the corridor, in DOOM, illustrating the blockage caused by the sunken floor—the alcove switch is just visible at the right edge of the figure.

Figure 16.10.
*A view from the sunken section
of the corridor.*

ALCOVE OFF SUNKEN SECTOR

In DOOM and DOOM II, this alcove uses SW1GSTON on its rear wall, with its lower unpegged flag set. This line is tagged to the sunken sector with a special attribute of 18 (S1 Floor: up to next higher) to provide the switch action. The floor of the alcove sector itself provides the new level, 24 units up from the sunken sector's current setting—enough to make the remaining step up to the next sector feasible. Only the side walls require the Y-offset from the table.

This alcove should be built the same way as the two previously described switch alcoves—use the METL2 texture and a Wall Torch.

RAISED CORRIDOR SECTION

Wall protrusions have been added to the raised section of the corridor too. These use GSTLION [GRNBLOK3] textures on their faces (centered as before). Again, don't make the gap between them so small that players cannot pass through.

CORNER SECTION (CEILING TRAP)

The corner sector will act as the ceiling trap described earlier. The textures used give some warning of this trap; the side wall on the outside of the bend uses MARBFAC3 [SKULLSB1]—as already noted, this line will need to be the right length to carry it. Additionally, the lighting level in this sector will be elevated compared to surrounding sectors. The short wall section opposite the marble face will look as though it is the source of illumination. To produce the right effect, this inner wall section needs some special treatment. It should be parallel to the outer wall and also divided into three parts, with the outer sections each about 12 units long and having SUPPORT3 [WOODWL] on them. Between them, the middle section carries SKULWALL [STNGLS1] with an X-offset to keep the texture central in the gap. This will produce an effective border on each side of the central (bright) texture.

 Readers using DOOM II will need to find a replacement for the SKULWALL texture; something like SLOPPY2 would do.

MARBLE3 [GRNBLOK4] is used on the upper essential between this sector and its neighbor to the southwest; a Y-offset of 32 is used to make the detail along the top of this texture visible.

The change this sector will undergo as the ceiling trap is activated produces some latent essential textures and generates some pegging requirements. The eastern face of the sector should have MARBFACE [DOORSTON] on its outward facing upper, and the southwestern face uses GSTONE1 [GRNBLOK1]. All the side wall lines of this sector have their lower unpegged flags set to prevent them moving when the ceiling comes down.

REMAINING CORRIDOR SECTIONS

The sections of the corridor leading east from the ceiling trap corner have little of note in them. NUKE24 [METL1] is used on all essential lower textures here, with GSTONE1 [GRNBLOK1] on any uppers. Upper textures are generally unpegged and need the Y-offset appropriate to their sector.

SWITCH ALCOVES

The pair of switch alcoves by the bottom step out of the long corridor use SW1GSTON [METL2] on their rear walls. These textures have their lower unpegged flags set, as do all of the alcoves' side walls, which use the ubiquitous GSTONE1 [GRNBLOK1]. The northernmost alcove has its rear wall tagged to the corner section of the corridor, with a special attribute of 41 (S1 Ceiling: move down to floor)—it is here that the ceiling trap is activated. The MARBLE3 [DOORSTON] texture is used as the upper essential over this alcove, with its upper unpegged flag set, as a visual warning (not that many players will notice it!).

 Once again, in Heretic this pair of switch alcoves should be built by using the METL2 texture and Wall Torches. In addition to the upper unpegged flag being set, the DOORSTON texture over the northern alcove will also require a Y-offset of –60 to align the skulls of that texture in the wallspace.

The southern alcove is tagged to the door sector at the eastern end of this corridor, with a special attribute of 103 (S1 Door: open). This opens the door, allowing the player into the arena—or allowing whatever is out there into the corridor!

THE DOOR TO THE ARENA

Finally, the door sector at the end of this corridor uses BIGDOOR7 [DOORWOOD] on both faces and DOORTRAK [WOODWL] on its side walls, with the lower unpegged flag set, as is usual for doors.

ADDITIONAL DECORATIONS (HERETIC)

The Heretic version of the WAD will benefit from a little extra ornamentation in the form of Serpent and Skull Torches placed at intervals along the corridor and in various corners, with maybe a Demon-Brazier here and there, too. This will distract the player from immediately noticing the Wall Torches in the alcoves and associating them with switch actions. Figure 16.11 shows the effect these produce.

Figure 16.11.
A view of the completed lower corridor in Heretic.

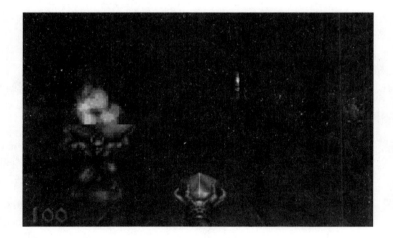

TRYING THE MODIFICATIONS

That completes the modifications to the corridor beyond the lift. If you have made these changes, you might like to try the WAD out and see how well it works. (It is available on the CD-ROM as WAD19.WAD (DOOM), D2WAD19.WAD (DOOM II), and H1WAD19.WAD (Heretic).) You may discover that, as it stands, the WAD has several nasty traps for the player—some of which were not intended and need rectification.

A WORD ABOUT TRAPS

No one doubts the need for traps in a WAD. They add a mental challenge to the game, making players keep an eye open for things other than the obvious and giving them something more than an exercise in grabbing the goodies and shooting the monsters. However, it is easy to have traps backfire on you as the designer and turn what seemed a nice idea at the time into a major irritation that detracts from play rather than contributes to it.

Consider, for example, the ceiling trap that has just been added to the WAD. Its main aim is to cut off the line of retreat down the corridor, forcing the player to face whatever is out in the arena once the next door is opened. In this sense, this trap works well; however, it has some unfortunate side effects.

First, it makes it necessary for the player to find another way out of the arena, since this exit is closed. Now, you made another way out earlier: the lift up to the window of the platform room. This works fine—if the window was previously opened! If not, the player is trapped here for good.

Second, it is just possible for a fast player to make it back under the closing ceiling. Any players doing this gain nothing, however, for the ceiling will still close and will now deny them access to the arena (and whatever it contains). The game will need to be restarted before the arena can be entered—an annoyance, to say the least.

The important lesson to learn here is that traps need to be examined carefully for all possible ramifications. Remember that not everyone plays in the same way; what may seem to you a logical way of proceeding through a WAD may never occur to other players. As a designer, you need to foresee every action your players might try and consider all possible sequences in which these actions will be carried out.

KEEPING TRAPS UNDER CONTROL

The key to the successful management of traps is to plan around the WAD as a whole, not around the traps you fancy using. Do not be seduced by neat traps and tricks. Consider rather what constraints you want to put on the players, and use traps to bring these about.

Remember, too, that traps limit a player's options. You should use them only to force players into taking particular paths you want them to go down. If you force them down too rigid a pathway, prescribing their play in too much detail, you prevent players from finding their own solution. The result is bored players.

In planning your areas for particular playing methodologies, always allow for others. Only use traps if you want to close off particular (easy) options. The traps that the WAD developed in the sorties so far have been added with little regard for the playability of the WAD as a whole; they have largely been illustrative of the techniques. This has made the WAD into a bit of a mess.

EXAMINING THE PROBLEM HERE

Look at the details of the current predicament, starting with the window. The intention in having this area closed at the start of the game was to make the opening of the window a surprise for the player climbing towards the platform—just one more thing to worry about while busy dealing with whatever the platform room contains.

If the player decides to pass straight through the platform room and the subsequent corridors down to the arena below, though, that surprise is no longer needed. There is, therefore, nothing to be lost by allowing this window to be opened from its arena side if it's still closed when the player reaches it. You may want to let the player do this manually—locating the switch could be a further puzzle here—or have it happen automatically by using suitably placed trips (on the approach to or exit from the arena lift, for example).

Second, look at the ceiling trap. As already noted, the purpose of this trap is to force the player who trips it to face whatever lies ahead. There is no good reason to have this prevent him from returning along this corridor later, once the arena has been cleared. You might want to provide a switch somewhere in the arena to open this section of corridor again from there, something to bear in mind when that area comes to be developed. More immediately useful, perhaps, would be offering some means of opening it from its other side, just in case a player makes it back there.

REPAIRING THE WAD

You should, therefore, make some minor repairs to your WAD to correct the current glut of traps. Start by adding some mechanism to open the platform room's northern window from the arena side. Then, allow the lower corridor's corner section to be opened from its southwestern side when a player returns here after the ceiling trap has been sprung. A standard manual door action on this section would allow any player back through this blockage but would still have it close again in case the arena monsters hadn't been dealt with!

Save your final, corrected WAD as WAD19A.WAD to stay in step with my WAD numbering.

NOTE: I am aware that the maze section of the WAD still has no exit. This will be dealt with in future sorties—have no fear.

CRUSHERS

The floor and ceiling movements examined so far have all been delayed (or temporarily reversed) by players or monsters who become caught up in their actions. No harm is done to players or monsters when this happens. There are two categories of actions that work very differently: the crushing floors and the crushing ceilings.

CRUSHING FLOORS

Crushing floors operate by moving up to eight units below their sector's ceiling, catching anything in the sector and crushing it. The crushing action does considerable harm to whatever is caught in the action and is usually fatal for players and smaller monsters. Barrels (or Pop-pods) caught in the action will explode, adding their quota of damage to anything nearby.

A floor crusher's motion continues to completion even when things are caught in it; anything caught is quickly pinned to the ceiling. Monsters not killed are unable to move or fight. The floor travels at standard mover speed, so players will need to shift rapidly to escape the pinning action.

 NOTE: The F_SKY1 ceiling "texture" is as fatal as any other here!

Other sector actions can be applied after this action is finished, although if anything remains trapped and alive in the crusher, stopping the action, the sector will not be available to take part in any further floor or ceiling movements until the obstruction is removed (which usually means the player killing it).

Table 16.7 gives the special line codes to set up crushing floors.

Table 16.7. Special line codes for setting up crushing floors.

Action	Activation Category			
	W1	WR	S1	SR
Crushing floor	56	94	55	65

CRUSHING CEILINGS

Crushing ceilings operate somewhat differently from the crushing floors. Whereas the floors move once, from their starting position to just below the ceiling, the crushing ceilings, once activated, continue to operate, cycling between their starting height and eight units above their sector's floor. They become what is termed a *perpetual mover*. The next section examines perpetual movers in detail.

PERPETUAL MOVERS

Most of the actions initiated by lines' special attributes operate for a finite time only. Once they terminate, the actions are deemed to be over and the affected sectors are free to participate in further actions. Perpetual mover actions do not function like this; their actions never terminate.

PERPETUAL ACTIONS

It is important to realize that it is not the movement initiated by these actions that is perpetual, but the action itself. This means that the game engine regards these actions as ongoing for the rest of the game, even if the movement has been stopped. Perpetual movers are, therefore, never free to participate in any other sector-changing action (except adjustments to the lighting levels, which always occur whether or not other activities are taking place).

The action is judged as ongoing because the motions these special lines trigger are cyclic in nature, without logical termination. Additional special line-types stop the motions of perpetual movers, but they only *pause* the action. Any further triggering of this action will cause the mover to continue in its original cycle of movement, starting up again from where it was paused.

Perpetually moving platforms do, of course, consume processing power, and they contribute to the count of surfaces in motion. It is a sensible idea, therefore, to make sure you include lines in your map to suspend their motion as the player moves away from them. If you want to give the player the impression that their motion is indeed continuous, you can always arrange multiple on/off trip-wire arrangements, as were used for the lights in the previous chapter.

PERPETUAL CRUSHERS

The crushing ceilings are all classed as perpetual crushers. They begin their cycle of movement by moving downward from their starting height. This initial height is the uppermost limit of their travel. The lower limit of their travel is eight units above their sector floor.

Crushing ceilings operate at two speeds: fast and slow. The fast crushers move at the same speed as standard lifts and doors; the slow crushers move at the speed of a mover. With one exception, they all make the standard mover sound. The exception is the new crusher introduced in DOOM v1.666, the so-called silent crusher. This fast crusher is silent during its travel. It does makes a clunk sound as it starts to move, though, and at each end of its travel.

The fast crushers continue in their motion regardless of whether anything is caught in them; slow crushers, on the other hand, reduce their speed of descent drastically when something is caught in them, reverting to normal speed as the motion reverses. As both types of crusher hold on to anything caught, inflicting harm for as long as it takes them to move from the object's height to their lower limit of travel and back, slow crushers will do considerably more damage per crush than will fast crushers.

Table 16.8 gives the line-type codes for the crushing ceilings.

Table 16.8. Special line codes for setting up crushing ceilings.

	Activation Category		
Action	W1	WR	S1
Start/resume slow crushing ceiling	25	73	49*
Start/resume fast crushing ceiling	6	77	-
Start/resume slow, silent crushing ceiling	141*	-	-
Pause crushing ceiling	57	74	-
Actions marked * available only in DOOM v1.666 and above.			

As perpetual movers, sectors started as crushers never become free to participate in any subsequent action that might try to affect their floor or ceiling. All the start/resume triggers will operate on these sectors, however, causing the crushing motion to resume, even if they are triggers for a different type of crushing action. The action that resumes is always of the original type.

PERPETUAL LIFTS

The other type of perpetual mover is the continuously operating lift. Once activated, this lift operates by moving its floor continuously up and down from one extreme of its travel to the other, moving at about half the speed of standard lifts. There is a three-second pause as the direction of travel reverses. These lifts make the same sound as ordinary lifts as they start, reverse, and stop their motions.

A perpetual lift gets *both* extremes of its motion from adjacent sectors (or its own starting floor level, if this is beyond either of these extremes). The range over which the lift operates is calculated once, at the point when the perpetual motion is first initiated. From then on, the action operates over this range regardless of whether adjacent sectors' floors subsequently move.

The initial direction of travel is determined by the lift's starting location within its range of motion; the lift always starts by heading away from the closest extreme of travel. If initiated when positioned exactly in the middle, it starts by moving up. If positioned anywhere other than at the lower extreme, motion begins immediately after the action is initiated. If started at its lower extreme, the lift will pause for three seconds (its usual turnaround period) before moving.

Like any perpetual mover, if the action is paused, any retrigger of the action will cause the lift to resume the motion that was underway when it was interrupted, with the lift operating over its full range, as before, no matter what changes may have taken place around it.

Table 16.9 gives the line-type codes for perpetual lifts.

Table 16.9. Special line codes for setting up perpetual lifts.

Action	Activation Category	
	W1	WR
Perpetual lift start/resume	53	87
Perpetual lift pause	54	89

Like standard lifts, these lifts automatically reverse their travel if players or monsters become caught between their floors and its own or adjacent ceilings. This causes no harm to player or monsters.

WAD SORTIE 20: ADDING A CRUSHER

NOTE: This sortie builds on the WAD produced in the previous one. If you did not produce that WAD, you should use WAD19A.WAD (DOOM), D2WAD19A.WAD (DOOM II), or H1WAD19A.WAD (Heretic) from the CD-ROM as your starting point. [Heretic variations are noted in brackets.]

This sortie will concentrate on adding a single crusher.

A SETTING FOR THE CRUSHER

The crusher will be located in a new area south of the southern courtyard, in a corridor linking the secret room with the sniper's den.

New sectors making the connection between the two existing areas will provide the following:

- Another hidden door, shot-activated, giving access from the western hidden room
- A short corridor
- A perpetual crushing ceiling
- A longer corridor
- A further door, admitting to the sniper's den

In addition, a recess will be needed beyond the door just inside the sniper's den. Figure 16.12 shows how these new areas link in.

Figure 16.12.
New lines south of the courtyard.

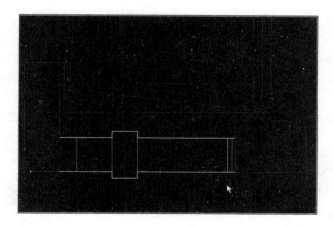

ADDING THE NEW AREA

Both the secret room and the sniper's den may need some extending or reshaping to allow convenient connection of the new areas, which should be drawn using WOOD3 [SNDCHNKS] as the default wall texture.

Table 16.10 gives the settings for the new sectors.

Table 16.10. Settings for the sectors around the crusher [Heretic settings in brackets].

Area	Lighting	Ceiling	Floor
West door	144	0 FLOOR4_1 [FLOOR27]	0 FLAT5 [FLOOR06]
West corridor	144	128 FLOOR4_1 [FLOOR27]	0 FLAT5 [FLOOR06]
Crusher	112	104 FLOOR4_1 [FLOOR27]	0 FLAT5 [FLOOR06]
East corridor	144	128 FLOOR4_1 [FLOOR27]	0 FLAT5 [FLOOR06]
East door	192	16 FLAT5 [FLOOR27]	16 FLAT5 [FLOOR27]
Recess	192	128 FLOOR4_1 [FLOOR27]	16 FLAT1_1 [FLOOR20]
Sniper's den	192	136 FLAT5_5 [FLOOR27]	16 FLAT1_1 [FLOOR20]

Table 16.11 gives details of the lines where WOOD3 [SNDCHNKS] is not used.

Table 16.11. Texture settings for surfaces in the crusher corridor.

Surface	Texture Details
Outer face of western door	BROWN1 [LOOSERCK] with Y-offset of –8
Inner face of western door	BIGDOOR7 [SNDPLAIN]
Faces of crusher	WOOD4 [SANDSQ2]
Sides of crusher	DOORTRAK [WOODWL] with lower unpegged flag set
Crusher recess reveals	SUPPORT3 [WOODWL] with lower unpegged flag set
Inner face of eastern door	WOOD4 [SNDPLAIN] with Y-offset of –48 [0]
Outer face of eastern door	BROWN1 [SNDPLAIN]
Wall over door recess	BROWN1 [SNDPLAIN] with upper unpegged flag set
Inner sides of door recess	BROWN1 [SNDPLAIN] with Y-offset of 8
All walls of sniper's den	BROWN1 [SNDPLAIN]

In addition, make sure that BROWN96 [CSTLRCK] remains on the outer surface of the sniper's wall. It will now be needed on an additional texture slot here and have its upper and lower unpegged flags set to allow for the changes to the sector behind it.

Make the western door an impact-activated door, in the usual way, and make the eastern door capable of being opened from the corridor side only. Have it latch open, once activated.

BUILDING THE CRUSHER

To set up the crusher itself, use the inner surface of the new area's western door to start the motion; this line should be tagged to the crushing sector with a special attribute of 73 (WR Crusher: slow start/resume). Remember that you need to make sure perpetual movers are turned off as players leave this area. Use line-type 74 (WR Crusher: pause) on suitable lines to achieve this. Remember also that you will need to cover both halves of the new area to allow for players leaving by either route. I suggest using the sniper's wall itself, and one of the lines in the southwestern courtyard recess. Any one of these lines that is not currently active will do, if it's not so close to a spacebar-activated trigger that it will stop that trigger from working.

Finally, save this WAD as WAD20.WAD and try out this latest area. Of course, you'll have to get in there first.

EXIT: MOPPING UP AND MOVING ON

In this chapter, you encountered several more types of active sectors: lifts, simple moving floors and ceilings, and crushers. You were shown how each of these operate and how to construct them in your own WADs.

The next chapter contains yet more active sectors and shows you how to manage complex active-sector arrangements.

COMPLEX MOVING SECTORS

In recent chapters, you have encountered the actions that single sectors can undergo when activated by the special lines. In this chapter, you will see how a group of active sectors will operate in concert. You will also be shown how sectors can be made to change their special characteristics, and you will see how some active sectors drag others along with them in their actions.

The WAD developed in earlier WAD sorties will be extended again with further sorties in this chapter. First, the single crushing ceiling added at the end of the previous chapter will acquire some neighbors; together these will act as a chain of crushers through which players will need to time their dash carefully if they are to survive. Additional sorties will add sectors that move and change and some actions that drag lots of sectors along, to provide some of DOOM's most complex multi-sector actions—the donut-eater and self-raising stairs.

ALL TOGETHER NOW

When you were first introduced to remotely activated sectors several chapters ago, you were told it's possible to tag more than one sector to a single trigger. So far, though, you have not seen how these grouped, active sectors behave.

GROUPING ACTIVE SECTORS

When more than one sector is tagged to a single trigger, there are three ways in which the resulting group of sectors may respond to the trigger's activation:

— *By Steve Benner*

- As a united group, with each member of the group changing to the same new setting.
- As a loose assemblage of sectors, with each member largely doing its own thing, but with occasional actions in one sector affecting some of the other members of the group.
- As a set of individual participants in an action, with each unaware of the actions of the others.

Just which of these modes of behavior applies to the group depends on the specific action being triggered. For the majority of actions, the third type of grouping will apply.

ACTING IN UNISON

The only actions that cause groups of sectors to act in unison are those affecting the sectors' lighting levels. If there is more than one sector tagged to a lighting-effect trigger, then all the sectors within the grouping will have their lights brought to the same level. Those actions that refer to adjacent sectors for the new value will get that value from the neighbors of only *one* member—the lowest numbered—of the group. The neighbors of the other members of the group are *not* considered at all. If you are not careful, this can result in some undesired results, with the entire group refusing to change or changing to an unexpected level. Figure 17.1 illustrates how this could come about.

Figure 17.1.

An arrangement of dark and bright sectors.

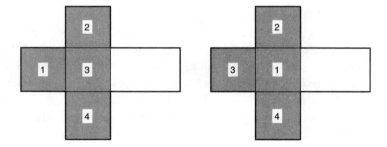

In Figure 17.1, the four shaded sectors are grouped to a single trigger somewhere of type 80 (WR Lights: match brightest adjacent level). These sectors all have the same brightness level, lower than the other sectors in the figure. Note that if these sectors had been created in the order indicated by the numbers in the left half of Figure 17.1, then the group's lowest numbered member (sector 1) has only one neighbor from which to take the new light-level value: sector 3. Because this sector is itself part of the group (and therefore already at that group's brightness level), no visible change will result.

It would require the sectors to be numbered as shown in the right half of Figure 17.1 for any change to occur when the trigger was activated. Only with this ordering of sectors does the lowest numbered member of the group have a neighbor outside the group itself. Note that few editors enable you to control the numbering of your sectors. You usually need to have drawn the sectors in the correct order when laying out the WAD. Bear this in mind, then, when planning areas that will use lighting effects involving grouped sectors.

LOOSE ASSEMBLAGES OF SECTORS

Loose assemblages occur when multiple sectors are in motion as slow crushers. Ordinarily, crushers move independently of each other, moving at a constant speed between each extreme of their travel. Slow crushers, you will recall, slow their motion further when something becomes caught in their downward travel. When several slow crushers are in motion together, the slowing of one can affect the motion of others. DOOM may pass the slowing of the action on to any other crusher also moving downward while the crush occurs. Just whether the slowing effect is transmitted is determined randomly for each separate crush and is completely outside the WAD designer's control.

> **NOTE:** The term "randomly" is used here to mean "unpredictably." DOOM's game engine does not generate or use random events—it merely seems to.

INDEPENDENT ACTIONS

With the exception of the two categories of action just described, tagging more than one sector to a single trigger will not create any significant grouping of participant sectors. Most of the time, what you achieve with such multi-tagged lines is using a single line to initiate the same action in more than one location simultaneously, with each sector responding to the action independently of all others. If any member of the group is not available to participate for some reason, then that particular sector will simply not be activated. This non-participant will not prevent any other sector from joining in the action. Similarly, any sector that has its action cut short for any reason will not affect concurrent activity going on elsewhere.

END POINTS OF INDEPENDENT ACTIONS

It is important to appreciate that the end points of normal independent sector movements are calculated from the conditions pertaining to the point of initiation, without regard for any other changes that may be in progress at the time. By way of illustration, consider three sectors side by side, in a line from west to east, as shown in Figure 17.2.

Imagine first of all (case *i* in Figure 17.2) that the floor heights in these three sectors, in order from west to east, are 64, 24, and 0 units and that the western and central of these sectors are both tagged to a single trigger somewhere of type 82. This trigger brings its target sectors' floors down to their lowest adjacent floor level.

Consider what happens when this line is triggered. At the point of activation, the western sector's lowest adjacent floor is to its east, at 24 units, and the central sector's lowest adjacent floor is also to its east, at 0 units. These are the heights to which these floors will move on the first triggering of this action. You should be able to see that a subsequent triggering of this action will bring the western sector's floor down to 0 with no movement from the central sector. After that, further activation of the line will have no effect.

Now imagine the same arrangement of sectors and trigger but with different starting heights for the floors of 64, 64, and 0. (Case *ii* in Figure 17.2.) On the trigger's first activation, the central sector will descend to the level of its eastern neighbor, as before. The western sector will not move, however, because at the point of activation it has no neighbor at a different height. A second activation of the trigger is needed to make this sector's floor move down to join the neighboring floor at its new level.

Figure 17.2.
Various configurations of grouped moving floors.

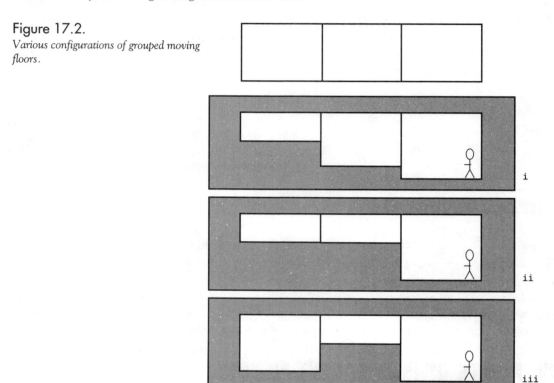

Note this well: It is a common mistake to group sectors like this in the hope that the tagged pair will move in unison to the lower level. They will not. DOOM considers the movement of each member of the group individually.

Finally, consider what happens if the floors start out at heights of 24, 64, and 0, as shown in case *iii*. The first time the line is triggered here, the western sector will move *up* to 64 units—the height of its lowest neighbor at the time of activation. This movement will occur instantaneously. (If you don't remember why, you may wish to review the previous chapter's discussion of movers.) The central sector will move down, at the normal speed, to level 0. Once again, the western sector will move its floor to 0 in the normal manner on the second triggering of the action.

COORDINATING AND SYNCHRONIZING MULTI-SECTOR ACTIONS

It is common to want several sectors to operate together as a single coordinated or synchronized unit, usually in chains of crushers and other perpetual movers. As you have already seen, though, when moving freely, each participating sector in a multi-sector action will take as much or as little time as it needs to finish its own action without regard for the movement of any other sector. The only way to achieve synchronization, therefore, is to use the same travel distance for each component.

Bear in mind, too, that slow crushers and perpetual lifts can be delayed in their action as a result of players and monsters becoming caught up in them. When this occurs to single members of a chain of such movers, it will wreak havoc with any synchronization of motion you had set up.

If you want perpetual movers to remain in phase with each other, you will need to ensure that the range of travel of each participant is the same. With crushers, though, it is often better to make the range of travel different for each component, so that they drift in and out of phase with each other, making it harder for players to time their dash through the entire chain. The next WAD sortie lets you try a crusher chain out for yourself.

> **NOTE:** The following WAD sortie builds on the WAD produced in WAD Sortie 20 of the previous chapter. If you did not accompany me on that sortie but would like to come along on this one, you should use WAD20.WAD (DOOM), D2WAD20.WAD (DOOM II), or H1WAD20.WAD (Heretic) from the CD-ROM as your starting point.

WAD SORTIE 21: BUILDING A CRUSHER CHAIN

In this sortie, you will add two more crushers alongside your existing one to complete the secret area located to the south of the southern courtyard.

AMENDING THE CURRENT CRUSHER ROOM

Figure 17.3 shows the arrangement you are aiming for in the modified crusher corridor.

The new areas are easy to add. You need to split each of the long eastern corridor walls, putting four new vertices where each end of a crusher will appear. By repositioning the inner pair of these vertices, you can reshape the sides of the corridor to provide the required recess. Repeat the operation for each new crusher recess, and finally add the new cross-corridor lines that make the faces of the crusher. You should not need to create any further vertices to add these extra lines.

Figure 17.3.
Lines for the complete crusher chain.

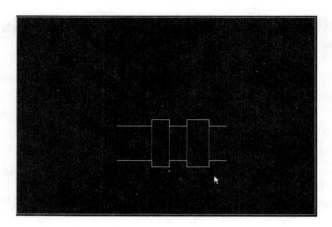

When you have made the rearrangements and drawn the new lines, you can create all the necessary new sectors, matching everything to the existing settings and textures. Connect the two new crushers to the same triggers as the original to have them operate as a group; in WADED, select one of the existing crusher activation lines and then, with this line selected, right click each of the two new crusher sectors in turn. This assigns the same tag number to all three of these sectors, so that they will be affected by all of the same lines. Users of WadAuthor will need to determine the tag number used by the triggers and set the new sectors' tag field accordingly.

Finally, decide on suitable settings for each of the crushing sectors. In addition to their heights, you might like to experiment with the overall size of each crusher, as well as the spacing between them. Save and play a few variants to find the best result. Observe how the slow crushers behave as a group when you become caught in one of them. (You will use God Mode, won't you?)

You could try out the room with faster crushers, too. When you are happy with the arrangement, tidy up the texture alignment and name your final wad WAD21.WAD.

NOTE: Remember, with DOOM v1.666 or later (or DOOM II), you have the so-called silent crusher at your disposal, too.

Figure 17.4 gives a view of the completed crusher room.

Figure 17.4.
The completed crushers.

RINGING THE CHANGES

The next group of sector actions to consider are the *changers*: sectors that change their appearance and behavior as they move.

THE MOVEMENT OF CHANGERS

All movements associated with changer actions affect only the target sectors' floors. In this aspect of their operation, changers behave just like movers. Where they differ is in the alterations their sectors undergo while moving.

THE CHANGES

As well as moving their floors to new locations, changer actions affect their target sectors in two further ways:

- **The sector's floor texture changes:** This provides sectors that can sink into other areas and vanish or rise up out of a large area of one floor texture and acquire a new texture to differentiate them from their surroundings.
- **The sector's special characteristic alters:** All changers alter the special characteristic of the sector they affect. Some reset it to 0, canceling out any special effect that the sector was using. This can turn a sector from a damaging area into a harmless one. Other changers can be made to copy a special characteristic from elsewhere, so that sectors can be turned into harmful ones.

THE ROLE MODEL

The changes wrought by these actions are determined partly by the code of the action and partly through the involvement of an additional sector, known as a *role model*. The function of the role model is to give DOOM a source for the new settings the changing sector will acquire.

The game engine uses two different methods to determine which sector will act in this capacity, depending on which special line-type initiates the action:

- **The trigger method:** Trigger-method changers take the sector on the right side of their action's *trigger line* as the role model for the changing sector.

- **The first-neighbor (or numeric) method:** Changers in this category use a more complicated method of locating a sector to act as a role model. They examine the changing sector itself to find its lowest numbered two-sided linedef, taking the sector on the other side of this—the changing sector's first neighbor—as the role model.

NOTE: A sector's first neighbor is usually the one it gained earliest in the creation of the WAD.

When triggered, a changer action will use whichever role-model method is appropriate to its own operation to locate the role-model sector. This sector's floor texture and, if applicable, its special characteristic are then copied to the tagged target sector as that sector moves.

Figure 17.5 shows these two types of changer in action on the same sector (S). At the top is shown the layout of sectors and floor patterns before activating any changers. The numbers on the lines of the tagged sector show the order in which these lines were drawn (in the WAD as a whole). The lower parts of the figure show the following:

i. The effect of a trigger-method changer, activated from line T. Notice how the floor texture from the sector on the right side of line T has been transferred to the active sector;

ii. The effect of a first-neighbor changer, activated from the same line as the preceding. Notice how the new floor texture for the active sector has been acquired from its first neighbor.

You could get different results here, of course, by drawing the lines of the tagged sector in a different order.

These actions may seem complicated to use, particularly those involving first-neighbor method changers. Fortunately, in practice, they are rarely so. Areas that will use such changers do need to be planned carefully in advance, however.

Figure 17.5.
The effects of the different role-model methods.

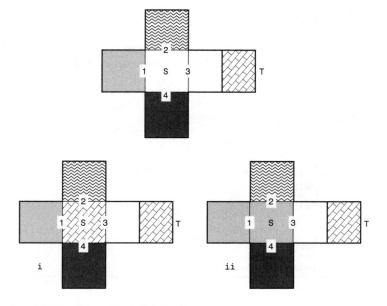

CHANGES TO THE SPECIAL CHARACTERISTIC

Not all values of a sector's special characteristic can be transferred to a changing sector. Table 17.1 indicates which ones can.

Table 17.1. Special sector characteristics that can be transferred by appropriate changer actions.

Code	Characteristic
4	High damage and blink; only the damaging aspect of this characteristic transfers
5	Medium damage
7	Low damage
9	Award secret credit
11	High damage and end level
16	High damage

If the role model has other values from those shown in Table 17.1, the moving sector acquires a special characteristic of 0.

CHANGER EFFECTS

Table 17.2 gives details of the available changer actions. Note that the majority are of the simpler, trigger-model variety and that not all these actions will transfer a special characteristic from the role model, even if it is of the permitted variety.

Table 17.2. Available changer codes.

Floor Movement	Role-Model Type	Special Transferred	Activation Category				
			W1	WR	S1	SR	G1
Up to next higher	Trigger	0	22	95	20	68	47
Up 24 units	Trigger	0	-	-	15	66	-
Up 24 units	Trigger	X	59	93	-	-	-
Up 32 units	Trigger	0	-	-	14	67	-
Down to lowest adjacent	1st Neighbor	X	37	84	-	-	-

NOTE: Changers that do not transfer the special characteristic from the role-model sector do still change the special characteristic of their target sector. They set it to 0, nullifying any damaging characteristic the sector may have had.

Movements occur in an identical manner to the corresponding mover actions.

WAD SORTIE 22: USING CHANGERS

NOTE: This sortie builds on the WAD produced in the previous one. If you did not produce that WAD, you should use WAD21.WAD (DOOM), D2WAD21.WAD (DOOM II), or H1WAD21.WAD (Heretic) from the CD-ROM as your starting point. [Readers working with Heretic will find appropriate variations given in brackets.]

This WAD sortie will show you how to use each of the two categories of sector changers. First of all, though, it will show you how you can use a changer as a straightforward mover, thereby expanding the range of available floor-moving actions at your disposal.

ALTERATIONS BEYOND THE LIFT

In my opinion, the sunken area of corridor in the green stone passageway is a little less than perfect in its operation. The small section of corridor immediately before the sunken section is fine while the sunken section is at its starting height, but it looks odd after the sunken section has been raised. It seems strange to have a lower section of corridor between the newly raised sunken section and the corridor leading back to the lift.

The special line used to raise the sunken corridor currently invokes an action that raises the floor to the next higher adjacent floor—in this case, the floor of the alcove housing the switch. The immediately adjacent corridor section—the one that is upsetting me so—is currently used to isolate the sunken sector from the long corridor, which is only 16 units above the starting height of the sunken floor. If this were the sunken floor's next higher floor, it would not rise enough to enable the player to go on.

It would be nice to have the ability to raise the sunken floor by a fixed 24 units, rather than having to worry about arranging neighbors at suitable heights. However, the actions to do this are available only as walk-through triggers, and I'd like to keep this operation on a switch. Line-type 15 (S1 Change floor: trigger-model; up 24) will work, though; it provides a sector change in addition to the movement, but that will not matter here. Indeed, it won't even be noticed. This action uses the trigger-method to find the role model; because the sector that houses the trigger for the sunken sector currently has the same floor-texture setting, no visible change will ensue.

All that is needed here, then, is to change the special attribute of the appropriate trigger line (at the back of the small alcove off the sunken sector) to the value 15. After this modification, the offending short section of corridor can be raised 16 units to –320, so that its floor is no longer lower than the long corridor's. Put NUKE24 [METL1] on the new texture surface that this exposes.

STARTING THE ARENA DEVELOPMENT

The remainder of this sortie will concentrate on developing the open arena at the northern end of the WAD. Figure 17.6 shows how this area needs to be divided up. As you can see, there are a lot of additions here, even though this is but the first stage of the arena's development. This sortie concentrates mainly on the arena's western half. Each new area is detailed shortly.

Figure 17.6.
The first additions to the arena.

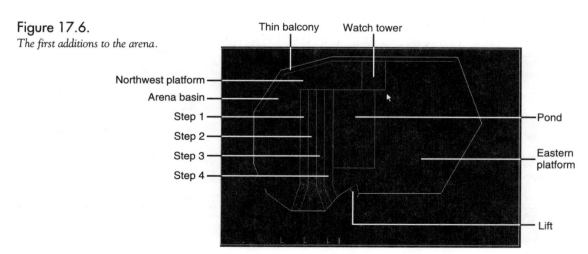

ADDING THE NEW AREAS

Start the modifications in WADED by using MULTI in LINES mode to change all the major wall textures of this arena to WOOD5 [TRISTON2 in Heretic]. Leave the faces of the lift in the southern wall as they are for now, though, so that it remains easy to find. Then enter Draw mode, select STARTAN1 [SNDCHNKS] as the default drawing texture, and add the lines for a thin balcony running inside the northern rim of the arena.

 Readers using DOOM II should substitute BRICK5 for STARTAN1 throughout this sortie. (It's a much nicer texture, anyway!)

Next, draw the square area that meets this northern balcony midway across the arena. (In Figure 17.6, the cursor is pointing to this area's southeastern corner). This sector will eventually form a lookout tower. Follow these lines with those marking out the platform area to the west of the tower. Then mark off the area at the extreme west of the arena; this will form the low arena basin. East from this are four wide steps, formed from lines running between the northwestern platform and the southern wall of the arena; add these next. The steps will lead up from the arena basin, the top step adjoining the large eastern platform and a rectangular pond. The player's progress from the west will be halted here through the use of an excessive step height.

Make all these sectors before going on. The settings are given in Table 17.3.

Table 17.3. Sector settings for the first additions to the arena [Heretic settings in brackets].

Area	Lighting	Ceiling	Floor
Balcony	255	216 F_SKY1	152 FLAT1_2 [FLOOR04]
Watch tower	255	216 F_SKY1	104 FLOOR4_8 [FLOOR04]
Northwest platform	255	216 F_SKY1	−144 FLAT1_2 [FLOOR04]
Southwestern door recess (from earlier sortie)	255	−128 FLOOR4_8 [FLOOR19]	−264 FLAT1_2 [FLAT506]
Arena basin	255	216 F_SKY1	−264 FLAT1_2 [FLAT506]
First step	255	216 F_SKY1	−240 FLAT1_2 [FLAT506]
Second step	255	216 F_SKY1	−216 FLAT1_2 [FLAT506]
Third step	255	216 F_SKY1	−192 FLAT1_2 [FLAT506]
Fourth step	255	216 F_SKY1	−168 FLAT1_2 [FLAT506]
Eastern platform	255	216 F_SKY1	−128 FLOOR0_1 [FLOOR04]
Pond	255	216 F_SKY1	−200 NUKAGE1 [FLTSLUD1]

The northern balcony walls need WOOD5 [TRISTON2] on their essential textures to make them look like part of the main arena walls. Use WOOD5 [CTYSTCI4] on the watchtower's essentials textures, BROWN144 [SNDCHNKS] on the risers of the steps, and STARTAN1 [SNDCHNKS] on all remaining essential textures.

The southwest door's sectors should be changed a little from their earlier settings. Use GSTONE1 [GRNBLOK1] on the side walls of the door sector itself as well as the outer door recess. Apply a Y-offset of –16 to these wall sections. WOOD5 [TRISTON2] is required on the upper over the outer door recess, with its upper unpegged flag set. Put GSTONE1 [GRNBLOK1] on the lower essential below the outer face of the door.

DIVIDING UP THE POND

The nukage-slime pond in the middle of the arena is the area that will use the changers. The next step, then, is to add the additional sectors within the pond. Figure 17.7 shows the arena again, with the new areas required for the pond.

Figure 17.7.
Details within the arena pond.

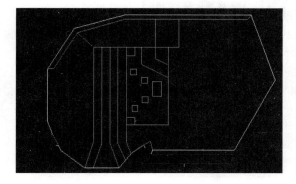

Start by adding the five shapes that are entirely contained within the pond. These are four square stepping-stones, 64 units or so in size, that lead out across the pond to a slightly larger rectangular island. The stepping-stones will seem to offer a way across the pond but will, in fact, sink below the surface when the player steps on them. (I'll explain just how this works in a moment.)

Make the sectors for these areas, using Make Sector on the pond sector itself again, afterwards. Then put line-type 37 (W1 Changer: down to lowest adjacent) on each line of each stepping-stone (but not the larger island—this will be somewhere for the player to stop and think). As you set its special attribute, tag each of these lines to its own stepping-stone sector; this way, the sector will sink regardless of which of its boundary lines the player crosses.

The floor settings for each island sector should be FLOOR0_1 [FLOOR05] at a level of –176. Set the brightness and ceiling values to match all the other sectors in this area.

HOW THE STEPPING-STONES WORK

The stepping-stones will operate as follows. Special line-type 37 is a walk-through trigger, which invokes a first-neighbor model changer. This changer lowers a sector's floor to the height of the lowest adjacent floor, at the same time transferring a floor texture and special characteristic from an adjacent sector.

All the stepping-stone sectors are completely surrounded by the main sector of the slime pond. No matter which of their lines was drawn first, therefore, their first-neighbor will be this pond sector. The main nukage-slime pond will thus act as the role-model sector, so that each stepping-stone will acquire the pond's texture as well as its damaging special characteristic as it moves.

Of course, being the only adjacent sector means that the main pond will also provide the new floor setting for the tagged sector. The net effect, therefore, is that as a player steps onto one of the stepping-stones, it will sink to the level of the pond floor. This, combined with its texture change, will cause it to vanish into the slime.

LETTING THE PLAYER OUT

The main pond sector is currently 32 pixels below the arena's top step, its lowest adjacent sector, so there is no escape from the pond. With such a clear invitation to enter it, players will find it annoying in the extreme if they are caught there until they die. An escape route is needed here.

Escape shouldn't be too easy, though, so make it possible only from the very corners. Add the two corner sectors, as in Figure 17.7, shown previously, using a floor height of –192 and a texture of FLOOR0_1 [FLOOR04]. Once again, use STARTAN1 [SNDCHNKS] as the essential texture for all these new areas.

ADDING THE FINAL AREA

Finally, add another changer to offer an eventual means of progress across the pond to the eastern platform (and then the lift). An angled causeway across the northeastern corner of the pond will provide this. It will lead from the northwestern platform (accessible from the top step), across the pond to the eastern part of the arena. Initially, though, it will seem to be part of the pond.

If you are using WadAuthor, the addition of this new sector is straightforward: Simply create it as a new six-sided polygonal sector within the pond sector, joining two of its sides with (specially split) sections of two sides of the pond.

In WADED, things a just a little more complicated. Start by adding the lines for this new sector and use Make Sector on it as usual but do *not* use Make Sector to repair the pond sector. Notice how adding the new causeway sector has cut away a small corner of the original pond sector, isolating it from the main body of this sector. Ordinarily, this would be turned into a new sector and given identical settings to the original. There is no need to do that, though—DOOM does not insist that all parts of a sector be contiguous, merely closed.

There is nothing to prevent the small northeastern corner from belonging to the main pond sector. If you move the mouse cursor over the main pond sector with Make Sector active, you will see that the original lines of this corner piece do indeed light up at the same time. (Moving the pointer into the main pond sector in WadAuthor will show that this editor is happy to create a split, or *disjunct*, sector itself.)

Unfortunately, it is beyond the capabilities of Make Sector to find these isolated lines and gather them back into the fold, so you will need to do this manually using Sec Define. Before choosing Sec Define, though, you will need to enter LINES mode and make each of the new lines of the causeway sector two-sided by setting their two-sided flag. Then you can return to Draw mode, select Sec Define, right click somewhere in the pond sector (even in the isolated northeastern corner), then click each of the four new lines of the causeway sector in turn to add their left sides to the now disjunct pond sector.

Having done this, you should give the new causeway sector the same settings as the pond sector, making sure that both have a special characteristic of 7 (Low Damage).

CREATING THE CHANGER

Finally, make the new angled piece into a suitable changer. Choose a convenient line to use as the trigger for this action—it doesn't matter which at the moment, because it is only a temporary arrangement to test the mechanism—and put a switch texture on it so that you will be able to find it easily when you play the WAD. Assign a special attribute of 20 (S1 Changer: Raise to next higher) to this line, tagging it to the causeway.

Special line-type 20 provides a switch-activated trigger-model changer that will raise the floor of the tagged sector to the next higher floor level. The floor texture of the sector on the right side of the trigger line is transferred to the sector that is moved. The special characteristic is not transferred, but any existing special value is reset to 0.

The angled sector's next higher neighbor is the western platform sector. This sector, therefore, provides the new height for the moving sector's floor, just 16 units below the large eastern platform floor—close enough to allow the player onto it.

The causeway's new floor texture will be whatever is on the right side of the switch-line that triggered the change. You can confirm this by putting a distinctive floor texture next to the switch and observing that the angled sector acquires it when it is activated. If you were to place the switch action on one of the pond's enclosing lines that has its right side facing into the pond, then the causeway's floor texture would not change as it rose. (I don't recommend you do this; I'm merely pointing out possibilities!)

The harmful effect of the angled sector's special characteristic is nullified by the changer (whatever the role model is), making it safe for the player to walk across the new causeway.

The movement of the angled sector will generate some essential textures. Fix these by applying STARTAN1 [SNDCHNKS] to them.

TRYING OUT THE ADDITIONS

You are now ready to save the WAD (as WAD22.WAD) and try it out. Try running over the stepping-stones to the island and back. It's all fine as long as you keep moving, isn't it? Activate the causeway and confirm that it acquires the correct texture and becomes safe to walk over.

Did you manage to remember all the essential textures? Figure 17.8 shows a view of the completed pond in my WAD22.WAD.

Figure 17.8.
Pond, causeway, and stepping-stones.

DRAGGING OTHERS ALONG

The final group of remote-controlled actions that produce moving sectors are the *entrainers*. These actions affect more than just their target sector.

DOOM'S DONUT

The first of the entrainers is, in effect, an extended changer. It works in a more complicated way than those described earlier, though. It is known as the *donut-eater* or *equalizer*. This action entrains an additional sector in its effect, as follows.

DOOM begins the action by inspecting all the lines that make up the boundary of the tagged sector to find the linedef with the lowest number (the first-drawn line of this sector). If this line is single-sided, nothing further happens.

If the line is two-sided, however, DOOM inspects it to see which way it faces. If the right side faces *into* the tagged sector, then this sector's floor is moved to the level of the floor on the other side of the line. Motion downward occurs at standard mover speed; movement upward occurs instantaneously. Any special characteristic of the sector *adjacent* to the tagged sector is removed. The action then ends.

If, on the other hand, the first-drawn line's right side faces *away* from the tagged sector, then this neighboring sector is taken to be a "donut" sector. It is this sector that will be consumed (its settings, that is, not its extent; this will be explained shortly). Note that this sector doesn't actually need to be donut shaped—it can be any shape at all—but it usually will be, with the tagged sector acting as the "hole" at the center. Figure 17.9 shows the usual arrangement: a central sector with a donut sector around it. The first-drawn line of the central sector is shown with its right-side tick.

Figure 17.9.
A DOOM donut.

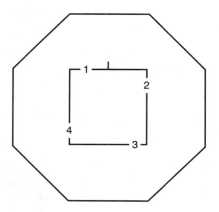

FINDING A ROLE MODEL

Having found a sector to be the donut, DOOM will proceed with the action by examining *this* sector to determine its lowest numbered linedef, *excluding* any that are shared with the original tagged sector. The sector on the other side of this further line (whichever way it faces) becomes a role model for the actions that follow.

USING THE ROLE MODEL

At this point, DOOM has all the information it needs to consume its donut (you're relieved, I'll bet!) It does this by transferring the floor texture of the role model to the floor of the donut sector (*not* the original tagged sector, note), setting the donut's special characteristic to 0 at the same time.

Figure 17.10 illustrates this with a simple example: The central tagged sector acts as the hole to its surrounding sector's donut. This in turn supplies a role model through its lowest numbered linedef. The donut gains the role model's floor texture.

Figure 17.10.
Consuming the donut.

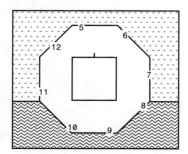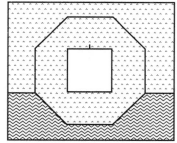

EQUALIZING THE FLOORS

At the same time the floor texture and special characteristic are being changed, the game engine moves the donut sector's floor up to match the role model's. The original tagged sector's floor moves down to the same height. In common with all movers, any motion in the opposite direction to the one expected will occur instantaneously.

CAUTION: If the engine does not find a role model for this action (because there is no sector on the other side of the donut's first-drawn line), all hell will break loose! Well, not quite, but random settings are taken for the role model—with suitably unpredictable consequences.

THE DONUT CONSUMED

The net result of this action is that both the tagged sector and its surrounding donut end up at the same floor height as the role-model sector, usually the sector that surrounds the donut itself. The donut's floor texture is changed and any harmful effect it had is nullified in the process. You have no doubt seen many instances of this effect in use. It is commonly used to place goodies out of reach on a central platform, surrounded by a damaging sector, which is consumed when the appropriate switch is pressed.

Figures 17.11 and 17.12 show the result of a well-known donut-eater's action.

Figure 17.11.
Before…

Figure 17.12.
…and after.

CREATING A DONUT-EATER

The easiest way to ensure that donut-eaters work correctly is to draw the whole structure at one time. These are the steps in the process:

1. Start by drawing the complete inner donut-hole. The first line you draw must have its right side facing out from this sector, so draw this sector in an counterclockwise manner. (If using a sector-based editor, you will probably need to select and flip all this sector's lines.)

2. Draw the outer donut sector next, starting with the line that will border the sector acting as a role model.

3. Avoid splitting any of these lines in future edits. Most editors will assign new (that is, more recent) line numbers to the new lines created—this can mess up DOOM's identification of both the donut sector and its role model.

4. Locate a suitable switch line for the action; the donut-eater is available only as a single-activation, spacebar-operated action. Tag this line to the inner donut hole sector. Set the line's special attribute to the value 9.

FAULTY DONUTS

There are a number of problems that can occur to stop the donut from operating correctly. The causes of common faults are listed in Table 17.4.

Table 17.4. Common donut faults and their causes.

Symptom	Cause
The switch refuses to operate.	The switch is not tagged to any sector, or the lowest-numbered line of the tagged sector is single-sided.
Only the tagged sector moves (although the donut sector loses its damaging effect).	The lowest-numbered line of the tagged sector has its right side facing in.
The donut operates but finishes at the wrong level and/or with the wrong floor texture.	The lowest-numbered line of the donut sector borders the wrong sector.

SELF-RAISING STAIRS

DOOM's other entraining action is the self-raising staircase. This action drags further sectors along with it, using an entraining method similar to the donut-eater's.

FINDING THE STEPS

The action starts, as always, with the tagged sector. This sector will become the first step of a new staircase. DOOM then looks for a two-sided line that has its right side facing into the tagged sector. If there are more than one of these, the one with the lowest number is taken. The sector on the other side of this line becomes the second step of the staircase.

This process is repeated until one of the following conditions occurs:

- No two-sided line has a right side facing into the current sector.
- A sector is met with a different floor texture.
- A sector is encountered that is already part of this action.
- A sector is encountered that is currently locked out of floor height changes.

The sectors selected by this process all take part in the action that follows.

Figure 17.13 illustrates this entrainment process in operation. In each case, the sector marked with the solid circle is the initial tagged sector. The upper part of the figure shows a simple arrangement of sectors. The action's selection of sectors is brought to a halt by the lack of further inward-facing right sides after four sectors.

Figure 17.13.

The entraining of sectors in a rising-staircase action.

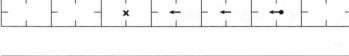

The lower portion of the figure shows a more complicated arrangement of sectors. The entrainment process has been made easier to follow here by carefully manipulating the way the lines face. Each participating sector has only one two-sided line with its right side facing into it—an arrangement that I recommend you adopt when building these structures yourself. Notice how the selection of sectors in the lower example is terminated when a sector that is already part of the action is revisited.

MOVING THE STEPS

The tagged sector's floor provides the reference height from which all of the other sectors' final floor heights are calculated. This first sector will be raised by a standard step-height—8 or 16 units, depending on the type of staircase in use—from its starting position. Each sector in the sequence after this will finish one step-height above the previous.

Once the sectors for the entire staircase have been located, and their final floor heights are determined, DOOM starts the floors of all these sectors moving simultaneously, accompanied by appropriate sound effects. The result is a block of sectors moving together, with each successive sector stopping as its floor reaches its allotted height. Any sectors of the staircase that start out above their finishing height are instantly moved to their new height.

Self-raising stairs will operate as crushing floors, doing harm to anything caught in the closing gap between their floor and ceiling. They are also capable of driving their floors up through their ceilings; it is probably not a good idea to let them.

Hexen has expanded the capabilities of self-raising staircases greatly and also completely changed the method by which sectors are entrained into the structure. Details are given in "Hexen's Special Codes," a chapter on the CD-ROM.

BUILDING SELF-RAISING STAIRWAYS

From their description, self-raising stairs might sound complex to build. In reality, they are generally quite easy. The main steps (sorry!) involved are as follows:

1. Draw the sectors for the staircase, starting with the bottom step and working up.

2. Again starting from the bottom step, select each sector in turn, making sure that the line bordering the next step in the sequence has its right side facing into the selected sector. Make sure that all other two-sided lines have their right sides facing out from the sector. This saves you from having to worry about the numbering of lines, which is often beyond your control, anyway. Leave single-sided lines with their right sides facing in, of course.

3. Make sure that all the two-sided lines of the last sector in the sequence have their right sides facing into *other* sectors.

4. Make sure that all the sectors of the staircase have the same floor texture.

5. Decide on a suitable activation line for the staircase. You can use either a switch or a trigger. Set this line's special attribute to the appropriate value. (See Table 17.5.)

6. Tag the trigger line to the first sector to move: the bottom step of the staircase.

7. Apply textures to all the latent essential lowers—the risers that will be exposed as the action operates.

If you find that your staircase fails to operate correctly, check the direction of all of its lines—and watch out for those floor-texture changes!

SUMMARY OF LINE-TYPES FOR ENTRAINERS

Table 17.5 gives the codes for the donut-eater and self-raising stair actions.

Table 17.5. Entrainer codes.

Action	Activation Category			
	W1	WR	S1	SR
Donut eater	-	-	9	-
8-unit, slow stairs	8	-	7	-
16-unit, turbo stairs	100* [106] -		127* [107] -	

*Turbo stairs require DOOM v1.666 and above, or Heretic (using the codes given in brackets).

WAD SORTIE 23: USING ENTRAINERS

NOTE: This sortie builds on the WAD produced in the previous one. If you did not produce that WAD, you should use WAD22.WAD (DOOM), D2WAD22.WAD (DOOM II), or H1WAD22.WAD (Heretic) from the CD-ROM as your starting point. [Heretic variations in this sortie are noted in brackets.]

This sortie will develop the eastern end of the outdoor crescent-shaped area that lies beyond your blue-keyed door. It adds a new room with a donut-eater; a self-raising stairway will also provide another connection to the embryonic maze area.

ADDING THE DONUT EATER

Figure 17.14 shows the general location of a new room at the eastern edge of your WAD.

Figure 17.14.
The general location of the new room.

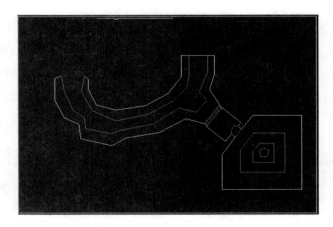

The new room will be entered through a short passageway, connected by a new keyed door, to an alcove area towards the eastern end of the crescent. Figure 17.15 shows all the new lines needed for this area, with the cursor arrow pointing to the southeastern corner of the sector that will become the donut.

ADDING THE NEW DOOR AND ENTRANCE PASSAGE

Start this new development by building a red-keyed door [green-keyed, in Heretic] off the crescent. It should have outer and inner recesses, as usual. Make the door as close to 256 units wide as you can for best alignment of the door texture. Don't forget to apply suitable textures to the side-walls of the recess (or use suitable door-gizmos) to tell the player that the door needs a key. Use BIGDOOR2 [DOORWOOD] on the door itself.

Next draw the two sectors of the entrance passageway. Use GRAYVINE [MOSSRCK1] on the walls of the larger of these; DOORBLU2 [WATRWAL1] on the short walls of the small one beyond.

Figure 17.15.

Detailed lines for the environs of the donut-eater.

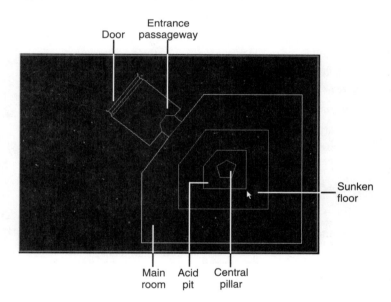

THE DONUT ROOM

Next, draw all the new lines for the main room and donut. Use GRAY7 [SQPEB2] as the default line-drawing texture for the outer walls of the room. When you come to make sectors here in WADED, start with the central one and work outward.

Table 17.6 gives the settings for all the new sectors in this area. Note that some of the sectors use special characteristics, mostly of a damaging variety.

Table 17.6. Sector settings in the new area [Heretic settings in brackets].

Area	Lighting	Ceiling		Floor	
Outer door recess	176	128	FLOOR7_1 [FLOOR27]	0	FLAT1_2 [FLOOR03]
Door	128	0	FLOOR7_1 [FLOOR27]	0	FLOOR7_1 [FLOOR27]
Inner door recess	224	128	FLOOR7_1 [FLOOR19]	–8	FLOOR7_1 [FLOOR19]
Outer passageway	128	120	FLAT22 [FLOOR05]	–16	FLOOR7_1 [FLOOR05]
Connecting sector	240 [192]	88	FWATER1 [FLTWAWA1]	–40	FWATER2 [FLTWAWA1]
Main area of room	176	168	FWATER3 [FLOOR09]	–24	FLAT14 [FLOOR09]
Sunken floor area	192	168	FWATER3 [FLOOR09]	–48	FLAT14 [FLOOR09]
Donut pit	192	168	FWATER3 [FLOOR09]	–80	FWATER1 [FLTWAWA1]
Central pillar	240	168	FWATER3 [FLOOR09]	32	FLOOR1_1 [FLOOR09]

Area	Special	
Inner door recess	13	Synchronized blink off
Connecting sector	4	High damage with blink on [16 High damage]
Donut pit	16	High damage

Use GRAY1 [CTYSTCI4] on all essential textures, except for the lowers of the central pillar. In DOOM, the central pillar should have mostly GRAY1 on its lowers, with GRAYDANG on just a couple of them. (DOOM II does not have GRAYDANG, so stay with GRAY1 there.) Use SQPEB2 in Heretic.

Finally, split one of the room's outer walls by adding another vertex 64 units from one of the corners, and put the SW1GRAY [SW1OFF] texture on the new short length of wall. (Don't worry about the alignment and vertical repetition of this texture—it is only a temporary arrangement.) Set the special attribute of this line to 9 (S1: Donut) and tag it to the central pillar sector. Make sure that all the lines of the central pillar face out— this saves the worry about which is the lowest numbered—and the donut-eater is finished. Simple, in the end, wasn't it?

In Heretic, you might like to embellish the area a little by adding an Environmental waterfall sound close to the small sector that acts as an entrance to the donut room. A sprinkling of Teleport glitter looks good here, too.

Before adding the stairs, you might want to save the WAD (as WAD23.WAD) and try out the donut-eater. Don't forget to place an appropriate key close to the new door so that you can easily get into the new area.

SELF-RAISING STAIRS

The area with a self-raising staircase will also be off the crescent-shaped courtyard. It will connect this courtyard to the embryonic maze area. Figure 17.16 shows what I am planning here.

Figure 17.16.
Connection from the crescent to the maze.

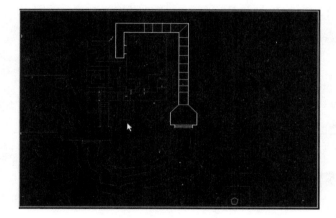

ADDING A NEW DOOR

Start by adding another red-keyed [green-keyed] door off the currently closed northeastern end of the crescent, drawn to match the door's blue counterpart at the other end with BIGDOOR2 [DOORWOOD] on the door face and suitable recesses [and gizmos]. You may need to rearrange the end of the crescent a little to get the door 256 units wide and to have it line up properly for a connection beyond it. Figure 17.17 shows a close-up view of the lines for new door, with recesses on each side of it.

Make the new door operate by using a special attribute of 28 (MR: Red [Green] Door: open and close) on the outer side, facing the crescent. The door should be one-way, however, so put no special attribute on its other, inner face. Use the DOORSTOP [METL2] on the side-walls of the inner recess as an indicator that the door doesn't open from this side. Then draw and make the sector beyond the inner recess using STONE2 [SPINE2] as the default texture. Apply the settings in Table 17.7 to the sectors you have so far.

Figure 17.17.
Details for the new door.

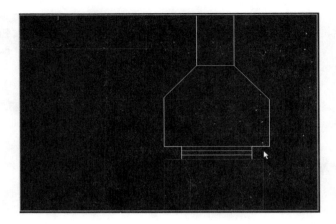

Table 17.7. Sector settings for the end of the crescent.

Area	Lighting	Ceiling		Floor	
Outer door recess	144	144	CEIL3_5 [FLAT516]	0	FLAT1_2 [FLOOR03]
Door	144	0	CEIL3_5 [FLAT516]	0	FLAT5_5 [FLOOR27]
Inner door recess	128	112	FLAT10 [FLAT516]	0	FLAT5_5 [FLOOR27]
Funnel-shaped sector	112	128	FLAT10 [FLAT516]	0	FLAT5_5 [FLOOR27]

CONSTRUCTING THE CORRIDOR AND STAIRS

Figure 17.18 shows the number and arrangement of sectors beyond the funnel-shaped corridor section. They should all be drawn with the STONE2 [SPINE2] wall texture.

Figure 17.18.
Sectors for a corridor with self-raising stairs.

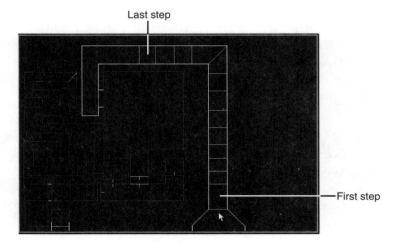

Last step

First step

Make the first of these sectors, setting its lighting level to 96. All its other settings should be the same as the neighboring funnel-shaped sector. This will be the first step of the self-raising stairway

You can now start making the other steps. Note that the number of sectors used here is important, if the fully risen staircase is to end at the correct height. Another twelve sectors will be used, so that the final floor height of the top step will be $13 \times 8 = 104$ units above the current floor height.

Draw and make the next five sectors, taking the ceiling of the last of these up to 160 to increase the available headroom. Then make the additional sectors up to the corner where the ceiling needs to go up again, this time to 192. Make the last four staircase sectors, once again taking the ceiling up on the last of these, this time to 224. Notice how the ceilings here rise steadily to prevent the player from being crushed as the stairs rise. The increment used for the ceiling step is 32 units to ensure that the wall texture (which has a 32-pixel pattern repeat) stays aligned.

Now draw and make the last of the corridor sectors, taking its ceiling up to 256. This sector will not be part of the rising staircase, so its floor needs to be at a suitable height. Set it to 112 to match the floor of the maze area close by. The top step will end its movement just eight units below this, leaving a final step up to the end corridor section.

Now, to make the staircase work, go into LINES mode and select the line marking the entrance into the narrow area of the corridor. (The cursor arrow is pointing to this line in Figure 17.18.) Put a special attribute of 8 (W1 Stairs: 8-unit rising) on here, tagging the line to the first step sector to its north. Check that this line has its right side facing into the sector to its south, otherwise you will find the wrong sector becomes entrained into the raising staircase.

If you now examine all the lines marking the risers for the remaining steps of the staircase, you should find that they already have their right sides facing into the step below them. This is what you want. Put STEP3 [SPINE2] on the lower-right texture slots of all these risers—they are latent essentials, remember. The line connecting the last step with the end section of the corridor needs to be flipped so that its right side faces away from the last moving step. This will end the entrainment of sectors into the rising stair. Put STONE2 [SPINE2] on the essentials of this line. Locate the lines where you changed the ceiling height, and put STONE2 [SPINE2] on the upper essentials here, too.

That completes the construction of the staircase, but you need to finish off the area before you can try it out.

FINISHING THE CORRIDOR

Make a short sector to connect your new corridor to the right half of the maze area. You will find that as you do this, the new sector inherits a tag. Don't worry about this; this is what you want it to do. This sector's lighting level will now follow the right-half of the maze's. Set the new sector's ceiling to 112 (the same as its floor) and put a special attribute of 1 (MR Door: open and close) on the corridor face of this new door. Remember that this line-type does not need to be tagged to a sector, but it does need the line to face the correct way.

Put texture STONE3 [SPINE1] on its upper texture facing the corridor (with a Y-offset of 16. You want a slight change of texture, not a lurch in the alignment). Use a texture on the other side of the door to match its neighbors, so that it is not noticeable from the maze. Do not provide any method of opening the door from this side, however, because I do not want the player to be able to leave the maze by this route. Complete the door by setting its side walls' lower unpegged flags, again using Y-offsets of 16.

MAKING AN EXIT FROM THE MAZE

This finishes the additions to the map. Given the right keys, a player can now pass through the crescent section, up the new stairs, and into the maze—only to become trapped, of course, at the top of the marble stairs.

Now arrange for players entering the maze by this route to trigger the removal of the impediment of the one-way stairs. You will recall that the trap on this staircase was created by placing two ceilings at special heights, so you need something to trigger the raising of these ceilings. Line-type 40 provides a walk-through action that raises a ceiling to the height of its highest adjacent ceiling. Position two of these triggers as you feel appropriate on suitable risers of the new back stairs into the maze.

 NOTE: Special line-type 40 is incorrectly categorized in WADED. It can be found in the FLOORS-3 list!

You will need to order these triggers correctly and space them out enough to allow one ceiling to have moved fully before the other is triggered. And you will have to tag them to the correct marble staircase sectors, of course. Don't forget, too, that this will create a latent essential texture somewhere on the marble stairs. Use MARBLE1 [DOORSTON] on this.

When you've done this, you can save the WAD (as WAD23A.WAD) and try it out.

SUGGESTED FURTHER MODIFICATIONS

There are a number of additional modifications that spring to mind for the areas you have just added.

MAKING THE STAIRS LESS OBVIOUS

You can make the presence of the corridor containing the rising stairs less obvious by raising the floor of the first step to 48. (You'll have an essential texture to deal with if you do this.) Use a special line-type of 23 (S1 Floor: lower to next adjacent) on one of the short walls next to the door (the cursor arrow points to this in Figure 17.17, shown previously), with a suitable texture (SW1SATYR [SPINE1], perhaps?) and tagged to the newly raised sector.

A LITTLE JOKE?

To balance the areas around the door, you may wish to use the same (or another) switch texture on the other wall at the side of the door. There isn't much for this switch to do, but line-type 41 (S1 Ceiling: move to floor) tagged to the inner door-recess would convince the player that there really was no way out here. If you add this modification in DOOM or DOOM II, change the upper texture over the recess to BROWN144 to match better with SW1SATYR. There are a couple of lower unpegged flags to set, too. In addition, you will need to tag this sector to another trigger to raise it again, in case the player ever comes back through the door from the other side! You can do that by adding a trigger of type 40 (W1 Ceiling: raise to highest adjacent) to one of the stair risers.

TIDYING THE STAIRS

Raising the ceilings to remove the one-way stair trap leaves the stairway's walls a little messy in the DOOM versions of the WAD. You might want to try tidying them up. Anything you do will be a compromise, however—it's just about impossible to have this perfect for all contingencies here.

The sample WAD23B.WAD (D2WAD23B.WAD for DOOM II, H1WAD23B.AD for Heretic) on the accompanying CD-ROM has these modifications added.

EXIT: MOPPING UP AND MOVING ON

In this chapter, you learned about the most complex of DOOM's active sectors. You have learned how sectors behave when they are asked to move together; you have learned about role model emulation by sectors that move and change; and you have seen and used crusher chains, moving and changing platforms, donut-eaters, and self-raising stairs in your own WAD. In fact, you have now seen all the active line-types that DOOM provides for sector movement and change.

The next chapter, "Let's Get the Hell Out of Here!," will present the few remaining special line-types—those that act on the player, rather than on elements of the map. Its WAD sorties will have you adding some of the final components of the DOOM world to your almost completed WAD.

LET'S GET THE HELL OUT OF HERE!

Recent chapters have concentrated on special line attributes that cause changes in targeted sectors. This chapter will look at the remaining special types of lines and also revisit the sector's special characteristic. None of the actions examined in this chapter result in changes to sectors, however; they all act on players, monsters, or both—with one rather odd exception.

The WAD that has been building in preceding chapters will be developed further in this chapter in three more sorties. The first of these will finally add an escape route to the embryonic maze area added several sorties ago. The second will add an exit to the WAD as a whole, and the last will sort out the awarding of credits for the discovery of the WAD's secrets.

This chapter starts, though, with a trip through DOOM's teleport, or "transporter."

TELEPORTS

You will already be familiar, no doubt, with the way a DOOM teleport operates: The player steps into it, vanishes, and rematerializes somewhere else. You have probably guessed by now that a teleport's action is caused by yet another special type of line. This is indeed the case. DOOM needs more than just the line, though, to create a functioning teleport.

COMPONENTS OF A TELEPORT

To build a teleport, three things are required:

■ **A teleport trigger line:** This is the line that the player steps over to "enter" the teleport and trigger the transportation action.

— By Steve Benner

- **A destination sector:** This is where the player rematerializes.
- **A landing spot:** This marks the precise location within the destination sector where the rematerialization takes place.

Each of these three items must be in place and properly set up for a teleport to operate, so first look at how each of these three items is provided.

HERETIC Readers familiar with Heretic's teleports might also expect pulsating floor textures and colored glitter to be required. As with most other magic tricks, though, such things are mere trappings, designed to fool the gullible into believing that things are more complicated than they are!

TELEPORT TRIGGERS

Teleport triggers are provided through special line-types. (As the only really active component of a teleport, these lines are often just termed "teleporters.") Table 18.1 gives the codes for the available teleport triggers.

Table 18.1. Codes for teleport triggers.

Action	Activation Category	
	W1	WR
Player/monster teleport	39	97
Monster-only teleport	125*	126*

*Monster-only teleports are available only in DOOM v1.666 and above and not in Heretic.

Hexen As with most other types of active lines, Hexen extends DOOM's teleporter capabilities. Details of the way this variant handles the teleport action are given in "Hexen's Special Codes," a chapter on the CD-ROM.

These triggers act much like any other walk-through trigger line, with the action taking place as it is crossed. The familiar teleport "pads" are simply sectors with all their passable boundaries set up as teleport triggers. When anything steps into the sector, it crosses an active line and is whisked away to the appropriate destination. This arrangement creates the illusion that the pad itself is active.

Unlike other walk-through actions, teleport lines can be triggered from only one side: their right. If you think about it, this makes a lot of sense. It allows a teleport pad to act as the destination from another teleport (a common arrangement) without having one of that pad's own teleport lines transport the player somewhere else as soon as they try to step from it.

To make a teleport pad active on entry and not on exit, all its active lines should be arranged with their right sides facing out from the pad sector.

TELEPORT DESTINATION SECTOR

Like other special lines, each teleport trigger needs be tagged to a sector—in this case, to act as a destination. Each trigger should be tagged to only one sector; a player cannot be sent to multiple destinations simultaneously. If a trigger is tagged to more than one sector, DOOM will take the lowest-numbered one to be the destination.

It is possible, however, to have more than one teleport trigger tagged to the same sector. This allows all a teleport pad's active lines (or several different teleports) to deliver to the same location.

TELEPORT LANDINGS

DOOM needs to know more than just the sector in which rematerialization will occur, though—it needs the precise spot. This is marked by placing a special category of Thing within the destination sector: the teleport landing. Each teleport destination sector must have one of these, or the teleport will not operate.

Teleport landings use the same attributes and flags as all other categories of Thing. The facing-angle attribute is used to determine which way players and monsters will face as they materialize. The skill-level flags can be used to indicate whether individual teleport landings are present (or absent) at particular difficulty settings of the game. DOOM will consider only those present at the game's current skill setting when looking for a particular teleporter's destination. This can be used to vary the precise location (and facing angle) of a teleport landing with skill setting.

If a destination sector has more than one teleport landing, the one with the lowest number (usually the first placed) will be used. If no teleport landing can be located within the destination sector at the game's current skill setting, the teleport remains inactive.

BUILDING A TELEPORT

Here is a summary of the steps involved in building a fully operational teleport:

1. Choose a line or lines to act as the teleport trigger. If you are using a particular area as a teleport pad (and you don't have to, of course) then make sure you use all the passable lines surrounding the pad—unless you want players and/or monsters to be able to walk onto the pad from some directions without teleporting.

2. Flip all the chosen trigger lines so that their right sides face the direction from which you want the line to be triggered. Typically, this will mean that all the passable lines surrounding a teleport pad will have their right sides facing out.

3. Place a teleport landing where you want materialization to occur. Make sure there's enough headroom for players to arrive at this spot. Decide which way you want players and monsters to be facing when they arrive here, and adjust the teleport landing's facing angle to suit.

4. Tag each of the teleporter lines to the sector containing the teleport landing.

These are the *essential* steps in producing a functioning teleport. You can, of course, arrange for more complex teleport pads that have their component triggers tagged to different sectors. Such teleports will then deliver to differing locations, depending on which line is crossed. And, of course, you can add whatever trappings you feel are necessary to make the teleport look like a teleport to the player.

TELEPORT TRAPPINGS

Teleports may be as conspicuous or as invisible as you feel is appropriate in your WAD. It is often a good idea to mark teleport destination points with distinctive patterns, especially in WADs that are designed for multi-player use. This gives players at least some warning of potential tele-frag spots and discourages them from lingering there.

If you want your teleports to *look* like teleports in DOOM, the GATE_ series of flats offers the classic set of ceiling and floor textures used in id Software's own levels. (See Figure 18.1.) There is no special trick to using them. Simply make your teleport pads a standard 64 units square, aligned precisely along grid lines, and place a GATE_ texture on the floor and ceiling.

Figure 18.1.
The GATE series of floor/ceiling textures.

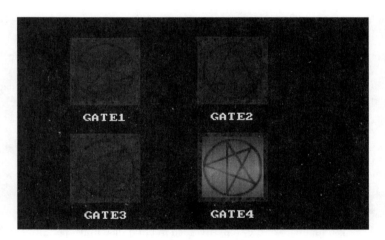

GATE4 tends to be used for teleporter landing pads that aren't active teleports, but there is, of course, no requirement that it be used in this way.

Heretic offers a similar dedicated teleporter pad texture, in this case the animated FLTTELE1 series. It also supplies extra trappings in the form of teleporter glitter: red for standard teleports and blue for teleports that end the level. Place these items as you would any of the game's Things; they are merely decorative. Figure 18.2 shows a typical Heretic teleport.

 Heretic's End-of-level teleporter is not really a teleporter at all, but an exit masquerading as one. It will be covered later in this chapter.

Figure 18.2.
A typical Heretic teleport.

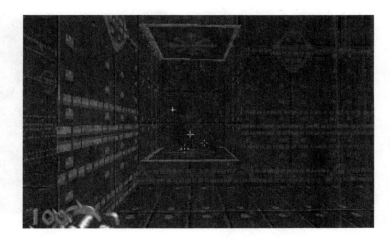

MONSTERS IN TELEPORTS

DOOM v1.666's monster-only teleporters are useful for letting monsters move around a WAD in a way that prevents players from following them. A discussion of using these, and other useful techniques for using teleports as monster-laden traps, appears in the next chapter, "Populating Your Nightmare."

NOTE: The following WAD sortie builds on the WAD produced in the last sortie of the previous chapter. If you did not accompany me on that sortie but would like to come along on this one, you should use WAD23B.WAD (DOOM), D2WAD23B.WAD (DOOM II), or H1WAD23B.WAD (Heretic) from the CD-ROM as your starting point.

WAD SORTIE 24: USING TELEPORTS

Teleports are useful devices for getting players out of sticky situations without requiring a lot of additions to a WAD. To demonstrate this, this sortie shows you how to add a simple way out of the maze. After that, I'll also show you how to use teleporter lines to make life a little trickier for the players.

A STRAIGHTFORWARD TELEPORT

Start by adding a teleport as an exit from the maze for players who have entered via the one-way marble staircase. Decide where you would like this to be. I've put mine at the end of one of the twisting areas in the left part of the maze, as shown in Figure 18.3, but it could be almost anywhere. All it needs is a single 64 × 64-unit grid square.

Figure 18.3.
Location for a teleporter in the maze.

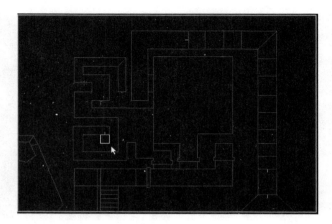

Be careful how you add to the maze in WADED, by the way. It is easy to wreck the special lighting operations here. If you add lines internally across an existing sector, you should incorporate the new lines into it using Sec Define, rather than Make Sector. This will ensure that the sequence of sector numbers isn't changed. (Grouped-sector lighting effects are sensitive to this, remember.)

When you have your new teleport sector properly defined, apply appropriate settings to it—you will need to use a lighting value of 144 to keep the lighting tricks working, remember—with one of the GATE_ textures on the floor and the ceiling. Use whatever wall textures you fancy, wherever they are needed.

 Heretic users should use FLTTELE1 on the floor and ceiling. You might also like to place some Teleport Glitter in the sector, too, to give the player the full Heretic transporter experience!

Next, make sure that all the entrance lines to your new sector have their right sides facing out from it. Put line-type 97 (WR: Teleport) on them all, tagged to a suitable destination sector. This could be anywhere, but I feel it should be somewhere that the player has already visited, so that the teleport is viewed as a means of escape from the stair-trap, not as a way on to new locations. I recommend using the starting sector—the hexagonal room.

Finally, place a Teleport Landing Thing somewhere in the destination sector. Save the WAD as WAD24.WAD, and then give it a whirl!

 NOTE: Teleport landings are termed *teleport destinations* in many editors.

SOME TELEPORT TRICKS

A more elaborate arrangement of teleports can be used to make whatever is located within the donut harder to get. Figure 18.4 shows five new areas around the sides of the donut room.

Figure 18.4.

New areas around the donut room.

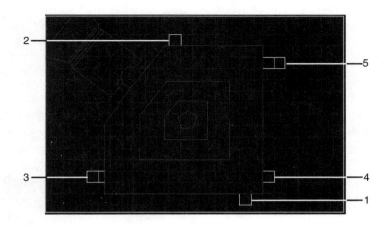

These new areas use an array of teleporters and switches to give the player a little puzzle. This operates as follows:

1. The switch to operate the donut-eater is in plain view on the rear wall of this alcove. This is also the only alcove the player can enter from the floor of the room. All the others are either raised too high or hidden behind doors. The problem is that the entrance line to this alcove is a teleporter line. As players enter, they are immediately transported to Area 2, without any hope of reaching the switch.

2. This alcove has a switch on its rear wall to activate a small sector next to Area 3 as a lift. The player will have to run across the room to catch this lift before it goes back up. The floor heights of areas 2 and 3 are such that the player cannot enter either of them from the main room's floor.

3. This area can be entered only by using the lift activated from Area 2. The alcove contains no switch, but it does have a teleport trigger across its entrance from the lift, which transfers the player to Area 4.

4. This alcove houses another switch, this time to raise the door that has been hiding Area 5 (which is not in view from here!). The player has 5 seconds to find it and get through it before it closes.

5. Behind the secret door raised by the switch in Area 4 is another teleporter. This takes the player (finally!) back to Area 1 and the switch to consume the donut, which the player may have forgotten after all that.

Creating this puzzle is not complicated, merely a little tricky to keep track of. Start by drawing and making each of the new areas. Area 5's two floors should both be at the same height as the main room floor. Set the floor height for the first alcove 24 units higher; all the others need to be even higher so that they cannot be entered directly. Choose the remaining sector settings for yourself. You may wish to consider how many of the teleports you want to have looking like teleports. Make sure you leave enough headroom for players not to become stuck when they materialize.

Use wall textures (with appropriate pegging) for all of the new walls to match well with the room's existing walls. There are a couple of suitable switch textures to choose from in DOOM and DOOM II. Don't forget that the door in front of Area 5 needs to be hidden. Careless texture alignment will give its location away.

Work on each of the switch and teleporter lines, placing appropriate special attributes and tags and making sure that each of the teleporter lines faces the correct way. Be sure to use repeatable actions for each of the switches that require the player to run to finish the next stage of the puzzle. Also, don't forget to disconnect (and hide) the temporary switch for the donut-eater before connecting in the real one.

Finally, place teleport landings in each of the destination sectors. Arrange these so that they face out from the alcoves into the room. This means that the switches will always be behind the player as they materialize. Figure 18.5 shows the location of each of the teleport landings required. Note that the numbers in this figure show which of the areas in Figure 18.4 (shown previously) have trigger lines tagged to the indicated sector.

Figure 18.5.
Teleport destinations and other tagged sectors in the donut room.

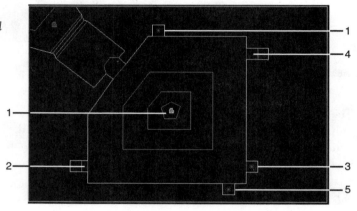

Notice that I've also added a key as the reward for solving the puzzle—a yellow one.

Save the WAD as WAD24A.WAD and see how well you did. Did you solve the puzzle of building it? How well does it play? Make whatever adjustments and changes you feel are necessary before going on. You might like, for instance, to reverse the way that the teleporter line of Area 3 faces. This will enable players to enter the sector without being teleported immediately. They will then probably hunt around in vain for some switch. Only when they give up and decide to leave will they be teleported on.

NOTE: Readers with DOOM v1.666 or later might like to make this room harder by using the turbo lift and door actions.

ENDING THE LEVEL

The final category of special line-types are the exits. These bring about the termination of the level, displaying the appropriate intermission screen with its tally of kills and so on. Besides using special lines, DOOM has another method of ending a level. Before looking at that, though, first examine the way lines are used to signal the exit from a level.

EXIT SWITCHES AND TRIGGERS

There are two mechanisms for ending a level with lines: walk-through exits and switch-activated exits. Naturally, these lines can only be activated once. Table 18.2 gives the codes available for producing exits.

Table 18.2. Exit codes.

Exit Type	Activation Category	
	W1	S1
Standard exit	52	11
Secret exit	124* [105]	51

*The walk-through secret exit code 124 is available only in DOOM v1.666 and later. Heretic uses a different code.

Heretic's walk-through secret exit is generally used in a teleporter-like way in Raven Software's own levels. Don't let this fool you into thinking that this is therefore a teleport line; it is a straightforward level exit.

STANDARD EXITS

Standard exits take the player to the next higher level number (after the intermission screen) except for the last mission of the episode, of course, which ends the episode. Mission 8 is the last of each DOOM and Heretic episode; Level 30 ends DOOM II. If an external patch WAD doesn't have the subsequent map, DOOM will load the original from the IWAD file.

Yet again, things are very different in Hexen; see "Programming the Action," a chapter on the CD-ROM.

SECRET EXITS

Secret exits take the player on to the appropriate secret level (again, after the intermission screen). In DOOM and Heretic, this is always Mission 9 of the current episode. DOOM II allows access to secret levels only from those levels offering such access in the game's original version. Attempts to access secret levels from levels other than these result in the player being returned to MAP01.

All exits from the secret missions are hard-coded to return the player to the same subsequent map as in the original game.

FATAL EXITS

A final way of ending a level is provided with one of the special sector characteristics—11. This setting applies the high rate of damage to reduce the health of a player in the sector. When it falls below 11 percent, the level ends. Most WADs make it impossible to escape such a sector to ensure that the mission does indeed end as a consequence of the player reaching this spot.

Although this action operates as a standard exit, taking the player on to the next mission, it makes more sense to use it as a device to end a complete episode—just as id Software does.

Fatal exits are not available in Raven Software's adaptations of the DOOM engine.

THE NEED FOR EXITS

It is desirable for all levels (especially those intended for single-player use) to have an exit; otherwise, players will not know whether they have finished it. This may sound trivial, but remember that it is only through triggering an exit action that players are given their tally. Without this tally, they will not know whether all secret locations have been found, all monsters disposed of, or all goodies collected. Such things are less important in WADs designed primarily for Deathmatch play, but most players still like to see exits and use them to end the game.

Exits are also vital in multi-level WADs, of course, to enable the player to progress to the next mission. You can have as many exits in each map as you consider necessary.

MAKING EXITS OBVIOUS

In the view of most player, it is also important that the role of a switch ending a level be obvious *before* it is pressed. There is nothing more frustrating than pressing a switch you have fought hard to gain in the belief that it opens a door, only to discover that it ends the level instead! Few players will be impressed with exits such as this.

Once again, the designers at id Software have provided several textures for you to use to make your exits conspicuous. DOOM's most obvious is, of course, the large red exit sign. Less obvious, perhaps, but still recognizable to most DOOM players, is the distinctive techno-door texture that id Software's designers use on the doors to most of their exit anterooms. This is the EXITDOOR texture, shown (alongside the equivalent texture from Heretic) in Figure 18.6.

Notice how the EXITDOOR texture is a multifunction texture. The pattern for the face of the door takes up only one half of the pattern; the remainder includes three additional textures. These are intended for use on the reveals of the recesses to either side of the door. Figure 18.7 shows these in use. Note the symmetrical form of the patterns to the side of the door.

Figure 18.6.
DOOM's EXITDOOR and Heretic's
DOOREXIT wall textures.

Figure 18.7.
EXITDOOR textures in use—three
times, here.

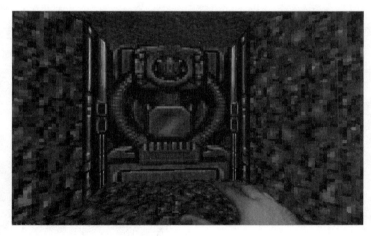

You get the pattern for the left reveal by using an X-offset of 64 pixels into the EXITDOOR texture; the pattern for the right reveal appears when you use an X-offset of 88 pixels. The lines for each reveal must be precisely 24 units long, of course, to take these patterns. If the lines are too long, the patterns will not repeat; there will merely be spillover into the next part of the texture.

The last 16 pixels of the EXITDOOR texture provide another lighting-panel pattern. Use an X-offset of –16 to apply this to any suitably sized line. Incidentally, notice that the EXITDOOR texture is only 72 pixels high; therefore, it won't tile correctly if applied to spaces that are too high for it.

Heretic offers nothing comparable to DOOM's EXITDOOR texture in terms of graphical richness. Its DOOREXIT texture (shown previously in Figure 18.6) should be recognized by most Heretic players for what it is, though, and you are encouraged to use this (and the other textures carrying the blue trident symbol) to signal exits, the way Raven Software does. Note that DOOREXIT is also a short texture, only 96 units high.

WAD SORTIE 25: ADDING AN EXIT

NOTE: This sortie builds on the WAD produced in the previous one. If you did not produce that WAD, you should use WAD24A.WAD (DOOM), D2WAD24A.WAD (DOOM II), or H1WAD24A.WAD (Heretic) from the CD-ROM as your starting point. [Heretic variations in this sortie are indicated in brackets.]

This WAD sortie will add an exit to your WAD to allow a player to end the level and move on to the next. This exit will be located in an area off the outdoor crescent, just to the west of the donut room. It will be located beyond a new yellow-keyed door, requiring the player to successfully finish the donut-room's puzzle before being permitted to leave this level.

BUILDING THE WAY OUT

Figure 18.8 shows the location and form of this new area.

Figure 18.8.
The exit from the level.

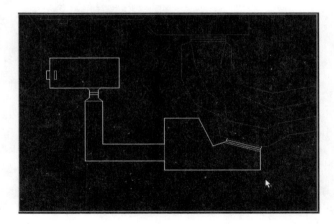

THE APPROACH

Start by building a yellow-keyed door off the southwest end of the outdoor crescent. Use suitable recesses, textures, and decorations, with a door width of 256 units to make the door match the other doors off this area. Use whatever wall textures and sector settings you feel are appropriate for the areas beyond the door—an open chamber and a corridor leading on toward the exit room itself. My DOOM WADs (WAD25.WAD or

D2WAD25.WAD) use ASHWALL for the walls of the chamber and STONE2 for the corridor. In Heretic, I've used RCKSNMUD on most of the walls, with occasional stretches of SPINE2. The corridor floor is 16 units below the chamber floor and has a much lower ceiling. I've also set the lighting levels quite low.

The corridor ends in a funnel-shaped sector (see Figure 18.9) designed to bring the corridor width down to 64 units and the height down to 72 to allow the EXITDOOR [DOOREXIT] texture to be used on the door ahead. (The cursor arrow points to the face of this door in Figure 18.9.)

Figure 18.9.
Close-up of lines for the exit door and final room.

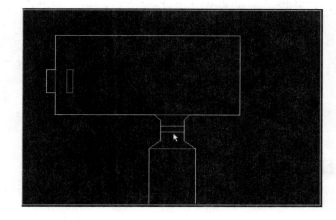

EXIT ANTEROOM WITH CHARACTERISTIC DOOR

In my DOOM WADs, the two walls of the funnel-shaped recess sector use the EXITDOOR texture on them where they abut the door. The lines for these have been made 24 pixels long (they run north-south aligned to make this easier to arrange) and have the appropriate X-offsets to use the symmetrical door-reveal patterns of this texture, as previously discussed. The face of the door itself also carries the EXITDOOR texture on its upper texture slot. Figure 18.7, shown previously, is, in fact, a view of this door in my WAD25.WAD.

Both sides of this door should be special type 1 (MR Door: open and close). Beyond the door (and an inner door-recess sector) is the main exit anteroom itself. The recess on this side of the door has short walls abutting the door sector. These are 16 units long and use the rightmost portion of the EXITDOOR texture.

Since Heretic's DOOREXIT texture cannot be usefully divided, my Heretic WAD has to forego the refinements around the door just described.

The short lines that connect the inner recess to the main anteroom in the DOOM WADs use the STONE2 texture, as do the rest of the walls beyond the door. Ceiling and floor heights for the areas around the door to the anteroom are given in Table 18.3. You may need to adjust these (or those of the approach areas to the south) to provide a better tie-in with your corridor. The room heights should be maintained if you want the wall textures to align correctly.

Table 18.3. Ceiling and floor heights for main exit anteroom and door (DOOM/DOOM II).

Area	Ceiling Level	Floor Level	Height
Recess south of exit door	48	-24	72
Exit door	-24	-24	0
Recess north of exit door	48	-24	72
Exit anteroom	72	-32	104

HERETIC Because the exit symbolism is rather different in Heretic, the exit anteroom has been arranged a little differently in the Heretic version of my WAD. I have used FLOOR23 (for its blue trident pattern) on floor and ceiling in this room, with METL1 on most of the walls. These patterns dictate that the room's walls be aligned on the 64 × 64 tiling grid and that they be 128 units high.

THE EXIT SWITCH

The switch that will trigger the end of the level is placed in an alcove in the western wall of the anteroom. In DOOM and DOOM II, this can a standard 64-unit wide switch alcove with the SW1STON1 texture on its back wall and its lower unpegged flag set. The alcove should be 72 units high, with the same floor height as the rest of the room.

In Heretic, the alcove should be 96 units high with SW2OFF on the rear wall. The unpegged flag can be left clear in this case.

Place a special attribute of 11 (S1: Exit) on the back line of the alcove. No tagging is necessary. This creates the exit switch.

AN EXIT SIGN

The fact that this is an exit switch needs to be signaled to the player. In the Heretic WAD, the presence of the blue trident symbols should be enough. In DOOM and DOOM II, there is a choice of method. The EXITSTON texture could be used on the wall over the alcove—it provides the red EXIT lettering on the appropriate stone texture—or you could make a sign suspended from the ceiling. I prefer this latter solution. To create it, another sector is needed just east of the switch alcove. This sector should be 64 pixels wide by 16 pixels deep and located close to the western wall as seen in Figure 18.9, shown previously.

This sector has the same settings as the main room, except for the ceiling, which has been lowered 16 units to create a set of essential upper textures around it. The 16-pixel high EXITSIGN texture is used on all these essentials, with X-offsets applied so that the appropriate parts of this multifunction texture appear correctly on each face (−16 on all faces).

FINISHING OFF

Finally, to save you from having to run around like crazy in the donut room to get the yellow key just to test this new area out, place another one in the crescent by the yellow-keyed door. Save the WAD as WAD25.WAD, then go try it out. You should now be able to progress from your WAD to the standard second level of the game.

SECRET AREAS

Among the items reported on a level's final tally screen is the percentage of the secret areas of the map that the player successfully located. You may have noticed that no matter how many of your own "secret" areas you visit when you play your WAD, your secret tally is always 0 percent when you trip the exit switch. This is because DOOM does not yet know that your level has any secrets!

MAKING SECRET AREAS

You have seen the ways in which areas can be kept hidden from players. However, simply hiding doors and other entrance points to these areas does not make them "secret" as far as DOOM or its variants are concerned. An area's secret nature must be notified to the game engine if it is to be included in reckoning the final tally. This is done by setting a sector's special characteristic to the value 9. A player entering a sector with this special value will be credited with the discovery of a secret area.

Note that the use of their special characteristic in this way precludes such secret sectors from possessing other special characteristics, such as fluctuating light levels or damaging properties.

TALLYING SECRETS

The game engine calculates the final tally of secrets that have been located by counting up the total number of sectors with a special characteristic of 9 and determining what proportion of these have been entered by the player during the game.

Heretic presents the player with the absolute figures, rather than expressing it as a percentage—much kinder on those players who hate mental arithmetic.

To give the player a useful indication of what proportion of secret locations have been found, you should apply the secret credit characteristic carefully. Generally, you should only use one occurrence of the special value for each *area* that is hidden. Remember that players are generally unaware of the distribution of sectors—they see only rooms and such. A room consisting of three sectors behind a hidden door should not grant more than one secret credit.

Furthermore, credits should be awarded sooner in an area, rather than later. The best location would be either the entrance sector itself or the first sector beyond it. This way, the player is not forced to walk all around a secret area just to collect the credit for its discovery. Watch out, too, for secret areas that have more than one possible way in. Make sure that players will pass into the credit-awarding sector no matter what entrance they use.

You should also ensure that players are given good reason to enter a secret area. If a player opens a secret door but does not enter because the small room beyond appears empty, DOOM will consider this room as an undiscovered secret area when the mission finishes. This will result in frustrated players wandering around trying to locate that last secret, which they have, in fact, already found. Placing a few bonuses in the room would have prevented this.

COMPULSORY SECRET DISCOVERIES

It is important for the correct feel of a game that players easily equate the secret credits they have been awarded with the locations they have found. You should not award secret credits for areas that players are forced into locating because of traps. Such areas are rarely seen as "secret" by players, so you will disturb their own mental count of how many secrets they have located by awarding credits unnecessarily. Finding a hidden exit from a room in which a player has been locked is usually its own reward!

Finally, even if your level doesn't use any secret locations, you should make sure that one sector does award a secret-discovery credit if your level is for DOOM or DOOM II. Use either the start sector or the one with the exit switch—one that the player is guaranteed to pass through. This ensures that the tally screen reports 100 percent of secrets located, rather than 0 percent when the level ends. This simple addition to your WAD will save players much frustration from wandering around looking for secrets that are not there. (If only id's designers had taken this advice with DOOM II!)

WAD SORTIE 26: AWARDING SECRET CREDITS

NOTE: This sortie builds on the WAD produced in the previous one. If you did not produce that WAD, you should use WAD25.WAD (DOOM), D2WAD25.WAD (DOOM II), or H1WAD25.WAD (Heretic) from the CD-ROM as your starting point. You should be aware that this sortie assumes some familiarity with the layout of this WAD. If you have not been following these sorties in detail, you might want to take a quick run through this WAD to familiarize yourself with its features and layout.

This final sortie of the chapter examines the WAD that you have built and makes recommendations about which of your current sectors should award secret credits. Try walking through the WAD now and take a look…

SETTING THE SECRET AREAS

Some of the WAD's candidates for awarding secret-discovery credits are the following:

- The one-way staircase
- The hidden room at the top of these stairs
- The platform room
- The southern courtyard
- The hidden room in the southwest corner of the courtyard
- The crusher room
- The sniper's den
- The hidden room off the southwest staircase
- The string of rooms behind the shot-activated doors off the blood/lava pool
- The room north of the blood/lava pool
- The causeway across the pond
- The ledge outside the northern window of the platform room

Consider the case for each of these areas in turn. To make a sector award a discovery credit, simply set its special characteristic to the value 9 (Award Secret).

THE ONE-WAY STAIRCASE

These stairs are currently located behind a secret door activated from a rather obvious switch. Currently, this area of the map is away from the main flow of the WAD. Decide for yourself whether it warrants inclusion as a secret area. If you decide in favor of it, I recommend using the entrance from the southwest passageway as the credit-awarding sector.

THE HIDDEN ROOM AT THE TOP OF THE STAIRS

This room is hidden only in the sense that players may not notice it as they pass. Its opening is triggered from further along the corridor, at which point they will definitely discover its presence! They may not be able to fathom the way to get in there, though. On balance, I would award a secret-discovery credit here.

THE PLATFORM ROOM

The entrance to the platform room is currently semi-hidden and its switch is not too obviously attached to it. It seems a little generous to award a discovery credit for this, though.

THE SOUTHERN COURTYARD

This area can be gained only when the player has located and tripped the switch in the hidden room. The area is hardly secret, however. How you view secret areas will determine whether you mark this as one. I probably wouldn't.

THE ROOM IN THE SOUTHWEST CORNER OF THE COURTYARD

This strikes me as a perfect candidate for a secret-discovery credit. By awarding a secret credit here, credit is effectively given also for finding the courtyard itself, because this credit cannot be collected until the way into the courtyard has been found.

THE CRUSHER ROOM

The string of crushers is located behind a door that is hidden and shot-activated. I would probably award a secret-discovery credit here. I would also let the entrance sector be the one that awards the credit. The discovery is awarded then, even if the player doesn't run the gauntlet of the crushers. (Just call me generous.)

THE SNIPER'S DEN

I would also award a credit here, too—that way the player earns extra credit for braving the crushers and noticing the door beyond. (Not that it's hidden, though. I said I was generous, didn't I?)

THE ROOM OFF THE SOUTHWEST STAIRCASE

The case for this room is similar to that for the room at the top of the one-way staircase. It is easier to get into, though—its door latches open—and there is the added complication that the special characteristic will already be in use if you left this area with flashing lights. Since this particular room contains the switch that will permit access to other areas already marked as secret, there seems little point in awarding a separate credit here. I'd leave this area out of the secrets list.

THE CORRIDOR BEYOND THE BLOOD/LAVA POOL

The discovery of these areas is a vital step in completing the arena section of the WAD. There is little point in awarding discovery credits here, in my opinion.

THE ROOM NORTH OF THE BLOOD/LAVA POOL

The opening mechanism for this room is not obvious in its purpose and is far enough from the room itself for careless players to miss it. It is not central to the overall scheme of the WAD, so I suggest that this room should award a credit.

THE CAUSEWAY

There seems to be no point in awarding credit for finding the causeway across the pond. As things stand, this is the only escape from the lower area of the arena.

THE LEDGE

It might not be immediately obvious why I have included the ledge north of the platform room in the list of secret areas. Bear in mind, though, that this area starts out hidden from the platform room. Also, if the lift up to it from the arena were to be made less conspicuous (or removed altogether in Heretic), players might take a while find this ledge. So far, no secret credits will accrue to the player who makes it to this area of the map, despite the need to locate and operate several switches successfully. All things considered, I would probably award a secret-discovery credit to players who do manage to reach this ledge as bonus for completing all of the puzzles on the way. (I may change my mind later, though!)

COLLECTING THE CREDITS

When you have decided which areas are to award credit for their discovery and have set all the appropriate sectors' special characteristic, you should save your WAD as WAD26.WAD. Check that your Player 1 Start position is back in its normal location in the hexagonal room, and take a run through your empty WAD to check that you can collect all of the secret credits. You may want to revise your original opinions as to what should be secret after you've been to them all.

THE TIME SCORE

In testing out your latest WAD, you might have noticed that DOOM reports a ridiculously short Par Time for finishing this level. This is because these times are hard-coded into the game engine itself and cannot be changed by anything in the PWAD file. If you want your levels to give more reasonable Par Times, you will need to build levels that match the originals pretty closely in completion times. Most players, however, are used to DOOM's unreasonable expectations here and habitually ignore this element of the score.

Raven Software (wisely) chose to dispose of the Par Time altogether.

SPECIAL EXITS AND ENDINGS

If you've played DOOM and DOOM II through all levels to the end, you will know that there is another rather special kind of ending used in some of id Software's own levels. This is the kind where it is necessary to kill certain monsters to finish the level and open an exit somewhere. Unfortunately, these particular effects arise from special code in the executable itself, leaving little scope for you to put these devices to much use in your own levels. The effects themselves are achieved by using either special tags or special Boss monsters.

BOSS TAGS

There are two so-called Boss Tags that produce special endings to a level. The first is Tag 666. If a sector has its tag field set to a value of 666, then that sector will move its floor to the height of the lowest adjacent floor when the last Boss monster in the level dies. To use this feature of the game, you will need to use a map editor that will give you direct access to sector tags. Also—and here's the catch—you can use the feature only in the same maps that use it in the original game! It can be used in E1M8 and E3M8 of DOOM, and MAP07 of DOOM II *only*, which rather limits its usefulness.

> **NOTE:** What constitutes a Boss monster is not fully known. The Baron of Hell seems to be the master Boss; if this type of monster is used in a level, the sector will trigger only on the death of the last one. If no Barons are present, though, other Boss monsters can be used: Cyberdemons and the Spider Mastermind both work in DOOM, and Mancubus works in DOOM II. Others may, too—why not experiment, if you're interested?

DOOM II also provides another similar special tag value: 667. This works only on MAP07 and has the effect of raising the sector's floor 16 units when the last Arachnotron dies.

BOSS THINGS

DOOM II also introduced two special Things that, when killed, cause the termination of a level. One works only on MAP32; the other works everywhere. These are Things 72 ("Billy") and 88 (the Boss Brain), respectively. They are of limited use outside their correct settings.

EXIT: MOPPING UP AND MOVING ON

In this chapter, you learned about the last few types of active line and saw how to create teleports and exits using them. You also learned how to make areas award secret-discovery credits.

By now, the geography of your WAD should be nearing completion. There are a few areas that need some final development, but you should be able to finish these for yourself by drawing on the knowledge you have acquired so far. There will be some hints about how these may be developed and instructions for some specific additions in the next chapter, though.

The main shortcoming with your WAD now is that it has little to fight, nothing to fight with, and little to collect beyond some credits for locating the secret areas. The next chapter will concentrate on putting these deficiencies right. It will review the types of enemies your players can expect to meet on their way to your new exit. (See Figure 18.10.) It will also lead you through the process of placing these enemies, and, of course, it will show you how to handle providing weapons, ammunition, and other goodies that your players will need to survive their ordeal.

Figure 18.10.

All it needs now are some monsters!

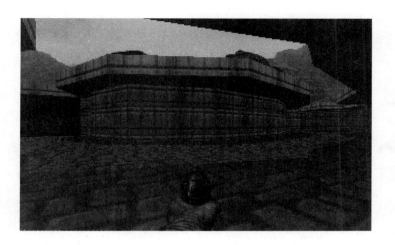

POPULATING YOUR NIGHTMARE

By now you should have a WAD in which the map is nearly complete. The map will not yet have much of a population, though, except a few monsters on the higher skill levels to help you test out some areas, an occasional piece of armor, and a few keys.

This chapter will set about changing that. The range of monsters available in each variant of the game will be examined and individual monster's characteristics reviewed. This chapter will also discuss the way DOOM's creatures behave in general and explain the way sound propagates through a WAD and offer tips on using this feature of the game to control the way monsters behave.

Finally, this chapter's WAD sortie will build on those of previous chapters by showing you how to build a sound-activated monster cache capable of spewing Hell-spawn around your players as soon as one of them puts so much as a trigger finger wrong!

KNOW YOUR ENEMY

Many designers spend hours drawing the geography of their playing arena, getting the layout and appearance just right, only to spoil everything with careless selection and positioning of enemies and resources. The distribution of the creatures and artifacts that players will encounter is at least as important—many designers would say more so—as the layout of the geography.

As always, the key lies in the planning. You should aim to

- Plan carefully
- Progress logically
- Play test thoroughly

— By Steve Benner with additional material by David Bruni

Apply these guiding principles to the populating of your WAD and to every other aspect of WAD design.

The first step in planning a WAD is knowing what is available for use within it. Previous chapters have detailed what is available for the building of the playing spaces. Now you'll learn what is available for populating a WAD, starting with the main occupants: the monsters.

Each variant of the game provides a different set of monsters to pit against your players. The original set, provided by DOOM, is a good starting point for studying the monsters.

THE DENIZENS OF DOOM

In many ways, DOOM still provides one of the most balanced series of monsters for pitting against players. Not one of DOOM's monsters was removed for DOOM II.

FORMER HUMAN TROOPERS

The *Former Humans* (Troopers) are the easiest of DOOM's monsters to kill and never pose much of a threat to players. They are fairly slow and usually take only one or two shots to kill. They are quite versatile, though, and four or five of them can give the player a good fight. When they die, they always drop a clip of bullets, so they can be useful suppliers of emergency rounds. These guys are good scattered throughout a WAD, especially at the beginning, where they can provide a warm-up for things to come. They are useful also for stirring things up in large monster groupings because their aim is often poor, and they frequently hit other monsters when aiming for the player. They are easily distracted, too, shooting at anything that fires at them. Troopers will fight with any sort of monster, though they tend to not last very long against anything. They will happily scrap amongst themselves until only one survives (see Figure 19.1).

Figure 19.1.
Former Humans doing your job for you.

FORMER HUMAN SERGEANTS

The *Former Human Sergeants* are similar in appearance and actions to the Troopers. They are a little bit tougher to kill, but not much; they can usually be stopped with a shotgun blast or one or two well-placed pistol shots. They move somewhat faster than Troopers; their aim is better; and, being armed with shotguns, they do more damage. In general, they can be used in a WAD in a similar way to Troopers, but remember that they drop a shotgun when they are killed and are often viewed by players as an easy source of that weapon and its ammo.

IMPS

Imps are spiked, scaly critters that are not at all nice to know. They don't carry weapons, but with their ability to spit fireballs and their razor-sharp claws, they hardly need to! Their aim is impeccable, and their fireballs can hurt a player considerably. Fortunately, they move slowly, and their fireballs are easily dodged. In close quarters, Imps physically attack the player and can inflict just as much damage with their claws as with their fireballs.

One shotgun blast can usually take care of an Imp, but it takes quite a few pistol shots to kill one. Imps die without leaving anything of benefit to the player, except a slightly less hostile environment. They are good to put on ledges because they can shoot a long way and are hard to kill from a distance. They are good also in groups because they are immune to fire from their own kind and therefore do not distract each other from their main task—toasting the player. In fact, Imps are generally difficult to distract from this task at all, although their fireballs can draw a lot of fire their way from bigger monsters, who will often make short work of them. If you want Imps to remain effective, they are best not mixed with more-powerful monsters.

DEMONS AND SPECTRES

The grotesque, pink *Demon* and its partly invisible cousin, the *Spectre*, have no weapons nor any other means of firing at their quarry. They prefer to rush right up and chew great chunks out of anything that annoys them. Players annoy them real fast. These monsters are harder to kill than Imps; two or three shotgun blasts or a lot of bullets will be needed to bring them down. The chainsaw is very effective on them, though. Demons move fairly quickly but are still easily out-run or out-maneuvered in open areas. They are effective in small, enclosed areas, especially in large numbers. Spectres are particularly effective in dark areas or against granular or animated textures because they are much harder to see in these situations. Unlike Imps, Demons and Spectres are easily drawn from the player by cross fire, but they never attack each other.

LOST SOULS

Lost Souls are one of two flying monsters in DOOM. These flying, flaming skulls move rapidly and can inflict a lot of damage on a player very quickly if the player lets them get close. Individually they are quite easily disposed of and therefore are best used in packs of half a dozen or so. Place them either in small, confining rooms where they can quickly overwhelm a player or in large rooms with high ceilings where they can move around a lot and attack from many angles. Lost Souls do not mix well with other monsters. They seem to like Demon-flesh in particular—almost as much as that of players.

CACODEMONS

Cacodemons are the first of the tough monsters. They're big, they're bad, they fly, and they spit fireballs straight from Hell! They take at least four shotgun blasts to kill. Their main weaknesses are that they can't move very fast and are fairly easy to kill at close range—all the player has to do is get in their face and keep shooting, and they'll die pretty much without a fight. They are also easily distracted into fighting other things. Cacodemons are most effective in large open areas, but they can also squeeze into small openings and walkways—a surprise attack or ambush at close range by even a single Cacodemon can be deadly. If you use a lot of these monsters in one room, be sure to arm the player with at least the shotgun or chaingun and plenty of ammo; otherwise, a couple of fireballs from the Cacos will quickly bring play to an end.

BARONS OF HELL

Barons of Hell are the first of the so-called Boss Monsters. These monsters are very tough. They don't move particularly fast, and their fireballs can be sidestepped with a little practice, but it takes at least 15 shotgun blasts, 100 bullets from the chaingun, or a well-placed rocket or two (or five!) to kill one. And up close, a player will soon succumb to a Baron's claws. Barons should be used sparingly unless your WAD is stacked high with ammo. Even then you should never pit more than two or three of them against a player at any one time, unless you also throw in enough other monsters to keep the Barons busy; they are easily distracted from fighting the player. They seem to particularly despise Cacodemons, but then, who can blame them? (See Figure 19.2.)

Figure 19.2.
Cacodemons and Barons of Hell scrapping it out.

OTHER BOSS MONSTERS

The *Spider Mastermind* and the *Cyberdemon* are the hardest monsters to kill in DOOM. These creatures are so big and powerful that they should be used only in special situations and under the right circumstances. They are usually so difficult to kill without cheating that if you do use them in your WAD, you should make sure that you have supplied a complete stockpile of munitions and power-ups to give your players a chance. Providing suitable geography is important, too: Offer plenty of shelter from which to fire or space through which to dodge and weave to provide the player with a challenge, not merely an ordeal.

DOOM II'S DEADLIER FOES

In addition to all the old favorites from DOOM, DOOM II provides eight new monsters. They're all bad news for the unsuspecting player.

FORMER HUMAN COMMANDO (A.K.A. THE CHAINGUN DUDE)

The *Former Human Commando* is much like the Former Sergeant except that he packs a chaingun (see Figure 19.3), which means that he can quickly do real damage to a player. Fortunately, the Chaingun Dude moves slowly, makes a nice fat target, and is easily killed. And when one dies, he leaves a chaingun behind for the player to collect, making the provision of chainguns in levels that contain these dudes almost unnecessary.

Figure 19.3.
The Chaingunner chaingunning.

Chaingunners are best placed in quiet, out-of-the-way ambush spots, preferably where they remain hard to see even after they have started firing. Keep them away from other monsters, too; they kill former humans who get in the way without so much as blinking and distract the powerful monsters. They work well in pairs but operate best when they can keep things personal between themselves and players.

HELL KNIGHTS

The *Hell Knights* are kid brothers to the Barons of Hell. They look and act very similar to their siblings but are somewhat easier to kill. You can use them just about anywhere that you would use a Baron of Hell, but you can use them in almost double the quantity. The Hell Knights fit in well as an intermediate-type monster. They are not as tough as a Baron, but they are tougher than lesser monsters such as pink Demons. If you use Hell Knights in your level, make sure that you give the player at least the assault shotgun or the chaingun to deal with them.

PAIN ELEMENTALS

The *Pain Elemental* is one of DOOM II's nastier monsters. Similar in form and behavior to the Cacodemon, the Pain Elemental is not confined to the ground but can fly through the air to give players a bad time. Like the

Cacodemon, it can enter small spaces and makes an excellent ambush monster. The Pain Elemental rarely attacks the player directly; its power lies in its habit of spitting out Lost Souls as fast as a player can shoot them. Fortunately, Pain Elementals can be disposed of with three or four shotgun hits. As a parting shot, though, a dying Pain Elemental explodes into three final Lost Souls for the player to handle.

Large, open areas with high ceilings are the place to put these monsters. The Pain Elemental itself doesn't move fast, but the Lost Souls it generates do and are harder to hit in large rooms. And while a player is busy dealing with Lost Souls, the Pain Elemental can fly around, producing new Lost Souls from other locations.

MANCUBUS

The *Mancubus* is another difficult monster to tackle. He's not comparable to any monster in DOOM (see Figure 19.4). Both of his arms end in prosthetic guns that spray fireballs around, shooting six at a time at the player. The Mancubus is also a pretty big guy, so you'll probably want to use him in large open areas. Fortunately for the player, the Mancubus isn't very fast and can be avoided without too much trouble (although dodging his fireballs is trickier). A Mancubus is reasonably difficult to dispatch, requiring 10 shots or so from the shotgun or four or five rockets to kill it. The plasma gun seems to be the best weapon to use against him; only a few blasts are needed to lay him low. Plan on giving players a decent weapon to use against these guys.

Figure 19.4.
A Mancubus about to turn ugly.

REVENANT

The *Revenant* is a rocket-launching, walking skeleton that packs some heavy firepower (see Figure 19.5). A single one of his rockets can take out a player without much problem. Dodging the rockets is tricky because they are capable of homing-in on a player. Up close, the Revenant will also pound the player with his fists. These characteristics make Revenants good for use in both small rooms and large areas. The Revenant is a little easier to kill than the Mancubus—it takes only four shotgun blasts or a rocket or two. Three or four Revenants are generally all a player can handle at once, though. Like the Mancubus, the Revenant is not a good monster to use around other bad guys. Stray shots from the Revenant and Mancubus tend to do too much damage for other monsters to survive long in the company of either of them. Mixing a Revenant with other monsters may leave little for the player to do but dodge.

Figure 19.5.

A Revenant making things hot for you (while an Arch-Vile conjures up a spell).

ARACHNOTRONS

The *Arachnotrons* (or Baby Spiders) look like little Spider Masterminds, but instead of having chainguns, they are equipped with plasma guns. They can be hard to deal with because in addition to being tough, they move fast, can shoot long distances, and cannot be easily approached without serious consequences. Luckily, they are nowhere near as hard to kill as Spider Masterminds. Successful use of these monsters requires carefully thought-out geography. The best areas provide a lot of open space for the monsters to move around in, with narrower spaces to allow players some cover. Well-designed interconnections can help: Let players take shortcuts but require the larger Arachnotrons to take longer routes through the wider corridors. Be sure to supply plenty of ammo if you expect players to face many Arachnotrons in your levels.

ARCH-VILE

The *Arch-Vile* (seen previously in Figure 19.5) is a real badass. Not only does it summon up an almighty whirl-wind of fire that comes from nowhere and can blast players from their feet, but, even worse, if it encounters any dead monsters, it will bring them back to life (see Figure 19.6). You'll not normally want to use many of these guys in your levels. To make full use of those you do include, it's best to arrange for them to stay out of the player's direct path for a while after they wake up, to give them a chance to do their resurrection bit. One thing an Arch-Vile won't resurrect, by the way, is another Arch-Vile, which is either a shame or a relief, depending on your point of view.

Figure 19.6.
An Arch-Vile brings a Revenant back for another tour of duty.

FINAL BOSS

The *Final Boss* on level 30 of DOOM II may or may not be considered a real monster. It is really just a mechanism for spawning monsters around the player and bringing the whole shooting match to a spectacular conclusion. Depending on what you want to achieve in your WADs, you may or may not want use this "monster." If you decide to use it (and who can resist?), you will find the necessary details in Chapter 34, "Essential Thing Information."

GUEST APPEARANCES

As a final note, remember that DOOM II added two Wolfenstein 3D levels, which include the SS *guards.* These guys look the same as they always have, complete with their machine guns and everything else. They even sound the same as they used to. If you want to add some variety to your WAD file, add a few of these guys to it.

A few other guest appearances in DOOM II can be added to your WADs for a bit of fun. These characters are amusing when you come across them in DOOM II for the first time but not many times thereafter. They're not really monsters, but you can shoot them up if you feel like it. Now, you're not going to tell me that you haven't come across Billy and John, are you?

HERETIC'S HELL-SPAWNED HORDES

In Heretic, DOOM's demonic forces of darkness were replaced with a bestiary from a bizarre fantasy world of wizards and warriors. An added complication in this variant of the game is that many types of monsters look the same but have different attack behaviors so that players don't always know what it is they're up against. This section will review what these monsters might be.

GARGOYLES

Gargoyles are half-demon, half-bat and aren't half unpleasant as they drop from the sky. They come in two types: plain Gargoyles and Fire Gargoyles. Plain vanilla Gargoyles can attack a player only with their claws. They are easily killed if the player can spot them and is fast enough to shoot at them as they attack from overhead. They are roughly equivalent to DOOM's Lost Souls but take less damage before dying. The *Fire Gargoyles* (or Gargoyle Leaders) look identical to their weaker brethren but are capable of hurling fireballs at the player. Their aim is deadly, and their fireballs travel fairly fast and can be tricky to dodge. Fire Gargoyles are still quite easy to kill, though. If you're a DOOM player, imagine a flying Imp, and you've got a Fire Gargoyle.

GOLEMS

Golems (walking rocks) also come in two varieties: plain Golems and Nitrogolems. Like plain Gargoyles, the plain Golem is easy to dispatch—a few hits from the Elvenwand is usually enough to see one off, releasing the captive spirit which drives it. Golems are no hazard until they get close enough to give the player a smacking. Use them as you would Troopers in DOOM: to give the player a warm-up. A Golem will occasionally drop a Wand Crystal, but you should generally not expect Heretic's monsters to supply a player with many items of use. *Nitrogolems* (or Golem Leaders) are like standard Golems but are capable of casting blazing skulls at their foes, which do a fair amount of harm. The blazing skulls can be dodged or shot quite easily (and unlike DOOM's Lost Souls, if they miss a player, they do not return). Nitrogolems are as easy to kill as standard Golems. They are good to introduce amongst the standard ones (although these two types will in-fight) to keep players on their toes and encourage them to tackle Golems from farther away than they otherwise would (see Figure 19.7).

Figure 19.7.
A Nitrogolem suddenly reveals itself for what it is.

Golems and Gargoyles fight amongst themselves if left to their own devices, so it's best not to mix these types too much.

UNDEAD WARRIORS

Heretic's *Undead Warriors* are fast-moving monsters with an infinite supply of magic axes that they hurl at players with deadly accuracy. The axes are easily dodged if the player isn't too distracted fighting other monsters at the time. Undead Warriors can be dispatched quickly with a few shots from the crossbow, if the player is up quite close. They are much harder to kill from a distance. Undead Warriors occasionally drop a few magical arrows, but never as many as it took to kill them.

SABRECLAW

Sabreclaws are Heretic's equivalent of DOOM's Demon. They move faster, though, and do damage more quickly if the player lets them get close enough to use those meat cleavers they have for hands. You can use Sabreclaws as you would Demons and Spectres in DOOM, but give them more space and hence the player more space to get away from them!

WEREDRAGON

Although *Weredragons* are large and fast-moving and have breath that will fry any player who comes within range, they are surprisingly easy to kill—a few hits from the crossbow is usually enough. For some strange reason, these critters occasionally drop a supply of Ethereal Arrows when they die. I wonder where they had them? Weredragons can be used much as Hell Knights in DOOM II.

OPHIDIAN

The trident-wielding *Ophidian* is reasonably easy to dispose of if the player is properly armed—something more powerful than the crossbow wouldn't go amiss. Ophidians are neither particularly strong, nor especially fast. The blast of energy that they fire at players can be hard to avoid, though, quickly turning anything it hits to toast. In small quantities, Ophidians can be dealt with quite quickly, but it's probably best to offer your players some potential shelter if you use many of these characters in your WAD.

DISCIPLE OF D'SPARIL

As students of D'Sparil's dark magic, *Disciples* will blink in and out of existence before a player's eyes. They are fairly weak characters, though, and can be dispatched quickly if they can be kept in view long enough. Getting up close is often the best way to dispose of Disciples, although they will rarely allow players the chance. (See Figure 19.8.) Because they drift through the air and can vanish and reappear at will, they are not constrained much by a WAD's geography. The barrage of magic missiles that they hurl at a player has a wide spread to it—similar to the fireballs of the Mancubus—that can rarely be dodged and does a lot of damage. A well-designed level can usually support three or four Disciples of D'Sparil without taxing the player too greatly. You'll need to supply a fair amount of ammunition, though, because much of it will probably go to waste firing at empty air. In recompense, a Disciple will occasionally drop a Claw Orb when it dies. Big deal!

Figure 19.8.
A Disciple of D'Sparil about to impart learning upon the player.

IRON LICH

Heretic's *Iron Lich* is without parallel in DOOM or DOOM II. This giant floating helm packs a devastating whirlwind of air or fire capable of lifting players high into the air and spinning them around. Iron Lich is a difficult foe to fight because it quickly does a lot of damage to a player and keeps the player from fighting back. If the player can get some shots in on this abomination, though, it will rapidly collapse to a heap of scrap metal. One of these monsters is difficult to deal with, and two at a time would be almost impossible without a lot of space to run around in and some low passageways where they could not follow.

MAULOTAUR

The *Maulotaur* is the closest thing that Heretic has to the Cyberdemon. Big, powerful, fast-moving, and just as devastating close up (see Figure 19.9) as from afar (see Figure 19.10), the Maulotaur is as hard to kill as a Cyberdemon (and harder to avoid). Keep these beauties to an absolute minimum in your WADs, and make sure your players are fully prepared before they encounter one.

Figure 19.9.
The Maulotaur about to demonstrate the origin of its name.

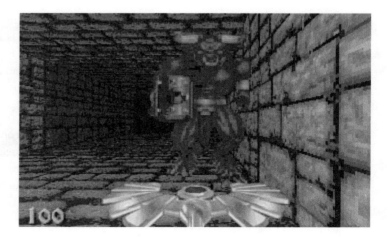

Figure 19.10.
The Maulotaur demonstrates the powers of its hammer.

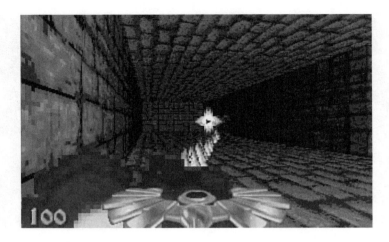

D'SPARIL

Heretic's big final showdown monster is, of course, the evil Serpent Rider *D'Sparil*—complete with Chaos Serpent mount! D'Sparil is, not surprisingly, an extremely difficult opponent to defeat. First of all, his mount moves with incredible speed for such a large creature and delivers a devastating blast of fire itself. By the time the serpent has been disposed of, the player's ammo supplies and health are likely to be running low, but this is not the end of D'Sparil.

The evil master wizard always survives the death of his mount and continues to fight on, using the full might of his magical power. He summons his Disciples to fight at his side. He vanishes whenever a player manages to bring fire to bear upon him, rematerializing at will around the player. Or so it seems. In fact, the wizard's materialization spots are under the WAD designer's control. In addition to placing D'Sparil in the level, you should place a few D'Sparil Spots around the WAD. These spots are the locations that the beleaguered wizard will hop off to as soon as the player fires at him. You can place spots close to the final encounter room to keep things hot for your player or scatter them far and wide around the WAD to make the player hunt the wizard (and ammunition) anew.

If you use D'Sparil in your WAD (and somehow a Heretic WAD is incomplete without him), bear in mind that he is extremely difficult to kill, the more so the further he is allowed to elude the player via his rematerialization spots. Getting the WAD design right to allow the introduction of this master of Heretic's monsters is one of the greatest challenges a Heretic WAD designer can face.

GHOST FORMS

As an added twist, many of Heretic's monsters are available in Ghost Forms (see Figure 19.11). In Ghost Form, monsters are virtually the same as in their "normal" form, but they are semitransparent, making them harder to spot. The Heretic manual claims that Ghost Forms are harder to kill than their non-Ghost equivalents, but I can't say that I've ever noticed this. Ghost Forms are available for four Heretic monsters:

- Golems
- Nitrogolems
- Undead Warriors
- Weredragons

Figure 19.11.
A *collection of Heretic's ghosts.*

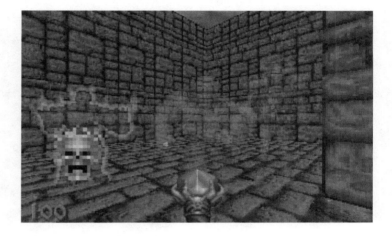

HEXEN'S HORRORS

The monsters in Hexen are a great improvement on the ones in Heretic: They look better, they move better, and they are generally more challenging to fight—and more satisfying to kill! Using monsters in Hexen is also a greater challenge for the designer because allowance must be made for the fact that players can choose their characters' abilities. This fact increases the complexity of monster layout because a mix of monsters that provides a good fight for a Fighter, say, might totally overwhelm a Cleric. You need to balance monster toughness and attack style with the strength and range of each possible player class. The next chapter will review the abilities and limitations of each of Hexen's player classes, but first you need to learn about the types of monsters Hexen players might be asked to face.

ETTIN

The *Ettin* is Hexen's equivalent of the Trooper. These two-headed monstrosities are slow-moving but fairly strong. They can inflict damage quickly, especially on the weaker player classes, if allowed time to get close enough to wield their spiked maces. Fortunately, Ettins are quite easily killed by all players, although the Cleric will need to be fairly nippy and dodge those maces. You might want to make more health or other power-ups available to this class of player.

AFRITS

Afrits are Hexen's new and improved Fire Gargoyles. These winged creatures can now hurl a stream of fireballs at a player, if allowed the time. They are easily dispatched, though, either with darts from the Sapphire Wand or a good punch from a Fighter. Once again, the Cleric will have the hardest time with these monsters until some weapon stronger than the Mace of Contrition has been obtained. Figure 19.12 shows an Afrit and an Ettin getting along like a house on fire.

Figure 19.12.
An Afrit and an Ettin becoming acquainted.

CENTAURS

Bearing a passing resemblance to the mythical beast of the same name, *Centaurs* cause damage at a high rate to any player who comes within range of their swords. They can also deflect missiles with their shields, reducing the advantage that players who can fire at them might have. As soon as Timon's Axe or the Frost Shards spell has been obtained, though, Centaurs aren't hard to kill. Once again, the Cleric tends to have the hardest time disposing of these creatures, so you might want to reduce the numbers that this class of player has to face.

SLAUGHTAURS

The *Slaughtaurs* (or Centaur Leaders) are a tougher form of Centaur capable of spewing magical fire from their shields. They are not much harder to kill than their lesser minions—just harder to survive long against!

WENDIGO

The *Wendigo*, or Ice Yeti, is a great lumbering beast who fires icy shards that quickly reduce a player's health. The icy blasts are difficult to avoid, so a player needs to dispose of these beasts quickly. Fortunately, Wendigos are easily killed by all player classes.

REIVERS

Reivers are Undead creatures who retain only the upper parts of their bodies. They fly through the air and summon up fireballs, which they hurl at players to devastating effect. They move quickly but are easily destroyed by all player classes. *Reiver Leaders* are sneakier versions of standard Reivers who lurk unseen, emerging from the ground when they spot their foes. Apart from this sneakiness, their behavior and characteristics are the same as standard Reivers.

STALKERS

The *Stalkers*, or Slime Monsters, also lurk out of sight and rise out of the slime to attack players. They can also sink back into the slime and slither around at high speed beneath the surface, emerging at will to surprise (and savage) players. (See Figure 19.13.) *Stalker Leaders* show the same behavior but can also fire slime projectiles at the player. Both types are dispatched with reasonable ease while they are visible.

Figure 19.13.
A Stalker stops stalking!

TIP: In Raven Software's own levels, Stalkers are confined to swampy areas and do not pursue players onto dry land. You can constrain these creatures to specific areas in your own WADs by surrounding the area with sectors with floors raised above the level of the Stalkers' area. These creatures will not step up any distance at all.

DARK BISHOPS

Dark Bishops are Hexen's equivalent of Heretic's Disciples of D'Sparil. Their circling projectiles of magical jade are even harder to avoid than Disciples' blasts, especially because these projectiles can track a player. Dark Bishops are frail, though, and are easily dispatched if their fire can be avoided. Don't mix Bishops with monsters that fire at players, or the players might have some of their work done for them.

CHAOS SERPENTS

Identical in form to D'Sparil's mount in Heretic, Hexen's *Chaos Serpents* come in two forms: the *Fire Serpent* and the *Gas Serpent*. The Fire Serpent delivers fiery blasts, whereas the Gas Serpent belches poisonous green gas. Fortunately, both varieties are easier to kill than D'Sparil's mount, although you'll need to make sure that all player classes have acquired at least one weapon before meeting any of these creatures.

DEATH WYVERN

Hexen's *Death Wyvern* (or *Dragon Lich*) is a very difficult monster for players to deal with. It is tough, fast, and very powerful. Keep these creatures to a minimum in your levels (or out of them all together), and make sure that your players are fully prepared if they have to meet one. (See Figure 19.14.)

Figure 19.14.
The Death Wyvern has its usual effect.

CAUTION: Unlike other Things, Death Wyverns cannot simply be placed into a Hexen level; they have to be correctly set up, with additional supporting Map Spots. Failure to place them correctly will result in either the Wyvern refusing to attack the player or in a complete hang of your computer system. Details on the correct way to use a Death Wyvern are given in Chapter 34, "Essential Thing Information."

HERESIARCH

The *Heresiarch* is one of Hexen's most powerful monsters. Fighting one of these is a lot like fighting D'Sparil himself in Heretic. With an array of powerful spells at their disposal, Heresiarchs can blast the player in a variety of ways, all of which are hard to avoid and cause serious harm. Heresiarchs can also summon Dark Bishops to their aid to make life really difficult for their foes. Along with this creature's almost infinite capacity to take damage, these characteristics make the Heresiarch an extremely difficult opponent to face. Consequently, you might want to reserve this character for levels intended for Cooperative play. You should also make sure that your players are properly armed by the time they encounter one and have plenty of health and other power-ups handy. (See Figure 19.15.)

Figure 19.15.
The Heresiarch making things personal.

THE THREE LEADERS

The Three Leaders—*Zedek*, Marshal of the Legion; *Traductus*, Grand Patriarch of the Church; and *Menelkir*, Arch-Mage of the Arcanum—are each available as the Nemesis for each player class to meet. And, boy, do these guys move fast! Naturally, each player is best matched to their former leader. All three Leaders are equally easy (read "hard") to kill by each class (given a completed multi-part weapon and sufficient mana) so you don't need to make each leader available only to the corresponding player class. There is also no real reason why you can't use more than one of each leader, other than through faithfulness to the storyline.

KORAX

Hexen's greatshowdown monster is the evil master *Korax*. As you would expect, this character is extremely difficult to defeat and is a fitting climax to the game. Whether you really want to put something this powerful in your WADs is for you to decide. It goes without saying that you'll have to provide players with a full complement of weapons and power-ups for them to prevail, doesn't it?

CAUTION: Korax requires special handling in a Hexen WAD. If you simply place a Korax Thing, Hexen will crash shortly after your player encounters the monster. The correct way to use Korax is covered in Chapter 34.

GHOST FORMS

Like Heretic, Hexen also has ghostly forms of some of its monsters: the two forms of Chaos Serpent, the Ettin, and the Centaur. These creatures act much as their usual counterparts but are easier to dispose of. When they are "killed," they simply vanish, leaving no corpse.

These monsters cannot be placed directly into a WAD as standard Things but have to be specifically *spawned* by a special control action. Their use is described in detail in "Hexen's Special Codes," a chapter on the CD-ROM.

CONTROLLING THE ENEMY

Having reviewed the range of monsters available for each variant of the game, it is worth looking at the standard ways all DOOM monsters behave as well as the ways this behavior can be controlled through the layout of a WAD. This discussion will lead to a better understanding of the best ways to use monsters in your levels and will help to make the process of deploying them throughout your WAD less tedious and error-prone.

STANDARD MONSTER BEHAVIOR

As you will know from playing, the basic behavior of DOOM's monsters is to stand at their posts asleep until something awakens them. Once awake, they will stand still no longer and will start to track the player. If a player is in sight, monsters who are capable of it will sooner or later start firing.

Three events will awaken a "sleeping" monster:

- Catching sight of a player
- Hearing a noise made by a player
- Being hit by fire

 Hexen introduced the idea of Dormant Monsters. These monster can be awakened only by special events. See "Programming the Action" on the CD-ROM for more details.

Once awakened, monsters do not normally go back to sleep, unless a player resumes a saved game—a common form of cheating!

 Hexen provides a special way to put monsters back to sleep. You'll find more details in "Programming the Action."

LINES OF SIGHT AND MONSTER FACING ANGLE

Very little in the world of DOOM works equally for players and monsters. You have been told earlier that monsters can see through all two-sided lines, regardless of texture. In fact, it goes further than that: Monsters can see through all two-sided lines that have any air gap at all between their adjacent sectors, regardless of vertical displacement. Therefore, of the three configurations of adjacent sectors illustrated in Figure 19.16, only in case *iii* is the player (at upper right) out of sight of the monster (at lower left).

Figure 19.16.
Unequal lines of sight.

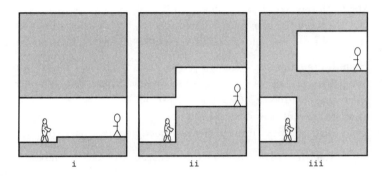

i ii iii

Players in cases *i* and *ii* of Figure 19.16 will awaken the monsters and will come under fire (although the fire will not reach the player in case *ii*). This trait will betray the presence of any monsters that you attempt to hide in trenches and such; bear it in mind when placing monsters.

TIP: The Reject Map can be used to disable monsters' lines of sight between particular sectors, removing the inequalities of this aspect of DOOM. This method is discussed in Chapter 23, "Reject Table Tricks."

To a certain extent, you can use a monster's initial facing angle to compensate for this effect. Monsters look forward with a field of vision of about 30 degrees to either side. Monsters do not stand perfectly still, though, even when asleep, and they will move a little from their starting angle as the game progresses.

USING DEAF MONSTERS

To prevent monsters from awakening when they hear a sound, you can use the monster's deaf-guard option. Setting this flag will cause monsters to ignore all sounds so that they awaken only when they catch sight of a player or are hit by fire from either a player or one of their fellows.

This option is also called the ambush option because it creates enemies that stay resolutely where they were placed (in hiding, usually), ignoring the sounds of combat around them and surprising the player later. Most of the time, you will not want to set this option; you will want to draw monsters from immediately adjacent areas to make combat come to a player no matter how the level is tackled.

You will usually not want to draw monsters from too far away, though. It would be undesirable, to say the least, to have all the enemies in a WAD zero in on the player's first pistol shot! To learn how to control the way sounds draw monsters into the fray, you need understand DOOM's principles of sound propagation.

SOUND PROPAGATION

In keeping with monster-player inequality, the way monsters hear noises differs from the way a player hears them. Monsters hear sounds made only by a player's weapons discharging, including the chainsaw and the fist. Monsters will not hear players grunting as they walk into walls or jump off high platforms. They are immune also to the sounds of doors and lifts operating and to their fellows firing or crying out in pain.

Sounds from a player's weapons propagate through the DOOM world in a standard way. First, a sound will immediately fill the player's current sector, awakening every non-deaf monster within it. It then travels across every line that has the Two-Sided flag set and where the arrangement of ceilings and floors leaves an air gap into an adjacent sector. Sound will not pass into sectors that are completely obstructed, such as a closed door or a sealed-off lift, or through any two-sided lines that have their Two-Sided flag clear.

Clearly, if left to its own devices, this propagation of sound could quickly have most of a WAD's monsters awake and on the trail of the player. Fortunately, DOOM provides a mechanism to prevent sound from propagating wildly throughout an entire WAD and awakening your monsters prematurely: a line's Blocks Sound flag. Lines with this flag set impede the progress of sound from one sector to another.

This flag does not operate in the same way as the Blocks Monsters or Impassable flag, however. It will not always prevent sound from crossing the line. First of all, it can't stop sound from spreading through an entire sector. Lines with the Blocks Sound flag set that are not between sectors will be entirely ineffectual. This flag is examined by the engine only when it determines whether sound can be propagated into an adjacent sector.

Further, sound is stopped only at the second Blocks Sound line it encounters. Therefore, sound will always pass into the sectors adjacent to the player's sector, given a suitable air gap.

These lines are intended to allow sound to fade away through a level rather than completely isolate sectors sonically from their neighbors. They also have no effect on the sound that the player hears while playing the game; that is handled completely differently.

TRACKING TALENTS

Yet another inequality between monsters and players is the monsters' ability always to sense the direction in which players lie. They use this sense to home-in on players and track them through the WAD. Fortunately (for the player), this ability is a straightforward homing talent that often leads monsters to dead ends.

You might want to impede monsters in their player-tracking and contain them in particular areas by setting the Blocks Monsters flags of some lines of your WAD. Remember, though, that such lines block the movement of all monsters, including the flying ones. If you want to stop only ground-based monsters from tracking through certain areas, consider using raised or sunken floors instead. Hexen's Stalkers, for instance, can be stopped with as little as two units of height difference between sector floors.

USING SOUND-PROPAGATION RULES AND THE TRACKING TALENT

The sound-propagation rules can be used also to awaken monsters that otherwise would never be awakened. This option can be combined with monsters' player-tracking abilities to create monster caches that deliver monsters into the game, either at irregular intervals to the keep the player on guard or in a rush to overwhelm the player at inopportune moments.

This technique is used in many of id Software's own levels. Take a look at the extreme northwest corner of DOOM's E1M9 for an example of the latter type of cache. (See Figure 19.17.)

Figure 19.17.
DOOM's E1M9 monster cache.

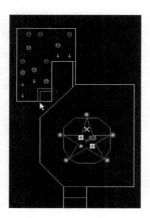

In this area, a thin open sector acts as a sound conduit into a room that is otherwise isolated from the rest of the WAD. The conduit carries the player's sounds into the isolated room to awaken the horde of monsters waiting there. In the starting condition, the monsters are no threat to the player because, apart from the thin conduit, the room is sealed.

A player who is lured into the room just to the south by the sight of the goodies there is in for a surprise, though. The edges of the star-shaped sector are tagged to open the thin sector in the corner of the monster-filled room (indicated by the cursor arrow in the diagram). This arrangement causes a teleport in the corner of the monsters' room to become accessible as soon as a player has stepped into the star-shaped sector. When this situation occurs, their ability to track the player will draw the monsters one by one over the teleporter lines to materialize in the room with the player.

Such sound conduits are not always necessary to carry sound into a monster cache, though. The next WAD sortie shows another way to achieve the same effect by using the sound-propagation rules in a different way.

RESPAWNING BEHAVIOR

The respawning of monsters in the hardest difficulty settings of the game is handled automatically by the game engine; the designer cannot alter this aspect of the game.

Hexen provides the designer complete control over its monsters' respawning through the use of its action control scripts. Details are given in "Hexen's Scripting Language," a chapter on the CD-ROM.

SUMMARY OF MONSTER-PLACEMENT CONSIDERATIONS

You should remember five main points when placing monsters in a WAD:

- Use monsters' facing-angle option to have them watch (or not) the entrances to areas so that the monsters are awakened as the player passes particular points in each area.
- Set a monster's deaf-guard option if you want it to wait until it sees a player before awakening.
- Use a suitable array of lines with the Blocks Sound flag set to prevent all non-deaf monsters in your open combat areas from awakening at the first sound the player makes.
- Use level changes or lines with the Blocks Monsters flag set to contain monsters within certain areas and prevent them from tracking the player in an undesirable way.
- Consider how the rules of sound propagation and monsters' player-tracking abilities can work to provide sudden monster releases or a steady stream of monsters into areas that players think have been cleared.

The next WAD sortie gives some practical examples of these ideas in use.

NOTE: The following WAD sortie builds on the WAD produced in the last sortie of the previous chapter. If you did not accompany me on that sortie but would like to come along on this one, you should use WAD26.WAD (DOOM), D2WAD26.WAD (DOOM II), or H1WAD26.WAD (Heretic) from the CD-ROM as your starting point. [Variations to be used when working with Heretic are noted in brackets.]

WAD SORTIE 27: A MONSTER CACHE

This sortie adds a new development to the growing WAD: a monster cache. Figure 19.18 shows the form and location of this element.

ADDING THE MONSTER CACHE

Notice where the new room is located, in the open space left by the curve of the western green stone corridor, beyond your first lift. To add this area in WADED, you should begin by drawing the main rectangle of the new room using GSTONE1 [GRNBLOK1 in Heretic] as the wall texture, but do not use Make Sector to turn it into a new sector. Instead, you should add the new lines to an existing sector. I've used the short corner sector of the corridor, indicated by the mouse pointer in Figure 19.18.

Figure 19.18.

The new monster cache.

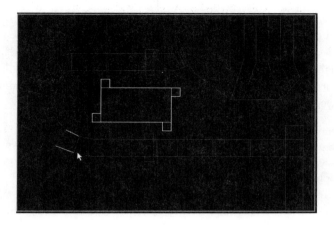

To add the new lines to this sector in WADED, choose Sec Define, right click in the chosen corridor sector to highlight it, and then left click in turn on each of the new lines. You now have another disjunct sector, like the slime pond in the arena. Of course, this new area requires no sector settings changes; it shares the settings of its disjunct part in the corridor. If you change one area's settings here, you will change the other's; remember that is all one sector.

Adding the New Sector in WadAuthor

To add the new sector in WadAuthor, start by adding a new rectangular sector in the space on the map indicated in Figure 19.18. Then move your mouse pointer into the corridor corner sector, noting its sector number shown in the status bar at the bottom of the WadAuthor window. Now double-click in your new sector to bring up its Properties dialog box. Click on the Linedefs tab in this box to see the settings for all the new lines. Edit the Sector field on this property sheet to match the number of the corner sector of the corridor just noted. That's all that is necessary to create a disjunct sector in WadAuthor.

Because this is all one sector, any sound reaching the corridor section of this sector will immediately propagate through to its disjunct part. Sound from any shots the player fires in the green stone corridor—or even out in the arena beyond, if the door is open—will therefore penetrate through to the new area and will awaken any non-deaf monster that you place there.

TIP: If you want sound to propagate through doors even when they are closed, add a recess on each side of the door as usual, then use the technique you have just seen here to make both of these recesses into one sector. Any sound reaching one side of the door will pass immediately to the other side, without any need to pass through the intervening door sector.

To make use of the new monster cache, you'll need to add a route out of the new room for monsters that have been awakened. Draw and make additional sectors off the four corners of the new room as shown in Figure 19.18. Make the lines across the entrances of these into teleporters, delivering monsters to various locations around the WAD. Make some of these teleporters deliver to points nearby and others to locations farther away. Use your knowledge of the way monsters in this room will follow the movements of the player to decide where each teleporter will deliver.

As an additional twist, allow the player to vary the way in which this monster cache delivers its load. Start by making the heights of the ceilings of the two teleport sectors that deliver farthest from the corridor the same as their floors. Then tag each of these sectors to the switch line in the unused (southern) alcove located in the corridor near the bottom of the lift. Put the special attribute of 103 (S1 Door: open) on this switch. Now, until this switch is thrown, the new room will deliver monsters closer to rather than farther from the corridor. It might take quite a while for a player to figure out what the switch achieves and whether it is useful or not.

Finally, populate the new room with some monsters and place a few columns in the room to stop the monsters from moving too freely along the walls. This addition should slow down their arrival at the teleports. If you want players to be able to get into the room and take a look at it, turn one of the lines of the corridor into an active teleport line that will take them there. Figure 19.19 shows the room with three Imps, four green columns, and a teleport destination to permit player access. Three of the room's own teleport delivery points can be seen in nearby corridor sections.

Figure 19.19.

Layout of Things in the new monster cache.

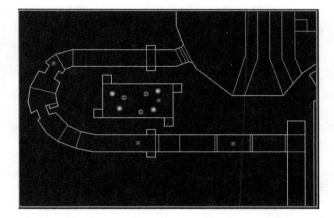

Notice, incidentally, how the addition of the monster cache has turned the corridor ceiling trap into something of a two-edged sword. Is it worth cutting off the line of retreat before entering the arena to prevent the propagation of sound to the new room? Probably. The last thing a player will need here is an additional attack from behind, which will occur if that ceiling is left up! This method provides players with an unexpected gain from an apparent trap. I wonder how many times they will need to play before they learn this, though?

When you've saved the WAD (WAD27.WAD) and seen how it works (you should hear the monsters wake up when you fire a shot in the bottom corridor), reload it into the editor and remove the temporary teleport line from the bottom corridor. Leave the teleport landing in the new room, though—tagged instead to all the lines surrounding the yellow key at the center of the donut. This change will cause any player who grabs the yellow key to be whisked away to the monster cache. (I just hope the monsters were enticed out earlier!) The yellow key should be close enough to the lines to let the player reach it just before a teleporter line does its stuff.

EXIT: MOPPING UP AND MOVING ON

In this chapter, you learned more about the different types of DOOM creatures and their basic behavioral patterns and about the rules for sound propagation through a WAD. You were also shown how to construct monster caches in your WAD.

The next chapter looks at the remaining items available to the WAD designer for use in a level: DOOM's weapons, power-ups, and other artifacts. It presents a strategy for populating and play-testing a complete WAD and shows you how to put the finishing touches on your new creation.

FINISHING TOUCHES

The preceding chapter reviewed the monsters available for players to fight in DOOM and each of its game variants. This chapter looks at what materiel players can be supplied with to help them through their ordeal. You will also be led through the steps involved in populating your WAD for real. You will be shown a strategy for deploying the enemy forces and for laying out caches of arms and other supplies for dealing with them. Methods for implementing different difficulty levels are discussed, and mention is made of other uses for the game's difficulty settings.

Finally, the last of the WAD sorties of this mission will provide you with practical experience in the initial stages of the process of populating your DOOM world.

KNOW THYSELF

Before discussing the weapons, armor, and other artifacts that can be made available to the player in each of the main DOOM game variants, it is worth taking a little time to review the capabilities and limitations of the DOOM gaming persona and its interaction with the artifacts of DOOM.

ACQUIRING AND USING ARTIFACTS

Each variant of the game made changes not only to the range of items available but also to the way these items could be acquired and used during play. Let's take a look at the differences that exist between these variants, paying particular attention to the way these differences might have a bearing on the strategies a designer needs to adopt in laying out a WAD.

— By Steve Benner with additional material by David Bruni

HANDLING ITEMS IN DOOM/DOOM II

One of the things that changed the least between DOOM and DOOM II was the playing methodology. The player has the same strengths and abilities in each. All of these games' weapons and artifacts can be taken and used by all players. If a player doesn't need (or can't carry) an item as it is encountered, that item remains behind for later use; otherwise, it is gathered up and either applied immediately (if it is a power-up) or added to the stocks (if it is a weapon or ammunition). This style of item acquisition meant that weapons and ammunition could be made available gradually as a level progressed. Players can acquire these items to carry and use as necessary in future encounters. Health and other power-ups, on the other hand, must be placed close to where they will be needed. Otherwise, these items might be wasted—because they must be used as acquired and their effects are short-lived—or else players have to spend a lot of time backtracking to replenish lost strength after major encounters. Generally speaking, DOOM levels need to be designed carefully with this characteristic of the game's artifacts in mind.

> **NOTE:** This chapter considers the general principles that apply to the populating of DOOM WADs. WADs intended for multiplayer use—especially Deathmatch WADs—have additional considerations. These are covered in Chapter 26, "Designing for Deathmatch."

HERETIC'S INVENTORY

In Heretic, the way items are used has changed. The acquisition and selection of the basic weapons and ammunition supplies, as well as the application of the minor health-replenishing Vials, remain the same as their DOOM equivalents, but other items of power are no longer applied automatically as encountered. Instead, the Heretic player gathers power-ups into an inventory and has the ability to select and use items from this inventory later, at will. This adds greatly to the realism of the game and provides the WAD designer with greater flexibility in WAD layout. It is now possible to place power-up artifacts further from their intended area of use than is possible in DOOM. This in turn obscures their intended use from players, encouraging a greater degree of experimentation during play. Thus the designer can make puzzles more complex. But it makes the maintenance of those puzzles harder, too; suddenly it is possible for players to use artifacts laid out for the solution of one difficulty to solve another too easily! This aspect of puzzle design in Heretic WADs is one that you will find needs careful watching. More will be said about this later.

Bear in mind too, when designing for Heretic, that power-ups acquired in one level and not used there can be taken to the next. Even though Heretic reduces the number of any such carryovers to a maximum of one of each kind, this still means that when you are making multilevel WADs, you have to remember what special artifacts were made available on the preceding level and design the next level accordingly.

FURTHER DEVELOPMENTS IN HEXEN

Hexen treats objects in much the same way as Heretic. This game does add a whole new complexity to their use, however, by introducing the concept of player class. In Hexen, each type of player not only has different capabilities, but also needs to use different weapons. Artifacts also change their function with player-type.

These changes impose a new dimension on WAD design. Hexen WADs need to be built for play by three types of players with different needs, abilities, and limitations. This affects all aspects of WAD layout: monster encounters need to be rethought for each player class, as does the availability of weapons and ammunition, health, and other power-ups.

Take a brief look at Hexen's three player classes, to consider what aspects of a WAD's design need special consideration in each case.

HEXEN'S CHARACTER CLASSES

Hexen enables a player to select from three classes of characters whenever a new game is started. This class determines the basic strengths and weaknesses of the player and determines what kind of weapons and armor the player can use.

BARATUS, THE FIGHTER

When playing as a Fighter, the player starts out stronger and with more armor than players in the other classes. Fighters can also move faster than any other class of player, all of which puts them at a greater advantage during hand-to-hand combat. The price to be paid is that Fighters cannot use long-range weapons and so are forced into close-range fighting more than the other classes. These players can build their armor class higher than other players—and need to in order to survive the dash into the melee that is so often required of them.

DAEDOLON, THE MAGE

The Mage is the weakest and slowest of the player classes. Mages are also not permitted strong armor, so players opting to play as Mages should make full use of the long-range weapons available to them. Mages can be pitted against monsters with long-range defenses sooner than can the other classes, because they are armed with a ranging weapon from the outset. Another penalty paid by those in this player class is that their slower running speed prevents them from being able to jump as far, laterally, as the other classes. This might deny them access to some areas of a WAD that Fighters, say, can enter with comparative ease. You might want to compensate for this limitation by providing Mages with alternative means of access—the Wings of Wrath, for instance.

PARIAS, THE CLERIC

Clerics are intermediary in their capabilities between Fighters and Mages. They are required to take part in hand-to-hand fighting until they have found their first weapon. Their medium speed and strength puts them at something of a disadvantage against most of Hexen's monsters while they have only the Mace of Contrition, but they can quickly overcome this disadvantage when they have a weapon at their disposal. You need to consider the mix of monsters and power-ups available to this class of player carefully, though, during the design of your WAD; it is the hardest to achieve a good balance for.

THE ARSENAL

One of the most important aspects of single-player and Cooperative-mode DOOM WAD design is achieving the correct balance of power between players and monsters. To help you appreciate the possibilities, I'll review the arsenal from which your players can draw their armament. Once again, each game has a different set from which to draw.

DOOM'S WEAPONS AND AMMUNITION

DOOM's weaponry is all appropriate to a Space Marine operating on a remote moon of Mars.

FISTS AND BERSERK PACK

The DOOM player's emergency backup weapon, for use when all else is unavailable or out of ammo, is his (or her) *Fists*. The beauty of this weapon is that it never runs out of ammunition. Of course, it doesn't do much damage, either, unless combined with a *Berserk Pack*. Although not generally classed as ammunition, the Berserk Pack can be considered ammo for the fists, enabling the player to do much more damage with them. It makes a useful addition in an area where Demons and Spectres are the only monsters and close encounters are a feasible battle plan. The effects of a single Berserk Pack last for the entire duration of a level and do not wear off with the red haze. Many players feel that a Berserk Pack should be made available in all levels as a matter of course!

CHAINSAW

The *Chainsaw* makes another good backup weapon, because it, too, can never run out of ammunition. After this weapon has been acquired, though, the fists can no longer be used, except immediately after picking up a Berserk Pack—a good reason to supply more than one Berserk Pack per level. Many players like to use the chainsaw to preserve ammo when dealing with Demons and Spectres, so if you provide one (hidden away somewhere, maybe) you can cut down on the amount of other ammo you supply. (See Figure 20.1.) It is also useful against most monsters weaker than Barons. And the chainsaw can be a popular Deathmatch weapon—there are DM WADs with no other weapons in them—so be sure that yours has one!

PISTOL AND BULLETS

When a WAD file first starts, the player already has a *Pistol* and a supply of *Bullets*. Extra bullets can be supplied in *Clips*, which hold a few bullets, or *Ammoboxes*, which hold a lot, the exact numbers varying with the difficulty setting. Firing single rounds, the pistol is useful only against the lesser monsters—Troopers, Sergeants, and Imps—so unless you keep the monsters that way, you should provide the opportunity to obtain a better weapon quite quickly. Troopers take fewer bullets to kill than they yield as they die, so theoretically at least, a player could complete a WAD populated only with Troopers without any additional weapons or ammo. The WAD is unlikely to be much fun, though!

Figure 20.1.

"Well, it's a choice of doing this or wasting the shotgun shells…"

SHOTGUN AND SHOTGUN SHELLS

The *Shotgun* is probably the best all-round weapon in DOOM. It can handle all but the most powerful of monsters. The player can carry enough shells to go a long way with this weapon, especially if a backpack has been provided too. Ammo for the shotgun can be supplied in two quantities: as a few *Shells* or as a *Box of Shells* (again, the exact quantities supplied each time vary with the difficulty level). You can make the shotgun available directly or use Sergeants as a supply of both the weapon and its shells. Sergeants certainly make a good supply of ammo for the shotgun, with the number of shells that their shotguns yield also being tied to the difficulty setting at which the game is played.

COMBAT SHOTGUN

DOOM II's new double-barreled *Combat Shotgun*, or Super Shotgun, is a great weapon made even better! The Combat Shotgun fires two shells at once but always seems to do more than twice the damage of the standard shotgun. Of course, it uses up the ammo twice as quickly (and it can't be fired when down to its last shell), and it has a longer reload time (see Figure 20.2). For most players of DOOM II, however, this is their weapon of choice most of the time. DOOM II still provides a standard shotgun, and you should generally make both of these weapons available in your DOOM II WADs if you want to keep most players happy.

CHAINGUN

The *Chaingun* is useful against just about all the monsters except the Boss monsters. Its biggest drawback is that it uses up a player's bullets very quickly, so if you supply one, you should consider supplying a backpack (and bullets by the boxload) too. Or you might not, if you want to keep your players hunting for ammo. The Chaingun is a good weapon to use to tempt Deathmatch players out into the open to collect.

In DOOM II, you can supply Chainguns (and bullets) by way of the Former Commandos. This means you'll probably have to make a shotgun available first to give the player a chance to collect it, though.

Figure 20.2.

The Combat Shotgun being reloaded.

ROCKETS AND ROCKET LAUNCHER

The *Rocket Launcher* is an excellent long-range weapon. The *Rockets* it fires are very powerful and can take out just about any of the monsters in DOOM (eventually, in some cases). It can also take out its user if it's fired carelessly! (See Figure 20.3.) Forcing the use of the Rocket Launcher in confined spaces can be a good way of testing your players' dexterity—or of driving them away from your WADs for good if you overdo it! Without the backpack, a player cannot carry many rockets, so if your WAD requires extensive Rocket Launcher use (through the presence of powerful monsters, for example), either provide some extra carrying capacity or maintain a steady supply of ammo. Rockets are available singly or in boxes.

Figure 20.3.

Oops!

The Rocket Launcher is regarded by many as one of the best weapons for use in a Deathmatch. One shot from the Rocket Launcher and your opponent is toast. Some of the best Deathmatches have centered around fights over the Rocket Launcher. Some people think it's too powerful a weapon for use in Deathmatch, though, because it can quickly unbalance the WAD. The best solution might be to make sure that all players stand an equal chance of acquiring one.

PLASMA RIFLE AND ENERGY CELLS

The *Plasma Rifle* is one of DOOM's most powerful weapons, being effective against everything except possibly the Cyberdemon. Before making a weapon such as this available in your WADs, therefore, you should consider whether it is really necessary. Of course, you can always limit its effectiveness by limiting the supply of the ammunition it requires. This can be supplied as single *Energy Cells* or in *Cell Packs* of 20.

BFG 9000

The previous comments are also true for the *BFG 9000*. DOOM's BFG (Big F——, er, Fragging Gun) can make quick work of all the monsters in DOOM, including the Cyberdemon. It can make short work of a full quota of Energy Cells, too! The BFG might be good for clearing a room full of lesser monsters, but it is not a useful general-purpose weapon, because of its slow firing action and the speed with which it drains energy cells. Ideally, the BFG 9000 should be considered only for single-player WADs, when the player will be facing very tough opposition. Or you can supply one to make a player use up a limited supply of plasma cells that much quicker. Or in Co-op games, in which players need to take care where they use it!

THE BACKPACK

At one level, the *Backpack* can be viewed as merely a supply of additional ammunition, because it contains additional supplies of each ammunition type. It also acts as a power-up for the player, of course, by increasing the amount of ammunition that can be carried. Supply a backpack if your level requires the player to go through a lot of ammunition. Withholding backpacks is a good way of making players more frugal with the ammunition they have been given, and is also a good way of preventing players from stockpiling arms and then sitting in one spot to pick off opponents in Deathmatch. If you make no backpacks available, players need to keep on the move to keep their frag count up.

HERETIC'S MAGICAL WEAPONS

In Heretic, all of DOOM's mundane (and high-tech) weaponry is replaced by the arcane and magical devices of the heretical Sidhe. Nonetheless, clear parallels remain visible between the capabilities of these devices and those of DOOM.

STAFF

The *Staff* is what the Heretic player has to use after all other weapons are out of ammo. It's a stick that does just about as much damage as the DOOM player's fists.

GAUNTLETS

Heretic's *Gauntlets* are equivalent to the Chainsaw in DOOM. For the gauntlets to be used, the player needs to get in close, but they never run out of charge. (See Figure 20.4.)

Figure 20.4.
"Come and get it…"

ELVENWAND AND WAND CRYSTAL

The *Elvenwand* is Heretic's pistol. Powered by *Wand Crystals*, each shot from this weapon does only small amounts of damage, sufficient to down Gargoyles and Golems after three or four hits but mostly ineffective on anything else. The player always starts with the Elvenwand, so you only need to supply the Crystals in a WAD, either as Wand Crystals (providing 10 shots) or as *Crystal Geodes*, capable of delivering 50. Golems occasionally drop a Wand Crystal, but this behavior cannot be relied on to keep a player supplied.

ETHEREAL CROSSBOW AND ARROWS

The *Ethereal Crossbow* is similar to DOOM's shotgun in its versatility and usefulness. Firing three magical discharges at each shot, the Crossbow is a powerful close-range weapon that is also capable of hitting multiple targets at a distance (although the spread is quite narrow). This weapon is effective against all but the most powerful of Heretic's monsters. The Arrows can be supplied as 5 *Ethereal Arrows*, or in *Quivers* of 20. Some monsters occasionally drop the odd supply of Ethereal Arrows, but never frequently enough to benefit the player much.

DRAGON'S CLAW AND CLAW ORBS

The *Dragon's Claw* feels like a hybrid of two of DOOM's weapons. It does damage at about the same rate as the Chaingun, with a firing cycle about as long as that of the Rocket Launcher. The barrage of magical power that it discharges disposes of many of Heretic's monsters quite quickly. Just like the Chaingun, it can quickly use up the player's supply of *Claw Orbs*. Unlike DOOM's Chaingun, though, using it does not deprive any other weapon of ammo! And unlike with the Rocket Launcher, careless use of the Dragon's Claw does not harm the player. Ammo refills can be supplied in units of 10 (Claw Orb) or 25 (*Energy Orb*).

HELLSTAFF AND RUNES OF POWER

Heretic's *Hellstaff* is a quick-fire weapon that really rips through its ammo (and anything it's fired at) in no time! Its *Runes of Power* can be supplied as *Lesser Runes*, which are good for 25 shots, or *Greater Runes*, providing 100. This weapon is roughly equivalent to DOOM's Plasma Gun in terms of its firing rate and effect.

PHOENIX ROD AND FIRE ORBS

The *Phoenix Rod* is Heretic's Rocket Launcher. When it's fired, its recoil is sufficient to push the player backward. If the weapon is fired at close range, the blast seriously hurts the user. The Phoenix Rod can be replenished with *Flame Orbs* (one shot each) or *Inferno Orbs* (10 shots).

FIREMACE AND MACE SPHERES

The *Firemace* is Heretic's most powerful weapon. It hurls explosive *Mace Spheres*, which make short work of anything they hit. This weapon has no equivalent in DOOM and, in any case, is a bit of an oddball (if you'll pardon the pun). In fact, I think there is something altogether strange about this weapon, and I can never quite take it seriously! I think it's the sight of those Spheres bouncing along. If you decide to make this weapon available to your players, ammunition is available as Mace Spheres (20) or Piles of Mace Spheres (100). Each shot requires 3 Spheres.

CAUTION: Another strange thing about the Firemace is that a level can never contain more than one of these weapons. If you add more, all except the last placed Firemace will appear as Disciples of D'Sparil when the level is played. Weird! (This feature has always been described as a bug. I rather think it's actually a joke! If you use more than eight Firemaces, though, the game crashes back to DOS as the level starts—whereupon the joke becomes less funny!)

BAG OF HOLDING

Heretic provides its players with a backpack just like DOOM does. Heretic calls it a *Bag of Holding*, but everyone knows it's really a backpack. It even *looks* like a backpack.

HERETIC'S EXTRA MUNITIONS

Powerful though many of Heretic's weapons are, in their standard state, none is capable of totally overwhelming monsters of even moderate strength. Heretic has no weapons of a power equivalent to the DOOM's BFG 9000. In addition, many of Heretic's monsters move with a speed that makes them difficult to hit, especially (ironically) with the more powerful weapons. For a player to make it through even a moderately populated Heretic WAD, additional power-ups are needed. Some of these add considerably to a player's store of weaponry. Let's take a look at these first.

TYKETTO'S TOME OF POWER

One of the artifacts that can be stored in a Heretic player's inventory and used when required is *Tyketto's Tome of Power*. This artifact provides a short-lived effect, but while active, the Tome of Power provides extra power to all a player's weapons. When weapons are powered up in this way, the effectiveness of all weapons is greatly increased, causing them to do more harm to whatever they hit. Some weapons consume ammo faster when powered up; others operate differently. The Firemace, for instance, combines three Mace Spheres into one and starts firing giant spheres when powered up. The Dragon's Claw fires faster, and its fire rebounds from whatever it hits as spinning iron-clad balls—fortunately, these do not harm the user, because they are difficult to avoid. (See Figure 20.5.)

Figure 20.5.
Dragon's Claw on power-up (with ricochet).

The Hellstaff sets up a falling rain of fire, killing almost any monster that steps into it (again, the user is immune). The best effects, though, are applied to the Phoenix Rod and to the Gauntlets. The Phoenix Rod turns into a flame thrower, pouring out a steady stream of flame, which can safely be used at close quarters (but which doesn't need to be, because it is an effective medium-range weapon too). The player does need to keep an eye open for the power-up wearing off, though! The powered-up Gauntlets are even better: they draw enemies in toward the player, draining their life energy and using this to replenish the player's—useful where Health power-ups are in short supply!

Most WADs of any difficulty need at least two or three Tomes of Power in them unless you provide a lot of Health and Ammo.

DELMINTALITIR'S TIME BOMB OF THE ANCIENTS

The *Time Bomb of the Ancients* is exactly what it sounds like: a device that can be left lying around to explode later. In this case, it is only a few seconds later—just long enough for a player to place it and run. These devices can be provided to give the player more choices in dealing with monsters. They are not particularly effective against any type of monster, but they can buy the player a bit of breathing space when the going gets tough. These weapons are also difficult to use effectively—getting the timing right is quite tricky—and can be a useful way to tax your players' abilities.

TORPOL'S MORPH OVUM

The *Morph Ovum* is a great "weapon" for players to have at their disposal. You'll find nothing like this in DOOM. When used, this device turns anything it hits into a chicken for a short time. The chicken can then be killed without difficulty. Naturally, these things are great for getting rid of even the most stubborn opponents, so don't make too many of them available.

These devices are also great fun in Deathmatch—just make sure that everyone can get one—and in games intended for Cooperative play. When morphed into a chicken, players can still participate in the game, but they temporarily lose access to their weapons and other artifacts—they can give an opponent a nasty peck, but that's about all! They are much more vulnerable when in this state, of course. They are also a lot smaller. This means that if you make areas with low ceilings that can be entered only when the player has been morphed into a chicken—either by an opponent or by a teammate in a multiplayer game—players can use this situation to turn a disadvantage into a potential advantage by gaining access to areas that would otherwise be unattainable. There is plenty of scope here for bizarre Cooperative setups, or hilarious Morph Ovum dueling tourneys.

HEXEN'S ARMORY

In keeping with Hexen's new player classes, the provision of weapons and ammunition has been rethought for this variant of the game. Players can only use the weapons appropriate to their particular class, each being provided with a range of four weapons. Fortunately, the supply of ammunition for these weapons is greatly simplified. Weapons are powered by sources of magical energy called Mana. Mana comes in two varieties, blue and green. Each class of player can have a weapon that requires one of the following:

- No Mana
- Blue Mana
- Green Mana
- Both green and blue Mana

At first sight, this might seem to make the WAD designer's task somewhat more complex. In reality, however, it does not. Each weapon type is roughly equivalent, between the classes, allowing for the different fighting styles of the three player classes. I'll look at what is available in a little more detail.

THE NO MANA WEAPONS

Hexen's base weapons require no Mana. They are equivalent to the standard fall-back weapons of earlier game variants, in that the player starts the game with them and always has them at hand if everything else fails. They tend to be more effective than the fall-back weapons of the other games, though. The following are the starting weapons:

- **Spiked Gauntlets:** Enable the Fighter to deliver quite a punch.
- **Mace of Contrition:** Gives the Cleric some means of defense, but not a lot.
- **Sapphire Wand:** Fires an unlimited supply of magical darts, giving the Mage a rather more effective base weapon than the Cleric.

THE BLUE MANA WEAPONS

The weapons powered by Blue Mana alone are the least effective of the weapons requiring charges:

- **Timon's Axe:** Enables the Fighter to mete out more harm than with the Gauntlets, but still only at close range.
- **Serpent Staff:** Provides the Cleric with a distance weapon, but not a very powerful one.
- **Frost Shards Spell:** Enables the Mage to start casting spells. These turn opponents into blocks of ice—eventually (see Figure 20.6).

Figure 20.6.
A Frost Shards Spell does its stuff.

THE GREEN MANA WEAPONS

The weapons powered solely by Green Mana are fairly powerful weapons, roughly equivalent to the Rocket Launcher in DOOM in terms of the damage they inflict (but very different to use!). Green Mana weapons consume charge more quickly than do Blue Mana weapons. These are the weapons:

- **Hammer of Retribution:** Enables the Fighter to deliver a blow strong enough to kill most foes outright, if used at close range. Used from afar, the hammer hurls a magical blow through the air at an opponent.

- **Firestorm:** Lets the Cleric summon a gout of fire from the earth. This is an effective close- or medium-range weapon, but it cannot be used from afar.

- **Arc of Death:** Provides the Mage with a spell that summons up columns of supercharged energy which quickly dispatch all but the toughest monsters. Again, this is most effective as a medium- or close-range weapon.

THE DUAL MANA WEAPONS

Hexen's most powerful weapons not only require the player to have a supply of both colors of Mana, but also must be acquired in installments! Each of these weapons consists of three parts, all of which must be obtained before the weapon can be used. All three of these multipart weapons are extremely powerful. They also consume a lot of Mana! These are the weapons:

- **Quietus:** The Fighter's three-part sword slices through most opponents like butter and hurls bolts of energy through the air at those foes sensible enough to stay away (see Figure 20.7).

Figure 20.7.
Quietus slicing through the Mana.

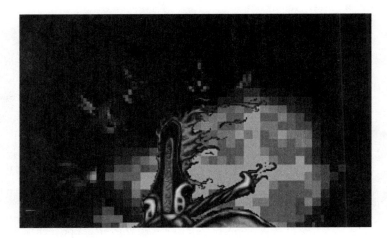

- **Wraithverge:** The Cleric's three-part staff summons the hungry spirits of the dead to hunt out and feed on the souls of the forces of evil.

- **Bloodscourge:** The Mage's three-part staff shoots spheres of searing fire that can track their targets (though not as well as spirits released from Wraithverge). It is not advisable to use this weapon near dry trees! (See Figure 20.8.)

Figure 20.8.
"I'm sure it moved…"

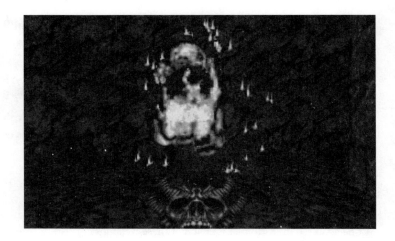

MANA CHARGES

Hexen's new ammunition is a great improvement over the complex array of different types used in Heretic. Supplies of Mana are available in just three types:

- Green Mana charges
- Blue Mana charges
- Combined Mana charges

This makes the supply of ammunition in a Hexen WAD far less complicated to arrange.

In addition, the *Krater of Might* artifact gives a full supply of both colors of Mana.

HEXEN'S EXTRA MUNITIONS

Like Heretic, Hexen provides players with several additional artifacts that can be used against opponents.

FLETCHETTE

The *Fletchette* (a flask of green potion) can be thrown at opponents. Its effect varies, depending on the player class of the user. For the Fighter and Mage, it behaves as an explosive missile; for the Cleric, it produces a cloud of poison gas that persists for a minute or so, poisoning anything that wanders into its orbit (including the player).

BANISHMENT DEVICE

The *Banishment Device* transports its target to the start of the level. Using this device on a monster activates that monster's death script and thus invokes any action that normally occurs when the creature dies (see "Programming the Action," a chapter on the CD-ROM, for more details).

THE DARK SERVANT

The *Dark Servant* summons a Maulotaur that defends the player for 30 seconds or so. Opponents are advised to stay well clear!

THE PORKELATOR

The *Porkelator* is Hexen's equivalent to the Morph Ovum. It isn't quite as much fun, but it can still have its (unusual) uses. In this book, however, I prefer not to mention such things.

DOOM'S POWER-UP ARTIFACTS

In addition to the stocks of weapons and ammunition that can be collected during play, DOOM supplies various other artifacts to help the player fight the good fight. Some of these replenish lost health or provide a boost to super-human condition, whereas others provide additional protection in the form of armor, or special abilities.

HEALTH BONUSES

The weakest of the health bonuses are the blue bottles that provide *Health Potions*. Although each of these increases a player's health by only 1 percent, they can always be taken, and they boost health past the normal 100 percent. Acquisition of these items also counts toward the bonus tally at the end of the level, so some should be included in single-player WADs to let the player clock up a bonus score during play. Clusters of half a dozen of these potions can also make the difference between life and death in some WADs, especially if other health-giving power-ups are kept to a minimum.

The *Stimpacks*, which are little medical kits, provide a 10 percent boost in health, as long as health is below 100 percent. The *Medikits* are even better; they give the player a 25 percent increase in health. Neither of these items can be taken if a player's health is already at 100 percent or over, nor do they count toward the game's bonus tally. The Berserk Pack can also be used as a health restorative: it not only gives the player super punching ability but also provides 100 percent health. Some tips on working out how many of these health bonuses to use in a WAD are given later.

The blue, hovering *Soul Sphere* (or Supercharge) gives the player a health increase of 100 percent. This is usually reserved as a prize after a very hard-fought battle to boost not only the players' health but their morale as well. You could, instead, insert one before the big battle room to boost players' health to the maximum for the ensuing fight. Generally, though, a level shouldn't contain too many of these health bonuses, or you run the risk of making it too easy to play. Soul Spheres also count toward the bonus tally.

DOOM II added a new health bonus: the *Mega Sphere*. In addition to providing a 100 percent health boost like the Soul Sphere, this artifact takes a player's armor class to 200 percent. The Mega Sphere was probably added to DOOM II to give the player a better chance against all the new and tougher monsters. You might want to supply a few if you're building a tough WAD yourself.

ARMOR BONUSES

DOOM players start without any special protection and must acquire armor to gain it. Armor comes in three types. Each piece of *Spiritual Armor*, the official term for the helmets, gives the player a protection-factor increase of 1 percent. Spiritual Armor does, however, enable the player to go up over the 200 percent level, and each piece collected counts toward the bonus tally at the end of the level. Treat Spiritual Armor as the protective equivalent of the Health Potion.

The green *Security Armor* takes the player to 100 percent armor level. A player is usually pretty vulnerable until one of these has been obtained. The blue *Combat Armor* is the heavy-duty armor that takes a player to an armor level of 200 percent. DOOM II's Mega Sphere combines the effect of the Soul Sphere with that of Combat Armor in one artifact.

The *Blur Artifact*, or Invisibility Sphere, makes the player invisible for a short time. This protects the player from monsters by making the monsters less sure in their aim. These artifacts are good in large rooms that have a lot of monsters in them.

The most powerful of the armor bonuses in DOOM is the *Invulnerability Sphere*. These are usually necessary in levels where there is either a Cyberdemon or the Spider Mastermind. This bonus gives the player a reasonable chance of defeating them. Using it in other situations just isn't in the true spirit of DOOM. (It isn't much fun either—see Figure 20.9.)

Figure 20.9.
Playing hard to hit (Invulnerability in DOOM).

Just as with health bonuses, armor bonuses should be matched to the hazards in a WAD. If you don't supply sufficient armor bonuses, your WAD might be unplayable; overdo their availability, and the WAD will be too easy. A strategy for getting this aspect of your WAD just right will be discussed later.

OTHER SPECIAL POWER-UPS

DOOM has other special power-ups that can be made available to help the player overcome certain hazards and difficulties in a WAD.

Radiation Suits might be needed wherever you have acid pits that the player must cross. This is particularly true if you're using the High Damage sector characteristic for these areas, because it won't take long for a player to die crossing sectors of this type. If your design is such that the player must enter the acid pit more than once, you might need to put two or more radiation suits in the area. Also keep in mind that the radiation suits don't last long. So if your acid pit is a large area or contains monsters that will delay your players' passage, you'll need to adjust the number of suits accordingly.

Light Amplification Visors can be provided for areas in your WAD that you have made very dark. They also are of time-limited use, but they could just enable your players to clear an area of its guardians, or locate that switch hidden in a dark recess somewhere. Use these items at your discretion.

The *Computer Map*, when picked up, shows the player the entire layout of the level. Areas that haven't been visited are shown in gray. The usual strategy with this power-up is to make it available in one of the final areas of a WAD, to enable the players to locate the last few secret locations that might have eluded them previously. This prevents the players from having to revisit every single room in your WAD, shooting and punching walls at random, to obtain that final secret bonus credit. Making this artifact available too soon can defeat the object of creating secret areas in the first place. It can just make locating the entrance to them all the more tantalizing, however, especially if you've devised a really sneaky trip-wire somewhere!

HERETIC'S POWER-UPS

Heretic's health and armor power-ups are very similar in function (even if very different in name and form) from those provided in DOOM. They fall into the same categories.

HEALTH BONUSES

Heretic's *Crystal Vials* work exactly as DOOM's Health Potions, except that they add 10 points to a player's current health. They cannot be added to the inventory and are used only if the player's health is less than 100. The *Quartz Flask* is equivalent to the Medikit, adding 25 to a player's health score. These items can be added to the inventory for use by the player when required, so you might not need to supply as many of these as you normally would Medikits—you can safely assume that a player will be carrying all that have been encountered. The *Mystic Urn* replaces DOOM's Soul Sphere, taking the player to full health. Because Mystic Urns can be carried in the inventory and applied as needed, they do not increase the player's health above 100.

ARMOR BONUSES

Heretic's *Silver Shield* is the equivalent of DOOM's Security Armor, working in exactly the same way. Similarly, the *Enchanted Shield* replaces the Combat Armor. Neither of these items can be added to the inventory but have to be used as encountered.

The *Shadowsphere* is Heretic's Blur Artifact, turning the player invisible for a time. Invulnerability is conferred on the player by *Valador's Ring of Invulnerability*. Both of these devices can be carried by the player and used as required.

OTHER SPECIAL POWER-UPS

Heretic's *Torch* performs the same function as DOOM's Light Amplification Visor, lighting dark areas (fancy that!). The *Map Scroll* gives a player the map of the whole WAD, whether visited or not, just the way the Computer Map does in DOOM. Of these two, Torches can be added to the inventory, whereas the Map Scroll is immediately effective.

Additionally, Heretic provides two new power-up artifacts with no equivalents in DOOM or DOOM II. *Darchala's Chaos Device*, when used, whisks the player back to the level's start location. You can make one of these available, if you like, in tough levels, in case things get too tough. They are also sneaky things to make available in Deathmatch.

Inhilicon's Wings of Wrath are many Heretic players' favorite. When used, this device imbues players with the ability to fly. This, of course, enables players to gain access to all sorts of places that would otherwise be denied to them. You should deploy this power-up with care in a WAD, because it can affect the way the WAD plays drastically—more will be said of this later. The Wings of Wrath add greatly to Deathmatch play and should be made available in most WADs of this type. Make sure that all players have a reasonable chance of acquiring them, because they confer a considerable advantage while they are active.

HEXEN'S ARTIFACTS

Hexen provides many of the same power-ups and other artifacts as Heretic. Most of these operate in the same way, although some have changed use slightly.

HEALTH BONUSES

Hexen's player health scheme is identical in all respects to Heretic's.

ARMOR BONUSES

Hexen's range of armor has been extended to cater to the needs of the different player classes. Each piece of armor contributes a different number of points to a player's armor class. Table 20.1 gives the points awarded to each player class by each type of armor artifact in Hexen.

Table 20.1. Armor points awarded by each of Hexen's armor artifacts.

Armor Artifact	Fighter	Cleric	Mage
Mesh Armor	5	2	1
Falcon Shield	4	5	3
Platinum Helm	3	1	2
Amulet of Warding	1	4	5

In addition, Hexen provides various time-limited improvements to a player's fighting chances.

The *Dragonskin Bracers* provide a short-lived addition of 4 points to a player's armor class, and the *Boots of Speed* cause a player to move faster for a while. The *Disc of Repulsion* repels most monsters, projectiles, and spells for a while. None of these artifacts is so powerful that you risk disturbing the balance of power in a WAD by introducing them.

Hexen's *Icon of the Defender* is equivalent to DOOM's Blur artifact and should be used in the same way. Hexen also provides Heretic's *Torch*, for lighting the darkness; the *Chaos Device*, to return a player to the start of the map in the case of emergencies; and the ever-popular *Wings of Wrath*, which now stay around for the duration of an entire cluster of maps. (The concept of map clusters is discussed in "Programming the Action" on the CD-ROM.

OTHER THINGS

Finally, in this roundup of items that a designer can leave lying around in a WAD for players to discover are a couple of additional scenery elements which are worth a closer look.

ADDITIONAL DECORATIONS

In addition to the floor, ceiling, and wall textures available for painting the various "hard" surfaces of your WAD, various decorative items can be added to a WAD. These do more than just provide atmospheric environments in which to do battle, however. They can introduce additional obstacles that make combat trickier by restricting player (and monster) freedom, and they might even constitute hazards in themselves.

HAZARDS

DOOM's exploding *Barrels* are the principal hazardous scenery item. These can produce such a devastating blast that many designers argue that they should be classed as additional ammunition for the players. Of course, strategically placed, they can make good ammunition for the monsters too!

DOOM II's burning barrels are entirely decorative and in no way hazardous.

Heretic's equivalent to DOOM's Barrel is the *Pop Pod*. You can use these in exactly the same way. Heretic provides one additional hazard in the form of the *Volcano*. These spurt fireballs out at frequent intervals.

Hexen's main hazard is the *Exploding Mushroom*. Again, this is equivalent to the DOOM's Barrel in that it is usually safe unless hit by fire, whereupon it leaves a cloud of poisonous gas that lingers for a couple of minutes.

OBSTACLES

Most of DOOM's remaining scenery elements act as obstacles, blocking the progress of players and monsters, who must find a way around them. These types of items can be used in large open rooms to restrict player and monster movements, or in narrow places to constrict them further. The choice of obstacle is largely a matter of personal taste. A full list of what is available in each game variant is given in Chapter 34, "Essential Thing Information."

NONBLOCKING DECORATIONS

Some of DOOM's decorations do not impede player or monster progress. These items act purely as decorative features, although they can be used to hide switches, power-ups, or even monsters, of course. Again, a full list of these items is given in Chapter 34.

SOUNDS

A new type of "decoration" introduced in Heretic is the Sound category. There are two types of Sounds: atmospheric or ambient sounds and environmental sounds. Both types are implemented as Things. *Ambient sounds* can be placed anywhere in a level. They are played at a constant volume at random intervals for as long as the map is in play. *Environmental sounds* are associated with the particular map location at which they are placed, and they sound louder the closer a player is to their source.

Hexen! Hexen also makes use of Sound Things but to a much lesser extent than Heretic. Even though Hexen has a reasonable number of Sound Things specified, only one of them (Wind Blowing) operates. All other Hexen Sound Things are silent. In fact, sounds in Hexen are controlled by means of Action Control Scripts and so are covered in "Hexen's Scripting Language," a chapter on the CD-ROM.

KEYS AND PUZZLES

Keycards are, of course, essential to the player's ability to complete a WAD. If you are using any of the key-operated doors, it is essential that you make the keys available somewhere in your WAD. I will have more to say about this aspect of laying out a WAD shortly, but first I'll just review what keys are available in each variant of the game.

DOOM'S KEYS

DOOM and DOOM II have six different keycards. These are available in three colors—red, yellow, and blue—and in two styles—standard keycards and skull-cards. There is, in fact, no difference between the standard and skull types; each opens a door of the appropriate color.

HERETIC'S KEYS

In recognition of the fact that there are only three kinds of door locks, Heretic offers only three keys, one of each color—yellow, green, and blue.

HEXEN'S KEYS

Hexen provides a much bigger range and variety of keys—11 in all! Their names are given in Chapter 34 and details of how they are used in "Hexen's Special Codes," a chapter on the CD-ROM.

HEXEN'S PUZZLE PIECES

As well as extending the number of available keys (and, thereby, the number of areas in a level that can be locked against a player), Hexen has a number of further devices for controlling the order in which players can do things. One of these devices you have already seen: the multipiece weapons. The component parts of these weapons can be distributed widely around a WAD to ensure that players have visited many distant areas of a WAD before being strong enough to tackle its stronger monsters (who presumably guard the ultimate goal).

Hexen's second mechanism for providing puzzles and ordering actions is the supply of so-called *puzzle pieces*. There are many of these items, ranging from mechanical components such as Clock Gears, through Gemstones and Spell Books, to Masks and Skulls! All of these items actually do nothing, most of the time. In fact, the only thing they do by default is display the message You cannot use this item here on-screen whenever the player tries to use one of them.

To make these items useful to the game, you must set them up correctly to perform whatever function you have in mind for them to perform! They can, in fact, be made to do almost anything. Before you're shown how this can be achieved, though, you need to know much more about Hexen's extended programmability, and that is the subject of other chapters. Details of how to set up the puzzle pieces is therefore deferred until "Hexen's Special Codes" on the CD-ROM.

PLANNING THE POPULATION

Like every other aspect of WAD design, populating a WAD with monsters and the means to dispose of them needs careful preparation and planning. Let's take a look at what's involved.

PREPARING TO POPULATE A WAD

By the time you start populating your WAD, you should have a clear picture in mind of the way you want the WAD to play. You should know what each of the areas in the map is like and what function each is to serve in the grand scheme of your level. You should have a fair idea of what is to happen in each area and in what order events should occur. If you don't know these things before you start laying out the denizens and artifacts of your WAD, they are unlikely to contribute much to the way it plays.

So before you start placing any items, take a good look at the geography of your WAD, clearing up in your own mind how you want each area to contribute to the level as a whole. Sketch out the way you feel play should progress. Then take a run through your empty WAD, trying to visualize the way it will all work. Only when you're confident that you know what you want should you set about trying to achieve it.

THE NATURAL ORDER OF THINGS

The secret to laying out a WAD successfully is largely one of sequence. One of the main difficulties in populating a WAD is achieving a balance between the forces that players will encounter and the means of disposing of them. You will find that it is much easier to achieve this balance if you do things in the right order. This is the sequence of placement I recommend:

1. **Player starts and keys:** Begin by laying out player-start positions and keys. This placement determines the flow of the WAD from the outset.

2. **Essential obstacles and artifacts:** Next, place those obstacles (and any artifacts) that are essential to the control of flow. These can be regarded as part of the geography. Leave out the decorations at this stage.

3. **Enemies:** When the flow of the WAD has been established, place enemy forces in the principal combat areas. This enables you to see how the forces you envisaged behave in the space you have provided for them.

4. **Weapons and ammunition:** After you are happy that the monsters behave as you'd like, concentrate on providing the players with the weaponry needed to dispose of them.

5. **Power-ups:** Having provided your players with creatures to fight, and the means of fighting them, you should now make sure that they can live long enough to do it.

6. **Bonuses:** Most players see collecting the bonuses as secondary to slaying the monsters. Lay these out, therefore, after the main battle scenarios have been completed.

7. **Decorations:** Add any final atmospheric decorations that you feel enhance your WAD. Don't overdo it!

8. **Extras:** When you're happy with the main areas of your WAD, consider adding a few wandering extras to the enemy's principal forces, just to keep your players on their toes.

Each of these stages in the laying out of a WAD will be examined shortly. Between each stage, test thoroughly and don't be afraid to go back a stage or two if need be to change or refine things you have doubts about.

EFFECTS OF OVERPOPULATION

Before you dash off to start filling your WAD with monsters, you should be aware of the consequences of overpopulating your DOOM world. Placing too many Things around your map can overload DOOM in two ways. The first way is through *Sprite overload*. This occurs when too many Things are in view at one time. The second problem you might encounter is *save buffer overflow*. This occurs when a WAD has just too many changeable items.

SPRITE OVERLOAD

Sprite overload is an unpleasant effect that can occur in areas that use a lot of Things, such as hordes of monsters all attacking simultaneously, or lots of decorations, or both. In laying out a WAD, you should always bear in mind that DOOM can handle the display of only 64 Sprites—enemies, decorations, ammunition (either on the ground or in flight!), bonuses, and so on—simultaneously. If there are any more than this, you will find that they all wink in and out of existence during play. The more Sprites there are, the longer each is invisible.

Avoid this effect by limiting the number of Things in view at any one time. Cut down on the number of monsters (you can make combat tougher by reducing armor, ammo, and health availability, or by increasing the toughness rather than the number of enemies). In addition, resist dense pockets of unnecessary decorations.

A maximum of 64 Sprites in view might sound like a major restriction to the more bloodthirsty of you, but remember that, generally, the game engine will have slowed to a crawl in trying to keep track of all of these Sprites long before this limit is reached! If, however, you really want these quantities of monsters, take steps to keep them spread out around the player so that they can never all be in view at the same time. The game will still slow down, but the WAD should not suffer from the disconcerting effect of winking Sprites!

SAVE BUFFER OVERFLOW

The buffer that DOOM uses when writing a saved game to disk is not very large (although it has been increased in later versions of the game). If your WAD provides the game engine with too many items that can change during the course of the game—basically any items that the player can acquire, kill, destroy, move, or change in any way—you risk causing this buffer to overflow. The result is a game that cannot be saved—and some very frustrated players!

It is difficult to gauge how big a WAD can get before causing this condition, mostly because it is impossible to judge precisely how much space DOOM will need. Developing your WAD by degrees, and regularly trying to save games while in play, will keep you assured that you are not over-stretching the engine's capabilities in this area.

USING THE DIFFICULTY SETTINGS

It is common for WADsters to feel that it is not necessary to create a design for each of DOOM's difficulty levels. They argue that most players will be using the hardest difficulty setting anyway, so why bother? In my opinion, such a view is misguided.

Certainly there is little point in implementing an easy version of your WAD for first-time players. You can reasonably expect all the users of your WAD to be seasoned DOOM players. (Otherwise, why would they be playing an add-on WAD?) Remember, though, that not all players have the same abilities or preferences. Your WADs will be better received if it is possible to vary the level of difficulty to suit a range of playing skills and styles.

Bear in mind, too, that you are not constrained to using DOOM's difficulty-level settings merely to vary the WAD's survivability. Used imaginatively, Things' skill-level flags can work constructively to prolong the useful life of your WAD by providing players with scope for more varied play than graded WADs can provide.

GRADED PLAY

As already noted, the provision of graded play can make a WAD appeal to a wider audience. When you're working on such a WAD, it is often best to lay it out at skill-level 1 ("Hurt Me Plenty"/"Bringeth Them Oneth"/ Normal) and to play-test this level first. Make this setting hard enough to push your own DOOM-playing capabilities—it should be a struggle to complete the level. Work out next what should appear at skill-level 0 ("I'm Too Young To Die" and "Hey, Not Too Rough") to produce something that is a comfortable play for you. Finally, work on skill-level 2 ("Ultra-Violence" and "Nightmare"), making this level very difficult for you to play.

Laying a WAD out like this can be time-consuming and tedious. But you should find that the result is a WAD that has at least one level to suit any player. Some tips on what you can do to give your players a harder time are given in later sections of this chapter.

NOTE: Remember, there are only three difficulty-level settings as far as Things are concerned.

VARIED PLAY

If you are more interested in producing a WAD that is uniformly tough to play at all difficulty settings, you can still use Things' skill-level flags to introduce other variations into your WAD. You can use the flags to control or vary the occurrence of most Things with skill level. Remember that this applies to obstacles, keycards, and teleport destinations, as well as the more obvious categories of monsters, weapons, and power-ups.

You can therefore use these settings to change the flow of a WAD completely from one difficulty setting to the next. You can use obstacles at some levels of difficulty to block corridors that are open at others; move the keys around and generally employ the skill-level flags as a cheap way of producing three different designs within the same basic map. This technique can greatly increase the lifetime of your WAD, providing its players with three WADs in one, with the need to find new ways of tackling each difficulty level.

You can also vary the game style, while at the same time keeping the play tough enough for even the most seasoned DOOMster. Use different mixes of monsters, weapons, and power-ups at each skill level to provide another element of variety for your WAD's players to select.

POSITIONING THE MISSION IN THE EPISODE

Another point you might need to consider when planning the population of your WAD is where it will be played within an episode. Most PWADs replace an episode's opening mission—few people will want to play all the way through a familiar mission to begin a new one. You might, of course, be building a new multimission WAD either from scratch yourself or by contributing one mission to a collaborative project.

Planning for players arriving from earlier levels can be tricky. You do not know whether players will arrive barely alive and in need of some power-ups pretty quickly, or whether they will arrive fully armed and super-fit, having saved the preceding level's Soul Sphere for last.

Usually, though, you will know what weapons were available to the player on the preceding level. Generally speaking, you should assume that these weapons have been obtained, and you can plan your own WAD around this assumption. If having those weapons then becomes vital to the completion of your own WAD—it doesn't have to, of course—you should make sure that your WAD will supply additional weapons for players who missed them earlier.

The safest option is to make it immaterial how a player is equipped on arrival and to provide everything necessary to complete your own level.

DEVELOPING A DEPLOYMENT STRATEGY

A suggested sequence for laying out the creatures and artifacts in a WAD was presented earlier in this chapter. Each step outlined then will now be examined in more detail, to enable you to see the overall strategy for the successful population of a WAD. You'll start by considering a map's flow of play.

CONTROLLING FLOW

Hopefully, your geography has been planned with consideration of its general flow in mind. Before you come to populate in earnest, though, it is worth taking a final run through the map, looking at the way it all interconnects and imagining how the player might progress from one area to the next.

Consider what order players might choose to do things in. Can they vary the order in which they tackle the areas? If they do, will this alter the way in which your planned encounters occur? It is easy to lose sight of the big picture when you are working on the geography of each room. Take the time, then, to try to imagine each area in use and how it fits in with what should happen in other areas; this method enables you to refine your thinking (and hence your design) of each area and maybe the WAD as a whole.

PLAYER START POSITIONS

When you are reasonably happy with the layout of the lines, decide where a player is to start—you should really have planned this from the outset, but you might want to revise your thinking after walking through the WAD a couple of times. Unfortunately, you cannot use the skill-level flags of Player 1 Starts to have the player begin the level in different places. If you attempt this action, DOOM uses only the last of the Player 1 Starts that you placed, no matter what difficulty level is selected. Each of the other positions is occupied by a static "projection" of the player. (See Figure 20.10.) These projections do not participate in the game—monsters appear not to be able to see them—but be warned that any harm they take is passed on to the "real" player!

NOTE: This restriction on the use of the skill-level flags applies to the other Cooperative-mode player starts too. It does not apply to Deathmatch starts, however.

Figure 20.10.

Seeing double? I wouldn't pull the trigger if I were you!

KEYCARDS

Use keyed doors to divide a WAD into self-contained areas, or to control the flow of play so that areas are tackled in an appropriate order. In this way, you ensure that the tougher monsters are not encountered until a player has had a chance to acquire some heavy weaponry, for instance, or to prevent a player from leaving until all the WAD's puzzles have been solved.

Lay out the keycards in the positions they need to occupy to facilitate the flow pattern you envisage. The locations of keycards can be made to vary with skill level. Utilize this capability either to make the cards harder to obtain at higher skill levels or to spring different traps as cards are acquired. If you want, you can even alter the flow altogether by changing the order in which the cards can be obtained.

OTHER ESSENTIAL ARTIFACTS

At this stage you should also lay out any obstructions that are important to the flow of the game. You can use certain items of decoration—firesticks, columns, and so forth—as obstructions in gaps that you want to let players shoot through but not pass through. Once again, you can control the use of these obstructions at the different skill-level settings, thus blocking off some corridors and opening others to change the interconnections of your WAD.

Consider also whether any special power-ups might be needed for the successful playing of certain areas of your geography—Light Intensifying Visors for the dark areas, for instance, or Radiation Suits. Place these items at this stage to help your play-testing. Again, the skill-level flags can be used to control the available quantities as well as the locations of these items. You might want to reduce their availability (or remove them altogether) at the higher difficulty settings.

TESTING THE FLOW

After you have laid out the various items that will control the flow of the game, try taking another run through it. Aim to make your way as quickly as possible from start point to exit, taking whatever route is required to collect all the keys and make it to the exit. Doing this at this stage might well identify areas that the player doesn't need to visit—and that therefore contribute little to the flow of the game. If you had intended those areas to figure more prominently in the game, you might need to redesign the flow. Try moving the keys around, or changing the way the doors are keyed, for instance. Or maybe you just want to use those areas for the positioning of secrets. (Players shouldn't need to go everywhere to complete a mission, of course—only to complete it with a full score.)

After any redesign, run through your level again to check that everything flows as you had intended. Try to imagine the sequence of predicaments that players might find themselves in as they work through the WAD. After you have done this a few times, you should have a clear picture of the way your WAD is going to work and where most of the monsters should be.

DEPLOYING MONSTERS

The choice and deployment of the forces that your players will encounter require not only a full appreciation of each enemy's individual characteristics, but also an understanding of the basic behavioral patterns common to all monsters. Some of this knowledge you should already have gained from playing the game itself (as well as from elsewhere in this book). Some additional factors that influence the movements of monsters during play, and the options open to the designer for controlling them, will be covered in a later part of this chapter. For now, though, I will just discuss in general terms tactics for the deployment of monsters in battle zones.

CHOOSING THE TYPES

The bulk of a WAD's monsters should be introduced in a structured way. Work around your WAD, implementing the main battle areas first. For each zone, determine the principal type of combat you want to inflict on your player. Decide the main mix of monsters and their quantities, taking into account their basic behavior and characteristics, the way they mix (or don't) with each other, and how much space they have around them in which to fight.

If the structure of your WAD forces areas to be tackled in a particular sequence, be sure to keep this feature in mind as you place the monsters. Try to make each encounter harder than the preceding one, and don't present players with the tougher monsters too early unless you intend them to have acquired some heavy weaponry as well.

GRADED ENCOUNTERS

When using monsters to produce graded play, don't assume that just throwing more and tougher monsters into the fray will always make things harder for the player. It might, but more often than not, it won't. This tactic frequently produces an unstable mix of monsters who are happy to spend their time fighting each other rather than the player. Often a player will have little to do apart from keeping out of the way and picking through the corpses afterward!

There are better ways of making levels tougher than by loading them up with extra monsters, and you should resist the temptation to do this. In particular, don't use the skill-level settings simply to satisfy players who might want a bloodfest. Let them use "Nightmare" mode.

Remember, too, that giving some players certain types of monsters to fight simply supplies them with additional ammunition and weapons! Most players view Sergeants as just another supply of shotgun shells, for instance. On the other hand, Imps used in large quantities give players a hard time. These are frequently employed because of their tolerance of their own kind's poor aim—and the fact that they provide the player with nothing afterward.

As you populate each area, therefore, it is imperative that you try out the WAD to see how the mix of monsters you are using behaves.

TESTING THE MIX

Testing your mix of monsters should not consist of wading into battle with the full protection of degreelessness and lots of very happy ammo, just to see how easy it is to waste everything in sight. Rather, you should mostly be running among the baddies, shooting at them just enough to keep them interested in you, and observing how they behave together.

Use God Mode to stay alive while you see whether any sort of status quo is maintained if you don't fight. Try to determine whether the monsters will quickly surround and overwhelm a player during proper play. Or will their buddies do all the dirty work if a player can just keep moving? Check that you are giving the player the sort of hard time you had planned.

ADDING VARIETY

When you think you have one area right, you can move on to populating the next. Aim for variety in encounters with monsters—not only in the types and quantities of enemies, but also in the character of the fight. Your geography should already have been designed to vary the sizes of combat arenas and to provide a mix of light levels. Make the most of these variations in your monster deployments. As well as rooms full of foes, arrange for some monsters to hunt for players while others lie in wait. (I'll look at some ways to arrange this situation shortly.)

Above all, don't make everything predictable—leaving a dark and twisting corridor altogether devoid of monsters can be a very effective way of raising a player's pulse rate. Aim to balance the suspense, the surprises, and the episodes of total carnage. Try to avoid the kind of shoot-'em-up WAD that bores players with its predictability long before they finish it.

WEAPONS AND AMMUNITION SUPPLIES

When you have most of the major battle zones populated with monsters, you can turn your attention to the weaponry required to deal with them.

GAUGING SUPPLY

One way to find out how much ammo you need to supply is to play each area in turn with the IDKFA code invoked (and IDDQD if necessary), taking note of your ammunition stocks before and after each main combat event. This gives you a chance to try the effects of fighting with different weapons, too. You might find that certain weapons make fighting easier, whereas others are a positive hindrance (such as the Rocket Launcher in confined spaces). Use this information to decide what weapons to make available at each difficulty level. Make levels harder by limiting the power or suitability of weapon supplies, as well as by reducing availability (and accessibility).

RELEASE RATE

Once again, consider the flow of your WAD in deploying weaponry. Use the secret places for the real goodies so that the more observant players benefit the most. Make sure, though, that players can obtain the weapons necessary for survival if they look and work hard enough for them.

In higher difficulty levels, you might want to leave it entirely to the monsters to supply ammunition and certain weapons such as the shotgun (and, in DOOM II, the Chaingun). You can also make things tougher by limiting the amount of ammunition players can carry—do not provide backpacks. This is a far more effective way of increasing the difficulty of a mission than increasing the monster count—half a dozen Imps can be quite a challenge if a player is down to bare hands!

ADDITIONAL ITEMS IN THE ARSENAL

This stage of laying out the WAD is often an appropriate time to consider the placement of barrels. These are important elements of the players' (and the enemies') arsenal. Not only do they act as a powerful weapon, but barrels also represent extra hazards in confined spaces. They are useful for creating temporary obstructions that players can move (if they think to) and are a good way of preventing players from being able to creep about the WAD without waking any monsters who might be around.

Barrels are useful devices for creating variation across the skill settings. Place them close to monsters to favor the players—or next to likely hiding places to make players' lives more hazardous.

TEST IT ALL AGAIN

When you've completed the layout of your WAD's arsenal, try playing it again using only what you've laid out. Use the God Mode as necessary to stay alive, but don't award yourself any additional ammo. Refine your monster placings and oil-drum spacings, and adjust the weaponry available until the WAD is satisfying to play.

You can then start thinking about the power-ups.

POWER-UP ARTIFACTS

Power-up artifacts are necessary for your players to survive the ordeals of your WAD. The correct deployment of these can often make or break a WAD.

GAUGING WHAT'S NEEDED

You can determine the amount of health that players are likely to expend in their battles by using the same technique you used to determine ammunition requirements—play the WAD without the IDDQD code, and note how much health is consumed in each encounter. Lay a temporary stockpile of health power-ups somewhere central in your WAD so that you can grab a quick boost between each encounter. Berserk packs are good here, because they give 100 percent health. (Don't forget to remove these power-ups when you've finished with them.)

Consider where you might place Stimpacks and Medikits to provide major replenishment of players' health. Decide whether you want to provide players with a health boost before a heavy encounter—this event often acts as a warning of something bad ahead—or whether you want to make them wait until they have survived the ordeal before offering the chance.

Generally, you should reserve the major bonus items, such as Soul Spheres and blue Combat Armor, as rewards at the end of large-scale combat, or tuck them away in secret locations.

Make levels harder by reducing available health. Provide a single large power-up quite early, say, and then only smaller boosts from then on. Players then must sustain little damage if they want to make it to the end of the mission.

SPECIAL POWER-UPS

Some of your planned encounters might require the more powerful artifacts, such as Blur or Invulnerability. Make sure that these artifacts are positioned appropriately (which is not to say that they're easy to find or to easy to obtain, of course!). Do this at this stage, if you didn't do it earlier.

It is often a good idea not to place these artifacts too close to where the action that you think requires them will occur. Let them be squandered the first few times the WAD is played, by encouraging players to take and use them too soon. You can achieve this outcome by positioning such artifacts in junctions or close to secret connections to the appropriate battle area. This method prevents players from associating the artifacts with the route to any particular area. Make it ambiguous how such artifacts might be needed. Give players the opportunity to try out their use in different ways. Don't forget to try out all of these different ways for yourself too, of course!

BONUSES

After the major items are in place, the Spiritual Armor and Health Potion bonuses can be sprinkled around as you feel necessary—usually in secret locations, as an incentive to enter and collect the secret credit, or as a quick boost before the next major combat. Generally, you can set the same bonuses on all skill levels—they might be all that will keep the player alive in the upper settings! Indeed, you might already have placed most of these items when you laid out your medical supplies.

ADDITIONAL DECORATIONS

Finally, any additional decorations that you feel are necessary for atmosphere can be positioned around the WAD. You can add these purely for effect or to serve some other purpose—as warnings, for example. Pools of blood beneath crushers are common in many WADs, as are corpses outside particularly hazardous areas (or just scattered around to make players nervous!). Mostly, what you use will be a matter of personal taste. Use whatever you feel fits into the general design of your WAD, but, as always, don't overdo it. Avoid too much decoration in areas with many monsters, or you run the risk of Sprite overload or of just slowing down the WAD to the point of unplayability.

At this stage of the design, try to avoid adding any items classed as Obstacles (see Chapter 34 for a list of these items), unless they are well away from the main action. Otherwise, you risk upsetting the balance of play that you have worked so hard to produce. If you particularly want decorative elements to contribute to the hazards of a level, add them early, rather than late in the design, so that they are in place while you are testing the layout of their areas.

CAUTION: Many items of gore are available in both obstructing and non-obstructing versions. Choose which items you use carefully.

EXTRAS

At this stage, your WAD should be just about ready. Try playing it from beginning to end without any cheat codes. Ask yourself how it works as a whole. Is there enough variety? Are things distributed correctly? Are there any unnecessary holes in the action? Refine the way it plays by adjusting any of the elements already in place. You might also want to add a few new items to break up any unevenness in the way the WAD plays.

To add a little unpredictability to a WAD, you might consider introducing a few wandering monsters. Such monsters—when placed where they will be awakened early, by either seeing or hearing the player, but in an area where they will take a long time to appear—can be made to pop up unexpectedly in a slightly different place each time. (Ways of achieving this action are discussed after the next WAD sortie.)

FINAL REVIEW STAGE

When you are completely happy with the way your WAD is playing, pass it to some others to play, and ask for their comments. If you can, watch the way they play it—you'll get a better feel for whether your traps and signals are working as you expected them to. If you can't be there to watch their game, ask them to record a demo of it. Watch this demo a few times, making notes of which aspects of the WAD are working as you intended and which still need improvement.

Don't keep asking the same play-testers to look at your levels after each minor change, though—they most likely will just get bored and will not give it a full workout. Pass it on again only when you have made all the significant improvements you can think of and feel you have things as good as they can be.

> **NOTE:** The following WAD sortie builds on the WAD produced in the last sortie of the preceding chapter. If you did not accompany me on that sortie but want to come along on this one, you should use WAD27A.WAD (DOOM), D2WAD27A.WAD (DOOM II), or H1WAD27A.WAD (Heretic) from the CD-ROM as your starting point. If you have not been following the development of these sample WADs in detail, you might want to take a complete run through the WAD to familiarize yourself with its layout before participating in the sortie.

WAD SORTIE 28: CHECKING THE FLOW

By way of preparation for the real populating of the WAD, this sortie looks at the steps involved in checking the flow of play through your WAD. It starts by considering the placing of the keys for those keyed doors.

> **HERETIC** Readers working with Heretic might feel that they have been abandoned in this sortie. This is because I think that they can now fend for themselves much better than in earlier sorties. The entirely DOOM-based details presented in this sortie easily translate into Heretic equivalents, however, so you should not experience any difficulties out there on your own. Remember: if in doubt, experiment!

THE INTENDED FLOW

It is time that I revealed to you my intended control of flow through the WAD you have been building. The keyed doors are already in place; I should tell you now where I have planned to place the keys.

Currently, players can explore west from the starting room by passing through the platform room, whence the whole of the western half of the map is accessible. Alternatively, a player might start by venturing east into the maze. The remaining areas of the map are locked away behind the blue-keyed door off the southeast passageway. One of the two accessible areas needs to hold a blue keycard, therefore.

In reality, two keys are needed before a player can progress much further. The blue keycard grants access only to the outdoor crescent area—all further doors are locked with red or yellow cards. I have used this arrangement to force players to tackle both the maze and the western area of the map before proceeding anywhere else.

The yellow key needs to be acquired before players can locate the exit from this level. The planned positioning of the keys is as described here:

- **Blue key:** Located just outside the north window of the platform room. This key will be accessible only after the player has successfully negotiated both the bottom corridor and the arena.

- **Red key:** Hidden in the maze. By locating the key to the "back entrance" of the maze in the maze itself, you'll make it impossible for a player to use the back stairs until the maze has already been visited. Measures will be taken to ensure that the player does not leave the maze without having first located the red key—read on!

- **Yellow key:** Located in the donut room, the yellow key will require that room's puzzles to be solved before it can be acquired. Before that, though, player must obtain the two other keys, to gain access to the donut room itself.

After all three keys have been found, the player is free to leave the level.

It is worth considering the rationale behind the placing of these keys in a little more detail.

THE BLUE KEY

The blue key will be placed where a player will quickly see it—reaching it will prove to be the problem here. Offering an early sight of a key in this way provides players with an incentive to explore the area further. This key needs to be positioned where it will be visible from within the platform room—provided that the northern window is open, that is! Call the locating of this key a reward, then, for approaching the upper level of the platform.

In my WAD (WAD27.WAD and D2WAD27.WAD), the key has been placed on a pedestal so that it is conspicuous through the window of the platform room. It can be reached from the Imp ledge—if the player makes it that far, of course!

THE RED KEY

The red key is also to act as a lure—this time in the more usual way, to entice players over a trigger line. This trigger will not perform the expected trick of opening a monster pen; in fact, it will be used to open the teleport that acts as an exit from the maze. To achieve this effect, a slight modification to the current WAD is required. The teleport sector needs to have its ceiling lowered to its floor. This change ensures that the player cannot leave the maze without both taking the key and locating the teleport.

Maybe the trigger should open a monster pen as well, to mask the sound of the teleport opening.

After the teleport in the maze has been found, it provides the area with an easy exit, making the trips on the back stairs that open the one-way staircase redundant. They can be used, though, to add another little twist here. Consider what would happen if you were to add another trigger action to the self-raising stairs, this time to close the teleport sector again.

Remember that these stairs cannot be reached without the red key. Anyone entering the maze by this route will, therefore, already know about the teleport and, in all likelihood, the trap of the one-way stairs. After arriving back in the maze by this route, a player will in all probability head straight for the teleport. Unfortunately, it won't be there any more!

A player's next logical move will be to head back to where the red key was located to try to reopen the teleport by retriggering the appropriate line. That approach needs to be foiled too. The line that opens the teleport sector as the red keycard is taken needs to be a once-only walk-through trigger. This technique will force the marble stairs to be used as the exit on this second visit to the maze—when the player eventually thinks of trying them.

THE YELLOW KEY

The yellow key is already in place as the prize for solving the puzzles in the donut room. No further consideration needs to be given to this item's contribution to the flow of the WAD.

TRYING OUT THE FLOW

You might want to place these various keys now, with suitable modifications to the appropriate areas of your own WAD.

When you've done this, see how it affects the flow of the WAD as a whole. Try running through from start to finish, visiting just those locations that are necessary to attain the exit.

Note that two areas do not need to be visited: the southern courtyard and the back stairs to the maze. The southern courtyard contains several secret areas. Their credits will remain uncollected until the player visits them. The player is not penalized for not using the back entrance to the maze, however. Figure 20.11 shows how this situation has been remedied by the addition of some further secret areas, with a cache of goodies off the corridor at the top of the self-raising stairs.

Figure 20.11.
Extra development to entice the player up the back stairs to the maze.

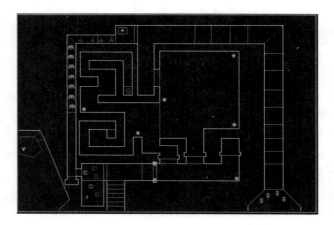

Also conspicuously undeveloped are the maze itself and the large open arena (which also still has temporary switching arrangements in place for the causeway across the pond).

ARENA DEVELOPMENT

Figure 20.12 shows how the arena might be developed further, as in my WAD27A.WAD (or D2WAD27A.WAD). The development here concentrates around the watchtower, north of the pond. A lift has been added to permit access to this watchtower, activated from a nearby switch. From the tower, an additional step provides access to the arena's northern balcony. The top of the watchtower has two switches. The more conspicuous of these switches raises the ceiling trap in the green stone corridor, should that have been tripped. The second, hidden round the back of the first, is the proper switch for raising the causeway from the pond—it replaces the temporary switch that was installed for testing purposes.

Figure 20.12.
Development of the watchtower in the arena.

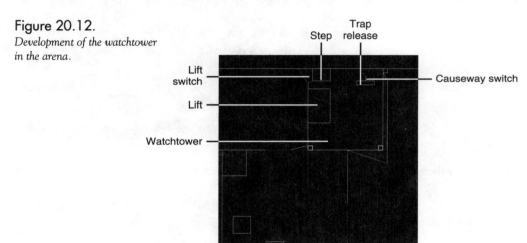

Allowing players onto the watchtower and the balcony compromises the impediment to progress caused by the pond—there is nothing to prevent players from simply leaping down from here. To rectify this problem, the southern and eastern edges of the watchtower and the south side of the balcony need to be set as impassable.

To explain the blockage, my WAD uses the MIDGRATE texture on both of the main textures of these lines. This creates railings to stop the player from jumping down to the eastern section of the arena. Additional sectors have also been placed around the watchtower to provide pillars to terminate these railings and to bring the ceiling down around them so that they look right from both sides. Figure 20.13 shows a view of the top of the new watchtower, looking east through the railings.

If you want to see this area in detail, examine WAD27A.WAD (D2WAD27A.WAD for DOOM II) from the CD-ROM. As well as trying it out to see how it plays, take a look at it in the editor to assure yourself that you understand how it operates.

PUSHING THE LIMITS

Before going on to begin populating your WAD, add whatever further developments you want to the arena and the maze. Note, though, that with the watchtower development just described, the arena is now about as complex as DOOM will permit. WAD27A.WAD will push v1.2 of DOOM over its maximum number of visible edges in this area—and some views within it will produce HOM, especially those that include all the edges around the pond (with its stepping-stones). DOOM v1.4 and above should be OK for a little while longer.

Figure 20.13.
On top of the watchtower.

Figure 20.14 shows how the eastern platform of the arena needs only a few tasteful decorations to complete it.

Figure 20.14.
Tasteful enhancements to the arena's eastern platform.

A TRIAL MONSTER DEPLOYMENT

The final section of this sortie considers an initial trial distribution of monsters throughout the WAD. It is meant to suggest the kind of monster layout I had in mind when I designed the geography of the WAD. Add monsters at skill-level 1 first. Resist temptations to vary the forces until you've tried it out like this.

HEXAGON ROOM

Leave the starting room as it is, with just a suit of armor on the platform. There will be plenty to fight later.

SOUTHEAST PASSAGEWAY

Place a couple of Former Humans here. (The player still has only a pistol, remember.) Position one of them so that he will see the player heading for the suit of armor.

ONE-WAY STAIRS

Players heading up the marble stairs will need a better weapon to face what's up there. You'd better have a Former Human Sergeant guarding the bottom of the stairs to supply a shotgun!

SECRET ROOM AT THE TOP OF THE STAIRS

This room should have a good mix of nasty beasties in it: some Imps, a Demon or two, and some Spectres, perhaps. Place at least one Spectre, with its deaf-guard option set, hiding in the depths of the room. (You don't want the player to empty the room completely from the corridor, do you?) Put a Chaingun in the depths of the room, too—the player will need it later.

MAZE

The maze isn't finished yet, so it is not a good place to populate right now. You might want to set some sound-blocking lines across the entrance to it, though. Then, when the maze is used, it won't empty too quickly as a result of the fight that is likely to occur in the corridor outside.

Return now to the western part of the map.

PLATFORM ROOM

Remember that players can enter the platform room before venturing anywhere else, and they might still be armed with only a pistol. Place some Former Humans around the floor level, along with a Sergeant or two, either on the platform or around the room. There should be some Former Humans on the platform too, to encourage the player to go up there.

OUTSIDE THE PLATFORM ROOM'S NORTHERN WINDOW

Some Imps should already be waiting for the platform room's northern window to be opened. Set their Level 1 flags to bring them into the game.

SOUTHERN COURTYARD AREAS

The southern courtyard and its associated areas should still be populated from the test games. Change their skill-level flags to bring these Imps into the game too, along with the sniper in his den. Put an Imp (or two) in the secret room off the southeast corner of the courtyard, with some barrels about the place. Leave the crushers as the only hazard in the southern corridor, at least for now.

Place another Chaingun in the sniper's den, in case the player comes this way instead of going up the marble stairs. Put some barrels here too.

 If you're using DOOM II, try putting a Former Commando here as the sniper. That'll have your players dodging!

SOUTHWEST STAIRS

Try a couple of Lost Souls in the secret room off the southwest stairs, and maybe a Spectre or a Demon. Decide whether you want them to see the player as the door is tripped, or whether you'd rather have them wait until the player returns—or shoots to open the doors at the end of the corridor. Set one of them deaf anyway.

Leave the rest of the corridor empty.

STRING OF SHOT-ACTIVATED DOORS BEYOND THE BLOOD POOL

Place an Imp or two behind a couple of the doors beyond the blood pool. Don't let them get too close to the lift, though; you don't want to risk the monster cache being triggered too soon.

BOTTOM CORRIDOR

Leave the bottom corridor empty. Any shots fired here spring the monster cache, remember.

ARENA

The arena is planned as the main combat area. Start it with a couple of Hell Knights: one on the northwestern platform, guarding the lift, and another on the eastern platform. Put some Imps and a Former Human or two in the basin and on the steps by the pond. You could put some Imps on the balcony and maybe on the watchtower, but you need some monster-blocking lines to prevent them from coming down on the lift.

Finish this first attempt with a deaf Cacodemon hiding behind the watchtower to catch players after they've found and crossed the platform.

Don't forget to set up a sound block between the arena and the platform room; otherwise, you'll have these arena monsters awake long before the player makes it down there—which will spoil the layout. Don't forget that you need two lines between the platform room and the arena to block the sound. You'll know whether you put them in the right place as soon as you open fire in the platform room.

GOING ON

After you've placed all of these items, save the WAD (WAD28A.WAD) and see how the areas work. There are no extra ammunition or health stocks out yet, of course, so you'll need some cheat keys to make it to the end.

After you've looked at the way this WAD operates—pay particular attention to the way the arena plays and to the way the monster cache delivers up its occupants—I'll leave it to you to decide what more it needs and where. From now on, in fact, this WAD is entirely in your hands. Feel free to add whatever you think it lacks. Good luck and have fun!

You'll find my final populated WAD (with one or two little additions!) on the CD-ROM as ARENA.WAD (or D2ARENA.WAD). Enjoy.

EXIT: MOPPING UP AND MOVING ON

In this chapter you have seen the range of weapons, armor, and other artifacts available for distribution around a WAD to help your players to fight the good fight against the powers of evil, or even against their friends! You have been presented with a strategy for putting the finishing touches on your WAD and getting it ready to present to the world—providing that you're working with DOOM, DOOM II, or Heretic. If you're aiming to work only with these variants of the game, your apprenticeship is over. You can move straight to the next mission of this episode and head toward the land of the DOOM Gods. Fare thee well on thy chosen path.

If, on the other hand, you want to learn more of the special knowledge needed to begin the longer road to the mastery of Hexen, you must stay awhile before becoming a journeyman WADster. There are still dark arts that you must master before you venture on. In the next chapter you will discover the first secrets of those dark arts: details of the programmable nature of Hexen and the changes that have been wrought on it to accommodate that new nature. So, bidding farewell to your DOOM-bound friends, turn the page and come with me: There are wonders still to behold.

CHANGING THE FACE OF DOOM

In this mission, we will explore some of the more advanced techniques available to the WAD designer, enabling you to continue your tentative steps towards the Land of the Gods. The techniques discussed in this mission require utilities with capabilities beyond the basic Map Editor covered in the preceding mission.

In this first chapter of the mission, we examine the various types of graphics used in DOOM and, more important, discuss how to replace some of these with your own creations.

INTRODUCTION TO DOOM GRAPHICS

Graphics are a very important element of DOOM because they define your environment and add the gritty realism that makes DOOM so convincing.

Achieving the unique atmosphere, or "look," you want in a level can range from difficult to downright impossible using the normal graphics of DOOM, despite their vast range. Being able to use your own custom graphics is an obvious (and extremely powerful) solution. Fortunately, every graphic that appears in DOOM can be replaced with one of your own design. Not even the sky is the limit!

TYPES OF DOOM GRAPHICS

Graphics in DOOM fulfill many functions. Some are pasted onto walls as texture, others onto floors and ceilings. A series of images can make up the animation frames of the monsters and artifacts. Yet further graphics are used

— By Justin Fisher and Steve Benner

for more general purposes, such as contributing to the make-up of the player status bar or the opening title screen, and so on. Technically, there is no real difference between any of these images. In fact, they are interchangeable—an Imp image could be used as part of a texture on a wall, for example, should you wish to make the change. However, there are considerable differences in how graphics images are used and how replacements are imported into DOOM. The following distinctions are required:

Textures: *Textures* are the images that cover the walls. They can have transparent areas when used on two-sided linedefs and can be either a single image or a composite of several. The component graphical elements of textures are called *patches*. The "sky" backdrop used in outdoor areas is also a texture, despite its apparent use on ceilings. It is a special case, though, and will be dealt with separately.

Flats: *Flats* are the images that cover the floors or ceilings. They cannot be made out of patches the way textures can.

Sprites: *Sprites* are the images of things that populate the levels: monsters, scenery, power-ups, and so on. An object such as the Medikit has only one sprite, but something that is animated, such as a burning torch or flamestick, has several sprites that are continuously cycled through.

A monster has many sprites—some for each activity in which it might be engaged, as well as for each angle from which the activity can be viewed.

Miscellaneous Graphics: All the images used for anything else in the game—the player status bar, the title screen, the help screens, menu text, the text and image at the end of each level, and so on—can be grouped together and termed *miscellaneous graphics*.

NOTE: This chapter concentrates on the theoretical elements of DOOM graphic replacement. The mechanics of actually putting your finished DOOM graphics into a WAD vary from utility to utility and so are touched on only briefly here. For more details of the practicalities, see Chapter 30, "Synthesis Tools."

BASIC CHARACTERISTICS OF GRAPHICS

Now that the basic differences are out of the way, what do all these graphical elements have in common? All graphics in DOOM are 8-bit bitmaps that use a set palette. That is, the images are made up of pixels using colors picked from DOOM's predefined palette of 256 colors. (Although the list of colors can be extracted with WinTex and edited, this complex procedure is seldom worthwhile. The existing color selection is good, and changing the palette will worsen the look of any existing DOOM graphics you use.)

Some graphics can be *masked*. This means that an area within the graphic will be made transparent when that area is displayed. For example, consider one of the sprites used to represent an Imp, shown in Figure 21.1. This sprite is a rectangular image, even though an Imp is not. The area of bitmap surrounding the Imp therefore needs to be masked. This masking is done simply by filling the areas that shouldn't be displayed with a special color from the palette—cyan (palette entry 247).

Figure 21.1.
A rectangular DOOM sprite.

CAUTION: When making images for graphical types that do not support masking, be careful not to put any cyan in the image, or you will get odd effects when the image is displayed in DOOM.

SETTING UP

The first thing you need in order to edit graphics for DOOM (other than a computer) is a graphics (painting) program that will edit 8-bit (256-color) images, a program that works in 24-bit (True Color) and cuts down to 8-bit later, or both.

For Windows, Paint Shop Pro is a good choice that is available as uncrippled shareware. For DOS, Image Alchemy is an equally valuable tool. It uses a command-line interface but can be run from a batch file. As a result, you can set up Image Alchemy to work through large sequences of images (useful for a set of 24-bit monster sprites) instead of having to load, edit, and save each image individually.

On top of the basic requirements, you can layer as much extra equipment as you can get your hands on. (You might add a scanner, a video-capture card, 3D rendering software, a drawing tablet, and so on. Find some friends in high-tech places…)

WORKING WITH DOOM'S COLOR PALETTE

Remember that to be displayed correctly in DOOM, an image must fit DOOM's palette of colors. If you import a graphic into DOOM that does not use the same palette, the image will be converted during the process, and the result displayed by DOOM might look awful. It is best, therefore, to have your graphics fit the palette before you import them, so you won't be in for any nasty surprises when you see them in DOOM.

If you are working in 8-bit in your painting software, you can work within the DOOM palette itself and so never encounter color problems during graphic importing. To do this, export an image (any image) from DOOM (using WinTex or some other exporting software). Load the image into your painting program and use the program to save this image's palette. You can then reload the saved palette whenever you begin a new graphic confident in the knowledge that your design will convert for DOOM flawlessly.

If you are working in 24-bit, the program will usually have an option to lower the color depth to 8-bit. With luck, when you use this option, you will be able to arrange for a conversion to the colors of a custom palette—in this case, a copy of the previously saved DOOM palette.

NOTE: DOOM and DOOM II have the same color palette. Heretic has a different palette, and Hexen has yet another. All palettes can be loaded from images exported from the appropriate game.

The quality of the processes of color reduction and color remapping can vary drastically between software. Generally, you must expect some loss in quality when reducing and remapping the colors of an image. If the results seem particularly bad, you might be using the wrong settings. On the other hand, you might be attempting to use an image that is just not compatible with the game's palette (there are some heavy color biases in DOOM that make the use of some types of images impractical). If you have the option, make sure you set the remapping to choose the nearest color in the custom palette. Do not try to simulate the exact color using dithering. At the resolution of DOOM's sprites and textures, only the most subtle dithering will go unnoticed. In general, dithering will ruin the image. If you cannot get good results, it is time to look at getting extra software to handle this task (or rethink what you are wanting to achieve).

The Effects of Diminishing Light

Remember that the images you create, once imported into DOOM, will look like the original images only when fully illuminated. In dim rooms, or as they recede from the player, images will be darkened by having their colors replaced with similar, but darker, colors. Sometimes DOOM makes seemingly odd decisions in choosing which color is the closest darker color by shifting to another range of colors. (Note how the Demon is brown in dim rooms, only becoming pink as it approaches the player.)

ANTI-ALIASING

The sprites and textures in DOOM are not high-resolution. Therefore, when they are scaled up as you get close, the game's graphics can become hideously blocky unless they are heavily anti-aliased. Think of anti-aliasing as the slight softening of those particular areas of contrast that highlight the pixelation of the image. Anti-aliasing is different from smoothing (blurring), which softens all areas of contrast.

The differences between anti-aliasing and smoothing are illustrated in Figure 21.2. This figure shows the same basic shape against two types of background: dark (black) and light (white). The left-most image in each case is the shape, in its "pure," low-resolution form. The central images show the same shape, anti-aliased around its edges. The right-most images are the shape again, this time heavily smoothed. The shape in this figure was anti-aliased to the dark background. Notice how doing this has helped to hide the pixelation, provided the shape remains against a dark background. Against the light background, matters have been made worse!

Figure 21.2.
Anti-aliasing and smoothing in operation.

Most methods of creating or capturing images automatically anti-alias as you work. With 8-bit painting programs that don't anti-alias, however, applying a *light* blur filter once the image is finished is the next best thing. You might also find that you can do a better job of anti-aliasing by manually drawing in the effect, especially if you are trying to achieve something more complex than drawing a line, such as creating an illumination or shine effect or a colored glow. Anti-aliasing by hand is a very laborious process, though. A similar method is manually applying a heavier blur with a brush tool. Hopefully, you will quickly discover which techniques work the best for you.

As well as using anti-aliasing within a sprite to reduce the apparent pixelation, you can apply anti-aliasing around a sprite to smooth any jagged edges. Because neither sprites nor backgrounds remain static in DOOM, be careful to apply this latter kind of anti-aliasing to a background color that is close to the colors that the sprite is likely to be seen against during play. Figure 21.2 showed the reasons for this. In DOOM, the best color to anti-alias to is usually dark gray.

TIP: Be careful not to let the software accidentally anti-alias your sprites to the cyan masking color surrounding them. To avoid this when working on sprites, work over a dark gray background and then use a color-fill tool to change the background to cyan when you are finished.

WORKING WITH DOOM'S GRAPHICS

Now that you have seen some general guidelines for working with graphics intended for use in DOOM, it's time for a closer look at the specific things you need to know about working with each of the main types of DOOM graphics.

EDITING TEXTURES

Textures are the easiest graphics to replace because there are none of the WAD importing complications of the other types.

Changing Textures

When you want to change the textures for DOOM's walls, remember that what is generally referred to as a "texture" is actually a composite structure. There are therefore two ways you can change what appears on a WAD's walls. You can add new patches—new graphics—or you can add new texture resources (or edit the existing ones) to create new assemblages of patches. In addition, you can combine these two: you could add a couple of new patches and then define half a dozen different ways to combine them through the use of six new textures.

You should already know some of the rules that govern the structure of textures. If you have read Chapter 11, "The Lowdown on Textures," you know that textures cannot have a height larger than 128 pixels. On walls of greater height than this, the texture is simply tiled vertically. If you force DOOM to tile a texture of less than 128 pixels high, the result will be Pink Bug. If the texture contains any cyan, the cyan areas will be transparent on two-sided linedefs. Textures with such transparent areas cannot be used on single-sided linedefs without incurring Tutti Frutti.

In addition, there are some points to bear in mind for making textures that look good in the game:

- Avoid small areas of high contrast.
- Avoid large areas of flat color.

Read on to learn the reasons for these tips.

SMALL AREAS OF HIGH CONTRAST

As a wall recedes into the distance in DOOM, the texture on it is scaled down. This is done by the graphic engine removing rows and columns of pixels. So, to scale a texture down to 80 percent of its original size, every fifth row and column of pixels is removed. Although large areas of high contrast (such as a large black square on a white background) will have their form preserved, small areas of high contrast (such as a letter "L" written black on white, but only one pixel thick) will be drastically affected. In the example just cited, the vertical bar of the "L" might disappear altogether, leaving just a confusing horizontal bar, or vice versa, or the whole letter might vanish. At any rate, the result is that walls twinkle as detail appears and disappears.

Take a close look at the DOOM textures, particularly the ones that work well (such as STARTAN3, shown in Figure 21.3), and you will see that changes in the detail take place over a number of pixels. In this way, these details can still be seen coherently when many of the pixels are missing. Smoothing any problem areas will fix them, but you might lose some texture detail in the process because it becomes blurred. It is generally best to work to avoid this from the start.

Figure 21.3.
DOOM's STARTAN3 texture.

LARGE AREAS OF FLAT COLOR

Large areas of flat color—areas filled with exactly the same shade of color—look poor because they are feature-less and deprive the player of the feeling of movement and depth. They also highlight the brightness divisions where the light diminishes into the distance. If a texture has large areas of a single color, try applying a little "noise" to give some hint of surface texturing. (Again, look at the DOOM textures to see how the designers at id Software have done it.)

EDITING THE SKY TEXTURE

The sky textures can be considered a special case for a number of reasons. In purely graphical terms, there are three important things to note. First, the sky texture is never scaled down, only up (and then only slightly).

Second, it is never affected by light changes, and, finally, it is fairly high resolution. In practical terms, this means the sky texture is perfectly suited for the use of a scanned photograph or rendering with minimal fuss. In DOOM-editing terms, as a texture, there are no complications when putting the sky texture in a PWAD. From an aesthetic standpoint, of all the textures in DOOM, the sky has the biggest effect on the feel and look of the level. Because you need replace only a single patch with just the color remapping to worry about, changing a sky texture is a very quick way to make a major difference to the atmosphere of a level. (Naturally, you'll need to have some outdoor areas to show it off!)

EDITING FLATS

Flats are always 64×64 pixels and are not made up of patches. This means that the entry name of a flat in a WAD will be the name of the flat in your level editor. Unlike textures, though, flats cannot simply be added to a PWAD without fuss, and the PWAD will probably require some form of installation before playing. The exact particulars depend on the software used for the job.

As you know, flats are tiled to fill the sector area. Because flats are fairly small images, most of the work in making a good flat goes into ensuring that it tiles well in all directions without leaving any obvious seams and without the repetition really being noticeable. For example, making a metal floorplate is fairly easy. If you've seen one floorplate, you've seen them all—a player won't be surprised if they all look alike. Making a rusty metal plate is a lot harder. The rust is a noticeable detail that should be unique to each plate. Unfortunately, in DOOM, the tiling of each flat will repeat the same rust pattern every 64 pixels across the entire area of the sector that uses it.

Clone (sometimes called Stamp) tools in painting programs are very good for making an image tile nicely, whereas simply blurring the edges together is often noticeable. Some software packages support some kind of *wrap-around mode*, which is a setting to tile the image 9+ times on-screen, thereby enabling you to edit the areas where an image tiles badly and have all the tiled images update as you do this. If your software doesn't have this capability, you can use cut-and-paste effectively to split the image. You can then swap the halves to make the edges meet in the center where any areas of poor tiling can be plainly seen and edited out. (The process then needs to be repeated vertically.)

The two general rules presented earlier for making good textures also apply to flats. Small, contrasting details should be avoided even more with flats than with textures. If the flat is used on a large area, only the subtlest of texturing will look good at a distance. It is also a good idea to have all the colors in the flat fairly similar; otherwise, the result will be distant ground that twinkles noticeably as the player moves.

EDITING SPRITES

Creating new sprites is perhaps the most challenging of graphical activities because it usually involves sequences of images. These can often be very large sequences, and every image must be consistent with the rest, so replacing the game's sprites can involve a lot of work. But sprites are what fill the game, so changing them to populate a level with your own creations is both worthwhile and rewarding if you're at all interested in making your own mark on DOOM.

DOOM's Sprites and Frame Sequences

The terminology associated with DOOM's sprites and their animation sequences can be confusing, largely because the word *sprite* can mean several different things. Strictly speaking, sprite refers to a single image. What makes an image a sprite is that it usually is a member of a *family* of related images, all depicting one object within the game. Unfortunately, *sprite* is sometimes used to refer to this family of related graphics rather than just a single image. Such usage is generally avoided in this book.

Many of DOOM's objects require more than one image to represent them, in order to make them appear animated. This can include some objects that you might think of as stationary. Figure 21.4, for example, shows the three images that constitute Heretic's WATR family of sprites used to depict that game's Wall Torch. These particular three sprites make up a complete animation *sequence*, which when displayed in succession, will produce the illusion of a flickering flame. Each step in this animation sequence is termed a *frame*. The images shown in Figure 21.4 are thus the sprites that contribute each of the frames of the Heretic Wall Torch's normal animation sequence.

Now, the Wall Torch is not a particularly active object. Other objects—principally weapons and monsters—can undertake several activities at various stages of the game. The player's current weapon, for instance, may be at the ready, in which case it could be either a single, static image or a sequence showing it pulsating in some way. On the other hand, the weapon may be firing, at which time the game engine will need to run through the images showing the weapon's firing and recharge sequence. Similarly, monsters may perform all sorts of activities, from simply marching on the spot to stalking the player and (usually) dying in some suitably spectacular manner. All these activities will require their own animation sequences if you intend to replace any of DOOM's active elements with your own creations.

Finally, some objects look different when viewed from different angles. The angle from which an object is viewed is termed its *rotation*. DOOM uses eight rotations for monsters, giving the graphical engine eight different viewing angles from which to choose. This means that a player moving around a stationary monster will see eight different views of that monster during one circuit. If the monster is animated (as monsters usually are), there will need to be eight sprites for each frame of the animation to allow the animation to be seen from the eight possible viewing angles.

Objects that look the same from all angles, such as the Wall Torch, are said to have no rotations.

Animation is central to the use of sprites simply because nearly all sprites are part of at least one animation sequence. Hence, the name given to each sprite describes how that sprite takes part in the animation sequence. Understanding this simple code is the first step to successful sprite manipulation.

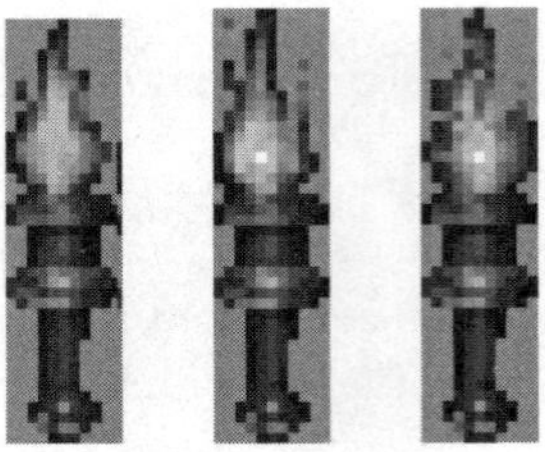

Figure 21.4.
The three frames of the normal sequence of the WATR sprite-family.

SPRITE NAMES

The name of a sprite entry follows this template:

nameXYXZ

or

nameXY

where

- *name* is a four-letter name identifying the family (or set) of sprites to which the image belongs. As an example, SARG is the name for DOOM's Demon sprite-set. (The logic of id Software's sprite-family names is long lost in the mists of time!)

- *X* is a letter that indicates where in the animation sequence the image falls, which is referred to as the *frame* of the animation. In the standard Demon animation, SARGB will be displayed after SARGA and before SARGC.

- *Y* (and *Z*) are digits that indicate which rotation of the object the particular sprite represents (if *Y* is 0 there are no rotations for that object). A more detailed explanation of rotations follows.

ROTATIONS AND REFLECTIONS

The *Y* and *Z* rotation codes within a sprite name can be a little tricky to master. Each is a number from 0 to 8. A 0 indicates that the sprite has no rotations and will look the same from all angles. The Demon's death sequence, for example, consists only of the sprites SARGI0, SARGJ0, SARGK0, SARGL0, SARGM0, and SARGN0. Whatever angle a player shoots a Demon from, therefore, it will always turn to face the player before falling over backward away from the shot. The final frame of this sequence, SARGN0, is the Demon corpse. Now you know why DOOM's corpses turn on the spot as you walk around them!

If a frame has rotations, the values 1 to 8 are used to indicate which viewing angle the image represents. A value of 1 indicates that the view is from straight ahead. Subsequent values indicate further increments of 45 degrees, clockwise—that is, the successive views a player would see when moving counterclockwise around a stationary thing.

Figure 21.5 shows the four frames of the Demon's walking sequence when viewed from the side (rotation 3). Note the animation of the legs and how the last frame is designed to be followed by the first frame to produce a seamless walking motion when looped.

Figure 21.5.
The four frames of rotation 3 of the walking Demon sprite.

Notice also that these sprites use the first form of the naming template shown previously. This form of the name enables sprite designers to take a shortcut when preparing certain frames. A sprite name such as SARGA3A7, for example, tells DOOM that there is no SARGA7 sprite. When a graphic of this name is required—to display the object from the appropriate angle—SARGA3A7 will be used instead, but mirrored. In this way, instead of having to create eight different sprites for the one frame—one sprite for each viewing angle—only five are needed. The front and back views (1 and 5) need to be unique, but directions 2, 3, and 4 can nearly always double as 8, 7, and 6, respectively. Figure 21.6 shows this shortcut being employed.

Figure 21.6.
The five sprites that make up the rotations of one frame of the Demon's walking sequence, with three reflections.

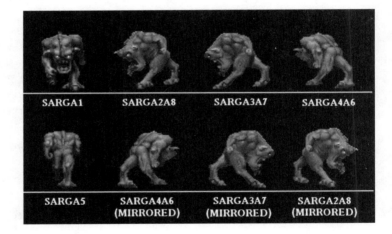

USING REFLECTIONS

The reflections shortcut is useful for cutting down on the number of images required for a complete sprite-set, but it has limitations. If you browse the sprites in the main DOOM.WAD, you will see that it is rare for the sprites of the monsters' attacking motion frames to be optimized in this way. This is because most of DOOM's monsters are symmetrical only when walking. When attacking, they are highly asymmetrical, demonstrating a definite "handedness." During an attack, one arm might be raised, whereas the other moves out sideways for balance, for example. If mirrored sprites were used in such cases, and the player happened to move during the attack sequence, the effect would look very odd, as a right-handed monster suddenly became left-handed. In attack frames, therefore, all eight sprites are usually required. In Heretic, the asymmetrical nature of most of the monsters, many of which carry weapons, means that the reflections shortcut can rarely be used. You should bear in mind the extra work required to portray asymmetrical monsters when you begin designing your own replacements.

MASTERING SPRITE NAMING

The easiest way to master DOOM's sprite naming convention is to take a long, hard look at the main IWAD sprites and note how they are named. You should also attempt to reconstruct each of the various animation sequences for yourself, noting where shortcuts have been taken. Compare the walking sequences of the Baron of Hell, Hell Knight, and Archvile, for instance. Then, to gain a better understanding of the relationship between monster behavior and the frames that display it (and hence the frames that are needed), use DeHackEd to look at how frame sequences are called by activity and how they are constructed in the frame table.

 NOTE: The use of the tools required to perform the tasks suggested here is presented in Chapter 30, "Synthesis Tools."

You might also notice that although it was indicated earlier that the reflections shortcut can be used only within the same frame, this is not strictly the case. Have a look at the movement sprites of the Archvile to see how the shortcut has been used to optimize a more detailed walking animation. (For example, VILEA3D7 is used for frame A and mirrored for use in frame D.)

SIZING UP THE TASK

With all these frames, and all these sprites for each frame, you might be wondering how many images are needed to depict a monster. There is, in fact, no simple answer. The Demon in DOOM, for example, has 14 frames. The first four frames are the walking sequence, with each frame consisting of five sprites. The next three frames are the attack sequence, followed by the pain frame, with eight sprites each. The next six frames are the death sequence (ending with the corpse), each frame having just one sprite each (SARGI0 through to SARGN0). The Demon has no alternative death sequence like the Former Humans have, so the grand total is 58 sprites. Ouch! In addition, the number of sprites varies with each object: Lost Souls have 30 or so, the various firesticks each have 4, whereas the Archvile has an amazing 145!

With so many sprites per monster, drawing them individually suddenly becomes a daunting task, and you might desperately seek an easier way. The method you adopt will depend on your particular skills and on your available resources. Among the things to consider is that sprites should be heavily anti-aliased. The method also needs to be suitable for easy animation. Photographing a model, for instance, will not be easy if the model cannot have its pose changed between frames.

Also remember that sprite animation looks best when each new frame is a completely new image. In reality, few parts of a body remain exactly the same when it moves. As people walk, for example, their whole body moves, at least partially. If you are using rendering software, it usually takes very little extra time to ensure that the whole body is in motion, and the result will look much better than if you accidentally leave the torso, say, in exactly the same place for two consecutive frames. With other methods, it can actually be worthwhile to reuse parts of a sprite over multiple frames, if you think the time saved by not completely redoing each sprite can be used to raise the overall quality of the animation by more than the loss incurred. (Be careful not to leave a section of a sprite dormant for an entire cycle of frames, though, because this looks much worse than motionless areas that last for only a few frames of the cycle.)

Another sprite shortcut you can use to gain time to boost overall quality is to re-use entire frames. Compare the walking cycle of the Baron of Hell to that of the Hell Knight again for a good example. You will find that the Baron has a four-frame walking cycle similar to that of the Demon, whereas the Knight has only two separate frames that are simply repeated to make a four-frame cycle. Have you ever noticed that the Hell Knight has fewer frames or seems to walk strangely compared to other monsters when playing DOOM II? I certainly didn't notice before finding this out, and I suspect most other players never do notice.

NOTE: Unlike many other graphics, sprites to replace the originals cannot simply be added to a PWAD—doing this will effectively remove all of the game's sprites, replacing only those present in the external WAD. There are numerous solutions to this, and you should check the documentation of the particular utility you are using to introduce your own sprites for advice on how to proceed.

EDITING MISCELLANEOUS GRAPHICS

Because DOOM's miscellaneous graphics (the components of the player-status bar and so on) are never scaled, they are similar to the sky textures in being straightforward for scanned or rendered images. Generally, your only worry will probably be whether the images you use will look good in the DOOM palette at VGA resolution. Like wall textures, these graphics can be imported into the game via a PWAD without complications.

Several file naming conventions are used for the various miscellaneous graphics: one for the series of faces for the player status bar, another for the series of numbers for the status bar, another for the letters of the font, another for the series of level names on the end-of-level screens, and so on. I won't attempt to detail them all here; they are not difficult to discover using WinTex (or similar software). Some of these graphics must be a particular size and shape (the face on the status bar, for example), which means that changing these graphics without regard for their size will crash DOOM. Fortunately, most are not limited in this way and can be changed quite freely.

Of all the graphics in the IWAD, these are the easiest to edit and change, so even for small projects it can be worth a little experimentation. If your level (or levels) starts on Episode One, for example, you could easily replace the graphic "Knee Deep in the Dead" with the name of your new level. This quick change can be quite helpful (especially to those players who don't read your text file) as well as adding a touch of distinction to your WAD.

EXIT: MOPPING UP AND MOVING ON

In this chapter you learned enough to ensure that your graphics convert and run as well as they can in DOOM. After a bit of practice you'll look over your first creations in disdain, as you rapidly get the hang of the techniques described here and begin to develop your own. Even if you aren't prepared to put in the effort required to produce graphics of a progressively better quality, you'll still never have to make do with those familiar old textures again. And for those with the patience to persevere, whole new worlds lie ahead!

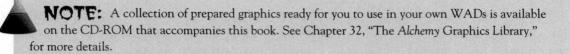

NOTE: A collection of prepared graphics ready for you to use in your own WADs is available on the CD-ROM that accompanies this book. See Chapter 32, "The *Alchemy* Graphics Library," for more details.

22

HACKING THE DOOM CODE

Previous chapters of this episode have all concentrated on the creation of new DOOM worlds through the building of PWADs. Although much of the way DOOM looks can be changed through the agency of the Patch WAD, there are certain parts of DOOM that cannot. Some features of the way the game plays are determined by data tucked away inside the DOOM executable code (DOOM.EXE) itself. This chapter examines which aspects of the game are controlled in this way and what steps can be taken to alter these aspects. It also looks at some of the effects that can be achieved this way.

BACKGROUND INFORMATION

Before changing the DOOM code, you need to learn something of what it contains.

ANATOMY OF AN EXECUTABLE FILE

DOS executable files such as DOOM.EXE consist of several parts that all work together to create the program you see when you run them. Without getting too technical, the DOOM.EXE file consists of three main sections: the DOS extender, the code section, and the data section.

The DOS extender is a program added to the beginning of the DOOM.EXE file that makes use of more advanced 32-bit instructions to manage the large amounts of memory that DOOM requires. This part of the executable should be left alone!

The code section is the heart and brains behind DOOM; it controls everything that is displayed on-screen. Hacking into this section without access

— By Steve Benner and
Gregory A. Lewis

to the original source code can generally be regarded as foolhardy, unless you're the kind of individual who can immediately make sense of screens full of assembler!

The data section is where an executable file's internal data is located. It contains many pieces of information, often in no particular order, to which the code section refers whenever it needs to know something about its own operation. This is the section of the DOOM executable that is of most value if you're looking to alter some of the fundamental behavior of your copy of DOOM.

 CAUTION: Hacking at id Software's executable code is an activity specifically prohibited by DOOM and DOOM II's license agreements. If you do change any of the data in the DOOM.EXE file, you must not distribute the changed file.

DOOM DATA SECTION

Within the DOOM executable's data section, there are countless pieces of information. These are the parts that have the most impact on the actual playing of the game:

- The Thing table
- The Frame table
- The Weapons table

In addition, there are areas holding miscellaneous DOOM details, such as the placement of menus, the cheat codes, and some precalculated math tables. But you often have little to gain from attacking these, unless you're intent on a complete conversion—a topic that's left until later in this book.

 CAUTION: Before embarking on any alterations to executable files, always make sure that you have the means to restore the file to its original condition should you alter something that renders the file unusable.

USEFUL INFORMATION IN DOOM.EXE

I'll give you a closer look at the information contained in the main tables of the DOOM executable file.

NOTE: Naturally, the precise contents, layout, and locations of data within an executable file can vary greatly with each version of the executable. The description given in this chapter is known to be accurate for versions of DOOM up to v1.9 and DOOM II. Heretic, as a close derivative of DOOM, is believed to follow this pattern closely too. Hexen, on the other hand, might well deviate greatly from it. That game variant's greater programmability provides an easy method for changing game play, however, and reduces the need to hack the executable directly.

THING TABLES

DOOM's Things have by far the most information concerning them in the executable file. Twenty-three pieces of information (*fields*) have been found by patient hackers. One of those fields, the Bits field, contains, coded in it, information for another 30 or so attributes! It is in this table that many people begin (and end!) their DOOM executable hacking. Many interesting effects can be achieved with only the slightest of changes here. Table 22.1 contains information on all the known fields of the Thing table. Entries in this table are identified by their position in it, starting with Thing 1, the Player.

Table 22.1. Information fields in DOOM's Thing tables.

Field Name	Description
Thing ID	The Thing's identification number used in level development (WAD files).
Attribute Bits	A collection of single-bit (on/off) attributes, such as whether or not the Thing is a projectile. These attributes will be detailed shortly.
Hit Points	The amount of damage this Thing can sustain before dying.
Speed	The speed at which the Thing moves. Do not be tempted to set this value very high. If you do, movement becomes very erratic and unpredictable. Projectiles have their speed multiplied by 65,536 during play. Regard a value of about 50 as a sensible maximum for high-speed projectiles; they tend to drift off-target if higher figures are used.
Width	The width of the Thing, expressed as a radius (as explained in Chapter 12, "Putting Sectors to Work"). The narrower a Thing is, the harder it is to hit.
Height	The height of the Thing. This value is used only for determining whether moving Things can enter sectors with reduced floor-ceiling gaps, or to determine when moving ceilings contact the Thing. All Things with their Obstacle bit set (explained shortly) behave as though infinitely tall in all game variants except Hexen, as far as inter-Thing collision detection is concerned.
Missile Damage	The amount of damage a projectile does when hitting a target. Some monsters (Lost Souls, for example) have this value nonzero, because they are treated as projectiles when attacking.
Reaction Time	Reaction time for monsters. The lower this value, the quicker the Thing is to attack.

continues

Table 22.1. continued

Field Name	Description
Pain Chance	The probability that a monster's attack will be interrupted if it is injured. A setting of 255 makes it certain; lower settings decrease the chances of the particular type of monster being distracted from attacking the player.
Mass	The Thing's mass, which determines its inertia. Set a Trooper's mass to 1 and watch him fly every time he's shot! The Cyberdemon has a high mass; rockets don't budge him much.
Alert Sound	The number of the sound (in the Sound Table) played when a monster first spots the player or when a projectile is launched.
Attack Sound	The sound played during an attack by a monster, such as the Demon "chew" sound.
Pain Sound	The sound played when a monster is injured.
Death Sound	The sound played as the Thing dies (or explodes, if it's a projectile).
Action Sound	The sound played at random when the monster is nearby.
Normal Frame	The first frame of the sequence displayed for inactive Things or monsters that are not yet active. This entry is simply a number, indicating the position of the specified frame within the Frame table (as explained shortly).
Moving Frame	The first frame of the sequence displayed when a monster becomes active.
Injury Frame	The first frame displayed when a monster is shot and injured.
Close Attack Frame	The beginning frame depicting the close attack sequence of a monster, such as an Imp clawing at the player.
Far Attack Frame	The first frame of the distant attack sequence of a monster, such as an Imp winding up to throw a fireball.
Death Frame	The starting frame of the sequence shown for a Thing's death.
Exploding Frame	The first frame of the series for an exploding death. This is available only for projectiles, Imps, the player, and the Former Human characters, because only these Things can have an exploding death.
Respawn Frame	The first frame shown when a Thing is resurrected by the Arch-Vile. This field does not exist in versions of DOOM earlier than v1.4.

NOTE: Note that DOOM uses the Player entries a little differently from the other entries in the Thing table. The standard fields for Speed and Hit Points are not used. These characteristics are controlled elsewhere in the executable and are not easily accessible. Most of the rest of the Player entries, though, can be changed as with any other Thing.

THE LOWDOWN ON ATTRIBUTE BITS

Table 22.2 lists a Thing's attributes controlled by the Attribute Bits field in the Thing tables.

Table 22.2. Explanation of the bit fields.

Bit Field	Name	Description
0	Gettable	If this bit is set, the Thing, such as an Ammo Clip, can be picked up by the player.
1	Obstacle	If this bit is set, the Thing cannot be walked through.
2	Shootable	If this bit is set, the Thing will take damage. Barrels have this bit set because they can be shot.
3	Total Invisibility	The Thing cannot be seen in any way. It won't even show up on the auto-map with the cheat codes.
4	Can't Be Hit	This bit is set for Things that can collide with something themselves but cannot be hit by anything else. Rockets, for example, have this bit set. They can collide with other Things (obviously) but cannot be shot down.
5	Semi-Deaf	Types of monster with this bit set will be activated only by the sounds that players make if they are in a direct line-of-sight of the player at the time.
6	In Pain	This bit is used internally by DOOM.
7	Steps Before Attack	This bit determines whether the monster will take a step before attacking the player.
8	Hangs From Ceiling	This bit is used for those gory, mangled, hanging bodies. This setting determines whether the height at which the sprite displays is determined by the sector's ceiling or its floor height.
9	No Gravity	Things with this attribute will not be subjected to gravity. The Cacodemon has this bit set, for example.
10	Travels Over Cliffs	Setting this bit stops the particular class of Thing from caring how big a drop there is from one sector to another. Rockets, for example, have this bit set. If you set this bit on the Imp, say, they will happily jump off high ledges to track the player.
11	Can Pick Up Items	This Thing can pick up Things flagged as Gettable. Normally, only the player has this bit set. If it is set for Things that have no internal code to tell them what to do with the Things they get, the game crashes.

continues

Table 22.2. continued

Bit Field	Name	Description
12	No Clipping	This bit enables this type of Thing to pass through solid walls and pass over triggers without activating them.
13	Slides Along Walls	This flag sounds fun but, sadly, has never been used in DOOM and is disabled in all releases.
14	Floating	This bit is used for floating monsters, such as the Lost Soul or Cacodemon.
15	Semi-No Clipping	Things with this bit set can walk up cliffs of any height. Also, walk-over linedefs are not triggered.
16	Projectile	This bit is set for Things that are projectiles. Without this bit set, rockets fired by the player would explode as soon as they appeared, because they are spawned "inside" the player's body.
17	Disappearing Weapon	This bit is used in multiplayer mode for Things such as the shotguns that Sergeants drop when they die, which disappear when picked up in multiplayer games. It is normally used only internally by DOOM but can be used to control spawning in -altdeath play.
18	Partial Invisibility	This bit creates the Spectre effect. (Spectres are just Demons with this bit set!)
19	Puffs (versus Bleeds)	When this bit is on, the Thing shows a puff mark when shot; otherwise, a blood spot is produced. Inanimate objects normally have this bit set, whereas monsters don't.
20	Sliding Helpless	Another bit that sounds more useful than it is, Sliding Helpless is as inoperative as Slides Along Walls.
21	No Auto-Leveling	Valid only for Floating Things, this bit enables flying monsters to attack without needing to adjust their altitude to match the player's. This makes it quite unfair for the player!
22	Counts Towards Kill	This Thing counts as part of the Kill score displayed at the end of a level.
23	Counts Towards Items	This Thing counts as part of the Item score displayed at the end of a level.
24	Running	This bit's use is not known. It might have something to do with the use of the Shift key during play, or then again, it might not!

Bit Field	Name	Description
25	Not in Deathmatch	This bit denotes a Thing that is not present in Deathmatch mode, such as keys and normal player starting spots.
26, 27	Color	The four values specified by combinations of these two bits determine what color will be used during play for the greens in the Thing's sprites. These bits are normally used only for Player sprites but could be used in your own sprites to economize on the number of sprite families needed to represent groups of related monster types. These are the four color substitutions caused by these flags:

	00	Greens (sprite unchanged)
	01	Browns
	10	Indigos
	11	Dark Reds
	28–31	Unused

THING ACTIVITY FRAMES

You saw in the preceding chapter that animation sequences in DOOM consist of a series of frames defining each view in turn. In fact, all the actions carried out by the Things in DOOM are controlled by their own particular *activity sequence* within the main executable file. These activity sequences consist of a series of activity frames that determine what happens at each step of the activity, what the player sees, and what happens next. These activity sequences are controlled through the executable's Frame tables. Table 22.1 shows how the Thing table contains entries associating particular activities of Things with entries in the Frame tables. Table 22.3 describes the information present for each frame in the Frame tables.

Table 22.3. Description of a frame's entries in the Frame tables.

Entry	Description
Sprite Family	Is a code number used to retrieve a four-character string from the Sprite table. This four-character string identifies the family of sprites to which the frame belongs.
Sprite Sub-Number	Identifies which individual picture of the sprite family to use for this frame. During play, the sprite sub-number is translated into a letter (0=A, 1=B, and so on) and is added to the sprite family code together with a final value determined by the angle at which the player views the action. This calculation determines the actual graphic used to portray this frame of the activity sequence, as explained in the preceding chapter.

continues

Table 22.3. continued

Entry	Description
Bright Sprite	Determines whether a frame's sprite is always displayed at its full brightness, even in dark areas (a single-bit attribute).
Duration	Specifies how long this frame is shown before moving on to the next one.
Code Pointer	Is an offset into the code section of the executable file telling the game engine what specific actions are associated with this frame of the activity sequence.
Next Frame	Indicates which frame to move to after this one has played.

It might not be immediately obvious just how much can be achieved by manipulating the information in Frame tables, but in fact, this is the heart of nearly all of DOOM's actions and therefore very rich ground for the hacker, as you will see.

SPRITE IDENTIFICATION

The Sprite Family and Sub-Number fields both narrow down exactly how the frame should appear on-screen. For example, say that a frame has a Sprite Family value of 42 and a Sprite Sub-Number of 7. A quick check of the 42nd element of the Sprite Table might reveal this to be the BOSS Sprite (the Baron of Hell). The frame's Sprite Sub-Number of 7 gives the letter H, which is then appended to the Sprite name, giving the name BOSSH. All sprites beginning with this sequence of characters show the Baron of Hell in pain. DOOM then appends a suitable viewing angle code as previously explained, to determine the precise graphic to display whenever this frame is called for—whenever the Thing is shot. You can therefore use these two fields to change the way Things appear as they go about their business—especially if you substitute sprites from other sprite families.

FRAME DURATION

Reducing frame durations can be a more effective way of speeding up monsters than increasing their speed settings in the Thing table, because this method ensures that all frames will be used correctly, in sequence.

USING THE CODE POINTER

Each frame's Code Pointer indicates to the game engine what special action (if any) needs to be taken at that point in the activity sequence. Because this field points into the heart of the DOOM executable code itself, it is not always easy to know what any particular value of it might mean, although sometimes this can be guessed, or determined by experimentation. Frame 811, for example (part of the sequence of a Barrel exploding) has a pointer to the routine that causes damage to be done to anything standing near the barrel. You could therefore use the same code pointer value in, say, an Imp's Close Attack Frame to make Imps do the same damage as an exploding barrel when close to a player. Ouch!

CAUTION: Change code pointers with care. If you set this entry to point to incorrect locations in the executable, you will almost certainly crash the game engine (and probably DOS as well). The safest way to try out code pointer changes is to use only those values that are in use elsewhere in the Frame tables and so are known to be valid entry points (even if not necessarily suitable).

CHANGING FRAME SEQUENCING

The Next Frame field is one of the most useful for changing DOOM's behavior. To see why, take a look at how activity sequences are controlled in DOOM. Consider the injury sequence for an Imp. When an Imp is injured, DOOM looks at the Thing entry for an Imp and finds the Injury Frame (455 in DOOM 1.7). That frame (showing an Imp in pain) is played for a certain time (specified by the Duration of Frame 455), and then DOOM moves to the next frame. For Frame 455, the Next Frame is 456, so DOOM moves on to that frame and plays it. The Next Frame of 456 is 444, which is also the first frame of the Imp's Moving sequence. In this way, every time an Imp is injured (but not killed), the injury sequence automatically leads back to the walking sequence as it completes. DOOM continues showing the cycle of frames of an Imp walking until another event occurs, such as the Imp deciding to attack or being shot again. (See Figure 22.1.)

Figure 22.1.
The Imp's Moving (top), Injury (center), and Attack sequences.

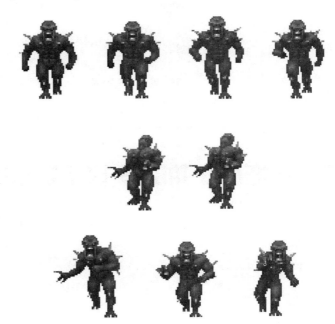

By using the Next Frame field, you can easily make DOOM change its course of action. You could, for example, change the Next Frame of Frame 456 (when the Imp is injured) to 452, the first frame in the Imp's attack sequence. Then, whenever an Imp is injured, it will immediately attack its opponent.

THE WEAPONS TABLE

The Weapons Table determines what each of the game's weapons looks like and what ammunition it uses (but, sadly, not the amount of damage each does per shot). Table 22.4 gives a short explanation for the fields in the DOOM executable's Weapons table.

Table 22.4. Weapons table entries.

Field Name	Description
Ammo Number	The ammunition type for this weapon (0=bullet; 1=shell; 2=energy cell; 3=rocket; 4=unused; 5=no ammo needed).
Max Ammo	The starting maximum capacity for the type of ammo this weapon uses. Acquiring the backpack allows the carrying of double this quantity.
Ammo Per Item	The amount of ammo gained when a standard power-up of the current ammo type is picked up. The larger ammo packs always give five times this quantity.
Deselect Frame	The first frame shown when another weapon is selected and the current weapon drops off the screen.
Select Frame	The first frame shown when the player switches to the current weapon and it rises on-screen.
Bobbing Frame	The first frame of the current weapon during the player's standard walking sequence.
Shooting Frame	The first frame of the weapon's firing sequence.
Firing Frame	The first frame of an additional sprite that accompanies the Shooting Frame to show any flames or flare coming from the weapon.

MISCELLANEOUS TABLES IN THE DOOM EXECUTABLE

In addition to the main tables just described, many other items of information are scattered throughout the DOOM executable whose locations have been determined. These include the following items:

- Sound information
- Sprite-name look-up tables
- Text look-up tables
- Cheat codes
- Players' armor class
- Monster in-fighting control

Also included are many other items of minor importance as far as the code-hacker is concerned. Specific details of these can be found in the documentation of whatever EXE-hacking tool you opt to use.

SAMPLE CHANGES TO THE EXECUTABLE

Virtually limitless changes can be attempted within the DOOM executable. Here are a few suggestions to set you off experimenting for yourself.

CAUTION: Don't forget that by editing the executable code itself, you are not merely providing a patch WAD to alter the playing of the game for one session, you are actually changing the way the game plays altogether. This means that the changes you make will be permanent (until such time as you undo them, anyway) and will operate in every WAD you play, including the main game WAD itself. Make sure that you have a copy of the executable files somewhere safe before you start.

CHANGING TELEPORTER EFFECTS

The distinctive sounds and visual effects associated with teleports often give away their presence when the players' lot would be much tougher if they didn't. It doesn't take much hacking to cure this difficulty. Thing 40 is the Teleport Flash. You can make this invisible by setting its Total Invisibility attribute, and you can silence it by changing Frame 131 as shown here:

    Next Frame: 0 (usually 131)
    Duration: 1 (usually 6)

Alternatively, you can disguise the Teleport Flash by substituting other frames for its Normal Frame, such as 117 (BFG Shot Frame) or 142 (Item Respawn Frame). Try changing its sound too, to one of the monster Alert Sounds, for example.

MAKING THINGS BLOODIER

You can make DOOM's monsters spookier by making their blood glow in the dark! Just set the Bright Sprite bit for Frames 90, 91, and 92 (the Blood Spurt sequence). With this change, you'll definitely know when you hit things in darkened rooms!

While playing with the Blood Spurt settings, why not change Frame 92 (the last frame in Blood Spurt) to have a Next Frame entry of 895? This causes each Blood Spurt to leave a Pool of Blood behind. (Don't forget to change the Bright Sprite bit for Frame 895 if you want this blood to glow in the dark too.)

You can also utilize DOOM's automatic color-changing facility to create an interesting effect with Barrels. Just make these changes to the attributes field of Thing 31 (Barrel):

    Puffs vs. Bleed: Off
    Color: 4 (both bits on)

Instead of barrels of green slime, you suddenly have exploding barrels of blood.

CHANGING MONSTER BEHAVIOR

You can no doubt see that the basic behavior of monsters can easily be changed totally. Imps in particular are a popular target for hackers of the DOOM executable, in many more ways than one.

CHANGING WHAT IMPS FIRE

Thing 32, the Imp Fireball, can be altered in various ways to make Imps tougher opponents:

■ Set the projectile bit of Thing 32. This makes the Imps' fireballs travel at the speed of a projectile, becoming nearly invisible and much harder to dodge.

■ Set the Death Frame of Thing 32 to 127 (a Rocket's normal death frame). This makes Imps' fireballs explode on impact, giving them a damage radius like rockets have.

■ Alternatively, copy the settings of Thing 34 (Rocket) into the Thing table entry for Thing 32 and have Imps fire rockets, for real. This is dangerous for players—and also for other Imps!

It's also quite fun to make Imps hurl barrels rather than fireballs. (See Figure 22.2.) Again, you just need to make a few changes to the entries for Thing 32:

Normal Frame:	806 (usually 97)
Death Frame:	808 (usually 99)
Width:	10 (usually 6)
Height:	42 (usually 8)
Death Sound:	82 (usually 17)

Figure 22.2.
What will those Imps be up to next?

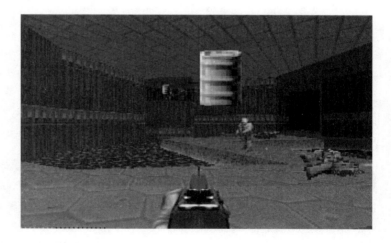

DISGUISING IMPS AS SOMETHING ELSE

You've already seen one change that can be made to Thing 31, the Barrel. Here's another rather more fiendish one. Copy most of an Imp's entry into Thing 31 to create a Barrel that transforms into an Imp when it wakes up:

Thing 31:

Hit Points:	60 (usually 20)
Speed:	8 (usually 0)
Width:	20 (usually 10)
Height:	56 (usually 42)
Pain Chance:	200 (usually 0)
Pain Sound:	27 (usually 0)
Death Sound:	Leave as 82 if you want the Imp to turn back into an exploding Barrel when it dies; change to 62 for regular Imp death sound
Action Sound:	76 (usually 0)
Injury Frame:	455 (usually 0)
Close/Far Attack Frames:	452 (usually 0)
Death Frame:	Leave as 808 if you want the Imp to explode like a Barrel as it dies; change to 457 for regular Imp death sequence
Exploding Frame:	(Change to 462 for Imp exploding, or leave at 0 for regular Barrel explosion)
Puffs vs. Bleeds:	Off (usually on)
Semi-Deaf:	On
Counts Towards Kills:	On (usually off)

CHANGING IMPS' ATTACK STRATEGY

Another popular modification to Imps is to turn them Kamikaze:

Thing 12 (Imp):

Close Attack Frame:	127 (usually 452)
Death Frame:	127 (usually 457)
Far Attack Frame:	0 (usually 452)

This prevents Imps from attacking from afar, but causes them to explode as a rocket when they get within close attacking range. Of course, you'll also need to take measures to allow them to get in close to a player, so you might want to bump up either their Speed or their Hit Points, or both.

CREATING GHOSTS

Finally, here's another very popular change: a ghost monster that's created as something dies. To create this change, you need to use an object that is spawned by the game engine as another object dies. The best object to use is generally the Ammo Clip dropped by a dying Trooper, although the Shotgun dropped by a Sergeant, or the Chaingun dropped by a Commando, would serve equally well.

The basis of the change is to turn the spawned item (the Ammo Clip) into a ghostly copy of the original monster (the Trooper). Here are the changes needed:

Thing 64 (Ammo Clip):

Hit Points:	1000
Speed:	8
Height:	56
Width:	16
Pain Chance:	0
Mass:	1
Alert Sound:	36
Attack Sound:	1
Pain Sound:	27
Death Sound:	59
Action Sound:	75
Normal Frame:	174
Moving Frame:	176
Injury Frame:	187
Close Attack Frame:	0
Far Attack Frame:	184
Death Frame:	189
Exploding Frame:	194
Respawn Frame:	203
Gettable:	Off
Shootable:	On
No Clipping:	On
No Gravity:	On
Floating:	On
Travels Over Cliffs:	On
Puffs vs. Bleeds:	On
Partial Invisibility:	On

Most of these settings are straight copies of the Trooper settings, except for the higher Hit Points, which makes them difficult to kill, and their rather ghostly attribute settings! Now instead of dropping Ammo Clips, Troopers give rise to Ghost Troopers when they die. These are much harder to kill. They can drift around, passing through walls, and follow the player everywhere. (See Figure 22.3.) They don't even shoot one another anymore!

An unfortunate side effect of this change is that all Ammo Clips placed in the level beforehand will also become Ghost Troopers, of course. If you really want to use Ammo Clips in your levels as well as have Ghost Troopers, you can achieve this outcome in the following way: Choose an unused Thing, such as the Chaingunner in DOOM, or an item that you don't anticipate using (or don't mind losing), such as some decoration in DOOM II. Copy all the Ammo Clip's usual entries to this Thing, including the Thing Id of 2007. Now change the Thing Id of the original Ammo Clip (Thing 64) to –1. You can now safely use Ghost Troopers as well as Ammo Clips in your WAD. This technique works because whereas startup Things are identified by their Id codes, Things spawned during play are identified by their positions in the tables. Thus, when Troopers die, the game engine continues to generate Things of type 64, not Things of Id 2007; hence they continue to spawn ghosts.

Figure 22.3.
Haunted DOOM?

EXIT: MOPPING UP AND MOVING ON

This chapter has introduced you to the wonderful (and at times, wacky) world of DOOM executable hacking. With the information here, you can try out all sorts of changes in the way your copy of DOOM works. The game will certainly never be the same again!

The next chapter shows you some less drastic ways of changing the way DOOM's monsters behave. In particular, it explains how to make monsters unaware of players in certain locations and introduces other tricks that can be performed using a PWAD's reject table.

23

REJECT TABLE TRICKS

This chapter considers a single small part of a DOOM WAD: the reject table. It explains the purpose and form of this table (also called the reject *map*) and then goes on to show you how you can use the reject table to introduce some interesting special effects into your WADs.

THE REJECT TABLE

The main role of DOOM's reject table is to speed up the part of the game engine that is responsible for deciding each monster's actions during play. As you know, the standard behavior of a DOOM monster is to remain at its post until wakened. Monsters can be wakened by hearing shots (provided they have not been made deaf) or by spotting a player. Now, checking all of a level's monsters at every refresh of the game, working out just what they can and cannot see, is a time-consuming process (and the more monsters there are, the more time would be consumed). The reject table helps out here by providing the game with instant information about certain lines of sight. This enables the game engine to make a rapid decision about many of its monsters.

What the reject table contains is, in effect, a map of which *sectors* can see which other sectors and which sectors are totally unsighted from each other. With this information supplied, the game engine need only

1. Look to see which sector the player occupies.

2. Determine (from the reject table) which areas of the level have a view of this sector.

3. Consider only monsters in those areas to ascertain (by performing a true line-of-sight check) which monsters can see the player at any given moment.

This ensures that the game does not waste time examining lines of sight for monsters who stand no chance of being able to see a player.

— *By Jens Hykkelbjerg*
and Steve Benner

As well as determining whether a sleeping monster wakes, the same line-of-sight calculations will decide whether a monster will attack a player. Monsters never attack players they cannot see—they simply hunt the players down!

To demonstrate how the reject table contributes to the game, I take a look at its structure.

STRUCTURE OF THE REJECT TABLE

Within the reject table, the pre-calculated line-of-sight information is stored on a sector-by-sector basis as a series of bits, which may be thought of as a table, arranged as in Table 23.1.

Table 23.1. A generalized reject table.

Sector the Monster Is in	Sector the Player Is in					
	0	1	2	3	4	etc....
0	b	b	b	b	b	etc....
1	b	b	b	b	b	etc....
2	b	b	b	b	b	etc....
3	b	b	b	b	b	etc....
etc....						

The value of each bit, b, has the meaning:

   0   player's sector can be seen (at least in part) from monster's sector

   1   player's sector cannot be seen at all from monster's sector

NOTE: The game engine uses this table only to determine the feasibility of *monsters* spotting players. It never uses the table to determine what the player can see.

A simple example should make this clear. For the map shown in Figure 23.1, for example, the reject table would be as given in Table 23.2.

Table 23.2. Full reject table for the sample WAD.

Monster Sector	Player Sector		
	1	2	3
1	0	0	1
2	0	0	0
3	1	0	0

Figure 23.1.

A simple WAD.

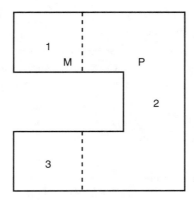

This reject table tells the game engine that from sector 1 it is possible to see into all sectors except sector 3; that all sectors are in view from sector 2; and that from sector 3, only sector 2 and sector 3 can be seen. In this example, the reject map is effectively saying that the engine need not look further to determine whether monsters in sector 1 could see a player in sector 3—they cannot.

THE MEANING OF ZERO

Note that the reject table tells the game engine only what definitely cannot be seen, not what can. For the example just cited, for instance, the fact that the reject table indicates that sector 2 is in sight from sector 1 does not mean that a monster at position M, say, in sector 1 will actually be able to see a player at position P in sector 2. The reject table merely tells the game that such a sighting should be feasible. The sighting may not actually occur for any number of reasons—indeed, you should be able to see that there are places in sector 2 where a player would be hidden from a monster at M. This means the game engine will need to determine the actual line of sight between point M and point P at game time.

You can see that only the presence of 1s in the reject table will affect the way the game plays. Each 1 in the table reduces the number of sectors where monsters' sightlines need to be considered. Of course, for a simple map such as that in Figure 23.1, the savings involved in having the reject table is small. For real maps, though, savings can be considerable. In most maps, any one sector can, in all likelihood, see into only a small percentage of the total number of sectors.

OPTIMIZING THE REJECT TABLE

The usual aim in constructing a reject table is to speed up the frame rate of the playing of a WAD by reducing the work the game engine has to do between those frames. To that end, a reject table will usually be *fully optimized*. In other words, the reject table will accurately reflect the feasible lines of sight between sectors within a WAD so the game engine never has to perform unnecessary line-of-sight calculations.

NOTE: The creation of a fully optimized reject table for anything but the simplest of WADs is a nontrivial activity. For this reason, most map editors do not generate one but provide a completely empty table—one with 0s everywhere. As already shown, such a map will not affect monster behavior in any way. The game may play slowly, however, because the speed-up that the reject table is designed to produce will be lost.

A specialist utility called a Reject Builder is required to create an optimized reject table. One such utility, RMB, is described in detail in Chapter 30, "Synthesis Tools."

Rather than focus on the business of optimizing the reject table, though, I'd like to consider ways this element of a WAD can be used to introduce special effects. Some of the special effects achievable by manipulating the reject table can be quite subtle; others can be pretty spectacular!

MANIPULATING THE REJECT TABLE

Normally, the reject table is structured so that it has no effect on the running of the game beyond providing a speed enhancement. Careful manipulation of the table can lead to changes in the behavioral patterns of a level's monsters, though. I'll explain why.

At the beginning of this chapter, I outlined why DOOM needs to perform line-of-sight calculations between monsters and players. Basically, these calculations determine whether:

- A sleeping monster should wake
- An awakened monster should attack a player

By introducing changes to the reject table, you can begin to influence these two aspects of monster behavior yourself. You can create monsters that stay asleep longer or are more reluctant (even downright unwilling) to attack players.

The practical outcome of this is that it becomes possible to make areas of a WAD where players gain an unusual advantage over DOOM's monsters—a rare occurrence that can enhance a WAD, if used sparingly. Alternatively, monsters can be made to seem more patient (and therefore more deadly) in their ambush strategy.

For example, look back to Figure 23.1. Consider what would happen if instead of the "correct" reject table shown in Table 23.2, the structure given in Table 23.3 were used.

Table 23.3. Falsified reject table for the sample WAD.

| Monster Sector | Player Sector | | |
	1	2	3
1	0	1	1
2	0	0	0
3	1	0	0

Now, these two tables differ by only one entry (shown in boldface type in Table 23.3 to make it easier for you to spot). This single bit tells the game engine that monsters in sector 1 cannot see players in sector 2. This has an interesting effect: Any monster at location M on the map will now be completely unaware of a player at location P. This results in the player being safe from the monster for longer because the monster will let the player get closer before it either wakes or attacks.

Below are other examples of the effects that can be introduced through simple changes of the reject table.

SPECIAL EFFECTS WITH THE REJECT TABLE

Special effects created by reject-table manipulation all operate in the same way: through falsified entries in the reject table. In particular, these effects rely on extra 1s entered into the table that make the game engine turn a blind eye to certain sector-to-sector views. These tricks divide into only a few types, but you can be amazingly versatile in applying them.

THE SELF-BLIND SECTOR

Take a look at Table 23.4 and consider how it will affect the way the sample level will play (again, the changed entry is shown in bold).

Table 23.4. Reject table for a self-blind sector.

Monster Sector	Player Sector		
	1	2	3
1	0	0	1
2	0	1	0
3	1	0	0

Here, the entry creates a sector (2) that is deemed by the engine to have no sight of itself. This is termed a *self-blind* sector. Monsters within such a sector will be completely oblivious to players in it with them! In this example, players can come under attack only from monsters in sector 1 or 3.

Such "safe" sectors can be very unnerving for players to encounter. Try out level E2M1 of the sample WAD, REJDEMO.WAD, on the accompanying CD-ROM to see this effect. Figure 23.2 shows a scene from this level, but you really have to experience this to appreciate it!

THE TOTALLY SAFE SECTOR

As already noted, the safety a player experiences in a self-blind sector extends only to monsters sharing the same sector. The sector may still come under fire from monsters in other sectors. You can create totally safe sectors—where the player will not be attacked by anything, anywhere—by setting a complete *column* of 1s in the reject table, as shown in Table 23.5.

Figure 23.2.
Demons mill around aimlessly in a "safe" sector.

Table 23.5. Reject table for a totally safe sector.

Monster Sector	Player Sector		
	1	2	3
1	0	1	1
2	0	1	0
3	1	1	0

Here, a player in sector 2 is completely immune from attack. Incorporating such sectors into an otherwise chaotic battle arena can be a good way to make a seemingly impossible task easy. All you then need to do is find some way of providing the player with a hint that the sector exists, without making it too obvious.

THE BLIND SECTOR

In addition to the totally safe sector, you can create completely *blind* sectors: sectors from which monsters will never spot players. These sectors can be useful for creating hordes of monsters that will be drawn out of their lairs only by the sound of fighting, not by the sight of a player. You can use blind sectors to make players think areas are safe, but blind sectors are actually safe only as long as they are approached quietly. Table 23.6 shows how a blind sector is made: by setting an entire *row* of the reject table. This example shows monsters in sector 1 made blind to all sectors.

Table 23.6. Reject table for a blind sector.

Monster Sector	Player Sector		
	1	2	3
1	1	1	1
2	0	0	0
3	1	0	0

CAUTION: Designing a totally blind sector and populating it with monsters having their Deaf Guard attribute set will create a horde of monsters who will wake up only when hit by shot. But this probably gives players too much of an advantage!

COMBINING EFFECTS

In practice, these extreme applications of reject-table manipulations are less use than intermediary applications. You are more likely to want to reduce the range of monsters' powers of sight a little, rather than make them totally blind. For this, you need a fairly sophisticated reject builder, one that is aware of the types of special effects that designers are likely to want. To demonstrate why, I'll take a moment here to consider the use of effects that will reduce what monsters can see.

APPLYING REJECT-TABLE TRICKS

It may not be immediately obvious how having some monsters incapable of seeing as far as usual may, in fact, benefit the monsters more than it does the player. The best way to appreciate the use of such visually impaired monsters is to think about the uses for deaf monsters in DOOM.

GIVING MONSTERS THE EDGE

The existence of deaf monsters allows the designer to create surprises for players by making these monsters wait until they see a player before moving. Reducing monsters' visual range will mean that they can be encouraged to wait even longer before moving, not attacking until the player is right on top of them.

Of course, to have such monsters surprise a player and not merely behave as sitting targets, you will need to hide them a little better than simply around the nearest corner.

Generally, to hide a monster, one of the following places or strategies can be used:

- In the dark
- Around corners or in alcoves
- Behind two-sided walls with texture on at least one side
- High up where the player can't see

You also can use a combination of these tactics.

Normally, a hidden monster will wake up the instant it sees a player, but, by applying the reject-table tricks you have just seen, it is possible to construct much more fiendish ambushes. For example, you can make monsters delay their ambush until the player enters the sector of your choice. Usually, you will want to make monsters hold their fire until the player is in a really difficult position—halfway across a narrow bridge, for instance.

This type of special effect makes life harder for the player. But it's also possible to design other kinds of special effects to make the player's life a little easier.

EVENING THE SCORE

When I started playing DOOM, I thought the monsters sometimes were unfair. It seemed that they had perfect vision, no matter how dark it got. As I stumbled along a dark corridor, finding it difficult to see the end of my own shotgun, the monsters still were able to shoot at me with remarkable precision. By applying reject-table adjustments, it is possible to redress the balance and provide a degree of safety to players that standard DOOM WADs cannot offer. Such realistic special effects may include:

- Safety behind two-sided walls with texture
- Improved safety in trenches
- Improved safety in the dark

This list is by no means complete, but it gives you some idea of what is possible. I'm sure you will be able to think up plenty more effects on your own.

EXAMPLES OF SPECIAL EFFECTS

The reject table also can help you incorporate some useful special effects into your WADs. Not all of the possible uses for these effects are covered here, but just enough to whet your appetite and make you want to start experimenting for yourself. To implement any of these effects you will need to use a special tool such as RMB. For now, I mostly address just the theory.

SAFETY BEHIND A TWO-SIDED WALL

In a Deathmatch WAD, two-sided walls with textures on only one of the sides can be used for great ambush spots. Monsters can normally look through any two-sided wall, though, regardless of texture. You can use the reject map to redress this imbalance. All you need to do is mark sectors on the textured side of the line as incapable of seeing into sectors on the other side of the line. Your players can then enjoy the delights of ambushing the monsters for the first time! (See Figure 23.3.)

Figure 23.3.
The player ambushing frustrated monsters in a modified E1M1.

> **TIP:** RMB provides the LEFT and RIGHT options to achieve effects such as this.

SAFETY IN TRENCHES

Making a trench where a player can shelter is easy. Persuading monsters that they shouldn't attack a player in the trench is harder—with standard map-making techniques, that is. Using a reject builder, though, you need only specify that sectors at a certain range from the trench cannot see into the trench to have DOOM prevent monsters in those sectors from shooting at players in the trench. This action alone is likely to be sufficient to encourage the monsters to wander around until they find other sectors from which they can attack—provided they haven't been picked off in the meantime by the player in the trench!

TIP: Never give players the edge totally, or you will quickly bore them. It is better to provide a momentary advantage, which is lost if not taken quickly, than to provide complete safety. Make sure, therefore, that players who simply hide in the trench don't gain from this. Allow the monsters to attack if they get close or achieve some other objective. In this way, players learn that they must act quickly or risk losing the advantage that the trench affords them.

RMB's SAFE option will allow you to build quite sophisticated areas of relative safety in your WADs.

SAFETY IN THE DARK

In dark areas you may want your monsters to have limited visual range just like your players have. To achieve this effect, make all sectors that are more than a certain distance from a dark sector unable to see into that sector. Provide a few dark patches like this around a very busy room to give your players an unprecedented degree of safety from the rest of the room's occupants. Of course, your players will need to stand still in these areas long enough to benefit from them. Figure 23.4 shows another scene from REJDEMO.WAD—this time E2M3. Only the Imp right up close is aware of the player's presence—an awareness that won't last much longer!

Figure 23.4.
Lurking in the shadows.

 TIP: Again, RMB's SAFE option allows the easy production of areas of safe shadow such as those in REJDEMO.WAD.

TRAPS FOR THE PLAYER

Hopefully, by now you can see that making traps for the player with reject-table tricks is simplicity itself. Mostly this consists of creating monster-laden sectors that are blind to all sectors but specific ones where the player is more vulnerable. You can use tricks such as this to delay monster attacks or to coordinate grouped monster attacks from several directions. The advantage of using reject-table tricks to achieve these effects, rather than the more common "trip-wire" approach with special lines, is that there will be no sounds of doors opening to alert the player. Instead, the player will be surprised by the sudden noise of angry foes!

The sample WAD on the CD-ROM (REJDEMO.WAD) has several such traps. Experience them for yourself. The RMB option file that produced the WAD is also supplied. Read this file in conjunction with the description of that package given in Chapter 30, "Synthesis Tools" (or the manual supplied with the program and contained on the CD-ROM), to see how all the effects were achieved. Then go build your own custom game!

EXIT: MOPPING UP AND MOVING ON

This chapter introduced you to the WAD's reject table and showed you how it can be used to create special effects in your WADs. The next chapter takes a closer look at some other special effects that can be used to make your WADs really stand out.

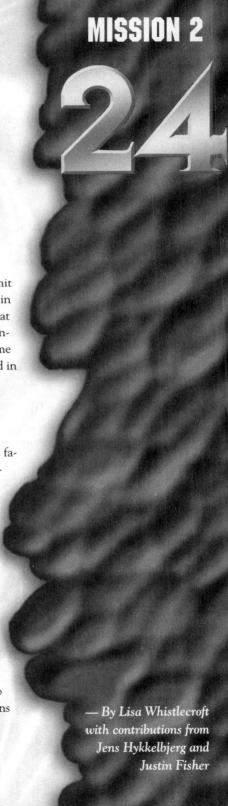

SPECIAL VISUAL EFFECTS

This chapter describes how to push DOOM's graphics engine to its limit (and sometimes a little beyond) to create some special visual effects in your WADs. All the special effects can be found on the CD-ROM that accompanies this book. Some are in the game WAD "The Unholy Trinity," by Steve McCrea, Simon Wall, and Elias Papavassilopoulos; some are in WADs built specifically for this chapter. Most can also be found in SPECIAL.WAD by Jens Hykkelbjerg.

SWITCHING THE TEXTURES

The first section of this chapter looks at ways in which you can make familiar DOOM features appear to behave in unfamiliar ways by replacing original graphics patches with your own.

MULTIPLE-ACTION SWITCHES

If you redefine the textures associated with trigger lines, you can create switches that appear to behave in novel ways. You should remember from Chapter 15, "Remote-Control Sectors," that trigger lines can have only one action associated with them and that to give the impression of multiple actions, you must place trigger lines close together and arrange for them to be used in turn. The problem with the sample WAD (SW5.WAD) presented in Chapter 15 is that the switch does not change its appearance until the last time it is activated. This is because all the earlier triggers in front of it are on lines that carry no texture. To fix that problem, what is needed is a switch texture that turns

*— By Lisa Whistlecroft
with contributions from
Jens Hykkelbjerg and
Justin Fisher*

transparent as the line is triggered. DOOM does not provide such switch textures, but you can easily make them. For a simple multi-action switch, the patches should be the same switch design in different positions. A nice variation on this idea is a guarded switch, in which the cover must be shot away before the switch can be used in the normal way.

To implement these switches, you first need to draw new switch designs for pairs of SW textures. The SW1 form will look like a switch, and the SW2 form will be transparent (using cyan). Then you must redefine existing switch pairs as single-patch textures and replace the original textures with your own.

CAUTION: You must redefine your switches as single-patch because you are going to place them on two-sided lines. You have to redefine an existing switch pair because you cannot create additional ones. Remember that after you have redefined such a texture, you cannot use the original in the same WAD.

Let's look at a multi-action switch first. To build this switch, simply place a number of lines (say, three) very close to each other across the back of an alcove. The lines should be only a pixel or so apart. Put your new switch textures on the two-sided lines and a standard switch texture on the back wall of the alcove. Tag each line to a different action, and remember to make them face the correct way.

To build the guarded switch, you need to make your switch designs slightly different. Make the SW1 texture look like a switch cover and the SW2 partner like a cover with a hole in it (suitably blackened and bent if you want perfection). Use cyan just in the "hole." Put your new texture on the front line of an alcove, give it line type 47 (G1: Mover, Raise floor to next higher), and tag it to the alcove—which should have the same floor height as the main room to ensure that this switch has nothing to do. Put any standard switch texture on the back of the alcove, with a normal spacebar action, and make sure that the switch is aligned with the hole.

While you're creating new, shot-activated switch texture pairs, how about one that looks like frosted glass and a partner that looks like broken glass? You could even put it in a window frame!

Some examples of unusual switches can be found in SPECIAL.WAD through the door marked "SWITCHES."

NEW PERSPECTIVES

NOTE: The perspective dodges described in this section were developed by Justin Fisher. Examples of appropriate graphics can be found in the *Alchemy* Graphics Library and NEMISIS.WAD on the CD-ROM.

One of the most striking changes you can make to a WAD is to move away from DOOM's very square visual universe and create angled or—even more dramatic—curved shapes to use as archways and window frames. Sometimes these can be quite difficult to incorporate into a WAD because the perspective techniques employed by id Software are designed to work well with the tiling methods used to paint the flat surfaces in DOOM. If you create archways, you need to persuade the graphics engine to draw the curved surfaces that they bound.

The first requirement for an archway, porthole, or other nonsquare opening is, of course, a new graphical texture that can be applied to two-sided lines. This texture will be rectangular like any other but will portray the arch around a curved transparent area. This provides the near surface of the wall with the arch in it. For realistic wall thickness, you need another texture of the same shape to put on the far side of the doorway sector. The problem then arises of how to deal with the through-wall textures. Without special treatment, the opening will look like a square hole with two cardboard archways propped up in it. This is because the default drawing methods are carefully designed to help the viewer perceive a 3D world on the flat monitor screen. This effect is achieved though two simple perspective techniques:

- The textures are rendered smaller the further they are into the picture.
- The textures are rendered darker the further they are into the picture.

To give the impression of a smooth surface on the inner walls of arches—that is, to remove the clues which tell the viewer that there is a square opening between the curved facades—it is necessary to neutralize these two perspective devices. The simplest way to get realistic curves, therefore, is to take the following actions:

- Use dark, flat, featureless textures on the inner walls and on the further arch outline texture. These textures do not alter as they are drawn smaller and so give no impression of being further away.
- Set the light level in the arch sector to 255 to minimize the effect of darkening with distance. This setting might cause problems in dimly lit rooms, in which case a compromise might be needed. The other giveaway—texture detail—is less noticeable under dim lighting anyway.

An example of a very convincing curved window is shown in Figure 24.1. This is a view from a high ledge in NEMISIS.WAD.

Figure 24.1.
A curved window in NEMISIS.WAD.

Having looked at substitution of textures, let's now consider what happens when textures are not drawn at all.

SKY TEXTURE TRICKS

As you know, you must put texture on all single-sided lines to avoid the Hall of Mirrors effect that results when the DOOM graphics engine cannot find anything to draw on-screen. As a general rule, you should also put texture on the so-called essential upper and lower parts of two-sided lines, for the same reason. In many circumstances, however, omitting these textures does not result in HOM. Some of these you might have already come across and treated as a fault—all are of interest because they are the basis of some special effects. Consider first the way sky ceiling textures work with transparent walls.

OUTDOOR WALLS, PARAPETS, AND SHEER DROPS

You might remember that the sky texture is rendered on-screen in a different way from both ceiling flats and wall patches. Specifically, it is always rendered at maximum brightness, it is never scaled, and it is always painted from the top of the screen downward until another texture, usually a wall, is encountered. The one remaining characteristic of sky painting is that if adjacent sectors have sky (F_SKY1) on the ceiling, any upper textures are not painted—even if you specify a texture for them, they are left transparent. Instead, sky is painted in a continuous flow from the top of the screen down to the first "solid" surface. Because it is unscaled, it always appears to be at an infinite distance, as sky should.

The simplest use for this is to produce lower walls around an outdoor courtyard area, as was done in WAD Sortie 7 of Chapter 11, "The Lowdown on Textures." If you create narrow sectors along the edges of an outdoor area and reduce their ceiling heights a little, the walls will be less high, and more sky will become visible as DOOM carries on flooding the sky texture further down the screen. If you reduce the ceiling height of the edge sectors to the same as the floor, sky will be painted all the way down to the floor level, giving a courtyard without boundary walls (and without any sign of the edge sectors too, which is one reason for making them thin!). Players who try to jump off the edge of the world, however, will find that the wall is still quite solid!

Figure 24.2 shows a typical rooftop view with sky "over the edge."

Figure 24.2.
A view from the roof.

NOTE: Some of the sky effects described in this chapter use sky down to floor level (or lower). With the normal DOOM sky textures, this effect looks great from a distance but is very disconcerting when the player moves up close, because the sky pattern repeats. SPECIAL.WAD uses the default textures, so you can see this effect there. If you replace the texture with, say, a starry sky in which the repeat doesn't show, the result can be stunning. The demonstration WAD, FINGERS.WAD, uses a beautiful tileable texture by Justin Fisher.

If you take the thin edge sector and, as well as lowering its ceiling level, you raise the floor level to meet its ceiling, you can give the impression of thickness to your boundary walls, creating a parapet, as shown in Figure 24.3. This is the first indication of an unexpected (but very useful) characteristic of the order in which DOOM decides what to draw. When the floor levels are the same, the sky runs down to the near edge of the boundary sector floor, hiding it; when the floor of the boundary sector is raised, however, the sky runs down to its *far* edge, leaving it visible. This fact opens up several exciting WAD design possibilities.

Figure 24.3.
A wall, a parapet, and a sheer drop.

SKY DOORS, INVISIBLE DOORS, AND FORCE FIELDS

The two effects just described can be used on doors. Where you place these in a WAD, of course, depends on the geography of your WAD and the effect you want to create, but the method is simple. For a Sky Door, create a normal door between two sectors. Put sky on all the ceilings and ensure that all the floor heights are the same; DOOM does the rest. Rather than a door, your players see an abrupt end to the floor, with nothing but sky beyond it. When they press the spacebar, the area beyond snaps into view. The only sign that there is a door opening is the rising side walls and the sound. (A Sky Door that opens more naturally will be described later in this chapter.)

TIP: A particularly fiendish variation on this sector arrangement is to make the "door" sector have its ceiling start in the raised position and place a Start Crusher action on its lines instead of a door action. Line-type 141 (W1: Start Silent Crusher) available in DOOM v1.4 and later is an especially vicious choice. With this, you create an invisible, silent crusher!

If you raise the floor level of the door sector by a little (8 or 16 pixels enables you to use a good step texture on the essential lowers you create), you get a totally different effect. When the edge sector of the courtyard was raised, you gained a parapet because the drawing engine rendered all that was visible through the upper texture (in that case, just the floor) before it filled in the sky. For some unexplained reason, the graphics engine does the same here and also shows the whole of the area beyond. The door itself is transparent because it is composed entirely of upper essentials—not painted because there is sky on all the ceilings. You also see sky to the floor on the walls of the door sector; these fill as the door opens. Put a suitable texture onto these sides and leave them pegged. You then have a totally new-looking barrier, one that prevents the player from passing until the rising screens cut off its effect—not at all like a door!

A fun use for this invisible barrier is to create a Monster Pen, as shown in Figure 24.4. Players can see the monsters but cannot shoot through the barrier (which actually absorbs rockets without a trace!). Even more puzzling is the fact that the monsters are totally oblivious to the players. By the time the players have run out of ammo, they might think to open the door. If, on the other hand, you prefer the monsters to wake up when a player enters the area, you could leave an air space between the floor and the ceiling of the door sector, or you could use a single disjunct sector on either side of it if you want only gunfire to wake them.

Figure 24.4.
"How could I miss?"

NOTE: You can see a Sky Door and a Force Field barrier in FINGERS.WAD on the CD-ROM. You can also see a more interesting Sky Door in SPECIAL.WAD. It is labeled, although you are not likely to miss it. There might be more sky beyond this door than you expect. Some of the additional effects are described later; you can examine the more extreme cases of sky everywhere by using a map editor.

The transparency phenomenon used for the invisible door has dramatic implications, as described next.

TRANSPARENT SURFACES INDOORS

Consider the transparent door for a moment. The upper textures were turned transparent by DOOM's sky painting method. The view beyond, however, is drawn because of what appears to be a bug in the graphics engine, which, if the floor of a door sector is raised, looks beyond the door and paints any DOOM space before filling in the sky. (The same effect is noticeable on the auto-map even with ordinary doors if they have raised floors. After the door has been seen, the map beyond it is shown as though the door were transparent, even if the door is marked as Secret on Map.)

This feature can be used wherever a raised door or similar sector is placed, even indoors. Obviously, you can't create a Sky Door without some sky around, but the force field works just as well indoors as out—just leave the textures off the surfaces of the door sector. Of course, you don't actually have to make it into a door either. You do need to be extra careful about avoiding HOM, especially around the sides of doors. Get around this problem by adding two small sectors across the edges of the door, with the same floor and ceiling heights as the rooms. The normal textures on their walls are visible in the same way that the sector beyond the door is. A suitable arrangement is shown in Figure 24.5.

Figure 24.5.
Sector arrangement to prevent HOM around transparent doors.

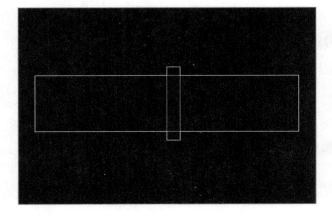

CAUTION: Invisible Doors do need to be totally transparent. If you put a grid or grating texture on the surface of your invisible door, you will get Tutti Frutti. Sad, but there it is.

It's time to formalize what you know about the use of transparent textures, because there are some simple working rules for their use.

HOW IT WORKS

Under some circumstances, DOOM enables the player to see through areas of void space into game space beyond. The condition under which this effect can occur indoors is quite strict: the door sector's floor must be higher than the floors on either side (it can be just one pixel higher if you don't want an obvious step). Any other floor-height combination produces HOM.

If this condition is met, then if there is something to see through the void, it is visible; if there is nothing to see through the void, the usual HOM results. Only two-sided lines can ever become transparent, and there must be a properly constructed sector beyond the void for anything to be visible. The lines that bound the void area become transparent in pairs and effectively behave just like the normal texture of a two-sided line. The difference is that, instead of seeing straight through a single line into the next sector, the player is seeing through two lines bounding an area of void space. Monsters cannot see "back" through it because it is an illusion caused by the drawing engine—monsters can see only through true air gaps.

INDOORS-OUTDOORS

Combinations of sky and ceiling can be used to good effect—after all, it is logical to have conventional openings such as doors and windows from buildings to outdoor areas.

DOORS

The Sky Door can be particularly effective on such a transition. You can arrange for the room beyond to appear gradually as the door opens, instead of flashing into view when the door starts to open. To do this, you need to have one area open to the sky and the other roofed. The door's ceiling should also be sky.

 CAUTION: It is generally essential for the door sector to have its floor higher than the sectors on either side, except in all-sky areas. Two combinations of floor heights always produce HOM, even outdoors. These are shown in Figure 24.6.

Figure 24.6.

Floor height combinations guaranteed to produce HOM along the far surface of the transparent door sector.

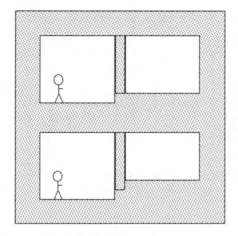

Examine FINGERS.WAD for examples of combinations that work, and then build transparent structures into your own WADs to puzzle and frustrate your players.

WINDOWS

As well as doors, WADs benefit enormously (in an aesthetic way, at least) from windows. If you want these to use the Sky Door effect, you need a slightly more complex arrangement of sectors. Visually, you want the indoor area to meet the outdoors, but structurally, you need adjacent sectors with sky on their ceilings. The effect therefore requires three sectors: the window frame with standard wall, floor, and ceiling textures; a truly outdoor sector beyond, to provide some sky; and a "closed" sector beyond that, also with sky on its ceiling. All three sectors should have their floors at the same height; the outermost sector's ceiling should also be at this height.

WATER

Let's now turn to a different set of visual effects. You will have noticed in DOOM that the player always runs around on the surface of any area. You can partially create the impression of ponds and pools by placing them a small distance below the surrounding area, but when the player steps into that area, the sense of drop is only as far as the surface of the new area. Water is, in effect, no different from blue carpet! It is possible, however, to create the impression of depth in your water or other liquids (or even in carpet—great for BOARDRM.WAD!).

CHEAP DEEP WATER

If you worked through some of the early WAD sorties, you might remember that the DOOM graphics painting process actually copes with some missing essential textures that should exhibit HOM. If you omit a texture from the essential texture over a doorway or along a step, DOOM continues the ceiling or floor texture from the room beyond the doorway, over the gap in texture, until it meets the start of the ceiling or floor in the nearer sector. This situation can be used to create a rough impression of water with depth. Build your pool sector. Then put another, slightly smaller, sector inside it, and give this sector a lower floor. Put the same water texture on the surface of both sectors, but do not put texture on any lower essentials. The player will be able to see the "join" between the sectors, but the effect is usable; there's no visible step in the water level, but the player can move down into the inner sector. This technique is very useful in one situation—the Tunnel.

THE TUNNEL

A nasty trick to inflict on your players is to create an area of damaging fluid through which they must wallow to get under a low area of ceiling. The construction of such a tunnel can best be seen from a map view, as shown in Figure 24.7.

Figure 24.7.

Sectors for a tunnel and trench.

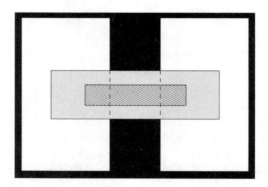

The left part of the figure shows a room with the start of a shallow pool with a deeper channel down the middle. Both pool sectors should have the same water (or slime, or lava) texture on the floor but no textures on the sides of the steps. The right part shows an identical arrangement on the other side of a wall (void space, shown black in the figure). The middle section of the plan shows the tunnel formed from three sectors with a much lower ceiling height, situated between the ends of the walls. These sectors continue the properties of the pool and trench. Only in the trench is there enough headroom for the player to pass under the wall.

A well-known example (from TRINITY.WAD) is shown in Figure 24.8. In this example, even the join in the textures looks quite good because it enhances the swirl of the lava over the step.

TRANSPARENT TEXTURES UNDER WATER

The techniques described earlier to create invisible doors can be used to dramatic effect when combined with the floor texture filling phenomenon just described.

Figure 24.8.

Trinity's lava trench.

THE PIT TRAP

From the sides, this looks like a perfectly normal pool, but it contains a deep shaft down which the player will fall—never to return, unless you provide some escape route.

The building process, once again, requires a set of concentric sectors. In this case, you must have four. What is crucial here is the way the relative heights are arranged, and which sectors have textures on the walls. Figure 24.9 shows the arrangement of sectors and the side view of the construction you are making.

Figure 24.9.

Sector arrangement for a pit trap.

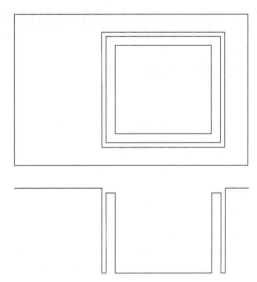

The largest sector is the room in which the trap is located, so give it an ordinary floor texture. Next in is a very narrow sector—the narrower, the better, really. Its floor should be very low indeed, preferably at least 400 units below the room, and should normally have the floor texture you want at the bottom of your pit. Put whatever wall texture you fancy on the lower essential that bounds the floor of the room—a brick texture or something slimy are probably what you want here. The next sector in provides the slime. Put its floor at a few units, 8 or so, lower than the room, and put a slime texture on its floor. Put nothing on either of the lower essentials that border this sector. Finally, set the floor of the innermost sector to match the floor of the narrow slot, and give it the same floor texture as the narrow slot.

The vital characteristics of this trap are the very low floors (so that the player cannot see them from the side of the pool) and the absence of textures on the sides of the raised ring. These missing textures serve two functions: First, from the outside, they cause the surface texture of the raised ring to flood across the whole pool, giving it its innocent appearance. And second, while the player is in the hole, the missing textures behave in the same way as in the invisible door. The transparent walls of the pit enable the player to see the outermost walls of the pool.

An example, called SLIMEPIT.WAD, can be found on the CD-ROM. I've chosen a variety of textures to show the various themes you can follow—you can make your pits all wet (as in one wall of the example) or resembling a dry room hidden under a false surface (as in the other three walls). I've added some gutters for the slime, but that's optional, of course. Actually, liquids don't have to be involved at all—tiger traps use branches! There is a way out of my trap—if you can find it—and I also added a wee surprise (not a tiger!) for the intrepid explorer.

WEIRD SECTORS—THE SWIMMING POOL

The swimming pool is actually one of the strangest effects described in this chapter. It uses methods that have not previously been mentioned in this book, but it illustrates a technique that is the basis of other (dry) special effects which will be described shortly. These effects all use nonstandard sector settings to achieve quite startling results.

Normally, when you create a sector inside another sector, the lines defining the inner sector have their inner sides assigned to the inner sector, and their outer sides assigned to the sector that surrounds them. If you change this setup so that the outer sides as well as the inner sides of these lines belong to the inner sector, an interesting effect arises. The graphics engine renders the entire area of these two sectors using the settings of the outer one. The player, however, walks around at the floor height of the *inner* sector—again over the whole combined area.

So to build a simple swimming pool, create a map with one sector inside another. Put a suitably watery texture on the floor of the outer sector. Set the floor height of the inner sector to be up to 40 units below that of the outer sector. Then change all the outer sidedefs of the lines that bound the inner sector so that they belong to the inner sector.

CAUTION: You have now produced a totally nonstandard line-sector relationship, and the nodes builders of most editors cannot cope with this situation. You should save the WAD without attempting to build the nodes tree and then use a separate, specialist nodes builder such as WARM. See Chapter 30, "Synthesis Tools," for more information about this utility.

The self-referencing sector arrangement just described can be nested, with each inner sector's lines belonging only to itself. In such cases, the sector settings used for rendering the scene are taken from the outermost sector, whereas the player's actual viewing height is determined by reference to the next inner sector.

This is, therefore, by far the most effective way to produce deep water. The surface appears unbroken and without awkward joints between sectors. When in the pool, however, you will find that the player's viewpoint lowers and the water surface gets closer as each step is descended. Note, incidentally, that because of the way in which each sector affects the view from the one further out, the viewpoint drops when a player steps into the pool, even if the first "wet" sector is actually at the pool-side level.

If you want the player to be able to walk out of your pool, you must have step sizes of 24 units or less between each sector. Don't have a total water depth greater than 46 units, though—if the player's head goes under the surface, HOM results as the unpainted essential lower texture comes into view.

If you fancy a swim in someone else's pool, load SPECIAL.WAD and take your player through the door marked SWIMPOOL.

HOW IT WORKS

The reason DOOM doesn't even try to draw the floors of the inner, self-referencing sectors is that the drawing routine assumes that the floor height will not change across a line with the same sector reference on both sides (you can't change floor height within a single sector, remember). So when the floor textures are drawn, these linedefs are ignored, the sector edges have no effect, and the floor is drawn between the last points where sector edges were seen—the edges of the pool. Why the player appears to walk at the level of the inner sector is less easy to say!

NOTE: You cannot use this Deep Water method to create the Tunnel. Because you can't change the floor *or ceiling* height within a single sector, DOOM's drawing routine assumes that neither of these will change across a line with the same sector reference on both sides. As a consequence, these linedefs are ignored when floor, ceiling, lower, and upper textures are drawn, so the floors and ceilings are painted at a constant height. Because the whole idea of a tunnel is to make the ceiling height lower while the liquid level stays the same, forcing the player to wallow about in it, this technique is no use here.

UP, UP, AND...

As well as being useful for holes, the self-referencing sectors just described can also be used to get your players high.

FLYING WITHOUT WINGS

If you create a simple, annular, two-sector map, as for the simplest swimming pool, but make the inner, self-referencing sector much higher than the outer one, you can give players the impression that they are flying. Try setting the floor to 70 units above the surrounding sector (with a suitably high ceiling to both sectors, of course). Gain access by using a teleport or the start of a level if you want to this to be a complete surprise. Or, if you like the walking-on-air effect, build the invisible stairs or invisible lift described next.

INVISIBLE STAIRS

Invisible stairs are really just a row of small platforms like the one just described. Build a row of sectors in the form you want for your stairs. In each sector, make another, smaller sector. Make all these inner sectors self-referencing—all the sidedefs should belong to the inner sector they bound. Set the floor height of all the outer sectors to be the same as the surrounding room. Now set the floor height of each inner sector to sensible step values. Increments of anything up to 24 are fine because you don't need to worry about correct placement of textures.

To climb some ready-made invisible stairs, load SPECIAL.WAD and take your player to the door marked INVISIBLE STAIR. A collection of stairs is in the room beyond, although mostly you can't see them, of course!

TIP: As you know, DOOM is not truly three-dimensional, so you cannot build bridges. You can, however, make something that looks a bit like a bridge that your player can walk over (but not under) by covering the top surfaces of an invisible staircase with non-obstructing Things that look like bricks. Put some support pillars in appropriate places and be certain to get the alignments perfect if you want it to look at all realistic.

INVISIBLE SELF-RAISING STAIRS

Now that you know how to make invisible stairs, you're bound to want the self-raising version sooner or later.

Invisible self-raising stairs need a set of steps just like the static, invisible staircase. Set all the inner sectors to be self-referencing, and then set *all* the sectors' floor heights to the height of the surrounding room. Now, to work, self-raising stairs need to be made of neighboring sectors, and the steps in your set of stairs must be isolated or the invisibility trick will not work. The answer is to create a set of neighboring sectors somewhere close but out of sight (in the void behind a nearby wall, for example). Make sure that all the lines face the correct way for self-raising stairs, and edit the sectors so that each has the same sector number as its invisible step's inner sector's counterpart. See Figure 24.10 for an example. (The sectors for the working model are in the void to the left; their disjunct parts are the triangular areas to the right.) Now, choose a suitable trigger line and tag it to the sector that is to act as the bottom step of your stairs.

Figure 24.10.
Sectors for a flight of invisible self-raising stairs.

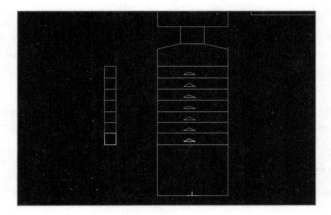

CAUTION: The algorithm for determining the order in which the stairs rise looks for lowest numbered linedefs. It is vital, therefore, that the model sectors are bounded by lines with lower numbers than any of the lines in the invisible staircase. To achieve this effect, it is wise to build the model before the "real" one.

The stairs out in the void will rise correctly when they are triggered. Because they share sector numbers with the invisible steps, they will drag these disjunct parts of themselves along in their motion. These then act like the "normal" invisible steps—the whole step takes the height of the inner sector as far as calculating player viewpoints is concerned, even though they are all still painted at floor level. The sound of the stairs rising comes from the model stairs out in the void, which is why they must be close by if you want them to be heard.

CONVERTING A LIFT

The invisible lift works in much the same way as the invisible self-raising stairs, in that it uses an invisible moving floor and model sectors out of the way somewhere.

TIP: An invisible lift in a lift-shaft looks pretty silly. It is best to convert an open lift adjacent to an exposed wall—like the one developed in the arena of the WAD built in the WAD sorties earlier in this book.

Assuming that you already have a lift, I'll take you through the steps necessary to make it invisible.

First, build two new, neighboring sectors somewhere where they will never be found. These are to provide models for the lift movement. Returning to your lift, create a self-referencing sector in the middle of the lift sector floor. Give this sector the same sector number as one of the model sectors, and set it to the upper level of the lift's travel. Set the rest of the lift sector's floor, and the other model sector, to the lower position of the lift. Then change your lift triggers so that they are tagged to the self-referencing sector.

The lift platform starts at its top level as usual. When triggered, it moves to the level of its lowest neighbor. The self-referencing sector has no neighbors but its disjunct part in the void has—and moves accordingly, taking the real lift with it. It returns as a normal lift would. The floor of the lift platform, however, always is drawn at the height of its outer part which remains at the lower level.

A sample lift can be found in SPECIAL.WAD. Jens has added some minimal textures so that you can see what is happening.

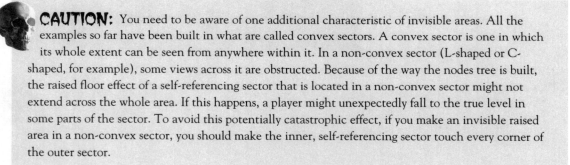

CAUTION: You need to be aware of one additional characteristic of invisible areas. All the examples so far have been built in what are called convex sectors. A convex sector is one in which its whole extent can be seen from anywhere within it. In a non-convex sector (L-shaped or C-shaped, for example), some views across it are obstructed. Because of the way the nodes tree is built, the raised floor effect of a self-referencing sector that is located in a non-convex sector might not extend across the whole area. If this happens, a player might unexpectedly fall to the true level in some parts of the sector. To avoid this potentially catastrophic effect, if you make an invisible raised area in a non-convex sector, you should make the inner, self-referencing sector touch every corner of the outer sector.

EXIT: MOPPING UP AND MOVING ON

In this chapter you have learned how some of the world builders created their own, unique special effects by taking advantage of quirks in the DOOM graphics engine. You now can incorporate these extra formulae into your own WADs to give them added spice and sophistication.

In the next chapter, you'll see how the techniques that have been described in this episode so far can be brought together, to take the first steps toward a total DOOM conversion.

TOWARDS A TOTAL CONVERSION

Although it may seem that everything that can be done in DOOM has already been done by others, this is, in fact, far from the case. Indeed, even within what may seem like familiar, well-trodden territory, there are vast tracts of the DOOM engine that remain completely unexplored. Beyond the familiar horizons lie uncharted regions aplenty—areas you may need to explore when you tackle a total DOOM conversion.

Naturally, it is impossible to provide a foolproof road map of uncharted ground. Nevertheless, in this chapter I attempt to direct your first footsteps in this area and warn you about some of the known pitfalls. Hopefully, this information will keep you out of the mire long enough for you to become a TC alchemist in your own right.

WHY GO FOR TOTAL CONVERSION?

A *total conversion* is, as the name suggests, a patch containing enough information to change the face of DOOM completely. It will add new monsters, scenery, textures, sounds, messages, and, of course, new maps designed to bring these elements together into a coherent whole, no longer recognizable as DOOM but seen by all as something new.

For many, making a DOOM conversion is the very pinnacle of DOOM editing. When nearly all facets of DOOM are being altered together, there is little that you cannot do. Your control over every detail of the way the game plays, looks, sounds, and acts allows unrivaled freedom of creation (see Figure 25.1). On the other hand, a DOOM conversion takes a lot of effort and time, and brings its own problems. Like other pinnacles in life, many may aspire to its heights, but few will achieve them.

— By Justin Fisher with additional material by Steve Benner

Figure 25.1.
Familiar ground—or is it?

In this chapter, you will discover the various options and problems involved in the creation of a total DOOM conversion. You can then decide whether you want to tackle the dizzying heights of such a project, or whether you'd rather stay plodding around copying others' WADs.

THINGS TO THINK ABOUT BEFORE YOU START

There are a lot of things to consider before you set off down the total conversion pathway. Complete preparation is essential. Although many decisions may be made for you by your particular circumstances, other choices may remain open for you to choose at your leisure. Let's take a look at the important choices you face.

GO IT ALONE OR TAKE A TEAM?

Precisely what can be tackled will depend upon the time (and abilities) of those working on the project.

If you intend to tackle the entire conversion yourself, the time commitment is going to be very large, but you will be the undisputed authority for all decisions. Your notes also won't need to be legible to anyone but you. The advantages of the team approach are equally obvious: A divided workload can lead to faster production, the team can benefit from each member's special skills and abilities, and, of course, more brains will be available to work on the problems. The main disadvantage of a team is that continually distributing updated files and information can be very time-consuming. In addition, possible aesthetic disputes and the extra organization required to bring the team together from time to time (even if only electronically over the Internet) may dishearten all but the most determined.

It is impossible to present one general answer here, of course. You will have to be guided by your own feelings and circumstances. But if it feels right, go with it! What have you got to lose (except maybe your friends)?

GAUGING THE SIZE OF THE PROJECT

The extent and scope of the conversion will be limited only by the amount of time you (all) have to spend on it. A rule of thumb I have found handy is to imagine the size of the task ahead of you and multiply this by ten to arrive at a more accurate estimation. Double this if there are two people involved. Double it again if there are three, and so on. All these doublings allow for the extra problems involved with communications between team members. If the final time estimate frightens you, that's good! It's meant to. Tackling a total conversion should not be undertaken lightly.

Let's take a look at what else you need to consider.

MAKING PLANS

Assuming you've decided to go ahead and take the plunge, you need to make some very careful plans before doing anything else. Planning is an even more important aspect of your preparation for TCs than it is with ordinary WAD design. In particular, you need to plan:

- **The scope of the conversion:** How much will be changed? (How total is total?)
- **The role of each participant:** Who will do what? (If you're on your own, it won't take long to decide.)
- **An order of attack:** What gets done when?

To focus on these elements, though, you need to decide something else first. You need to choose a theme (see Figure 25.2).

Figure 25.2.
A famous TC theme.

THE THEME

Your early planning should revolve around picking a theme for your conversion. As well as helping you to focus on the conversion's requirements, if you've opted to take the team approach, this stage of the planning will involve all the team members. This will get everyone engaged and enthused and ready to work together—or bring out the fact that maybe the team isn't able to work together! It also should iron out any difficulties of coordination and communication within the team before any real work has been started and ensure that information flows quicker once work has begun.

Choosing a theme isn't just a good way to get your team working together quickly, though. Choosing a theme is just as important to a solo attempt. The theme should determine your entire approach to the conversion. It will dictate how much has to be changed and in what way—to be convincing, every aspect of your conversion must remain true to the theme. The theme is the heart of your conversion (see Figure 25.3).

Figure 25.3.

Staying true to the theme: the landing pads.

CHOOSING A THEME

In deciding upon a theme, you need to consider whether it should be an adaptation of a favorite film, TV show, book, or other work or whether you're going to strike out and produce something entirely original.

The advantages of creating an original theme for the conversion are frequently overlooked, which is a shame, as this approach has much to commend it. First, with an original theme you are not restricted by having to copy, rather than create, the universe. The result, being entirely your own creation, can be more satisfying. There are added complications with basing a conversion on the work of others, too: Issues of copyright may leave you with a conversion that looks great but that the original copyright owners forbid you from distributing (or, worse, insist that you destroy). By using a popular film or book as a basis for the conversion, you may feel that you will automatically have a waiting audience of fans. Total conversions are so rare, though, that you will find that there is a waiting audience of players eager for *any* new DOOM conversion. If the theme is good, and the conversion well made, people will play it and like it. If the theme appeals to you, then it is likely to appeal to others as well. I recommend that you play it safe: Be original.

PLANNING THE REST

By the time you have a theme decided, you will find that much of the rest already will have fallen into place, particularly in a team effort. There will still be many details to pick over and decide on though, so the next step is to work toward some grand design, an overview of how your conversion is going to look.

THE GRAND DESIGN

Almost by definition, one goal in making a DOOM conversion is that the result be a unique experience rather than a superficial change—DOOM not only in new clothes, but also with a new attitude. The ways a conversion can be made different from DOOM are limited by little other than imagination, but one good method is to give a new plot to the game. Often the plot will arise out of your chosen theme. Within the conversion, you can convey and reinforce the plot in various ways.

FORCE GOAL COMPLETION

With forced goal completion, the player must complete goals (perhaps outlined in a level briefing before the game) consistent with the storyline to complete the level.

You have been chosen to infiltrate a sophisticated alien stronghold. A scouting team has acquired basic structural information; from this we have decided that you first have to enter the complex via a waste chute on the east side. From the waste processor you should be able to reach the power source of the complex without alerting the security bunker. Shutting off the power will put the alien troops on alert, but it will also disable the internal security devices, so you should be able to proceed to the security bunker itself without facing organized resistance. Once there, you should plant a bomb: the timer will give you 5 minutes to clear the compound before the detonation.

Which in turn allows a troop ship to land safely near the installation and disgorge its cargo…Well, you get the idea.

THE TREASURE HUNT

Another approach is to have your game reveal clues about what to do as the player moves about the level. When pieced together, these clues give the required information for completing the level. The means of revealing information can take many forms:

- A mural on the wall depicting what the player must do (or depicting a map of the level, showing the location of that secret tunnel)
- A wind that seems to whisper something as it rushes through the trees
- Words carved into a stone cliff face
- A prisoner who gives some advice when you free him from his shackles
- A warning scrolling across a computer terminal

The possibilities are endless. The information given might simply reveal a hidden passage that could not be spotted without the clue, or it might warn that the level exit is guarded by a creature or robot that cannot be harmed by any weapons except one the player does not have. Of course, more information is needed to find this new weapon, and so on…

MULTIPLE OUTCOMES

A third approach is to have player actions on one mission determine what the next mission will be.

As you make your way out of the waste processing unit, you come to a junction in the maze of corridors. You dash off confidently down the corridor to the left, not noticing the cameras overhead. Suddenly, doors are closing around you, while others are opening. The lights go out, plunging you into darkness. You hear strange alien laughter. Fearing the worst, you slip your phaser back into its holster and reach for the pulsed disrupter. You look around and see that the way back is sealed. If only you'd turned right…but it's too late for regrets. You take another step through the darkness and—whoosh! Now where are you?

By spreading the scenario to span two levels, you can use the secret level to interpose a tougher infiltration level for players who don't follow the clues you lay out for them.

INVOLVING THE PLAYER

All these examples are possible and all require the player to become involved in the grand design. No longer can a player complete the level simply by shooting everything that moves. Although this sort of thing will be different from DOOM, whether it is as much fun depends a great deal on how it is implemented. It is up to you, then, to implement it well! To do this, you have to keep your wits about you. You have to stay true to your theme (see Figure 25.4). But you also have to maintain an awareness of your conversion's roots.

Figure 25.4.
Involving the player in the theme!

WORKING WITHIN DOOM

Even though a total conversion will differ from DOOM in look and feel, you will still be working with the same game engine. Some aspects of the game can be changed more easily than others and these will, of course, be the principal candidates for your ministrations. You can do an amazing amount of alteration without diving too deep into virgin territory. Next is a discussion of the most effective changes you can make, for minimum effort.

CHANGING THE LOOK

One of the easiest changes to make to DOOM is to change the way it looks. Chapter 21, "Changing the Face of DOOM," looked at this topic in detail, and little needs to be added here. The more graphics you change, the more total your conversion will seem. Remember, though, that this can involve a tremendous amount of work very quickly. You may find that many of the standard textures can be adapted very quickly with just a few additions and some clever lighting effects to produce a very different feel to the game (see Figure 25.5).

Figure 25.5.
Another scene from Nemisis.

TIP: DOOM II's graphics, in particular, lend themselves much more to adaptation than do those of DOOM or Heretic. Look at Figure 25.6 to see how well a few new textures can add new life to a DOOM II level.

Of course, the more sprites you change, the greater will be the players' belief that they are playing a new game.

Figure 25.6.
A little change goes a long way in DOOM II.

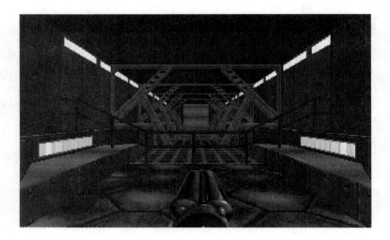

IF IT MOVES, CHANGE IT!

I've noticed that many players will (instinctively?) try to relate what they see in a conversion back to DOOM. Be mean and nasty! Don't just rehash traditional monsters in new forms, allowing the player to deal comfortably with your "new" monsters as they have with thousands of others. Use your imagination and make something really new. If players have to invent new tactics and learn how to combat a new type of monster, then your conversion will be providing the spice they were hoping for as they waited for your megabytes of conversion to download.

NOTE: Read Chapter 22, "Hacking the DOOM Code," to learn more about changing the way monsters behave.

Experienced DOOM players may remember the moment of panic when they met their first Pain Elemental in DOOM II. This is something that no amount of previous DOOM experience really prepares you for. I would like to think that people's first encounters with any of the new monsters in *Aliens* TC evoke a similar response (see Figure 25.7).

Tools exist that will enable you to create such vastly different foes, so there is no reason not to. Why stop at the monsters? The same principle applies to everything in the conversion: the less familiar ground the player has to work from, the more intense, edgy, and ultimately immersive the experience will be. Don't forget that you can change the cheat codes, too!

CAUTION: Even if you do intend to change every aspect of the way DOOM looks and plays, be careful not to tamper with id Software's copyright notices—or Raven Software's, if you're working on Heretic or Hexen. Not only would that be illegal; it would also be very inconsiderate!

Figure 25.7.

"Do I shoot, or will I regret it?"

PUSHING THE LIMITS

Although there are limits to what can be done with DOOM, it is best to pretend that there aren't. Even if some things cannot be done, most can be simulated (albeit clumsily at times). Obviously, a good understanding of the limits of DOOM is essential, but don't let those limits restrict your thinking.

The impossibility of putting rooms on top of one another is a good example. Some levels are so well designed that it would simply never occur to you that they were limited in this fashion. There are other levels that give the impression of rooms on top of one another by moving floors while the player isn't looking. Various optical tricks that simulate the effect can be used, too. In other words, if the effect you want to achieve is impossible, don't just give up on it. Start thinking laterally and find a way around this minor setback.

Other chapters of this mission cover many of the special effects you can consider for your conversion. Try Chapter 23, "Reject Table Tricks," and Chapter 24, "Special Visual Effects," in particular.

STARTING OUT

With most of your ideas planned and the major decisions made, you can start to map out a strategy for tackling the conversion itself. Some general tips might help you with this.

ORDERING THINGS

When making your first conversion, you may be tackling many tasks for the first time. In such circumstances it is very important to remember to do the most important things last. Let me explain: If you are making a DOOM conversion about infiltrating an alien stronghold, say, the first thing you might be tempted to do is to set about making the sprites for the aliens—to find out whether you can do it, whether it will work, and so on.

Beware: This approach is a trap! By the time the conversion is nearing completion, you will find that your skills—in designing graphics, in building sprites, in matching and balancing colors—will have grown considerably.

The first things you did—the aliens, in this case—will probably look downright shabby compared to their more recently created environment. You are then left with the harsh choice of including "substandard" work in the conversion or of discarding them, in the full knowledge that you will need to spend many more hours re-creating them.

Although the latter option is actually a desirable course of action, in terms of the final quality of your work, it will be a difficult course to take, especially if time is short. To achieve a good balance between time and quality, a partial solution is to work on the unimportant things first and tackle the important things later, when your skills have improved. That way, you can include early work, even if it is "substandard," without hurting the overall quality. It doesn't matter nearly so much if a light fitting, say, has the wrong perspective, or bad shading, or whatever. The players' attention will be on the important things—which are probably bearing down on them at speed, giving them no time to admire the decor—and these will look great! (See Figure 25.8.)

Figure 25.8.
Some minor details for starters.

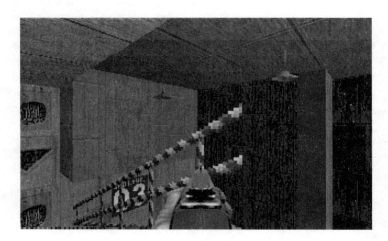

A similar situation exists with building the levels for your conversion. It is tempting to start this stage early, because it's an easy task. It's also natural to want to work "across the board": spending a few hours making levels, then working on a sprite or two, and then adding some sounds, perhaps, before going back to add to the map. This approach may quickly result in completed levels, but you probably will find that they have to be reworked later as your conversion takes shape. Your new monsters may require more space to move than your architecture allows, your new textures may turn out not to work quite right in the chosen light levels, some decorative items may have been changed into new things, and so on. Obviously you'll need a level to test your changes on, and many ideas and new requirements occur as a result of level building, but it can be a mistake to do too many levels too soon.

KEEPING TRACK OF IT ALL

Due to the sheer quantity of things that need to be changed and the need to keep track of all of these, you should develop the habit of continually making notes. I find this is vital. It is especially important to keep track of details such as which textures and things have been replaced, which sprite frames have been used for what, and so on. No matter how obvious and easily remembered you may think your changes are, by the time they have started to pile up, many of the earlier details may become forgotten. Hacking into your own work trying to find what you did with a particular frame or where you inserted an image is very time-consuming, not to mention irritating and moderately embarrassing!

THE TOOLS OF THE TRADE

Much of this book is devoted to the various DOOM editing tools and utilities available, so you have all the information at your fingertips to help you decide for yourself what suits you best. If you are tackling a total conversion, you're likely to need at least one of every basic type of utility. Rather than recommend any in particular, I would simply urge you to consider learning to use more than one utility for any one task. Even though it is unlikely that you would miss out on anything by using only one utility, there is sometimes a tendency to restrict your thinking to the methodology that the particular utility employs and neglect alternative approaches to solving a problem. There are also gains to be had from being able to use the strengths of one utility to cover the weaknesses in another.

The tools you will need include:

- **A level or map editor:** You will need to lay out new levels to give your players a new environment. One that allows you to change the names given to the things is useful, as this saves you from having to remember (or constantly refer to your notes to find out) that you need to place a Cacodemon when you want an alien pod on your map.

- **An external nodes builder:** This may be necessary if you have decided to incorporate any special effects that require strange, nonstandard arrangements of sidedefs.

- **A reject-table builder:** If you want to create any special tricks using the WAD's reject map, you will need a specialized reject-table builder.

- **A general WAD composition tool:** You will need to be able to introduce new elements beyond standard map components to your WAD. Sound effects; music; new graphics for floors, ceilings, walls, and game objects; and message screens may all be needed.

- **An executable hacking tool:** To change the way monsters and other objects behave, you will need to access the data fields tucked away in DOOM's executable files.

- **A WAD conversion utility:** To apply your conversion to other game variants, you may want to employ the services of a WAD conversion utility. Why stick at one total conversion when, for a little extra effort, you can have two?

In addition to these specific DOOM editing tools, you also will need general-purpose tools for the preparation of your new materials: graphics and painting programs, music and sound editing facilities, and so on. Just learning to use all these tools can be a sufficiently daunting task even before you think about the conversion itself!

THE ELEMENTS OF THE CONVERSION

Most of the elements of a total conversion have specific chapters in this book that cover them: level editing, graphic editing, DOOM.EXE hacking, and so on. It is worth mentioning some of the more important aspects to consider as you complete your final planning of the conversion, however.

SOUNDS

One of the most important yet underutilized elements for conveying the atmosphere and feel of your world is *sound*. If you have explored the eerie swamps in Hexen, you will know what I mean. It is all too easy to think of sound as support for the graphics, or one of the less important things to be changed, but sound is a very powerful tool in your arsenal and, if used properly, is almost a guarantee of success. Any trepidation a player feels at the sight of a half-eaten corpse dangling from a rafter will pale in comparison with what the player feels when nothing threatening can be seen, but something *very* threatening is obviously *very* close. Do you remember the first time you reached E2M8 of DOOM? I think it fair to say that many people are happy to live with fewer monsters in *Aliens* TC for the special sound effects that this sacrifice allowed.

HACKING THE EXECUTABLE

DOOM.EXE editing is another technique that tends to be under-used. Although most conversions include a little editing, often only minor or few changes are made. Editing the DOOM.EXE gives the freedom to change all the basic rules of the game—without telling the player!

Extensive DOOM.EXE editing is a very effective way to avoid any feeling of superficiality to the conversion. This vein is particularly rich if you are tapping DOOM II—here you will find a huge variety of frames, sounds, functions, objects, and so on at your disposal.

PAY ATTENTION TO THE MAP

The most important aspect of a conversion, though, remains the maps themselves. These tie everything together. Good and imaginative level design is of overwhelming significance, and no amount of clever tricks or fancy graphics will ever be a substitute for this.

PLANNING THE DISTRIBUTION

Planning the distribution of a conversion before you've even started its construction may seem a little strange, but it is important to give this matter some thought at the outset because it can have a bearing on the way you proceed.

Making a reliable installation system is not as easy as it seems. No matter how perfectly the system is made, someone somewhere is bound to have a hardware/software combination that causes problems. If that person is unaware that a problem occurred with installation, the semi-operational version of your work will give entirely the wrong impression of both you and your conversion.

You can take a few simple steps to avoid this. The easiest is to alter the start of the first level of your conversion so that if any part of the installation failed, the fault becomes obvious. You can usually safely assume that levels, textures, and sounds will work flawlessly. These require no installation, just that the PWAD containing them be present. DeHackEd patches, sprites, and flats (and demos, as these are version-specific) are the most likely items to be missing if installation fails. A possible option, then, would be to surround the player start position with standard DOOM objects that are impassable, such as firesticks, or to place the player on top of such an object so movement is impossible. Have an early patch create some monsters with a spot-player sound that says something like, "Installation has failed, consult text/help file." Place one or more of these looking at the player at startup. As a final part of your conversion's installation, arrange for another DeHackEd patch to turn the blocking items invisible, thereby removing them from the game, and turn the monsters into some innocuous (and silent) decoration. If you use this approach and an installation fails, the player cannot move and is told what has happened. If installation succeeds, the game proceeds as normal.

Arranging an installation procedure like this can be a little tricky, but it's worthwhile to attempt if you value your reputation!

EXIT: MOPPING UP AND MOVING ON

So, that's really all there is to it. All that remains is for you to start work on your conversion!

Once you've started the project, it should rapidly become unique, and for me to give generic advice after the planning stage becomes difficult. Ultimately, you will have to become the greatest expert on your particular conversion.

As I said at the start of this chapter, much of what is possible in a DOOM conversion is still uncharted territory, waiting for you to enter, explore, and return with your finds. Hopefully there is sufficient information in this chapter for you to take the first steps into the unknown.

Your imagination and creativity are the keys. Remember, you have an entire world to create and work with—the ultimate work of art! I look forward to seeing (and playing) the fruits of your endeavors.

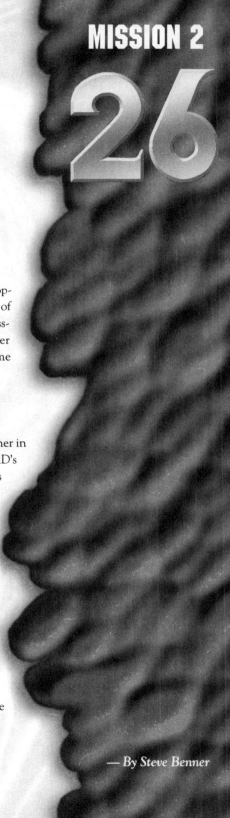

DESIGNING FOR DEATHMATCH

So far in this book, I have made little distinction between the development of WADs for single players to tackle alone and those for groups of players to tackle together. In this chapter, I go some way toward redressing the balance, as I look at the features that mark good multiplayer WADs—particularly Deathmatch (DM) WADs—and provide some pointers toward creating your own.

MULTIPLAYER MODES

Many players of DOOM prefer to play in groups, rather than alone, either in Cooperative play, where they gang up on the monsters and solve the WAD's puzzles together, or in Deathmatch, where the creatures and the puzzles can go hang. (Why frag a monster when you can frag a friend?)

Each of these two types of multiplayer games has its own particular requirements and imposes an extra layer of design criteria on the WADster.

COOPERATIVE PLAY

Many single-player WADs can be immediately suitable for Cooperative play. All you may need to do is check that all four cooperative starts have been added to your WAD. Monster and power-up ratios can often be left as they are. Your single-player testing should have ensured that little spare health or ammunition is lying around. In Cooperative play, these resources have to go further—balancing out the additional ease with which the monsters may be dispatched.

— *By Steve Benner*

BATTLING COOPERATIVELY

Ironically, battles often are not easier for players in Cooperative mode. Making sure their buddies don't get caught in friendly fire means they have to take a little more care where they spray their lead. The additional slight hesitation that results can make all the difference to the player's own survival.

TRICKS AND TRAPS

One aspect of a game that changes totally as soon as more than one player is at large in a WAD is the possible flow through its areas. Many flow-control features—one-way staircases, trip-wire traps, and so on—rely on knowing where the player is at the point that a trap is triggered, as well as where the player has been before-hand. In Cooperative play, the location of other players when one player springs a trap cannot be known or predicted. Some traps can become disastrous in Cooperative mode, creating the need for the designer to be extra careful when adding traps and tricks to WADs intended for Cooperative play.

TACKLING PUZZLES COOPERATIVELY

The preceding comments apply to puzzles, too. Puzzles that are difficult in single-player mode can become trivial in Cooperative play. The donut room in the sample series of WADs produced in Episode 2, Mission 1, "A Hell of Your Very Own," is a good example. With a little modification, this room could be made into a puzzle that requires Cooperative play: If you make it impossible for a single player to run from one of the switches to the lift or the door, the WAD suddenly needs two players to solve it.

Other little multiplayer twists could be added here, too. You could make it necessary for the yellow key to be acquired to leave the donut room very easily. Just make the door out of the room require a yellow key from the inside. This change would make it essential for the donut room's puzzle to be solved before players could move on. If the puzzle required two players to solve it, single players venturing here without their friends would be-come trapped until they were rescued—a good way to ensure that the WAD is indeed played cooperatively.

Another sneaky Cooperative mode trick would be to arrange for each teleport line around the donut's center to deliver to different teleport destinations. Cooperative players may not always notice which side of this sector their buddies passed through in grabbing the key. When they try to follow, they could find themselves some-where completely different! (This particular modification also would bring an interesting little twist to the single-player game, of course.) WADs that make the team work together but that work hard to keep them apart are by far the best Cooperative-play WADs (see Figure 26.1).

Figure 26.1.

We're all in this together…

Further possibilities for interesting (or at least amusing) cooperative tactics arise from the fact that when turned into chickens in Heretic, or pigs in Hexen, players change size. You could therefore produce tunnels that normally would be too small for a player to enter but that could be entered with ease by one who had been suitably morphed. If the tunnel led to a crucial switch, say, you could force the team to expend a Morph Ovum to send one of its members off to perform the task. It would then be up to the rest of the team to protect the weakened member until the effect wore off. I wonder how long it would take team members to think of this idea.

Remember, too, that in Hexen, pigs can be clambered over. A Porkelated player could therefore provide the rest of the team with a real piggy-back ride—enough of one to help them up that extra-large step, at any rate!

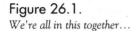

Giving cooperative players the need to work together as a team in this way can make play much more rewarding. It also may wreck the WAD as a single-player WAD, of course. You will need to decide which is more important to you.

DEATHMATCH

Many of the points just discussed in relation to Cooperative play apply equally well to Deathmatch mode. In Deathmatch, however, the situation is complicated by the very different nature of the play. DM players will be less interested in solving puzzles and are likely to have little patience for traps and tricks. First and foremost, these players will want to find each other and start trading lead.

Deathmatch DOOM is used to provide a virtual-reality environment where players set their own targets (usually their buddies!) and their own objectives. The designer's job is to provide the environment but not the objectives. From this point of view, Deathmatch WADs can be easier to design and implement than single-player WADs. The designer does not need to consider flow or provide puzzles. Give the players a space to run around in, some weapons, and some ammo, and then leave them to it. If only it were that simple…

DEATHMATCH DESIGN CONSIDERATIONS

Single-player WADs rarely convert well to Deathmatch scenarios. If you want to design for Deathmatch games, it is usually better to concentrate on that aspect of a WAD's design and develop a DM-only WAD. This prevents you from having to compromise both single- and multiplayer aspects, which is what usually happens with WADs intended to be used in either mode.

To put a good Deathmatch WAD together, you need to have an understanding of what makes a good Deathmatch arena. DM design can be every bit as challenging as (and some would say much more rewarding than) producing a single-player WAD. The remainder of this chapter provides an overview the more important points to consider if you wish to venture into this area of WAD design.

BALANCE

The overriding requirement in any Deathmatch WAD is to provide and maintain balance. Keep things equal for each player—which is not to say that you must keep things the *same* for each player. Strive to ensure that no player gains an unfair advantage over any other or is unfairly disadvantaged in any way. Sacrifice all other aspects of the design before compromising this principle. If you get this aspect of your design right, most players will forgive all of its other shortcomings. If you get it wrong, your WAD will probably be consigned to a black hole.

Keep this warning in the back of your mind as you consider the main design features of your WAD.

Hexen Deathmatch design for Hexen has the added complication that players may each choose to fight as a different class. Keeping things balanced under such circumstances calls for extra care. You may need to adjust certain aspects of your design to minimize the advantages offered to any particular class of player. You will be alerted to specific aspects of Hexen WAD design that can lead to player imbalances as this chapter progresses.

THE PLAYING SPACE

The playing space of a Deathmatch WAD needs to be given a lot of thought. As already stated, DM players like to get into action quickly. They also like to be able to ambush each other and to be capable of disappearing and reappearing suddenly in other places. This creates a number of design requirements and possibilities.

RANGE

In planning the extent of a Deathmatch WAD, keep the players' range in mind. DM players are unlikely to want to spend much time exploring the WAD itself. They will want to be able to appraise the immediate area quickly, grab some weapons, and then go in search of their opponents. Few players enjoy trudging for miles before they catch sight of anything.

Remember, though, that DOOM can support up to four players at once. Games with three or four players may need a bigger playing area than games with only two. And, of course, the more familiar players become with the geography, the smaller it will start to seem to them.

If it is a large WAD, you might want to place all your DM starts fairly close together, so that everyone starts out in the same general area. You can then lay out some (similar strength) weapons in a way that draws the players together. Once they have located their opponents, players can decide for themselves whether they want to enter the fray right away or spend time hunting out some different weapons.

INTERCONNECTIONS

Deathmatch WADs must dispense with the largely linear design that can often benefit single-player WADs. You should provide geography that enables your players to move around in a large number of ways. Provide lots of interconnections between the areas of the WAD, but keep the interconnections short to enable players to travel through them quickly.

SYMMETRY

One of the best ways to ensure that the terrain favors no one regeneration spot is to maintain a high degree of symmetry in your WAD. This has the added advantage that if many of the respawn places look similar, it will take regenerated players a little while to orient themselves.

Figure 26.2 shows an excellent example of the points made so far: CASTLE.WAD for Heretic by Alfred Svoboda. Although this particular WAD has its shortcomings, as the basis for a Deathmatch arena it has much to commend it. Notice the provision of ample interconnections, giving rich and varied hunting (and hiding) grounds. The WAD is compact without being confining, and the overall symmetry provides equality of spawn spots with a good degree of disorientation.

HEIGHT VARIATION

As well as avoiding linear spaces, try to keep your thinking away from the purely horizontal. Use variations in height levels to produce areas that allow plentiful ambush spots and make players keep their eyes open. (Take a look at DOOM's E1M4 for a good example from the masters.) Again, use short interconnections between the various levels. Use steep stairs and lifts rather than gradual level changes down long corridors. Provide players with an interesting and varied hunting ground.

Figure 26.2.
An example of good Deathmatch terrain.

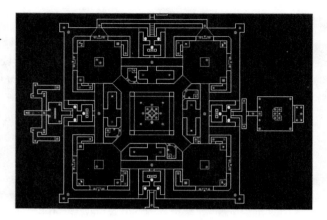

Use of the vertical dimension is particularly important in those variants of the game that allow players to look up and down as well as to actually fly. Hunting opponents is so much harder when they can be quite literally all around! (See Figure 26.3.)

Figure 26.3.
More good Deathmatch hunting ground.

If you have acquired the habit of adjusting the relative floor heights and separation distance of sectors onto which players must jump, remember that there are differences in the maximum running speeds between the various player classes in Hexen. This means that different classes of players can jump different lateral distances. Don't adjust sectors so finely that you deny one class of player access to particular areas unless you also supply that class with a different advantage elsewhere.

HIDING PLACES

The provision of hiding places is an important consideration in the design of Deathmatch WADs. Provide plenty of them (the interconnections and height variations of a DM level can be helpful here). Be careful, though. Secure hiding places overlooking exposed areas (particularly ones that players are forced to cross) encourage players to spend their time there in the hope of picking off their opponents in safety (see Figure 26.4). Such features make for boring (or frustrating) play.

Figure 26.4.
A secure hiding place—something to avoid in Deathmatch design.

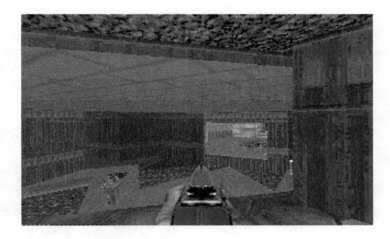

OPEN SPACES

Open spaces are useful for the exposure they can bring to players crossing them. Do not make them too large, though, or you make it impossible for the exposed player to work out where distant and better-hidden players are firing from.

Make sure that open spaces do not work in favor of particular starting positions. You may wish to keep open spaces toward the center to maintain the symmetry of your layout. DM regeneration locations can then be positioned in similar areas around the edges of the map, making it necessary for all players to cross the central spaces to hunt the others. Be careful, though, that such areas do not prevent regenerated players from getting back into the game.

CHOICE OF TEXTURES

When choosing textures for walls in WADs intended for Deathmatch play, remember that each player is given a different colored suit: green, brown, indigo (black, actually), and red, in DOOM and DOOM II. Take care not to give any one player an unfair advantage by using textures against which that player can hide. Also be aware of placing any player at a distinct disadvantage by having him or her conspicuous wherever he or she goes.

In DOOM, the indigo player is virtually invisible against the ashwall texture, for example. The green player has a decided advantage against the marble wall textures, which the red player will hate.

Keep players' colors in mind as you design your WAD, and try to vary the surfaces so you have no single, overall color scheme. If you want areas that are predominantly one color, try to balance the WAD by providing areas that offer similar advantages to each of the other players. Heretic and Hexen are easier to design for in this respect.

LIGHTING LEVELS

Use can be made of lighting levels in Deathmatch WADs just as in single-player WADs, but bear in mind that the player in the dark is now the one at the advantage, rather than the opposite way around. Brightly lit areas tend to be unpopular in Deathmatch WADs, as this makes hunting the other players a lot less fun than wandering around in the half-light. A good Deathmatch WAD will make use of the lighting levels by placing weapons and other goodies in pools of light within an otherwise dark room. This way, several players may edge around a room, wondering whether to risk showing themselves to grab whatever is on offer, as shown in Figure 26.5.

Figure 26.5.
Is it worth the risk?

OTHER MAP FEATURES

Elements of the map that a designer of single-player levels takes for granted can gain new significance in Deathmatch WADs. Many standard features need to be reappraised if they are to be used successfully.

DOORS

Many Deathmatch players dislike the presence of doors, because they slow progress from one area to another. They also signal a player's whereabouts through the sounds they make as they open and close. Certainly you should not include doors simply for the sake of the appearance of your WAD. They can be a useful feature, however, because of the risk players can face from opening them.

You could provide a choice of tactics by connecting the same areas in different ways, such as a short interconnection using a door and a longer one without. Players can then either take the longer route quietly or risk signaling their presence to any opponents within earshot by taking the shorter one. Such arrangements also enable doors to be used as decoys and distractions: A player could open the door and then run around the long way in the hope of fragging from behind any opponents on the other side of the door.

KEYED DOORS

The presence of keyed doors is completely irrelevant to DM players, who always start out with all necessary key-cards in their possession. This feature also can be used to aid in the adaptation of a single-player WAD to Deathmatch use: If a WAD does not utilize one of the three colored keys in its single-player mode, then that color becomes available to supply an additional series of doors that only DM players can open. These extra doors can be used to bypass areas of the map that are unsuited to Deathmatch play or simply to provide extra connectivity, breaking up the enforced linear flow of the single-player game.

If you do use such a feature, you should not use the appropriate color-coding by the side of the door to indicate that a key-card is required to open it. This would confuse single players, who will think there is still a key somewhere for them to find. Instead, use the doorstop texture to suggest to the single player that the door is merely decorative. (Although, of course, DOOM will tell them otherwise if they try the door—as most players will!)

An alternative way of preventing single players from being confused by these doors is to provide them with the extra key once the WAD has been completed in the "prescribed" manner. The interconnection provided by the door might as well be used in the single-player game, too, rather than leaving it as just so much wasted space.

TELEPORTS

Teleports are great devices for improving the interconnection of areas in Deathmatch WADs. Remember, though, that the sound and sparkle of a teleport in operation are conspicuous to other players. You may want to vary the exposure of teleport destinations with the skill level of the game by placing the lower skill-level teleport landings behind alcoves in the destination sector, for example.

Hexen's teleports provide the facility to move between maps. It is best to avoid too many of these in Deathmatch WADs, as they will disrupt play considerably.

DAMAGING SECTORS

Areas with harmful special characteristics or crushing ceilings tend to be unpopular with DM players. Many feel that these features get in the way of Deathmatch play. Newer versions of the game have addressed the problem of suicides, but it is generally best to remove the temptation by keeping damaging areas in a Deathmatch WAD to a minimum.

DECORATIONS AND OBSTACLES

Decorations and obstacles can be used in Deathmatch WADs much the same way as in single-player games. Their use is governed by more or less the same rules. DM-only obstacles can be used to convert parts of a single-player WAD for DM play by blocking off areas that would not work well in multiplayer games. Make sure that areas that need to be blocked off have the obstacles properly placed and that players cannot work their way around their edges, or just bludgeon their way through.

Remember not to use barrels (or pop pods) as such obstacles, as they can be quickly disposed of. Also remember that barrels do not regenerate in -altdeath play. Generally, though, barrels can be employed much as they can in single-player games: to make areas more hazardous and to discourage players from hiding around particular corners.

SPECIAL FEATURES

As is the case with standard map elements, many of a WAD's special features need to be reappraised for Deathmatch use. DM WADs generally do not benefit from some of the features used to enliven single-player WADs, but instead need their own particular special aspects.

PUZZLES, PROBLEMS, AND TRAPS

As already noted, Deathmatch players rarely have the patience to solve puzzles and problems, whether to make progress through a room or to obtain the items they might be interested in (their weapons and ammunition). Traps that are intended to catch individual players can become a nuisance in Deathmatch WADs. Either keep such traps out altogether or, again, if you're aiming for a multipurpose WAD, make sure there are alternative ways around the traps for DM players.

Single-player WADs also can cause traps for DM players unintentionally. Doors that single players could only approach from one side may not have an opening mechanism from the other side. These doors will bar the exit of DM players who regenerate on the wrong side of them. If you lock your players in areas where there is nothing for them to do except wait until someone comes along and frags them, they are unlikely to be impressed.

It is a good idea to make sure every door can be operated from both sides (unless this defeats the design, of course) even though this might appear to introduce some redundancy.

SECRET AREAS

Whereas single-player games commonly have the majority of the goodies tucked away in secret locations, this is usually a bad idea in Deathmatch WADs. This method can give any player who has a greater familiarity with the layout of the WAD a major advantage over the others. If you hide weapons, for example, the player who has played the WAD before will know where to dash to grab them all before the other players have even oriented themselves. Newcomers to the WAD will quickly become bored with it if they are fragged repeatedly while they spend time hunting for a weapon so they can join in against their more experienced colleagues.

Although it can be argued that prior knowledge will always be to a player's advantage, this can be minimized by placing in plain view everything that is available. This doesn't mean that *obtaining* all items has to be easy—only finding them.

SIGNALS

Many DM players like features that signal the location of their opponents. This can be something as simple as the operation of doors and lifts giving audible signals or the glitter and fizz of a teleport (or regeneration event). It also can involve more complex arrangements, such as trips in one area triggering events in another—turning the lights on and off in one area to warn of a player in another or the triggering of remote lifts, for example.

These features enable players to assess the whereabouts of their opponents and to plan interceptions, ambushes, or just a good old-fashioned chase to gain their frag. If you want to demonstrate your abilities as a DM WADster, dispense with single-player traps and tricks and aim for these sorts of features instead. Be aware, though, that these features do tend to favor the more experienced players of your WAD. Once again, make them obvious, so players with a knowledge of your WAD's features do not gain an unfair advantage over newcomers.

OBJECT PLACEMENTS

The layout of objects in a Deathmatch WAD is far more critical than it is in a single-player WAD. It is crucial that you keep an eye open for any imbalance you might be creating as you distribute items through the level. Don't have single, large caches of items such as weapons or health, as you might in a single-player WAD, or you could end up in a situation where one player will begin near a weapons cache, another will get the armor, and a third will begin in the middle of nowhere with only a pistol and some useless stimpacks.

Once again, take care to provide for all three player classes, making sure that if you supply all three puzzle pieces for one class, for instance, you do so for the others as well.

Symmetry of design can help here, enabling you to present each player with a similar array of objects wherever he or she starts.

STARTING POSITIONS

Deathmatch games can have up to 10 DM start/regeneration positions per difficulty level. Make sure you have at least four, or DOOM will not be able to start a four-person session with your WAD. It is recommended that you use all 10 DM start positions so as to provide a greater variety of starting conditions for your players, and to make the restart process less predictable.

As previously noted, the shimmer of a player's DM regeneration is conspicuous to the other players, and you may want to take this into account when you position the DM start positions. In contrast to single- and cooperative-player starts, you can use the skill-level flags of DM rebirth positions to change their locations with the difficulty level of the game. Use this to shelter the regeneration of players using the lower skill settings or to place them nearer to available weapons or armor.

In positioning regeneration spots, remember to allow your players to get back up to a reasonable strength quite quickly. If you don't do this, you will unfairly favor the players who make the early frags. Let regenerated players back into the game quickly, or you will find that they tend to leave for good.

WEAPONS AND AMMO

Acquiring weapons and ammunition will be the principal goal of most DM players—when they're not actually fragging the opposition, that is. Don't get carried away with the weapons you make available to DM players, though. Most players will want something more powerful than the pistol fairly quickly, but you should limit the power of what you provide.

A popular tactic is to make a shotgun readily accessible from all DM start positions. There should be greater risk involved in reaching more serious weapons, such as the chaingun and rocket launcher. (Risk, in DM terms, usually means exposure.) Weapons such as the chainsaw can be made available, too. The very powerful weapons such as the plasma guns—and the rocket launcher, some would argue—should be available only at the lower difficulty settings of the game, if at all (and preferably only then at considerable risk to the player). These weapons quickly destroy any balance the WAD had by making long-distance or indiscriminate kills too easy.

HERETIC Readers working with Heretic should have no difficulty equating the preceding comments about DOOM's weaponry to their variant of the game. There is a fairly clear correspondence, as indicated in Chapter 20, "Finishing Touches." Many designers prefer to make nothing more than the gauntlets and the crossbow available. And maybe a mace to lure people out into the open…

Hexen The provision of weapons for Deathmatch WADs in Hexen may seem complicated by the fact that so many of the mage's weapons are ranged, whereas the fighter's are not. It can be tempting to provide the fighter with some more powerful weapons by way of compensation. Don't. The designers of Hexen took great pains to get the player classes very carefully balanced. The fighter's greater speed and strength are adequate compensation. If you allow all players to equip to the same level of weaponry, you should find that balance is maintained quite well. It is generally not a good idea to make the multipart weapons available in Deathmatch, for the reasons already outlined in the discussion about powerful weapons. Making some parts of each weapon available can be a useful ploy to tempt newcomers to your WAD out into the open. The trick won't work again once they realize that the final part isn't available, of course, but they may take awhile to discover this fact!

Similarly, ammunition needs to be distributed carefully in Deathmatch WADs. Keep players on the move to hunt for ammunition by spreading it around the WAD in small quantities. In addition, limit the players' ability to stockpile ammunition by depriving them of backpacks. This will prevent a player who has a plentiful supply of ammo from settling down in a good ambush spot and just picking off everyone who appears.

MONSTERS

Monsters serve a very different purpose in Deathmatch WADs from the roles they play in single- and cooperative-player games. Many players prefer to have no monsters in the way while they stalk their buddies; others like to have monsters around as a supply of weapons and ammunition. The presence of monsters also provides additional signals for players. Monsters either can act as lookouts for carefully positioned players or, more usually, will provide clues to the whereabouts of other players through the noise and flashes of combat.

It is largely a matter of personal preference whether you use monsters or not. Use them in limited quantities, though, and confine yourself to the weaker types. The principal players should not find themselves upstaged by appearances of Cyberdemons and such. Use monsters only to make the main play a little trickier or to provide a steady stream of ammunition.

As always, aim to keep things balanced, making sure that no particular start position will subject a player to more (or less) than his or her fair share of monster encounters. Players will not take kindly to discovering that their opponents have been waiting, weapons at the ready, while they fought their way past the hordes of Hell. Nor will the other players be happy to be robbed of their rightful frag if the hordes win.

BONUSES AND POWER-UPS

The distribution of power-ups is also more critical in DM WADs than in those intended for single-player use. Once again, an uneven distribution of these items will lead to an imbalance. Too much health or armor—or the correct quantity poorly distributed—can lead to unfair advantages (especially in -altdeath play), while too little of either can be disastrous for all players.

It is usually better to use more of the smaller power-ups than to provide large ones, although you may want to supply some security armor as standard close to each regeneration point, at least at the lower skill levels.

As with weapons, you may want to place a few of the more powerful artifacts in exposed positions, maybe more as bait than as anything else. Aim for balance by providing an even distribution of them. In general, though, avoid the excessive power-ups such as Combat Armor, Blur, and Invulnerability Artifacts.

Again, Heretic users should be able to translate the preceding DOOM-based analysis of useful power-ups into Heretic terms. The Time Bomb of the Ancients is a fun item to offer for Deathmatch, and many players feel that the Morph Ovum and Wings of Wrath are essentials (I'd be inclined to agree—see Figure 26.6). It is probably unwise to make too many Tomes of Power available unless you have limited the weaponry severely. A mix of nothing but gauntlets, the Time Bomb, and a Tome of Power can produce an interesting contest!

Figure 26.6.

Prepare to die, human!

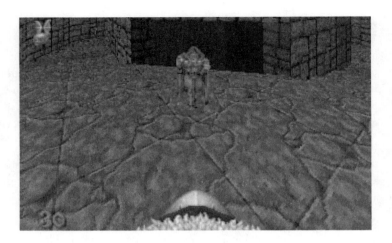

It is always better to distribute a lot of the smaller power-ups, such as the stimpacks and bonus items, throughout much of your WAD, rather than use the bigger medikits or spheres. Unlike with structured single-person WADs, remember that you can't predict players' hunting patterns through your WAD; you can only guess at the likeliest encounter spots.

Once again, the designers of Hexen have worked very hard to make sure all the standard power-ups provide a good balance of power between the player classes in Hexen. All you have to do is limit the availability of the really powerful ones and make sure everything you do supply is available to all. Once again, the Winds of Wrath and the Porkelater should be provided as standard.

TESTING

The testing of DM WADs can be more involved than that of single-player WADs, largely because of the problems involved with hunting oneself. You can usually inspect only the technical aspects of the WAD with simple walkthroughs. To really test how it works as a Deathmatch arena, you will need to make contact with other players and arrange some test sessions. If you're at all involved in DM play, though, this shouldn't be too difficult to arrange.

After you've had several test sessions, play-testing and refinement are similar to the testing of single-person WADs: Get people to play it and listen to their comments.

Don't be put off, though, if your play-testers initially complain that the level is too complex or too large. Wait until they've been trying it out for a while and have grown more accustomed to its playing space before you start to take that particular criticism seriously.

EXIT: MOPPING UP AND MOVING ON

The production of Deathmatch WADs can be a major test of your abilities as a WADster. Provided that you keep in mind the requirements of Deathmatch play, it need not be more difficult than the production of any WAD. As usual, plan your work, pay attention to the detail as you work, and try to arrange a test for playability at every stage. Aim to maintain balance throughout the WAD. The production of a Deathmatch level can be one of the most challenging as well as rewarding WAD-building experiences. You could even enjoy playing the WAD yourself!

EPISODE

MISSION 1: GENESIS

MISSION 2: SYNTHESIS AND METAMORPHOSIS

3

THE TOOLS OF THE GODS

WADAUTHOR

This chapter presents full details of the capabilities and operation of the map editor package WadAuthor from Williston Consulting. This is a Windows-based editor that enables the building and modification of WAD files for DOOM, DOOM II, Heretic, and Hexen. Readers who want to embark upon the WAD sorties presented in Episode 2, Mission 1, "A Hell of Your Very Own," using a Windows editor rather than the DOS editor presented in that mission might want to peruse this chapter as part of their pre-mission preparation.

Details on how to install WadAuthor on your computer are presented in Chapter 4, "Using the CD-ROM." The version of WadAuthor on this CD-ROM is a pre-registered version of this shareware program. You cannot distribute this version to anyone else.

GETTING STARTED

When starting out with new software, the familiar urge to toss the manual aside and begin clicking often rears its ugly head. This urge usually subsides after the third or fourth incomprehensible error message leaves you wondering if the program was written by a space alien. This is the place to start reading when you decide that WadAuthor falls into that category.

THE WADAUTHOR EXECUTABLES

WadAuthor ships with two separate executable files. One, WAUTHR16.EXE, is compiled for 16-bit operation under Windows 3.*x* or Windows for Workgroups. The other, WAUTHOR.EXE, is compiled for 32-bit operation under Windows 95 or Windows NT.

Users running Windows 95 or Windows NT should always use the 32-bit version of WadAuthor to take full advantage of the 32-bit environment.

— By John Williston

Users running Windows 3.*x* or Windows for Workgroups 3.*x* are encouraged to run the 32-bit version using the latest version of Microsoft's Win32s subsystem. The Win32s subsystem enables access to most of the benefits in the 32-bit version, while running within 16-bit Windows.

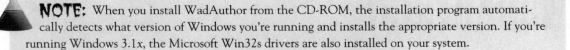

NOTE: When you install WadAuthor from the CD-ROM, the installation program automatically detects what version of Windows you're running and installs the appropriate version. If you're running Windows 3.1*x*, the Microsoft Win32s drivers are also installed on your system.

GETTING HELP

WadAuthor ships with a detailed help file that provides assistance and information for most of the features in the program. Help can be obtained through several different methods. Reviewing these should serve as a good introduction to the WadAuthor help system.

CONTEXT-SENSITIVE HELP

Context-sensitive help is almost always available in WadAuthor. To invoke it, press the F1 key. The help file topic corresponding to the current location within the software is displayed. Many topics provide links to other related topics to provide more information.

Context-sensitive help for dialog boxes usually contains a graphic image of the dialog box, enabling the user to click various controls in the image for more information. Help is also available for all prompts and error messages. If you don't understand any given message, press the F1 key and examine the help topic for a more detailed description.

THE HELP CURSOR

A graphical environment's greatest strength can also be its Achilles heel. After all, who can remember what all those little toolbar bitmaps mean? The help cursor provides a safe way to find out what the various elements of the user interface do without invoking the command.

To use the help cursor, press Shift+F1. The cursor changes to a pointer overlaid by a question mark. Clicking a menu item, toolbar, toolbar button, status bar, or other user interface element displays the appropriate help file topic, as shown in Figure 27.1.

Figure 27.1.
WadAuthor's help cursor in use.

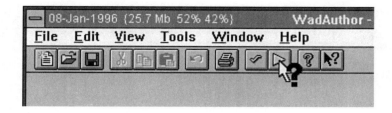

THE HELP MENU

The WadAuthor Help menu provides quick access to several of the most frequently useful topics in the help file. A short description of each relevant item is provided here:

- **Contents:** Displays the contents page of the help file. This page is like the contents page of a book, providing a high-level breakdown of the major help file sections.

- **Search For Help On:** Displays the Help Topic Search dialog box. This dialog box enables the user to enter text, dynamically updating the list of topic search keywords that match the text.

- **How To Use Help:** Displays the help file provided with the operating system designed to assist users in learning to use the help system.

- **Tutorial:** Displays the help file tutorial. The tutorial is designed to help a beginning author through the process of creating a first map.

- **Troubleshooting:** Displays the troubleshooting help file topic. This topic contains a list of common problems and questions.

- **What's New?:** Displays detailed information about the bug fixes, enhancements, and new features in the current version of WadAuthor.

INITIAL CONFIGURATION

When WadAuthor is started for the first time, the user is often prompted for information before initialization can complete. WadAuthor provides support for multiple games (DOOM, DOOM II, Heretic, and Hexen) by using a different WAD-game configuration file (WCF file) for each of the games.

WadAuthor uses the WCF file to determine where the game files are located. The game files are then used to load various data used later during editing. If WadAuthor cannot locate the WCF file or any of the required game files, it prompts the user for the correct data.

The WAD-game Configuration dialog box enables the user to specify the location of the main game WAD file if WadAuthor cannot locate it. If you wish to use a different WCF file, click the Cancel button to display the WCF Selection dialog box. Otherwise, simply correct the path to the main game WAD file before clicking the OK button.

> **NOTE:** If you wish to select a different WCF file after the initial configuration process, choose the Select Configuration File option from the File menu. Because WadAuthor maintains the current WAD-game data in memory, any open documents must be closed before this menu option will be available.

If the various games are installed in their default directories, the WAD-game Configuration dialog box never appears. Once WadAuthor has completed initialization, it is ready for use.

UNDERSTANDING THE INTERFACE

As a Windows program, the WadAuthor interface should be immediately familiar to anyone comfortable with the Windows environment. There are, however, a couple of items specific to WadAuthor that bear explaining.

TOOLBARS

WadAuthor provides a *standard toolbar* by default. The standard toolbar, shown in Figure 27.2, contains shortcuts for the most basic commands in WadAuthor.

Figure 27.2.
WadAuthor's standard toolbar.

The standard toolbar buttons, listed from left to right, can be used to perform the following operations:

- Create a new document
- Open an existing document
- Save the current document
- Cut the current selection to the clipboard
- Copy the current selection to the clipboard
- Paste from the clipboard
- Undo the last action
- Print the current map
- Check the current map
- Run the current map
- Display the help file contents topic
- Invoke the help cursor

TIP: All the toolbar buttons in WadAuthor supply ToolTips. To find out which command a button executes, place the mouse cursor over it and wait. Within a few seconds, a brief description appears in a small window, accompanied by a more verbose explanation in the status bar.

The 32-bit version of WadAuthor also supplies two other toolbars that can be selectively enabled or disabled from the WadAuthor Options dialog box (discussed later). The *view toolbar*, shown in Figure 27.3, provides shortcuts for the most frequently used view configuration and editing commands in WadAuthor.

Figure 27.3.
WadAuthor's view toolbar.

The view toolbar buttons, listed from left to right, can be used to perform the following operations:

- Create a new rectangular sector
- Create a new polygonal sector
- Create a new Thing
- Zoom in
- Zoom out
- Set the zoom to best fit the map to the available display area
- Increase the grid
- Decrease the grid
- Toggle Thing bitmap display
- Toggle grid display
- Toggle the snap-to-grid option

The *user tools toolbar*, shown in Figure 27.4, provides shortcuts for launching the user-defined tools (discussed later). Each button launches the command whose position on the Tools menu corresponds to the button number.

In the 32-bit version of WadAuthor, all the toolbars are of the multi-dockable variety. What does this mean? It means that if you don't like where a toolbar is, you can move it.

To move a toolbar, use the mouse to grab the toolbar by pressing and holding the left mouse button within a portion of the toolbar outside the buttons and the caption (if visible). When the toolbar is dragged near the edge of the application frame, the toolbar wire frame changes to indicate that the toolbar can be docked by releasing the mouse button.

Toolbars can be docked to any of the four sides of the application frame, or they can float freely—much like a sort of tool palette. Toolbars can even be multi-docked when floating. For example, dragging the view toolbar and releasing it on top of the floating standard toolbar combines the two toolbars in a single floating window.

Figure 27.4.

WadAuthor's user tools toolbar.

STATUS BAR

WadAuthor uses the status bar to display messages, provide some information about the current view settings, and identify the current object. The status bar, shown in Figure 27.5, uses several different panes to achieve this.

Figure 27.5.

WadAuthor's status bar.

Thing: Enemy : Imp at (1984,2608) facing E on 345 (number 42)   DOOM II: Hell On Earth   None   12345DM 64   1828,2802

The panes, listed from left to right, are as follows:

- **Message Pane:** Displays useful messages and provides identification for the current object.
- **WAD-game Pane:** Displays the name of the current WAD-game (determined by the current WCF file).
- **Object Filter Pane:** Displays the current object filter setting (None, Vertex, Thing, Linedef, or Sector).
- **Thing Display Pane:** Displays the current Thing display attributes setting.
- **Grid Spacing Pane:** Displays the current grid spacing setting.
- **Cursor Position Pane:** Displays the current cursor position.

TIP: Clicking a toolbar or status bar with the right mouse button displays a menu of available control bars from which the user can select. If all the control bars are disabled, the Options dialog box is the only way to re-enable them.

The 32-bit version of WadAuthor correctly saves the toolbar and status bar settings when shut down, restoring them on startup. Once the environment is properly customized, it stays that way.

IMAGE PREVIEW CONTROLS

Whenever possible, WadAuthor supplies a graphical preview of the object being edited. The property editing dialog boxes (discussed later) provide good examples of this. In almost every case, clicking an image preview control with the left mouse button invokes the Image Browse dialog box, enabling graphical selection from a complete list of the available options.

IMAGE LIST CONTROLS

Wherever the name of an image can be edited, WadAuthor uses an image list control to supply some additional features. An image list control looks just like a normal Windows edit control, but it is usually associated with an image preview control. The image list control supplies the following keyboard commands for choosing an image:

- **F2:** Invokes the Image Browse dialog box for full-size, side-by-side graphical selection.
- **Up Arrow:** Selects the previous image.
- **Down Arrow:** Selects the next image.
- **Page Up:** Selects the image one page above the current image.
- **Page Down:** Selects the image one page below the current image.
- **Ctrl+Home:** Selects the first image in the list.
- **Ctrl+End:** Selects the last image in the list.

RELATIVE CHANGE CONTROLS

When editing numeric values such as sector ceiling heights or a lighting value, WadAuthor uses relative change controls to allow some flexibility in setting new values. Relative change controls handle double and triple plus and minus sign characters, as listed here:

- **++/−−:** A double plus or minus prefix adds or subtracts the specified value from the original value. For example, when setting a sector light level, entering a value of ++10 increases the existing value by 10 units.
- **+++/−−−:** A triple plus or minus prefix adds or subtracts the specified value relative to an appropriate reference value. For example, when setting a sector ceiling height, entering a value of +++128 makes the ceiling 128 units above the floor. The triple plus or minus prefixes are meaningful only when a reference is available. For example, a floor can be adjusted relative to the ceiling, but a lighting level has no reference—a triple plus or minus would be interpreted the same way as a double plus or minus.

DOCUMENTS AND VIEWS

Internally, WadAuthor uses a separation of documents and views to separate data presentation from the data itself. The current version of WadAuthor supports a single type of document (a WAD file) and a single type of view (the map editing view). For now it is enough to recognize that the term *document* refers to a WAD file, whereas the term *view* refers to a map editing view.

WORKING WITH DOCUMENTS

The purpose of this section is to highlight some of the important features WadAuthor supplies for working with documents and views.

CREATING A NEW DOCUMENT

Creating a new document is the first step in creating a new map to play. To create a new document, select the New option from the File menu or select the appropriate button in the standard toolbar. You are greeted with a new empty map, as shown in Figure 27.6.

Figure 27.6.

An empty WadAuthor map editing window.

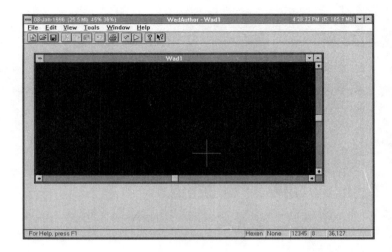

OPENING A DOCUMENT

As soothing as it might be to stare at a blank window, WadAuthor is pretty useless without an open document. To open a document, select the Open option from the File menu. This invokes the File Open common dialog box, enabling you to select a WAD file for editing. Select a file and click the OK button, or click the Cancel button to abort the procedure.

CHOOSING A MAP

When WadAuthor opens a WAD file, it opens the first map it finds within the WAD file. If the WAD file contains more than one map, a different map can be selected by choosing the Select Map option from the View menu. If any changes have been made to the current map, WadAuthor asks if the changes should be saved prior to loading the new map data.

SAVING A DOCUMENT

To save a document under the current filename, select the Save option from the File menu or click the appropriate toolbar button. To save a document under a different filename, choose the Save As option from the File menu and provide a new name in the resulting dialog box. Clicking the OK button saves and re-opens the WAD file with its new name.

It is important to understand how WadAuthor saves a file. For maximum safety, WadAuthor copies the entire WAD file during the Save operation, even if file backups have been disabled. This guarantees integrity of the disk-based data even if the Save operation fails for some reason. This can, however, cause some minor confusion.

For example, if you were to open the main Hexen WAD file, change the attributes for a single Thing object, and click the Save button, the operation can take a long time. This is because WadAuthor is creating a complete copy of the entire WAD file. It might be a bit slower than necessary in certain situations, but it can be quite handy when another program crashes the system in the middle of a Save!

PRINTING A DOCUMENT

WadAuthor supplies the kind of standard printing facilities users expect from a Windows application. WadAuthor provides "What You See Is What You Get" (WYSIWYG) printing with a couple of small caveats listed here:

- Thing bitmaps are not used for printed output.
- The portion of the map actually printed can vary slightly from the portion displayed by the current view. This is due to differences in aspect ratio between the screen and the selected output device.
- The printed output contains a brief header and footer in addition to the map view.

Perhaps the more technically accurate phrase would be "What You See Is Almost What You Get."

NOTE: Try using Print Preview to make sure your document will print as desired. To access the Print Preview feature, select the Print Preview option from the File menu.

WORKING WITH VIEWS

The map editing view is the primary interface in WadAuthor. As such, learning to use it well can pay great dividends in the overall quality and enjoyment of a WAD-editing project. Many keyboard shortcuts are available for working with the views. For a complete list, consult the help file "Keyboard Interface" topic.

ADJUSTING THE ZOOM

WadAuthor supplies fairly flexible zoom configuration through a few simple commands. When a new view is first created, it zooms and centers itself to provide a best fit for the entire map. The user can always return to a best fit view by selecting the Best Fit option from the View menu, by pressing the Home key, or by clicking the appropriate button on the view toolbar.

Zooming in increases the degree of magnification, allowing work of greater detail. Zooming out, not surprisingly, decreases the degree of magnification. These two zoom commands are available from the View menu and the view toolbar, and they have keyboard shortcuts assigned as well (the + and – keys).

Constantly zooming in and out can be quite tedious, not to mention slow, on old hardware. Because of this, the WadAuthor object zoom feature can be very useful. To zoom a given object on the map, move the cursor over it and press the Z key. WadAuthor calculates the zoom setting required to best display the object, centering the view on it in the process.

Object zoom can be applied any number of times. To quickly restore the settings prior to the first object zoom, press Shift+Z. These simple keystrokes make it much easier to switch quickly between high-level and low-level views of the current map.

NOTE: Each map editing view maintains its own zoom setting (and grid setting, as seen later) independent of all other views—even views into the same document.

ADJUSTING THE GRID

The grid setting within WadAuthor is used for a variety of purposes. In general, lower settings are more favorable for highly detailed work, whereas higher settings are more favorable for less detailed work. The current grid setting can be changed by selecting the appropriate items from the View menu, clicking view toolbar buttons, or using the keyboard shortcuts (] or Shift+Plus to increase; [or Shift+Minus to decrease).

USING THING BITMAPS

One of the most attractive features of the Windows environment is its graphical nature. WadAuthor uses bitmap representations of Things within a map whenever possible, unless instructed otherwise. Thing bitmaps are displayed only at the highest zoom settings to avoid problems with overlap due to scaling difficulties. (See Figure 27.7.)

On old hardware, displaying a map's Things as bitmaps can degrade performance to an unacceptable level, in spite of the lengths to which WadAuthor goes to achieve good video performance. If repainting Things within the map is too slow, simply turn this feature off via the View menu option or the appropriate view toolbar button.

THING DISPLAY OPTIONS

The Thing display options provide a way to quickly determine which of the Things within a map are present at different difficulty levels and modes of play. Things not present based on the current Thing display settings are outlined on the map with a dotted pen. To set the Thing display options, choose the Thing Display item from the View menu, or use any of the keyboard shortcuts discussed in the reference section of the help file.

Figure 27.7.

WadAuthor's display of Things in the map editing view.

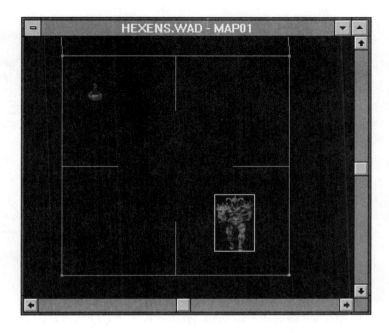

SNAP TO GRID

The grid feature of WadAuthor can be very useful when trying to design geometrically symmetrical architecture; it can also be very annoying when trying to do otherwise. Fortunately, it can easily be disabled via the View menu option or the appropriate view toolbar button.

THE CURRENT OBJECT

As the cursor is moved around the map editing view, the object immediately underneath is highlighted, making it the current object. The current object is the object affected by operations like clicking the mouse or object zooming. (A Player 1 Start is the current object in Figure 27.7.)

If the current object has a valid tag number assignment, the other objects within the map that share the tag are highlighted as well. This enables you to see quickly which objects share tags. More information is given about working with tags later.

To set the current object to a specific number, press the F2 key to invoke the Center on Object dialog box, shown in Figure 27.8. This dialog box enables you to specify the type and number of the desired object. Clicking the OK button centers the map on the specified object, making it current.

MULTIPLE WINDOWS

Here is where the power of the WadAuthor document/view architecture really begins to show. WadAuthor can provide fully synchronized editing of a single document across multiple views in separate windows.

Figure 27.8.
WadAuthor's Center on Object dialog box.

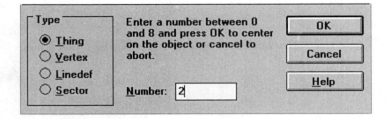

A new window into the current document can be created by selecting the New Window option from the Window menu. The new window contains a new view into the current document, separate from all other views.

This feature can be a very powerful aid. For example, you can open a second view into the current document, setting it to a best fit of the current map, while the original view is kept at maximum zoom for detailed work. The display across the two views maintains perfect synchronization as different editing operations are performed.

BASIC EDITING

To make the best use of WadAuthor, it is important to understand the basic design philosophy. WadAuthor was designed to work on a room-by-room basis, rather than requiring the user to create and link vertices or draw linedefs. WadAuthor generally works best when you first create the general architecture sector by sector, joining them as desired. Once the basic layout is complete, populating the map can be quickly accomplished.

TIP: WadAuthor provides an Undo feature for all editing operations that alter data. The Undo buffer, by default, is unlimited, meaning it expands as necessary within the limits of system memory. If a mistake is made, simply select Undo from the Edit menu, click the appropriate button on the default toolbar, or press Ctrl+Z or Alt+Backspace from the keyboard.

SELECTION

WadAuthor uses the familiar "select then operate" metaphor common in contemporary software. This means you must first select something to work with it. Selecting map objects in WadAuthor can be done with the mouse or with the keyboard, although most users will probably find the mouse to be the easier method.

SELECTING A SINGLE OBJECT

To select a single object, place the cursor over the object to make it current, then click the left mouse button. The spacebar can also be used in place of the mouse click.

SELECTING MANY OBJECTS

To select many objects at once, WadAuthor provides a rubber-band selection. While holding down the Shift key, click the left mouse button at the anchor point for the selection rectangle. Then simply drag the mouse until the desired objects are completely enclosed within the selection rectangle. When the mouse button is released, all objects completely enclosed within the rectangle are selected.

MODIFYING THE SELECTION

To add or remove an object to or from the current selection, place the cursor over the object, hold down the Ctrl key, and click the left mouse button. This toggles the selection state of the current object. As before, the spacebar can be used in place of the mouse click.

USING THE OBJECT FILTER

WadAuthor goes to great lengths to support modeless operation. This means that WadAuthor enables the user to work with all object types at once; you are not required to change any mode setting to work with a different type of object.

This does require extra processing time, however, and can impair performance on old hardware. If moving the mouse to a different object does not quickly highlight the object, try setting the object filter. The current object filter is displayed in the status bar and can be set by selecting the Object Filter option from the View menu or using the keyboard shortcuts (N, V, T, L, or S).

USING DISAMBIGUATION

Quite frequently, many objects are crowded in a very small area of the map. When this occurs, it can be very difficult to pick a single object out of the crowd. The object filter can be very helpful in these situations, but it can be inconvenient to keep switching between the different object types.

WadAuthor provides object disambiguation as an alternative solution. To use this feature, hold down the Alt key while performing a single-object selection. WadAuthor displays a dialog box listing up to one object of each type that is closest to the cursor position. You can then select a specific object from the list.

DRAG AND DROP

Dragging and dropping selected objects is a basic operation that enables you to move objects around the map quickly. To initiate drag and drop, click and hold the left mouse button on a selected object.

While continuing to hold the mouse button, move the cursor. Notice how WadAuthor provides a wire frame representation of the objects during the drag operation. This provides an exact reference for the final drop location. When the objects are in the desired new location, release the mouse button to complete the move operation.

If, while dragging, the mouse cursor moves beyond the bounds of the current map editing view, the view scrolls toward the cursor. The scroll rate is slow at first, increasing toward a moderate maximum within a few seconds.

 NOTE: Drag and drop, like virtually all other mouse operations in WadAuthor, can be aborted by pressing the Esc key.

THE CONTEXT MENU

The context menu is, not surprisingly, a context-sensitive menu that provides access to the most powerful features in WadAuthor. To display the context menu for a given object, move the mouse over the object and click the right mouse button.

The list of available choices is different depending on the type of object clicked, other selected objects, and the surrounding objects. The context menu provides access to functions for which no other method of invocation exists, so it is important to learn to use it correctly.

 NOTE: The context menu adheres to the new Windows 95 interface guidelines, popping up after the right mouse button has been released. Keyboard users can invoke the context menu by pressing Shift+F10.

CREATING SECTORS

WadAuthor supplies functions to create rectangular (square, actually) or polygonal sectors. (Math majors, please take note: I realize that a rectangle is a polygon—the difference refers to the degree of design flexibility.)

To create a new sector, invoke the context menu at the desired sector location and select one of the two aforementioned options. Alternatively, click the appropriate button on the view toolbar to achieve the same result. When using the toolbar, WadAuthor needs to ask for the desired location of the sector to be created before continuing.

Rectangular sectors can be created to match the current grid size or a user-specified size. The mouse position is first snapped to the current grid setting (if snap-to-grid is enabled) before the vertices are created.

Polygonal sectors are created based on a user-supplied radius and number of sides. This makes it very simple to create more advanced shapes. Circles, for example, can be closely approximated by supplying a large number of sides. The vertices for this type of sector are not snapped to the current grid setting; otherwise, distortions in the desired polygonal shape would result. The center point, however, is snapped to grid if snap-to-grid is enabled.

When creating a new sector, WadAuthor uses the specified point as the center of the new sector. If this point already lies within another sector, WadAuthor creates a sector whose linedefs are all two-sided. If the point lies in an unused portion of the map, a stand-alone sector with one-sided linedefs is created.

> **NOTE:** Any object that WadAuthor knows how to create can be inserted into the map using the keyboard alone. Press the Insert key to invoke the Object Insertion dialog box, select the desired object type, define the object parameters, and provide the location as prompted. The remainder of the process is no different from using the mouse.

CONNECTING SECTORS

Two sectors are connected if they share a common linedef; this arrangement usually means that the player can pass between the two. WadAuthor connects sectors by joining linedefs or vertices. To join two sectors, take the following steps:

1. Select the linedef to be moved.
2. Add to the selection the linedef to which the first linedef should be joined.
3. Invoke the context menu by clicking the right mouse button on one of the two selected linedefs.
4. Select the Join Linedefs option from the context menu.

WadAuthor joins the two linedefs into one, creating a two-way connection between the two sectors. The player can pass freely between the two sectors unless further editing is performed.

Vertices can be joined in a similar manner. WadAuthor must perform a bit of extra work, however, during each vertex join to check if the resulting join eliminates a linedef or connects two sectors. For this reason, the linedef join method for connecting sectors is recommended, because it is more reliable.

Joining objects is also possible via drag and drop. At the end of a drag-and-drop operation for a single linedef or vertex, WadAuthor checks to see if the object has been dropped on another of the same type. If so, WadAuthor asks if the objects should be joined.

MODIFYING SECTOR LAYOUT

A sector is initially created as a symmetrical polygon of a given size and number of sides. What if you would rather have a highly asymmetrical shape instead? WadAuthor provides several tools to modify the shape of an existing sector.

ROTATING AND SCALING

To rotate or scale a sector around its center (as defined by the average of all its vertex coordinates), select the sector, invoke the context menu, and choose the appropriate option: Rotate Sector(s) or Scale Sector(s).

The resulting dialog box enables the user to specify the parameters for the operation. Optionally, the final vertex positions can be snapped to grid, and the Things within the sector can be included in the operation. Including Things in the operation can greatly increase the time required, so use this option wisely. Doing so, however, can be a real time-saver when a pre-populated sector needs to be adjusted by a few degrees.

As implied by the menu option that provides this function, the operation can be performed on multiple sectors. In this case, the center point is calculated based on all the vertices for all the sectors. This means that all the sectors rotate around a common point, rather than each around its own individual center.

ADDING VERTICES

Rotating and scaling are useful sector transformations, but what if the actual shape of the sector needs to be changed? WadAuthor provides the capability to add more vertices to a given sector. Coupled with the capability to drag and drop vertices, this enables the user to make a sector of virtually any shape.

Adding vertices is accomplished by splitting one or more of the linedefs in a given sector. To perform the operation, select one or more linedefs, invoke the context menu, and choose the Split Linedef(s) option. A new vertex is inserted at the center of each linedef in the selection.

WORKING WITH TAGS

WadAuthor provides a special tool for adding, removing, viewing, and changing tag assignments within the map. To invoke the tool, select the Tags option from the Tools menu, or press Ctrl+T from the keyboard.

The Tags dialog box lists the current tag numbers in use, along with the objects sharing the currently selected tag number. Changing the selected tag number updates the list of objects, and changing the selected object highlights the object within the map view. The object itself is highlighted as the current object; all other objects sharing the same tag number are highlighted in a different color.

Clicking objects on the map with the left mouse button adds them to or removes them from the list. Thus, to tag a linedef to a sector, add or select the desired tag number and click the two objects on the map. Many of the normal editing functions are unavailable when the Tags dialog box is displayed.

CREATING SPECIFIC MAP COMPONENTS

Users often want to create certain standard components of a WAD-game map. WadAuthor currently provides automatic creation of two types of sector: the door and the staircase.

CREATING A DOOR

Although you can always use the editing features of WadAuthor to create a door manually, it is much simpler to convert an existing sector into a door. WadAuthor can convert a sector into a door in a single operation, provided the sector meets the following criteria:

- The sector has exactly four linedefs.
- One pair of opposite linedefs is one-sided.
- The remaining pair of opposite linedefs is two-sided, each sharing only the sector to be converted.

To perform the conversion, select the sector to be converted and choose the Convert Sector To Door option from the context menu. WadAuthor prompts the user for a motif to use during conversion. (Door motifs are covered in more detail later.) After you select a motif and click the OK button, WadAuthor converts the sector to a door.

CREATING A STAIRCASE

As with doors, manual creation of staircases is perfectly possible in WadAuthor, but it is tedious. It is much simpler to use WadAuthor's built-in option to convert an existing sector to a staircase for you. To do this, you first need a rectangular sector. To turn this into a staircase, select the sector and choose the Convert Sector To Stairs option from the context menu. You are prompted for a direction, number of steps, and a motif to use during conversion. (Stair motifs are covered in more detail later.)

After you select a motif and click the OK button, WadAuthor converts the sector to a staircase. The number of steps determines how many times the existing sector is divided; the motif determines what changes are applied for each step; and the direction determines from which end of the original sector to start.

NOTE: The configuration of the original sector linedefs determines the configuration of the linedefs created for the steps. For example, the linedefs created in the direction of travel face the same direction as the starting linedef, whereas the top and bottom linedefs created for the steps face the same direction as the originals.

CREATING THINGS

Creating Things is quite similar to creating sectors. You invoke the context menu at the location where the Thing is to appear and select the Create New Thing option, or click the appropriate view toolbar button. The location of the new Thing is snapped to grid if snap-to-grid is enabled.

To make populating the map more efficient, WadAuthor remembers new Thing settings. This same data is used across all WAD games because, with the exception of Hexen, many of the Thing settings are shared. When switching between Hexen and any of the other games, pay careful attention to the settings when creating a new Thing.

EDITING PROPERTIES

One of the most powerful editing features in WadAuthor is its capability to edit multiple properties of multiple map objects in a single operation. For example, if you use the rubber-band selection technique to select several Things, linedefs, and sectors, their properties can all be edited simultaneously using a property sheet (also known as a tabbed dialog box).

To edit the properties of the current selection, invoke the context menu and choose the Properties option. The resulting property sheet contains up to three property pages: one each for selected Things, linedefs, and sectors, as shown in Figure 27.9.

Figure 27.9.
WadAuthor's Map Object properties sheet.

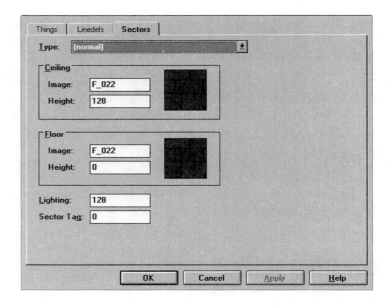

Properties in common across all objects of a given type are set initially to the common value; otherwise, the field is left blank. Attributes are a special case, displaying instead a three-state behavior consisting of On (marked with a crossed box), Off (marked with an open box), and Indeterminate (designated by means of a shaded box). Clicking the OK button sets only those properties for which a value is specified. If one or more objects change as a result of the editing, an Undo transaction is generated and the new data is stored. Each object type property page has a few special features worth mentioning.

THINGS

The Things property page features an image preview control that displays the sprite associated with the given Thing. An example is shown in Figure 27.10. As with most image preview controls, the user can click the left mouse button to invoke the Image Browse dialog box. This enables graphical selection of the Thing from the list of all available Things, as illustrated in Figure 27.11.

Figure 27.10.
WadAuthor's Things property page.

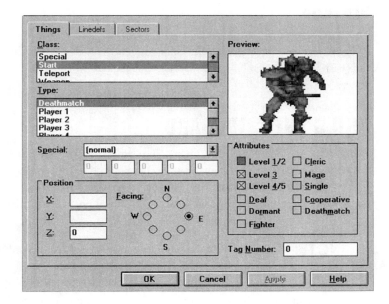

Figure 27.11.
Browsing Things in WadAuthor.

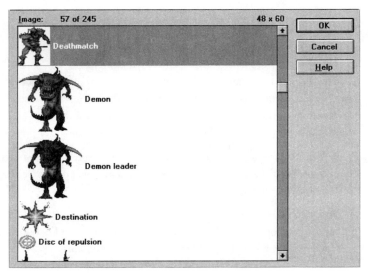

LINEDEFS

The Linedefs property page features image preview controls with associated image list controls for selecting the textures applied to each side. The user can click the left mouse button to invoke the Image Browse dialog box. This enables graphical selection of the desired image.

SECTORS

The Sectors property page features image preview controls for the floor and ceiling textures as well as relative change controls for the floor height, ceiling height, and light level. The user can click the image preview controls with the left mouse button to invoke the Image Browse dialog box. This enables graphical selection of the desired image.

USING THE CLIPBOARD

WadAuthor uses the standard Windows clipboard to provide data transfer from one map to another, and even from one game to another. Objects can be cut or copied to the clipboard, then pasted. When pasting from one WAD game to another, it might be necessary to convert the data for the destination game. In this case, not all the data is pasted, but the basic architectural details should be left intact.

NOTE: When two-sided linedefs are pasted from the clipboard, the second sector reference is set based on the surrounding sector. If there is a surrounding sector, the linedef remains two-sided; otherwise, it is set to one-sided to prevent the HOM effect within the game. If necessary, WadAuthor even flips linedefs to prevent problems when pasting into an unused portion of the map.

CHECKING THE MAP

WadAuthor tries to minimize the number of errors that occur during the creation and editing of a new map, but they usually manage to creep in anyway. In this context, an error does not mean a software error, but rather a problem with the map data itself. To check the current map, select the Check Map option from the Tools menu, click the appropriate button on the standard toolbar, or press Ctrl+K from the keyboard.

WadAuthor examines the map for a variety of common problems. If none are detected, a message box to that effect is displayed. Otherwise, the Check Map dialog box opens (see Figure 27.12). The Check Map dialog box can be a big help when things are not as they seem.

A list of potential problems is provided, along with a more detailed description of the selected problem. If the problem is one for which WadAuthor has a default fix, the Fix button can be used to apply it. Buttons are also provided to view a specific problem, fix as many problems as possible, and recheck the map.

Figure 27.12.

WadAuthor's Check Map dialog box.

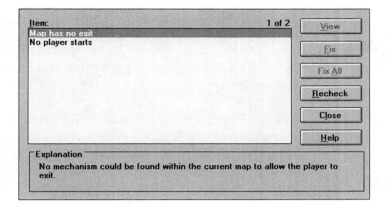

NOTE: The default fix that WadAuthor applies is not always the correct one. For example, if a given Thing is set so as not to appear at any level of play, WadAuthor fixes this by setting all the relevant attributes. This might not be what was desired.

RUNNING THE MAP

One of the features that makes WadAuthor an incredibly productive environment is its capability to actually play-test the current map without leaving the Windows environment. To run the current map, select the Run Map option from the Tools menu, click the appropriate button on the standard toolbar, or press Ctrl+R from the keyboard. WadAuthor launches a DOS session with the command-line arguments required to run the current map, first prompting you to save any changes made.

All the WAD games supported by WadAuthor are quite demanding of the system hardware. As a result, there are several important points of which you should be aware when using this feature:

- A minimum of 8MB of physical RAM seems to be required when running under Windows 3.*x* or Windows for Workgroups 3.*x*. A minimum of 12MB seems necessary under Windows 95, and 16MB under Windows NT.

- Sound support is disabled by default to avoid crashing. Most sound card drivers do not support access from a DOS session under Windows 3.*x*, Windows for Workgroups 3.*x*, or Windows NT.

- To avoid problems with differing startup directories, WadAuthor switches to the WAD-game directory before launching the DOS session. If the game directory name violates the MS-DOS 8.3 character convention, the game might not work properly.

NOTE: The process of running a map is actually pretty complicated, in order to provide the same function for all the different games under Windows 3.*x*, Windows for Workgroups 3.*x*, Win32s, Windows 95, and Windows NT. To simplify one aspect of the feature, WadAuthor stores the command executed when launching the map in the Run entry of the Wadgame section in the current WAD-game configuration file.

Most users of Windows 95 should find that they can enable the sound if they like, depending on their hardware. To find out, make a backup of the WAD-game configuration file and edit it manually using Notepad or some other text editor. Remove the -nosound parameter from the Run entry, then try running the current map. If it works, your hardware can probably support it; if it crashes or fails in some other way, your hardware probably cannot support it.

ADVANCED EDITING

It is now time to acquaint you with some of the most powerful aspects of WadAuthor. Understanding the features detailed in this section is not necessary for creating basic maps. At the same time, it is not possible to fully utilize WadAuthor without them.

RAW DATA EDITING

Many of the features in WadAuthor have been designed for the beginning WAD author (pun intended). WadAuthor tries to accomplish this without blocking power users from getting the job done. In fact, WadAuthor provides the ultimate level of detail for editing gurus: access to the raw map data itself.

Whenever the context menu is invoked on a single selected object, the Edit Raw Data option is available. Selecting this option invokes a dialog box that provides access to the actual data written to the WAD file during a Save operation.

WadAuthor works hard to prevent errors no matter what a user enters. Just because it works within WadAuthor, however, is no guarantee the map will still run. You should use this feature with caution, because it can quickly render a map unusable.

RENAMING THE MAP

WadAuthor uses the default new map name specified by the current WAD-game configuration file when creating a new map. If the name of a map needs to be changed, WadAuthor provides a feature for doing so. Click the right mouse button on an unused portion of the map to invoke the context menu, and choose the Map Name option.

WadAuthor displays the Map Name dialog box to enable the user to specify the new name. If the map name supplied does not exist in the main WAD file, WadAuthor provides an appropriate warning and enables the operation to be aborted. Otherwise, the new map name is assigned.

NOTE: Like any other WadAuthor editing operation, the map renaming can be undone. The new map name is not actually written to disk until the next Save operation.

USING MOTIFS

WadAuthor provides some powerful features for creating architecture within a map. Just as a good architect designs new structures around a single dominant theme, the best WAD files exhibit this same consistent unity of design. WadAuthor consolidates this aspect of WAD file development in motifs.

WadAuthor uses a different motif file for each WAD game, enabling the user to develop architectural themes appropriate to the look and feel of a given game. For example, one of the high-tech wall panels from the original DOOM would look a bit out of place in Hexen.

A motif file contains different kinds of motifs: sector motifs, door motifs, and stair motifs. The motifs present within the current motif file can be viewed and edited by selecting the Motifs option from the Tools menu.

NOTE: The current motif file "remembers" each of the last-used sector, door, and stair motifs between editing sessions. The appropriate one of these is used as the default whenever a motif is required. To change the default motif, switch to the appropriate property page, select the desired motif, and click the OK button.

Like the Property Editing dialog boxes, the Motif Property pages make use of image list controls and relative change controls where appropriate. This serves a dual purpose, making motif editing easier and providing much greater flexibility in motif application. As always, pressing F2 within an image list control invokes the Image Browse dialog box to enable graphical selection.

SECTOR MOTIFS

Sector motifs are actually used for several purposes. As mentioned earlier, they are used during sector creation. They can also be applied to a group of selected sectors, and they can be used by WadAuthor when correcting texture-related map errors. A sector motif defines the following data:

- Textures for the linedefs within the sector. The controls for editing these values are image list controls.
- Ceiling height, floor height, and lighting values. The controls for editing these are relative change controls.
- Ceiling and floor images for the sector. The controls for editing these values are image list controls.

The relative change controls for ceiling height, floor height, and lighting enable sector motifs to provide some advanced features. For example, by leaving the floor height blank and setting the ceiling height to +++256, the motif, when applied, forces the ceiling height of the sector to be 256 units above the floor. This makes it possible to create interesting motifs for commonly used sector features.

To apply a motif to a sector, select the sector and choose the Apply Sector Motif option from the context menu. Select the desired motif in the resulting dialog box and click the OK button to continue.

 TIP: When applying a sector motif, only the sides of the linedefs actually facing the sector are affected by the above (or upper), main, and below (or lower) textures. This prevents the application of a motif from changing the linedef as seen from an adjacent sector.

DOOR MOTIFS

Door motifs are used for one purpose only: creating doors. When converting an existing sector to a door, the user is prompted for a door motif to use during the conversion process. A door motif defines the following data:

- Door, base, and track images. The controls for editing these values are image list controls.
- The type of door being created.

The door, base, and track images refer to the images applied to the visible surface of the door, the bottom of the door (the door sector ceiling), and the image applied to the one-sided linedefs in the sector being converted, respectively. The door types available depend somewhat on the game for which the map is intended.

STAIR MOTIFS

Stair motifs, like door motifs, are used for one purpose only: creating stairs. When converting an existing sector to a staircase, you are prompted for a stair motif to use during the conversion process. A stair motif defines the following data:

- Ceiling, floor, and stairwell images. The controls for editing these values are image list controls.
- Ceiling height, floor height, and lighting increment values.

The ceiling, floor, and stairwell images refer to images applied to the step ceiling, the step face, and the sides of the stairwell, respectively. For example, when converting a subsector to a rising staircase, it is usually necessary to set the below textures for the side linedefs; WadAuthor uses the stairwell image for this purpose.

The ceiling height, floor height, and lighting increment values lie at the heart of the stair conversion routine. These changes are applied at each step in the staircase. For example, supplying a floor increment of 8 units while leaving the others blank creates a staircase rising 8 units with each step. The values can be positive or negative, allowing quite a bit of flexibility in staircase generation.

ALIGNING TEXTURES

Quite frequently, particularly when working with irregularly shaped sectors, it is necessary to adjust the image offsets for a given linedef to make the wall textures tile seamlessly. WadAuthor can adjust these values to exactly align textures across multiple linedefs.

To use this feature, select a group of connected linedefs, invoke the context menu, and select the Align Linedef Textures option. WadAuthor invokes the Texture Alignment dialog box to let you select which of the linedef's textures to use.

TIP: WadAuthor uses the first linedef in the list to determine the available textures and sizes. Keep this in mind when selecting the list.

WADAUTHOR OPTIONS

The WadAuthor Options dialog box, shown in Figure 27.13, is actually another property sheet containing several property pages used to configure various aspects of WadAuthor's behavior. To display the Options dialog box, select Options from the Tools menu. Each available property page of this dialog box is covered in some detail in the following sections.

Figure 27.13.
WadAuthor's Options dialog box, Files page.

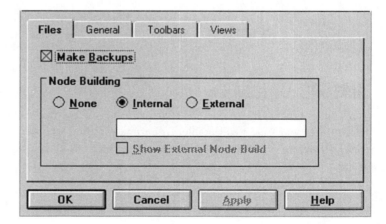

FILE OPTIONS

The Files page enables the user to configure some of the aspects of WAD file handling in WadAuthor. The Make Backups option determines whether WadAuthor retains the previous version of a WAD file at the completion of a Save operation.

The Node Building options require a bit more explanation. By default, WadAuthor uses its own internal node building code to generate the various precalculated data required by the WAD game at runtime. Power users, no doubt, will want to use their own favorite node building tool—to allow a finer degree of control over the final product, or if using certain special effects that need special treatment during node building.

To accommodate this requirement, WadAuthor enables node building to be disabled completely or handled by an external tool that can be specified in the supplied field. When you use an external node builder, WadAuthor launches the specified command and waits for its completion before continuing with the Save operation. Various replaceable parameters are available for use as command-line arguments. Consult the help file topic for more information about the available parameters and what they mean.

GENERAL OPTIONS

The General page of the Options dialog box contains options that really do not belong on any of the other pages. The Restore Main Window Position option determines whether WadAuthor will occupy the same screen position during different editing sessions. The Unlimited Undo option determines whether WadAuthor will enable Undo only for the last operation, or whether it should use memory as necessary to maintain a complete list of all editing operations.

 TIP: If memory is tight, you can save some by disabling the Unlimited Undo feature. Because this limits the Undo list to a single operation, however, this should be considered only as a last resort. It is probably a better idea to save more often, because a Save operation releases the memory associated with the Undo list back to the operating system. Frequent saving is a good habit to adopt anyway.

TOOLBAR OPTIONS

The Toolbars page is one of the few elements of the user interface that differs between the 16- and 32-bit versions of the WadAuthor executable. Unfortunately, the 16-bit version cannot support the multi-dockable toolbars that are such a nice addition to the 32-bit version. Rather than compromise the 32-bit version, WadAuthor supplies only the standard toolbar and status bar in the 16-bit version.

Thus, the options that appear on this page are different, depending on which version of the executable is running. In either case, you can enable or disable each of the toolbars by clicking the available options.

VIEW OPTIONS

The Views page of the Options dialog box is shown in Figure 27.14. This page enables you to set the default behavior for various view operations. Most of the options provided can be customized on a view-by-view basis as necessary. The options and their meaning are as follows:

- **Start Maximized:** Determines whether new view windows are initially maximized.

- **Show Thing Bitmaps:** Determines whether new views initially show Thing bitmaps.

- **Use Drag Cursor:** Determines whether the single- or multi-drag cursor is used in place of the normal cursor during a drag operation. At some zoom settings, the different cursors can make the wire frame display difficult to see.

- **Show Grid:** Determines whether new views initially show the grid.

- **Snap To Grid:** Determines whether new views initially snap to grid.

- **Default Grid:** Determines the initial grid setting for new views.

Figure 27.14.
The Views page of WadAuthor's Options dialog box.

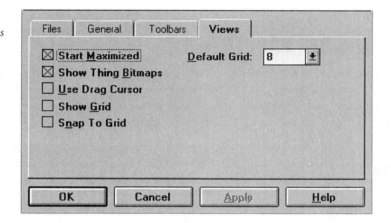

USER-DEFINED TOOLS

WadAuthor was never intended to be the ultimate WAD file editing tool. Many features have been deliberately omitted simply because other fine tools already exist. It is, however, designed to be a tool that works well with others.

The user-defined tools feature provides a mechanism for linking with external tools. You can define up to nine external tools that can be invoked with the press of a single button or selection of a menu item. To view and edit the list of available tools, select the Customize option from the Tools menu.

The list of available tools is displayed in the order in which they appear on the Tools menu. To change or remove one of the existing tools, select the desired tool and change the data or click the Remove button. To add a new tool, click the Add button and fill in the fields with the appropriate data. Replaceable parameters can be used for command-line arguments. Consult the help file topic for more information about the available parameters and what they mean.

HEXEN-SPECIFIC CHANGES

DOOM, DOOM II, and Heretic were constructed around the same basic game engine, with each new variant requiring only minor modifications. With the introduction of Hexen, this trend seems to have ended. Hexen introduces some tremendous new features for the aspiring WAD file designer, greatly increasing the flexibility of the game engine.

WadAuthor provides full support for Hexen in the same familiar Windows environment, just as for the other games. At the same time, however, the changes in Hexen are significant enough to require modification of the affected portions of the user interface. The following sections describe some of the specific differences when working with Hexen.

LINEDEF PROPERTIES

WadAuthor supports all the new specials in the familiar class/type breakdown used for the other WAD games. The main difference is that specials can take up to five arguments to provide greater control over the desired action. These arguments can be entered in the fields immediately beneath the special type list. Only the fields for arguments relevant to a given special are enabled for editing.

All the new linedef attributes are supported through additional attribute controls. As always, if the box is checked, the given attribute is applied. Veteran WAD file developers should take special note of the new Repeatable attribute, because this aspect of linedef behavior used to be tied to the specific action to be taken.

In the other WAD games, the method by which a linedef is triggered was also tied to the specific action to be taken. Hexen changes this as well, de-coupling the activation from the action. WadAuthor supports this new feature through the addition of the Activate control, enabling the user to specify the condition under which the special is triggered.

THING PROPERTIES

Hexen (and therefore WadAuthor) supports assignment of specials to Things as well as linedefs. In addition, some Thing attributes are used a little differently from other game variants.

THING SPECIALS

As with linedefs, a Thing's special arguments can be specified in the fields immediately beneath its special type control. Only the fields for arguments relevant to a given special are enabled.

Some of the Thing types in Hexen have pre-assigned interpretations for the special arguments. For example, Things that spawn other Things typically require the numeric identifier of the Thing to be spawned. For these Things, special assignment is not allowed, but the appropriate arguments for the pre-assigned behavior are available for editing.

POLYOBJECT ANCHOR FACINGS

To use polyobjects correctly, the Anchor Spot must be associated with the Start Spot. This association is made using the Thing property normally interpreted as the angle at which it initially faces. An additional field is available when working with Hexen to manually specify the number used for the Thing angle. Clicking the angle buttons updates the field with the value corresponding to the selected direction.

ADDITIONAL THING ATTRIBUTES

All the new Thing attributes are supported through additional attribute controls. As always, if the box is checked, the given attribute is applied.

In Hexen, Things can have an initial altitude above the floor of the sector in which they are located. WadAuthor enables editing of this property through the addition of a Z Coordinate field.

Finally, Hexen adds the concept of Thing identifiers (tids). WadAuthor treats these as just another tag, which enables the familiar tag tool to be used with Hexen Things, just as with sectors and linedefs. The Thing identifier can also be changed via the new Tag Number field in the Thing Property dialog box.

CREATING A DOOR IN HEXEN

Doors are also handled somewhat differently in Hexen. Unlike the other game variants, no distinction of class is made for local doors and remote doors. Each of the door specials simply requires a tag number to identify the door sector. Specifying a tag number of 0, however, causes the door special to operate on the sector owning the linedef. When converting a sector to a door, WadAuthor takes advantage of this to avoid using a tag number. To make the door special affect a different sector, use the Tags dialog box to perform any necessary tag assignment.

HEXEN SCRIPTS

The Scripts dialog box represents the most powerful addition to WAD file editing yet. The Hexen game variant can execute compiled action code scripts (ACS for short). The scripting capabilities present in Hexen enable truly unprecedented flexibility in WAD file creation.

To invoke the Scripts dialog box, click the right mouse button in an unused portion of the map to invoke the context menu, and choose the Scripts option. (This is available only when working with a Hexen WAD-game configuration file.) WadAuthor displays the Scripts dialog box for the current map. This dialog box supplies a simple integrated development environment similar in purpose, if not in features, to those used by professional programmers.

It is important to understand where the script code is stored within the WAD file, because no standard currently exists. WadAuthor adheres to a standard originally proposed by the author of another popular editing tool. For each map, WadAuthor stores the script code in a SCRIPTS lump immediately following the BEHAVIOR lump.

If the current WAD file was not created by WadAuthor, it is quite possible that no SCRIPTS lump exists; this is, after all, only one of many proposed standards. If WadAuthor cannot locate a SCRIPTS lump, the existing BEHAVIOR lump is decompiled into script code. WadAuthor cannot re-create the original comments or variable names, but the logical structure of the code is preserved. This feature can be of great assistance in learning how to write good script code.

If the current map does not have any compiled script code in its BEHAVIOR lump, WadAuthor loads the script code present in the DEFAULT.ACS file distributed with WadAuthor. This code contains a sample script for the breaking glass effect used throughout Hexen. For more information on using it, consult the associated help file topics.

The Scripts dialog box enables the user to export the existing script code to a disk file, import script code from a disk file, choose a custom font for displaying the code, edit the existing code, and compile the code. Any errors that occur during the compilation are displayed in the results window, with the associated line (if any) highlighted within the script code control. These features make the Scripts dialog box a powerful tool for developing Hexen script code.

TAGS IN HEXEN

Hexen's new Thing identifier permits the identification of a Thing or group of Things for scripting purposes (or as an argument to a special). As I already stated, rather than provide a separate interface for working with the identifiers, WadAuthor uses the familiar Tags dialog box for setting and removing Thing identifiers.

The Tags dialog box, therefore, when working with Hexen, includes Thing objects in the list of map objects possessing a given tag. These can be added to or removed from the list of tagged objects by simply clicking the representation of the Thing in the map editing view. Selecting from within the list of objects performs the same highlighting as with other map objects, enabling the user to quickly see which objects possess a given tag number.

THE WADAUTHOR VALUE PACK

The WadAuthor Value Pack (WAVP for short) is made available to all registered users of WadAuthor. It provides some handy DOS utilities for manipulating WAD files, as well as a Windows-based image viewing utility. The WAVP also provides a glimpse into the origin of WadAuthor; the code developed for the WAVP utilities was later used as the foundation for WadAuthor. This section acquaints you with the tools available in the WAVP and provides some practical examples of how they might be useful in actual editing situations.

 TIP: All the DOS-based utilities take command-line parameters. For a listing of the valid parameters, along with some examples of their use, run the utility without any parameters.

WADDIR: WAD FILE DIRECTORY LISTING

The WAD file directory utility, WADDIR.EXE, probably represents the common starting point for all editor authors. It dumps a textual listing of the directory entries into a WAD file, providing resource numbers, names, sizes, and file offsets. This data can be useful when using the other utilities.

WADDUMP: WAD FILE DUMPING

The WAD file dumping utility, WADDUMP.EXE, provides a textual description for many of the map-related resources within a WAD file. It dumps a textual listing for the vertices, Things, linedefs, sidedefs, sectors, and other resources that define a map. This utility was very useful in determining how the map objects were related after the file structures had been determined.

WADEXT: WAD FILE RESOURCE EXTRACTION

The WAD file resource extraction utility, WADEXT.EXE, enables you to save the raw data within a WAD file resource to an external file, optionally removing the resource from within the WAD file. This utility was very helpful in developing a disassembler for the Hexen behavior resource.

A good practical use for this utility would be to remove the script code from a WAD file prior to distributing it. For example, if you use WadAuthor to develop a WAD file named AWESOME.WAD that contains some very fancy scripts, you might not want to pass on the original script code. Executing the following command would remove the SCRIPTS resource from the final WAD file:

```
WADEXT.EXE AWESOME.WAD SCRIPTS AWESOME.ACS DELETE
```

This command removes the resource named SCRIPTS from the AWESOME.WAD WAD file, saving its data in an external file named AWESOME.ACS. The utility does not remove a resource from a WAD file without first saving it to an external file.

WADINJ: WAD FILE RESOURCE INJECTION

The WAD file resource injection utility, WADINJ.EXE, is the natural counterpart to the extraction utility. It enables you to append, insert, or replace resources within a WAD file with data from an external file.

Continuing with the previous example, assume that the user finds it inconvenient to keep removing the SCRIPTS resource prior to distributing AWESOME.WAD. Or perhaps the user simply prefers an external text editor to using WadAuthor. In any event, the script code could be externally compiled, creating an AWESOME.O file from the AWESOME.ACS file. The following command could then be used to replace the existing BEHAVIOR resource with the newly compiled data:

```
WADINJ.EXE AWESOME.WAD REPLACE BEHAVIOR AWESOME.O
```

CAUTION: This utility should be used with caution. If used incorrectly, it could quickly damage a WAD file beyond recovery. Always make backups before replacing existing WAD file resources.

WADMERGE: WAD FILE MERGING

The WAD file merging utility, WADMERGE.EXE, enables the combination of multiple WAD files into a single output WAD file. This utility can be very helpful for creating a final distribution WAD file from separate WAD files used during development.

For example, if WadAuthor has been used to develop three separate maps for the original DOOM—E2M1, E2M2, and E2M3—it is normal to provide the end user with a single WAD file, rather than supplying three. Assuming the three maps are currently stored in E2M1.WAD, E2M2.WAD, and E2M3.WAD, executing the following command combines the three WAD files into a single output WAD file named AWESOME.WAD:

```
WADMERGE.EXE AWESOME.WAD E2M1.WAD E2M2.WAD E2M3.WAD
```

WAD file developers might want to use this utility early in the development process to combine multiple WAD files. It can make playing, editing, and maintaining the individual maps much easier via the support for multiple map WAD files built into WadAuthor.

WADZADJ: WAD FILE SECTOR HEIGHT REPORTING AND ADJUSTMENT

The WAD file sector height reporting and adjustment utility, WADZADJ.EXE, enables you to query the vertical extents of all sectors in a given map, optionally applying an offset. This utility has been very helpful in working around a bug in the original DOOM engine.

The bug, as veteran WAD file developers will no doubt attest, causes the game engine to behave in an undesirable fashion when selecting the nearest floor or ceiling from a sector whose floor or ceiling is at a negative altitude. In short, old versions of the engine scan only in the positive direction to find the nearest floor or ceiling. This utility enables the application of an offset to all sectors, thus solving the problem. For example, if AWESOME.WAD contains a problem sector whose floor is at –64, the following command adds an offset of 64 units to all sectors:

```
WADZADJ.EXE AWESOME.WAD /O:64
```

Of course, you could always use WadAuthor to select all the sectors within the map, then apply the 64 unit offset from the Sector Properties dialog box. When the need first arose to fix this kind of problem, WadAuthor did not exist.

WIMGVIEW: WAD FILE IMAGE VIEWING

The WAD file image viewing utility, WIMGVIEW.EXE, permits the viewing of all the images within a game's main IWAD file. This utility started as a research project to discover how to display the image data within a WAD file. Since then it has been enhanced to enable saving of the images in the standard Windows bitmap file format. The utility is a Windows application that requires no command-line arguments. Its use should be fairly obvious.

EXIT: MOPPING UP AND MOVING ON

This chapter presented the main capabilities of WadAuthor. WadAuthor is not perfect, but it can be a very powerful tool when understood properly. If you want to find out more about it and its capabilities, extra information is provided in its online help. The best way to discover its true potential is to unleash it, though. Experiment with it, try out some different ideas, and above all else, have fun!

WADED

This chapter examines the map editor WADED, by Matthew Ayres. This is an intuitive and easy-to-use DOS-based map editor for DOOM, DOOM II, and Heretic. It features heavily in the series of WAD sorties presented in Episode 2, Mission 1, "A Hell of Your Very Own," earlier in this book. This chapter provides a full reference to the WADED program for those readers who prefer to explore the editor on their own. You can find details of how to install WADED on your computer in Chapter 4, "Using the CD-ROM."

OVERVIEW

As one of the easiest editors to use, WADED includes many features that make level-editing and level-building a snap. Let's take a quick tour of its general features.

CONFIGURING WADED

The first time you use WADED, it brings up a setup screen for you to supply the locations of your DOOM, DOOM II, or Heretic game files (see Figure 28.1). To work, you must supply WADED with the locations of the main IWAD files of each game variant you want to use.

Once in the setup screen, you can have WADED search your hard drive for main game files by hitting F9, the quick-search key. If WADED is unable to find a registered copy of DOOM, DOOM II, or Heretic, it leaves all three fields blank. If that happens, you have to type in the paths manually. Once you have supplied WADED with the location of your games, hit the F10 key to save this information, and start up WADED.

— By Matthew Ayres and Kirk Yokomizo with contributions from Steve Benner

Figure 28.1.
The WADED setup screen.

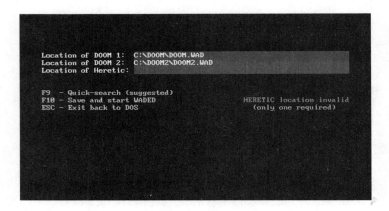

```
Location of DOOM 1:  C:\DOOM\DOOM.WAD
Location of DOOM 2:  C:\DOOM2\DOOM2.WAD
Location of Heretic:


F9  - Quick-search (suggested)
F10 - Save and start WADED                    HERETIC location invalid
ESC - Exit back to DOS                          (only one required)
```

NOTE: You need to give WADED the location of only one of your games. Before starting, WADED checks that you are using registered copies of the specified games. WADED does not let you proceed unless you have at least one of the games that it can work with.

If at any later time you need to tell WADED a different location of your game, you can load the setup program from the command line by typing `waded -c`.

TIP: The locations of all your games are stored in the WADED.CFG file. Rather than start WADED with the `-c` command-line switch, you can merely edit this file if you prefer. WADED still checks that the specified files are part of the registered release of the game.

If you have configured WADED to use more than one variant of the game, you can start WADED up directly from the command line to work that particular game. This is achieved with the command-line switches in Table 28.1.

Table 28.1. WADED's command-line switches for controlling the game to work with.

Game	Switch	Example
DOOM	(none)	`waded mywad.wad`
DOOM II	-2	`waded -2 mywad2.wad`
Heretic	-3 (or -h)	`waded -3 mywadh.wad`
		`waded -h mywadh.wad`

Note: WADED does not work with Hexen.

SWITCHING GAMES

WADED can work with only one game at a time. You can either bring up the desired game from the command line (as described previously) or you can switch to another game after WADED has been loaded into memory. Switch to other games by clicking the game button directly below the arrow buttons, as shown in Figure 28.2. The name on this button is the current game you are working with. When you click it, WADED brings up the list of games that are available.

Figure 28.2.
Switching to other games.

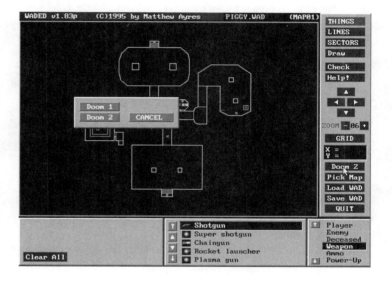

Switching games erases all that is currently on the screen. WADED asks you to confirm that this is really what you want to do before proceeding. If you want to switch to work on an external PWAD for a different game variant, you need to load the new variant's IWAD file before loading your new external file.

OTHER FILE OPERATIONS

To load external WAD files, click the Load WAD button, or press the **L** key on the keyboard. WADED brings up a list of all the files in the current directory with the extension .WAD. Simply click the required WAD name, or press the **L** key again to type in the complete path and name of the WAD file.

Whenever you load a WAD that has multiple levels in it, WADED brings up a menu of all the available maps contained in the WAD. Select the level you would like to see first by clicking the appropriate map name. If you subsequently want to work with another map from the same WAD, click the Pick Map button to bring up the list of levels again.

CAUTION: Clicking the Load WAD or Pick Map buttons clears the currently displayed map. Make sure that you have saved it before using these buttons if you want to keep any changes you have made.

To save a map that you have been working on, click the Save WAD button or press the **S** key. WADED brings up the Save window, shown in Figure 28.3. This is where you tell WADED what you want to call your map file and what level to save it as: for example, E1M1 (Episode 1, Mission 1). When saving a WAD, you can have WADED build the nodes before saving or you can choose not to. If you are not sure which way to go, leave WADED to work this out for itself—it usually knows when a rebuild is necessary.

Figure 28.3.
WADED's PWAD Save window.

CAUTION: WADED can save only one level to a PWAD file. If you have loaded a map from a multilevel file, take care to supply a new name when you save the file; otherwise, the other maps are overwritten.

TIP: If you are working on a multilevel WAD, it is recommended that you keep each level in a separate file until you are ready to distribute the finished WAD. You can then use the utility WADCAT (described later in the chapter) to glue your various WADs together into one big WAD.

The file is saved in the current directory unless you change the path field. Click in it or press the **P** key to gain access. If you are saving over an existing file, WADED warns you and asks you to confirm that you want to proceed. If you do save over an existing WAD file, WADED renames the old file with a .BAK extension. (Any existing .BAK file with the same name is deleted.)

TIP: You will find WADED more convenient to use if you save your WADs in the WADED directory.

To exit WADED, click the Quit button. You can also exit with the **Q** and Esc keys. Before exiting, WADED asks you if you are sure you want to exit. Click Yes to exit or Cancel to return to WADED.

MAP MOVEMENT

When you are editing a level in WADED, it is helpful to be able to move around in the map you are working on. You can move in the four basic directions: up, down, left, and right.

If you prefer using the keyboard to the mouse, you can use the arrow keys on your keyboard. Press any of the keys to scroll the map in that direction just a little bit. Hold down a direction key to scroll around quickly.

If you like to stick with mouse operation, you can use the movement buttons located on the right-hand side bar (see Figure 28.4). Simply click the appropriate direction-arrow button. Click and hold to move around quickly.

Figure 28.4.
WADED's right-hand side bar.

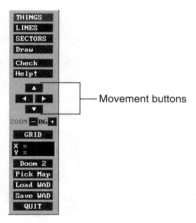

To make WADED center your map on the screen, just press the Home key.

If you want to get in closer to your map for more precise editing, use the plus key (+) to zoom in to the map. The minus key (–) zooms back out. Alternatively, you can use the ZOOM buttons located on the right-hand side bar, immediately under the movement buttons. Between the ZOOM buttons is an indicator showing the current ZOOM factor. WADED enables 15 different levels of zoom.

THE GRID

WADED's GRID button enables you to turn on or off the display of the game's 64×64 pixel grid that determines how flats align. WADED shows this grid in blue. It can be useful when arranging sectors that have particular floor or ceiling textures in use and you want to make sure that your walls don't cut them oddly. It can also be used to quickly check the size of a sector. Much of the time, you might prefer to work with it switched off to make the screen less cluttered.

WADED'S MODES

To work with the elements of a WAD in WADED, you need to select the correct working mode. WADED has four working modes, each accessible from the appropriate button in the right-hand side bar:

- Things mode
- Lines mode
- Sectors mode
- Draw mode

The rest of this chapter concentrates on each of these modes in turn.

THINGS MODE

To work with DOOM's Things, you must first switch WADED into Things mode. Do this by clicking the THINGS button in the right-hand side bar. In this mode, all the Things that a map contains are shown by symbols at the correct locations.

Many Things in WADED use a small depiction of the corresponding item within the game. Some do not, and these are shown simply as circles or squares shaded in particular ways. Weapons and ammunition are shown as shaded red circles if they don't have a depiction. Each different type of enemy has a different color in WADED. Some have a white box around them, because there are more types of enemies than colors to choose from. At higher zoom levels, all enemies have an arrow in them that points in the direction they face at the start.

> **NOTE:** The particular symbol that WADED uses to depict a Thing is determined by the contents of the WADED.T file located in the WADED directory. You can change the way Things are categorized, as well as the names WADED uses for them. If you edit this file, though, be sure you have a backup of it in case of accidents.

INSERTING A THING

Before you insert a Thing, you need to choose the type of Thing you would like to insert. Do this by first selecting the category of Thing in the category selection window, located at the bottom right of the screen. Once you have selected the category of your choice, the Thing selection window, located to the left of the category selection window (see Figure 28.5), enables you to pick the actual Thing to be inserted.

Figure 28.5.

WADED's various Things mode windows.

Having selected the type of Thing, move the cursor onto the map area and click the right mouse button wherever you would like the Thing to appear during play.

> **CAUTION:** Be sure not to click an existing Thing because this deletes it.

A green highlight box is shown around the Thing to show that it is the currently selected Thing. The newly inserted Thing's attributes are displayed in the bottom-left information window, shown in Figure 28.5.

CHANGING A THING'S ATTRIBUTES

WADED's Things information window might need a little explanation.

At the top left of this window is a copy of the currently highlighted Thing's symbol. Just to the right of this is its name; farther right is the type number for that Thing. (This is the actual number that DOOM uses to keep track of Things; you need not worry too much about it.) Below all this are the X and Y coordinates of the Thing on the map. You can change a Thing's X and Y coordinates only by moving it around on the map.

In the middle of the Things information window are eight small buttons arranged around an arrow showing the current orientation of the Thing you have highlighted. Click any of the eight buttons to change the direction that the arrow points. The direction you select here tells DOOM which way to face the item at the start of a game.

The right half of the Things information window is taken up by five more small buttons. These are all toggles that can be turned either on or off. Buttons that are toggled on are marked with a small white square within them. The first three toggles are marked 1+2, 3, and 4+5. The settings of these buttons determine the difficulty levels at which the selected Things appear in the game. The last two buttons in the Things information window are marked DM and Deaf. The setting of the DM button determines whether the selected Thing appears only in multiplayer games, whereas the Deaf button enables you to set whether a Thing is deaf.

SELECTING THINGS

To select a Thing already on your map, simply click its symbol. A green highlight box appears around the Thing. Once a Thing is selected, its type and attributes are shown in the Thing information window, as just described.

MOVING THINGS

To move a Thing, click and hold down the left mouse button while the cursor is over the Thing. As long as you continue to hold down the mouse button, moving the mouse drags the Thing around the map. Release the mouse button to drop the Thing at its new location.

REMOVING SINGLE THINGS

Deleting Things is simple. You can delete Things by either clicking the right mouse button on a Thing or by selecting a Thing with the left mouse button and then pressing the Delete key.

CLEARING ALL THINGS

Within the Things information window is a button marked Clear All. Click this and it does exactly what it says! It clears all Things from your map. A confirmation window pops up first, just in case you accidentally hit this button and didn't mean to (see Figure 28.6).

Figure 28.6.

The Clear All Things confirmation window.

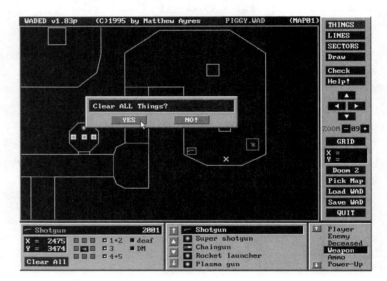

LINES MODE

Click the LINES button to enter WADED's Lines mode. In this mode, WADED hides all the Thing symbols, showing only its lines. Use Lines mode to select lines and modify their attributes. WADED lets you assign textures to walls, set special actions, and tag special lines to sectors.

NOTE: WADED uses the term *line* to mean the combined linedef and sidedef(s) structure contained within the WAD file. With WADED, you never need to know that, though!

LINE COLOR CODES

Lines in WADED are colored differently depending on some important factors. Single-sided lines are bright white. Two-sided lines appear gray. Lines representing locally active doors are bright cyan. The currently selected line is red, and any of its tagged sectors are green.

SELECTING A LINE

To select a line, simply place the mouse cursor over it and click. The selected line shows red. When selected, a line is shown with a small tick-mark on one of its sides. This marks the line's right (or front) side; the side without the tick is its left (or back). (To select more than one line at a time, you need to use WADED's Multi mode, which is explained later.)

LINE ATTRIBUTES

When a line is selected in Lines mode, information about the line appears in another information window at the bottom of the screen. This window is shown in Figure 28.7.

Figure 28.7.
WADED's line information window.

Using the controls and information fields within WADED's line information window, you can change all the attributes of the selected line. You can do the following:

- Change the line's flag settings
- Apply a special attribute to the line
- Apply textures to either side of the line
- Remove textures from any part of the line
- Apply texture offsets to either side of the line
- Work with more than one line at a time

NOTE: The length, angle, and identifying number of a line displayed in the line information window can be changed only by moving the line in WADED's Draw mode, which is described later.

CHANGING A LINE'S FLAGS

A large proportion of the line information window is taken up by attribute buttons like those in the Thing information window. These are the line's flag settings. You can set or clear any of these flags independently of each other just by clicking them to toggle their current setting. When the button shows white, the appropriate flag is set; otherwise, the flag is clear.

CAUTION: Take care when changing a line's flags. In particular, note that changing a line's two-sided flag in WADED not only changes the state of the flag, but also adds or removes the line's left sidedef. Used incorrectly, this action can render the map incapable of being played.

SETTING A LINE'S SPECIAL ATTRIBUTE

To set a line's special attribute (to activate doors, lifts, and so on), you can adjust the Special value (which appears at the far left side of the line information window) using the adjacent + and – buttons. If you don't know the code number for the action you require (and who does?), click the LIST button just beneath the Special value. WADED brings up a list of all the specials available for you to choose from. The specials are divided into categories by function—doors, floors, lifts, lights, ceilings, stairs, and miscellaneous—as shown in Figure 28.8. Switch between these categories using the buttons beneath the list.

Figure 28.8.

One of WADED's Special Line lists.

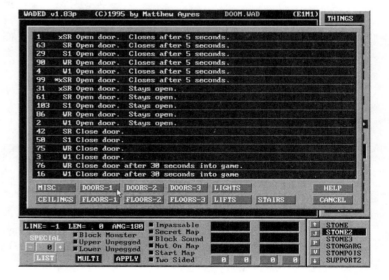

In front of every special on the list is a set of numbers and letters. The numbers indicate the Special value required to achieve the described action. The letters indicate how the line is activated and whether it can be activated more than once. These codes match those used in Chapter 36, "Special Line Types."

To select a special action for a line, simply click in the appropriate line of the list. The chosen value is copied into the appropriate field of the line information window.

NOTE: If you set a line's Special attribute, you might need to tag the line to one or more sectors. The way to do this is explained shortly.

ASSIGNING TEXTURES TO LINES

The right side of the line information window is taken up with six boxes (refer to Figure 28.7). These are the line's texture boxes. They are divided into two groups: the left and the right. The right-hand group represents the three texture slots of the line's right side; the group on the left represents those on the line's left side (if it has one). The texture boxes are arranged as are the textures on the line: the top boxes are for the line's upper textures; the central boxes are for the line's main textures; and the bottom boxes are for the line's lower textures.

If any of the six boxes are highlighted red, this means they are essential textures, and an error occurs in the game if they are left clear.

CAUTION: The main right texture of a single-sided line should always have a texture defined, no matter what. WADED assumes that you know this, however, and does not give you additional warning.

To assign textures to a texture slot, you have to select a texture from the texture list, which appears at the far right of the line information window. (Again, refer to Figure 28.7.) Once you have the texture selected, you can click in any of the six texture boxes to transfer the selected texture name to it.

TIP: There are a few shortcuts you can use when looking for a texture in the texture list window. These are described shortly.

CLEARING TEXTURES

You can clear any of the texture slots by clicking with the right mouse button. The texture name is replaced by a – symbol, indicating that the texture is transparent.

APPLYING TEXTURE OFFSETS

The four blue buttons that appear beneath the texture fields of the line information window (refer to Figure 28.7) indicate the X- and Y-offsets in force on each side of the line. These values can be changed by means of the Change Linedef Texture Offsets window, shown in Figure 28.9. This window can be summoned by clicking any of the offset buttons of the line information window. Use the appropriate + and – buttons of the Change Linedef Texture Offsets window to increase or decrease any of the line's X- or Y-offsets in steps of four units.

Figure 28.9.
WADED's Change Linedef Texture Offsets window.

CHANGING MULTIPLE LINES

WADED features a simple way to manipulate attributes of multiple lines. To start, click the MULTI button. All attributes shown in the line information window are reset. (Your lines remain unchanged, however.) The attribute toggles contain small green marks, and the texture boxes contain Xs.

Use the mouse to select all the lines you would like to change. Each line you select is highlighted red in the usual way. Click a line again to deselect it.

Now you can tell WADED which changes you want to make on all the selected lines. Change the attributes in the line information window as for single lines. Touch only the attributes that you want changed on all the selected lines. Any attributes you leave untouched (green mark for attribute toggles, Xs in value boxes) will remain as they are when you apply the changes.

Once you are satisfied with your selections, click the APPLY button to make the changes take effect (see Figure 28.10). If you don't want to make the changes, click the MULTI button to cancel the whole operation.

NOTE: You can change all line attributes in MULTI mode except the X and Y texture offsets. These can be changed only in single line mode.

Figure 28.10.

Applying COMPBLUE to a whole room.

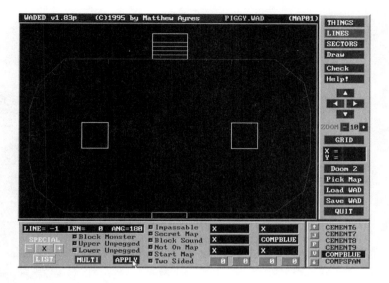

BROWSING TEXTURES

As well as enabling you to select a texture to apply to your lines, the textures list at the bottom right of the screen in Lines mode lets you view any of the wall textures available in the particular game variant you are working with. To do this, select the texture with the left mouse button, then click the V button, or simply click the texture name using the right mouse button. WADED clears the screen and shows a preview of the selected texture. Within this preview, you can scroll through the textures using the right and left arrow keys or leave the preview screen by pressing Esc (or **Q**).

In addition to the scroll arrows, some useful buttons in the texture list box help you move around the list quickly. The J button lets you jump to a certain part of the list (see Figure 28.11). When you click this button, WADED prompts you for the first letter of the texture you want to scroll the list to. If you type **C**, for instance, WADED jumps to the first texture that starts with the letter C—CEMENT1 in DOOM II.

If you click the P button, WADED brings up a large texture list, where you can pick (or preview) the texture you want to use. (See Figure 28.12.)

TURNING LINES AROUND

If you want to change a line's direction, this is easily achieved in Lines mode: Select the line on the map and press the **F** key. WADED flips the line over, taking all side information with it. It maintains correct sector referencing, so you don't need to worry about that.

Figure 28.11.

Using the J button.

Figure 28.12.

The main textures list.

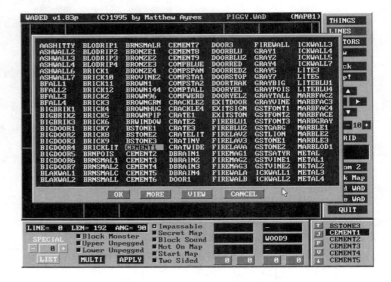

NOTE: Maps that have had lines flipped need to have their nodes rebuilt before they can play. Unfortunately, WADED doesn't know this and might offer the wrong default when you next save the map.

TAGGING LINES TO SECTORS

If a line has a non-zero special attribute, you might need to tag the line to one or more sectors. To do this, simply use the right mouse button to select a target sector for the currently highlighted line. You can click in additional sectors to tag more than one to the line if you like. Tagged sectors show in green on the map whenever the trigger line is selected. Click the right mouse button on a green sector, and WADED removes the tag between the line and that sector.

SECTORS MODE

WADED's Sectors mode, chosen with the SECTORS button in the right-hand side bar, is used to assign or change attributes of the sectors in your map. When you are in Sectors mode, you can change ceiling and floor heights, assign special characteristics, and change the textures of the ceilings and floors.

SELECTING A SECTOR

To edit a sector's attributes, you must first select it. To do this, click anywhere within the sector. When selected, a sector is outlined with flashing red lines. If the sector you have selected has any special lines tagged to it, those lines appear green on the map. The attributes of the selected sector are displayed in the sector information window at the bottom of the screen, as shown in Figure 28.13.

Figure 28.13.
WADED's sector information window.

Using the controls and information fields within the sector information window, you can change all the attributes of the selected sector. You can do the following:

- Change the lighting level
- Apply a special characteristic to the sector
- Change the floor and ceiling heights
- Change the floor and ceiling textures
- Work with more than one sector at a time
- Automatically configure the sector to be a door
- Select another sector

EDITING NUMERICAL ATTRIBUTES

To change any of the sector's numerical attributes, either use the + and – buttons next to the appropriate box (these change the values in steps of eight in most cases) or simply click the box containing the value and type in a new one, pressing Enter when you have finished.

ASSIGNING SPECIAL CHARACTERISTICS

Changing or adding sector specials can be done in the same way as changing any other numerical value. Alternatively, you can summon up a list of the effects by clicking the LIST button—just as with lines' special values—and choosing from this.

ASSIGNING FLOOR AND CEILING TEXTURES

Textures are assigned to the ceiling and floor of a sector in a similar fashion to the way they are placed on lines. First select the texture you want to use from the textures list. (This list works in exactly the same way as the line textures list box discussed earlier.) You can now click the left mouse button in the ceiling texture box or the floor texture box. If you want to use the sky texture, F_SKY1, you can simply click the right mouse button in the floor or ceiling texture box, rather than hunt for this texture in the list.

CHANGING MULTIPLE SECTORS

Editing multiple sectors is similar to editing multiple lines. Simply click the MULTI button to enter Multi mode. Texture settings are Xed out and numerical fields are marked with **. As previously, these indicate fields that will not be touched when changes are applied. Now select all the sectors that you want to be affected just by clicking in each in turn. Selected sectors are highlighted in flashing red. After the sectors are selected, you can edit the attributes you want to change. When all changes have been marked, click the APPLY button, and the changes are implemented. To cancel changes before they are applied, click the MULTI button again.

MAKE DOOR

To make a door out of any four-sided sector, select the Make Door button in the sector information window. Then click anywhere in the sector that you want to make into a door. WADED does its best to turn the designated sector into a door.

 CAUTION: Do not use this function if you are working with Heretic. WADED puts DOOM textures on your lines: this crashes the game when you try to play the map.

DRAW MODE

WADED's Draw mode is used for editing existing maps by changing vertices, lines, and sectors. Draw mode is also used for creating levels from scratch. While in Draw mode, you can add, move, and delete vertices, lines, and sectors. Draw mode also contains utilities to create sectors in your map from existing lines and vertices. To enter Draw mode, click the Draw button in the right-hand side bar.

WIPING THE SLATE CLEAN

To start a new map, click the Scratch button. This clears all Things, lines, sectors, and vertices from the map, ready to start fresh. You are asked to confirm that this is what you want to do.

CREATING NEW MAP ELEMENTS

There are two ways to draw new parts to your map. These are the (single) Line and (multiple) Lines drawing submodes, accessed by using the appropriate buttons in the Draw column of the draw button bar at the bottom of the screen, shown in Figure 28.14. (The Room button in the same column is not used in the current version of WADED.)

Figure 28.14.
Drawing in WADED's Draw mode.

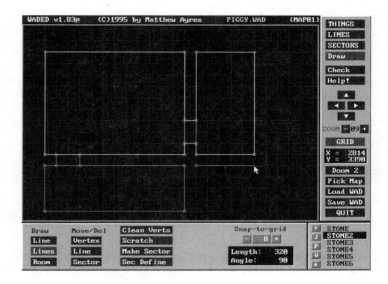

DRAWING SINGLE LINES

WADED's Line facility is used to draw a single line from one point to another on the map. This drawing mode is mainly used to add a line to connect two existing vertices or lines, or to carry out minor modifications to the map. It works in the same way as drawing multiple lines (described next), but drawing ceases when you finish the line.

DRAWING MULTIPLE LINES

WADED's Lines facility is used to draw whole sequences of lines on a map, usually to mark out an entire future sector. When you are in the Lines drawing mode, click (and release) the left mouse button at the point where you want to start a line. Move the mouse pointer to a new location (see Figure 28.14) and click where you want to end the line. When you next move the mouse, WADED automatically starts drawing a new line. You can continue to move the mouse to new locations, clicking to terminate each line and start a new one. To complete any drawing in Lines mode, move the mouse until it is over an existing line or vertex. (The line turns red as you approach.) Once over an existing line, the next click of the mouse terminates the drawing, connecting the current line to the existing line (or vertex). This drawing technique helps to ensure that you draw only closed shapes, in compliance with DOOM's sector defining rules.

MOVING AND DELETING MAP ELEMENTS

WADED's Draw mode also enables you to move and delete existing vertices, lines, and entire sectors. Select the type of move (or deletion) you want to perform from the buttons in the Move/Del column of the draw information window. To move a specified object, simply drag it to its new location using the mouse. Movements carried out this way maintain all existing connections. The particular element being moved has its size, orientation and, in the case of a sector, shape preserved.

If you move a vertex to the same location as another existing vertex, WADED asks you if you want to merge these vertices. Merging vertices simply combines the vertices into one, disposing of any line running between them.

 CAUTION: When moving map elements, be sure not to create any overlapping or crossing lines, because these cause problems with making sectors and building nodes later.

Deletion of map elements is controlled with the same series of buttons in the lower draw bar. Select the type of deletion you wish to perform and then right click the object to cause the deletion.

Take care with deletions. The interdependence of vertices, lines, and sectors means that what you intended to be a single deletion might, in fact, force the removal of several other items. Deleting a vertex results in the deletion of all attached lines. Deleting lines or sectors might leave one or more sectors open. These could crash both WADED and DOOM if left in this state.

NOTE: While in Move/Del: Vertex mode, you can also add vertices to the map. You might want these as reference points for later drawing, or to split an existing line. You can place vertices on the map by positioning the cursor and clicking the right mouse button. To add a vertex to an existing line, move the mouse cursor over a line on the map. The line flashes red. Clicking the right mouse button adds a vertex to the selected line. You can now move this new vertex to make two lines from the original one.

CLEARING EXTRANEOUS VERTICES

If you want to get rid of all those excess vertices (the ones not attached to any lines), simply click the Clean Verts button and WADED removes them all. Be sure to rebuild the nodes if you do this, however, because this button removes all the vertices associated with the nodes tree (which WADED does not normally show) as well as any unattached vertices that are left over from your own editing.

USING SNAP-TO-GRID

WADED's snap-to-grid feature is used to control how vertices that you create are aligned. WADED makes sure that all vertices that are drawn have their X and Y coordinates at an integral multiple of the current snap-to-grid setting. To turn snap-to-grid off, simply set its value to 1. (The setting is doubled on each click of the + button and halved on each click of –.)

NOTE: Also, do not confuse snap-to-grid with the function of the GRID button. This latter shows DOOM's 64×64 pixel grid used for alignment of flats. If snap-to-grid is set to 64, it coincides with this grid, so this setting can be used to draw areas where you want whole ceiling or floor tiles to be used. Most of the time, though, a value of 8 is a more useful snap-to-grid setting.

CREATING SECTORS

WADED provides two ways to create sectors out of the lines on your map: an automated way, for quick results, and a manual way, for fine tuning.

USING MAKE SECTOR

After you have drawn a shape on the map, you will want to use WADED's Make Sector feature to turn it into a new sector (see Figure 28.15). In Figure 28.15, the mouse is over an undefined sector. All the lines of this sector appear purple in color. When the left mouse button is clicked in this position, a new sector is defined, consisting of all the lines that surround the space the cursor is over. If you move the mouse around the map, WADED highlights each existing sector that it passes over. If your mouse is over an area, and the lines defining it do not show red, or only certain lines are highlighted, this indicates that the sector is incomplete. You need to use Make Sector to fix the sector. To do this, just click inside the affected area. Your newly defined sector then highlights red. You should continue in this way until all purple lines are gone from your map, indicating that all sectors have been created.

Figure 28.15.
WADED's Make Sector feature.

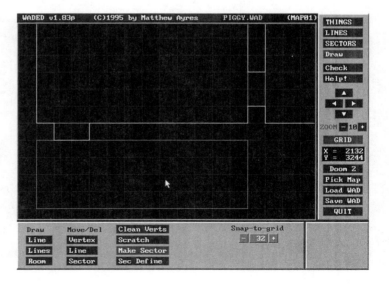

CAUTION: Do not try to use Make Sector on an open-ended figure or one that has overlapping lines. Doing so crashes WADED. All sectors must be closed polygons.

Sectors created with Make Sector take various default settings, usually derived from an adjacent sector. Make Sector can sometimes take a while on complex or large sectors, so you might need to be a little patient. Clicking in the area outside the existing map does nothing.

MANUAL FINE TUNING OF SECTORS

You should find that most of the time WADED's Make Sector facility is all you need to create the sectors of your map. Occasionally, though, you might need to carry out some manual fine tuning of sector assignments, either to work around the limitations of WADED's automatic sector creation or to introduce some unorthodox arrangement of your own. For this, WADED provides a manual sector defining facility. This is accessed by means of the Sec Define button.

This facility enables you to adjust which lines belong to a particular sector. Having clicked the Sec Define button, right click inside the sector you want to adjust. Then click any line, using the left mouse button to reassign it. WADED asks you which side of the chosen line you want to add to the selected sector. Repeat the operation for each line you want to add or remove from the selected sector.

KEYBOARD EQUIVALENTS IN WADED

Although the easiest way to use WADED is with the mouse, most operations have keyboard shortcuts. Table 28.2 lists the global keyboard button equivalents. Table 28.3 lists the commands that are available only from the keyboard. Table 28.4 gives the keyboard commands available for editing lines. Table 28.5 lists the keyboard commands for editing sectors.

Table 28.2. Global WADED commands.

Key	Equivalent Button
F1	THINGS
F2	LINES
F3	SECTORS
F4	Draw
F5	Draw: Line
F6	Draw: Lines
F7	Draw: Room

Key	Equivalent Button
F9	Move/Del: Vertex
F10	Move/Del: Lines
F11	Move/Del: Sectors
C	Check (not implemented)
H	Help! (not implemented)
arrow keys	Scroll map
–	ZOOM –
+	ZOOM +
G	GRID
M	Pick Map
L	Load WAD
S	Save WAD
Q (or Esc)	Quit

Table 28.3. Keyboard-only commands.

Key	Command
Home	Center map
B	Build nodes
I	Information on level
R	Redraw/reset mouse

Table 28.4. Line keyboard commands.

Key	Command
P	Pick texture from list
V	View textures
F	Flip line
T	Make line two-sided
Del	Delete selected item

Table 28.5. Sector keyboard commands.

Key	Command
P	Pick floor/ceiling tiles
V	View floor/ceiling tiles
Del	Delete

USING WADCAT

Included with WADED is a DOS-based utility program called WADCAT. With this program you can easily put multiple levels into one main WAD file. This is extremely useful if you are making a set of levels that you want to follow each other, as in an episode. Use of this program is very simple. When invoked from the DOS command line, the program prompts for all the information it requires.

SPECIFYING FILES

First, you must supply a name for the file you want to create. After that, WADCAT asks for a list of source WADs. These should contain the levels to be assembled into one WAD. It doesn't matter what level designations are used in the source WADs, because WADCAT enables you to change them. They could all start out as E1M1, or MAP01, or any other map at all. You don't need to supply the WAD filenames in any particular order, although you will find it easier to work with WADCAT if you give them in the order in which you want them to play in the final WAD. Terminate the list of input WADs by pressing Enter without supplying a name.

CAUTION: When supplying WAD names to WADCAT, you must omit the .WAD file extension. If you do not, WADCAT does not create the output file.

DESIGNATING LEVELS

After supplying WADCAT with an empty source file name, the program reads each of the files you have specified, examining each to determine what levels it has within it. WADCAT tells you as it starts processing each file. As it encounters a level, it stops to ask for the designation that is to be given to the level in the final WAD. Type the new numbers, or press the spacebar to leave a level as it is.

TIP: WADCAT can take multilevel WADs as input as well as single-level WADs, and it can process all the levels found within it just as if they had come from separate files.

After the last file has been processed, WAD creates the new output file and quits.

> **NOTE:** You can ignore the final `File not found` message that WADCAT displays just before it says `Done`. It is normal.

MIXING GAME TYPES

WADED performs no checking of the WADs it accepts as input. It accepts levels that use either the `ExMy` or `MAPxx` designations. It happily mixes these two map types into a single final WAD. Why might you want to do this? Because this way you can produce a single WAD that works on either DOOM or DOOM II! Awesome!

> **CAUTION:** Although WADCAT happily enables you to mix game types in a single WAD, it performs no conversions: it is up to you to ensure that the mix is compatible. You cannot normally mix DOOM and Heretic WADs, for example—although you could, if you set your DOOM levels to play as Episode 1, say, and your Heretic levels as one of the other Episodes. Of course, you would have to warn users of your WAD what you had done, because trying to play a DOOM WAD in Heretic or vice versa is guaranteed to crash the game. (If you want to learn more about converting WADs between the game variants, see Chapter 31, "WAD Metamorphosis.")

EXIT: MOPPING UP AND MOVING ON

This chapter presented the full working details of the DOS-based editor, WADED. There are, of course, a whole host of other DOOM-genesis tools available. Some of the more important ones are discussed in the next chapter.

OTHER GENESIS TOOLS

Previous chapters of this mission examined in detail the two editors that are provided in pre-registered versions on the CD-ROM which accompanies this book. These are by no means the only DOOM map editors available, of course; they are not even necessarily the best! Many other editors are available for use with most variants of the game. Each offers a different set of features and operational methodology. You should try several different editors before making a final choice. You might find that it is impossible to make a final choice and instead opt to use several editors, switching between them in order to take advantage of their individual strengths.

To help you in your selection, this chapter describes briefly some of the other DOOM map editors that are available to you. All these editors are on the CD-ROM that accompanies this book. You can find full documentation on the use of these editors (as well as complete tutorials, in some cases) on the CD-ROM with the software. If you want to install any of these utilities on the hard disk of your computer, see Chapter 4, "Using the CD-ROM," for full details on how to proceed.

DEU

The DOOM Edit Utility, known as DEU, was the first DOOM level editor and is probably still the most popular. The DOOM-editing community has awaited Version 5.3 of DEU more eagerly even than Quake! DEU was originally written by Raphaël Quinet (based on a Things editor by Brendon Wyber) and has since become an extensive collaborative operation as other people have contributed to its coding and ported it to additional platforms. Although generally classed as a DOS-based editor, DEU also has versions available for Windows, OS/2, UNIX, X-Window, Linux…where will it end? Versions for most of these operating systems are supplied on the CD-ROM.

— By Jason Hoffoss, Ben Morris, Raphaël Quinet, Jeff Rabenhorst, Jack Vermeulen, and Lisa Whistlecroft

DEU works with DOOM, DOOM II, The Ultimate DOOM, and Heretic, and it's entirely free. It comes complete with source code, so if you don't like the way it operates or think it lacks some features, you can modify things to your liking.

DEU's main features include the following:

- Automated polygonal-sector building
- Cut-and-paste capability between maps
- Single-file grouping of several levels
- Scale and rotate capabilities for objects
- Floor and ceiling heights distribution
- Automated texture alignment
- Automated staircase generation
- Sprites viewing during Thing editing (see Figure 29.1)
- Facility for WAD resource replacement through the inclusion of raw binary data in a WAD
- Full manual operation for creating non-standard settings for special effects
- Consistency and error checking
- Fully documented source code in C

Figure 29.1.
DEU's Edit Thing dialog box.

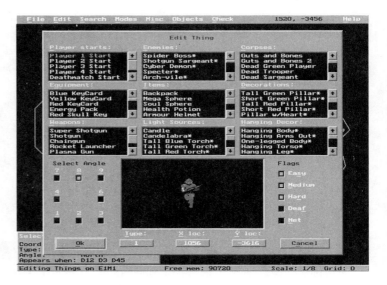

DEU has very few limitations—if you can live with the way it handles the screen and shows its lines at times (see Figure 29.2). It is a little lacking in features when compared with some more recent editors, but for most users, its sheer power and versatility more than makes up for that.

The documentation included with DEU provides full information about modifying the code and adding new features. The authors ask that you pass along your new features so that they can consider them for inclusion in future releases, thereby sharing the work (and the fun!).

Figure 29.2.
Joining lines in DEU.

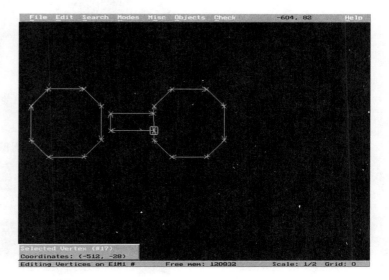

DEEP

DeeP is a professional-quality level editor for DOOM, DOOM II, The Ultimate DOOM, Heretic, and Hexen written by Jack Vermeulen. It runs under DOS but is fully compatible with Windows 3.x, Windows 95, and OS/2 Warp. At first glance, it seems very similar to DEU, but if you look deeper, you find it has many more sophisticated features.

- Built-in graphics texture drawing capabilities to personalize your level without invoking other graphics packages or WAD composition tools. (See Figure 29.3.)
- Powerful interactive WYSIWYG (What You See Is What You Get) drawing tools.
- Sophisticated cut, copy, paste (even between different levels), and (best of all) undo!
- Convenient setup of defaults. (See Figure 29.4.)
- Dynamic game switching to edit all the game variants in one program.
- True one-step linedef/sector drawing with no guesswork involved.
- Accurate gamma correction for easy viewing of dark textures.
- Extensive and totally configurable error checker.
- Convenient map and texture browsers.
- Extensive online help always available.
- Definitions for many predefined structures—windows, stairs, and so on.

Figure 29.3.

Changing a texture composition in DeeP.

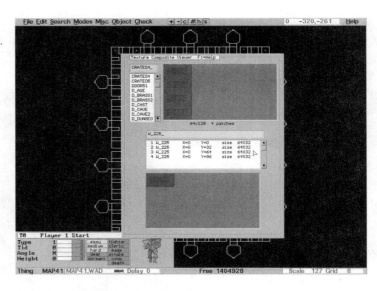

Figure 29.4.

DeeP's fully graphic default setup screen.

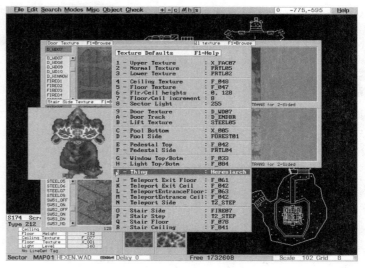

DeeP's principal limitation is that the Heretic and Hexen textures are incorrect in the current version. You can easily change them using the Fix Missing Textures facility. Plans for a future release include a conversion utility for Heretic and Hexen. DeeP is shareware for which registration is required.

The CD-ROM that accompanies this book contains an extensive, illustrated introduction to DeeP. In addition, the documentation that is supplied as standard with the program includes a full tutorial and a sample WAD containing examples of the predefined structures.

DMAPEDIT

DMapEdit is a full-featured map editor for DOOM and DOOM II written by Jason Hoffoss. Version 4.0 runs under DOS, and its aim is to be both very powerful and very easy to use—giving the user complete control over the map but automating as many tasks as possible.

Its main features include the following:

■ Multi-map operation, allowing work on several maps at once.

■ Simple manipulation of map objects or groups of map objects with cut and paste between maps.

■ Predefined structures such as staircases (see Figure 29.5).

■ 3D previewing of all or part of a map with solid or transparent rendering of walls (see Figure 29.6).

■ Compact icons used for Thing placements, providing an uncluttered display with convenient facing arrows for perfect monster positioning (see Figure 29.7).

■ Extensive error detection and correction.

■ Fast and reliable nodes builder.

■ Capability to run DOOM from within DMapEdit for easy testing of levels.

Figure 29.5.

Automated staircase construction in DMapEdit.

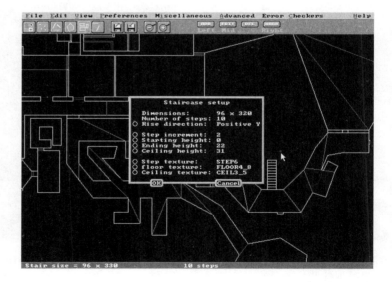

The CD-ROM that accompanies this book contains a full introduction to DMapEdit; the documentation included with the program caters to both beginning and advanced users. In addition, the package comes with extensive tutorials, which include free-running demos of each of the program's main features. DMapEdit's main limitation is that it does not currently support Heretic or Hexen, but plans for a new version include that support. It is also incompatible with some video cards (check the documentation files for details). DMapEdit is freeware.

Figure 29.6.
A 3D preview in DMapEdit.

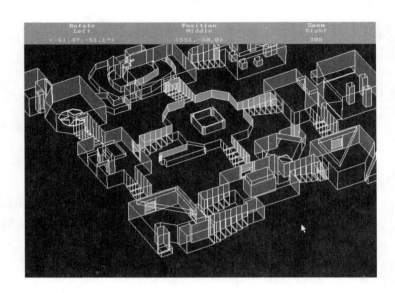

Figure 29.7.
DMapEdit's Thing mode.

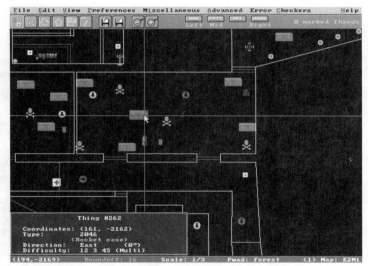

EDMAP

EdMap is a DOS-based map editor for DOOM, DOOM II, and Heretic written by Jeff Rabenhorst. Its features include the following:

- Automated lift, door, stair, and teleport building.
- Manual override on all automated building features.

- Facility for user-defined sector styles.

- Capacity for handling externally added graphics patches.

- Enhanced 3D map option with full editing control (see Figure 29.8).

- On-screen help with search facility.

- Batch file for nodes tree building with WARM (which is bundled).

- Simple converter from DOOM to DOOM II and DOOM to Heretic.

- Pop-up calculator.

- Support for total conversions.

- Capability to play the map from within EdMap.

- Error and consistency checking.

EdMap's main drawback is that its presentation of some information can be confusing (see Figure 29.9), although many people like the full control that this editor's information bars give them.

Figure 29.8.

Editing sidedefs in EdMap with 3D mode enabled.

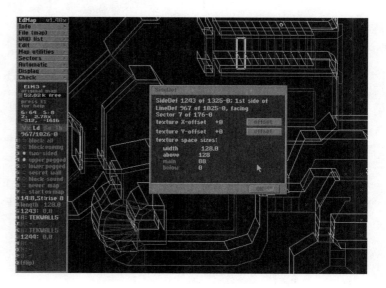

Figure 29.9.

EdMap's Vertex mode.

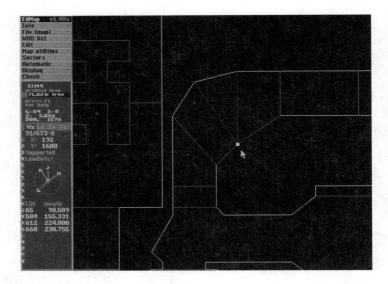

DCK

DCK (DOOM Construction Kit) Version 2.2, written by Ben Morris, is a DOS-based graphical editor for creating maps for DOOM, DOOM II, and Heretic. Its unobtrusive automated tools take care of many of the mundane tasks involved in creating maps yet still afford complete control over the design of your levels.

Its main features include the following:

- Texture display and search facility.
- Capability to run each game from within the editor.
- Support for textures in external files (files other than the IWAD).
- Automated and manual texture alignment.
- Clipboard with cut, copy, and paste—even between files.
- Full drag-and-drop functions.
- Capability to create huge maps.
- Graphical display of Things.
- Capability to rotate and scale objects to any size.
- Comprehensive consistency checker (DCK can even fix most consistency errors unaided).
- 256-color SVGA, 32-bit Protected Mode operation.

DCK also has a lot of other helpful features such as the following:

- An automated tag set function.

- A format painter that enables you to copy an object's attributes to any number of marked objects. Copy sector appearances and heights, line types and tags, Thing skill levels, and so on.

- Motifs—series of defaults that DCK uses to decorate new sectors and lines. You can define many motifs for each game and switch between them with a few keystrokes.

Although DCK does not attempt to hide any of the complexities of map editing, it reduces the learning curve by providing an easy-to-understand interface for every element of level design. DCK Version 2.2 is freeware; there is no registration required.

HCK

HCK is the Hexen equivalent of DCK from the same author. It naturally contains a lot of Hexen-specific enhancements.

- Pop-up choices for arguments where appropriate.

- Built-in support for the ACS script compiler.

- Capability to edit your map's script right from HCK, using your favorite DOS editor.

- Highlighting for the relationship between Thing identifier fields and lines whose specials reference them.

In addition, the editor has the following changes:

- No more built-in node builder, so you can use whichever you prefer.

- "Drag-and-align" texture alignment. Besides having a crafty name, this feature is very useful; HCK displays the texture you want to align and enables you to drag a crosshair to exactly the point that you want DOOM to start displaying the texture.

- Integrated vertex and line modes! No more switching back and forth in order to make structural changes.

- A totally new user interface. It looks and acts more like Windows and is much easier on the mouse hand.

HCK's main disappointment is that it is no longer free! It is now a shareware product and requires a registration fee.

PURPLE FROG MISSION EDITOR

The Purple Frog Mission Editor (PFME), written by Robert Forsman, is a UNIX/X-Window-based mission editor for DOOM, DOOM II, and Heretic. It can edit multiple maps simultaneously with cut-and-paste between maps. It can also display multiple, editable views of the same map with different magnifications (see Figure 29.10). Of course, as PFME runs in an X-Window, you can even do real work at the same time you're editing DOOM levels!

Figure 29.10.

Multiple PFME windows.

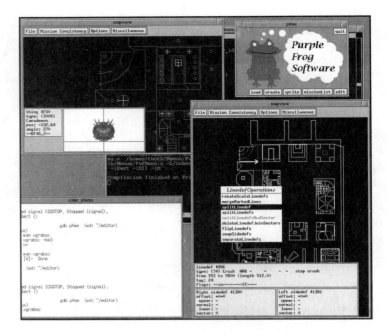

Its features include the following:

- Robust algorithms that generate correct results even with map elements which upset many other editors. For example, self-raising staircases still build properly even when other marked sectors are adjacent. You can even use it to construct self-raising stairs across sectors with varying floor textures!

- No problems with non-contiguous sectors, which figure in many advanced special effects.

- Automated texture alignment across any selected sidedefs.

- Sidedef editing mode for the ultimate in wall painting control.

- Consistency checking detects about 60 percent of known error classes. (Because Robert Forsman is a renowned expert in consistency checking, that means 80 percent by most people's standards!)

PFME has a number of limitations:

- It has no built-in node or reject builder.

- It does not yet support multiple editable windows spread across separate X-displays for cooperative multi-person editing (but then what does?). The feature is planned, however, for a future release (one day).

- It only supports 8-bit PseudoColor visuals, so 16-bit true-color displays aren't supported.

- Only SunOS 4 and Linux binaries are currently available.

If you have suitable flavors of UNIX available, you might like to give this powerful (but under-sung) editor a try. It is supplied free of charge.

EXIT: MOPPING UP AND MOVING ON

This chapter concludes our round-up of some of the editors supplied in the CD-ROM with this book. I hope that it encourages you to try out some of them (or maybe even all) to find one that suits your needs (or just your tastes). This also concludes our look at tools designed for the creation of new DOOM worlds from scratch. In the next mission of this book, we examine some of the tools available for the further synthesis of special components of DOOM WADs and the metamorphosis of existing maps into others of a (potentially) very different character.

SYNTHESIS TOOLS

The preceding chapter reviewed some of the tools available for building a DOOM world from scratch or editing the layout of an existing WAD. In this chapter, we review some of the tools that you can use to assemble and manipulate WAD resources beyond simple map elements. These tools allow the synthesis of completely new DOOM worlds where more than the mere layout of walls, rooms, and monsters are changed. All of the utilities described in this chapter are available on the CD-ROM that accompanies this book. For details on how to install any of them to your computer's hard disk, consult Chapter 4, "Using the CD-ROM."

NWTPRO

New WAD Tool Pro (NWTpro) is a powerful DOS-based utility for DOOM, DOOM II, Heretic, and Hexen written by Denis Moeller. A resource-based WAD-file editor, NWTpro uses a text-mode, menu-based system to enable you to view, play, edit, copy, move, create, and delete any type of DOOM WAD resource.

FEATURES OF NWTPRO

NWTpro's main features let you do the following tasks:

- View, play, and edit resources
- Copy, move, create, and delete resources freely between two open WADs
- Export resources to GIF, PCX, WAV, VOC, RAW, WAD, and TXT file formats
- Import GIF, PCX, WAV, VOC, or RAW data into any WAD
- Easily edit new and old textures, as well as create, copy, move, and delete textures

— By Steve Benner, Jens Hykkelbjerg, Gregory A. Lewis, Denis Moeller, and Olivier Montanuy

- Add and delete patches (edit pnames list)
- Use new sprites and flats with NWTpro's command-line ADD and MERGE features
- Perform advanced WAD editing with the command-line WAD cleaner and WAD joiner

WORKING WITH RESOURCES IN NWTPRO

Figure 30.1 shows the opening screen of NWTpro. It shows the main IWAD resources in the left window and an open PWAD's resources in the right window. If you wish, you could open a second PWAD in the left window, keeping the main IWAD open in the background.

Figure 30.1.

NWTpro's opening screen.

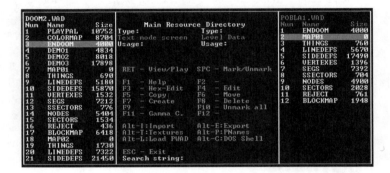

To work with any kind of resource in NWTpro, move the highlight to the resource name and press the appropriate key, as described in Table 30.1.

Table 30.1. NWTpro's key commands.

Key	Description
F1	Provides help information
Enter	Presents the selected resource in the most appropriate way
Tab	Flips between the left and right side of the screen
Spacebar	Marks and unmarks entries
F4	Edits resource(s)
F5	Copies resource(s)
F6	Copies and deletes resource(s) in one action
F7	Creates new, empty resource

Key	Description
F8	Deletes entry or entries
F10	Unmarks all entries on the selected side
F11	Performs gamma correction (use this if your display is too dark)
Esc	Leaves any opened box and exits to DOS
Alt+L	Loads new WAD on the selected side
Alt+C	Presents a DOS shell

NWTpro provides the capability to view animations; just mark the frames you want to be displayed and press Shift+Enter. While viewing the animation, you can speed it up by pressing + and slow it down by pressing –. To end the animation, press Esc.

EXPORTING AND IMPORTING RESOURCES

In order to work on many WAD resources, you must export them for editing with an appropriate utility and then re-import the new version. NWTpro allows the export (and import) of any of a WAD's resources. It supports GIF and PCX formats for graphic resources, WAV and VOC formats for digital sounds, and the RAW format for any resources that don't need further conversion—DOOM demo-files (.LMP) or music files (.MUS), for example. NWTpro handles all conversions automatically as long as you attempt only sensible operations (you shouldn't try importing music as graphics, for example). Some points are important to consider when you're importing files into WADs, however.

NWTpro generally reads all standard GIF and PCX files, but as explained in Chapter 21, "Changing the Face of DOOM," you should make sure that the graphics you import are in 256 colors (8-bit) and use the same palette as the game. NWTpro does not let you import pictures of a greater color depth than 8-bit. If your palettes don't match, NWTpro tries to adapt the imported palette to that of the game. Such a substitution will probably turn out okay because brown will still be brown, but it might not look exactly as you expected.

NWTpro also expects an imported image to have the color cyan (red=0, green=255, blue=255) somewhere in its palette. This color is mapped correctly onto DOOM's color #247 for correct rendering of transparent areas. If you don't have this color, your images might not import correctly.

EDITING RESOURCES

NWTpro has a very powerful Edit function, which you invoke by pressing F4. The exact operations that are available vary with the particular resource you're editing, of course. To give you a taste of editing with NWTpro, the next section discusses the process of changing a WAD's wall textures.

WORKING WITH PATCHES AND TEXTURES

To work with wall textures, you must also work with their component parts, the patches, which are contained in a resource called the *pnames* resource.

VIEWING AND EDITING THE PNAMES RESOURCE

To view or edit the pnames resource, locate it in the WAD's resource list. Then, simply press Enter to open the resource and see a list of all of the pnames (patch names).

If you want to view any of these patches, you can highlight the name of the patch and press Enter. Press F7 to select a (graphics) file to import as a new patch or F8 to delete any you don't want.

PNAMES AND ALIAS NAMES

Most graphic resources (whether in pnames or elsewhere) have names that are difficult to remember or relate to—names such as WALL42_3, for example. NWTpro makes using these names easier by providing an Alias list. The idea is simple; every patch has an Alias name. WALL42_3, for instance, is also known as METALBAR, which is more descriptive. This Alias list is contained within a simple text file that you can edit to suit your own needs (and new patches).

VIEWING AND EDITING TEXTURES

To view textures, first locate a Texture resource. (There are two, TEXTURE1 and TEXTURE2, which keep the textures in the shareware game separate from the textures reserved for the registered version.) With the cursor on one of the texture resources, press Enter to open it. NWTpro lists all available textures on the left side of the screen. On the right side is the list of patches of the currently selected texture. (See Figure 30.2.)

Figure 30.2.
NWTpro's Textures Directory screen.

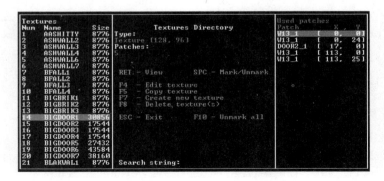

You can use NWTpro's standard editing keys to edit (F4), copy (F5), move (F6), or delete (F8) a texture. Resources can be copied (or moved) into a file of their own (.RAW or .TXT format) or into another WAD file. NWTpro prompts you for a filename whenever you select one of these options before it proceeds with the operation.

NOTE: NWTpro's copy, move, and delete operations operate only on entries that have been *marked* beforehand with the spacebar.

When you press F4 (or F7 to create an entirely new texture entry), you are prompted for a file into which the completed texture should be saved. You can specify a new file or the currently loaded WAD file if you want the texture to be immediately available to this WAD. After supplying the name of the file, you see the texture composition screen (see Figure 30.3) where you assemble patches to make up your new texture. In this screen, you can do the following tasks:

- Preview patches by pressing Enter.

- Add a patch at the end of the patch list by pressing the spacebar. NWTpro switches into graphics mode for you to position the patch. Use the cursor keys to position the patch and press Enter to place it in the texture. The patch appears overlaid on all the others, so build your textures from the back. You can abort the positioning of a texture by pressing Esc.

- Reposition a patch in the texture by pressing F9. (Be sure to flip to the right side list before doing this.)

- Insert a patch into the texture by pressing F7. The selected patch from the list on the left side will be inserted at the position of the right cursor. If this is on the first entry, the new patch is placed before all the others.

- Delete a patch from the texture by pressing F8. (Be sure to flip to the right side list before doing this.)

- Clear the texture by pressing F4. NWTpro deletes the patch list on the right side and you can start your texture anew.

- View the texture with all the patches you have added to it by pressing F3. NWTpro switches into graphics mode and displays your assembled texture. If you have done nothing else since you created a new texture, you see a beautiful black screen.

Figure 30.3.
NWTpro's texture composition screen.

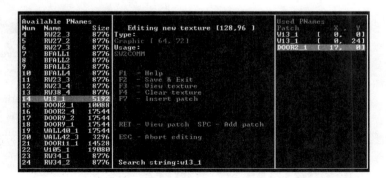

Once you have the texture composed to your satisfaction, press F2 to save it into the file you specified before you started editing. (You can abort editing without saving by pressing Esc.) If you save it into the currently loaded WAD file, your texture is listed on the left side along with all the others.

NWTPRO SUMMARY

NWTpro has many other capabilities, but there is insufficient space to present them all in detail here. If you are looking for a powerful and yet friendly DOS-based WAD resource editor, then look no further.

WINTEX

WinTex 4.1 is a Windows-based WAD resource editor for DOOM, DOOM II, The Ultimate DOOM, Heretic, and Hexen by Olivier Montanuy. It can have up to 20 WAD files (for any one game variant) open simultaneously, as well as cut, copy, and paste between them. WinTex is a rather more complex tool, at first sight, than NWTpro. Figure 30.4 shows its opening window with the important control areas marked.

Figure 30.4.

WinTex's opening window.

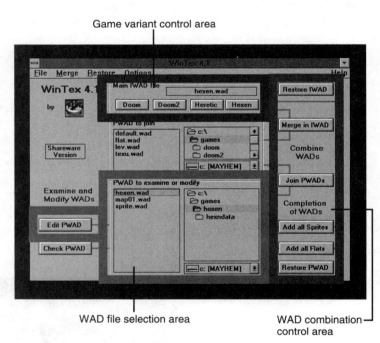

Game variant control area

WAD file selection area

WAD combination control area

Most of the time, you need only concern yourself with the Game variant controls (to select the particular game you want to work with) and the WAD file selection area (to select the WAD file you want to work on). You won't often need the other areas for advanced operation of the program.

CAPABILITIES OF WINTEX

WinTex offers many of the same capabilities of NWTpro. Essentially, you can examine, export, and import any WAD resource, all within a graphical working environment. In addition, WinTex lets you look at some of the more unusual aspects of your WAD in a graphical way. It enables you to see at a glance the ramifications of your WAD's Reject map, for example, by showing you what is in view from any chosen sector (see Figure 30.5). It even displays a WAD's nodes tree, should you ever have the need to examine this.

Figure 30.5.
WinTex's Reject map viewer.

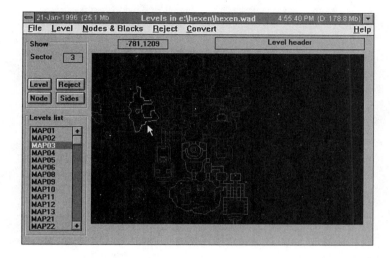

WINTEX SUMMARY

You will find that WinTex 4.1 provides all you would expect of a modern WAD resource editor operating in the Windows environment. Its use is not entirely intuitive, however, and you should carefully study the help and documentation files included with the program to get the most out of this utility.

DEHACKED

DeHackEd (pronounced dee-hak-ed) is a DOS-based DOOM.EXE Hack Editor written by Greg Lewis. It enables the alteration of such things as enemy hit points and the monsters' speed and appearance by changing a few specific values in the EXE file. It provides easy access to all the main executable's data tables (outlined in Chapter 22, "Hacking the DOOM Code") and all the known minor ones too. Version 3.0 of DeHackEd works with DOOM v1.666 and later, all releases of DOOM II, and The Ultimate DOOM. It also includes mouse support.

THE DEHACKED PATCH PHILOSOPHY

Modification of the DOOM.EXE would not be much fun if the changes could not be saved and used again at a later date. DeHackEd saves the changes that are made to the DOOM.EXE file to *patch* files, which contain only the information extracted from the DOOM.EXE that DeHackEd edits.

NOTE: Do not confuse DeHackEd's patch files, which normally have the extension .DEH, with the PWAD patch files. DEH files can only be used by DeHackEd, which applies these patches to the executable code before DOOM is started.

By using patch files and applying only those that you want, you can easily patch and re-patch your DOOM code as often as you like, building up change after change. Of course, it is sensible to start by having DeHackEd save the contents of your original, pristine DOOM executable to another patch file that you can use to restore the game's correct behavior at any time.

SETTING UP DEHACKED

Before using DeHackEd for the first time, check the entries in its .INI file.

DEHACKED.INI

The DEHACKED.INI file enables you to customize your copy of DeHackEd for your personal use. Put a copy of this file in each of your DOOM game directories (if you intend hacking at more than one) and edit it to reflect the way your machine is set up. The .INI file has ample comments (each starting with the # symbol) to indicate what each entry is for.

The doomexe and doomwad parameters tell DeHackEd where it should look for the main DOOM files on your computer. You might want to make a copy of your DOOM.EXE file (calling it something like DOOMHACK.EXE) and then refer to that file in the DEHACKED.INI file. That way, there is always a clean copy of the DOOM.EXE file to use under its normal name, and yet you can still edit a copy to your heart's desire. The DOOM.WAD file reference must also be correct or DeHackEd will not run. (DeHackEd requires access to the WAD file for two reasons: to make sure that you are using a registered or commercial version of DOOM and to play or show the Sounds and Frames when required.)

SAVING A BACKUP PATCH

Once you have the .INI file set up, you can take a backup copy of the original .EXE file's settings by typing the following line:

```
dehacked -save filename
```

CAUTION: Even making a backup patch file is not a 100 percent guarantee that you can return your DOOM.EXE file to its original state. The updates that id Software releases to upgrade DOOM from one version to another also check the date and time of the DOOM.EXE, which will not be correct even if you load the backup patch. Always make sure to keep a copy of your DOOM.EXE file safe somewhere so that you can use it whenever you need an original copy of the EXE file.

USING DEHACKED

You can use DeHackEd in two modes: an interactive screen mode to build up new patches or a batch file or command-line mode to apply (or undo) ready-made patches to the executable. Let's look briefly at the uses of each mode.

INTERACTIVE MODE

You start DeHackEd in interactive mode by simply typing the following line at the DOS prompt:

```
dehacked
```

DeHackEd's 50-line VGA screen layout makes its use easy and highly intuitive. The opening screen is the main Thing editing screen (see Figure 30.6), which allows the editing of the executable's Thing table. To edit a field in this table, use the cursor keys to highlight it and press Enter or click it with the mouse pointer. You can select a new Thing to edit by clicking (or pressing Enter) on the ID# entry field. This brings up a scrolling (descriptive) list of all known Things.

Figure 30.6.
DeHackEd v3.0's opening Thing editing screen.

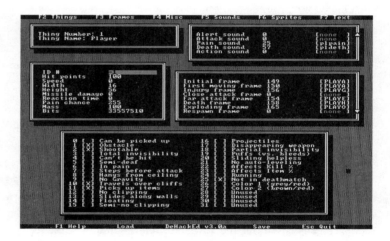

In addition to the Things screen, DeHackEd also provides screens for editing the following items:

- The Frame tables
- Miscellaneous information, including the Weapons table and various player and game behavior information
- The Sound tables
- The Sprite tables
- The executable's Text entries

You select these editing screens through simple function-key presses or from a top menu by using the mouse. The bottom of the screen acts as a menu bar too, providing quick access to the program's Load and Save functions, as well as Help and Exit.

By pressing the A key at any time (or clicking the program's name on the bottom line of the screen), you can bring up an About box that displays the credits for DeHackEd and a small status summary. The latter information tells you where the patch files are saved and which version of DOOM you are editing (if you have more than one).

EXAMINING MORE INFORMATION IN INTERACTIVE MODE

DeHackEd would be a superb tool even if all it did was allow you to change the values in the executable's tables. In fact, it goes one step further by providing the means to examine the main WAD resources that you are working with. When you're working with the Frame editor, for example, a simple press of the spacebar (or left mouse click) displays the sprite associated with the selected frame. Subsequent presses of the spacebar move you on to the next frame of the current sequence until a sequence is exhausted.

In a similar way, you can play sounds while in the Sounds editor and view long text strings in their entirety in the Text editor.

DeHackEd's editing screens usually present information in decimal format. If you prefer to work in hexadecimal notation, however, the program will accommodate you; simply press the H key (or D to revert).

WORKING WITH PATCHES

DeHackEd does not actually write any of the changes you make to the DOOM.EXE until you instruct it to. This gives you the chance to abort without making changes if you think you've made a mess of things. Having designed your new killer patch, you can opt to Save the changes to a patch file for later use or Write them straight to the .EXE to try them out. You can also Load previously saved patches to build up new patches with combined effects. DeHackEd's new patch file format means that it only writes the changed settings to the patch file, not all of them, meaning that additive patch effects are easy. A new X keystroke also allows you to abandon all changes, restoring the .EXE to its original untouched state.

INTERACTIVE MODE KEYBOARD CONTROLS

Table 30.2 provides a complete summary of DeHackEd's keyboard controls.

Table 30.2. A summary of available keys.

Key	Action
Escape	Leaves input boxes and Help screens; exits to DOS
Enter	Edits the current field
Space	Views or plays the current field (when applicable)

Key	Action
C	Copies data from one object to another
D	Changes to the decimal number system
G	Goes to a specific Thing through an alphabetical list of Thing names
H	Changes to the hexadecimal number system
J	Jumps to the information in the current field, in its respective editor
L	Loads a patch file and replaces all information with the data from the file
M	Merges a new patch file with the information already in DOOM
R	Runs DOOM from within DeHackEd
S	Saves a patch file to a specified filename
U	Undoes all changes and returns to the most recently written version of the executable file
W	Writes all changes to the executable file
X	Restores the executable to its original state
F2	Switches to the Thing editor
F3	Changes to the Frame editor
F4	Brings up the Miscellaneous editor
F5	Goes to the Sound editor
F6	Changes to the Sprite editor
F7	Switches to the Text editor

USING DEHACKED FROM THE COMMAND LINE

DeHackEd was designed to be simple to use in batch files. The full command-line syntax is the following:

```
dehacked [doompath] [-load patch1 patch2 ...] [-save patch]
```

The [doompath] is optional. If you run DeHackEd in a different directory from the one DOOM is in, you can give the path to your DOOM directory here. This value overrides any path and name specified in your DEHACKED.INI file.

The -load option updates the DOOM.EXE file with the specified patches. The first patch is loaded normally, and all other patches listed after it (if there are any) are merged with it. The patch directory given in the .INI is the directory where DeHackEd checks for the files unless you specify an explicit path along with the filenames.

Conversely, the -save option saves the current DOOM.EXE status to the specified patch file.

DEHACKED IN SUMMARY

DeHackEd is the tool to use to develop your own hacks into the DOOM executable and to save these hacks as patches that can be distributed for other players to use. You will also need to use DeHackEd to apply patches to your DOOM executable. To do this, you need know nothing more than how to set up DeHackEd's .INI file and use its `-load` and `-save` command-line options.

RMB

RMB is a DOS-based Reject map builder (hence its name) written by Jens Hykkelbjerg. You can use RMB with WADs for all versions of DOOM, DOOM II, Heretic, and Hexen. In addition to being an excellent Reject map builder, RMB can also make all kinds of special effects by providing you with perfect control of your Reject map settings (and therefore control over what your monsters think they can see).

THE COMPONENTS OF RMB

RMB comes with two utility programs, INSPECT and EFFECT.

RMB'S INSPECT UTILITY

The INSPECT utility has two main uses; it can count the number of bits set in the Reject map and at the same time calculate the efficiency of the Reject table (the proportion of the table that has 1s in it). This enables you to see whether any reject optimization has already been performed on a WAD, whether any special effects might be in use, and whether any further speed-up might be possible.

RMB'S EFFECT UTILITY

The EFFECT utility allows you to apply simple special effects to WAD files through the Reject map. This command-line-operated utility enables the designer to specify sectors as wholly safe or blind. It is useful only for a very limited range of effects, but it can be handy if you don't want to get involved with the full use of RMB's option files.

RMB

You can use RMB itself in two main ways. At its simplest, the program can be invoked to process a WAD file for total optimization. When you do this, RMB reads in each map of the file and then works through each sector in turn, deciding precisely which sectors are in view. The more sectors RMB can identify as unsighted from other sectors, the faster your final WAD should play. You can even use RMB to improve the playing speed of id and Raven Software's original WAD files, which are not fully optimized already! (A ready-to-use batch file to do this comes with RMB. It takes some time to run, though!)

A more sophisticated use of RMB is to arrange for it to introduce some special effects to your WAD while it goes about its job of optimizing the rest of the file. To do this, you need to use it in conjunction with special option files.

RMB'S OPTION FILES

For complete control over your Reject maps, use RMB in conjunction with *option files*. These special files provide RMB with command-like controls over its operation. They enable the designer to specify the state of particular inter-sector lines of sight, which in turn permits the creation of the particular WAD tricks that are achieved only through Reject map manipulations (see Chapter 23, "Reject Table Tricks").

Table 30.3 gives a full list of the options available in RMB with a short explanation of the function of each. You can find the details about each option in the manual for the program, which is on the CD-ROM that accompanies this book.

Table 30.3. RMB options.

Option	Function
#	Marks a comment line in the option file.
BAND	Makes "bands" of blindness/safety.
BLIND	Makes sector(s) blind (or partially so).
BLOCK	Stops monsters from seeing through a pair of specified lines.
DISTANCE	Specifies how far (by lateral distance) monsters can generally see.
DOOR	Specifies the maximum number of doors that monsters can generally see through.
ExMy	Marks start of options for a particular DOOM or Heretic level.
EXCLUDE	Forces exclusion of the view from one sector to another.
GROUP	Merges sectors into one for the purposes of line-of-sight calculations. (Each sector in the group gets an identical reject entry.)
INCLUDE	Forces inclusion of the view from one sector to another.
INV BLIND	Makes sector(s) long-sighted.
INV SAFE	Makes sector(s) invisible to monsters nearby (but not to distant ones).
LEFT	Makes a two-sided line into one-way see-through (from left to right).
LENGTH	Specifies how far (by sector) monsters can generally see.
LINE	Makes a two-sided line impossible to look through for monsters.

continues

Table 30.3. continued

Option	Function
MAP*xx*	Marks start of options for a particular DOOM II or Hexen map.
NODOOR	Marks sector(s) as not being counted as a door. (Used only with DOOR option.)
NOMAP	Removes the graphical display; reports progress as dots instead.
NOPROCESS	Only applies special effects; no processing done (very fast).
ONE	Same as BLOCK but only operates in one direction.
PERFECT	Generates a perfect Reject map. (Forces processing of all sectors.)
PREPROCESS	Groups sectors to gain processing speed. (The efficiency drops.)
PROCESS	Forces processing of specified sector(s).
REPORT	Reports long lines of sight to file.
RIGHT	Makes a two-sided line one-way see-through (from right to left).
SAFE	Makes sector(s) invisible to distant monsters.
TRACE	For debugging only; use is not recommended.

RMB SUMMARY

RMB is the utility to use if you find that your WADs are playing slowly because of their size. You can also use it to introduce special Reject map effects to make monsters turn a blind eye to the presence of the player.

WARM

WARM (WAD Auxiliary Resource Manipulator) v1.5 is a DOS-based utility written by Robert Fenske, Jr. and ported to OS/2 by Mark K. Mathews. It works with WADs for all versions of DOOM, DOOM II, Heretic, and Hexen. Its main purpose is to build the nodes, ssectors, segs, blockmap, and reject resources for a WAD from the basic elements (vertices, linedefs, and sidedefs) that compose each level. Its principal features include:

- Lightning-fast nodes tree building
- Lightning-fast blockmap building
- Fully automatic reject building
- Manual manipulation of Reject map special effects

It also has various utility function options that perform the following tasks:

- Merge WADs and levels
- Extract resources

- Substitute resources
- Randomize Things
- Rename resources
- Pack/unpack WADs

WARM comes with full source code, which is known to compile and run successfully under MS-DOS, OS/2, SunOS 4.1.*x*, Solaris 2.*x*, Linux, FreeBSD, HP-UX, VMS, and Windows/NT. It is one of the few nodes builders that can cope with the special requirements of self-referencing sectors (needed for certain special effects) and so should generally be the nodes builder of choice if you find that you need something more than your editor's nodes builder offers.

EXIT: MOPPING UP AND MOVING ON

This chapter provided a brief overview of some of the more important tools for putting together the specialist elements of a WAD beyond the capabilities of most map editors. The next chapter looks at another specialist utility: a tool for transforming WADs written for one game variant into a WAD that can be played in another.

WAD METAMORPHOSIS

DM2CONV by Vincenzo Alcamo is a utility designed to convert WADs so that they can be used with variants of DOOM other than the one for which they were originally written. This chapter presents this utility in detail, showing you how to use it and why you might want to use it. You can find details on how to install DM2CONV on your computer in Chapter 4, "Using the CD-ROM."

INTRODUCTION

If you have been working through the earlier chapters of this book, you know that there are many differences in the WADs for the different variants of DOOM. Because of the way the game engine accesses PWADs, you cannot even load a PWAD that has been written for one variant into another without the game engine crashing. This is partly because the PWAD structures differ and partly because much of the vital information for rendering your DOOM world—all the graphics, the Thing information, and the special actions, for example—is stored in the main IWAD of the game.

So what do you do if you have just finished your best ever WAD in DOOM II and your friends tell you they can't play it because they prefer either The Ultimate DOOM or Heretic?

One option is to go through every line and sector of your WAD, checking the textures and special actions and altering them to fit another target game…and then doing the same for the monsters, the ornaments, the music, and so forth. "But that is going to be tedious in the extreme, and very prone to errors and oversights," I can hear you saying. Fret not! Help is at hand in the form of DM2CONV.

— By Lisa Whistlecroft

WHAT DM2CONV CAN DO

DM2CONV converts WADs written for DOOM, The Ultimate DOOM, DOOM II, and Heretic into WADs for any of the others—or, indeed, for the same game (you'll see why that might be useful shortly). This gives a total of 16 possible conversion routes, although you never need to convert DOOM WADs for The Ultimate DOOM because the latter runs all DOOM WADs without any need for change. In addition, DM2CONV is fully programmable, enabling you to choose precisely what replaces what during the conversion process.

CAUTION: Because of the fundamental differences among the four variants of DOOM, only conversions from DOOM to DOOM II or Heretic, and from DOOM II to The Ultimate DOOM are absolutely guaranteed to produce playable WADs. Many other conversions work perfectly well, but you should be aware that some special effects just cannot be transferred between games.

WHAT CAN BE CONVERTED

Several classes of DOOM elements need to be converted, depending on which games you are moving between, and some you might want to change just for fun. The full list comprises the following:

- **Level identification**: Episode-and-mission or level. DOOM and Heretic use ExMy to reference their maps; DOOM II uses MAPxx.

- **Line information**: Wall textures and triggers. Each game has a different set of wall textures available; some line triggers or special actions are different, too.

- **Sector information**: Floor and ceiling textures and special characteristics. Each game has different floor and ceiling textures; Heretic has many extra sector specials.

- **Thing information**: Decorations, monsters, and the difficulty levels and quantities in which they appear. You can decide exactly how you want your converted WAD to be populated.

- **Other WAD resources**: Special items, normally changed only in large-scale conversions. Their names might need changing when the WAD is converted.

- **The music**: You can shuffle the order while you do it, too.

As you can see, there are an enormous number of conversions you could make, just starting from one WAD. After all, there are a multitude of monsters to choose from every time you want to replace one. DM2CONV makes life easy for you at the outset by providing a set of sensible conversion mappings as a default. If you use the default setting, all monsters of one type in, say, DOOM WADs are always converted to the same new monster in conversion for Heretic.

GETTING STARTED

DM2CONV is a very powerful and flexible utility, capable of letting you customize the way your conversions are carried out. On the other hand, it can also be very simple to use, if you just want to carry out a quick conversion to enable you to try out a WAD in a different game variant.

SIMPLE USE

If you decide to start with the default settings, the command for using DM2CONV is very simple. Suppose you want to take Steve McCrea's TRINITY.WAD back into the medieval time of Heretic under the name of TRINITYH.WAD. To do this, you would type the following:

```
DM2CONV TRINITY.WAD TRINITYH.WAD @:DTOH
```

The @:DTOH tells DM2CONV that you want to convert from DOOM to Heretic. Using DM2CONV in this way requires you to remember only four abbreviations for the names of the various games. These are given in Table 31.1.

Table 31.1. Game abbreviation codes.

Game	Abbreviation Code
DOOM	D
The Ultimate DOOM	UD
DOOM II	D2
Heretic	H

If you really hate typing long commands, you can omit the file extensions and the TO and just type this:

```
DM2CONV TRINITY TRINITYH @:DH
```

NOTE: Strictly speaking, you do not need to specify the name of the file you want to create, either. If you don't, DM2CONV simply overwrites your source file. This is okay if you never, ever, experiment without first making a backup, but it is a rather risky practice!

MORE DETAILED USE

A fuller statement of the syntax of a DM2CONV conversion command is

`DM2CONV sourcefile [destinationfile] @[responsefile][:labelname]`

Let's look at each element of this command in turn, seeing what it is, how it is used, what it enables you to control, and what it requires you to provide for it to work effectively:

`DM2CONV`	This invokes the DM2CONV conversion program.
`sourcefile`	You must supply DM2CONV with a valid PWAD or IWAD file to work from.
`destinationfile`	This is where your new WAD is stored. If a file of this name already exists, it is overwritten; if you fail to specify this filename, your source WAD is overwritten.
`@responsefile`	This tells DM2CONV what Response file to use to determine the way the conversion runs. Response files are discussed in detail in the next section of this chapter. If you omit the filename here (typing only the @ character), DM2CONV uses its default file. This is called DEFAULT.RSP and must be kept in the same directory as DM2CONV. By using a different Response file (either by writing your own or modifying the default), you can customize your conversions.
`:labelname`	If you specify a label within the Response file, DM2CONV reads the Response file only from that label onward. In the Trinity example shown earlier, the `:DTOH` after the @ tells DM2CONV to start executing DEFAULT.RSP from the label DTOH. This enables you to provide with the program a single, comprehensive file that handles all the most likely conversions.

RESPONSE FILES

The reason the syntax for DM2CONV itself is so straightforward is that the program runs as an interpreter and the changes are specified in the Response file. At its simplest, the Response file needs to contain no more than the versions of the game that the conversion is running between, and substitutions for any elements of the source game that do not appear in the destination game. These are usually floor, ceiling, and wall textures, Things, and sector and line specials. The DM2CONV code itself takes care of the conversion elements over which you normally have no control. (This is one reason why you must specify the source and destination games. Another reason is that it needs this information to read and write the PWAD file structures correctly.)

Response files should have the file extension .RSP, but this need not be specified in the command to DM2CONV. If you don't keep your own Response files in the DM2CONV directory, you must specify the full path to them. A detailed discussion of the contents of Response files is given shortly.

NOTE: DM2CONV uses Response files in a similar way to DOOM itself. A description of their use is given in Chapter 2, "Running DOOM."

THE DEFAULT RESPONSE FILE

The Response file that is provided with DM2CONV, DEFAULT.RSP, allows for eleven conversion modes. You can go from any version of the game to any other, with the exception of DOOM to The Ultimate DOOM, where no conversion is necessary.

CAUTION: Because the level structure of DOOM II is radically different from that of the other variants of the game, multilevel PWADs can run into conversion problems. Specifically, the use of secret missions might get messed up.

The four possibilities that the default file does not allow for are conversions within one game. Such conversions require you to write your own Response files but then enable you to reuse the same map with different monsters and special effects. You can use these to simplify a favorite WAD for a beginner, for example, or to turn a bloodbath into a real nightmare!

A SIMPLE RESPONSE FILE

Let's look at a simple Response file. HEXAGON.WAD, which can be found on the CD-ROM accompanying this book, contains a simple one-room map. Figure 31.1 shows a view of this rather gray room. You might recognize this as the hexagonal room from the series of WAD sorties of Episode 2, Mission 1, "A Hell of Your Very Own."

Figure 31.1.
Recognize this room?

If you wanted to convert this room for DOOM II—changing its appearance as you did so—you could write a Response file such as the one given in Listing 31.1. The comments explain what each line does. (Everything after a semicolon is a comment. These are not executed by DM2CONV and can be omitted.)

Listing 31.1. A simple DM2CONV Response file.

```
SET FROM=DOOM TO=DOOM2              ;This specifies the source
                                    ;and destination games (without this
                                    ;info DM2CONV cannot do the conversion)
ECHO Converting from DOOM to DOOM II ;The Response file can tell you
                                    ;what it is doing (pretty trivial here
                                    ;but useful in branching Response files

[FLOORS]                            ;Tells DM2CONV that subsequent items
                                    ;are flats (which can, of course, be
                                    ;on either the floor or the ceiling
MFLR8_1=GRASS1                      ;all occurrences of MFLR8_1 will be
                                    ;changed to GRASS1
CEIL3_5=GRNLITE1                    ;CEIL3_5 will be changed to GRNLITE1

[TEXTURES]                          ;Subsequent items are wall textures
STONE2=SPACEW4                      ;STONE2 will be changed to SPACEW4

[THINGS]                            ;Subsequent items are Things
48=85                               ;These are the type numbers of the Things
                                    ;the Tall Techno-Column (48) will become
                                    ;a Tech Light Column Long (85)
ECHO Done
```

If you write this file for yourself, you need to save it with the extension .RSP. The easiest place to put it is in the DM2CONV directory on your hard disk. A copy, called HEXAGDD2.RSP, is on the CD-ROM with HEXAGON.WAD. To carry out the conversion using this file, type this:

```
DM2CONV HEXAGON.WAD HEXAGON2.WAD @HEXAGDD2
```

You can then take a look at it if you have DOOM II. (HEXAGON2.WAD is also on the CD-ROM with the other files.) Figure 31.2 shows how it should look.

Figure 31.2.
*The same room in a DOOM II-only
version.*

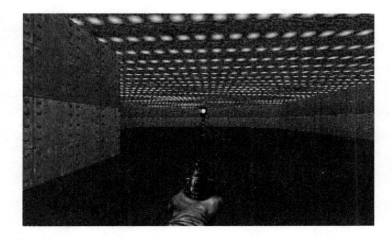

RESPONSE FILE COMPONENTS

The Response file you have just seen contains most of the elements that are permissible. Here are the components of a Response file in more detail:

- **Comments**: These must start with a semicolon and are not executed.

- **Labels**: These must start with a colon. They are used to designate starting points of the Response file. A label can be specified in the command line that invokes DM2CONV to have the program run the Response file from that point. Any part of the Response file can call another part by referencing its label, just like calling a subroutine in any programming language.

- **Commands**: There are four commands—ECHO, RETURN, ABORT, and SET—plus four conditionals—IFDEF, IFNDEF, ELSE, and ENDIF. ECHO enables the Response file to write to the screen while running. RETURN and ABORT are ways of terminating sections of the Response file. SET and the conditionals are used for Symbol control and program branching. These are discussed later in this chapter.

- **Section tags**: These act as headings for the different types of replacements.

- **Replacements**: These make up the bulk of the Response file and are the elements you will most likely want to write yourself. There are six types of replacement, which are examined in some detail later in this chapter. All of them take the form of a *replacement expression*, which simply states what element of the source game you want to replace, and what you want to replace it with. They look like an equation, thus: `element to be replaced = element to replace it with`.

NOTE: Real replacement expressions must never contain spaces. A space acts as a delimiter, enabling you to put multiple expressions on one line.

REPLACING DOOM ELEMENTS

As has just been said, the six types of replacement expression must be grouped together in sections, by type, preceded by a section tag. The sections are as follows:

- **[NAMES]**: WAD directory entry names
- **[FLOORS]**: Floor and ceiling flats
- **[TEXTURES]**: Wall textures
- **[SECTORS]**: Sector Specials
- **[LINEDEFS]**: Line Specials
- **[THINGS]**: Things

In addition to the six types of true replacements, there is an additional section for the definition of Things by name:

- **[OBJECTS]**: Thing names. If you define the names of Things, you can refer to them by name, instead of by their numbers, when you come to replace them.

NAMES

This is where conversions are done of the elements of the WAD that are not part of the map—the music, the demonstrations that play before you do, the sky textures, and so forth.

FLOORS AND TEXTURES

Both sorts of surface textures are handled in the same way. The replacement expressions take the following form:

```
texture1=texture2
```

For the replacements to work properly, the wall textures you substitute must fit properly into the spaces in the WAD that they are to fill. The source and destination textures must be of the same height, or the destination texture must be exactly 128 pixels high. This is to conform with DOOM's texture tiling method. You might remember that tiling of textures of heights other than 128 pixels results in the Pink Bug effect. (See Chapter 11, "The Lowdown on Textures," for more information on this subject.) Two-sided lines can have see-through textures on them, so all instances of these should be replaced by see-through textures. Do not use see-throughs as other substitutions, though, or you will get the Tutti Frutti effect on solid walls. Similarly, if the source texture is made up of a single patch, you should take care not to specify a complex or overlaid texture for the destination, in case the texture is used anywhere as the main texture on a two-sided line, where it invokes Medusa!

SECTORS AND LINEDEFS

Both types of special action are handled in the same way. The replacement expressions can take these forms:

```
code1,code2,...=code3
code1-code2,...=code3
```

The minus sign indicates all sector or line special codes in the range *code1* to *code2* inclusive.

> **CAUTION:** Remember that many special line-types are specific to particular games and might not be supported by the destination game. Turbo doors and 16-pixel self-raising stairs are two examples that can cause problems. Substituting ordinary doors for their turbo counterparts is straightforward and does not affect play of the resulting WAD. You cannot replace tall staircases with short ones, however. (Actually, you can, but you won't be able to get up the last step.) As a result, some WADs are inevitably unplayable after conversion.

THINGS AND OBJECTS

Let's look at DM2CONV's objects first because they can be used in Thing replacement. Object expressions are not replacement expressions. Their purpose is to define names that can then be used in replacement statements in the [THINGS] section.

> **TIP:** Rather than using an [OBJECTS] section in each of your Response files, a better method is to save all your object definitions in one separate Response file. A default version of this, called OBJECTS.RSP, is supplied with DM2CONV. Call this file by having the line @OBJECTS at the start of your Response files.

> **NOTE:** OBJECTS.RSP is not complete. It contains monsters and weapons but omits some decorations. The Tall Techno-column isn't in it, for example. See Chapter 34, "Essential Thing Information," for a full list of all Things and their reference numbers in all variants of the game.

The definition expression format used within the [OBJECTS] section takes this general form:

```
number=[(radius,height)]game,name
```

game is a compilation of the game codes given previously in Table 31.1. (The Ultimate DOOM is excluded, though, because it has all the same Things as DOOM.)

NOTE: The radius and height values are optional and are currently not used by DM2CONV.

Examples of object definitions are as follows:

```
1=DD2H.Player 1 Start
6=DD2 .Yellow Key Card
6=   H.Iron Lich
68= D2 .Arachnotron
85=   H.Silver shield
```

Spaces are allowed after the equals sign, in both the game field and the name field. Consequently, only one expression is allowed per line.

TIP: Reading an object's Response file is much easier if you use spaces to designate unsupported games, so the game field falls into neat columns.

In addition to all the Things in DOOM, DOOM II, and Heretic, Vincenzo Alcamo has defined two special objects in his default OBJECTS.RSP. These are as follows:

```
0=DD2H.REMOVE
9999=DD2H.MIX
```

Their use is described later in this chapter.

THING REPLACEMENT

Let us now look at Thing replacement in some detail because this is where the fun really starts—both in WAD conversion and in the possibilities that DM2CONV opens up.

CAUTION: You should be aware of one possible side effect of substituting one Thing for another. They can be of different sizes. This means that an obstruction might end up completely blocking a passage that it was meant merely to constrict. Or it might not completely cover something that was supposed to be secret. Additionally, if you put a large monster into a position that had held a small one, you might find that it gets stuck and cannot take part in the action. It is clear from the full syntax of the object definition expression that size-checking is planned for a future release of DM2CONV. Until then, you will have to think carefully about what you substitute for what, or be prepared to move a few things about with a map editor afterwards.

An additional problem is that some WADs require you to kill a specific monster to open the exit. If this monster has no counterpart in the destination game (and most do not) you can never finish the level. As a result, some WADs are unplayable after conversion.

SIMPLE REPLACEMENTS

The simplest form of the Thing replacement expression is

`thing1=thing2`

This replaces all instances of `thing1` with `thing2`. Things are specified by their number unless you have defined them as objects. You can abbreviate objects as long as they remain unambiguous. Examples of Thing replacement expressions follow:

```
48=85
TALLTECHNOCOLUMN=TECHLIGHTCOLUMNLONG
TALLT=TECHLI
```

Each of these expressions performs the same replacement, assuming that the objects used in the second and third expressions have been defined correctly.

NOTE: Because of the way DOS operates, you have to omit all the spaces in objects when you use them in the [THINGS] section of your Response file.

MULTIPLE REPLACEMENTS

Multiple replacements are allowed. The simplest forms are as follows:

`thing1,thing2=thing3`	All Things of type `thing1` and `thing2` are replaced with Things of type `thing3`.
`thing-thing2=thing3`	All Things in the range `thing1` to `thing2` are replaced with `thing3`.
`thing1=thing2,thing3`	All Things of type `thing1` are replaced by Things of type `thing2` or `thing3`. Replacements are chosen at random and in equal proportions.
`thing1-thing2=thing3-thing4`	You can specify any number of source and destination Things.

It is possible to specify absolute numbers or ratios of destination Things, and sensible defaults are used when the numbers don't work out right:

```
IMP=DEMON@5          ;5 imps become demons; any others remain imps

IMP=DEMON@5,SPECT@10 ;5 imps become demons, 10 spectres, rest stay as imps
                     ;if fewer than 15 imps, 33% become demons, 66% spectres

IMP=DEMON@5,SPECT    ;5 imps become demons; any others become spectres
                     ;if fewer than 5 imps, all become demons

IMP=DEMON@50%        ;half the imps become demons

thing1,thing2=thing3@5,thing4@20%,thing5 ;you can combine all these elements!
```

CONDITIONAL REPLACEMENTS

You can also set conditions under which a Thing can be replaced in a particular way, with an alternative for if the condition is not met. All commands using the conditional logic must start with a ?. A conditional substitution has three parts:

```
?condition
?ELSE
?END
```

The `condition` expression takes the form

```
thinglist relational-operator value
```

where the components are as defined in Table 31.2.

Table 31.2. Elements of the `condition` expression.

Element	Definition
`thinglist`	A selection of Thing codes such as `BARON@50%,FIRESTICK`
`relational-operator`	One of these: = <> > >= < <=
`value`	An integer in the range 0 to 16383

DM2CONV counts all the Things specified by the `thinglist` and compares this count with the given value. The replacements that are carried out if the condition is met follow straight after the `?condition` expression. The `?ELSE` command signifies the start of the replacements that are carried out if the condition is not met; it is optional. The conditional process must be terminated by the `?END` command. Nesting is allowed.

Some examples that use both Thing numbers and objects follow. The first deals with a WAD's Barons of Hell using just Thing numbers.

```
?3003>10            ;if there are more than 10 Barons of Hell
    3003=69@50%     ;convert 50% of them into Hellknights
?ELSE
    3003=64@1       ;else convert 1 of them into an Archvile
?END
```

Simple conditional replacements can be put into a single line, as in the following example, which ensures that a DOOM II WAD gets a Super Shotgun.

```
?82=0 2001=82@1 ?END    ;if there is no supershotgun,
                        ;convert one shotgun into a supershotgun
```

The principal use of conditional replacements is to ensure that there is a chosen number of a specific item in a WAD. The next Response file segment demonstrates how to make sure that a WAD has just two BFGs.

```
?BFG>2               ;if there are more than 2 Big Guns
    BFG=BFG@2,CELLPAC ;convert the rest into Cellpacks
```

```
?ELSE                       ;otherwise
    ?BFG<2                  ;if there are fewer than 2
        BFG,PLASMA,CELLPAC,CELLCHARGE=BFG@2
                            ;convert any 2 from these others into BFGs
    ?END
?END
```

SPECIAL SUBSTITUTIONS

DM2CONV has a number of special ways in which you can convert Things.

REMOVING THINGS AND (MAYBE) PUTTING THEM BACK

If you set a Thing's type-number to 0, it is ignored by the game engine, so it never appears when you play your WAD. DM2CONV has given this value the name REMOVE in OBJECTS.RSP, so you can remove Cyberdemons from a WAD simply by including lines in either of these formats:

```
16=0
CYBERDEMON=REMOVE
```

These items are still present in the WAD, however, and remain available for remapping into something else. If at the end of your conversion you have had to remove a few items that have no appropriate equivalent in your destination game, you can convert them all into power-ups at one go, thus:

```
0=81                ;Removed Things into Crystal Vials by their number
REMOVE=CRYSTALVIAL  ;or by Objects
```

OVERLAYING THINGS

There are other ways of reusing removed items. If a destination Thing is preceded by a plus sign (+), the source Thing is not altered. Instead, a removed item is converted into the new Thing and placed over the source Thing. This can be useful for livening up the action:

```
DEATHMATCHSTART=+SHOTGUN
```

> **NOTE:** Because DM2CONV cannot increase the number of Things in a WAD, you must ensure that sufficient items have been removed before you use this command.

MIXING THINGS UP

DM2CONV has a second special object in OBJECTS.RSP. It has the value of 9999 and is called MIX. This can be used to scramble the positions of Things specified in the source object list:

```
IMP,SERGEANT,BARON=MIX
```

This shuffles the placing of all the Imps, Sergeants, and Barons. Where there was a monster before, there will still be a monster after conversion—but you won't know which until you go and look.

DIFFICULTY SETTINGS AND OTHER FLAGS

DM2CONV recognizes, and can use, the flags that are associated with Things. These flags are shown in Table 31.3.

Table 31.3. Thing flags.

Flag	Function
1	Difficulty settings 1 and 2
2	Difficulty setting 3
3	Difficulty settings 4 and 5
D	Deafguard
M	Multiplayer mode only

The full statement of a Thing conversion expression, therefore, is as follows:

```
thing1[:flags]... =thing2[@quantity[%]][:flags]...
```

Things in an expression can carry more than one flag, although some are meaningless in certain situations and some take precedence over others. The following sections look at each of them in turn.

DIFFICULTY

If a Difficulty flag (1, 2, or 3) is specified in the source, only the Things marked for appearance at that difficulty setting are changed. Remember, though, that a Thing can be only one thing at once, so if a changed Thing also appears at other Difficulty settings, it will be changed there as well. For example,

```
IMP:1=STIMPAC
```

has the following effects in your new WAD:

- ■ Any Imp set to appear at Difficulty setting 1 is turned into a Stimpack.
- ■ If any of these Imps appear at other Difficulty setting, they are Stimpacks at these settings also.
- ■ Any Imps set only to appear at other Difficulty settings remain as Imps.

If a Difficulty flag is specified in the destination, the remapped Thing has that flag set and appears only at that Difficulty setting. To prevent the second effect just described, you need to type this:

```
IMP:1=STIMPAC:1
```

Now, higher difficulty settings still lose some Imps but do not gain the extra Stimpacks.

DEAFGUARD

The D flag has no meaning for Things other than monsters. Additionally, it has meaning only as a destination flag. In this position it causes converted monsters to become deaf.

MULTIPLAYER

When used as a source flag, M causes only Things set to appear in Multiplayer mode to be converted. As a destination flag, the converted Things appear only in Multiplayer mode.

> **NOTE:** DM2CONV is great for converting a single-player WAD for Deathmatch use because it enables you to remove the monsters and convert them into power-ups.

In addition to supporting the standard Thing flags used by DOOM, DM2CONV has defined a set of flags specific to its own Thing conversion operations. These are shown in Table 31.4.

Table 31.4. DM2CONV flags for additional Thing manipulation.

Flag	Function
0 (zero)	The Thing does not appear at all
A	All Things of this type are processed
O	Only Things of this type that have not already been converted are processed
C	Only Things of this type that have already been converted are processed

These flags can be used in addition to the standard Thing flags although, again, some are meaningless in some situations or are overridden by the standard flags. Some are used to override Symbol settings. (Symbols are discussed later in this chapter.)

ZERO

The 0 flag has meaning only as a destination flag. In this position it causes converted Things to be hidden at all Difficulty settings and in all player modes. The Difficulty flags override this, because its effect is just to clear all of them.

> **TIP:** The zero flag is useful for removing a Thing entirely from the action, without losing its identity. Note that you are not setting the Thing's type-number to 0, as in the REMOVE statement, so it remains in place and you can resurrect it later if you wish.

A, O, AND C

These are used to override the ONCE symbol. Symbols are discussed next.

SYMBOLS

Symbols perform two quite different functions in DM2CONV. The first of these is in the control of the Response file. As you have seen, the Response file can act like a set of subroutines. The grammar of the Response file language permits conditional branching and nesting (including nesting of further Response files), and the flow is controlled by the status of symbols. These can be set and cleared within the Response file or by optional command-line settings when you start the conversion running.

The full syntax of a DM2CONV conversion command, therefore, is as follows:

```
DM2CONV sourcefile [destinationfile]
        [/symbol[=[value]]]... @[responsefile][:labelname]
```

A symbol is defined by either of these commands:

```
SET symbolname
/symbolname
```

Its definition is removed by either of these:

```
SET symbolname=
/symbolname=
```

These symbols then control program flow by means of the set of conditional statements:

```
IFDEF symbol      ;if symbol is defined
IFNDEF symbol     ;if symbol is not defined
ELSE
ENDIF
```

NOTE: Symbols are not the same as variables. Response file branching is determined by whether the symbol is defined (if not, the ELSE branch is followed).

The second function of symbols is to carry information directly to the DM2CONV program. Symbols are given values by the command

```
/symbolname=value
```

in the command line that runs the program. The effects of certain permitted values are hard-coded into DM2CONV. The principal use of this mode of symbol function is to permit user control of the remapping of levels.

The use of symbols need concern you only if you want to write Response files that can make subtle changes in the way some WADs are converted. A hypothetical fragment of a file that uses a symbol to control its action follows. (Readers wanting to know more about the use of symbols should study the DM2CONV documentation files included with the program on the CD-ROM.)

```
SET FROM=DOOM TO=DOOM2

[THINGS]
IFDEF wimp
    2001=82      ;Shotgun to Super Shotgun
ELSE
    3005=71      ;Cacodemon to Pain Elemental
    9=65         ;Sergeant to Chaingunner
ENDIF
```

If this was an extract from a Response file called DD2.RSP, you would now be able to invoke it as follows to produce easier versions for beginners:

```
DM2CONV sourcefile destinationfile /wimp @DD2
```

ONCE

There is one symbol, however, that you should learn how to use. Its purpose is to prevent the sequential parsing of the conversion statements from totally messing up your intentions when you are converting between games that can contain the same Things. Without this symbol, you could end up with the monster distribution in total ruin! Take the Response file MAYHEM.RSP shown next, which was intended to make a WAD just a little trickier to play.

```
SET FROM=DOOM TO=DOOM2

[THINGS]
STIMPAC=IMP
IMP=DEMON
DEMON=CACODEMON
CACODEMON=PAINELEMENT
```

Because DM2CONV processes each of these lines in turn, the end result of running this Response file is a WAD full of Pain Elementals and not much else! To achieve the desired result of just increasing the trickiness of the WAD overall, you should set the ONCE symbol. This is done either by adding /ONCE to the command line that calls the Response file:

```
DM2CONV sourcefile destinationfile /ONCE @MAYHEM
```

or by adding the following line to the file itself before the substitution expressions:

```
SET ONCE     ;or you can use SET ONCE=1
```

The ONCE symbol can take other values. Their effects are shown in Table 31.5.

Table 31.5. Values of the ONCE symbol.

Value	Function
0	Everything is converted.
1	Only Things not already converted are converted.
2	Only Things already converted are converted.
anything else	Same as setting 1—hence, just defining the symbol with /ONCE (which actually gives it the value of "ONCE") defaults to 1, which is what you want.

NOTE: These effects are the same as those of the A, O, and C Thing conversion flags, which is why the flags can be used on single-line conversion expressions to override the effect of this symbol.

EXIT: MOPPING UP AND MOVING ON

This concludes the look at DM2CONV. Basically, you have seen that you can use the utility in two ways:

- Leave it using DEFAULT.RSP, throw your favorite WADs at it, play them and see how it goes—modifying anything you don't like with a map editor of your choice afterwards.

- Decide in advance how you would like a WAD to play in another variant of the game, plan the changes you would make—starting with the simpler (and more immediately rewarding) substitutions of textures, decorations, and monsters—and do a conversion of your own.

Either way you'll have a lot of fun and get a lot more playing time from your WADs.

THE ALCHEMY GRAPHICS LIBRARY

On the CD-ROM that accompanies this book, you will find a sizable library of graphics exclusively created for this book, designed specifically for use with DOOM. If you want to add a special extra touch to your level, give it a whole new look, or employ some of the ideas described in Chapter 25, "Towards a Total Conversion," this graphics library might be just what you are looking for.

This final chapter of the current episode gives an overview of what you can expect to find in the library, how to find what you're looking for, and in some cases, indications of ways to use what is there.

See Chapter 4, "Using the CD-ROM," for instructions on installing the graphics library to your hard drive.

INTRODUCTION TO THE GRAPHICS LIBRARY

Having access to a graphics library can be a great help, especially if you lack the time or equipment to create graphics yourself. I have tried to make this particular library of use to you in a number of ways. First, the graphics are fully optimized to the DOOM palette and will import flawlessly. The graphics themselves are all appropriate for use with the DOOM imagery but can also provide an interesting contrast. They are also presented in families of images, to enable you to use and develop particular themes in your WADs. Finally, due to careful organization and naming of the library's component files, it should be a simple matter to identify and locate the particular file you need.

— *By Justin Fisher*

HOW THE LIBRARY IS ORGANIZED

The *Alchemy* Graphics Library can be found on the CD-ROM in a directory called GRAPHLIB. Within this directory, the individual graphics files are categorized into directories according to their intended use. These categories match the five types of graphics used in DOOM and detailed in Chapter 21, "Changing the Face of DOOM"—textures, sky textures, flats, sprites, and misc.

Within each of these subdirectories, the individual files use a naming system appropriate to the type of images they contain. This is designed to make it easier for you to find the kind of image you want. Each directory is detailed shortly, but each has a text file index within it that lists the files in the directory with a brief description, plus any relevant notes. The name of the index file in each directory is INDEX.TXT.

The SPRITES directory is further divided into subdirectories, one for each set of new monster sprites. Because there can be upwards of 60 sprites to a monster, this avoids a lot of clutter.

GRAPHICAL FILE FORMAT

The graphics are all presented in GIF format and in the DOOM palette. Consequently, they import perfectly into DOOM or DOOM II. If you want to use them for Heretic or Hexen, however, you need to remap them—see Chapter 21 to find out more about this. Inevitably, because the graphics are optimized for DOOM, they look better in DOOM than when remapped for another game.

With this in mind, a copy of each image is also present as a 24-bit TIFF image whenever possible. These are the original pictures, before they were remapped (and possibly touched-up) for DOOM. If you need to remap an image, you should look to see if a TIFF version is available and work from that, rather than the 8-bit version prepared for DOOM.

CONTENTS OF THE GRAPHICS LIBRARY

I have tried to make this a useful collection of images. For replacing graphics in a game like DOOM, a clip-art style of selection—even a large one—is never particularly useful. Such graphics rarely have much in common and are difficult to use together coherently. Rather than produce an all-encompassing collection of random images, I decided to make a smaller selection of several sets of graphics. Each set contains graphics on a similar theme that can be used together and that enable some degree of choice and flexibility in their use. I present these by type.

THE TEXTURES DIRECTORY (GRAPHLIB\TEXTURES)

The textures in this directory include generic stone and brick textures, animated light effects, organic living walls, weathered industrial textures, and other generic themes, as well as some interesting individual textures.

The naming system used for the textures is pretty straightforward; each series of textures designed to fit together has the same name, distinguished by a number at the end. If a series of textures is part of a larger group on the single theme, it has a prefix shared by other textures on that theme. In addition, textures that are part of an animated sequence have a final letter designating their location (frame) within the sequence.

As an example, I_CRET3B.GIF (shown in Figure 32.1) indicates a texture within the I_ theme of textures (in this case, the Industrial theme) that is designed to be used with the other CRET textures. This is the third texture of the CRET family and is the second (B) frame of that texture. An individual, non-animated texture would simply be given a more descriptive filename, if there are no other similar textures.

Figure 32.1.
The I_CRET3B texture.

If this seems complex, you can just use the index file—the idea is simply that the textures of a similar theme be grouped together rather than scattered across the directory.

THE SKY TEXTURES DIRECTORY (GRAPHLIB\SKIES)

Because sky textures have a powerful effect on the feel of the level, I have supplied a selection of vastly different textures, from cold, misty mountains (see Figure 32.2) to desert sandstorms. Although all tile horizontally, some tile vertically as well, making them suitable for levels with tall towers and other places where the vertical-tiling join becomes visible.

Figure 32.2.
The R_FOREST replacement sky texture.

There is no need for a naming system for sky textures; each file is simply given a descriptive name.

THE FLATS DIRECTORY (GRAPHLIB\FLATS)

For the most part, the flats are simply generic textures (gravel, paving stones, metal plates, and so forth). The files use the same naming system as those in the textures directory, with the exception that although there are flats in the same theme, they all appear as individuals, not as part of a series.

THE SPRITES DIRECTORY (GRAPHLIB\SPRITES)

As well as two complete monster sprite sets (one of which is also suitable for replacing player sprites) you will find sprites for new weapons, and also for new scenery—particularly of the type that DOOM lacks, such as trees. There are also several other miscellaneous sprites, such as banners like that shown in Figure 32.3.

Figure 32.3.
The BANNER-M sprite.

The sprite graphics files use the same naming conventions as sprites in DOOM—a 4-character name with another 2 to 4 characters of animation information. If you are not familiar with it, the naming convention is detailed in Chapter 21. In many cases, the graphics are designed to replace an existing set of sprites in DOOM directly, in which case the filename is that of the sprite that it replaces, rather than a name more suited to the sprite set. Check the index file for details.

THE MISCELLANEOUS DIRECTORY (GRAPHLIB\MISC)

There are not many graphics in this category. For the most part they simply provide an alternative to standard DOOM graphics that are not part of the levels—the graphics at the end of a level, or the player's status bar, for example. Like some of the sprites, most of the graphics in the miscellaneous directory are given the filename that corresponds to the WAD entry name of the graphic they are designed to replace. They are unlikely to work properly anywhere else.

EXIT: MOPPING UP AND MOVING ON

So, there you have it. I hope you find the graphics library useful, especially as a quick means of adding a few new graphics to a basic PWAD. For information on actually importing the graphics into a WAD, read Chapter 21 as well as Chapter 30, "Synthesis Tools," and any documentation that is provided with whatever WAD software you decide to use.

This now concludes this episode, which has concentrated on the means at your disposal for building and modifying WADs to your requirements. In the next episode, you will find a complete dossier of information that should prove indispensable during your own unaccompanied forays into the world of WAD alchemy.

EPISODE

MISSION 1: DOOM DATA DOSSIER

MISSION 2: THE LAND OF THE GODS

4

THE DAY AFTER THE APOCALYPSE

THE ANOMALIES

By way of an introduction to this mission, this chapter provides a quick illustrated tour of the visual anomalies that can occur in DOOM. It looks at what can go wrong with your WADs, what causes the problems, and what can be done to prevent them.

DOOM'S VISUAL ANOMALIES

Many of the visual anomalies that can occur in DOOM have been covered in earlier chapters. Some that haven't been discussed before are introduced here, and some old favorites are reviewed again.

PINK BUG AND TUTTI FRUTTI

If you have worked through the WAD sorties of Episode 2, Mission 1, "A Hell of Your Very Own," you are familiar with the causes of the two graphical anomalies known as Pink Bug and Tutti Frutti. These two anomalies are very similar to each other. Pink Bug results from the use of short textures on spaces that are too large for them. In Figure 33.1, the 24-pixel texture STEPTOP has been used on a tall wall. Notice how the tiling on this wall has gone awry. Textures of heights other than 128 pixels do not tile correctly in DOOM.

— By Steve Benner

Figure 33.1.
A wall with Pink Bug.

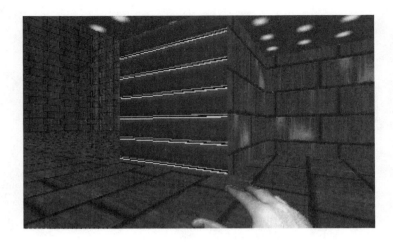

The Tutti Frutti effect results from the use of transparent textures on single-sided main textures. It is similar to Pink Bug but manifests itself in areas that should be see-through.

HALL OF MIRRORS

Perhaps the most infamous of all of DOOM's visual errors is the Hall of Mirrors (HOM) effect. It is unlikely that you have completed many WADs without encountering it somewhere. Figure 33.2 is an example of how this effect appears.

Figure 33.2.
A nasty attack of HOM.

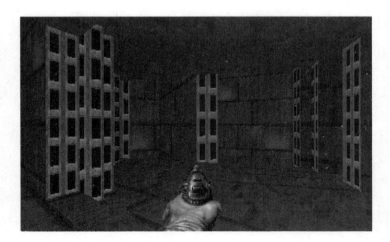

In DOOM and DOOM II, the effect of HOM is much more spectacular than this printed figure suggests. On a computer monitor, it flashes and flickers. (It isn't so bad in Heretic and Hexen, but it is still to be avoided!) This anomaly occurs when errors in the WAD result in DOOM having nothing to paint on part of the display. As a consequence, an area of the screen is left unrefreshed between updates of the view, and whatever was there before remains in the gap.

DOOM's video-buffering technique works by building several separate images in video pages out of sight of the player and cycling through these pages to produce a smooth screen representation of the player's changing view. When an area of the display is not refreshed completely between these cycles (as occurs when there are any unpainted areas), parts of earlier images will remain. These older images continue to flash before the player, causing the flickering effect associated with this anomaly.

There are a number of causes of the Hall of Mirrors effect, each producing a slightly different variation on the main theme.

HOM FROM MISSING TEXTURES

The most common cause of HOM is the omission of an essential texture—usually from a line's main (or normal) texture slot. The particular example shown in Figure 33.2 was caused by the omission of a texture on a door face's essential upper. While the door is closed—as in the figure—this texture slot acts in the same way as any of the adjacent main textures. When texture is omitted from this slot, the result is as you see in the figure.

HOM FROM EDGE OVERLOAD

The problem known as *edge overload* was mentioned briefly while discussing stairs in Chapter 12, "Putting Sectors to Work." The cause of this affliction is the graphics engine being given too many vertical surfaces to render in one update. The result is that it simply gives up after it has painted as many as it can, leaving the rest as they were. HOM results in the unpainted areas of the screen.

Versions of DOOM earlier than 1.4 exhibit this problem sooner than later versions do. Figure 33.3 illustrates how this problem is beginning to affect the sample WAD from the earlier WAD sorties (ARENA.WAD) when it is played with DOOM v1.2.

Figure 33.3.
HOM from edge overload.

The view shown here is from the extreme eastern edge of the arena balcony, looking back across the watch-tower and the pond. If you consider the map of this area, you see that there are a lot of small lines here for the engine to look through. Look carefully at Figure 33.3, and you can see that the problem is at its worst in the areas over the pond—especially over the stepping-stones—and in the section over the switch that operates the lift (note the sky directly above the player's index finger in the figure).

HOM caused by edge overload can be distinguished from the common effect of omitting texture by the inconsistency of the former's appearance. Edge overload manifests itself in different places as the player moves around (or merely looks around) an area of the WAD. HOM from missing textures appears only (and consistently) in the area of the screen that the missing texture should occupy.

In the example shown in Figure 33.3, when the player takes a single step forward from the point shown, the effect vanishes—presumably because the removal of the complex of lines making up the lift at the extreme left edge of the screen drops the number of edges in view back below the critical threshold value.

Edge overload can be difficult to avoid in large and complicated open areas like the arena, because of the vast number of lines in view. The problem is much reduced in later versions of the game, but the effect can still occur. When it does, the only solution is to cut down on those regions of a WAD that provide open vistas through the entire map, or to make your maps (or at least the views in them) less complex. Sorry, but that's the way it is.

CAUTION: If your WAD ever requires DOOM to display more than 128 distinct floor and ceiling surfaces (collectively known as *visplanes*) simultaneously, a more serious error occurs: DOOM crashes back to DOS with a `Too many visplanes!` message. This can arise from wide open views across many sectors—another good reason to limit such views. It can also occur if your sector shapes are too complex. The solution is usually to make your sector shapes simpler or limit how much of the map the player can see from any point.

SLIME TRAILS

Another cause of HOM (one that is, thankfully, becoming rare) is a faulty nodes tree. Nodes generators are much better than they used to be, but nodes-tree faults can still arise from time to time. The nodes tree is essentially the structure from which all views are derived, so it is understandable that display anomalies result from faults in this structure.

HOM can result from nodes-tree faults that leave holes in the display information. The result is similar to that caused by missing textures. These anomalies always occupy the same place—and are always present—but they can be distinguished from a missing texture error by virtue of their almost invariably narrow form. They tend to appear as thin strips of some visual anomaly (usually HOM) on odd walls, usually in areas of complex shapes.

In addition to causing HOM, a faulty nodes tree can give rise to spurious transparent areas on walls. Being thin, these effects usually show up as a silvery shimmer down a wall. This gives the effect its name—a *slime trail*.

One such example is shown in Figure 33.4. Notice how the player is pointing to a transparent strip that runs up part of the right-hand wall. The effect occupies only a small section of wall—much smaller than the smallest line used on the map hereabouts—ruling out an editing error.

Figure 33.4.

A slime trail down a solid wall.

This is, in fact, caused by a faulty build of the nodes in this area—in turn caused by the awkward angles at which all the walls run in this particular WAD. The faulty build has led DOOM to believe that there is something to display beyond this section of line. Fortunately, DOOM found something there in this case: the corridor beyond. Had there been void beyond this wall, HOM would have been the result—just as if a texture was missing.

As already noted, faults involving nodes builders are becoming very rare, especially with current state-of-the-art nodes builders. Some peculiar map layouts can just fool the logic of even the best of these builders, however, so these odd effects are always a possibility, albeit an unlikely one. If you suspect your nodes builder of causing problems, you can always test this by rebuilding the WAD's nodes tree using another nodes builder (either a stand-alone one, such as WARM, or one built into another editor). If the effect vanishes (or moves) then you have established the cause (and may well have solved the problem at the same time). If the effect is the same, however, the cause is most likely not related to the nodes tree, for very few nodes builders will produce the same tree as another nodes builder. If you find odd invisible missing or invisible walls recur in your maps, even after trying several nodes builders, then go back to checking your line layouts.

MEDUSA

An example of the dreaded Medusa effect is shown in Figure 33.5. This is caused by using overlapping or vertically tiled textures on a two-sided line's main texture. Some editors' consistency checkers will help you here by warning you about using these textures in this way. The precise form of this effect differs depending on the texture in use; Figure 33.5 is what happens when BROVINE is used. The other consequence of this effect is that the game slows down to an absolute crawl. The problem is more acute when more of the screen is taken up by the faulty texture. The best way of getting out of this if it occurs during play is to hit the Tab key to bring up the automap. You can then turn to face away from the offending wall and regain proper control of the game.

Figure 33.5.
The Medusa effect.

MOIRÉ, OR FLASH OF BLACK

Another effect that has not been discussed previously is an annoying, strange flash of black (or brown) across the screen that can occur as the player moves into a new sector. This happens when moving between sectors with large differences of ceiling height (more than 559 units in DOOM v1.2, much higher in later versions). The taller a sector becomes, the worse the effect—hence one of its names: the Tall Room Error. Figure 33.6 shows what the effect looks like if the player passes through it slowly enough: a brown pattern of moiré fringes that sweeps across the player's view.

Make the changes in your sector ceiling heights more gradual if you are plagued with this problem.

Figure 33.6.
A bad case of moiré.

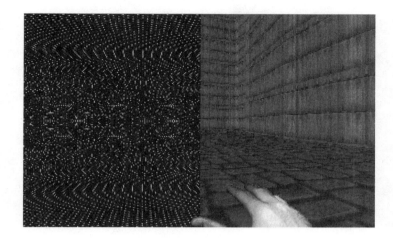

POLYOBJ OVERLAP

Finally, Figure 33.7 shows what can happen if you build your Hexen PolyObjs incorrectly. This figure shows the result of producing a mirrored pair on top of each other. Both members of the pair were, in fact, invisible until the action was triggered. Take care with the placing of your Start Spots to avoid this kind of visual anomaly.

Figure 33.7.
A case of overlapping PolyObjs in Hexen.

EXIT: MOPPING UP AND MOVING ON

The anomalies that can occur in DOOM are legion. Mostly, though, they occur irregularly, or as a result of breaches of the construction rules that have been explained elsewhere in this book. The further into DOOM editing you go, the more esoteric the errors and anomalies become. Some you can exploit and treat as deliberate features of your WAD. Mostly, though, you'll be more interested in identifying and eliminating the causes. I hope this chapter helps you out.

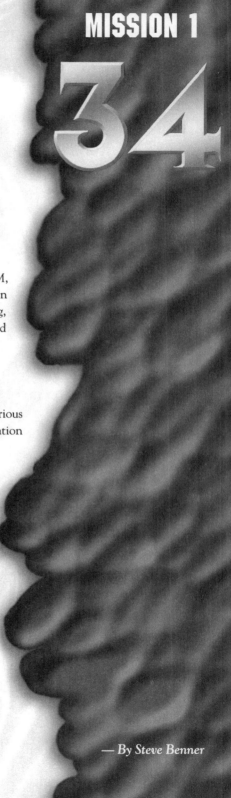

ESSENTIAL THING INFORMATION

This chapter provides detailed reference information for all DOOM, DOOM II, Heretic, and Hexen Things, organized by basic category. In addition, it includes general notes on the characteristics of each Thing, as well as specific information on the use of some of the more specialized ones.

NOTES ON THE TABLE ENTRIES

Each of the tables in this chapter gives information about each of the various Things that can appear on the map at the start of a level. This information includes the following:

- **The Thing's type-code number:** This identifies to the game engine what the Thing actually is. If DOOM does not recognize this code, the game crashes back to DOS as the level starts.

- **The Thing's four-letter sprite prefix:** This identifies the sprite family used to represent the Thing on-screen. Some of the tables also give the sequence of sprite suffixes used to represent animated objects. (These are not given where sequences are complex, as with enemies and some special Things.)

- **The Thing's basic characteristics,** as detailed next.

— *By Steve Benner*

BASIC CHARACTERISTICS

Some Things have particular gaming characteristics associated with them. Sometimes, these characteristics are common to a whole group of Things—all monsters can be killed and count toward the final Kills tally, for instance. Other characteristics are specific to individual Things, however; these are indicated by means of special icons in the tables that follow.

Things that count as bonuses are marked 🐾—any of these that remain uncollected at the end of a level are deducted from the Bonuses score. Things marked with 🦶 can be picked up by players and added to their inventory for later use. (These appear in Heretic and Hexen only, of course.)

Generally speaking, when a level starts, Things are standing on the floor of the sector in which they are located (or at a fixed height above it, determined by the form of their sprite). Some hug the ceiling instead; these are marked with 👃.

NOTE: DOOM map editors often have Things incorrectly described or oddly categorized. If you are in doubt about which Things are which in your maps, you should check the code numbers your editor uses (or build yourself a test WAD to see).

THINGS OF DOOM AND DOOM II

This section presents all the Things available for use in DOOM and DOOM II. All of DOOM's Things can be used in DOOM II, but many new items were added to DOOM II. These new items are marked in the tables with **DOOM II**.

PLAYER AND ENEMY START POSITIONS

The location of all players and enemies at the start of a level is determined by Player and Enemy Start Things. Table 34.1 gives the details of these.

NOTE: In DOOM and DOOM II, all players and enemies obstruct each other if their lateral extents coincide. For collision detection purposes, players and monsters are regarded as infinitely tall. (The dimensions of DOOM's Things are presented later in this chapter.)
All enemies can be killed and count toward the final Kill ratio.

Sprites of Things marked 🖌 use a substitution color to replace the greens of the stored sprite. (See Chapter 22, "Hacking the DOOM Code," for more details.) Table 34.1 also includes codes for the Things that affect the locations of player and monster materialization during play: teleport landings (which are covered in detail in Chapter 18, "Let's Get the Hell Out of Here!") and DOOM II's Boss Shooter and Spawn Spot (discussed next).

Table 34.1. DOOM/DOOM II player and enemy starts.

Thing	Code	Sprite Family	Characteristics
		Player Start Positions	
Player 1 start position	1	PLAY	
Player 2 start position	2	PLAY	
Player 3 start position	3	PLAY	
Player 4 start position	4	PLAY	
Deathmatch start position	11	PLAY	
		Enemy Start Positions	
Former Human	3004	POSS	
Wolfenstein 3D SS Officer	84	SSWV	DOOM II
Former Human Sergeant	9	SPOS	
Former Human Commando	65	CPOS	DOOM II
Imp	3001	TROO	
Demon	3002	SARG	
Spectre	58	SARG	
Lost Soul	3006	SKUL	
Cacodemon	3005	HEAD	
Hell Knight	69	BOS2	DOOM II
Baron of Hell	3003	BOSS	
Arachnotron	68	BSPI	DOOM II
Pain Elemental	71	PAIN	DOOM II
Revenant	66	SKEL	DOOM II
Mancubus	67	FATT	DOOM II
Arch-Vile	64	VILE	DOOM II
Spider Mastermind	7	SPID	
Cyberdemon	16	CYBR	
Boss Brain	88	BBRN	
		Miscellaneous	
Teleport landing	14		
Boss Shooter	89		DOOM II
Spawn Spot	87		DOOM II

CAUTION: Never have more than one of each of the Single and Cooperative Player Start positions in a level. This creates strange player clones that take hurt and pass it on to the real player but otherwise take no other part in the game. id Software also cautions against the use of more than ten Deathmatch Start Positions in one level—apparently, dire results can occur if you do this.

Using the Boss Shooter in DOOM II

Use of DOOM II's Shooter from the Icon of Sin level is not obvious and needs a little explanation. The functional parts of this special monster are the Boss Shooter Thing (#89) and the Spawn Spot Thing (#87). The Boss Shooter acts as a monster in that, when "awakened," it begins firing the spinning Spawning Cubes. These are fired toward a Spawn Spot, where they transform into standard monsters (chosen at random). The Spawn Spot can be placed anywhere in the level with the Boss Shooter; the Spawning Cubes can pass through all intervening walls to reach their target. If more than one Spawn Spot is used, the Boss Shooter chooses one at random for each new Cube.

The Boss Shooter itself is invisible; its Cubes appear to materialize out of nowhere. If you want to make it look as though they are being spawned by something in particular, you need to build that something around the Shooter.

The Boss Brain "monster" is unrelated to the Boss Shooter, except in name. If you know anything of id Software, you will recognize this as a joke! It is classed as a monster only because it can be killed and contributes toward the Kills score.

CAUTION: It is possible to use multiple Shooters in a level, in which case they each use all the Spawn Spots provided. This can be counterproductive, however, because if two Spawning Cubes reach the same Spawn Spot simultaneously, their resultant monsters become glued together. (See Figure 34.1.) This effectively blocks the Spot against all future materializations (monsters continue to materialize but are added to the growing amalgam). For this reason, it is wise to provide plenty of space around your Spawn Spots to enable monsters to move away from them quickly after materialization, and to limit the number of Shooters to one per level.

Figure 34.1.
The result of too many Boss Shooters for one Spawn Spot!

DOOM AND DOOM II WEAPONRY

Table 34.2 gives details of all the weapons and ammunition that can be laid out for players in DOOM and DOOM II WADs. All these items can be collected up to the player's maximum carrying capacity. None of them count toward the final Items score.

Table 34.2. DOOM/DOOM II weapons and ammunition codes.

Thing	Code	Sprite Family	Characteristics
		Weapons	
Chainsaw	2005	CSAW	
Shotgun	2001	SHOT	
Combat shotgun	82	SGN2	DOOM II
Chaingun	2002	MGUN	
Rocket launcher	2003	LAUN	
Plasma gun	2004	PLAS	
BFG 9000	2006	BFUG	
		Ammunition	
Ammo clip	2007	CLIP	
Box of Ammo	2048	AMMO	
Few shotgun shells	2008	SHEL	
Box of Shells	2049	SBOX	
Rocket	2010	ROCK	

continues

Table 34.2. continued

Thing	Code	Sprite Family	Characteristics
Box of Rockets	2046	BROK	
Cell charge	2047	CELL	
Cell charge pack	17	CELP	
Backpack	8	BPAK	

DOOM AND DOOM II POWER-UPS

Table 34.3 gives details of DOOM and DOOM II's power-ups. All of these can be picked up by a player, providing they can be used at that time. Some count toward the final Items score, but not all; those that do are indicated in the Characteristics column of the table.

Table 34.3. DOOM/DOOM II power-ups and key codes.

Thing	Code	Sprite	Sequence	Characteristics
		Power-Ups		
Spiritual Armor	2015	BON2	ABCDCB	
Security Armor	2018	ARM1	AB	
Combat Armor	2019	ARM2	AB	
Radiation Suit	2025	SUIT	A	(up to v1.2)
Invulnerability Artifact	2022	PINV	ABCD	
Health Potion	2014	BON1	ABCDCB	
Stimpack	2011	STIM	A	
Medikit	2012	MEDI	A	
Soul Sphere	2013	SOUL	ABCDCB	
Mega Sphere	83	MEGA	ABCD	
Berserk Pack	2023	PSTR	A	
Blur Artifact	2024	PINS	ABCD	
Computer Map	2026	PMAP	ABCDCB	
Light Amplification Visor	2045	PVIS	AB	

Thing	Code	Sprite	Sequence	Characteristics
		Keycards		
Blue keycard	5	BKEY	AB	
Red keycard	13	RKEY	AB	
Yellow keycard	6	YKEY	AB	
Blue skull key	40	BSKU	AB	
Red skull key	38	RSKU	AB	
Yellow skull key	39	YSKU	AB	

DOOM AND DOOM II DECORATIONS

DOOM's decorations fall into two categories: blocking and non-blocking. These are detailed in Table 34.4. Items marked 🔫 can be destroyed by firing at them.

NOTE: Blocking decorations are regarded as infinitely tall for collision detection purposes. The radius of these items is given in Table 34.5.

Table 34.4. DOOM/DOOM II's decorative Things.

Thing	Code	Sprite	Sequence	Characteristics
		Obstructions		
Barrel	2035	BAR1	AB	🔫
Burning barrel	70	FCAN	ABC	DOOM II
Tall green pillar	30	COL1	A	
Short green pillar	31	COL2	A	
Tall red pillar	32	COL3	A	
Short red pillar	33	COL4	A	
Candelabra	35	CBRA	A	
Short green pillar with heart	36	COL5	AB	
Short red pillar with skull	37	COL6	A	
Evil Eye symbol	41	CEYE	ABCD	
Floating Skull	42	FSKU	ABC	

continues

Table 34.4. continued

Thing	Code	Sprite	Sequence	Characteristics
Burnt gray tree 43	TRE1	A		
Stalagmite	47	SMIT	A	
Tall technocolumn	48	ELEC	A	
Large brown tree	54	TRE2	A	
Tall blue firestick	44	TBLU	ABCD	
Tall green firestick	45	TGRE	ABCD	
Tall red firestick	46	TRED	ABCD	
Short blue firestick	55	SMBT	ABCD	
Short green firestick	56	SMGT	ABCD	
Short red firestick	57	SMRT	ABCD	
Tall technolamp	85	TLMP	ABCD	DOOM II
Short technolamp	86	TLP2	ABCD	DOOM II
Floor lamp	2028	COLU	A	
Impaled human	25	POL1	A	
Twitching impaled human	26	POL6	AB	
Skull on a pole	27	POL4	A	
5-skull shish-kebab	28	POL2	A	
Pile of skulls and candles	29	POL3	AB	
Hanged victim, twitching	49	GOR1	ABCD	(rope)
Suspended victim	50	GOR2	A	(rope)
Suspended victim, 1-legged	51	GOR3	A	(rope)
Hanging pair of legs	52	GOR4	A	(rope)
Hanging single leg	53	GOR5	A	(rope)
Hanging victim, no guts	73	HDB1	A	DOOM II (rope)
Hanging victim, no guts/brain	74	HDB2	A	DOOM II (rope)
Hanging torso, looking down	75	HDB3	A	DOOM II (rope)
Hanging torso, open skull	76	HDB4	A	DOOM II (rope)
Hanging torso, looking up	77	HDB5	A	DOOM II (rope)
Hanging torso, no brain	78	HDB6	A	DOOM II (rope)
Hanging Billy	72	KEEN	*	DOOM II (rope) (pistol)

Thing	Code	Sprite	Sequence	Characteristics
		Non-Blocking Gore		
Candle	34	CAND	A	
Exploded player	10	PLAY	W	
Exploded player (as previous)	12	PLAY	W	
Dead player	15	PLAY	N	
Dead Former Human	18	POSS	L	
Dead Former Human Sergeant	19	SPOS	L	
Dead Imp	20	TROO	M	
Dead Demon	21	SARG	N	
Dead Cacodemon	22	HEAD	L	
Dead Lost Soul (invisible)	23	SKUL	K	
Pool of blood and guts	24	POL5	A	
Suspended victim, arms akimbo	59	GOR2	A	
Hanging pair of legs	60	GOR4	A	
Suspended victim, 1-legged	61	GOR3	A	
Hanging single leg	62	GOR5	A	
Hanged victim, twitching	63	GOR1	ABCD	
Pool of guts	79	POB1	A	DOOM II
Pool of blood	80	POB2	A	DOOM II
Brains and Spine	81	BRS1	A	DOOM II

TIP: Many of DOOM's hanging items of gore are provided in both varieties: blocking and non-blocking. Use the non-blocking type wherever there is room for a player to pass beneath the object; otherwise, your players encounter an invisible barrier as they try to move under it. On the other hand, if you hang these items in low-ceilinged areas, you should use the blocking variety for added realism.

SIZES OF DOOM AND DOOM II THINGS

Table 34.5 gives the sizes of most of DOOM and DOOM II's Things. Although these are quoted as a radius (or as a diameter—both figures are given here for convenience), don't forget that Things are really square in their extent.

Table 34.5. Vital statistics of DOOM/DOOM II Things.

Thing	Radius	Diameter	Height	Initial Health
Player	16	32	56	100
Former Human	20	40	56	20
Wolfenstein 3D SS	20	40	56	50
Former Human Sergeant	20	40	56	30
Former Commando	20	40	56	70
Imp	20	40	56	60
Demon	30	60	56	150
Spectre	30	60	56	150
Lost Soul	16	32	56	100
Cacodemon	31	62	56	400
Hell Knight	24	48	64	500
Baron of Hell	24	48	64	1000
Arachnotron	64	128	64	500
Pain Elemental	31	62	56	400
Revenant	20	40	56	300
Mancubus	48	96	64	600
Arch-Vile	20	40	56	700
Spider Mastermind	128	256	100	3000
Cyberdemon	40	80	110	4000
Boss Brain	16	32	16	250
Billy	16	32	72	100
Gettable items	20	40	16	—
Barrel	10	20	42	20
Large brown tree	32	64	*	—
Other obstacles	16	32	*	—

*For collision detection purposes, all obstacles are deemed infinitely high.

HERETIC THINGS

This section presents all the Things available for use in Heretic WADs. These divide into the same categories as DOOM Things, with the addition of Sounds.

HERETIC PLAYER AND ENEMY STARTS

The location of all players and enemies at the start of a Heretic level is determined by Player and Enemy Start Things in the same way as they are in DOOM. Table 34.6 gives details of the codes and sprites used in this game variant. It also includes the codes of the special Things used to control where player and monster materializations occur.

Table 34.6. Heretic Player and Enemy Starts.

Thing	Code	Sprite Family	Characteristics
Player Start Positions			
Player 1	1	PLAY	
Player 2	2	PLAY	
Player 3	3	PLAY	
Player 4	4	PLAY	
Deathmatch	11	PLAY	
Enemy Start Positions			
Gargoyle	66	IMPX	
Gargoyle leader	5	IMPX	
Golem	68	MUMM	
Golem ghost	69	MUMM	
Nitrogolem	45	MUMM	
Nitrogolem ghost	46	MUMM	
Undead warrior	64	KNIG	
Undead warrior ghost	65	KNIG	
Disciple of D'Sparil	15	WZRD	
Sabreclaw	90	CLNK	
Weredragon	70	BEAS	
Ophidian	92	SNKE	
Ironlich	6	HEAD	
Maulotaur	9	MNTR	
D'Sparil	7	SRCR	

continues

Table 34.6. continued

Thing	Code	Sprite Family	Characteristics
		Miscellaneous	
D'Sparil teleport spot	56	—	
Teleport Destination	14	—	
Blue Teleport Glitter	52	TGLT	
Red Teleport Glitter	74	TGLT	

 Heretic's Teleport Glitter is entirely non-functional, merely providing decoration. It is included in the tables for convenience.

Using D'Sparil and His Teleport Spots

If D'Sparil is used in a Heretic level, several D'Sparil Teleport Spots (Thing #56) are also needed. These determine where the D'Sparil monster rematerializes after vanishing when fired on by players. Do not have two D'Sparils active at once in a level, in case they both attempt to materialize simultaneously at the same spot.

HERETIC WEAPONRY

Table 34.7 gives details of the weapons and ammunition that can be placed in a Heretic WAD for use by the player.

Table 34.7. Heretic weapons and ammunition.

Thing	Code	Sprite Family
	Weapons	
Gauntlets	2005	WGNT
Crossbow	2001	WBOW
Dragon Claw	53	WBLS
Phoenix rod	2003	WPHX
Hellstaff	2004	WSKL
Mace	2002	WMCE

Thing	Code	Sprite Family
	Ammunition	
Wand crystal (10)	10	AMG1
Wand crystal (50)	12	AMG2
Crossbow bolts (5)	18	AMC1
Crossbow quiver (20)	19	AMC2
Energy orb (10)	54	AMB1
Energy orb (25)	55	AMB2
Hellstaff lesser runes	20	AMS1
Hellstaff greater runes	21	AMS2
Phoenix orb (1)	22	AMP1
Phoenix orb (10)	23	AMP2
Mace spheres (20)	13	AMM1
Mace spheres (100)	16	AMM2
Bag of holding	8	BAGH

HERETIC POWER-UPS

Table 34.8 presents details of Heretic's power-up artifacts. Some items are used immediately after they are acquired; others can be added to the players' inventory for use as desired. The latter are marked in Table 34.8 with the icon.

Table 34.8. Heretic power-ups and keys.

Thing	Code	Sprite Family	Characteristics
		Power-Ups	
Crystal vial	81	PTN1	
Mystic Urn	32	SPHL	
Silver Shield	85	SHLD	
Enchanted Shield	31	SHD2	
Map Scroll	35	SPMP	
Quartz flask	82	PTN2	
Morph Ovum	30	EGGC	

continues

Table 34.8. continued

Thing	Code	Sprite Family	Characteristics
Time Bomb of the Ancients	34	FBMB	
Chaos device	36	ATLP	
Invisibility	75	INVS	
Wings of Wrath	83	SOAR	
Ring of Invulnerability	84	INVU	
Tome of Power	86	PWBK	
Torch	33	TRCH	
		Keys	
Green key	73	AKYY	
Blue key	79	BKYY	
Yellow key	80	CKYY	

HERETIC DECORATIVE THINGS

Table 34.9 gives details of Heretic's decorative Things. As in DOOM, some block players' and monsters' movements, whereas others do not. In addition, some of these decorations also constitute hazards to players—see Chapter 20, "Finishing Touches," for details.

Table 34.9. Heretic decorations.

Thing	Code	Sprite Family	Characteristics
		Non-Blocking	
Hanging Moss (large)	48	MOS1	
Hanging Moss (small)	49	MOS2	
Chandelier	28	CHDL	
Skull on short rope	26	SKH4	
Skull on medium rope	25	SKH3	
Skull on long rope	24	SKH2	
Skull on very long rope	17	SKH1	

Thing	Code	Sprite Family	Characteristics
Hanging corpse	51	HCOR	
Wall torch	50	WTRH	
Blue Teleport Glitter	52	TGLT	
Red Teleport Glitter	74	TGLT	
Non-Hazardous Obstructions			
Stalactite (small)	39	STCS	
Stalactite (large)	40	STCL	
Stalagmite (small)	37	STGS	
Stalagmite (large)	38	STGL	
Barrel	44	BARL	
Small pillar	29	SMPL	
Brown pillar	47	BRPL	
Serpent torch	27	SRTC	
Demon brazier	76	KFR1	
Blue door gizmo	94	KGZB	
Green door gizmo	95	KGZG	
Yellow door gizmo	96	KGZY	
Hazardous Obstructions			
Volcano	87	VLCO	
Pop-pod	2035	PPOD	
Pop-pod Spawner	43	—	

HERETIC SOUNDS

Table 34.10 gives the codes for Heretic's final category of decorative Things: the Sounds. These fall into two categories: Environmental Sounds and Ambient Sounds. During play, Environmental Sounds are continuous and appear to emanate from the location at which they are placed. Ambient Sounds, on the other hand, are heard at random intervals during the game, and always at a constant volume so as to appear to follow the player around.

Table 34.10. Heretic sounds.

Thing	Code
Environmental Sounds	
Waterfall Sound	41
Wind Sound	42
Ambient Sounds	
Scream	1200
Squish	1201
Water Drops	1202
Slow Footsteps	1203
Heartbeat	1204
Bells	1205
Growl	1206
Magic	1207
Laughter	1208
Running Footsteps	1209

HEXEN THINGS

Hexen has a wider range of Things than earlier game variants. Its Things can also be a little trickier to use because of the way their control has been extended. Hexen's programmability through its Action Control Scripts has introduced another characteristic of Things that needs to be presented in the tables. This is their predefined Scripting Name by which each type of Thing is referenced in an Action Control Script. In addition, some Things can be spawned using the Thing_Spawn (and related) special actions. These actions require a code number that differs from the map code; this is also given in the tables, under the heading Spawn Code. (Details of the special action codes that spawn Things in Hexen are given in "Hexen's Special Codes," a chapter on the CD-ROM.)

Hexen also has a facility for setting the height above the floor at which a Thing is positioned when the level starts. In general, unless it is marked ⸸ in the tables, a Thing that is positioned at a nonzero starting height is subjected to gravity as the level starts. Some remain where positioned, however, for the duration of the level, and these are marked ⬤ in the tables.

HEXEN PLAYER AND ENEMY STARTS

One of the major changes between Hexen and earlier variants of the game engine is that blocking Things are no longer deemed to have infinite vertical extent. In Hexen, it is possible for players to jump over obstacles (including monsters and other players) that are positioned at suitable heights below them. Indeed, items that in other games were viewed as obstacles can now be used as steps up to otherwise inaccessible areas.

Table 34.11 gives details of Player and Enemy Start Things in Hexen, including the diameter and height of enemies.

Table 34.11. Hexen Player and Enemy Starts.

Thing	ACS Identifier	Map Code	Spawn Code	Sprite Family	Diameter	Height
		Player Start Positions				
Player 1 start	Player_1_start	1		*	32	56
Player 2 start	Player_2_start	2		*	32	56
Player 3 start	Player_3_start	3		*	32	56
Player 4 start	Player_4_start	4		*	32	56
Deathmatch start	Player_Deathmatch	11				
		Enemy Start Positions				
Ettin	C_Ettin	10060	5	FDMN	40	68
Centaur	C_Centaur	107	1	CENT	40	64
Ghost Centaur			103	CENT		
Centaur Leader	C_CentaurLeader	115	2	CENT	40	64
Chaos Serpent (Fire)	C_Demon	31	3	DEMN	64	64
Ghost Serpent (Fire)			101	DEMN		
Chaos Serpent (Gas)	C_Demon2	8080	—	DEM2	64	64
Ghost Serpent (Gas)			100	DEMN		
Reiver†	C_Wraith	34	8	WRTH	40	56
Reiver Leader†	C_Wraith2	10011	9	WRTH	40	68
Stalker	C_Serpent	121	6	SSPT	64	70
Stalker Leader	C_SerpentLeader	120	7	SSPT	64	70
Wendigo	C_IceGuy	8020	20	ICEY	44	75
Death Wyvern	C_Dragon	254	—	DRAG	40	65
Dark Bishop†	C_Bishop	114	19	BISH	44	65
Heresiarch	C_Heresiarch	10080	—	SORC	80	110
Zedek	C_FighterBoss	10100	—	PLAY	32	64
Traductus	C_ClericBoss	10101	—	CLER	32	64

continues

Table 34.11. continued

Thing	ACS Identifier	Map Code	Spawn Code	Sprite Family	Diameter	Height
Menelkir	C_MageBoss	10102	—	MAGE	32	64
Korax	C_Korax	10200	—	KORX	130	115
		Miscellaneous				
Map Spot	X_MapSpot	9001				
Map Spot with Gravity	X_MapSpotGravity	9013				
Teleport Destination	Player_TeleportSpot	14				
Teleport fog	Z_TeleportSmoke	140		TSMK		

*Player sprites vary with player class.

†Monsters marked with a dagger do not activate trigger lines of the Enemy Crosses category.

Hexen's teleports operate differently from those in other game variants. They require each Teleport Destination Thing to be directly tagged to its triggering action by means of its own tid field, rather than the tag field of the sector it occupies. See "Hexen's Special Codes" on the CD-ROM for details.

Hexen's Teleport Fog is entirely decorative and not necessary to the functioning of the teleport.

HEXEN MAP SPOTS

Hexen's various *Map Spots* have specific functions, associated with particular Special Actions and Things. The Death Wyvern, for instance, requires several Map Spots to determine its flight path. Other uses for Map Spots are covered in later sections of this chapter.

Using Hexen's Death Wyvern

Hexen's Death Wyvern requires special treatment in the layout of a WAD; otherwise, you risk causing the game to hang the computer during play. In addition to placing the Death Wyvern itself (Thing #254) on the map, you must also place a Map Spot (Thing #9001) with a tid set to match that of the Wyvern. When the Wyvern is awakened, it flies toward this Map Spot.

The Map Spot's arg fields (usually used to parameterize a Thing's special action characteristic) must then be used to specify the tids of up to five additional Map Spots. Each time the Wyvern visits this Map Spot, it chooses one of the further Map Spots to fly to next. Each Map Spot the Wyvern visits must provide at least one other Map Spot for the Wyvern to visit next.

This mechanism permits the designer to have some say in the flight path taken by the Wyvern. However, it does not fly directly from Map Spot to Map Spot but deviates to attack the player from time to time.

If the Wyvern ever reaches a Map Spot that does not specify further Map Spots in its argument fields, the game hangs. There is no limit to the number of times a Wyvern can visit any one Map Spot, so it is perfectly feasible to use a single Map Spot that simply references itself if you just want the Wyvern to fly around in circles.

Another Hexen Thing that makes use of the Map Spot is the final showdown monster, Korax. This is another of Hexen's Things that must be used correctly if you want to avoid crashing the game engine. Before looking at this, however, it is necessary to review the way Hexen's monsters can trigger special actions.

HEXEN MONSTERS AND SPECIAL ACTIONS

You recall from "Programming the Action" on the CD-ROM that Things in Hexen are capable of triggering special actions through their new Special Characteristic. All the monsters listed in Table 34.11 trigger this special action when they are killed (or banished, using the Banishment Device), with the sole exception of Korax, which uses seven special dedicated scripts, rather than a Special Characteristic. (Scripts and Hexen's ACS scripting language are described in detail in "Hexen's Scripting Language" on the CD-ROM.)

Using Korax in Your Hexen Levels

Korax (see Figure 34.2) requires more setting up even than the Death Wyvern. This is because this monster is extremely versatile in its capabilities and can be used to summon up virtually any sort of mischief that you fancy. Unfortunately, if you don't set everything up just right, the only sort of mischief you can rely upon is the game engine crashing gracelessly back to DOS!

The first requirement is that you provide Korax with several Map Spots (Thing #9001) in the level. Additionally, each of these Map Spots must have their tid field set to the value 249. Finally, you must include seven ACS scripts in your WAD, with the numbers 249 to 255, inclusive. These scripts are called by the game engine at various times during a player's fight with Korax (Table 34.12 gives the details) and provide the designer with an almost limitless number of ways to use Korax in a WAD.

Table 34.12. Scripts used by Korax.

Script	When Used
249	Runs when Korax's health drops below half
250 to 254	Runs at random by Korax during combat
255	Runs at death of Korax

Figure 34.2.

Korax: A nightmare for the designer as well as for the player!

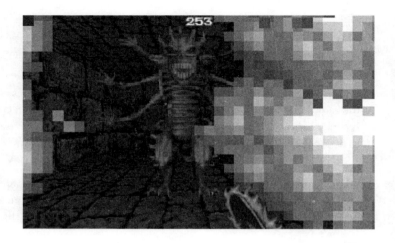

HEXEN WEAPONRY

Table 34.13 gives the codes and sprites for each of Hexen's weapons and sources of charges. Weapons can be acquired only by players of appropriate class.

Table 34.13. Hexen's weapons and ammunition.

Thing	ACS Identifier	Map Code	Spawn Code	Sprite Family
Fighter Weapons				
Timon's Axe	2F_Axe	8010	27	WFAX
Hammer of Retribution	3F_Hammer	123	28	WFHM
Quietus Hilt	4F_1Hilt	16	31	WFR3
Quietus Crosspiece	4F_2Crosspiece	13	30	WFR2
Quietus Blade	4F_3Blade	12	29	WFR1
Mage Weapons				
Frost Shards	2M_ConeOfShards	53	36	WMCS
Arc of Death	3M_Lightning	8040	—	WMLG
Bloodscourge Staff	4M_1Stick	23	39	WMS3
Bloodscourge Stub	4M_2Stub	22	38	WMS2
Bloodscourge Skull	4M_3Skull	21	37	WMS1

Thing	ACS Identifier	Map Code	Spawn Code	Sprite Family
		Cleric Weapons		
Serpent Staff	2C_SerpentStaff	10	32	WCSS
Firestorm	3C_Firestorm	8009	—	WCFM
Wraithverge Shaft	4C_1Shaft	20	35	WCH3
Wraithverge Cross	4C_2Cross	19	34	WCH2
Wraithverge Arc	4C_3Arc	18	33	WCH1
		Ammunition		
Blue Mana	Mana_1	122	11	MAN1
Green Mana	Mana_2	124	12	MAN2
Combined Mana	ManaCombined	8004	75	MAN3

HEXEN POWER-UP ARTIFACTS

Table 34.14 lists all of Hexen's special power-up artifacts. As in Heretic, some of these can be acquired only if needed (whereupon they are also used), whereas others can be stored in the players' inventory until required and used at will (and so are marked 🖛). Hexen also has several Puzzle Pieces that require special programming before they can be used. The use of these special artifacts is described in "Hexen's Special Codes" on the CD-ROM.

Table 34.14. Hexen's power-ups and other artifacts.

Thing	ACS Identifier	Map Code	Spawn Code	Sprite Family	Characteristics
		Power-Ups			
Crystal Vial	A_HealingWimpy	81	23	PTN1	
Quartz Flask	A_HealingHefty	82	24	PTN2	🖛
Mystic Urn	A_HealingComplete	32	25	SPHL	🖛
Krater of Might	A_BoostMana	8003	26	BMAN	🖛
Mesh Armor	Ar_Armor	8005	68	ARM1	
Falcon Shield	Ar_Shield	8006	69	ARM2	
Platinum Helmet	Ar_Helmet	8007	70	ARM3	
Amulet of Warding	Ar_Amulet	8008	71	ARM4	

continues

Table 34.14. continued

Thing	ACS Identifier	Map Code	Spawn Code	Sprite Family	Characteristics
Flechette	A_Flechette	8000	72	PSBG	
Torch	A_Torch	33	73	TRCH	
Boots of Speed	A_BootsOfSpeed	8002	13	SPED	
Dragonskin Bracers	A_Bracers	8041	22	BRAC	
Wings of Wrath	A_WingsOfWrath	83	15	SOAR	
Icon of the Defender	A_IconOfDefender	84	—	INVU	
Disc of Repulsion	A_Repulsion	36	18	ATLP	
Dark Servant	A_DarkServant	86	16	SUMN	
Chaos Device	A_ChaosDevice	10110	74	BLST	
Mystic Ambient Incant	A_HealRadius	10120	—	HRAD	
Banishment Device	A_Banishment	10040	17	TELO	
Porkelator	A_Porkelator	30	14	PORK	
		Keys			
Steel Key	K_Steel	8030	85	KEY1	
Cave Key	K_Cave	8031	86	KEY2	
Axe Key	K_Axe	8032	87	KEY3	
Fire Key	K_Fire	8033	88	KEY4	
Emerald Key	K_Emerald	8034	89	KEY5	
Dungeon Key	K_Dungeon	8035	90	KEY6	
Silver Key	K_Silver	8036	91	KEY7	
Rusted Key	K_Rusty	8037	92	KEY8	
Horn Key	K_Waste	8038	93	KEY9	
Swamp Key	K_Swamp	8039	94	KEYA	
Castle Key	K_Castle	8200	—	KEYB	
		Puzzle Pieces			
0: Yorick's Skull	ZZ_Skull	9002	76	ASKU	
1: Heart of D'Sparil	ZZ_BigGem	9003	77	ABGM	

Thing	ACS Identifier	Map Code	Spawn Code	Sprite Family	Characteristics
2: Ruby Planet	ZZ_GemRed	9004	78	AGMR	
3: Emerald Planet 1	ZZ_GemGreen1	9005	79	AGMG	
4: Emerald Planet 2	ZZ_GemGreen2	9009	80	AGG2	
5: Sapphire Planet 1	ZZ_GemBlue1	9006	81	AGMB	
6: Sapphire Planet 2	ZZ_GemBlue2	9010	82	AGB2	
7: Daemon Codex	ZZ_Book1	9007	83	ABK1	
8: Liber Oscura	ZZ_Book2	9008	84	ABK2	
9: Flame Mask	ZZ_Skull2	9014	—	ASK2	
10: Glaive Seal	ZZ_FWeapon	9015	—	AFWP	
11: Holy Relic	ZZ_CWeapon	9016	—	ACWP	
12: Sigil of the Magus	ZZ_MWeapon	9017	—	AMWP	
13: Clock Gear	ZZ_Gear	9018	—	AGER	
14: Clock Gear (Bronze)	ZZ_Gear2	9019	—	AGR2	
15: Clock Gear (Bronze Hub)	ZZ_Gear3	9020	—	AGR3	
16: Clock Gear (Bronze Ring)	ZZ_Gear4	9021	—	AGR4	

HEXEN DECORATIONS

Hexen is particularly rich in items provided merely to enhance the look of a level. For convenience, these items are divided into various categories in Table 34.15. The destructible items that you destroy by shooting in DOOM and DOOM II are also marked by 🔫 in this table; but in Hexen, you destroy by punching them—much more satisfying, in my opinion. Very rich environments can be assembled from Hexen Things, as shown in Figure 34.3. Take a look at the sample WAD called LEAVES.WAD on the CD-ROM that accompanies this book for a glimpse of the vast number of woodland items alone.

Figure 34.3.
Just some of Hexen's woodland decor.

Table 34.15. Hexen's decorative items.

Description	ACS Identifier	Map Code	Sprite	Diameter	Height	Characteristics
			Hanging Chains			
Short Chain	Z_Chain32	8071	CHNSA	8	32	
Long Chain	Z_Chain64	8072	CHNSB	8	64	
Chain with heart on hook	Z_ChainHeart	8073	CHNSC	8	32	
Chain with large hook	Z_ChainLHook	8074	CHNSD	8	32	
Chain with small hook	Z_ChainSHook	8075	CHNSE	8	32	
Chain with spiked ball	Z_ChainSpikeBall	8076	CHNSF	8	32	
Chain with skull on hook	Z_ChainSkull	8077	CHNSG	8	32	
			Gore			
Impaled Corpse	ZG_CorpseKabob	61	CPS1	20	92	
Sleeping Corpse	ZG_CorpseSleeping	62	CPS2	40	16	
Corpse (hanging upside down)	ZG_CorpseHanging	71	CPS3	12	75	
Hanged Corpse	ZG_CorpseLynched	108	CPS4	22	95	
Heartless Hanged Corpse	ZG_CorpseNoHeart	109	CPS5	20	100*	

Description	ACS Identifier	Map Code	Sprite	Diameter	Height	Characteristics
Sitting Corpse (chained)	ZG_CorpseSitting	110	CPS6	30	35	
Pool of Blood	ZG_BloodPool	111	BDPL			

Decorative Items

Description	ACS Identifier	Map Code	Sprite	Diameter	Height	Characteristics
War Banner	Z_Banner	77	BNR1	16	120	
Vase on pillar	Z_VasePillar	103	VASE	24	54	
Silver statue of winged demon with a skull in its hand	Z_WingedStatue	5	STTW	10	62	
Fire-skull	Z_FireSkull	8060	FSKL	10	10	
Brass Brazier	Z_BrassBrazier	8061	BRTR	12	35	
Iron Maiden	ZG_IronMaiden	8067	IRON	24	60	
Unlit Chandelier	Z_Chandelier_Unlit	8063	CDLR	20	60	
Lit Chandelier	Z_Chandelier	17	CDLR	20	60	
Barrel	Z_Barrel	8100	BARL	30	32	
Bucket	Z_Bucket	8103	BCKT	16	72	
Blue Candle	Z_BlueCandle	8066	CAND			
Spent Candle (short)	ZM_SmCandle	8503	TST4			
Spent Candle (tall)	ZM_LgCandle	8504	TST5			
Spent Candle with web	ZM_CandleWeb	8502	TST3			
Group of Candles	Z_Candle	119	CNDL			
Large Stein	ZM_LgStein	8500	TST1			
Small Stein	ZM_SmStein	8501	TST2			
Spilled Goblet	ZM_GobletSpill	8505	TST6			
Tall Goblet	ZM_GobletTall	8506	TST7			
Short Goblet	ZM_GobletSmall	8507	TST8			
Goblet with silver bands	ZM_GobletSilver	8508	TST9			
Meat Cleaver	ZM_CleaverMeat	8509	TST0			

continues

Table 34.15. continued

Description	ACS Identifier	Map Code	Sprite	Diameter	Height	Characteristics
		Trees and Forest Decor				
Deciduous Tree 1	ZF_TreeLarge1	78	TRE4	30	180	
Deciduous Tree 2	ZF_TreeLarge2	79	TRE5	30	180	
Fir Tree	ZF_Hedge	8068	XMAS	22	130	
Small Shrub	ZF_Shrub1	8101	SHB1	16	24	
Large Shrub	ZF_Shrub2	8102	SHB2	32	60	
Gnarled Tree	ZF_TreeGnarled1	80	TRE6	44	100	
Gnarled Tree with Vine	ZF_TreeGnarled2	87	TRE7	44	100	
Dead Tree Trunk	ZF_TreeDead	24	TRE1	20	96	
Dead Tree Trunk (as previous)	ZF_TreeDestructible	25	TRE1	30	128	
Dead Tree (Tinder dry)	ZF_DestructibleTree	8062	TRDT	30	180	🔫
Blasted Stump	ZF_StumpBurned	28	STM1	24	20	
Chopped Stump	ZF_StumpBare	29	STM2	24	20	
Swamp Tree 1	ZS_Tree1	27	TRE3	20	120	
Swamp Tree 2	ZS_Tree2	26	TRE2	20	150	
Swamp Branch	ZS_Vine	60	SWMV	16	80	
Swamp Log	ZS_Log	88	LOGG	40	25	
Small Swamp Stump	ZS_Stump1	37	STM3			
Swamp Stump	ZS_Stump2	38	STM4			
Hanging Moss 1	ZS_Moss1	58	MSS1			
Hanging Moss 2	ZS_Moss2	59	MSS2			
Blowing Leaves†	Spawn_Leaf	113	LEF			
Poison Mushroom	ZF_ShroomBoom	8104	SHRM	6	20	🔫
Large Forest Mushroom 1	ZF_ShroomLarge1	39	MSH1			
Large Forest Mushroom 2	ZF_ShroomLarge2	40	MSH2			

Description	ACS Identifier	Map Code	Sprite	Diameter	Height	Characteristics
Medium Cave Mushroom	ZC_ShroomLarge3	41	MSH3			
Tall Small Cave Mushroom	ZC_ShroomSmall1	42	MSH4			
Small Pale Cave Mushroom	ZC_ShroomSmall2	44	MSH5			
Small Cave Mushroom	ZC_ShroomSmall3	45	MSH6			
Small Forest Mushroom	ZF_ShroomSmall1	46	MSH7			
Small Forest Morel	ZF_ShroomSmall2	47	MSH8			
Ice Formations						
Large Icicle	ZI_IcicleLarge	89	ICT1	16	66	
Medium Icicle	ZI_IcicleMedium	90	ICT2	10	50	
Small Icicle	ZI_IcicleSmall	91	ICT3	8	32	
Tiny Icicle	ZI_IcicleTiny	92	ICT4	8	8	
Large Ice Spike	ZI_IceSpikeLarge	93	ICM1	16	66	
Medium Ice Spike	ZI_IceSpikeMedium	94	ICM2	10	50	
Small Ice Spike	ZI_IceSpikeSmall	95	ICM3	8	32	
Tiny Ice Spike	ZI_IceSpikeTiny	96	ICM4	8	8	
Cave Decorations						
Large Stalactite	ZC_StalactiteLarge	52	SLC1	16	66	
Medium Stalactite	ZC_StalactiteMedium	56	SLC2	12	50	
Small Stalactite	ZC_StalactiteSmall	57	SLC3	16	40	
Stal-pillar	ZC_Stalagmite_Pillar	48	SGMP	16	138	
Large Stalagmite	ZC_StalagmiteLarge	49	SGM1	16	48	
Medium Stalagmite	ZC_StalagmiteMedium	50	SGM2	12	40	
Small Stalagmite	ZC_StalagmiteSmall	51	SGM3	16	36	
Stone and Rock Formations						
Tiny Stone	ZC_Rock1	6	RCK1	40	16	
Small Stone	ZC_Rock2	7	RCK2	40	16	
Medium Rock	ZC_Rock3	9	RCK3	40	16	

continues

Table 34.15. continued

Description	ACS Identifier	Map Code	Sprite	Diameter	Height	Characteristics
Large Rock	ZC_Rock4	15	RCK4	40	16	
Large Brown Rock Formation	ZW_RockBrownLarge	97	RKBL	34	72	
Small Brown Rock Formation	ZW_RockBrownSmall	98	RKBS	30	50	
Gray Rock Formation	ZW_RockBlack	99	RKBK	40	40	
Rubble (1)	ZM_Rubble1	100	RBL1	40	16	
Rubble (2)	ZM_Rubble2	101	RBL2	40	16	
Rubble (3)	ZM_Rubble3	102	RBL3	40	16	
Graveyard Items						
Leaning Cross (RIP)	ZG_TombstoneRIP	63	TMS1	20	46	
Leaning Cross (SHANE)	ZG_TombstoneShane	64	TMS2	20	46	
Leaning Cross (plain)	ZG_TombstoneBigCross	65	TMS3	20	46	
Celtic Cross (BRIAN R) (BRIAN R)	ZG_TombstoneBrianR	66	TMS4	20	52	
Celtic Cross (plain)	ZG_TombstoneCrossCircle	67	TMS5	20	52	
Cross on pedestal (plain)	ZG_TombstoneSmallCross	68	TMS6	16	46	
Cross on pedestal (BRIAN P)	ZG_TombstoneBrianP	69	TMS7	16	46	
Gargoylia						
Stone Gargoyle	ZP_GargPortalShort	74	STT4	28	62	
Icy Stone Gargoyle	ZP_GargIceShort	76	STT5	28	62	
Stone Gargoyle on Pedestal	ZP_GargPortalTall	72	STT2	28	108	
Icy Stone Gargoyle on Pedestal	ZP_GargIceTall	73	STT3	28	108	

Description	ACS Identifier	Map Code	Sprite	Diameter	Height	Characteristics
Lava Gargoyle	ZP_GargLavaDrkShort	8049	GAR6	28	62	
Lava Gargoyle on Pedestal	ZP_GargLavaDrkTall	8045	GAR2	28	108	
Bright Lava Gargoyle	ZP_GargLavaBrtShort	8050	GAR7	28	62	
Bright Lava Gargoyle on Pedestal	ZP_GargLavaBrtTall	8046	GAR3	28	108	
Bronze Gargoyle	ZP_GargBrnzShort	8051	GAR8	28	62	
Bronze Gargoyle on Pedestal	ZP_GargBrnzTall	8047	GAR4	28	108	
Bronze Gargoyle on Corroded Pedestal	ZP_GargCorrode	8044	GAR1	28	108	
Steel Gargoyle	ZP_GargStlShort	8052	GAR9	28	62	
Steel Gargoyle on Pedestal	ZP_GargStlTall	8048	GAR5	28	108	

*The pool of blood that collects beneath the Heartless Hanged Corpse is not part of its sprite and always appears on the floor below it, regardless of the height of the sector it occupies.

†Use the Blowing Leaves' facing angle to determine which way the leaves blow.

HEXEN'S MISCELLANEOUS ITEMS

Hexen has two special items of decor that do not fall into any other category. These are listed in Table 34.16.

Table 34.16. Miscellaneous Hexen items.

Description	ACS Identifier	Map Code	Sprite	Diameter	Height	Characteristics
Glitter Bridge	Z_GlitterBridge	118	TLGL	32	2	
Bell	Z_Bell	8065	BBLL	56	120	

HEXEN SOUNDS

Table 34.17 lists the Sounds that are supposedly available in Hexen. Their existence is largely academic, however, because only the Wind Blowing sound Thing produces any sound. All the others are inoperative, although several of them can be found throughout Raven Software's own levels. It is believed that Raven discontinued the use of Sound Things in Hexen after developing the special ACS codes that can be used to trigger any of the sounds in the game. Details of the activation of sounds using ACS functions is given in "Hexen's Scripting Language" on the CD-ROM.

Table 34.17. Hexen's sounds.

Sound Name	Code
Stone	1400
Heavy	1401
Metal	1402
Creak	1403
Silent	1404
Lava	1405
Water	1406
Ice	1407
EarthCrack	1408
Metal2	1409
Wind Blowing	1410

SPECIAL HEXEN CATEGORIES

In addition to its richer set of standard items, Hexen has several special categories of Things that extend the game's use of Things beyond simple placement of objects. These all require either special treatment of their special arg (or parameterization) fields or to be used in conjunction with Hexen's special activation codes.

PARAMETERIZED THINGS

Some of Hexen's Things require their special parameterization fields to be set to particular values in order to operate as they should. Table 34.18 lists those Things that use their special parameterization fields to determine their appearance and behavior during play.

Table 34.18. Hexen's special effect Things.

Description	ACS Identifier	Map Code	Sprite
Bat Spawner	Spawn_Bat	10225	
Fog Spawner	Spawn_Fog	10000	
Small Fog Patch	Spawn_Fog_a	10001	FOGS
Medium Fog Patch	Spawn_Fog_b	10002	FOGM
Large Fog Patch	Spawn_Fog_c	10003	FOGL
Small Flame (timed)	Z_SmallFlame_Timed	10500	FFSM
Large Flame (timed)	Z_LargeFlame_Timed	10502	FFLG

Table 34.19 provides details of these Things' parameterization.

Table 34.19. Parameterization of Hexen's special effect Things.

Thing	Arg1	Arg2	Arg3	Arg4	Arg5
Bat Spawner	frequency	spread	—	lifetime	turn
Fog Spawner	speed	spread	frequency	lifetime	—
Fog Patches	speed	—	—	lifetime	moves
Timed Flames	lifetime	—	—	—	—

The meanings of these parameters are as follows:

frequency   A value in the range 1–10 that determines how often the spawned items appear. (The figure is a time interval, measured in octics—8 tics.)

spread   The angle of spread over which the spawned items appear. Values in the range 0–255 are permitted; 128 represents 180 degrees.

lifetime   The lifetime of the objects produced by the spawners (or the Things themselves, in the case of the fog patches and flames). This is measured in octics from the start of the level.

turn   The amount of turn on each move of the spawned object. Again, a value of 128 represents 180 degrees. (Keep this value small for realistic movement.)

speed   The speed of movement of the spawned object (or of the Thing itself, in the case of the fog patches). Values in the range 0–10 are permitted; 10 is the fastest.

moves   A Boolean that determines whether the Thing moves. If this parameter is 0, the object does not move, no matter what value the speed parameter is set to.

In addition to the Things described here, Hexen provides another group of parameterizable Things. These are the Hiding Place objects—Things that yield some contents when broken. These are listed in Table 34.20.

Table 34.20. Hexen's Hiding Place Things.

Description	ACS Identifier	Map Code	Sprite	Diameter	Height	Characteristics
Large Amphora	ZM_Pot1	104	POT1	20	32	
Medium Amphora	ZM_Pot2	105	POT2	20	25	
Squat Pot	ZM_Pot3	106	POT3	30	25	
Suit of Armor	Z_ArmorSuit	8064	SUIT	32	72	

To make these items yield an item when they are destroyed, set their first arg field to the spawn code of the desired object. The specified object is automatically spawned in the same place as the Hiding Place Thing upon the latter's destruction.

CAUTION: It is possible to have a Hiding Place Thing deliver any spawnable object. Take care, however, if you hide large, blocking items (such as monsters) this way. If the extent of the item being spawned overlaps with any other Thing (such as the player), they become glued together and unable to move. This can quite easily happen if the player has to approach close to the Hiding Place Thing to break it (as is usually the case). If you really want to hide Ettins inside suits of armor, make sure that the player must smash the armor from afar.

THINGS CAPABLE OF ACTIVATION

Hexen has a special group of Things that are capable of being affected by the Thing_Activate and Thing_Deactivate special codes. (See "Hexen's Special Codes" on the CD-ROM for more information about using these.) These special codes operate by converting their target into a different Thing. The Things that can be affected are generally provided in deactivated/activated pairs, as indicated in Table 34.21. For each of these pairs, the deactivated member can be activated to become the activated member, and vice versa. Sound effects usually accompany the activation event, whereas deactivation is always silent.

Table 34.21. Hexen's paired activatable/deactivatable Things.

Deactivated Item Activated Item	ACS Identifier	Map Code	Sprite Family	Width	Height
Minotaur Statue (no fire)	Z_FireBull_Unlit	8043	FBUL	20	80
Minotaur Statue (with fire)	Z_FireBull	8042	FBUL	20	80
Unlit Wall Torch	Z_Wall_Torch_UnLit	55	WLTR	20	16
Burning Wall Torch	Z_Wall_Torch_Lit	54	WLTR	20	16

Deactivated Item Activated Item	ACS Identifier	Map Code	Sprite Family	Width	Height
(Nothing)* Small flame (permanent)	Z_SmallFlame_Permanent	10501	FFSM		
(Nothing)* Large flame (permanent)	Z_LargeFlame_Permanent	10503	FFLG		
Unlit Twined Brazier	Z_TwinedTorch_Unlit	117	TWTR	10	64
Burning Twined Brazier	Z_TwinedTorch	116	TWTR	10	64
Cauldron (without fire)	Z_Cauldron_Unlit	8070	CDRN	12	26
Cauldron on a fire	Z_Cauldron	8069	CDRN	12	26
Hidden Spike†	Spike_Down	10090	TSPK		
Raised Spike	Spike_Up	10091	TSPK	20	128
Headless Golden-Winged Statue Golden-Winged Statue with head (no deactivation possible)	ZZ_WingedStatueNoSkull	9011	STWN	10	62
Pedestal Pedestal with gem (no deactivation possible)	ZZ_GemPedestal	9012	GMPD	10	40

*No Thing is available to provide a deactivated starting version of the two permanent Flames. If you want these items to start in the extinguished state, you need to add appropriate Thing_Deactivate functions to a script that runs as your map opens.

†Any player or monster standing on the spike as it rises is killed.

Other Things can be subjected to the Thing_Activate and Thing_Deactivate specials without causing them to change into other Things. The statistics for these items are given elsewhere in this chapter, but Table 34.22 gives the effects that result from applying these special codes to them.

Table 34.22. Simple Thing activations.

Thing	Activation Effect	Deactivation Effect
Bell	Tolls	—
Bat Spawner	Begins spawning	Ceases spawning

A sample WAD (called ACTIVES.WAD) demonstrating the use of activated Things is provided on the CD-ROM that accompanies this book. Figures 34.4 and 34.5 show the result of just one activation in this WAD.

Figure 34.4.
Before activation…

Figure 34.5.
…and after.

POLYOBJ THINGS

Three Things are provided to support Hexen's special Polygonal Objects. The details of these are given in Table 34.23. Their use is covered in detail in "Making Moving Scenery" on the CD-ROM.

Table 34.23. Hexen's PolyObj Things.

Thing	ACS Identifier	Map Code
PolyObj Anchor Spot	PO_Anchor	3000
PolyObj Start Spot	PO_StartSpot	3001
PolyObj Crushing Start Spot	PO_StartSpot_Crush	3002

EXIT: MOPPING UP AND MOVING ON

This chapter provided full details of all the Things available for use in maps for DOOM, DOOM II, Heretic, and Hexen. The next chapter provides similar reference tables for the special characteristics that can be given to sectors.

SPECIAL SECTOR TYPES

This chapter summarizes the codes used to provide special sector characteristics in each main variant of DOOM. The use of these characteristics was discussed fully in Chapter 13, "Special Sectors." The codes are presented here for easy reference. You usually need not remember all the code numbers for the various effects—most editors provide a more meaningful list from which to choose the effects. They are given here for the benefit of those readers who want to work with raw WAD data.

DOOM/DOOM II SPECIAL SECTOR TYPES

Table 35.1 lists all the effects available in DOOM and DOOM II through a sector's special characteristic.

Table 35.1. DOOM/DOOM II special sector types, ordered by code.

Code	Effect
0	Normal sector; no special effect
1	Blink off (random intervals)
2	Blink on (0.5-second intervals)
3	Blink on (1-second intervals)

continues

— *By Steve Benner*

Table 35.1. continued

Code	Effect
4	High damage; blink on at 0.5-second intervals
5	Medium damage
6	NOT IMPLEMENTED
7	Low damage
8	Oscillate lighting
9	Award secret credit
10	Close sector 30 seconds into level
11	High damage until player <=10% health, then end level/game
12	Synchronized blink on (1-second intervals)
13	Synchronized blink off (0.5-second intervals)
14	Open sector 5 minutes into level
15	NOT IMPLEMENTED
16	High damage
17	Flicker light on and off at random (DOOM v1.666 and later only)

Use of any other special sector setting (or any of the unused codes) causes the game to crash back to DOS when a player enters the sector.

HERETIC'S SPECIAL SECTORS

Heretic's special sector types are based largely on DOOM's, but they have been extended a little. Table 35.2 lists all of Heretic's special sector types.

Table 35.2. Heretic's special sector types, ordered by code.

Code	Effect
0	Normal sector; no special effect
1	Blink off (random intervals)
2	Blink on (0.5-second intervals)
3	Blink on (1-second intervals)
4	High damage; blink on at 0.5-second intervals; strong current to east
5	Medium damage

Code	Effect
6	NOT IMPLEMENTED
7	Low damage
8	Flicker lighting down at random intervals
9	Award secret credit
10	Close sector 30 seconds into level
11	Normal sector; no special effect
12	Synchronized blink on (1-second intervals)
13	Synchronized blink off (0.5-second intervals)
14	Open sector 5 minutes into level
15	Reduced floor friction
16	High damage
17, 18, 19	NOT IMPLEMENTED
20	Very slow current to east
21	Slow current to east
22	Normal current to east
23	Fast current to east
24	Very fast current to east
25	Very slow current to north
26	Slow current to north
27	Normal current to north
28	Fast current to north
29	Very fast current to north
30	Very slow current to south
31	Slow current to south
32	Normal current to south
33	Fast current to south
34	Very fast current to south
35	Very slow current to west
36	Slow current to west
37	Normal current to west
38	Fast current to west

continues

Table 35.2. continued

Code	Effect
39	Very fast current to west
40	Weak wind to east
41	Normal wind to east
42	Strong wind to east
43	Weak wind to north
44	Normal wind to north
45	Strong wind to north
46	Weak wind to south
47	Normal wind to south
48	Strong wind to south
49	Weak wind to west
50	Normal wind to west
51	Strong wind to west

Again, the use of any other value in a sector's special characteristic causes the game to crash back to DOS when a player enters the offending sector.

HEXEN'S SPECIAL SECTOR TYPES

Hexen's new programmability means that many of the old special sector actions are no longer necessary, and consequently they have largely been dropped from this variant of the DOOM engine. Table 35.3 lists the special sector types that exist in Hexen.

Table 35.3. Hexen's special sector types, ordered by code.

Code	Function
1	Manual phased lighting
2	Start lighting sequence
3	Continue lighting sequence 1
4	Continue lighting sequence 2
26	Stairs 1

Code	Function
27	Stairs 2
198	Indoor lightning (bright)
199	Indoor lightning (reduced)
200	Use alternative sky
201	Slow scroll north
202	Medium scroll north
203	Fast scroll north
204	Slow scroll east
205	Medium scroll east
206	Fast scroll east
207	Slow scroll south
208	Medium scroll south
209	Fast scroll south
210	Slow scroll west
211	Medium scroll west
212	Fast scroll west
213	Slow scroll northwest
214	Medium scroll northwest
215	Fast scroll northwest
216	Slow scroll northeast
217	Medium scroll northeast
218	Fast scroll northeast
219	Slow scroll southeast
220	Medium scroll southeast
221	Fast scroll southeast
222	Slow scroll southwest
223	Medium scroll southwest
224	Fast scroll southwest

As with all other variants, the use of any other code crashes the game engine.

CAUTION: Take care when using the automated phased lighting specials 2, 3, and 4. These codes are collected by Hexen's preprocessor as the level loads. They are subsequently replaced by appropriately calculated, phased lighting controls before being passed to the game engine proper. Any sectors that are not so changed (owing to the sequence being incorrectly constructed) cause a crash back to DOS when the player enters them. Consult Chapter 13, "Special Sectors," for information on how to use these codes correctly.

EXIT: MOPPING UP AND MOVING ON

This chapter has summarized, for reference purposes, the codes available for creating special sectors in DOOM, DOOM II, Heretic, and Hexen. The next chapter provides similar reference into these games' special line types.

SPECIAL LINE TYPES

This chapter provides a complete list of all the special line-types available in DOOM, DOOM II, and Heretic, for reference purposes. In earlier chapters of the book, you will find descriptions of the way these lines are used, as indicated throughout the tables presented here.

Table 36.1 provides the details of special line attributes, arranged by function; Table 36.2 provides a complete list ordered by action code.

In these tables, the following symbols and conventions are used:

*	Indicates that the action is provided only in versions of DOOM beyond 1.4. It is safest to assume that v1.666 is needed in these cases. These codes do not work in Heretic, although the function might be provided by new codes specific to Heretic.
**	Indicates that the action is provided only in versions of DOOM *earlier* than 1.4 (and all versions of Heretic).
[brackets]	Indicate codes that are specific to Heretic.
Italics	Indicate codes that do not use the sector tagging mechanism.
S	Indicates a spacebar-operated action.
M	Indicates a manually operated action (spacebar, without sector tagging).
W	Indicates a walk-through–activated trigger.
G	Indicates an impact-activated trigger.
1	Indicates a single-use trigger.
R	Indicates a repeatable action trigger.
†	Indicates that a trigger can be activated by monsters.

— *By Steve Benner*

Hexen The structure and use of special lines has been extended in Hexen to a system of special actions that can be invoked in various ways. These special action codes are the subject of "Hexen's Special Codes," a chapter on the CD-ROM.

NOTE: Virtually all editors remove the need for you to know the exact numbers used to trigger actions by providing meaningful descriptions of the actions themselves. These tables are provided here for the benefit of those readers needing an accurate list of the code numbers and the actions associated with them for their own purposes.

Table 36.1. Special attributes arranged by action.

Action	M1	MR	W1	WR	S1	SR	GR
				Activation Category			
Doors (See Chapters 14 and 15)							
Door: Open, pause, close	–	1†	4†	90	29	63	–
Door: Open and stay	31	–	2	86	103	61	46
Door: Close	–	–	3	75	50	42	–
Door: Close for 30s, open	–	–	16	76	–	–	–
Turbo door: Open, pause, close	–	117*	108*	105* [100]	111*	114*	–
Turbo door: Open and stay	118*	–	109*	106*	112*	115*	–
Turbo door: Close	–	–	110*	107*	113*	116*	–
Door: Open, close (blue)	–	26	–	–	–	–	–
Door: Open, close (red)	–	28	–	–	–	–	–
Door: Open, close (yellow)	–	27	–	–	–	–	–
Turbo door: Open (blue)	32	–	–	–	133*	99	–
Turbo door: Open (red)	33	–	–	–	135*	134*	–
Turbo door: Open (yellow)	34	–	–	–	137*	136*	–

Action	Activation Category		
	W1	WR	SR
Lights (See Chapter 15)			
Switch lights off (brightness level 0)	35	79	139*
Switch lights on full (brightness level 255)	13	81	138*
Switch light level to match dimmest adjacent	104	–	–
Switch light level to match brightest adjacent	12	80	–
Make light blink on every 1.0 seconds	17	–	–

Action	Activation Category			
	W1	WR	S1	SR
Lifts or Elevators (See Chapter 16)				
Standard lift	10	88	21	62
Turbo lift	121*	120*	122*	123*
Perpetual lift start/resume	53	87	–	–
Perpetual lift pause	54	89	–	–

Action	Activation Category				
	W1	WR	S1	SR	G1
Moving Floors (See Chapter 16)					
Raise floor by 24 units	58	92	–	–	–
Raise floor by 512 units (lift speed)	–	–	140*	–	–
Raise floor to match next higher floor	119*	128*	18	69	–
Turbo version of above	130*	129*	131*	132*	–
Raise floor by shortest lower texture	30	96	–	–	–
Move floor up to lowest local ceiling	5	91	101	64	24
Move floor down to lowest adjacent floor	38	82	23	60	–
Move floor down to highest adjacent floor	19	83	102	45	–
Move floor down to 8 units above highest adjacent floor	36	98	71	70	–
Move floor to 8 below ceiling, crushing	56	94	55	65	–

continues

Table 36.1. continued

Floor Movement	Role-Model Type	Special Transferred	W1	WR	S1	SR	G1
				Activation Category			
Changing Floors (See Chapter 17)							
Up to next higher	Trigger	0	22	95	20	68	47
Up 24 units	Trigger	0	–	–	15	66	–
Up 24 units	Trigger	X	59	93	–	–	–
Up 32 units	Trigger	0	–	–	14	67	–
Down to lowest adjacent	1st Neighbor	X	37	84	–	–	–

Action	W1	WR	S1	SR
	Activation Category			
Entraining Actions (See Chapter 17)				
Donut eater	–	–	9	–
Build 8-unit stairs, slow	8	–	7	–
Build 16-unit stairs, turbo	100* [106]	–	127* [107]	–

Action	W1	WR	S1	SR
	Activation Category			
Moving Ceilings (See Chapter 16)				
Move ceiling up to highest adjacent ceiling	40	–	–	–
Lower ceiling to floor	–	–	41	43
Lower ceiling to 8 above floor	44	72	49**	–

Action	W1	WR	S1
	Activation Category		
Crushing Ceilings (See Chapter 16)			
Start/resume slow perpetual crusher	25	73	49*
Start/resume fast perpetual crusher	6	77	–
Start/resume slow, "silent" crusher	141*	–	–
Pause crusher (any type)	57	74	–

Action	Activation Category	
	W1	WR
	Teleports (See Chapter 18)	
Player/monster teleport	39†	97†
Monster-only teleport	125*†	126*†

Exit Type	Activation Category	
	W1	S1
	Exits (See Chapter 18)	
Standard exit	52	11
Secret exit	124* [105]	51

Effect	Code
	Effects (See Chapter 14)
Scroll texture to left	48
Scroll texture to right	[99]

Table 36.2. Special attributes of lines, arranged by code.

Code	Activation	Sound	Speed	Effect
1	MR†	Door	Medium	Door: Open, pause, close
2	W1	Door	Medium	Door: Open and stay
3	W1	Door	Medium	Door: Close
4	W1†	Door	Medium	Door: Open, pause, close
5	W1	Mover	Slow	Floor: Raise to lowest local ceiling
6	W1	Crusher	Fast	Crusher: Start/resume (fast)
7	S1	Mover	Slow	Stairs: 8-unit
8	W1	Mover	Slow	Stairs: 8-unit
9	S1	Mover	Slow	Change Donut
10	W1	Lift	Fast	Lift: Down, pause, up
11	S1			Exit: Standard
12	W1			Lights: Match brightest adjacent

continues

Table 36.2. continued

Code	Activation	Sound	Speed	Effect
13	W1			Lights: On full
14	S1	Mover	Slow	Changer (Trigger): Raise floor 32, nullify special
15	S1	Mover	Slow	Changer (Trigger): Raise floor 24, nullify special
16	W1	Door	Medium	Door: Close for 30 seconds, then open
17	W1			Lights: Blink on every 1.0 second
18	S1	Mover	Slow	Floor: Raise to match next higher floor
19	W1	Mover	Slow	Floor: Lower to highest adjacent floor
20	S1	Mover	Slow	Changer (Trigger): Raise floor to match next higher floor, nullify special
21	S1	Lift	Fast	Lift: Down, pause, up
22	W1	Mover	Slow	Changer (Trigger): Raise floor to match next higher floor, nullify special
23	S1	Mover	Slow	Floor: Lower to lowest adjacent floor
24	G1	Mover	Slow	Floor: Raise to lowest local ceiling
25	W1	Crusher	Medium	Crusher: Start/resume (Slow)
26	MR	Door	Medium	Door: Open, pause, close: (Blue)
27	MR	Door	Medium	Door: Open, pause, close: (Yellow)
28	MR	Door	Medium	Door: Open, pause, close: (Red [Green])
29	S1	Door	Medium	Door: Open, pause, close
30	W1	Mover	Slow	Floor: Raise by shortest lower texture
31	M1	Door	Medium	Door: Open and stay
32	M1	Door	Medium	Door: Open and stay: (Blue)

ode	Activation	Sound	Speed	Effect
33	M1	Door	Medium	Door: Open and stay: (Red [Green])
34	M1	Door	Medium	Door: Open and stay: (Yellow)
35	W1			Lights: Off
36	W1	Mover	Fast	Floor: Lower to 8 above highest adjacent
37	W1	Mover	Slow	Changer (First Neighbor): down to lowest adjacent, special transferred
38	W1	Mover	Slow	Floor: Lower to lowest adjacent floor
39	W1†	Teleport		Teleport: Player/monster
40	W1	Mover	Slow	Ceiling: Raise to match highest adjacent
41	S1	Mover	Slow	Ceiling: Lower to floor
42	SR	Door	Medium	Door: Close
43	SR	Mover	Slow	Ceiling: Lower to floor
44	W1	Mover	Slow	Ceiling: Lower to 8 above floor
45	SR	Mover	Slow	Floor: Lower to highest adjacent floor
46	GR	Door	Medium	Door: Open and stay
47	G1	Mover	Slow	Changer (Trigger): Raise floor to match next higher, nullify special
48	–			Effect: Scroll texture left
49**	S1	Mover	Slow	Ceiling: Lower to 8 above floor
49*	S1	Crusher	Slow	Crusher: Start/resume (Slow)
50	S1	Door	Medium	Door: Close
51	S1			Exit: To secret level
52	W1			Exit: To next standard level
53	W1	Lift	Slow	Lift: Start/resume (Perpetual)
54	W1			Lift: Pause

continues

Table 36.2. continued

Code	Activation	Sound	Speed	Effect
55	S1	Mover	Slow	Floor: Move to 8 below ceiling, crushing
56	W1	Mover	Slow	Floor: Move to 8 below ceiling, crushing
57	W1			Crusher: Pause
58	W1	Mover	Slow	Floor: Raise 24 units
59	W1	Mover	Slow	Changer (Trigger): Raise floor 24, special transferred
60	SR	Mover	Slow	Floor: Lower to lowest adjacent floor
61	SR	Door	Medium	Door: Open and stay
62	SR	Lift	Fast	Lift: Down, pause, up
63	SR	Door	Medium	Door: Open, pause, close
64	SR	Mover	Slow	Floor: Raise to lowest local ceiling
65	SR	Mover	Slow	Floor: Raise to 8 below ceiling, crushing
66	SR	Mover	Slow	Changer (Trigger): Raise floor 24, nullify special
67	SR	Mover	Slow	Changer (Trigger): Raise floor 32, nullify special
68	SR	Mover	Slow	Changer (Trigger): Raise floor to match next higher floor, nullify special
69	SR	Mover	Slow	Floor: Raise to match next higher
70	SR	Mover	Fast	Floor: Lower to 8 above highest adjacent
71	S1	Mover	Fast	Floor: Lower to 8 above highest adjacent
72	WR	Mover	Slow	Ceiling: Lower to 8 above floor
73	WR	Crusher	Slow	Crusher: Start/resume (Slow)
74	WR			Crusher: Pause
75	WR	Door	Medium	Door: Close

Code	Activation	Sound	Speed	Effect
76	WR	Door	Medium	Door: Close for 30 seconds, then open
77	WR	Crusher	Fast	Crusher: Start/resume (Fast)
78				Does nothing
79	WR			Lights: Off
80	WR			Lights: Match brightest adjacent
81	WR			Lights: On full
82	WR	Mover	Slow	Floor: Lower to lowest adjacent floor
83	WR	Mover	Slow	Floor: Lower to highest adjacent floor
84	WR	Mover	Slow	Changer (First Neighbor): lower floor to lowest adjacent, special transferred
85				Does nothing
86	WR	Door	Medium	Door: Open and stay
87	WR	Lift	Slow	Lift: Start/resume (Perpetual)
88	WR†	Lift	Fast	Lift: Down, pause, up
89	WR			Lift: Pause
90	WR	Door	Medium	Door: Open, pause, close
91	WR	Mover	Slow	Floor: Raise to lowest local ceiling
92	WR	Mover	Slow	Floor: Raise by 24 units
93	WR	Mover	Slow	Changer (Trigger): Raise floor 24, special transferred
94	WR	Mover	Slow	Floor: Raise to 8 below ceiling, crushing
95	WR	Mover	Slow	Changer (Trigger): Raise floor to match next higher, nullify special
96	WR	Mover	Slow	Floor: Raise by shortest lower texture
97	WR†	Teleport		Teleport: Player/monster
98	WR	Mover	Fast	Floor: Lower to 8 above highest adjacent

continues

Table 36.2. continued

Code	Activation	Sound	Speed	Effect
99*	SR	Blaze	Turbo	Door: Open and stay: (Blue)
[99]	–			Effect: Scroll texture right
100*	W1	Mover	Turbo	Stairs: 16-unit
[100]	WR	Blaze	Turbo	Door: Open, pause, close
101	S1	Mover	Slow	Floor: Raise to lowest local ceiling
102	S1	Mover	Slow	Floor: Lower to highest adjacent floor
103	S1	Door	Medium	Door: Open and stay
104	W1			Lights: Match dimmest adjacent
105*	WR	Blaze	Turbo	Door: Open, pause, close
[105]	W1			Exit: To secret level
106*	WR	Blaze	Turbo	Door: Open and stay
[106]	W1	Mover	Turbo	Stairs: 16-unit
107*	WR	Blaze	Turbo	Door: Close
[107]	S1	Mover	Turbo	Stairs: 16-unit
108*	W1	Blaze	Turbo	Door: Open, pause, close
109*	W1	Blaze	Turbo	Door: Open and stay
110*	W1	Blaze	Turbo	Door: Close
111*	S1	Blaze	Turbo	Door: Open, pause, close
112*	S1	Blaze	Turbo	Door: Open and stay
113*	S1	Blaze	Turbo	Door: Close
114*	SR	Blaze	Turbo	Door: Open, pause, close
115*	SR	Blaze	Turbo	Door: Open and stay
116*	SR	Blaze	Turbo	Door: Close
117*	MR	Blaze	Turbo	Door: Open, pause, close
118*	M1	Blaze	Turbo	Door: Open and stay
119*	W1	Mover	Slow	Floor: Raise to match next higher
120*	WR	Lift	Turbo	Lift: Down, pause, up
121*	W1	Lift	Turbo	Lift: Down, pause, up
122*	S1	Lift	Turbo	Lift: Down, pause, up
123*	SR	Lift	Turbo	Lift: Down, pause, up

Code	Activation	Sound	Speed	Effect
124*	W1			Exit: To secret level
125*	1†	Teleport		Teleport: Monster only
126*	R†	Teleport		Teleport: Monster only
127*	S1	Mover	Turbo	Stairs: 16-unit
128*	WR	Mover	Slow	Floor: Raise to match next higher
129*	WR	Mover	Turbo	Floor: Raise to match next higher
130*	W1	Mover	Turbo	Floor: Raise to match next higher
131*	S1	Mover	Turbo	Floor: Raise to match next higher
132*	SR	Mover	Turbo	Floor: Raise to match next higher
133*	S1	Blaze	Turbo	Door: Open and stay: (Blue)
134*	SR	Blaze	Turbo	Door: Open and stay: (Red)
135*	S1	Blaze	Turbo	Door: Open and stay: (Red)
136*	SR	Blaze	Turbo	Door: Open and stay: (Yellow)
137*	S1	Blaze	Turbo	Door: Open and stay: (Yellow)
138*	SR			Lights: On full
139*	SR			Lights: Off
140*	S1	Mover	Medium	Floor: Raise 512 units
141*	W1	Lift	Fast	Crusher: Start/resume ("Silent")

EXIT: MOPPING UP AND MOVING ON

This chapter has summarized, for reference purposes, the codes available for producing special lines in DOOM, DOOM II, and Heretic. "Hexen's Special Codes" on the CD-ROM provides similar reference for Hexen's special action codes.

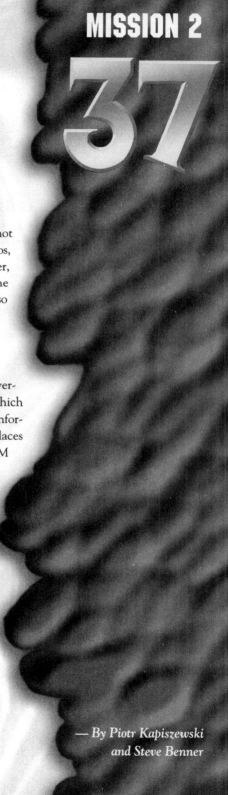

OUT AND ABOUT

Without doubt, part of the great success of DOOM can be attributed not only to an engine design that allows an almost infinite number of scenarios, but also to the distribution channels that have been used. In this chapter, you'll take a closer look at DOOM's main distribution channel—the Internet—and examine ways in which you can join in the fun. You'll also discover places you can visit on America Online and CompuServe.

DOOM AND THE INTERNET

DOOM has been on the Internet since its beginnings. The shareware version was first released there, and thus the craze began. The ease with which information can be exchanged over the Net has allowed a wealth of information sources to spring up. There are already countless interesting places to visit and people to talk to who are involved in all the aspects of DOOM you have seen in this book—and more. You will find people and places involved in design, distribution, coordination, and help services. The best part of the whole thing is that all of these resources are no further away than your computer screen.

SOURCES

Because the Internet is truly international—and consequently vast—it can often be hard to track down the best places to go, or people to contact. When the whole world lies at your feet (or, more accurately in this case, at your fingertips), deciding where to go first can be tricky. You therefore need to take a look at the routes available to you. The most important Internet sources of DOOM-related information, and channels for the distribution of your own work, are these:

— By Piotr Kapiszewski
and Steve Benner

- The World Wide Web (or WWW)
- Newsgroups (USENET News and other such groups)
- Internet mailing lists
- Internet Relay Chat (or IRC)
- FTP sites

Just which of these sources are available to you depends, of course, on the services offered by your Internet provider. In addition to these Internet services, numerous dial-up Bulletin Board Services (BBSs) are dedicated to (or dominated by) DOOM-related material. With the ever-increasing availability of Internet access, however, these are generally of less global importance than the Internet sources just listed. Before taking a look at where to go, though, I'll let you know just what you can expect to find.

WHAT'S OUT THERE

Let me give you some ideas of what is currently available.

- **Game utilities:** Editors, special effects programs, general-purpose DOOM utilities, and so on.
- **Game elements:** Including various patches to sound, music, graphics, characters, and scenarios.
- **Documentation:** In the form of Frequently Asked Question (FAQ) documents, cheats, technical specs, and so on.
- **Reviews:** Descriptions and evaluation of various add-on levels that are available.
- **DHT exams:** DOOM Honorific Titles and demos of famous tourneys or Deathmatches.

I'll look at each of these categories in turn.

GAME UTILITIES

Just as DOOM itself was distributed first on the Internet, so are many of the utility programs that have sprung up around it. You can acquire the latest updates to your favorite utilities, or get hold of the newest tools as they are released in free or shareware versions and uploaded to the various DOOM-related distribution sites around the world.

GAME ELEMENTS

Literally thousands of game elements are out there for you to acquire, free of charge, too. These include the following elements:

- **Levels:** By far the most common game element, new levels are available for every game variant.
- **Graphics:** New textures, flats, and sprites to enhance your own levels.
- **Sounds:** New sound effects to change the atmosphere of the game.

- **Music:** New musical sound tracks for you to scream along to.
- **DeHackEd patches:** Patches to enhance the weapons, alter monster behavior, change the appearance of various game elements, and much more.

With the Internet being a two-way information-distribution system, nothing can stop you from making your own contribution to this stock of goodies. I'll have more to say on that topic later.

DOCUMENTATION AND REVIEWS

The Internet is a great place for acquiring information. It is probably true to say that every single scrap of information in this book had its origin somewhere out there, in an FAQ, a technical documentation file, or simply an e-mail message!

In addition to technical information of the kind found in this book, there is also plenty of DOOM-related chat taking place. Much of this information can be readily tapped. And you can join in yourself, of course.

You will also find reviews of many of the items discussed earlier; read these reviews to see just what is worth its download time.

LMPS AND DHTS

Lastly, as well as sharing utilities, scenarios, and information with other DOOM fans, you can even share the experience of play itself. Quite apart from the capability to connect to other players' machines and do a bit of Deathmatch or Co-op play, you can share in the experiences of other players by downloading their LMP (demo) files and playing them back to see how others tackle those tricky bits. Or you can preview some of these add-on WADs you've heard so much about. In addition, there are regular Internet DOOM-playing contests that are judged from recorded demos. The winners of these are awarded DOOM Honorific Titles, and their names are publicized on the Internet.

So you see, there are plenty of ways of extending the DOOM experience over the Internet, and the Net offers endless potential for you to become famous yourself! Take a look now at some of the ways to access this gold mine and contribute to it yourself.

WORLD WIDE WEB

Unquestionably, the Internet's single most significant advance in recent years has been the development and implementation of the HyperText Transport Protocol (http). Http has enabled the creation of the information "structure" now known as the World Wide Web, or just WWW or Web for short. The proliferation of WWW pages has probably been the greatest explosion of information the developed world has seen since the invention of the printing press! To access this information, all you need is an Internet connection and a Web browser. Just about the whole world and their dogs (and, in some cases, their goldfish too) have their own Web page these days, and countless more pages appear daily. Fortunately, finding DOOM-related matter out there is easy. For this, thank the DoomWeb project.

DOOMWEB

Back in the dim and distant past (at the beginning of 1994), a group of people got together and decided to consolidate forces on development of a project they called DoomWeb. The aim was to link DOOM-related Web pages around the world, but connected to a central hub. The idea was that this hub would act as a common reference point for all of these pages and, they hoped, would become known as the first port of call for anyone seeking DOOM-related pages on the Web. That hub has now become a reality. It is called DoomGate. If you have a Web browser, you can find it at URL `http://doomgate.cs.buffalo.edu/`. The service is provided through a dedicated host on the Net, thanks to the generosity of numerous sponsors, and the help of Steve Young (`syoung@doomgate.cs.buffalo.edu`), Ken Smith (`kensmith@cs.buffalo.edu`), and David Milun (`milun@cs.buffalo.edu`).

Through DoomGate, the DoomWeb project provides information about all aspects of the game, along with information about Heretic, Hexen, and, as it becomes available, Quake.

Perhaps the most useful aspect of WWW is its capability to integrate not only textual information but also graphics and sound. Documents can be linked together across the world, creating a single resource, even though the actual data resides on many different computers. They can be maintained by different individuals who are sometimes thousands of miles apart geographically.

This certainly is the case with DoomWeb. Many of the people who participate in the project are literally on opposite sides of the planet. Only a few of us have ever met face to face, and the usual way of communication is via e-mail and IRC. As the results show, it is possible to create and maintain large-scale projects in such environments and to carry the ideas through without regard for distance or language barriers.

THE ORGANIZATION OF DOOMWEB NODES

It is nearly impossible to describe in detail the layout of each DoomWeb node because they are constantly changing. New updates to various documents, or changes based on user feedback, frequently force the Node-masters to update their pages. This is why I recommend that you approach DoomWeb through DoomGate. From there, you will find links out to the principal nodes, covering

- Forums
- Mailing list information
- DOOM-editing information
- Add-ons, including utilities and new levels
- The DOOM help service

You'll also find more information about DoomGate itself (including how to join us if you have interesting DOOM-related pages of your own), access statistics, and, of course, links out to the official pages of the great masters themselves. So surf on in!

NEWSGROUPS AND MAILING LISTS

Internet Mailing Lists and USENET News are two ways of keeping in touch with like-minded individuals.

NEWSGROUPS

USENET carries several newsgroups of interest to anyone interested DOOM-related matters. Following, you will find a list of the main ones. These newsgroups, which carry lots of useful information, should be available at most sites.

rec.games.computer.doom.announce

Subject: Assorted announcements (moderated).
Provides: Information, Frequently Asked Questions (FAQs) documents, and reviews about DOOM. A must for both new and adept players as well as developers. It carries all the latest updates to all important documentation that is available. It covers the original games and all game variants.

rec.games.computer.doom.help

Subject: DOOM Help Service (new players welcome).
Provides: Flame-free help and information for all players, new and old alike. Sample topics include these:

- How to solve a particular level, find a key, get 100 percent of the secrets, and so forth.
- DOOM setup questions. ("I get such-and-such an error when I start DOOM.")
- Non-DOS version (Linux, SGI, and so on) questions.
- Finding FTP sites, WWW sites, multiplayer BBSs, and so on.

rec.games.computer.doom.misc

Subject: Talk about DOOM, id Software, and related issues.
Provides: Lots of idle (but essential!) gossip, including these topics:

- Status of WinDoom, Jaguar, and other "ports" of the game.
- Quake, other id Software-related "in-development" topics.
- Previous id games (Wolfenstein 3D, and so on) and DOOM-engine games (Heretic and so on).
- "DOOM, the Movie," Ferrari Testarossas, other stuff about id.
- Comments about magazine/newspaper/TV stories about DOOM or id.
- GT Interactive, general DOOM sales/distribution topics.
- Piracy, viruses, and illegal copies of DOOM. (No, it doesn't provide them!)
- Commercial DOOM-related advertisements.
- DOOM-related hardware debates and so forth.

- Benchmarks and timedemos.
- Favorite music, monsters, weapons.
- Other topics not dealing with actual game playing or editing.

---

rec.games.computer.doom.editing

Subject: Editing and hacking DOOM-related files.
Provides: Technically oriented discussions on editing DOOM and DOOM-related files. Topics include these:

- Hacking the DOOM.EXE file, editing saved games and LMPs.
- PWAD design techniques.
- Design problems or limitations (HOM, Medusa, and so forth).
- Questions about the popular editors (where to get, bug reports, and so on).

 NOTE: Comments or questions about playing user-written PWADs (opinions, keys, secrets, and so forth) should not be posted here—post to rec.games.computer.doom.playing instead.

---

rec.games.computer.doom.playing

Subject: Playing DOOM and user-created levels.
Provides: Discussion on all aspects related to playing DOOM, including topics such as these:

- PWAD upload announcements, reviews of PWADs, PWAD lists, and so forth.
- Secrets, strategies, bugs of specific user-developed PWADs.
- Unusual experiences(!), Deathmatch strategies, boasts, LMPs, and so forth.
- Keyboard/mouse movement techniques.
- Side effects of playing DOOM.
- "Looking for another DOOM player in area code…"
- Lists of people wanting to play multiplayer modem/net DOOM.
- Tournament discussions and multiplayer topics.

 NOTE: Non-play-related topics (including Quake) go to the .misc group.

INTERNET MAILING LISTS

Internet mailing lists are lists of the e-mail addresses of individuals who share a common interest. You usually must *subscribe* to a list to join it. You normally do this by just sending a message to an automated process at a specific e-mail address. After you are on the list, you can e-mail all other members of it by sending a single message to the list itself. Most mailing lists are also available in digest form. This can be delivered at regular intervals or after a certain number of messages have been received and digested. Subscribe to whichever form is more convenient for you.

CAUTION: Unlike with the newsgroups, in which information is passed to you only when you request it, subscribers to a mailing list receive *all* the mail sent to the list for the term of their subscription, whether they want it or not. Before you subscribe to too many lists, therefore, you should ensure that you have sufficient space in your incoming mailbox to support the volume of mail the lists might generate, which can be as many of 50 messages per day on a fairly active list. Also, be sure to keep the instructions for unsubscribing from the list; these will normally be e-mailed to you as part of the automated welcoming process.

You should be careful not to mail to a list unnecessarily; remember that a couple of hundred copies of your mail might be winging their way around the world a few minutes after you send it. To justify this, you should try to ensure that you really have something to say before mailing! You might find yourself in trouble with both your Internet provider and the administrators of any lists you subscribe to if you don't use mailing lists responsibly.

Quite a few mailing lists are related to various aspects of DOOM. The more important ones are given next.

dooml

Address: dooml@doomgate.cs.buffalo.edu
Subscription details: Send mail to majordomo@doomgate.cs.buffalo.edu with the command subscribe dooml or subscribe dooml-digest in the body of the message.
Topics: This is the original general-purpose DOOM, DOOM II, Heretic, and Hexen discussion list. The digest goes out weekly.

doomgate-announce

Address: doomgate-announce@doomgate.cs.buffalo.edu
Subscription details: Send mail to majordomo@doomgate.cs.buffalo.edu with the command subscribe doomgate-announce in the body of the message.
Topics: Announcement-only list dealing with various new things that take place on DoomGate, such as new additions to the Web or FTP archives, as well as general changes and improvements that the DoomWeb group is bringing out.

doom-editing

Address: doom-editing@nvg.unit.no
Subscription details: Send mail to doom-editing-request@nvg.unit.no or to doom-editing-digest-request@nvg.unit.no (subject and body immaterial).

Topics: This is the advanced DOOM-editing list. This list carries heavy traffic and is generally intolerant of beginners' questions, although some of its members do offer a help service for beginners (details are sent when you subscribe). The best thing to do if you're thinking of joining this list is to subscribe first, then lurk silently for a time (at least a week) to see what kinds of mailings are acceptable. Most of the grand wizards who contributed to this book are members of doom-editing; much of the material presented here first saw light of day there.

hexen-editing

Address: `hexen-editing@jalad.globalnews.com`
Subscription details: Send mail to `hexen-editing-request@jalad.globalnews.com` with the word `subscribe` in the body of the message.
Topics: This list is interested mostly in matters pertaining to Hexen's scripting language, and other Hexen-specific material that is felt to be of little interest to the doom-editing list. Once again, there is low tolerance of beginners' questions here.

quake-editing

Address: `quake-editing@nvg.unit.no`
Subscription details: Send mail to `quake-editing-request@nvg.unit.no` or to `quake-editing-digest-request@nvg.unit.no` (subject and body immaterial).
Topics: This list will be up and running only after the release of Quake. You're all set and ready to go....

util-announce

Address: `util-announce@doomgate.cs.buffalo.edu`
Subscription details: Send mail to `majordomo@doomgate.cs.buffalo.edu` with the command `subscribe util-announce` in the body of the message.
Topics: Announcement-only list dealing with new utilities and add-on tools to help you stay informed.

wads

Address: `wads@doomgate.cs.buffalo.edu`
Subscription details: Send mail to `majordomo@doomgate.cs.buffalo.edu` with the command `subscribe wads` in the body of the message.
Topics: General discussion forum for issues related to new level development. Critique, comments, and reviews regarding existing and newly released levels.

irc-dooml

Address: `irc-dooml@doomgate.cs.buffalo.edu`
Subscription details: Send mail to `majordomo@doomgate.cs.buffalo.edu` with the command `subscribe irc-dooml` in the body of the message.
Topics: Discussion of various issues that take place on `#doom` on IRC.

IRC

The Internet Relay Chat is a replacement for (and also an improvement on) Talk. A traditional UNIX tool, Talk enabled two people to conduct a conversation in real time. IRC expands on the concept to enable literally thousands of people to talk to one another through various *channels*.

For DOOM-related topics, several active channels exist: #doom, #doom2, #heretic, and #doomgate. As the names imply, the channels deal with various aspects of each game. You will most likely find the most traffic on #doom, however. Here you will be able to meet not only people who play the game but also those who actively participate in DOOM development (including, on occasion, people from id Software).

FTP SITES

FTP sites are probably the single most important resource of the Internet. They enable you to access files on remote computers for both download and upload. This means that you can obtain files and deposit files at public places. To access one of these sites, you need, in addition to Internet access, an FTP-client program. Such programs are frequently bundled with modems and over networking products.

DOOM SITES

Currently, the primary site for all DOOM-related materials is ftp.cdrom.com. This machine is owned by Walnut Creek CD-ROM. From this main machine, many other sites *mirror* (or copy) its files to enable users all around the world to access them more easily. To distribute the load equally among sites, always connect to the site nearest to you geographically when you want to download files.

CAUTION: Always connect to the *primary* site if you want to upload files. If you upload a file to one of the mirrors, the file will be removed when the machine next updates its copy of the primary site. When downloading files, however, it is best to connect to a mirror site closest to you. This will usually give you the fastest connection (as well as easing the load on the primary site for people wanting to upload).

Table 37.1 lists the main DOOM-related ftp sites at the time of writing. Many of these are mirror sites of ftp.cdrom.com, to which connection is often easier when the primary site has reached its maximum number of permitted connections—currently 500.

Table 37.1. FTP mirrors of `ftp.cdrom.com`.

Location	Site	Directory
California	`ftp.cdrom.com`	/pub/idgames
Australia	`ftp.next.com.au`	/pub/mirror/
Austria	`flinux.tu-graz.ac.at`	/pub/doom
California	`ftp.pht.com`	/pub/games/doom
England	`ftp.dungeon.com`	/pub/msdos/games/doom
Germany	`ftp.uni-erlangen.de`	/pub/pc/msdos/doom
Kentucky	`ftp.iglou.com`	/doom
Kentucky	`ftp.thepoint.com`	/pub/msdos/games/infant2.doom
Montana	`ftp.coe.montana.edu`	/pub/mirrors/doom
Netherlands	`ftp.sls.wau.nl`	/pub/msdos/doom
Oregon	`ftp.orst.edu`	/pub/doom
Pennsylvania	`smb130.rh.psu.edu`	/pub/doom
South Africa	`ftp.sun.ac.za`	/msdos/doom
Sweden	`ftp.luth.se`	/pub/doom
Taiwan	`nctuccca.edu.tw`	/pub/PC/games/doom
Wisconsin	`ftp.uwp.edu`	/pub/games/id/home-brew/doom

THE DIRECTORY STRUCTURE ON FTP.CDROM.COM

It is the directory structure of any ftp site that mostly determines how much time you waste hunting for the material you want. The directory structure of the DOOM area of `ftp.cdrom.com` is carefully arranged to minimize this, and if you log in to this site, you should find the correct area very quickly. Figure 37.1 shows the upper levels of this site.

The contents of most of these directories should be obvious:

- **docs:** Various information and documentation files, further divided by subject.
- **graphics:** Replacement graphics for DOOM, DOOM II, Heretic, and Hexen.
- **idstuff:** Shareware versions and official game patches from id Software.
- **incoming:** Upload your files here (see next section).
- **levels:** Add-on levels for each game variant are stored here, further divided by game and then alphabetically to keep ftp file lists down to a manageable size.
- **lmps:** Demos from other users.

- **misc:** Everything that doesn't fit anywhere else.
- **music:** Well, now, I'm not sure what's in here.
- **newstuff:** Files that the caretakers have not had time to sort. There is often so much in here that there is also an oldnewstuff directory within it that everything still in newstuff is periodically moved into.
- **sounds:** New sound effects.
- **themes:** Large PWAD projects are kept here to separate them from smaller, individual WADs.
- **utils:** DOOM-related utilities, further divided as shown in Figure 37.2.

Figure 37.1.

The ftp.cdrom.com *directory hierarchy.*

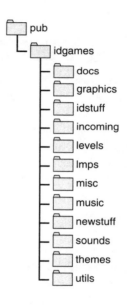

Figure 37.2.

The utils hierarchy.

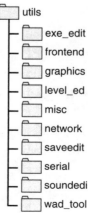

Because there is often little agreement over the categorization of some utilities, you might need to hunt around in these directories a bit before finding what you're looking for. It's well worth checking out all of these directories regularly anyway, if you're at all interested in the technical aspects of DOOM.

FTP BY E-MAIL

For those who do not have direct Internet access, a service is available that enables you to receive various DOOM-related files and documents by e-mail. A detailed document on how this service works is available in the form of a FAQ. It is maintained by John Van Essen (`vanes002@maroon.tc.umn.edu`) and is posted on a regular basis to rec.games.computer.doom.announce.

DISTRIBUTING YOUR OWN FILES

Whether it is a new level, a help file, or a review, each time anyone contributes something, many people benefit. You are therefore encouraged to distribute your own works by making them available either on the World Wide Web or on ftp sites such as `ftp.cdrom.com`. By doing this, your name becomes known throughout the world, and, ultimately, if you continue to provide the support or expertise, people turn to you for help or suggestions. And believe me, there is no greater feeling than when someone either thanks you for something you have done or asks you a good question, relying on your knowledge and expertise. Who knows, you might even be invited to write a book!

UPLOADING BY FTP

So your level is complete and you can finally share it with others. All you have to do now is upload the file to a well-known ftp site. As already indicated, the best place at the moment is `ftp.cdrom.com`, the main DOOM-related ftp archive. By common agreement, this site accepts uploads and then other sites mirror it; so your work will be all around the world within a day or two of your original upload.

> **NOTE:** Because of space constraints and changing fads, the primary DOOM site might change from time to time. In the event of a change, information will always be posted to all relevant newsgroups and mailing lists, so even if you only sporadically read some of the forums, you should always be able to find out what the current site is.

Uploading any file to an ftp site is a simple process. Before you do that, though, make sure that you have everything ready to deliver. Here are the steps to follow first:

1. Compress the file(s) you intend to upload into a single .ZIP file, using a utility such as PKZIP.

2. If you are going to upload a WAD, fill out a WAD Authoring Template. (You will find a sample template later in this chapter, and a blank for your own use on the CD-ROM that accompanies this book—it's called WAT.TXT.) It is crucial to have some standardized way of recording various aspects

of your level. This template is used by all authors, and it covers all aspects of your level in a consistent fashion. Save your template file with the same name as your .ZIP file but with the extension .TXT instead.

3. If it's a utility you're intending to upload, be sure to write a short description of it so that people will know what it does without having to wait for it to download to them first. Usually, the first page or so of the documentation written to accompany the utility suffices. (You did write some documentation for the utility, didn't you?) Save this short description to a text file with the same name as your .ZIP file but with the extension .TXT instead.

4. Now that you have two files, you are ready to connect to the ftp site to upload your files.

To carry out the delivery, you need to have access to the Internet and have an ftp-client program. With this, you simply log in to the appropriate site (`ftp.cdrom.com` in most cases) as user `anonymous`, giving your complete e-mail address as the password.

NOTE: Don't get disheartened if your connection is refused. Most DOOM sites are very busy at all times. Just keep trying—you will get through eventually. Try to pick a time in the early hours of the morning (Pacific Standard Time) for the best chances of connection to `ftp.cdrom.com`.

The only directory to which you have permission to write your files is /pub/incoming, so you should change to this directory before attempting an upload.

CAUTION: Do not attempt to put your files in what you consider to be the most appropriate directory; the ftp server will not let you.

Before sending your files, make sure that you change the mode to BINARY; otherwise, your (binary) .ZIP file will be corrupted by the transfer. After you've done this, you should be able to send your files. Connections to remote machines are often a little shaky, and you might find that a transfer terminates abruptly or simply jams up solid. You might need to try a couple of times before you achieve a successful upload. (This could involve re-establishing the connection to the ftp site.)

As each file is uploaded and transfer completes, you should receive a confirmation saying that the transfer completed successfully. It is important to check this so as not to upset others when they try to download your level only to find out that it doesn't work.

Now your files are on the primary distribution FTP site. Within a few days, they will be moved into the right place in the directory tree, and other people will be able to use them.

ANNOUNCING YOUR WORK

Because there are so many DOOM goodies out there, it is important—if you want yours to be noticed—to inform the DOOM community on the Internet about your upload. The best way to do this is to post the MYLEVEL.TXT file (or whatever) to the rec.games.computer.doom.announce newsgroup. You can also mail it to the wads@doomgate.cs.buffalo.edu mailing list. From there you will have to wait and see what the users think about it. Be patient—it sometimes takes a while before anyone decides to mail you or comment on your level on a public forum.

Listing 37.1. WAD authoring template.

```
WAD Authoring Template V1.4   (Clip this line)
==================================================================
Title               :
Filename            : xxxx.WAD
Author              : Your name here
Email Address       :
Misc. Author Info   :

Description         : Set the mood here.

Additional Credits to  :
==================================================================

* Play Information *

Episode and Level #  : ExMx (,ExMx,...)
Single Player        : Yes/No
Cooperative 2-4 Player : Yes/No
Deathmatch 2-4 Player : Yes/No
Difficulty Settings  : Yes/Not implemented
New Sounds           : Yes/No
New Graphics         : Yes/No
New Music            : Yes/No
Demos Replaced       : None/1/2/3/All

* Construction *

Base                 : New level from scratch/Modified ExMx/xxx.WAD
Editor(s) used       :
Known Bugs           :


* Copyright / Permissions *

Authors (MAY/may NOT) use this level as a base to build additional
levels.

(One of the following)

You MAY distribute this WAD, provided you include this file, with
no modifications.  You may distribute this file in any electronic
format (BBS, Diskette, CD, etc) as long as you include this file
intact.
```

```
You MAY not distribute this WAD file in any format.

You may do whatever you want with this file.


* Where to get this WAD *

FTP sites:

BBS numbers:

Other:
```

COMPUSERVE AND AMERICA ONLINE

Several areas on CompuServe and America Online feature DOOM-related files and information. Some of the areas offer mainly information, whereas others are good sources for downloading files. Table 37.2 lists the main areas to visit on CompuServe.

Table 37.2. CompuServe forums.

Forum Name	GO Keyword	Notes
Gamers forum	GAMERS	Offers several DOOM-related software libraries and message areas.
Action Games	ACTION	Includes several related software download and message areas.
Computer Gaming World	CGWMAGAZINE	Includes 3-D Gaming area (the main place to visit).
Hot Games	HOTGAMES	Provides mostly demos and limited play versions of games.
ZD Net Action Games	ZDACTI	Requires payment of additional fees.
ZD Net Software Center	CENTER	Requires payment of additional fees.

The main area to visit on America Online is the PC Games forum (keyword: PC Games). In the Message board, choose List Categories and then DOOM. To download files, visit the PC Games Software libraries and choose the DOOM area. You'll also find files in the Game Cheats and Editors and Game Hints and Fixes download areas.

EXIT: MOPPING UP AND MOVING ON

This chapter has introduced you to some of the places out on the Internet where you can continue the DOOM experience. It also has shown you how you can contribute to the growing corpus of DOOM material yourself, after you have finally attained wizard status. The next chapter takes a good look at some of the best that has been produced by those who have gone before you, to uplift and inspire you to even greater things yourself.

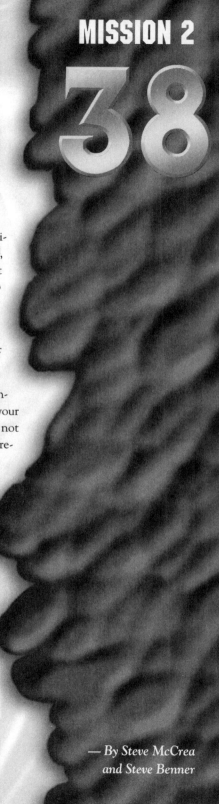

WORTHY WADS

The bulk of this book concerns itself with the technicalities and practicalities of creating your own add-on levels—WAD files—for DOOM, DOOM II, Heretic, and Hexen. To draw the book to a close, we present some of the best homemade WADs so that you can see what others who have walked this path before you have achieved. With only one exception, all the WADs presented in this chapter are available on the CD-ROM that accompanies this book. This chapter is designed to serve both as a guide to the best of the WADs on the CD-ROM and as a showcase of the current state of the art of WAD alchemy.

When you have seen the results, we hope that you will be inspired to continue your own designs and that you will pick up the gauntlet thrown at your feet, accepting the challenge to do better. If the task seems daunting, do not be disheartened. Remember that each of the WADs presented here was created linedef by painstaking linedef by someone just like yourself (although possibly with more spare time). A full list of the creators of each of the WADs on the *Alchemy* CD-ROM is given at the end of the chapter.

This chapter might spoil many of the surprises that these levels would otherwise supply—you might prefer to play them first. You can do this most easily using the DoomShell utility described in Chapter 5, "Playing New Levels."

THE GREATEST WADS OF ALL TIME

Certain WADs have taken the world by storm and have become firm favorites of nearly all players. Let's get this show on the road by taking a look at these.

— By Steve McCrea and Steve Benner

ALIENS-TOTAL CONVERSION

NOTE: For legal reasons, it is not possible to include the *Aliens*-TC WAD on the CD-ROM that accompanies this book. Check out the main DOOM archives on the Internet, listed in Chapter 37, "Out and About," to find a copy. By way of recompense, the author of *Aliens-TC*, Justin Fisher, has provided a specially created graphics library for use in your own WADs. You can find details of this in Chapter 32, "The *Alchemy* Graphics Library."

Aliens-Total Conversion, or *Aliens*-TC, is perhaps the most famous (or at least, infamous) homemade WAD of all. It is, to my knowledge, the only WAD to provoke a public (if not official) response from id Software when John Romero declared "*Aliens*-TC kicks ass!"

The scene is a landing pad outside a docking bay. The edges of the pad are rimmed with safety barriers that are painted with warning stripes. Lights course down short poles and along chevrons on the ground, to guide ships in. Toward the horizon, large brown stones are scattered on the earth.

The opening scene from *Aliens*-TC is indicative of the amount of work (and attention to detail) that has gone into this WAD. The big stones blend perfectly with the mountainous backdrop to give a real sense of depth to the landscape. The flashing pole is set up as a three-frame animation in the object table using DeHackEd, whereas the chevrons are new floor flats, replacing green slime.

A lift leads down into the bay, where barrels occupy the corners. Shooting a barrel results in a dribble of fluid running from a hole in the side. On a wall of the bay is the number 37, in bold print, its neon numbers flickering erratically.

The floor level number on the wall is in a narrow recess textured in steel with the random flashing attribute, covered by a transparent texture with cutouts for the digits—a brilliant stroke of design.

The lift sound is just one of 35 well-chosen sound effects from the film, all of which enhance the feeling that this isn't DOOM anymore.

Progressing down a darkened side passage, Apone barks, "Check those corners!" Entering a nearby room, the floor strewn with debris, Apone comments, "Sir, this place is dead. Whatever happened here, I think we missed it."

Incredibly, the first level has no enemies. In a very brave move by the author, the player instead wanders around a deserted complex, discovering the changes made by the defending humans and stumbling across evidence of alien activity. (They also have the opportunity to stock up on ammunition and armor.) Lighting is expertly controlled, with an exceedingly good mix of dim and slightly flickering areas.

Occasional outbursts of dialogue are actually triggered at appropriate moments. The "Check those corners" object is created by giving the dialogue to a monster as a wake-up cry and then editing the frame table to make this monster invisible and remove it from the game on waking up. Each time Sergeant Apone says "Check those corners," it is this type of object, placed nearby. A superb idea, and needless to say, the atmosphere it generates is tremendous.

The docking area is secure. An intermission screen indicates that the next objective is to rescue the colonists from the atmospheric processor. As the lift descends into an area that shows all the signs of heavy infestation, Apone reminds you that there might be survivors out there. Fibrous green matter hangs off the walls, and here and there corpses are stored near open eggs. (See Figure 38.1.)

Figure 38.1.

Finding some of the colonists by an opened alien egg.

The alien-infested regions are very cleverly done. Justin extracted some of the skin and flesh textures from the Inferno episode and recolored them dark green. He then cut bits of corpses from various textures and pasted them in. Rib-like objects are arranged along the edges to roughen the passage.

Finally, a dark shape rushes forward. The shotgun barks, and the alien explodes with a screech in a spray of deadly acid. The next one won't get so close. From the direction of a closed egg comes a gurgling sound, and suddenly a facehugger is scuttling rapidly into another shotgun shell. If only it weren't so dark…

Alien behavior is well implemented though a DeHackEd patch. Some are basically Demons, with only a close attack, whereas others (with some artistic license) are Imps who spit acid at you. Facehuggers do actually hatch from alien eggs and then behave like ground-based skulls.

The first eight levels loosely follow the plot of the film *Aliens*, ending in a cargo loader showdown with the alien queen in the Sulaco (see Figure 38.2).

Aliens-TC is the most complete add-on to DOOM ever written, evoking those old feelings of fear and trepidation you experienced when you first played DOOM. It is also a fine homage to the film!

Figure 38.2.
Aliens-*TC*. *Using the cargo loader in the Sulaco.*

DOOMSDAY OF UAC

Leo Martin Lim's Doomsday of UAC (commonly known just by its filename of UAC_DEAD) is a massive single level for DOOM. It weighs in at nearly 400KB for the level data alone, with a starry sky patch completing the file. (In comparison, the largest—and my favorite—level in DOOM, The Spawning Vats, is a mere 184KB.) The setting is the headquarters of the UAC corporation in Jakarta, which has (surprise, surprise) been overrun by assorted Hell-spawn.

You awaken inside a narrow aluminum container. The presence of three Medikits is somewhat disquieting, as is the total lack of visible features on the walls and floor. You throw open one of the walls to reveal a Demon and its Former Human Sergeant handlers in a narrow passage. Two or three Medikits later, you step out of the passage into a huge courtyard.

So far, nothing particularly inventive. It makes for a frantic start if the player is armed with only a pistol, as seen in a number of the original levels, such as The Spawning Vats. There are several more Spectres, Former Human Sergeants, and Imps around the end of the passage before the player has a chance to relax.

You glance back at the aluminum container. It is a truck trailer, turned on its side! The back door, emblazoned with the UAC logo, is hinged back, and the wheels are still spinning after the crash. Nearby are rows of similar trailers, in a more natural attitude.

Putting the trailer on its side was very clever, allowing the wheels and axle to be detailed immaculately with a single O-shaped sector. The tires are the DOORTRAK texture, given a scrolling effect to make them appear to spin. Rear lights on some of the other trailers are the thin, blue striplights in aluminum frames. However, this is just a warm-up for the spectacle to come.

Some distance ahead of the trailer you find the cab, also lying on its side with its wheels spinning. The engine cover has popped open to reveal a burning engine, but strangely, the headlights still cut a bright swath through the gloom. From the bloodstains, you guess that the driver has been dragged away though the shattered windshield. Angrily, you shoot the fuel tank.

It is hard to find fault in this piece of DOOM architecture, and very hard to believe that it is even possible, given the restrictions of the graphics engine. However, closer examination reveals that only one floor and one ceiling are visible in any one region of the truck. Excellent little touches such as the headlights and the barrel for a fuel tank complete the effect. Pools of blood are used throughout the level in a creative way.

You jog down a wide curving ramp to a circular courtyard, at its center a fountain filled with blood. You make short work of the Imps hiding behind the stone sculpture of the letters UAC, then waste the Former Human Sergeants lurking in a dimly lit underground parking lot down another curving ramp. Fluorescent tubes flicker erratically on all sides of the regular lines of concrete supports. (See Figure 38.3.)

Figure 38.3.
Picking off the Hell-spawn that are hiding behind the UAC statue.

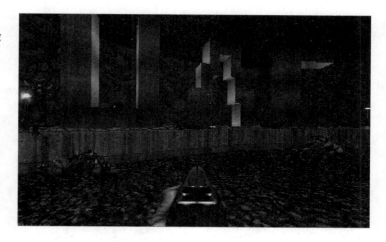

Similar floor and wall textures disguise the steps on the ramps, giving the immediate impression of a smooth slope. The center of the fountain includes a blood-drooling gargoyle texture. The UAC lettering again makes the player wonder how it is done. In contrast to *Aliens*-TC, the fluorescents are lit in the standard way, using a small flickering sector in front of the wall.

When you finally enter the headquarters buildings proper, a sudden urge overtakes you, probably because this place is making you nervous. You slip into a nearby room, and not wanting to squeeze between a line of soldiers, you start looking under the doors for an empty cubicle. When you get in, you find that all it contains is a box of bullets, which you have to use on the soldiers.

Leo has used the fact that doors can be initially partly open, here. In a subsequent level, called Cheese, the women's toilets contain not water but blood!

You stagger, relieved, into a tall marble lobby. Large cylindrical columns hang from the ceiling, supporting spotlights. Taking a moving walkway, you enter a long room containing a low rectangular table. As you approach the table, shutters over the windows rise to reveal a heavily populated balcony.

There is a board meeting in progress in the next room, and the board members are concentrating heavily on the meeting briefs laid before them on the circular table. The walls are brightly illuminated, highlighting monitors and maps. The doors behind you remain hinged open, but instead you open the secret door behind the speaker's podium and venture into the hellish passage beyond.

The architecture in this level is highly effective, with the rooms and furniture slightly larger than life, which has the effect of intimidating the player. The huge columns supporting the spotlights look as though they came directly from the lobby of an expensive hotel. The walkway does not actually carry the player along, but otherwise it is realistic. Similarly, the hinged doors are there even before the doors are opened, but the presence of a large collection of Cacodemons is a good distraction.

Narrowly avoiding falling into two deadly pits, you finally choose the correct path in the underground complex and step out onto a ledge above a huge lake of lava. Ahead of you, you can see pairs of candles floating in the air, marking what appears to be a path across the chamber. "The hell with it," you think, "it worked for Indiana Jones in the Last Crusade." So you step off the ledge and onto…an invisible staircase! (See Figure 38.4.) Running across, you cannot help but notice the poor guy hanging in the rock formation to your right. He certainly has lost a lot of blood.

Figure 38.4.
On the invisible staircase.

The invisible staircase is the trick in this level that made it so famous, and it is quite bizarre that it exists at all. If you have read Chapter 24, "Special Visual Effects," you should know how the effect is achieved. One must assume that Leo discovered this technique by accident, though, because John Carmack himself would have had a hard time predicting its existence. Leo certainly put it to good effect.

At the top of the staircase is a room, the door of which locks behind you. A Cyberdemon floats unmoving on the red keycard, surrounded by four skulls that hover above your dead buddies. Clearly, some kind of Satanic ritual is under way. As you approach the Cyberdemon, Barons of Hell suddenly appear and attack you. In its death throes, one of the Barons completes the incantation, which awakens the summoned creatures. (See Figure 38.5.)

The monsters in the room are surrounded by invisible blocks, just like the staircase, that reach up to the ceiling. These are marked with the sector tag 666 so that they lower when the last Baron dies. (This level is E1M8.) The clever tricks around the Cyberdemon make up for its inclusion in such a small room, which is usually considered to be inexcusable.

Figure 38.5.

The Barons do not appreciate you interrupting their Satanic ritual.

Exhausted from the struggle, you finally find an escape shuttle powered up at the end of a runway, its engines roaring against a blast wall. Hopping in, you take off the brakes, allowing the ship to race toward the cliff edge.

The level ends with another spectacular vehicle. At the other end of the runway is a sector with ceiling texture F_SKY1 and a ceiling height equal to its floor height. The dividing line has no upper texture, and altogether this creates a cliff edge.

Doomsday of UAC features solid level design and interesting gameplay. What sets it apart is that every location is big, bold, and dramatic, and guaranteed to impress or baffle. As with many add-on levels, though, a fast machine is needed for the full experience.

ETERNITY

Eternity, or Serenity II, by Bjorn Hermans and Holger Nathrath, is a full DOOM episode that replaces the Shores of Hell. This, I think you will agree, is a huge undertaking when you consider that they have already released a highly acclaimed replacement episode for Inferno called Serenity. Having gotten some of the more bizarre ideas out of their systems in Serenity (for example, mazes with walk-through walls), the authors have settled down and designed a beautiful, traditional episode with an emphasis on playability.

You emerge from the end of the pipe into a bloody reservoir. At your feet lies a shotgun, which you snatch up gleefully before quickly wading forth. Some cannon fodder in a pipe a few steps to your right guards a radiation suit, and you rapidly clear the blockage in the pipe off to the left that leads to the main part of the complex.

Here, the presence of the radiation suit fools the player into thinking that this bloody complex of passages is going to be huge and torturous to navigate. The immense simplicity is then a great and unexpected relief (as well as an excellent design decision). Having gone to the trouble of selecting appropriate wall and floor textures, most designers would have made this section overly large, immediately frustrating the player.

On a more general note, acid floors in the episode are handled sensibly and are mostly avoidable. The player is more likely to encounter one as punishment for falling off a ledge, for instance, than as an impediment to further progress. Where it is necessary to cross such areas, radiation suits are provided, often in hidden areas. The authors have also ensured that is impossible to get trapped anywhere.

Down a pair of symmetrical stairways a passage stretches away, its lights flashing rhythmically. Between the stairways, an alcove sports a huge marble engraving of a Baron, illuminated by a pair of striplights. As you venture down the passage, a door suddenly opens just ahead of you and its occupants stream out and attack.

Many of the rooms in the episode display partial symmetry, broken only by the passages in and out, adding an element of realism to the architecture. The authors are not afraid to borrow an idea or two from the original id Software levels, such as the passage with its alternately dark and flashing light levels.

There are many recurring decorations, one of which is the Baron engraving. In contrast to the id Software levels—where the presence of this icon symbolized the imminent appearance of a Baron and hence served to set the player's nerves on edge—in this episode it usually is just decoration. Similarly, the conventions of what are normally teleport pads have been upset, because quite often the pads are nothing more than placemats for keys. These and other details are at least consistent throughout and contribute to the unique feel of the levels (as well as serving to throw old hands off-balance from time to time).

In the majority of homemade WADs, when rooms full of bad guys open suddenly, those rooms are usually behind you, and Sergeants make short work of your back. Not so here. This is typical of the fair play of the enemy. It is a rare moment in this game when you are not given the opportunity to shoot first.

Beyond the strobing passage is a marble-walled room, the marble broken vertically at regular intervals by rusting iron beams. In the center of the room, brightened by a large rectangular skylight, the yellow skull-key rests atop a platform. When you throw the switch facing the platform, however, parts of the balcony drop into the floor, revealing stairs down into the lower regions of the room.

The marble-and-iron motif crops up repeatedly in the levels, and it is one of the many original and imaginative combinations of textures that breathe new life into the old id Software graphics. Holes in the ceiling are made to accentuate the dramatic look of a room, contrasting sharply the edges of the room and its center.

The playing sequence is not entirely predictable, but at the same time it is usually obvious what to do next. It is clear that the levels are designed almost exclusively for single-player rather than Deathmatch mode. Travel from one point to another in a level is by a specific route. The effect of the switch, although unexpected, is both visible and audible from the switch location, and hence rewarding.

A line of archways splits the lower area in two, and at each end lies a door. Through the archways, strips on the columns of the arch cast overlapping cones of light onto suspicious-looking panels. (See Figure 38.6.) You nudge a panel open and find the blue skull-key. Meanwhile, one of the other panels has slid open, releasing more of the usual beasts to roam amongst the archways. You take the key with one hand while you pump the shotgun with the other.

Wherever possible, the authors have added realistic lighting in the form of light coming in through windows and skylights, artificial light sources such as torches and wall strips, and the shadows cast by both. The effort they have expended was not wasted; indeed, the lighting is one of the most eye-catching features of the episode. (See Figure 38.7.)

Figure 38.6.

Lights affixed to beautifully constructed archways.

Figure 38.7.

The lighting was inspired by the starting room in DOOM's Spawning Vats.

Just before the exit you come across a capital R cut into the floor of a room and filled with glowing slime. The slime casts a faint reversed R on the ceiling. (See Figure 38.8.) Ignoring it totally, you sprint into the exit room, and having waited for the opposition to be crushed, you time your bid for the central column and freedom (at least until the next mission).

Each level has a letter prominently incorporated into one of the rooms in some way, so that over the eight levels the letters spell out *Serenity*. (From which you can deduce that the level just described was number three.) Fortunately, this did not influence the design of the levels, as the rooms in question are just tacked onto the map. The final level recapitulates the letters and then adds the Y, which is also used to make the Cyberdemon easier to deal with by raising and lowering just enough to block his rockets when raised.

Also of note on the final level is a beautiful semi-transparent stained-glass texture that looks terrific with the hellish red sky visible through the gaps. Perhaps coincidentally, Heretic also features stained glass textures, although not transparent and not so realistic (the Eternity graphic appears to be a scanned photograph).

Figure 38.8.
The trademark of the episode—a letter that forms the centerpiece of a room on each level.

Eternity comprises eight varied yet consistent levels that have a unique and enjoyable feel, with the style of play allowing a mainly offensive approach. The difficulty levels are sensibly chosen, with "Hurt Me Plenty" about equivalent to "Ultra-Violence" in the original DOOM and "Ultra-Violence" roughly the same as "Ultra-Violence" in DOOM II. A lot of care has been taken to make the levels look good and play better.

RETURN TO PHOBOS

When Michael Kelsey's Return to Phobos was released, it was one of the first full-episode replacements available, and it was eagerly received by the Internet community. There was much discussion about the excess of switches and puzzles (there are two new textures, both switches), but there was no disputing that id Software itself would have been proud of this one. To this day no one has so successfully recaptured the spirit of Knee Deep in the Dead and placed it in a WAD.

You are outside a huge slab of a building. From the front, with its columns and overhangs, it is highly reminiscent of a museum. (See Figure 38.9.) The central entrance is a door formed from a thin metal panel stretched between a pair of thick beams. When you try to open the door beyond, it sticks. After a few attempts, you open it enough to get under.

Doors in Return to Phobos are not always simply a rectangular sector with a picture of a door on it. Here is a door with a meaningful shape, followed by one with an unpredictable character. The sticking door is a clever trick, relying on the standard door behavior of rising to just below the lowest neighboring ceiling. There is a sector on the left of the door with a crushing ceiling. (The scraping sound is audible next to the door.) The sector is hidden by a DOORTRAK texture on the two-sided line separating it from the door.

Although there are no examples on this level, lifts are also made more interesting, for example, by having pillars with SUPPORT, DOORTRAK, or LITE textures cutting into the lift sector. After you have seen one of these types of lifts, standard DOOM lifts look plain and unrealistic.

Figure 38.9.
The spectacular facade of the main building in Return to Phobos.

You make it out the back of the building, past the huge shallow pool set among tall columns. A set of stairs leads to the upper floors, where from a window you can almost see over the perimeter wall. You take another flight of stairs even higher, and from here the view is spectacular. Beyond the wall, irregularly patterned agricultural land stretches away to the base of the mountains. (See Figure 38.10.)

Figure 38.10.
Looking out an upper window toward fields stretching away to the mountains.

The author has set aside almost one third of the area of the level for this one view out a window. The fields are just any green flats; at long range, the details of the ground are lost. The edge of the map has been carefully positioned to avoid the sky texture wrapping around vertically.

Returning to the main building, you enter a cavernous area, the extents of which are hidden in darkness. Above the watery floor, small dimly lit rooms are cut into columns, and steps lead variously up and down between them. As you move from column to column, you are knocked from a set of steps by an attacking skull. It is a short swim to the nearest teleport, which takes you back to one of the columns. (See Figure 38.11.)

Figure 38.11.

Fighting on the steps between rooms cut into a series of columns high above some water.

This is the most impressive location you will ever see in any DOOM level. The lighting is perfect; there is just enough to let you see the neighboring columns. The ground is far enough down that when there, none of the steps or little rooms can be seen. And it is great fun to rush up a set of stairs and blow an Imp out the far side of a column down into the water with the shotgun. To avoid the area slowing down excessively, it is irregularly shaped, with walls protruding from the edges and dividing the space into compartments.

You arrive on a wide balcony overlooking three sides of a large, chunky maze. From here you choose a route to the exit of the room and pick off its more obvious denizens before jumping in. Running swiftly to the end of the maze, you skip over some puddles of slime and throw a few switches, opening nearby doors. Only an Imp stands between you and the exit signs.

I never liked mazes, even when I was playing Wolfenstein 3D. (I hated secrets, too, but the DOOM approach to secrets has tempered my opinion somewhat.) The overview of the maze is a novel approach, though, and it works well. The acid puddles are just the right size so that you would be unlucky to be hurt when running over them, and even the switches are a lazy nod toward the designer's obsession with puzzles.

The first level is probably the worst offender in the puzzle department. To progress farther than the fifth room requires the execution of a bizarre series of jumps and button presses.

However, all the levels look excellent, thanks to good choice of textures and solid architecture. Everything feels right: columns are neither too fat nor too thin; passages are not overly cramped; doors are wide enough with tidy and functional-looking frames; stairs are never so steep as to make combat difficult; and transitions between textures on walls are always associated with an appropriate divider, such as one of the SUPPORT textures.

Once doors were doors, lifts were just plain ordinary lifts, and WAD files were just single levels. When Return to Phobos was released, it greatly influenced all that. Now, doors are often all kinds of shapes, lifts run on tracks or up pillars, and level designers long for the free time to finish their episodes-in-progress. Others should follow Michael Kelsey's example and reexamine the features that made id Software's original levels so great.

THE UNHOLY TRINITY

The Unholy Trinity, by myself (Steve McCrea), Simon Wall, and Elias Papavassilopoulos, started life as a rather pedestrian map of Trinity College, Cambridge. Somewhere along the line, I decided that that would not be enough, and I took a camera to the college. When the level was completed, nearly all its textures had been replaced by half a megabyte of scanned, retouched photographs and a few hand-drawn graphics. Add to this some entertaining tricks and challenging gameplay, and it could not fail. The original TRINITY.WAD was designed for use with DOOM. Versions are now available for DOOM, the Ultimate DOOM, and Heretic in single or multiplayer modes. The difficulty levels are fully implemented too.

You are looking out across a wide grassy courtyard criss-crossed by cobbled paths at a three-floor ivy-covered building with a sloping tiled roof. Next to it is a tan-colored stone building with tall, ornate windows. The sky is almost clear blue, with only a few scattered wispy clouds breaking the monotony.

The walls across the court are 384 units high, and although DOOM textures normally repeat every 128 units, these walls appear to have a 384-unit-high texture. The truth of the matter is that there is a sector behind the wall, a floor height of 128, and a ceiling height of 256. The upper, middle, and lower textures are each a part of the tall texture. The line of the wall is marked impassable so that skulls and Cacodemons cannot accidentally wander into the hidden sector and disappear. The lines making up the sector are marked as hidden, so they do not appear during the game in the auto-map.

SKY1 is redefined in the TEXTURE1 resource to consist of four patches, each 256 units wide. Therefore, the sky texture is 1024 pixels wide and is unique through 360 degrees. Each patch is aligned with a main compass point: the patch at 0 is east; the patch at 256 is north; the patch at 512 is west; and the patch at 768 is south. Note that this means the sky is mirrored left to right.

To your right, a dark rounded doorway leads into the Porters' Lodge, according to the calligraphy above the door. You dash into the plaster-walled room, open the wood-paneled hatch in the counter, and steal the porters' supply of shotgun shells. They have no need of them anymore, as their corpses are sprawled at your feet.

Darkening the doorway sector disguises the inherent squareness of the structure so that the rounded graphic with its black base fits in. The plaster and wood paneling are the two hand-drawn textures. The hatch is simply a lift that is set one unit lower than the rest of the counter to make it visible to the observant player. Unlike doors, lifts return exactly to their initial height, and the position of the hatch is not lost.

Back out in the main courtyard, there are gatehouses set into three sides, their octagonal towers standing above the rest of the buildings. On one of the gatehouses you see a clock face partially obscuring arched windows. Below the windows, a sculpture of Edward III stands in a small alcove. (See Figure 38.12.)

The towers protrude from the wall to disguise the essentially two-dimensional nature of the structure. For an example, look at the wall at the start of Inferno, which appears to be a big sheet of cardboard, and compare it with the doorway in the courtyard of E1M1, which looks very solid indeed. The sector dividing off the taller part of the wall is thin, because you can see through the lower F_SKY1 ceiling to the wall behind.

Figure 38.12.

The Edward III gate in the Unholy Trinity with the chapel on the right.

Details on each of the gatehouses are unique. Rather than having a full graphic for each of the walls, there are patches for windows, crests, statues, and the clock face, which are positioned over a plain stone background. Many of the textures in the level are handled this way, to save space in the WAD file. This level was the first to redefine TEXTURE1, and I had to write my own tools to do it. Now you have several to choose from! (See Chapter 30, "Synthesis Tools," for details of a selection of such tools available on the *Alchemy* CD-ROM.)

The chapel is packed with Imps arranging barrels under the supervision of a Former Human Sergeant. One or two shots takes care of them. On the altar lies one of your comrades. As you nudge the altar, the entire wall drops, revealing a hellish passage under the college. Down the passage is a chamber cut by a river of lava that runs between openings in the walls, and up to his waist in the lava stands a soldier.

There are several opportunities to kill monsters with barrels in the level, because I find it very satisfying when being attacked to single out and shoot the barrel in a horde of bad guys. It's almost as much fun as the chainsaw.

The channel is basically one of those hideous glitches involving missing textures put to good use. (If you want to know how it was done, look at Chapter 24, where it is explained in detail.)

When you attempt to go through a passage to the next court, the way is blocked by a door marked with the college coat-of-arms. Up some stairs, you find a Baron of Hell guarding a switch. The switch is slightly recessed into the plaster wall and flanked by copies of the same coat-of-arms. You throw the switch and return to the passage to find that the door has opened.

Identifying the switch with the coat-of-arms is a good way of associating it with the door. It is recessed into the wall to avoid having to redefine a switch texture to put a switch in a plaster-walled room. This is especially important if you want the level to be easy to include in a multi-author WAD file—for example, a series of good Cooperative levels. The alternative is to widen a standard switch texture and add your patches on the right-hand side. For some reason, all the switches in Heretic are recessed into the wall.

You enter a small, darkened room packed with soldiers in neat rows. Through a window in one wall is another player facing off against a Cyberdemon! During the scramble for the door handle, the words "CAMERA—PETER

MORGAN" *suddenly appear on the window, and the realization sinks in—it's only a movie. The player fires uselessly a few times before the Cyberdemon pulps him with a rocket.* (See Figure 38.13.)

Figure 38.13.
The Unholy Trinity cinema.

One of the centerpieces of the level is this cinema screen showing the credits for the level in a 27-frame animation. Each frame is defined in sequence between SLADRIP1 and SLADRIP3. DOOM looks for these two textures and animates whatever lies between them. The Cyberdemon, the player, and the rocket images seen in these textures are simply the game sprites applied as patches. DOOM does not distinguish between sprites and patches in textures, so it is a simple matter to apply them this way if you have access to a good WAD composition tool. The lettering had to be handled differently, though—each character was extracted and a new patch was made from it.

The Unholy Trinity was a ground-breaking level when it was first released because of the techniques it used, and thanks to the beauty of the buildings that it accurately portrays, it still looks good. As usual, however, complexity inevitably means it has a slow frame-rate in some areas. In "Ultra-Violence" mode, it is challenging to complete quickly, and even after some experience on the level, it still takes about 20 minutes to finish.

THE NEWCOMERS

As well as the classic WADs just described, there are always many new arrivals clamoring for attention, some of which might make equal claim to the title of Greatest WAD of all-time. A few of the front-runners are mentioned here.

OUTPOST 21

On the surface, Outpost 21 appears to be a peaceful complex that provides its small team of dedicated scientists with living quarters, research labs, and recreational facilities. When you arrive there, you are hardly expecting the hail of bullets that greets you. You dodge from building to building armed only with your standard issue sidearm, desperately seeking a way into the main building where there will surely be something better to defend yourself with.

Outpost 21, a DOOM level by Scott Amspoker, can hardly be classed as a newcomer. This WAD has been around since before DOOM II and although not as famous as many other WADs, it has long been a firm favorite of the cognoscenti. Designed for single-player only, Outpost 21 has its share of puzzles (none of them too difficult) and plenty of action. It has no special features to mark it out as innovative, but its excellent layout and masterful provisioning of weapons and ammo make for a good solid DOOM WAD to rank among the best. There are a lot of monsters to face in Outpost 21, arranged in such a way that they come in a more-or-less steady stream (and generally from all sides). You won't find a lot of surplus ammo, though, and the bigger weapons (and even armor) can be hard to come by. To survive, you'll need to do a lot of running and a lot of dodging. Don't combine this with too much shooting though, or you'll quickly be down to fists.

The government boasts that Outpost 21 is the home of scientific research that will benefit all humanity. Neither they nor the aliens who recently inhabited Outpost 21 are aware of the dark and dirty secrets that lie beneath.

Another feature that makes this WAD so popular is the attention paid to the lighting levels throughout. There is excellent integration of outdoor and indoor areas, with the lighting always just right for each situation. Scott is an absolute master with DOOM's lowest lighting settings, too. All apprentice WADsters would do well to study this WAD carefully.

BOOTHILL

Well, pardner, it seems like the townsfolk heard we was acomin', for they sure as hell have made themselves scarce. Everyone seems to have checked out of the hotel in a hurry, but it was nice of someone to leave their six-shooters behind—they'll come in handy. Not a soul in the bordello, or the saloon, either, though there's a pretty tune coming from the pianola. Guess no one'll mind if I help myself to a drink before I go look for Billy. I sure do hope for this town's sake that no harm has come to him…

Boothill, a Deathmatch-only WAD for DOOM II, is an absolute must for any fans of the Western genre. Tim Ash, Jason Kirby, and Dave King have done a great job recreating a classic Western set with new textures galore and new sprites to replace many of the standard DOOM power-ups. Most of the weapons have been redesigned to match the new scenario with altered firing sounds too. In fact, the level of detail that Boothill's designers have managed to cram into this WAD just has to be seen to be believed.

The layout of the WAD is extremely compact, but like a real town, it has a vast number of routes between the main areas—all buildings that you'd expect to find in an early Western town. One or two clever little tricks—such as a pianola (complete with scrolling piano-roll) that starts playing when a player approaches it—serve to keep everyone notified of player movements in certain areas. Theses touches make a level ideal for Deathmatch because no one can stay hidden for long.

The pianola effect is achieved by replacing the normal turbo lift sound with a sampled Western-style, honkytonk tune and then tagging each of the lines of the piano stool sector to another small sector (tucked away out of sight) with WR turbo lift actions. The hidden lift sector is partnered by another small, hidden sector, whose floor is positioned at the right height below the lift sector to make the sample play for just the right length of time. The bottles on the tables of the saloon are actually DOOM health potions, nicely redesigned.

The scale of the WAD and the excellent use of different floor levels make this a superb Deathmatch environment. The designers have introduced a degree of humor that works really well, too. There are jokes aplenty to lighten the mood, none of which really pall or come to irritate as such things so often can when seen or heard for the hundredth time. From the presence of Billy to the replacement of DOOM's armor bonuses and the intriguing way of finishing each level, much of this WAD is guaranteed to produce a smile or two.

It's been a long day, but it ain't over yet. I'm still here, but the Marshal and his men are still here too. The ammo's running low, and the light is fading. Looks like there's a long night ahead for one and all. I wonder how many of us will see the dawn…

Boothill replaces the first four levels of DOOM II. Each new level provides a similar Western town, although the layouts vary, with each more compact to ensure that the action never wanes. Each level is set at a different time of day, too. The first level is in the full light of day, but dusk is falling in the second level, and it's full night by time you reach level three. This level demonstrates excellent control of a WAD's lighting levels with expertly judged areas of shadow around the buildings. Level four is set at dawn, and the town has acquired a small park, beautifully designed and executed, complete with ceremonial cannon—quite a useful Deathmatch weapon, as it happens!

The only real fault that I can find with this WAD is that there isn't more of it! Sadly, Tim Ash has found life too busy to complete the addition of all the planned levels, but there is still plenty to both occupy and delight the Deathmatch player in Boothill. All in all, it is fair to say that no aspect of WAD design has been overlooked in making this a really fun level to play.

MEMENTO MORI

Right from the opening screen with its new logo, Memento Mori oozes quality. A full replacement for every level of DOOM II with full implementation of all difficulty settings in all modes of play (although Cooperative play is recommended), this WAD is surely one of the most important third-party WADs. It is certainly one of the most impressive. The result of four months of almost non-stop work by 22 of the most renowned WAD builders from around the globe, Memento Mori is what many people wanted DOOM II to be!

Suddenly you find yourself face to face with a horde of soldiers, all servants of the forces of the giant pentagram upon which they march. To you, they are nothing more than the source of a better weapon. Moving on, you quickly clear the circular corridor outside. Looking for a way on, you find a switch. You press it—and find yourself dropped into the midst of yet more Hell-spawn…

From the outset, Memento Mori is non-stop action, but it is also much more than that. Many of DOOM II's original textures have been expanded and improved, and there are incredibly large floor and ceiling details (such as the huge red pentagram on the floor inside the opening room)—every single one expertly crafted and faultlessly applied. The designers have used just about every novel design trick that they could lay their hands on (and many that they devised themselves). One of the early switches triggers the building of a *descending* staircase, for instance, resulting in the player being dropped instantly among a roomful of Imps. Fortunately, the Imps have their backs to the action, so they don't get too much of an advantage over the startled player!

This little trick is achieved by creating a self-rising staircase with all the stair sectors except the first initially set to the height of the *top* step. When the action is triggered, the steps drop to their finishing heights, rather than building upwards in the usual way. Because the player has to stand on the second step to press the switch, there is no avoiding the sudden plunge.

With so many different designers working on the levels, it is amazing how coherently the levels of Memento Mori follow one another. This has partly been achieved by the team working to a consistent story-line thread and partly by pooling and sharing new texture resources so that a consistent feel permeates all the levels. At the same time, each level is different so that variety is maintained and all possibility for boredom is firmly banished. It is also amazing how much excellent architecture has been squeezed into this WAD, with every level providing a visual feast. This WAD is undoubtedly destined to become one of the greatest DOOM II add-ons of all time.

Memento Mori is brought to you by Denis and Thomas Moeller, Michiel Rutting, David Davidson, Tom Mustaine, Jens Nielsen, Orin Flaherty, Eric Sargent, Marc Anthony Klem, Alden Bates, Eric Reuter, Mackay "Avatar" McCandlish, Florian Helmberger, Kurt Schmid, Eric Sambach, Henrik Rathje, Michael Rapp, Scott Lampert, Andy Badorek, Milo and Dario Casali, and William Sullivan.

OTHER WORTHY WADS

In addition to the classic WADs (and the classics-in-the-making) just discussed, there are many other WADs worthy of your attention. Unfortunately, there is simply not enough space to describe them all (or even list their names) in this book. Brief mention will be made, however, of a few WADs that come highly recommended, either for their overall design or for some particular feature that lifts them above the ordinary.

GALAXIA

Galaxia, a single-player level for DOOM, was Pavel Hodek's first WAD. Some players might find the presence of a Spider Mastermind in the first room a little off-putting and immediately dismiss the WAD as a typical first attempt. They would be over-hasty. By keeping your eyes peeled and your wits about you (and your finger on the Shift key!), it is possible to progress beyond the first room and go on to discover just how vast and richly furnished with new ideas the Galaxia WAD is. Pavel has made a number of subtle changes to various aspects of the game—such as new sounds for many monsters and weapons—thus keeping the player unsure of all that is happening.

DEIMOS SUBWAY

Deimos Subway, by Neal Ziring, is a replacement for DOOM's E2M1. Intended principally for a single player, this WAD places the action in a subway overrun by you-know-what! The WAD uses a range of replacement graphics that work well in the chosen environment. The subway scenario enables Neal to use a wide variation of lighting levels to good effect too, as well as providing an excuse for a long linear run of open sectors that give the monsters (as well as the player) lots of opportunities to roam around and keep popping up unexpectedly.

Neal employs few special effects in this WAD, preferring to supply a good solid design with the emphasis on playability and attention to detail. He also likes secret areas, providing a number of hidden passageways and switches secreted away in corners or behind obstructions. Many of these need to be located to make progress, although the WAD is so large and open that there is never any sense of frustration or feeling that one is trapped in an area with nothing to do but find the exit. The balance of weapons, ammo, and monsters is just about ideal, too—especially at Hurt Me Plenty level. The WAD is extremely difficult to complete at Ultraviolence level, though; don't waste any ammo if you play at this level.

The really special touches in this WAD are in the extra decorative detail that generally contributes little or nothing to play but makes the scenario so much more realistic and a real treat to explore. All in all, Deimos Subway is a positive gem of a WAD.

NECROMANIA

Necromania from Cerebral Software (James and Chas Blachly and Brendon Goza) is another large-scale DOOM II WAD, playable in all game modes. Complete with DeHackEd patch, this WAD changes many aspects of the game to lend something of a TC feel to the WAD. The levels are pure DOOM, however, with non-stop action for the trigger happy. It isn't killing all the way, though; there are plenty of puzzles and lots of route-finding challenges. Somehow, level designers James and Brendon manage to always keep one more surprise around the next corner—even those corners that you've turned half a dozen times already (or think you have).

Players who dislike tricks and traps will probably hate all fifteen levels of this WAD. I found that the thinking and the shooting (and the running) are very well balanced, though. Each time you think a trap has got the better of you, the way out suddenly becomes clear. The balance of monsters, weapons, and ammo is good, too, with power-ups appearing just when you need them (or ominously beforehand).

The design of the maps is imaginative and generally well-executed, with lighting and shading always handled well. I do hope that this WAD team finds the time and the energy to complete their projected additional fifteen levels. If they can maintain the high standard of this WAD, Necromania will become a truly worthy WAD.

WIZARD4

Wizard4, by Phil Burnham, is a replacement for Heretic's E1M7. It supports all play modes (although it's a less-than-satisfactory Deathmatch WAD because of its large size) at all difficulty settings. This WAD is worthy of note for the attention to detail that has gone into its design. Every texture is meticulously aligned (not always easy to achieve in Heretic) and the lighting levels are well-nigh ideal. The author has paid attention to good building design with a good balance of open areas and enclosed corridors.

Wizard4 contains plenty of surprises for the player (as well as a couple of new sounds to add variety; the new crossbow sound is particularly good). No new textures have been added, but Heretic's fairly narrow range has been fully exploited and used to good effect.

The balance of power in Wizard4 is better than in many of the original Heretic levels, although it is by no means easy at any difficulty setting! It takes a long time to explore this huge WAD. Some of the puzzles are a little tricky to solve, although nothing is impossible—just stick at it and be prepared to play this great level a lot before you beat it!

SHADOWX1

Shadowx1 is the first WAD for Hexen to be compiled by the Shadow BBS WAD team of Jay "Lasher" Darji, Alan "Talis" Willard, Kevin "Undertaker" Farley, and Donovan "Conqueror" Young. This is a Deathmatch-only WAD containing 15 levels, all based around the central opening Hub. This is a great idea because it enables players to select a level to play from within the game without ever having to quit. Each of the portals out from the Hub is indicated on the ground nearby to help players identify and select their favorite areas easily. The authors have also made clever use of Hexen scripts to run the credits for the WAD shortly into play.

Shadowx1 uses some great new sound effects, replacing many of the standard Hexen sounds. The WAD is let down only by its rather monotonous lighting levels and occasional poor use and alignment of textures. Most players will be too busy running around collecting the goodies and hunting their friends to worry too much about either of these aspects, though.

EXIT: CREDITS

Sams Publishing would like to thank all the people who contributed levels for the CD-ROM. They are Scott Amspoker, John W. Anderson, Mark Anderson, Shane Arnott, Tim Ash, James Atchison, Andy Badorek, Piet Barber, Nicholas Barnard, Alden Bates, Dusty Bedford, Nicholas Bell, Cimarron Benjamin, David Biggs, Mark Billingham, Robert Bingham, James and Chas Blachly, Vance Andrew Blevins, Daniel Bondurant, Doug Branch, Lawrence Britt, Gerry Browne, Antony Burden, Phil Burnham, Bill Campbell, Peter Captijn, Dario Casali, Milo Casali, Scott Coleman, Scott F. Crank, Michael Cullen, Garth Cumming, David Davidson, Jay Darji, Aaron Desilet, Colin John Dickens, Valter Di Dio, Scott Dougherty, Jason Dyer, Doug Dziedzic, Edgar Easterly, IV, Andrew Elliott, Jim Elson, Darrell Esau, Kevin Farley, Andrea Farnocchia, Barry Ferg, Glenn Fisher, Orin Flaherty, Kenneth S. Forte, Tom Frial, Jean-Serge Gagnon, Corrado Giustozzi, Brandon Goza, Mark K. Gresbach Jr., Daniel Griffiths, Magne Roar Groenhuis, Stefan Gustavson, Terry Hamel, Ryan Hare, Timothy Harris, Mark Harrison, Noah Haskell, Stephen Heaslip, Florian Helmberger, Bjorn Hermans, David J. Hill, Jan Hladik, Pavel Hodek, Shawn Holmstead, Lawrence Hosken, Joel Huenink, Drew Hurlstone, Steve Huskisson, Danny Hyde, Jim Imes, John Jablonski, Jawed Karim, Gerhard Karnik, Robin Charles Kay, Matthew E. Keller, Michael Kelsey, Andy Kendall, Dave King, Joseph King, Jason Kirby, Marc Anthony Klem, Christen David Klie, Jim Kugelman, Jeffrey Kung, Ricardo Lafaurie Jr., Scott Lampert, Sam Lantinga, Nelson Laviolette, Joe Lawrence, Leo Martin Lim, Phil Longueuil, Andre Lucas, John C. Lyons, Stefan Maes, Jon Mandigo, Michael Marsh, Brian K Martin, Fairfax Shield McCandlish, Mackay McCandlish, Bill McClendon, Steve McCrea, David McGruther, E McNutt, Jason Michelsen, Denis Moeller, Thomas Moeller, Olivier Montanuy, Larry Mulcahy, Gordon Mulcaster, Andrew Murphy, Dr. Roger MW Musson, Tom Mustaine, Holger Nathrath, Cameron Newham, Jens Nielsen, Chris Niggel, Michael Niggel, Rutger Nijlunsing, Pete Nilson, Andy Olivera,

Elias Papavassilopoulos, Denis Papp, Steven and Rand Phares, Joe Popp, Warren Racz, Michael Rapp, Henrik Rathje, Michael Reed, Eric C. Reuter, Steve Rice, Alex Rivero, Anthony Rocchio, Todd Rodowsky, Tim Rodreguez, C. Bradford Rose, Marc Rousseau, David Russell, Michiel Rutting, Doug Ryerson, Eric Sambach, Eric Sargent, Dave Sawford, Andrew Scarvell, Kurt Schmid, Klas Scholdstrom, Eric Severn, Lloyd Shelby, Ryan Shephard, Shane Sherman, Jimmy Sieben, Scott A. Smith, Richard Smol, Joe Sola, Craig and Brian Sparks, Glenn Storm, Phil Stracchino, William Sullivan, Alfred Svoboda, Dave Swift, Erwen Tang, Sam Taylor, Robert Teegarden, Dan Teeter, James Thompson, Paul Turnbull, M. Van der Heide, Jack Vermeulen, John Wakelin, Simon Wall, Russ Walsh, Larry Wangemann, Richard Ward, Phillip Wayne, Daniel Weed, Damien Wellman, Chris White, Keith Wilkins, Alan Willard, Matt Williams, Myles Williams, Ron Williams, Timothy Willits, Adam Windsor, Jim Wiscarson, Don Wood, Russell Wronski, Donovan Young, and Neal Ziring.

INDEX

SYMBOLS

A

Add to Your Sams Library Today with the Best Books for Programming, Operating Systems, and New Technologies

The easiest way to order is to pick up the phone and call

1-800-428-5331

between 9:00 a.m. and 5:00 p.m. EST.
For faster service please have your credit card available.

ISBN	Quantity	Description of Item	Unit Cost	Total Cost
0-672-30865-7		Virtual Reality Madness! 1996 (Book/3 CD-ROMs)	$49.99	
0-672-30562-3		Teach Yourself Game Programming in 21 Days (Book/CD-ROM)	$39.99	
0-672-30947-5		Visual Basic 4 in 12 Easy Lessons (Book/CD-ROM)	$45.00	
0-672-30637-9		Visual C++ in 12 Easy Lessons (Book/CD-ROM)	$45.00	
1-57521-049-5		Java Unleashed (Book/CD-ROM)	$49.99	
0-672-30661-1		Windows 95 Game Developer's Guide Using the Game SDK (Book/CD-ROM)	$49.99	
0-672-30507-0		Tricks of the Game Programming Gurus (Book/CD-ROM)	$45.00	
0-672-30697-2		More Tricks of the Game Programming Gurus (Book/CD-ROM)	$49.99	
1-57521-041-X		The Internet Unleashed 1996	$49.99	
❏ 3 ½" Disk		Shipping and Handling: See information below.		
❏ 5 ¼" Disk		TOTAL		

Shipping and Handling: $4.00 for the first book, and $1.75 for each additional book. Floppy disk: add $1.75 for shipping and handling. If you need to have it NOW, we can ship product to you in 24 hours for an additional charge of approximately $18.00, and you will receive your item overnight or in two days. Overseas shipping and handling adds $2.00 per book and $8.00 for up to three disks. Prices subject to change. Call for availability and pricing information on latest editions.

201 W. 103rd Street, Indianapolis, Indiana 46290

1-800-428-5331 — Orders   1-800-835-3202 — FAX   1-800-858-7674 — Customer Service

Book ISBN 0-672-30935-1

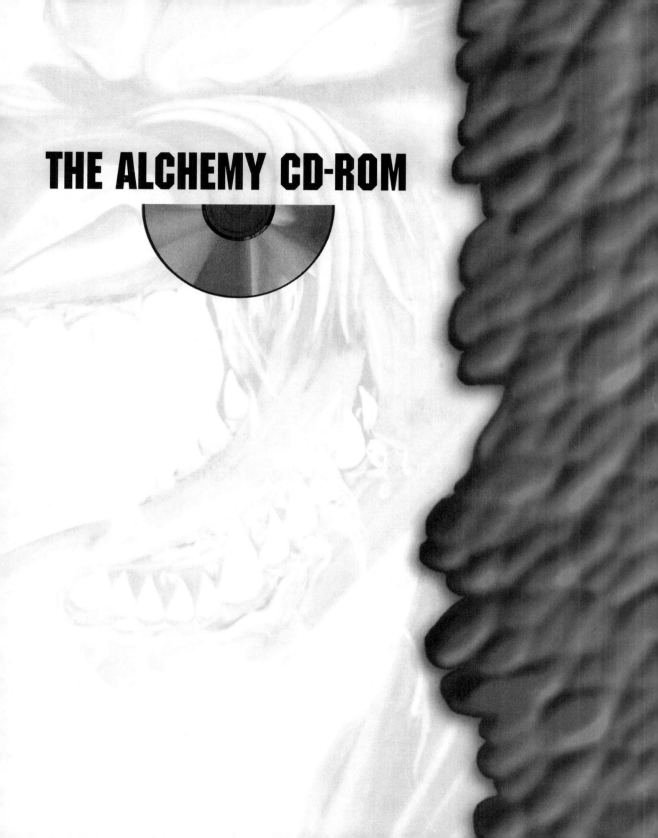

THE ALCHEMY CD-ROM

THE ALCHEMY CD-ROM

You'll find a wealth of software for DOOM, DOOM II, Heretic, and Hexen on the CD-ROM, including the following:

- More than 1,500 horror-drenched new levels, including single play, Deathmatch, and Cooperative levels.
- Fully registered version of WadAuthor 1.2, the Windows-based WAD editor—an *Alchemy* exclusive!
- DoomShell 5.0, the best program available for playing game levels—an *Alchemy* exclusive!
- *Alchemy* graphics library for game levels—an *Alchemy* exclusive!
- Special registered version of WADED 1.88, the DOS-based WAD editor.
- Sample files for the WAD-building lessons in the book.
- Special advanced WAD-editing documentation—an *Alchemy* exclusive!
- More than 50 of the best utilities for editing and hacking game levels.

 NOTE: See Chapter 4, "Using the CD-ROM," for detailed instructions on installing and using the software on this disc.

MINIMUM SYSTEM REQUIREMENTS

In order to use the software on the CD-ROM, your system should have the following:

- Registered version of DOOM, DOOM II, Heretic, or Hexen
- IBM PC-compatible computer
- 386 processor (486 or higher recommended)
- DOS 5.0 or higher
- Windows 95, Windows 3.1*x*, or Windows NT (required for WadAuthor)
- 4MB RAM (8MB recommended for some programs)
- SVGA 256-color graphics
- Sound card and mouse (recommended)